D1476939

Corrections in America

edition 12

Corrections in America
An Introduction

Annotated Instructor's Edition

Harry E.
Allen, Ph.D.
San Jose State University

Edward J.
Latessa, Ph.D.
University of Cincinnati

Bruce S.
Ponder
Allen Ponder Associates

Prentice Hall

Boston   Columbus   Indianapolis   New York   San Francisco   Upper Saddle River
Amsterdam   Cape Town   Dubai   London   Madrid   Milan   Munich   Paris   Montreal   Toronto
Delhi   Mexico City   Sao Paulo   Sydney   Hong Kong   Seoul   Singapore   Taipei   Tokyo

Editor in Chief: Vernon R. Anthony
Senior Editor: Eric Krassow
Editorial Assistant: Lynda Cramer
Director of Marketing: David Gesell
Marketing Manager: Adam Kloza
Senior Marketing Coordinator: Alicia Wozniak
Senior Managing Editor: Joellen Gohr
Project Manager: Steve Robb
Senior Operations Supervisor: Pat Tonneman
Operations Specialist: Laura Weaver
Senior Art Director: Diane Y. Ernsberger
Text and Cover Designer: Rokusek Design
Cover Image: Getty One
Manager, Rights and Permissions, Image Research Center:
Zina Arabia

Manager, Visual Research, Image Research Center:
Beth Brenzel
Manager, Cover Visual Research & Permissions,
Image Research Center: Karen Sanatar
Image Permission Coordinator, Image Research Center:
Richard Rodrigues
Photo Researcher: Kathy Ringrose
Media Editor: Michelle Chrurma
Media Project Manager: Karen Bretz
Full-Service Project Management: Emily Bush,
S4Carlisle Publishing Services
Composition: S4Carlisle Publishing Services
Printer/Binder: Quebecor World Color/Versailles
Cover Printer: Coral Graphics
Text Font: Minion, 10/12

10 9 8 7 6 5 4 3 2 1

Library of Congress Cataloging-in-Publication Data

Allen, Harry E.
   Corrections in America : an introduction.—12th ed./Harry E. Allen, Edward J.
Latessa, Bruce S. Ponder.
      p. cm.
   ISBN-13: 978-0-13-503439-2
   ISBN-10: 0-13-503439-6
   1. Corrections—United States. I. Latessa, Edward J. II. Ponder, Bruce S. III. Title.
   HV9304.A63 2010
   364.60973—dc22

                                        2009014818

dedication

To Grandfather Walter E. Allen (1851–1906)

Harry Allen

To my family—Sally, Amy, Jennifer, Michael, Allison, and Denise, for always being there for me

Edward Latessa

To Beverly, Fred, Marissa, and Steven

Bruce S. Ponder

The 12th edition of *Corrections in America* is supported by a complete package of instructor and student resources.

www.mycrimekit.com

MyCrimeKit offers text-specific learning objectives, chapter summaries, flashcards, practice tests, video clips, simulations, animations, and interactive activities to help students master the material presented in the textbook.

Also included in MyCrimeKit are tools to help with online research and career exploration in criminal justice.

• The Online Research Center includes access to the Cybrary, "The World's Criminal Justice Directory," featuring a searchable list of over 10,000 annotated crime and justice Web sites. Access to additional online search tools and a research tutorial are also available through access to Research Navigator.

• The Career Center includes information about dozens of career opportunities in criminal justice, criminology, and juvenile justice, and it features interviews with numerous professionals in the field.

Corrections in America, 12th Edition + MyCrimeKit Access Code Package 0-13-507801-6

INSTRUCTOR 12th SUPPLEMENTS

Instructor's Resource CD-ROM (Includes Instructor's Manual, PowerPoint Presentation, TestGen Electronic Test Item File, and Chapter Video Clips)	0-13-503448-5
Online TestGen Computerized Test Bank	0-13-503445-0
Online Instructor's Manual	0-13-503443-4
Online PowerPoint Presentation	0-13-503449-3
Online Blackboard/CourseCompass Test Item File	0-13-503451-5
Online WebCT Test Item File	0-13-503450-7

STUDENT SUPPLEMENTS

CourseSmart ebook	0-13-503440-X

ACCESSING ONLINE SUPPLEMENTS

To access and download supplements online, visit Pearson's Instructor Resource Center (IRC). Go to **www.pearsonhighered.com,** click the Instructor Resource Center link, and then enter the ISBN of the supplement you want to download.

To access the IRC, you will need an instructor access code. If you do not have one, you can register at the IRC site. Within 48 hours after registering, you will receive a confirming email including your instructor access code.

brief contents

contents

The field of corrections is undergoing rapid and significant changes, occasioned by court decisions, institutional overcrowding, and legislative mandates. The results are problems unforeseen in the history of corrections. In this edition, we identify those major change factors and the impacts they are having on the field. In addition, the authors project the effects of and changes in the developments of the field, including projections of impacts through the next three years. These improvements are designed to enhance student understanding and learning about this dynamic field. They include:

- More than twenty percent of the research cited is new. One-third of the photographs have been updated.
- New or expanded coverage is included on such issues as smoking in prison, death row exonerations due to DNA testing, boot camps, what works in corrections, and innovative solutions to institutional overcrowding.
- Some eighty percent of the charts, graphs, and figures are new, and almost all of those are projected to 2012.
- The textbook has been reorganized based on the comments from reviewers, including deletion of three chapters (Appellate Review, Imprisonment, and Futures of Corrections). Some twenty percent of the content of those earlier chapters is reintroduced in other chapters.
- A major reorganization of chapter placement closely reflects the systematic flow of the criminal justice system. The parts of the textbook include: Foundations, Community Corrections, Institutional Corrections, and Correctional Clients.
- A multimedia approach to pedagogy incorporates a companion Web page ("My-CrimeKit") that reinforces student learning. A separate Test Bank containing test questions is included in the Instructor CD that accompanies the Annotated Instructor's Edition. Also new is the Comprehensive Instructor's Guide just created for this edition.
- Over 700 PowerPoints are available to assist instructors in class presentation and reinforce student learning.
- Thirty streaming videotapes have been added, expanding coverage of recent changes, and correctional staff and inmate issues.
- The Glossary has grown to include definitions and descriptions of all Key Terms in this edition.
- The Annotated Instructor's Edition includes instructions and class activities, all of which can be found in the margins of all pages in the text.
- Page numbers are included for definitions and descriptions for every Key Term in the text.
- Finally, a CourseSmart ebook of this textbook is available.

acknowledgments

We would like to acknowledge the great assistance of people who merit special recognition in the twelfth edition of *Corrections in America*. Instructors, former students, colleagues, and doctoral graduates were generous in pointing out the strengths and weaknesses of the eleventh edition, and they made considerable suggestions for improving the textbook. Fortunately, we took them seriously and have benefited from their expertise. Our formal reviewers heaped praise where there might be praise and uniformly agreed on subjects deserving more attention. We would like to thank these conscientious reviewers: John Stuart Batchelder, North Georgia College and State University; Bruce L. Bikle, California State University, Sacramento; Pauline Brennan, University of Nebraska at Omaha; Johnny Cabrera, Buffalo State College; Phyllis Coontz, University of Pittsburgh; Charles J. Corley, Michigan State University; Alex del Carmen, University of Texas at Arlington; Ellen Eason-Montgomery, Harold Washington College; Connie Ireland, California State University, Long Beach; Robert F. Meier, University of Nebraska at Omaha; Chris Menton, Roger Williams University; Beth Pelz, University of Houston, Downtown; Cecil L. Willis, University of North Carolina, Wilmington; and Robert Worley, University of Texas of the Permian Basin. Tim Peyton is a great editor with whom to work, keeping us uplifted by humor and gently prodding for performance. His editorial staff contributed in many ways to the improvement of this twelfth edition, the longest continuously published textbook on corrections in the nation.

We wish to acknowledge and thank Clifford E. Simonsen, on whose shoulders we stand. Finally, we acknowledge our families, who shouldered much absence from us, humored us, handled our human needs, bolstered us in despondency, and were there when we needed them. We could not have done it without you.

Harry E. Allen

Edward J. Latessa

Bruce S. Ponder

about the authors

Harry E. Allen is Professor Emeritus in the Justice Studies Department at San Jose State University since 1997. Before joining San Jose State University in 1978, he served as Director of the Program for the Study of Crime and Delinquency at The Ohio State University. Previously, he served as Executive Secretary of the Governor's Task Force on Corrections for the State of Ohio, after teaching at Florida State University in the Department of Criminology and Corrections.

Professor Allen is the author or coauthor of numerous articles, chapters in books, essays, and textbooks, including the first editions of *Corrections in America* with Clifford E. Simonsen, the eleventh edition with Dr. Simonsen and Edward J. Latessa, and the first three editions of *Corrections in the Community* with Edward J. Latessa. He has been very active in professional associations and was the first criminologist to serve as President of both the American Society of Criminology and the Academy of Criminal Justice Sciences. He received the Herbert Block Award for service to the American Society of Criminology and the Founder's Award for contributions to the Academy of Criminal Justice Sciences. He is a Fellow in both the Western and American Society of Criminology. He currently is designing and instructing online courses for the University of Louisville in the areas of corrections, ethics, computer applications, substance abuse, community corrections, terrorism, and alternatives to incarceration.

Edward J. Latessa is Professor and Head of the Division of Criminal Justice at the University of Cincinnati. He received his Ph.D. in 1979 from The Ohio State University. Dr. Latessa had published more than 80 works in the area of criminal justice, corrections, and juvenile justice. He is coauthor of seven books, including *Corrections in the Community*, which is now in its fourth edition. Professor Latessa has directed more than 85 funded research projects, including studies of day reporting centers, juvenile justice programs, drug courts, intensive supervision programs, halfway houses, and drug programs. He and his staff have also assessed nearly 500 correctional programs throughout the United States. Dr. Latessa is a consultant with the National Institute of Corrections, and he has provided assistance and workshops in more than 40 states. Dr. Latessa served as President of the Academy of Criminal Justice Sciences (1989–1990). He has also received several awards, including the August Vollmer Award from the American Society of Criminology (2004), the Simon Dinitz Criminal Justice Research Award from the Ohio Department of Rehabilitation and Correction (2002), the Margaret Mead Award for dedicated service to the causes of social justice and humanitarian advancement by the International Community Corrections Association (2001), the Peter Lejins Award for Research from the American Correctional Association (1999), the ACJS Fellow Award (1998), the ACJS Founders Award (1992), and the Simon Dinitz Award from the Ohio Community Corrections Organization. He and his wife Sally have four beautiful children.

Bruce S. Ponder grew up in part on the raj of the Maharaja of Dharbhanaga and in Europe. He was a professional racecar driver in the 1970s, winning major competitions, including the "12 Hours of Sebring" (1972). He was formally trained in political science, computer information systems, and computer sciences. He has also studied terrorism extensively, and team-taught in-service training programs at the Southern Police Institute. Currently he is Internet coordinator and team instructor in a variety of courses in Justice Administration at the University of Louisville, particularly terrorism and corrections.

part 1

Historical Perspectives

Overview

A crucial question in corrections is, "Who are offenders and what shall we do with them?" Part 1 deals with the process by which punishment originated as a private matter between an offending party and the victim but later came to be an official state function. Significant changes over time are examined, starting with 2000 B.C. and continuing through contemporary efforts to construct places of punishment and reform. Behind each of the four major answers to the crucial question lay assumptions about the nature of offenders and what to do with them. Part 1 details these perceptions, assumptions, and answers, as well as corresponding correctional practices and fads that have emerged during the last 4,000 years.

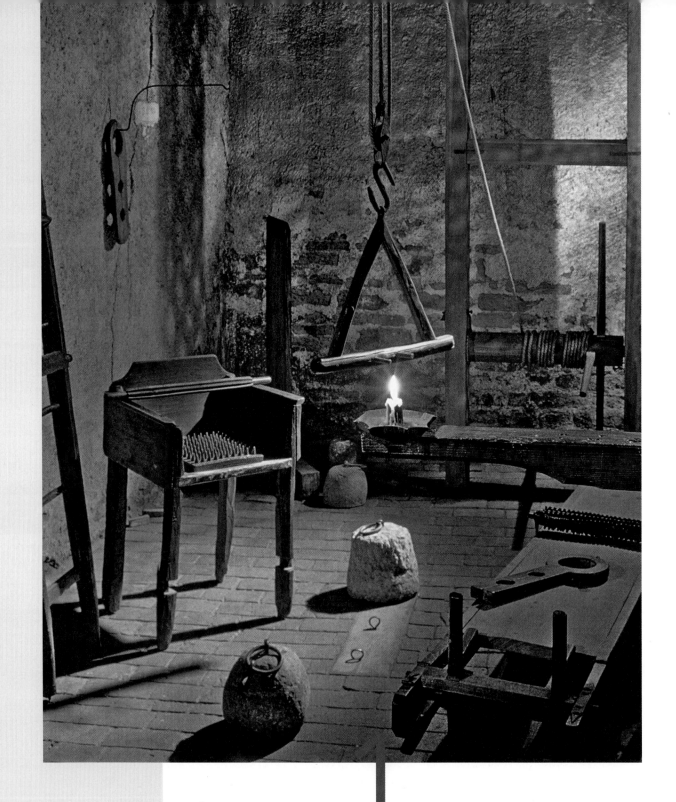

Early History
(2000 B.C. to A.D. 1800)

Outline

Redress of Wrongs
- Retaliation
- Fines and Punishments

Early Codes
- Babylonian and Sumerian Codes
- Crime and Sin
- Roman and Greek Codes
- The Middle Ages

Punishment
- Capital and Corporal Punishment
- Deterrence
- Emergence of Secular Law
- Early Prisons
- Workhouses

The Age of Enlightenment and Reform
- Montesquieu and Voltaire: The French Humanists
- Bentham and the Hedonistic Calculus
- John Howard

Houses of Correction, Workhouses, and Gaols

Transportation Systems
- Deportation to the American Colonies and Australia
- Hulks: A Sordid Episode

Early Cellular Prisons
- The Maison de Force at Ghent and the Hospice of San Michele
- William Penn and the "Great Law"
- The Walnut Street Jail

> *"The descent to hell is easy. The gates stand open day and night. But to reclimb the slope and escape to the upper air: this is labor."*
>
> —Virgil, *Aeneid, Book 6*

Overview

This textbook is not intended to be an in-depth history of corrections nor a dissertation on its legal aspects. It is helpful, however, to know at least a little of the fascinating historical background (legal and social) to gain an improved understanding of the concepts, practices, and operations that we will discuss later, and how we got to where corrections is today as we enter the twenty-first century. In describing this background, we avoid technical jargon to keep misunderstanding to a minimum. Where appropriate, specific individuals and events that have influenced the history of corrections are detailed in the chapter.

It is important to study the growing field of corrections for a variety of reasons. This dynamic field is undergoing rapid, mind-boggling change. In the interest of reducing crime, protecting children, salvaging redeemable offenders, and increasing citizen and society safety, the nation has entered into an unprecedented prison construction program. Every two weeks, the nation needs to construct and open a 1,600-bed prison and hire at least 200 new correctional officers. Corrections, as a major industry, needs to be able to find and hire competent, educated, and motivated persons.

key term

Retaliation
Act designed to repay (as an injury) in kind, or to return like for like, *especially* "to get revenge."

key term

Blood feud or Vendetta
Blood feud; an often-prolonged series of retaliatory, vengeful, or hostile acts or exchange of such acts.

key term

Lex salica
The custom of atonement for wrongs against a victim by payment to appease the victim's family.

key term

Wergild
The European word denoting *lex salica*.

key term

Friedensgeld
The practice of paying restitution for crime to both the victim and the Crown.

Never have so many Americans been in the arms of the law and under correctional control; never has the percentage of the citizenry incarcerated been as high as it is today. The size of corrections is rapidly increasing and—measured by the number of employees, offenders, and budgets—still undergoing significant growth.

Corrections affects the lives of ordinary people almost daily. Employees of prisons (as well as probation and parole officers) are in immediate contact with frequently violent and aggressive offenders, much more so than the typical municipal police officer who, in a busy week, may interact once with such an offender. The populace in general, and students of corrections in particular, must understand the dynamics that affect all forms of correctional work. They also must understand criminal behavior, to better cope with the variety of offenders and to deal effectively with problematic clients. These factors are explored throughout this textbook, and your instructor will help you gain the necessary knowledge to begin your journey into this fascinating field. We begin now by tracing the roots of corrections back to the early beginnings of civilization, as we know it.

REDRESS OF WRONGS
Retaliation

The earliest remedy for wrongs done to one's person or property was simply to retaliate against the wrongdoer. In early primitive societies, personal **retaliation** was accepted and even encouraged by members of the tribal group. This ancient concept of personal revenge could hardly be considered "law." Yet it has influenced the development of most legal systems, especially English criminal law, from which most American criminal law derives.

The practice of personal retaliation was later augmented by the **blood feud**, in which the victim's family or tribe took revenge on the offender's family or tribe. Because this form of retaliation could easily escalate and result in an endless battle or **vendetta** between the injured factions, some method of control had to be devised to make blood feuds less costly and damaging.

The practice of retaliation usually begins to develop into a system of criminal law when it becomes customary for the victim of the wrongdoing to accept money or property in place of blood vengeance. This custom, when established, is usually dictated by tribal tradition and the relative positions of power between the injured party and the wrongdoer. Custom has always exerted great force among primitive societies. The acceptance of vengeance in the form of a payment (such as cattle, food, or personal services) was usually not compulsory, however, and victims were still free to take whatever vengeance they wished. Legal historians Albert Kocourek and John Wigmore described this pressure to retaliate:

> It must not be forgotten that the right of personal revenge was also in many cases a duty. A man was bound by all the force of religion to avenge the death of his kinsman. This duty was by universal practice imposed upon the nearest male relative—the avenger of blood, as he is called in the Scripture accounts.[1]

The custom of atonement for wrongs by payment to appease the victim's family or tribe became known as ***lex salica*** (or ***wergild***, in Europe). It is still in effect in many Middle Eastern and Far Eastern countries, with the amount of payment based on the injured person's rank and position in the social group. The practice of paying restitution for crimes to the Crown, in addition to victims, was known as **friedensgeld**. With fines, the victim disappeared from the criminal justice system, becoming the ignored component of the crime. The victim has reappeared in the restorative justice movement, described in Chapter 5.

Fines and Punishments

How did these simple, voluntary programs become part of an official system of fines and punishments? As tribal leaders, elders, and (later) kings came into power,[2] they began to exert their authority on the negotiations. Wrongdoers could choose to stay away from the proceedings; this was their right. But if they refused to abide by the imposed sentence, they were declared to be outside the law of the tribe (nation, family), or an **outlaw**. There is little doubt that outlawry, or exile, was the first punishment imposed by society,[3] and it heralded the beginning of criminal law as we now know it.

Criminal law, even primitive criminal law, requires an element of public action against the wrongdoer—as in a pronouncement of outlawry. Before this element of public action, the backgrounds of criminal law and sanctions seem to have been parallel in most legal systems. The subsequent creation of legal codes and sanctions for different crimes either stressed or refined the vengeance factor, according to the particular society's values.

EARLY CODES

Babylonian and Sumerian Codes

Even primitive ethics demanded that a society express its vengeance within a system of regulations and rules. Moses was advised to follow the "eye for eye and tooth for tooth" doctrine stated in Exodus 21:24, but this concept of **lex talionis** is far older than the Bible; it appears in the Sumerian codes (1860 B.C.) and in the 1750 B.C. code of King Hammurabi of Babylon, compiled more than 500 years before the *Book of the Covenant* (1250 B.C.).

As early societies developed language and writing skills, they began attempting to record the laws of their nations. While most historians view the Hammurabic Code as the first comprehensive attempt at codifying social interaction, the Sumerian codes preceded it by about a century, and the principle of *lex talionis* was evident in both. The punishments handed out under these codes were harsh and based on vengeance (or *talion*), in many cases being inflicted by the injured party. In the Babylonian code, more than 24 offenses called for the penalty of death. Both codes also prescribed mutilation, whipping, or forced labor as punishments for numerous crimes.

The kinds of punishments applied to slaves and bonded servants have been cited by many scholars[4] as the origin of the punishments that in later law applied to all offenders. As stated by historian Gustav Radbruch:

> Applied earlier almost exclusively to slaves, [the mutilating penalties] became used more and more on freemen during the Carolingian period [A.D. 640–1012] and especially for offenses that betokened a base and servile mentality. Up to the end of the Carolingian era, punishments "to hide and hair" were overwhelmingly reserved for slaves. Even death penalties occurred as slave punishments and account for the growing popularity of such penalties in Carolingian times. The aggravated death penalties, combining corporal and capital punishments, have their roots in the penal law governing slaves.[5]

The early punishments were considered synonymous with slavery; those punished even had their heads shaved, indicating the "mark of the slave."[6] In Roman days, the extensive use of penal servitude was spurred by the need for workers to perform hard labor in the great public works. The sentence to penal servitude was generally reserved for the lower classes; it usually meant life in chains, working in the mines or rowing in the galleys or ships, or building the public works planned by the government. The sentences carried with them the complete loss of citizenship and liberty until they died, and were classed, along with exile and death, as capital punishment. Penal servitude, or **civil death**, meant that the offender's property

class activity

One of the major contributions of the Christian church was the concept of "getting right with God." Ask how this principle would contribute to the development of places in which offenders could repent.

key term

"Get right with God"
Directive that the offender must make peace with God through repentance and atonement.

was confiscated in the name of the state and that his wife was declared a widow, eligible to remarry. To society, the criminal sentenced to penal servitude was, in effect, "dead."

Crime and Sin

Punishment of the individual in the name of the state also included the concept of super-stitious revenge. Here crime was entangled with sin, and punishment in the form of wergild (payment to the victim) or *friedensgeld* (payment to the state) was not sufficient. If society believed the crime might have offended a divinity, the accused had to undergo a long period of progressively harsher punishment to appease the gods. As time passed, the zone between church law and state law became more blurred, and the concept of personal responsibility for one's act was combined with the need to "**get right with God**."[7] The early codes, even the Ten Commandments, were designed to make the offender's punishment acceptable to both society and God.

Roman and Greek Codes

In the sixth century A.D., Emperor Justinian of Rome wrote his code of laws, one of the most ambitious early efforts to match a desirable amount of punishment with all possible crimes. Roman art of the period depicts the "scales of justice," a metaphor demanding that the pun-ishment balance the crime. Justinian's effort, as might be expected, bogged down in the far-flung empire's morass of administrative details that were required to enforce it. The Code of Justinian did not survive the fall of the Roman Empire, but it left the foundation on which most of the Western world's legal codes were eventually built.

In Greece, the harsh Code of Draco provided the same penalties for both citizens and slaves, incorporating many of the concepts used in primitive societies (for example, vengeance, outlawry, and blood feuds). The Greeks were the first society to allow any of their citizens to prosecute an offender in the name of the injured party. This clearly illustrates that during the Greek period, public interest and protection of the social order were becoming more important than individual injury and individual vengeance.

The Middle Ages

The Middle Ages was a long period of general social disorder. Vast changes in the social struc-ture and the growing influence of the church on everyday life resulted in a divided system of justice. Reformation was viewed as a process of religious, not secular, redemption. As in early civilizations, the sinner had to pay two debts, one to society and another to God. The "ordeal" was the church's substitute for a trial by the leadership of the secular group, until the practice was abolished in A.D. 1215. In trials by ordeal, the accused were subjected to impossible, dan-gerous, or painful tests, in the belief that those who were truly innocent would emerge un-scathed, whereas the guilty would suffer agonies and die; this process determined guilt or innocence. The brutality of most trials by ordeal ensured a very high percentage of convictions.

The church expanded the concept of crime to include some new areas, still reflected in modern codes. During the Middle Ages, sexual activity other than for the purpose of procre-ation was seen as especially sinful. Sexual offenses usually involved either public or "unnatu-ral" acts, and they provoked horrible punishments, as did heresy and witchcraft. The church justified cruel reprisals as a means of saving the unfortunate sinner from the clutches of Satan. The zealous movement to stamp out heresy brought on the **Inquisition** and its use of the most vicious tortures imaginable to gain "confessions" and "repentance" from alleged heretics. Thousands upon thousands of persons died at the hands of the Inquisition in Spain and Hol-land, where these sometimes inhumane methods were the most extensively used. Punishment was not viewed as an end in itself, but as the offender's only hope of pacifying a wrathful God.

key term

Inquisition
A former Roman Catholic tribunal for the discovery and punishment of heresy; an investigation conducted with little regard for individual rights through a severe questioning.

The Inquisition was a tribunal, established by the Catholic Church in the Middle Ages, with very wide powers for the suppression of heresy. The tribunal searched out heretics and other offenders, rather than waiting for harges to be brought forward. Emperor Frederick II made the Inquisition a formal institution in 1224, and it lasted until 1834. The main contribution of the medieval church to our study of corrections is the concept of free will. This idea assumes that individuals choose their actions, good or bad, and thus can be held fully responsible for them. The religious doctrines of eternal punishment, atonement, and spiritual conversion rest on the assumption that individuals who commit sins could have acted differently if they had chosen to do so.

The early codes and their administration were usually based on the belief that punishment was necessary to avenge the victim, or to satisfy God. In early small tribal groups and less complex societies, direct compensation to the victim was used in place of revenge to prevent disintegration of the social structure through extended blood feuds. When those groups concentrated their power in a king or similar ruler with another title, the concept of crime as an offense against the victim gave way to the idea that crime (however lowly the victim) was an offense against the state and society in general. In the process, *wergild* was replaced by *friedensgeld,* and the administration of punishment became the responsibility of the king. Concentrating that power also led to a tendency to ignore victims and their losses, while concentrating on the crime and the criminal.

PUNISHMENT

Capital and Corporal Punishment

The most common forms of state punishment over the centuries have been death, torture, mutilation, branding, public humiliation, fines, forfeits of property, banishment, imprisonment, and transportation.[8] These acts, and numerous variations on them, have always symbolized retribution for crimes. (Imprisonment and transportation are relatively modern penal practices and will be discussed in later chapters.)

The death penalty (killing the offender) was the most universal form of punishment among early societies. There was little knowledge of behavior modification and other modern techniques to control violent persons, and often the feared offenders were condemned to death by hanging, crucifixion, burning at the stake, drowning, being drawn and quartered, and any other cruel and unusual method the human mind could conceive. As technology advanced, methods for killing offenders became more sophisticated. In the belief that punishment, especially capital punishment, would act as a deterrent to others, societies carried out executions and lesser punishments in public.

Torture, mutilation, and branding fall in the general category of **corporal punishment** (any physical pain inflicted short of death). Many tortures were used to extract a "confession" from the accused, often resulting in the death penalty for an innocent person. Mutilation was often used in an attempt to match the crime with an "appropriate" punishment. (A liar's tongue was ripped out, a rapist's genitals were removed, and a thief's hands were cut off.) Branding was still practiced as late as the nineteenth century in many countries, including America. Corporal punishment was considered to be an example and a deterrent to other potential offenders.

The public humiliation of offenders was a popular practice in early America, utilizing such devices as the stocks, the pillory, ducking stools, the brank, and branding. The most significant aspect of those punishments was their public nature. Offenders were placed in the stocks (sitting down, hands and feet fastened into a locked frame) or in the pillory (standing, with head and hands fastened into a locked frame), and then flogged, spat upon, heaped with garbage, and reviled by passersby.

The pillory was a way to provide public humiliation.
SOURCE: *Photo by Harry E. Allen, Ph.D.*

The skull crusher was used for interrogations.
SOURCE: *Photo by Harry E. Allen, Ph.D.*

key term

Brank
A bird-cage like instrument placed on the offender's head with sharp-edged iron plates that would cut tongues and mouth of the gossiper.

key term

"Cat-o'-nine tails"
Torture device for whipping or flogging.

class activity

Ask students if they know what "caning" is. Is it a form of corporal punishment? Would it be preferable for thieves to be caned rather than cutting off their hands? Assign students to use the Internet to examine "caning" and "corporal punishment" in Singapore and Saudi Arabia.

The ducking stool and the brank were used as common public punishments for gossips. The ducking stool was a chair or platform placed at the end of a long lever, allowing the operator on the bank of a stream to dunk the victim. The **brank** was a birdcage-like instrument placed over the offender's head, containing a plate of iron with sharp spikes in it that extended into the subject's mouth. Any movement of the mouth or tongue would result in painful injury.

Flogging (or whipping) became a common punishment in almost all Western civilizations. The method was used particularly to preserve discipline in domestic, military, and academic settings. It was usually administered by a short lash at the end of a solid handle about three feet long, or by a whip made of nine knotted wires, lines, or cords fastened to a handle (the famed **cat-o'-nine-tails**), sometimes with barbed-wire spikes worked into the knots. Flogging was a popular method of inducing confessions at heresy trials, because few victims could stand up long under the tongue of the lash. Caning remains a legal punishment in countries such as Malaysia, Saudi Arabia, Singapore, and South Africa.[9]

Deterrence

The extensive use of capital and corporal punishment during the Middle Ages reflected, in part, a belief that public punishment would deter potential wrongdoers—a belief that the passing years have refuted: "It is plain that, however futile it may be, social revenge is the only honest, straightforward, and logical justification for punishing criminals. The claim for deterrence is belied by both history and logic."[10] No matter how society tried to "beat the devil" out of offenders, the only criminals who seemed to be deterred were the ones who had been tortured to *death.* Later, enlightened thinkers began to seek more rational deterrents for crime by investigating its cause.

Emergence of Secular Law

The problem of drawing up a set of laws that applied to the actions of men and women in earthly communities was compounded by Christian philosophers who insisted that law was made in heaven. In the fourth century A.D., St. Augustine recognized the need for justice, but only as decreed by God. The issue was somewhat clarified by Thomas Aquinas in the thirteenth century, when he distinguished among three laws: eternal law (***lex eterna***), natural law (***lex naturalis***), and human law (***lex humana***), all intended for the common good.[11] The last was considered valid only if it did not conflict with the other two.

As time passed and the secular leaders (kings and other types of monarchs) became more powerful, they wanted to detach themselves from the divine legal order and its restrictions on their power. In the early fourteenth century, many scholars advocated the independence of the monarchy from the pope. England's lord chancellor, Sir Thomas More, opposed the forces advocating the unification of church and state and died on the executioner's block as a result. He refused to bend ecclesiastical law to suit the marital whims of his king, the fickle King Henry VIII. Sir Thomas More was out of step with his times in another sense as well. As an advocate of the seemingly radical theory that punishment could not prevent crime, he was one of the first to see that prevention might require a close look at the social conditions that gave rise to crime. In the sixteenth century, unfortunately, this line of thought was too far ahead of its time, but Sir Thomas More's ideas persisted and eventually contributed much to the foundation of modern theories in **criminology** and penology.

The early background of law and punishment points up the significance of social revenge as a justification for individual or societal punishment against an offender. This rationale allowed the development of penal slavery and civil death as retaliation for wrongs against the Crown. The idea of correcting an offender was entirely incidental to punishment. Imprisonment served purely for detention. Offenders who were condemned to the galleys or the sulfur mines suffered a form of social vengeance, often including the lash and other physical abuse, far more painful than was the loss of freedom alone. The offender was placed in dungeons, galleys, or mines to receive punishment, not as punishment.

The idea of punishment to repay society and expiate one's transgressions against God explains in part why most punishments remained cruel and barbarous. Presumably, the

The "rack" was used for punishment.
SOURCE: *Photo by Harry E. Allen, Ph.D.*

key term

Mamertine prison
An early place of confinement in Rome using primitive dungeons built under the main sewer.

key term

Sanctuary
Asylum that placed the wrongdoer in seclusion or arrest in cities.

key term

Bridewell
A workhouse created for the employment and housing of London's unemployed or underemployed working classes.

hardships of physical torture, social degradation, exile, or financial loss (the four fundamental types of punishment[12]) would be rewarded by eternal joy in heaven. Ironically, those punishments did little to halt the spread of crime: "Even in the era when extremely severe punishment was imposed for crimes of minor importance, no evidence can be found to support the view that punitive measures materially curtailed the volume of crime."[13]

Early Prisons

What kinds of facilities for imprisonment existed during earlier ages? It is important to examine some aspects of the first institutions as they are related to later correctional practices. Some form of detention for offenders, whether temporary or permanent, has been a social institution from the earliest times. Offenders were, of course, always detained against their will, but the concept of imprisonment as a punishment in and of itself is a fairly recent thought. Formerly, imprisonment was primarily a means of holding the accused until the authorities had decided on his or her real punishment, chosen from the variety just described. Even those condemned to penal servitude in the Roman public works must surely have been kept in some special place at night, regardless of how primitive. Unfortunately, little is known about this form of imprisonment. Most places of confinement were basically cages. Later, stone quarries and similar places designed for other purposes were used to house prisoners. The only early Roman place of confinement we know much about is the **Mamertine Prison** (*http://en.wikipedia.org/wiki/Tullianum*), a vast system of primitive dungeons built under the main sewer of Rome in 64 B.C.[14]

In the Middle Ages, after the fall of Rome, fortresses, castles, bridge abutments, and town gates were strongly and securely built to defend against roving bands of raiders. With the advent of gunpowder, however, those fortress cities lost much of the deterrent power of their walls and towers. The massive structures were then used as places of confinement. Many became famous as places to house political prisoners.[15] It was not until the twelfth century that prison chambers were specifically included in castle plans.

The Christian church had followed the custom of **sanctuary** or asylum[16] since the time of Constantine, placing the wrongdoer in seclusion to create an atmosphere conducive to penitence. This form of imprisonment was modified into more formalized places of punishment within the walls of monasteries and abbeys. Long periods in solitary confinement for alleged transgressions against canon law were common. The prisons built during the Inquisition were similar in concept, if not in operation, to later cellular prisons in America.[17] The idea of reformation through isolation and prayer had some influence on our first penitentiaries, but, in general, the impact of such practices in this respect remains hard to evaluate.

Workhouses

Bridewell, a workhouse, was created for the employment and housing of London's "riffraff" in 1557 and was based on the work ethic that followed the breakup of feudalism and the increased migration of the rural populations to urban areas (*http://www.workhouses.org/uk*). The workhouse was so successful that by 1576, Parliament required the construction of a Bridewell in every county in England. The same unsettled social conditions prevailed in Holland, and the Dutch began building workhouses in 1596 that were soon to be copied all over Europe.

Unfortunately, workhouses did not typify the places of confinement used for minor offenders and other prisoners in the seventeenth and eighteenth centuries. Most cities had to make prisons out of buildings erected for some other purpose. No attempt was made to keep the young from the old, the well from the sick, or even the males from the females. No food was provided for those without money, and sanitary conditions were usually deplorable. Exploitation of inmates by other inmates and jailers resulted in the most vicious acts of violence and degradation. "Jail fever" (a common term for typhus), which was spread easily in such conditions, soon traveled to surrounding cities and became the main method of keeping the country's population down. By the beginning of the eighteenth century, work-houses, prisons, and houses of correction in England and the rest of Europe had deteriorated into shocking conditions. Forcing criminals to exist in such miserable prisons became perhaps the most ruthless—if abstract—social revenge of all the punishments thus far described. "Out of sight, out of mind" was the watchword of that period, with the public seldom being aware of what happened behind the walls (ironically, a condition not unknown at the beginning of the last millennium).

lecture note

Explain the Inquisition. Ask students which issues led church leaders to initiate and then maintain this institution. Did the Inquisition achieve its goals?

THE AGE OF ENLIGHTENMENT AND REFORM

As suggested, the underlying principle of public revenge for private wrongs invariably tipped the scales of justice in favor of the state. Corporal and capital punishment were the rule. Executioners in sixteenth- and seventeenth-century Europe had at least 30 different methods of death from which to choose. These ranged from hanging and burning at the stake to more creative forms such as stretching the prisoner to death on the rack. Public punishment and degradation were commonly prescribed for even minor offenses. Imprisonment served only as a preface to the imposition of some gory punishment, carried out in the name of justice. With over 200 crimes in England punishable by death, that nation witnessed some 800 public executions a year. As the seventeenth century drew to a close, the concept of retributive punishment by the state (with its implication that pity and justice are forever locked in opposition) was firmly entrenched in the laws of England and many other European countries.[18]

The events of the eighteenth century are especially important to the student of corrections. For it was during this period, later known as the **Age of Enlightenment**, that some of the most brilliant philosophers of our history recognized humanity's essential dignity and imperfection. Such giants as Charles Montesquieu, Voltaire, Cesare Beccaria, Jeremy Bentham, John Howard, and William Penn led the movement for reform. The impact of their work, though not confined to any one area, was particularly constructive with regard to the treatment of criminals. Let us consider the contribution made by each.

Montesquieu and Voltaire: The French Humanists

The French philosophical thinkers Montesquieu (1689–1755) and Voltaire (1694–1778), along with Denis Diderot (1713–1784), epitomized the Age of Enlightenment's concern for the rights of humanity. In his essay *Persian Letters,*[19] Montesquieu used his mighty pen to bring the abuses of criminal law to public attention. Voltaire became involved in a number of trials that challenged the old ideas of legalized torture, criminal responsibility, and justice. The humanitarian efforts of those men paralleled the work of the most influential criminal law reformer of the era, **Cesare Beccaria** (1738–1794), founder of the **Classical School**. The best-known work of Beccaria is *An Essay on Crimes and Punishment,* a primary influence in the transition from punishment to corrections. It was the most exciting essay on law of the eighteenth century. It proposed a reorientation of criminal law toward humanistic goals and established the following principles:

1. The basis of all social action must be the utilitarian conception of the greatest happiness for the greatest number.
2. Crime must be considered an injury to society, and the only rational measure of crime is the extent of that injury.
3. Prevention of crime is more important than punishment for crimes; indeed punishment is justifiable only on the supposition that it helps to prevent criminal

key term

Age of Enlightenment
A philosophic movement of the eighteenth century marked by a rejection of traditional social, religious, and political ideas and an emphasis on rationalism.

profile

Cesare Beccaria
The founder of the Classical School of Criminology.

key term

Classical School
Approach to understanding crime and social policy for offenders.

conduct. In preventing crime it is necessary to improve and publish the laws, so that the nation can understand and support them; to reward virtue; and to improve the public's education both in regard to legislation and to life.

4. In criminal procedure secret accusations and torture should be abolished. There should be speedy trials. The accused should be treated humanely before trial and must have every right and facility to bring forward evidence on his or her behalf. Turning state's evidence should be done away with, as it amounts to no more than the public authorization of treachery.

5. The purpose of punishment is to deter persons from the commission of crime and not to provide social revenge. Not severity, but certainty and swiftness in punishment best secure this result. Punishment must be sure and swift and penalties determined strictly in accordance with the social damage wrought by the crime. Crimes against property should be punished solely by fines, or by imprisonment when the person is unable to pay the fine. Banishment is an excellent punishment for crimes against the state. There should be no capital punishment. Life imprisonment is a better deterrent. Capital punishment is irreparable and hence makes no provision for possible mistakes and the desirability of later rectification.

6. Imprisonment should be more widely employed, but its mode of application should be greatly improved through providing better physical quarters and by separating and classifying the prisoners as to age, sex, and degree of criminality.[20]

Although Beccaria himself did not seek or receive great personal fame, his small volume[21] was praised as one of the most significant books produced during the Age of Enlightenment. Four of his newer ideas were incorporated into the French Code of Criminal Procedure in 1808 and into the French Penal Code of 1810:

1. An individual should be regarded as innocent until proven guilty.
2. An individual should not be forced to testify against himself or herself.
3. An individual should have the right to employ counsel and to cross-examine the state's witnesses.
4. An individual should have the right to a prompt and public trial and, in most cases, a trial by jury.

Among the philosophers inspired by Beccaria's ideas were the authors of the U.S. Constitution. It seems we owe a great deal to this shy Italian writer of the eighteenth century.[22]

Bentham and the Hedonistic Calculus

Jeremy Bentham (1748–1832) was the leading reformer of the British criminal law system during the late eighteenth and early nineteenth centuries. He believed that if punishments were designed to negate whatever pleasure or gain the criminal derived from crime, the crime rate would go down. He strongly advocated a system of graduated penalties to tie more closely the punishment to the crime. As political equality became a dominant philosophy, new penal policies were required to accommodate this change in emphasis. As Thorsten Sellin stated:

> Older penal law had reflected the views dominant in societies where slavery or serfdom flourished, political inequality was the rule, and sovereignty was assumed to be resting in absolute monarchs. Now the most objectionable features of that law, which had favored the upper classes and had provided often arbitrary, brutal, and revolting corporal and capital punishments for the lower classes, were to be removed and equality before the law established. Judicial torture for the purpose of extracting evidence was to be abolished, other than penal measures used to control some conduct previously punished as crime, and punishments made only severe enough to outweigh the gains expected by the criminal from his

crime. This meant a more humane law, no doubt, applied without discrimination to all citizens alike in harmony with the new democratic ideas.[23]

Bentham believed that an individual's conduct could be influenced in a scientific manner. Asserting that the main objective of an intelligent person is to achieve the most pleasure while experiencing the least amount of pain, he developed his famous **"hedonistic calculus,"**[24] which he applied to his efforts to reform the criminal law. He, like Beccaria, believed punishment could act as a deterrent, but only if it were made appropriately relevant to the crime. This line of thought, adopted by active reformers Samuel Romilly (1757–1818) and Robert Peel (1788–1850) in the early nineteenth century, has been instrumental in the development of the modern prison.

John Howard

John Howard (1726–1790) gave little thought to prisons or prison reform until he was appointed sheriff of Bedfordshire in 1773. The appointment opened his eyes to horrors he had never imagined. He was appalled by the conditions he found in the hulks and gaols (jails) and pressed for legislation to alleviate some of the abuses and improve sanitary conditions. He also traveled extensively on the European continent to examine prisons in other countries. He saw similarly deplorable conditions in most areas, but was most impressed by some of the institutions in France and Italy. In 1777, he described those conditions and suggested reforms in his *State of Prisons.* In 1779, Parliament passed the Penitentiary Act, providing four principles for reform: secure and sanitary structures, systematic inspection, abolition of fees, and a reformatory regime.[25]

The Penitentiary Act resulted in the first penitentiary, located at Wyndomham in Norfolk, England, and operated by Sir Thomas Beever, the sheriff of Wyndomham. As we will see later, the principles contained in the act, though lofty in concept, were hard to implement in the prevailing atmosphere of indifference. It is ironic that this great advocate for better prison conditions did himself die of **jail fever** (typhus) in the Russian Ukraine in 1790. John Howard's name has become synonymous with prison reform, and the John Howard Society has carried his ideas forward to this day.[26]

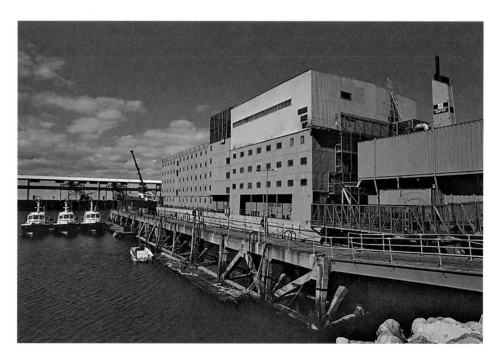

The HMP *Weare* prison boat, a contemporary hulk.
SOURCE: © *Richard Smith/CORBIS*
All Rights Reserved

key term

Workhouse
A house of correction for persons guilty of minor law violations; sometimes referred to as a "poorhouse."

key term

Gaols
Places of confinement in England for persons held in lawful custody; *specifically*: such a place under the jurisdiction of a local government (as a county) for the confinement of persons awaiting trial or those convicted of minor crimes.

key term

Banishment
To remove by authority from a state or country; the sentence to cast out of a local residence or country due to criminal behavior on the offender's part.

HOUSES OF CORRECTION, WORKHOUSES, AND GAOLS

The proliferation of Bridewell-style houses of correction in England was originally intended as a humanitarian move. As a result, in 1576, Parliament ordered that each county in England construct such an institution. They were not merely extensions of almshouses or poorhouses, but were actually penal institutions for all sorts of misdemeanants. Although the bloody penalties for major offenses were growing in number, not even the most callous would advocate harsh physical punishment for every offender. All sorts of rogues, from idlers to whores, were put into the Bridewells, where they were compelled to work under strict discipline at the direction of hard taskmasters. Today, the house of correction and the **workhouse** are regarded as synonymous. The workhouse, however, was not actually intended as a penal institution, but as a place for the training and care of the poor. In practice, however, the two soon became indistinguishable, first in England and later in America. Conditions and practices in such institutions were no better than those in the gaols by the turn of the eighteenth century.

The use of **gaols** ("jails") to detain prisoners has a grim and unsavory history. As the eighteenth century began, gaol administration was usually left up to the whim of the gaoler (jailer), who was usually under the control of the sheriff. Gaols were often used to extort huge fines from those who had the means, by holding those people indefinitely in pretrial confinement until they gave in and paid. The lot of the common "gaolbirds" (detained suspects and criminals) was surely not a happy one. Many of the prisoners perished long before their trial dates. The squalid and unhealthy conditions gave rise to epidemics of jail fever (typhus) that spread to all levels of English life. John Howard claimed that more people died from this malady between 1773 and 1774 than were executed by the Crown.[27] Ironically, prisoners, not prison conditions, were blamed for the spread of the deadly disease, and even more sanguinary penalties for offenses were devised. Robert Caldwell describes the typical English gaol:

> Devoid of privacy and restrictions, its contaminated air heavy with the stench of unwashed bodies, human excrement, and the discharge of loathsome sores, the gaol bred the basest thoughts and the foulest deeds. The inmates made their own rules, and the weak and the innocent were exposed to the tyranny of the strong and the vicious. Prostitutes plied their trade with ease, often with the connivance and support of the gaolers, who thus sought to supplement their fees. Even virtuous women sold themselves to obtain food and clothing, and frequently the worst elements of the town used the gaol as they would a brothel. Thus, idleness, vice, perversion, profligacy, shameless exploitation, and ruthless cruelty were compounded in hotbeds of infection and cesspools of corruption. These were the common gaols of England.[28]

It is depressing to think that John Howard, shocked into humanitarian reform efforts when he found himself responsible for one of those human cesspools, was the only sheriff to undertake action against such institutions.

TRANSPORTATION SYSTEMS
Deportation to the American Colonies and Australia

As noted, one of the earliest forms of social vengeance was **banishment**. In primitive societies the offender was cast out into the wilderness, usually to be eaten by wild beasts or to succumb to the elements. As we have discovered, imprisonment and capital punishment were later substituted for banishment. Banishment to penal servitude was, in effect, civil death. Banishment to the gaols, however, more often than not ended in physical death.

The wandering and jobless lower classes, in the period following the breakup of feudalism, were concentrated mostly in high-crime slums in the major cities. As economic conditions worsened, the number of imprisonable crimes increased to the point that the available prisons were filled. In England, from 1596 to 1776, the pressure was partially relieved by the deportation or **transportation** of malefactors to the colonies in America. Estimates vary greatly of how many original American settlers arrived in chains. Margaret Wilson estimates between 300 and 400 annually;[29] other authorities put the figure as high as 2,000 a year. The use of convict labor was widespread before the adoption of slavery in the colonies. And even though the entering flow of dangerous felons was somewhat slowed by the introduction of slavery, the poor and the misdemeanant continued to come in great numbers.

The American Revolution brought transportation to America to an abrupt halt in 1776; but England and Ireland[30] still needed somewhere to send the criminals overloading their crowded institutions. Captain James Cook had discovered Australia in 1770, and soon the system of transportation was transferred to that continent. It was planned that the criminals would help tame that new and wild land. More than 135,000 felons were sent to Australia between 1787 and 1875, when the British finally abandoned the system.

Transportation ships were hired transports employed to convey convicts from England to New South Wales. Private business entrepreneurs carried offenders to another country for a fee, essentially making a pound off the backs of offenders. Contractors received between 20 and 30 pounds per head. The more convicts carried, the greater the profit would be; thus, overcrowding on the ships was the rule, not the exception. As a result of such a state of confinement, the most loathsome diseases were common and the death rate was extremely high: 158 of 502 who were placed on the *Neptune* in 1790 for conveyance to Australia died en route; and 95 of the 300 placed into the holds of the *Hillsborough* in 1799 died during the voyage. Those who did arrive were so near dead that they could not stand and it was necessary to sling them like goods and hoist them out of the ships, and when first landed they died at the rate of 10 to 12 a day. The government attempted in 1802 to correct these evils by sending convicts twice a year in ships specially fitted for the purpose that were under the direction of a transport board and commanded by naval officers.[31] Although the transports continued to be crowded, health conditions apparently improved greatly because Sir T. B. Martin, head of the transport board, reported in 1819 that "within the past three years only 53 out of 6,409 convicts (a rate of 1 in 112) had died. Out of the 10 transports which had recently sailed only one or two had died"(http://www.genealogyandhow.com/lib/australia/prisoner-ships.htm).

Hulks: A Sordid Episode

From 1776 to 1875, even with limited transportation to Australia, the increased prisoner loads wreaked havoc in England's few available facilities. The immediate solution to that problem created one of the most odious episodes in the history of penology and corrections: the use of old **hulks**, abandoned or unusable transport ships anchored in rivers and harbors throughout the British Isles, to confine criminal offenders. The brutal and degrading conditions found in the gaols, houses of correction, and workhouses paled in comparison with the conditions found in those fetid and rotting human garbage dumps.

Those responsible for the hulks made no attempt to segregate young from old, hardened criminals from poor misdemeanants, or even men from women. Brutal flogging and degrading labor soon bred moral degeneration in both inmates and keepers. The hulks were originally intended only as a temporary solution to a problem, but they were not completely abandoned until 1858, eighty years later. (Hulks were used in California in the nineteenth century, and one state, Washington, considered the use of decommissioned U.S. Navy warships in 1976. New York used a floating jail for some time in the 1980s.) This episode in penal history becomes especially relevant when the problems of overcrowding in our maximum-security prisons are examined.

EARLY CELLULAR PRISONS
The Maison de Force at Ghent and the Hospice of San Michele

key term

Maison de Force
A Belgian workhouse for beggars and miscreants, designed to make a profit by an enforced pattern of hard work and both discipline and silence. An important rule: "If a man will not work, neither let him eat."

thematic question
Using the gaol as an example, discuss how the perceptions of the nature of offenders changed between the seventeenth and eighteenth centuries.

key term

Hospice of San Michele
A corrections facility designed for incorrigible boys and youth, and included silence, large work areas, and separate sleeping cells. Both expiation and reform were intended goals.

lecture note
Ask students how residents of gaols were able to eat when incarcerated. Explain the fee system, and ask how it would be possible to eat without visible means of support or relatives or friends.

profile

William Penn
Quaker leader who created the state of Pennsylvania and a system of justice that required compensation of victims and repentance to restore the offender to God's grace.

In his travels through Europe, John Howard was most impressed by Jean-Jacques Vilain's **Maison de Force** (stronghouse) at Ghent, Belgium, and by the Hospice (hospital) of San Michele in Rome. Although those institutions had developed along individually different lines, both made lasting impressions on Howard. Both served as workhouses, but otherwise they had little in common. Their differences were more important than their similarities.

Predecessors of the Belgian workhouses were those in neighboring Amsterdam, constructed around 1596. Most were intended to make a profit,[32] not to exemplify humanitarian ideals, and were seen as a place to put rogues and able-bodied beggars to work. The workhouses were modeled after the Bridewell institution in England and followed a similar pattern of hard work and cruel punishment. By the eighteenth century, Belgium, too, was faced with increasing numbers of beggars and vagrants, and the government called on administrator and disciplinarian Jean-Jacques Vilain for help. His solution—the Maison de Force built in Ghent in 1773—followed the basic workhouse pattern established in Holland and England, but in many respects it was far more just and humane.

Vilain's efforts at improving the administration of the workhouse earned him an honored place in penal history. He was one of the first to develop a system of classification to separate women and children from hardened criminals, and felons from minor offenders. Although he was a stern disciplinarian, he was opposed to life imprisonment and cruel punishment. Rather, he defined discipline by the rule, "If any man will not work, neither let him eat." Vilain's use of individual cells and a system of silence while working resembled the procedures observed at the Hospice of San Michele in Rome. His far-reaching concepts of fair and just treatment, when viewed against the harsh backdrop of that era, mark Vilain as a true visionary in the correctional field.

The **Hospice of San Michele** was designed for incorrigible boys and youths under age 20. As such, it is generally recognized as one of the first institutions to handle juvenile offenders exclusively. Prisoners were administered massive doses of Scripture and hard work in hopes that this regimen would reform them. The rule of strict silence was enforced through the flogging of violators. (The use of separate cells for sleeping and a large central hall for working became the model for penal institutions in the nineteenth century.) This concept of expiation and penance, as applied to corrections, was new and exciting to John Howard, and his Puritan ethic enabled him to see the value of repentance and hard work as demonstrated by the program at San Michele. Under somewhat different policies, the Hospice of San Michele is still used today as a reformatory for delinquent boys.

The main concepts that carried over from the early cellular institutions were the monastic regimen of silence and expiation, the central community work area, and individual cells for sleeping. The philosophy of penitence and monastic contemplation of past wrongs espoused by those institutions was reflected in the Quakers' early prison efforts in America.

William Penn and the "Great Law"

The American colonies were governed by the British under codes established by the Duke of York in 1676 and part of the older Hampshire Code established in 1664. These codes were similar to those followed in England, and the use of capital and corporal punishment was the rule of the day. Branding, flogging, the stocks, the pillory, and the brank were also used extensively.

William Penn (1644–1718), the founder of Pennsylvania and leader of the Quakers, brought the concept of more humanitarian treatment of offenders to America. The Quaker movement was the touchstone of penal reform not only in America, but also in Italy and England through its influence on such advocates as Beccaria and Howard. Compared with the other harsh colonial codes in force at the time, the **Great Law** of the Quakers was quite humane. This body of laws envisioned hard labor as a more effective punishment than death for serious crimes, and capital punishment was eliminated from the original codes. Later, in supplementary acts, murder and manslaughter were included as social crimes. Only pre-meditated murder was punishable by death, with other criminal acts treated according to the circumstances.

It is interesting to note that the Quakers' Great Law did away with most religious of-fenses and stuck to strictly secular criminal jurisprudence, a departure from the codes of other colonies and the earlier European codes. Under the Great Law, a "house of correc-tions" institution was established where most punishment was meted out in the form of hard labor. This was the first time that correctional confinement at hard labor was used as a punishment for serious crimes, and not merely as a preface to punishment scheduled for a later date.

The Quaker Code of 1682 was in force until 1718, when it was repealed, ironically, only one day after the death of William Penn. The English Anglican Code replaced the Great Law, and the mild Quaker philosophy gave way to harsh punishments. The new code was even worse than the previous codes of the Duke of York. Capital punishment was prescribed for 13 offenses,[33] and mutilation, branding, and other corporal punishments were restored for many others.

The influence of Montesquieu, Voltaire, Beccaria, Bentham, Howard, and Penn was felt throughout colonial America. Much of the idealism embodied in the U.S. Constitu-tion reflects the writings of those progressive eighteenth-century leaders. With their philosophies in mind, we can consider some of the major developments in correctional practice in that era of reform.

The Walnut Street Jail

As we have seen, the world of the eighteenth century had prisons, but they were generally used as places of detention for minor offenders and for pretrial confinement. One of the earliest American attempts to operate a state prison for felons was located in an aban-doned copper mine in Simsbury, Connecticut.[34] This underground prison began opera-tion in 1773 and quickly became the site of America's first prison riots in 1774. Although some have called it the first state prison, it was really not much more than a throwback to the sulfur pits of ancient Rome, and it did nothing to advance the state of American cor-rections. The prisoners were housed in long mine shafts, and the administration build-ings were placed near the entrances. Underground mine shaft prisons constituted one of several American attempts to provide a special place in which to house and work con-victed felons. The establishment of such a special facility was finally accomplished in Pennsylvania in 1790.

The Walnut Street Jail, until the innovation of solitary confinement for felons, was typical of colonial jails. They are described in David J. Rothman's *Discovery of the Asylum* (Boston: Little, Brown, 1971, p. 55). Jails in fact closely resembled the household in struc-ture and routine. They lacked a distinct architecture and special procedures. When the Virginia burgess required that county prisons be "good, strong, and substantial," and ex-plicitly recommended that they follow "after the form of Virginia housing," results were in keeping with these directions. The doors were perhaps somewhat sturdier, the locks slightly more impressive, but the general design of the jail was the same as for an ordinary residence. True to the household model, the keeper and his family resided in the jail, oc-cupying one of its rooms; the prisoners lived several together in the other rooms, with lit-tle to differentiate the keeper's quarters from their own. They wore no special clothing or

key term
_____

The Great Law
Body of laws of the Quakers that saw hard labor as a more effective punishment than death for crimes and one that demanded compensation to victims.

lecture note

Explain the role of the Quakers in the establishment of the penitentiary and their role in the contributions of religion to the field of corrections. Ask students to identify other religious groups that have made such contributions. Ask if "faith-based" programs in prison are effective in reducing recidivism. If the consensus is "yes," ask how that could happen (what are the theoretical bases of this program, and how do they lead to reduced recidivism?).

thematic question

Using the question of "who are offenders and what should be done with them," show how the conception of criminal offenders changed since the Code of Hammurabi.

class activity

Divide the class into two groups, and assign each side 15 minutes to organize an answer to the question: If transportation meant you were taken to a military camp in another country so you could not coordinate attacks on the victorious opponent, what could you expect in terms of treatment?

lecture note

Explain *banishment* as a punishment and *transportation* as a national policy of managing the problem of high volume crime. Ask students if drug abusers should be disabled by incarceration.

key term

Penitentiary
Originally a detention center in which inmates could do penance and repent or turn away from crime; now any larger penal institution for detention of inmates.

key term

Walnut Street Jail
First penitentiary created in Philadelphia by the Quakers.

uniforms and usually neither cuffs nor chains restrained their movements. They walked—not marched—about the jail. The workhouse model was so irrelevant that nowhere were they required to perform the slightest labor.

It is hard to imagine a time when there were no long-term penitentiaries for felons, but before 1790 that was the case. Ironically, in that year, the first **penitentiary** in America, the prototype of the modern prison system, was born in the same city that spawned the fledgling United States as a nation. Philadelphia, Pennsylvania, the home of the Declaration of Independence, is also—thanks to the Quakers—the home of the **Walnut Street Jail**, the first true correctional institution in America.

Originally, the penitentiary was a place where offenders reflected on their crimes and repented (or changed). Today the term refers to a major adult facility where felons are incarcerated as punishment.

Despite earlier efforts at prison reform, the Quakers had been thwarted in their humanistic goals by the repeal of Penn's Great Law in 1718. In 1776, the first American Penitentiary Act was passed, but its implementation was delayed because of the War of Independence. In 1790, with the Revolution behind them, the Quakers reasserted their concern with the treatment of convicted criminals.[35] After much prodding, they convinced the Pennsylvania legislature to declare a wing of the Walnut Street Jail a penitentiary house for all convicted felons except those sentenced to death.[36] Thus, although prisons, gaols, dungeons, and workhouses had been in existence for years, this wing was the first to be used exclusively for the correction of convicted felons.

Some of the concepts embodied in the Walnut Street Jail had their antecedents in the charter of William Penn in 1682. Those provisions, repressed by the harsh Anglican Code, were as follows:

1. All prisoners were to be bailable.
2. Those wrongfully imprisoned could recover double damages.
3. Prisons were to be free as to fees, food, and lodging.
4. The lands and goods of felons were to be liable for confiscation and double as restitution to injured parties.
5. All counties were to provide houses to replace the pillory, stocks, and the like.[37]

key term

Pennsylvania system
The system of prison discipline using isolation or solitary confinement with both a work requirement and moral and religious instruction.

Although not all of the idealistic reforms were adopted, the direction of change had been established. The system of prison discipline developed at the Walnut Street Jail became known as the **Pennsylvania system**. The Pennsylvania system was developed through the ideas and efforts of such reformers as Benjamin Franklin (1706–1790) and Benjamin Rush (1745–1813), building on the humanitarian ideals of Howard, Bentham, Beccaria, and Montesquieu. Patriot and war hero William Bradford (1721–1791), who drafted the codes that implemented the system, praised the European reformers in the state legislature.

As originally conceived, the basic element of the Pennsylvania system called for solitary confinement without work. It was assumed that this method would result in quicker reformations. Offenders could reflect on their crimes all day and would soon repent so they might rejoin humanity. The terrible effects of such isolation—physical and psychological—soon became apparent. Some kind of work had to be provided, as well as moral and religious instruction, to maintain the prisoners' mental and bodily health. The work schedule thus was from eight to ten hours a day, and the prisoner worked in isolation, usually on piecework or handicrafts.

Increasingly more convicts were sent to the new state prison, and overcrowding shattered early hopes for its success. Even the original system of separate areas for women and children broke down with the flood of inmates. But despite the ultimate failure of the Walnut Street Jail program, it represented a major breakthrough for penology. New prisons were soon in demand throughout America, and the Walnut Street Jail was copied extensively, in at least ten states and many foreign countries.[38]

class activity

Ask the students to argue for *free will* in criminal offending. If there is consensus favoring free will, ask how the drug abuser exercises free will after becoming addicted.

Summary

In this chapter, we initially observed the principle of punishment pass from an individual's response to a wrong, to a blood feud that involved the family, to an abstract action taken by some bureaucracy in the name of the state. The last approach to justice and punishment allowed the places of confinement to become human cesspools. It took the brilliant and dedicated reformers of the eighteenth century to establish the basis for modern penal philosophy.

As the eighteenth century drew to a close, a new feeling of vigor and energy sparked the move for prison reform. The decade after the opening of the Walnut Street Jail was full of hope for the concepts embodied there, however imperfectly. It would be an oversimplification to say that the Walnut Street Jail was the world's first real attempt at a prison for convicted felons. The eighteenth century produced many such attempts, both in Europe and in America. Some of the principles behind the Walnut Street Jail, however, had a permanent influence on the development of correctional institutions throughout the world. Connecticut's abortive attempt to establish a state prison at Simsbury failed because the mineshafts could not be made habitable and because there was little public enthusiasm for the project. The Quakers' compassionate efforts, though much more humane, were doomed to failure by the lack of public and political support, incompetent personnel, and enforced idleness. With the industrial age came overcrowded prisons, which forced the new administrators to consider much larger and more productive kinds of institutions. As America entered the nineteenth century, it also entered an age of expansion. The prison movement adopted this growth-oriented philosophy, and as we will see in the next chapter, the nineteenth and early twentieth centuries became the age of prisons.

Key Words

retaliation, 4	*lex eterna*, 9	workhouse, 14
blood feud, 4	*lex naturalis*, 9	gaols, 14
vendetta, 4	*lex humana*, 9	banishment, 14
lex salica, 4	Criminology, 9	transportation, 15
wergild, 4	Mamertine Prison, 10	hulks, 15
friedensgeld, 4	sanctuary, 10	Maison de Force, 16
outlaw, 5	Bridewell, 10	Hospice of San Michele, 16
lex talionis, 5	Age of Enlightenment, 11	William Penn, 16
civil death, 5	Cesare Beccaria, 11	Great Law, 17
"get right with God," 6	Classical School, 11	penitentiary, 18
Inquisition, 6	"hedonistic calculus," 13	Walnut Street Jail, 18
corporal punishment, 7	Jeremy Bentham, 12	Pennsylvania system, 18
brank, 8	John Howard, 13	
cat-o'-nine-tails, 8	jail fever, 13	

Review Questions

1. At what point in a society's development does retaliation begin to become criminal law?
2. What effect did the kings' increasing power have on punishment?
3. What was the first punishment imposed by society?
4. What is meant by civil death?
5. What is meant by free will?
6. What form of punishment has been most widely used?
7. What is meant by "deterrence as a result of punishment"?
8. What were some of the earliest forms of imprisonment?
9. From what does most American law derive?
10. What was Beccaria's main contribution to corrections?
11. What were John Howard's four principles for a penitentiary system?
12. Many reformers tried to improve prison conditions in the eighteenth century. Name at least three and describe their major contributions.
13. Why is it important to study corrections?

Endnotes

1. Albert Kocourek and John Wigmore, *Evolution of Law, Vol. 2, Punitive and Ancient Legal Institutions* (Boston: Little, Brown, 1915), p. 124. See also Jeffrie Murphy, "Two Cheers for Vindictiveness," *Punishment and Society* 2:2 (2000): 134–143.

2. Ronald Akers, "Toward a Comparative Definition of Criminal Law," *Journal of Criminal Law, Criminology and Police Science* (1965): 301–306.

3. Kocourek and Wigmore, *Evolution of Law,* Vol. 2, p. 126.

4. Thorsten Sellin, "A Look at Prison History," *Federal Probation* (September 1967): 18.

5. Gustav Radbruch, *Elegantiae Juris Criminalis,* 2nd ed. (Basel, Switzerland: Verlag fur Recht und Gesellschaft A. G., 1950), p. 5.

6. Slaves were also marked by branding on the forehead or by metal collars that could not be easily removed.

7. This religious requirement brought the two issues of sin and crime into the same arena and broadened the scope of the church courts. The offender was obligated to make retribution to both God and the state.

8. V. A. C. Catrell, *The Hanging Tree: Execution and the English People: 1770–1868* (New York: Oxford University Press, 1994). For an example of the American experience, see Robert Lilly, "Executing U.S. Soldiers in England, WW II," *British Journal of Criminology* 37:2 (1997): 262–288.

9. Editors, "Guards Get Jail and Cane for Prisoner's Death," *The Straits Times* (March 21, 1996): 2. See also Roger Mellem, "Government Violence in the War against Drugs," *International Journal of Comparative and Applied Criminal Justice* 18:1 (1994): 39–51.

10. Walter C. Reckless, *The Crime Problem,* 4th ed. (New York: Appleton-Century-Crofts, 1969), p. 497.

11. Harry Elmer Barnes and Negley K. Teeters, *New Horizons in Criminology,* 3rd ed. (Englewood Cliffs, NJ: Prentice-Hall, 1959), p. 286. For a more recent update on deterrence, see Stewart D'Alessio and Lisa Stolzenberg, "Crime, Arrests and Pretrial Jail Incarceration: A Test of the Deterrence Thesis," *Criminology* 36:4 (1998): 735–761.

12. Stephen Schafer, *Theories in Criminology* (New York: Random House, 1969), p. 25.

13. Edwin H. Sutherland, *Criminology* (Philadelphia: Lippincott, 1924), p. 317.

14. Reckless, *The Crime Problem,* p. 504. There is little evidence that increased use of incarceration will lead to lower levels of crime. See Rodney Hennington, W. Johnson, and T. Wells, "Supermax Prisons: Panacea or Desperation," *Corrections Management Quarterly* 3:2 (1999): 53–59; and Jesenia Pizarro and Vanja

Stenius, "Supermax Prisons." *The Prison Journal* 84:2 (2004): 228–247.

15. Norman Johnston, *The Human Cage: A Brief History of Prison Architecture* (Washington, DC: American Foundation, 1973), p. 5. See also John Britton and E. Brayley, *Memoirs of the Tower of London* (Littleton, CO: Fred Rothman, 1994); and Dana Priest, "U.S. Preparing for Lifetime Jailing of Terror Suspects," *Seattle Times* (January 2, 2005), p. 3.

16. Johnston, *The Human Cage,* p. 6.

17. The practice of granting a criminal sanctuary from punishment was generally reserved for holy places. It was abandoned in England in the seventeenth century.

18. For an historical view of the development of Western criminal justice systems up to the eighteenth century, see Herbert Johnson and Nancy Wolfe, *History of Criminal Justice* (Cincinnati, OH: Anderson, 2003), pp. 24–109.

19. The *Persian Letters* was a satirical essay by Montesquieu on the abuses of current criminal law. The essay greatly influenced Beccaria. This, along with Voltaire's activities, led Beccaria to write his *An Essay on Crimes and Punishment.*

20. Barnes and Teeters, *New Horizons in Criminology,* p. 322.

21. Cesare Beccaria, *An Essay on Crimes and Punishment* (Philadelphia: P. H. Nicklin, 1819).

22. Beccaria's contributions to corrections as the father of modern criminology have been called into question in recent years. See Graeme Newman and Pietro Morongu, "Penological Reform and the Myth of Beccaria," *Criminology* 28 (1990): 325–346. Nonetheless, he remains the central figure in liberal penology.

23. Thorsten Sellin, "A Look at Prison History," *Federal Probation* 31:3 (1967): 20.

24. *Hedonistic calculus* was a term devised by Jeremy Bentham to describe the idea that "to achieve the most pleasure and the least pain is the main objective of an intelligent man."

25. Barnes and Teeters, New Horizons in Criminology, p. 335. See also John Freeman, *Prisons Past and Present* (London: Heinemann, 1978), for an excellent set of papers celebrating Howard's contributions to prison reform, and Jacques Petit et al., "The History of Incarceration in Penal Populations," *Criminologie* 28:1 (1995): 3–147 (in French).

26. The John Howard Society is a nonprofit organization supported by contributions. It provides casework service to inmates and their families, and it also works to promote community understanding of prison

problems and offers technical assistance to correctional agencies (608 South Dearborn Street, Chicago, IL 60605). A biography of John Howard can be found at www.johnhoward.ca/bio.htm.

27. John Howard, *The State of Prisons* (New York: Dutton, 1929). For more background on Bridewells, see Leonard Roberts, "Bridewell: The World's First Attempt at Prisoner Rehabilitation Through Education," *Journal of Correctional Education* 35:3 (1984): 83–85. One example of Howard's influence can be found in the Wakefield Prison History, http://freepages.history. rootsweb.com/~wakefield/histpris.html (accessed January 9, 2005).

28. Robert G. Caldwell, *Criminology* (New York: Ronald Press, 1965), p. 494.

29. Margaret Wilson, *The Crime of Punishment* (New York: Harcourt, Brace and World, 1931), p. 224.

30. Bob Reece, *The Origins of Irish Convict Transportation to New South Wales* (New York: Palgrave, 2001).

31. Alexis Durham, "Origins of Interest in the Privatization of Punishment: The Nineteenth and Twentieth Century American Experience," *Criminology* 27 (1989): 107–139. See also the National Archives of Ireland, *Sources in the National Archives for Research into the Transportation of Irish Convicts to Australia (1791–1853): Introduction,* www.nationalarchives.ie/topics/transportation/transp1 .htm (accessed January 9, 2005).

32. For a discussion of contemporary punishment for profit, see David Shichor, *Punishment for Profit: Private Prisons, Public Concerns* (Thousand Oaks, CA: Sage, 1995); and Colorado Criminal Justice Reform Coalition, "For Profit Incarceration," www.ccjrc.org/ pdf/forprofit.pdf (accessed January 9, 2005).

33. Only larceny was exempt from capital punishment. All other major crimes were punishable by death. For a poignant view on contemporary flogging, see Azam Kamguian, *Why Islamic Law Should Be Opposed?* www .secularislam.org/articles/opposed.htm (accessed January 9, 2005).

34. For a short history of this facility, see Charles W. Dean, "The Story of Newgate," *Federal Probation* (June 1977): 8–14. See also Alexis Durham, "Newgate of Connecticut: Origins and Early Days of an Early American Prison," *Justice Quarterly* 6 (1989): 89–116; and Judith Cook, *To Brave Every Danger* (London, UK: Macmillan, 1993).

35. Barnes and Teeters, New Horizons in Criminology, p. 336.

36. Negley K. Teeters, *The Cradle of the Penitentiary* (Philadelphia: Pennsylvania Prison Society, 1955).

37. Donald R. Taft, *Criminology,* 3rd ed. (New York: Macmillan, 1956), p. 478.

38. Harry E. Barnes, *The Story of Punishment,* 2nd ed. (Montclair, NJ: Patterson Smith, 1972), p. 136.

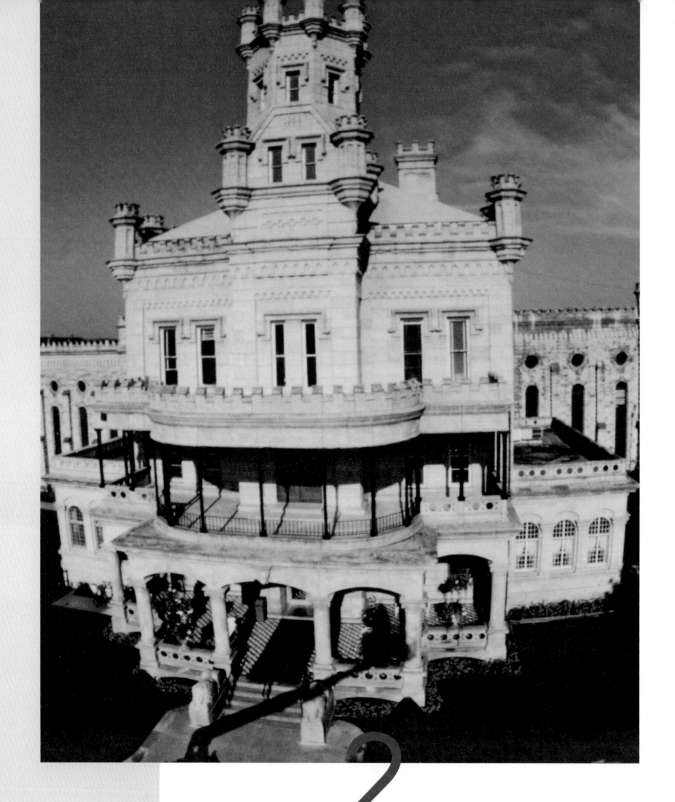

chapter 2

Prisons
(1800 to the Present)

Outline

"To the builders of this nitemare Though you may never get to read these words I pity you;
For the cruelty of your minds have designed this Hell;
If men's buildings are a reflection of what they are,
This one portraits the ugliness of all humanity.
IF ONLY YOU HAD SOME COMPASSION"

—On a prison wall

Overview

The first chapter acquainted the student with how corrections has grown from individual to group punishment, then from group punishment to legal codes and punishment applied by the country or state. We saw how the idea of reform by penitence in the Walnut Street Jail grew to be a whole new concept—the penitentiary. In this chapter we examine how this simple concept grew into the vast network of prisons across America by exploring the first two competing concepts or systems of prison design and construction in the United States.

The student should remember that corrections must always ask the question "Who are offenders and what are we expected to do with them?" Offenders are (1) evil and must be punished, (2) out of touch with God and need to repent, (3) uneducated and ill trained to function in modern society, and (4) sick and in need of being cured. The answers to these questions are commonly known as the punishment, reform, education, and medical models of corrections. In the final part of this chapter, we explore the philosophical foundations on which these models were constructed and explain some of the rationales underlying current correctional developments. It is essential for the student to understand why this nation has entered into an age of massive change in public acceptance of crime and criminal and prison operations, what goals are being sought, and what might be the implications of the adoption of new programs, operations, and facilities. We begin with the two major competing concepts or systems that evolved and fought for prison designs and construction in the United States for the majority of the twentieth century.

THE PENNSYLVANIA SYSTEM

With the advent of the nineteenth century and the social upheaval produced by the Industrial Revolution, the citizens of Pennsylvania led the way in developing the penitentiary system. The Walnut Street Jail had been fairly effective for a decade, and the earlier **Pennsylvania system** was copied extensively in both architectural design and administration. But when the Philadelphia Society for the Alleviation of the Miseries of Public Prisons[1] observed the many emerging problems at the Walnut Street Jail, a radically new kind of prison was proposed for the state. It was suggested by some that solitary confinement without labor continue to be used as the sole reformatory process.

The Western Penitentiary at Pittsburgh, built in 1826, was based on the cellular isolation wing of the Walnut Street Jail. Essentially, the Western Penitentiary amounted to a poor imitation of Jeremy Bentham's proposed prison (Panopticon), an octagonal monstrosity that originally provided for solitary confinement and no labor. The legislature amended the program in 1829, maintaining solitary confinement but adding the provision that inmates perform some labor in their cells. In 1833, the small dark cells were torn down, and larger cells with enclosed exercise yards (**outside cells**)[2] were built. The efforts influenced the development of what became the Eastern Penitentiary, located in Philadelphia.

The **Eastern Penitentiary** became the model and primary exponent of the Pennsylvania, or "separate," system. This prison was built like a square wheel, with the cell blocks arranged like spokes around the hub, or central rotunda. The routine at Eastern was solitary confinement, silence, and labor in outside cells. This arrangement clearly stressed the maximum and continuous amount of separation of each inmate from all the others.

Although the Pennsylvania system aroused great international interest, it was adopted by only two other states. The New Jersey State Penitentiary in Trenton began operations in 1837, along the lines of the separate system. It was soon abandoned, however, in favor of that used at Auburn, New York. Rhode Island followed the same pattern as that of New Jersey. Its first prison, built in 1838 along the lines of the Eastern Penitentiary, had abandoned the separate system by 1852. By contrast, many European countries wholeheartedly adopted the Pennsylvania model.[3]

Al Capone's cell in Eastern Prison.
SOURCE: *Tom Berault, courtesy of Eastern State Penitentiary Historic Site, Philadelphia.*

THE AUBURN SYSTEM

The major evils of the jails and other confinement facilities before 1800 were indiscriminate congregate confinement and enforced idleness. The rapid debasement of the prisoners when kept in filthy conditions, with men, women, and children thrown together under a regime of neglect and brutality, appalled the early reformers. The long-term prisons established in the last decade of the eighteenth century were not just a substitute for capital and corporal punishment; they were total administrative and custodial systems intended to remedy the evils of the old methods. In the first quarter of the nineteenth century, administrators experimented with many new systems. The leading contenders for the world's attention were the Eastern Penitentiary and the New York State Prison at Auburn, opened in 1819.

The Auburn prison administrators developed a system that was almost the opposite of that used at the Eastern Penitentiary. The building itself was based on a new **inside cell** design[4] and the cells were quite small when compared with those at Eastern. The small cells were designed to be used only for sleeping, not as a place for work. In addition, a new style of discipline was inaugurated at Auburn that became known as the **Auburn**, or "congregate," **system.**

In the early years of the Auburn prison, administrators tested the efficacy of the Pennsylvania system. They selected 80 of the most hardened convicts, placing them in solitary confinement and enforced idleness for two years, from Christmas 1821 through Christmas 1823. So many of those men succumbed to sickness and insanity that the experiment was discontinued long before the two-year mark. The Auburn administration thus claimed failure for solitary confinement when the method included idleness. Given the small inside cells in Auburn, their claim was no doubt a valid one. However, the Auburn experiment cannot be considered a fair comparison to the Pennsylvania system, because the latter system used large outside cells and provided for handicraft and other labor in the cells.[5]

key term
_____

Inside cells
Prison cells that do not touch the outside walls of the cell block.

key term
_____

Auburn system
Prison model consisting of small individual cells, large work area for group labor, and enforced silence.

Discipline at Auburn

An unfortunate by-product of the badly planned Auburn experiment was the use of solitary confinement as a means of punishment within the prison. The discipline regimen at Auburn also included congregate work in the shops during the day, separation of prisoners into small individual cells at night, silence at all times, lockstep marching formations, and a congregate meal at which the prisoners sat face-to-back.[6] There was great emphasis on silence. In the belief that verbal exchange between prisoners was contaminating, conversation was prevented by liberal use of the whip. An excellent description of the Auburn system in its early stages, drawn from a letter by Louis Dwight (1793–1854), who was an early advocate of the Auburn System, as quoted by Harry Elmer Barnes (1889–1968) follows:

> At Auburn we have a more beautiful example still of what may be done by proper discipline, in a prison well constructed. It is not possible to describe the pleasure which we feel in contemplating this noble institution, after wading through the fraud, and the material and moral filth of many prisons. We regard it as a model worthy of the world's imitation. We do not mean that there is nothing in this institution which admits of improvement; for there have been a few cases of unjustifiable severity in punishments; but, upon the whole, the institution is immensely elevated above the old penitentiaries. The whole establishment, from the gate to the sewer, is a specimen of neatness. The unremitted industry, the entire subordination and subdued feelings of the convicts, has probably no parallel among an equal number of criminals. In their solitary cells they spend the night, with no other book but the Bible, and at sunrise they proceed, in military order, under the eye of the turnkeys, in solid columns, with the lock march, to their workshops; thence, in the same order at the hour of breakfast, to the common hall, where they partake of their wholesome and frugal meal in silence. Not even a whisper is heard; though the silence is such that a whisper might be heard

through the whole apartment. The convicts are seated, in single file, at narrow tables, with their backs towards the center, so that there can be no interchange of signs. If one has more food than he wants, he raises his left hand; and if another has less, he raises his right hand, and the waiter changes it. When they have [finished] eating, at the ringing of a little bell, of the softest sound, they rise from the table, form the solid columns, and return, under the eye of the turnkeys, to the workshops. From one end of the shops to the other, it is the testimony of many witnesses, that they have passed more than three hundred convicts, without seeing one leave his work, or turn his head to gaze at them. There is the most perfect attention to business from morning till night, interrupted only by the time necessary to dine, and never by the fact that the whole body of prisoners have done their tasks, and the time is now their own, and they can do as they please. At the close of the day, a little before sunset, the work is all laid aside at once, and the convicts return, in military order, to the solitary cells, where they partake of the frugal meal, which they were permitted to take from the kitchen, where it was furnished for them as they returned from the shops. After supper, they can, if they choose, read Scripture undisturbed and then reflect in silence on the errors of their lives. They must not disturb their fellow prisoners by even a whisper.[7]

The Auburn system became the pattern for more than 30 state prisons in the next half century. Sing Sing Prison in New York followed the Auburn pattern in 1825. Wethersford Prison in Connecticut copied the Auburn system but used a more moderate form of brutal punishments. Later prisons modeled their disciplinary systems after Wethersford.

Auburn's structural design, with inside cells and wings composed of two to four tiers of cells (**cell blocks**), became the model for most prisons built in the following 150 years. Many variations and innovations on the Auburn concept were developed. The most popular of those types, first constructed in 1898 at Fresnes, France, became known as the "telephone pole" design. Regardless of the cell-block arrangement, the inside cell design became the most common model in America.

One of the more important, but less noted, aspects of early prison architecture was the grand scale and sheer size of the institutions. "Bigger is better" (and more cost effective) was the watchword of early prison builders. Huge gothic-style structures achieved an effect similar to that of the medieval castles or cathedrals of Europe. They made the people inside seem small and insignificant. This feeling was further enhanced by the stern discipline employed in these huge castles of despair. Size is discussed again in later chapters, but we should note here that the size of the early prisons gave rise to a subtle pressure to keep them filled with society's castoffs.

PRISON COMPETITION

The main theme in both the Pennsylvania and Auburn prison systems was the belief that a regimen of silence and penitence would prevent cross infection and encourage improved behavior in the prisoner. Supporters of the Pennsylvania system claimed it was easier to control the prisoners, gave more consideration to their individual needs, prevented contamination by the complete separation of prisoners from one another, and provided more opportunity for meditation and penitence. Another advantage they cited was that prisoners could leave the Pennsylvania system with their background known only to a few administrators, because they did not come in contact with other prisoners.

On the other hand, supporters of the Auburn or congregate system argued that it was cheaper to construct and get started, offered better vocational training, and produced more money for the state.[8] The persuasive power of economics finally decided the battle, and the **congregate system** was adopted in almost all other American prisons, even in Pennsylvania. The Western Penitentiary was converted in 1869 and finally, in 1913, the Eastern Penitentiary changed its system. The capitulation of the Pennsylvania system

---

key term

Cell blocks
Multitier living cells usually stacked one atop the other, built within a hollow building and not touching exterior walls.

class activity

Ask students to describe the Auburn or "congregate" system, as well as the architecture of those prisons. What types of products could reasonably be produced in this type of prison? At what cost?

key term

Congregate system
Prison modeled on the Auburn system with inmate work and feeding done en masse, in total silence.

followed many long years of fierce controversy between the two systems. "The only grat-ifying feature of the controversy was that both systems were so greatly superior to the un-speakable . . . system which they displaced that their competition inevitably worked for the betterment of penal conditions."[9]

PRISON RULES

As mentioned in Chapter 1, prisons can be viewed as yet another method to implement so-cial vengeance for wrongs against society. Europeans examining the Auburn and Pennsylva-nia systems made a keen observation on the American society and its prisons:

> It must be acknowledged that the **penitentiary system** in America is severe. While society in the United States gives the example of the most extended liberty, the prisons of the same country offer the spectacle of the most complete despotism.[10]

In this context, the individual citizen's sense of guilt when he or she inflicts brutal or cruel punishment on another is diffused by the need for revenge on criminal offenders as a class and for the protection of society. The "out of sight, out of mind" principle was espe-cially evident in the early-nineteenth-century prisons. Most of them were located far out in the countryside, free from either interference or inspection by the communities that sup-plied the prisoners. It is not too hard to understand why rules and procedures emphasized the smooth and undisturbed operation of the prison rather than the modification of the in-dividual prisoner's behavior. Administrators were usually judged by the prison's production record and the number of escapes, not by the number of successful rehabilitations. Because of this, rules were designed to keep prisoners under total control. It is those early and well-established prison practices that have been the most difficult to overcome in the emerging standards of good correctional practices.

Elam Lynds, warden of Auburn and later of Sing Sing (which he built), was one of the most influential persons in the development of early prison discipline in America. He is de-scribed as having been an extremely strict **disciplinarian** who believed that all convicts were cowards who could not be reformed until their spirit was broken. To this end he devised a system of brutal punishments and degrading procedures, many of which remained as ac-cepted practice until very recent times.

The imposition of **silence** was seen as the most important part of the discipline program. The rule of absolute silence and noncommunication was maintained and enforced by the im-mediate use of the lash for the slightest infraction. Lynds advocated flogging as the most effec-tive way to maintain order. He sometimes used a "cat" made of barbed wire strands, but more often a rawhide whip. The stereotype of the ex-con who is always talking out of the side of his mouth actually developed in the "silent" prisons to get around the silence rules.

Another bizarre form of discipline that was developed at Auburn was the **lockstep formation**. Prisoners were required to line up in close formation with their hands on the shoulders or under the arms of the prisoner in front. The line then moved rapidly toward its destination as the prisoners shuffled their feet in unison, without lifting them from the ground. Because this nonstop shuffle was "encouraged" by the use of the lash, any pris-oner who fell out of lockstep risked a broken ankle or other serious injury from the steadily moving formation. Breaking the rule of silence during formation was considered especially objectionable and was punished viciously.

The use of degrading prison garb was also initiated at Auburn and Sing Sing. Early prisoners were allowed to wear the same clothing as the free society did. At Auburn and Sing Sing, different colors were used for the first-time offenders and for repeaters. Bizarre outfits served to reveal the prisoners' classification at a glance, to institutionalize them further, and to facilitate identification of escapees. The famous **prison stripes**

key term

Penitentiary system
Prison designed to enforce penitence and prisoner anonymity, with individual manual labor in inmate cells.

key term

Disciplinarian
Prison administrator usually using harsh punishments to reinforce institutional rules.

key term

Silence
Absence of speech between inmates within early prisons.

key term

Lockstep formation
Lines of inmates marching closely behind their leader, with hands on top of shoulders or under the armpits. Requires shuffling and muteness in march from one area of the prison to another.

key term

Prison stripes
Prison uniforms with horizontal black bands and white stripes, frequently colored to designate inmate classification.

A modern chain gang crew helps with community cleanup in Phoenix, Arizona.
SOURCE: *Photo by Jerri Edger, courtesy of Maricopa County Sheriff's Department.*

came into being in 1815 in New York. The stripes were abandoned in most prisons but they have since been returned by the Mississippi legislature in 1994 and by many other local jails and prisons.

The methods used to prevent conversation or communication during meals were also humiliating. As mentioned, prisoners were required to sit face-to-back. They were given their meager, and usually bland and unsavory, meal to eat in silence. If they wanted more food, they would raise one hand; if they had too much they raised the other. Any infraction of the rule of silence resulted in a flogging and the loss of a meal. This kind of entrenched procedure, very resistant to modern reforms, has been the source of many prison riots. Earlier prisons also had **treadmills** on which inmates labored, sometimes for exercise but frequently as a form of physical punishment.

One of the earliest and most well-known forms of prison discipline was the "prison-within-a-prison," or **solitary confinement,** used as punishment for violation of institutional rules. Although the early experiment with total solitary confinement at Auburn showed it could not serve as the basis of a permanent prison system, the administrators saw its possibilities as a punishment for infractions of prison rules. Most of the prisons designed along the Auburn model therefore had a block of cells somewhere inside the walls, often referred to as the "hole." Usually, a sentence to solitary confinement was accompanied by reduced rations as well, consisting often of only bread and water. Solitary confinement is frequently used to discipline prisoners even today, although under much more humane conditions.

The many new prisons that were constructed in the century after the Eastern Penitentiary and the Auburn Prison made few, if any, contributions to the development of penology or corrections. The two greatest innovations, which persist today, were prison industries and the massive structures that used the interior cell-block design. Enforced silence was finally seen as a failure and abandoned. Cruel and barbaric punishments, though publicly decried, are still sometimes used—largely because most prisons are isolated from society and its controls. The development of corrections between 1800 and 1870, using policies, procedures, and philosophies that were unjust, still produced better results than did the universally accepted capital and corporal punishment that preceded it. And in the following era the swing toward a more realistic and humanistic correctional approach began.

CHANGE IN THE WIND

Maconochie and Crofton: A New Approach

The reformatory system in America owes a great deal to the work of an Englishman, Captain Alexander Maconochie, and an Irishman, Sir Walter Crofton. Together they laid the foundation for reformative rather than purely punitive programs for the treatment of criminals.

Maconochie and the Indeterminate Sentence

A "sweat box" punishment cell for solitary confinement.
SOURCE: *Photo by Peter C. Unsinger, courtesy of American Correctional Association. Reprinted with permission.*

In 1840, Captain Maconochie was put in charge of the British penal colony on Norfolk Island, about 800 miles east of Australia. To this island were sent the criminals who were "twice condemned": They had been shipped to Australia from England and then from Australia to Norfolk. Conditions were so bad at Norfolk that men reprieved from the death penalty wept, and those who were to die thanked God[11]—that was the kind of hell Maconochie inherited.

The first thing Maconochie did was to eliminate the flat sentence,[12] a system that had allowed no hope of release until the full time had been served. Then he developed a "mark system" whereby a convict could earn freedom by hard work and good behavior, thus creating the **indeterminate sentence**. This type of sentencing put the burden of release on the convict. As Maconochie said, "When a man keeps the key of his own prison, he is soon persuaded to fit it into the lock." The system had five principles:

1. Release should not be based on the completion of a sentence for a set period of time, but on the completion of a determined and specified quantity of labor. In brief, time sentences should be abolished, and task sentences substituted.
2. The quantity of labor a prisoner must perform should be expressed in a number of "marks," which he must earn, by improvement of conduct, frugality of living, and habits of industry, before he can be released.
3. While in prison he should earn everything he receives. All sustenance and indulgences should be added to his debt of marks.
4. When qualified by discipline to do so, he should work in association with a small number of other prisoners, forming a group of six or seven, and the whole group should be answerable for the conduct and labor of each member.
5. In the final stage, a prisoner, while still obliged to earn his daily tally of marks, should be given a proprietary interest in his own labor and be subject to a less rigorous discipline, to prepare him for release into society.[13]

It is a sad fact that Maconochie's visionary efforts toward rehabilitation were not appreciated or supported by the unenlightened bureaucrats above him. His results thus were disclaimed, and the colony fell back into its former brutalized routine almost as soon as he left it.

<u>key term</u>

Indeterminate sentence
A period of confinement with specified minimum and maximum length, allowing a parole board to release the inmate when rehabilitation has been achieved.

Crofton and the Irish System

Fortunately, Maconochie's ideas did reach beyond the shores of Norfolk Island. His successful use of the indeterminate sentence[14] showed that imprisonment could be used to prepare a convict for eventual return to the community. If this were true, then the length of sentence should not be an arbitrary period of time but should be related to the rehabilitation of the offender. Sir Walter Crofton of Ireland used that concept in developing what he called the "indeterminate system," which came to be known as the **Irish system**. He reasoned that if penitentiaries are places where offenders think about their crimes and can decide to stop their criminal misbehavior ("repent"), there must be a mechanism to determine that this decision has in fact been made, as well as a mechanism for getting the inmate out when penitence has been done. The indeterminate sentence was believed to be the best mechanism.

The system Crofton devised, like Maconochie's, consisted of a series of stages, each bringing the convict closer to the free society. The first stage was solitary confinement and monotonous work. The second stage was assignment to public works and a progression through various grades, each grade shortening the length of stay. The last stage was assignment to an intermediate prison where the prisoner worked without supervision and moved in and out of the free community. If the prisoner's conduct continued to be good and if he or she were able to find employment, the offender returned to the community on a conditional pardon or **ticket-of-leave**. This ticket could be revoked at any time within the span of the original fixed sentence if the prisoner's conduct was not up to standards established by those who supervised the conditional pardon. Crofton's plan was the first effort to establish a system of **conditional liberty** in the community, the system we know today as parole.

THE REFORMATORY ERA (1870 TO 1910)

Leaders in U.S. penology and prison administration met at the American Prison Congress of 1870[15] to discuss the direction that corrections practices should take. They were especially concerned about overcrowding, and they discussed what new kinds of prisons should be built to alleviate it. Many urged that Maconochie's and Crofton's plans be adopted in America. The members endorsed that idea, and the reformatory era in American corrections was born.

The first **reformatory** in America was built in 1876, in Elmira, New York, and became the model for all those that followed. **Zebulon Brockway**, the first superintendent, had introduced some new educational methods at the Detroit House of Corrections, and he expanded on that concept at Elmira. Elmira was originally built for adult felons, but it was used instead for youths from 16 to 30 years of age who were serving their first term in prison. One observer cited the following characteristics as the standards for Elmira, and many such characteristics reappeared in its imitators:

1. The material structural establishment itself. The general plan and arrangements should be those of the Auburn system, modified and modernized; and 10 percent of the cells might well be constructed like those of the Pennsylvania system. The whole should be supplied with suitable modern sanitary appliances and with abundance of natural and artificial light.
2. Clothing—not degradingly distinctive, but uniform, . . . fitly representing the respective grades or standing of the prisoners. . . . Scrupulous cleanliness should be maintained and the prisoners appropriately groomed.
3. A liberal prison diet designed to promote vigor. Deprivation of food, by a general regulation, is deprecated. . . .
4. All the modern appliances for scientific physical culture; a gymnasium completely equipped with baths and apparatus; and facilities for field athletics.

5. Facilities for manual training sufficient for about one-third of the population. . . . This special manual training covers, in addition to other exercises in other departments, mechanical and freehand drawing; sloyd [manual training] in wood and metals; cardboard constructive form work; clay modeling; cabinet making; clipping and filing; and iron molding.
6. Trade instruction based on the needs and capacities of individual prisoners. (Where a thousand prisoners are involved, thirty-six trades may be usefully taught.)
7. A regimental military organization with a band of music, swords for officers, and dummy guns for the rank and file of prisoners.
8. School of letters with a curriculum that reaches from an adaptation of the kindergarten . . . up to the usual high school course; and, in addition, special classes in college subjects. . . .
9. A well-selected library for circulation, consultation, and for occasional semi-social use.
10. The weekly institutional newspaper, in lieu of all outside newspapers, edited and printed by the prisoners under due censorship.
11. Recreating and diverting entertainments for the mass of the population, provided in the great auditorium; not any vaudeville or minstrel shows, but entertainments of such a class as the middle cultured people of a community would enjoy. . . .
12. Religious opportunities . . . adapted to the hereditary [and] habitual . . . denominational predilection of the individual prisoners.
13. Definitely planned, carefully directed, emotional occasions; not summoned, primarily, for either instruction, diversion, nor, specifically, for a common religious impression, but, figuratively, for a kind of irrigation.[16]

The only real differences between the programs at Elmira and those at the adult prisons were the emphasis on reforming youth, increased academic education, and more extensive trade training. Two significant features were adopted for the reformatories, though: the indeterminate sentence and a grading system based on marks that could lead to parole.

Elmira was copied, in one form or another, by 17 states between 1876 and 1913. Brockway's leadership produced the first attempt to offer programs of education and reformation to all inmates, adult or youth. Trade training, academic education, and the military type of discipline utilized at Elmira undoubtedly also influenced the programs of many of the older prisoners. Some aspects of the indeterminate sentence and parole concepts were finally extended to the state prisons. It is not surprising that in an era when public education was considered to be the answer to so many problems in the outside world, it was viewed as the answer to crime as well. But because the same physical environment and the same underpaid and poorly qualified personnel found in prisons were also found in reformatories, those institutions were soon reduced to junior prisons with the usual routine. The same-old "prison discipline" was still the most dominant feature in any penal program.

Although the two main contributions of the reformatory era were the indeterminate sentence and parole, the seeds of education, vocational training, and individual rehabilitation had been sown. Even though such radical ideas could not flourish in the barren and hostile environment of that period, they took root and grew to fruition in later years.

POST–CIVIL WAR PRISONS

The 16 states that built prisons between 1870 and 1900 were almost all in the northern or western part of the country. Their only claim to improvement was the introduction of plumbing and running water. All were of the Auburn type, and the only modifications in the older prison routine were the abandonment of the silent system and the use of the indeterminate sentence and parole.

In the South, devastated by the Civil War, the penitentiary system had been virtually wiped out. Some states attempted to solve their prison problems by leasing out their entire

class activity

Ask students to identify Captain Alexander Maconochie and explain the offender problems he faced. What were his solutions?

class activity

After the class discusses Maconochie, repeat the same questions for Sir Walter Crofton. Show how both implemented the indeterminate sentence solution.

class activity

Ask the students to define the *reformatory* and why the reformatory movement began. What challenges did such a movement face? Was it successful? If the consensus is "no," ask what could have been done to have made it successful.

lecture note

Explain the development of the federal Bureau of Prisons, and note the contributions of leadership, absence of prison plants, and availability of federal funds to the federal prison system. Why did it become a much-admired model?

key term

Lease system
The hiring of inmates to
perform work details managed
by private entrepreneurs,
either while out of or still
incarcerated in prison facilities.

convict population to contractors, which became known as the **lease system**.[17] Others took
in contract work or devised combinations of both leasing out prisoners and taking in contracts. Yet another group of slaves thus replaced the freed blacks: the convicted felons. The
South was unique in that many of its prisons ignored both the Auburn and reformatory systems. The South's agrarian economy made exploitation of cheap labor both easy and desirable. A large portion of the prison population in the South was composed of plantation
blacks who had no influence or resources, and they were treated with no mercy.[18] Leasing
was eventually replaced by prison farms in most southern states, but the practice was not
completely erased until the mid-1920s. This sordid period in penal history, brought to light
again in the 1960s in Arkansas,[19] simply confirms the depths to which even so-called civilized people can sink in the treatment of their castoffs. The correctional experience in the
South made only a negative contribution in regard to both procedure and discipline.

THE TWENTIETH CENTURY
AND THE INDUSTRIAL PRISON

class activity

Ask students what effects the
American Civil War had on
prisons and offenders. Focus
student attention on migration
of citizens to cities,
unemployment, and
entrepreneurial efforts to "make
a buck" off the backs of
offenders. If students perceive
contracting as profit-motivated,
ask them if there are any prisons
on the contemporary scene that
are private-sector prison
providers. Are they "making a
buck" off the backs of
offenders? If the consensus is
"yes," ask if correctional officer
unions are motivated by money
concerns.

The introduction of handicrafts into the solitary Eastern Penitentiary cells represented the origin of prison industries in America. In continental Europe and England, the infamous efforts
to provide labor in the workhouses and Bridewells had resulted in such fruitless activities as
the treadmill. The modern pressure to provide vocational training or earnings for inmates did
not concern early American prison administrators; rather, they wanted to make the prisons
self-sustaining. Toward this goal, the prison workshops were merely extensions of the early
factory workshops. When the factory production system was introduced into prisons and they
began to show actual profits from their output, legislators were quickly convinced that prison
industries were a sound operation. The Auburn system held out over the less efficient Pennsylvania system because it paid better returns on taxpayer investment. By the 1860s, the system of absolute silence had begun to fall apart because of the necessity for communication in
the industrial shops. Early prison industries, in effect, exploited the available free labor for the
sole purpose of perpetuating the institution itself. Some leaders in the field, however, saw that
a change in emphasis could make the industries an important factor in prisoner rehabilitation.

From the beginning of the twentieth century until 1940, the number of inmates in U.S.
prisons increased by 174%.[20] Ten new Auburn-style prisons and even one based on Bentham's Panopticon were built during this period—often referred to as the industrial era for
prisons in America, which finally reached its zenith in 1935. The new prisons were considered "as cold and hard and abnormal as the prisoners whom they were intended to persuade
toward better things."[21]

key term

Industrial prison
Any penal institution whose
main objective is the use of
inmate labor to produce
marketable products for prison
profit.

The **industrial prison** can credit its origins to the profits turned by the first state prisons. Early in the nineteenth century, however, mechanics and cabinetmakers began to complain about the unfair competition they faced from the virtually free labor force available
within prisons. The use of lease and contract systems aggravated the problem and led to a
series of investigations that reached national prominence in 1886. The emergence of the labor union movement, coupled with abuses of the contract and lease systems of prison labor, eliminated those systems in the northern prisons by the end of the nineteenth century.
They were replaced by piece-price[22] and state-account[23] systems. Opposition to prison industries resulted in enforced idleness among the increasing inmate population. This forced
the adult prisons to adopt reformatory methods in some measure but made self-sustaining
institutions a thing of the past.

key term

Hawes–Cooper Act
Federal legislation that forbids
the manufacture and
transportation of prison goods
by convicts and prisoners.

Because the story of the prison industry's battle with organized labor is a history in itself,
it is not covered here. The beginning of the end for large-scale prison industries, which kept inmates employed in some kind of work, was the enactment of two federal laws controlling the
character of prison products. The **Hawes–Cooper Act**, passed in 1929, required that prison

correctional **brief**

Hawes–Cooper Act, Chap. 79. (1929)

Be it enacted by the Senate and House of Representatives of the United States of America in Congress assembled, That all goods, wares, and merchandise manufactured, produced, or mined, wholly or in part, by convicts or prisoners, except convicts or prisoners on parole or probation, or in any penal and/or reformatory institutions, except commodities manufactured in Federal penal and correctional institutions for use by the Federal Government, transported into any State or Territory of the United States and remaining therein for use, consumption, sale, or storage, shall upon ar-

rival and delivery in such State or Territory be subject to the operation and effect of the laws of such State or Territory to the same extent and in the same manner as though such goods, wares, and merchandise had been manufactured, produced, or mined in such State or Territory, and shall not be exempt therefrom by reason of being introduced in the original package or otherwise.

Sec.2   This act shall take effect five years after the date of its approval. Approved, January 19, 1929.

---

products be subject to the laws of any state to which they were shipped. The **Ashurst–Sumners Act**, passed in 1935, essentially stopped the interstate transport of prison products by requiring that all prison products shipped out of the state be labeled with the prison name and by prohibiting interstate shipment where state laws forbade it. In 1940, the Ashurst-Sumners Act was amended to prohibit fully the interstate shipment of prison products.

The economic strains of the Great Depression, beginning with the Wall Street stock market crash in 1929 and spanning the period from 1929 to 1940, led 33 states to pass laws that prohibited the sale of prison products on the open market. Those statutes tolled the death knell for the industrial prison. With the exception of a few license plate and state furniture shops, most state prisons took a giant step backward to their original purposes: punishment and custody. Fortunately, another model was emerging at the same time: the "new penology" of the 1930s and the U.S. Bureau of Prisons under the leadership of **Sanford Bates**.

Sanford Bates is a legendary figure in American corrections. He served as the President of the American Correctional Association (1925), became the first superintendent of federal prisons (1929), and was selected as the first director of the U.S. Bureau of the Prisons (1930). Later he served as commissioner of the New York State Board of Parole, and then commissioner of the New Jersey Department of Institutions and Agencies.

key term

Ashurst-Sumners Act
Federal legislation requiring "truth of manufacturing, transportation and interstate shipment of prison-made goods" by requirement that the packages to be plainly and clearly marked.

profile

Sanford Bates
First director of the U.S. Bureau of Prisons

correctional **brief**

Ashurst–Sumners Act, Chap. 412 (1935)

Be it enacted by the Senate and House of Representatives of the United States of America in Congress assembled, That it shall be unlawful for any person knowingly to transport or cause to be transported, in any manner or by any means whatsoever or aid or assist in obtaining transportation for or in transporting any goods, wares and merchandise manufactured, produced, or mined wholly or in part by convicts or prisoners [except convicts or prisoners on parole or probation], or in any penal or reformatory institution, from one State, Territory, Puerto Rico, Virgin islands, or District of the United States, or place noncontiguous but subject to the jurisdiction thereof, or from any foreign country, into any State, Territory, Puerto Rico, Virgin Islands, or District of the United States, or place noncontiguous but subject to the jursidiction thereof, where said goods, wares, and merchandise are intended by any person interested therein to be received, possessed, sold, or in any manner used, either in the original package or otherwise

in violation of any law of such State, Territory, Puerto Rico, Virgin Islands, or District of the United States, or place noncontiguous but subject to the jurisdiction thereof. Nothing herein shall apply to commodities manufactured in Federal penal and correctional institutions for use by the Federal Government.

Sec. 2   All packages containing any goods, wares, and merchandise manufactured, produced, or mined wholly or in part by convicts or prisoners, except convicts or prisoners on parole or probation, or in any penal or reformatory institution, when shipped or transported in interstate or foreign commerce shall be plainly and clearly marked, so that the name and address of the shipper, the name and address of the consignee, the nature of the contents, and the name and location of the penal or reformatory institution where produced wholly or in part may be readily ascertained on an inspection of the outside of such package.

class activity

Ask students to describe the industrial prison in its heyday. Have the class focus on in-prison ("intramural"), inmate lease, and the piece-price programs. Is it better to have inmates idle or working to generate profits?

key term

Alcatraz

A supermax island prison for inmates in the San Francisco Bay Area and part of the U.S. Bureau of Prisons until its closing; also known as "the Rock".

key term

Lock psychosis

Term denoting overconcentration of prison administrators with security and community protection, to be accomplished through extensive use of locks, head counts, and internal control of inmates.

key term

Convict bogey

Irrational fear of prison inmates who can only be managed through head counts, locking, and recounting.

class activity

Ask students why the industrial prison waned during the Great Depression. What effects did its retrenchment have on prison administration?

THE PERIOD OF TRANSITION (1935 TO 1960)

The quarter century between 1935 and 1960 was one of great turmoil in the prisons. Administrators, stuck with the huge fortresses of the previous century, were now deprived of the ability to provide meaningful work for inmates. The Depression, influx of new immigrants, and criminal excesses of the 1920s and 1930s hardened the public's attitude toward convict rehabilitation at a time when behavioral scientists were just beginning to propose hopeful reforms in prisoner treatment. J. Edgar Hoover, director of the Federal Bureau of Investigation (FBI), led the battle against "hoity-toity professors" and the "cream-puff school of criminology." His war on crime helped give the world the supermaximum prison, **Alcatraz**. Located on an island in San Francisco Bay, Alcatraz was constructed to house the most hardened criminals confined in the federal prison system. When it was built in 1934, it was seen as the answer to the outrages of such desperate criminals as Al Capone, Robert Stroud ("Birdman of Alcatraz"), and Bonnie and Clyde. Eventually, the U.S. Bureau of Prisons abandoned this prison as too expensive to maintain.

Such notables as Bernard Glueck at Sing Sing between 1915 and 1920, Edgar Doll and W. G. Ellis in New Jersey in 1925, and A. W. Stearns in Massachusetts in 1930 pioneered early efforts toward diagnostic classification and casework. Sanford Bates introduced procedures into the U.S. Bureau of Prisons in 1934. Although sometimes "borrowing" principles from states across the nation, the U.S. Bureau of Prisons gradually emerged as the national leader in corrections, introducing many new concepts that have been copied by state systems. Two major contributions were diagnosis and classification and the use of professional personnel such as psychiatrists and psychologists to help rehabilitate inmates. The federal system also led the way to more humane treatment and better living conditions (see Chapter 11). But no matter how they were cleaned up, prisons remained monuments to idleness, monotony, frustration, and repression. Despite attempts to tear down the massive walls around some prisons, the forces of **lock psychosis** continued to hold out. Prison inmates were feared as the **convict bogey**, which could be dealt with only by locking and relocking, counting and recounting. Interestingly, the convict bogey is the unreasonable fear by prison administrators that leads them to lock prisoners behind several layers of barred doors and other barricades. Counts are usually conducted several times a day to ensure that all prisoners are locked up. (Modern correctional administrations use plastic wrist identifier bands for continuous inmate counting and location.)

It is not too surprising that the long hours of idleness, forbidding architecture, growing populations, and unnecessarily repressive controls created unbearable tensions among the inmates. The first riots in this country, as noted earlier, were at the mineshaft prison in Simsbury, Connecticut. (A riot is a violent, tumultuous disturbance within the prison or other correctional institutional involving seven or more inmates assembled together and acting as a common cause.) Riots at the Walnut Street Jail were reported in the early 1800s as well. The mid-nineteenth century, when prison industries provided extensive work for convicts, was a time of few riots. Presumably, either the inmates were too tired to riot or the control was too strict. As the prison industries died out, riots began to take place more regularly, adding evidence to the theory that enforced idleness causes restlessness and discontent among prisoners. There was a wave of riots in the prisons between 1929 and 1932. During World War II there were few problems, but in 1946 there was even a riot in Alcatraz, the superprison.

Whether neglect of prisons and lack of meaningful activities finally bore bitter fruit or whether the rising prosperity of the 1950s simply presented too sharp a contrast with the bleak life on the inside, there was an explosion of prison discontent during the early part of that decade. More than 300 prison riots have occurred since 1774, and 90% of those have occurred in the last four decades.[24] The American Correctional Association investigated the 1950s riots and reported what appeared to be the main causes:[25]

1. Inadequate financial support and official and public indifference
2. Substandard personnel
3. Enforced idleness
4. Lack of professional leadership and professional programs

5. Excessive size and overcrowding of institutions
6. Political domination and motivation of management
7. Unwise sentencing and parole practices

The explosion predicted from the conditions created by overcrowding, idleness, and lack of public concern erupted at Attica in the fall of 1971. The modern era became a period of seeking ways to prevent such events: Community-based corrections became the watchword for reform in corrections, and the "correctional filter" (discussed in Chapter 6) was supplied with more outlets for diverting inmates from seething, overcrowded prisons. Supreme Court decisions created further pressure for reform. The result, at least until the end of the 1970s, was a state of uneasy status quo. The status quo was broken in the beginning of the 1980s by riots at a New Mexico prison, which resulted in numerous brutal deaths and public outrage. Prison riots continued; in 1996, there were four prison riots over three days in federal prisons. In 2001, several inmates were injured in a California prison riot, and, in 2004, there was a riot in a privately run correctional institution in Kentucky.[26]

It appears now that some of the programs designed to relieve the problems in the overcrowded fortress prisons have in fact contributed to many of the conditions and made them even riper for violence. Prison gangs (institutional threat groups) elevate tension, conflict, and riots. The fortress prisons are still here, they are even more overcrowded, and their maximum-security clients are now the "bottom of the barrel" regarding behavioral problems. This has caused an abandonment of the medical model and steady movement toward a model emphasizing custody and control over everything else in a futile effort to keep peace in the institutions and "protect society." The problem of selecting a philosophy or ideology that is effective and reflective of society's mood is a problem administrators will have to confront in the next decade. To comprehend the current issues in corrections, we must examine the decision process and options available to the prosecution, judiciary, and releasing authorities.

class activity

Ask the class to describe what happened to prison administration from 1920 through the 1960s, focusing on the Bureau of Prisons' contributions, the events immediately after World War II, and prison riots.

THE MODERN ERA

The "modern era" of corrections is generally considered to have begun about 1960, and it was characterized by a pattern of change that was to highlight the next decade. The 1960s era in the United States was noted for turbulent and violent confrontations at almost every level of activity affecting human rights. The forces for change at work in the overall society were also reflected in great pressures for change in corrections. The dramatic reinterpretations of criminal law, the civil rights movement, violent and nonviolent demonstrations in the streets, the assassinations of a popular president and two other important national figures, the continuation of the longest and most unpopular war in American history—all of these outside pressures were also felt inside the walls of the nation's prisons. Reaction took the form of periodic violent prison riots and disorders. The U.S. Supreme Court emerged as the primary external agent for the enforced recognition of the basic rights of those swept up in the criminal justice system. This external pressure was generated by a long series of significant judicial interpretations. In addition, leadership and funding by the federal government were given to correctional administrators and planners at the state and local levels, enabling them to create, implement, and evaluate new standards, policies, and practices. Unfortunately, aspiring politicians and the media have collectively generated and nurtured inaccurate stereotypes about offenders, blunting correctional gains and giving rise to more intractable problems.[27] The conservative movement in the political arena continues to cause a steady move to the right in corrections, wreaking havoc with the shrinking efforts at rehabilitation, which works. The turmoil continues.

INTERNALLY SOUGHT REFORM

Early prisons were less secure than modern ones, and escape was far more common. It was easier to "disappear" into early American society with a new name and a new start. Inmate

class activity

Ask the class to explain the civil rights movement that began in 1955 and how it affected prisons. Focus student discussion on decisions by the U.S. Supreme Court.

lecture note

Explain the concept of the "standards of human decency that mark the emergence of a maturing society" and how the federal judiciary became a major force of correctional reform.

homework

Assign students to read "How Hollywood Reformed the Georgia Prison System" (http://www.trouparchives.org/burns.html) and write a one-paragraph answer to the question: How did Robert Elliott Burns contribute to the reform of corrections in Georgia?

k e y   t e r m

Ombudsman
Correctional overseer who investigates reported complaints (as from inmates, prison personnel, and prison staff), reports findings, and helps to achieve equitable settlements.

k e y   t e r m

War on Drugs
A criminal justice program focusing on reducing the manufacture, use, sale, or trafficking of drugs.

security and control, improved in recent years, have made escape from prisons difficult; and systems of identification and control, including computer banks of data on each of us, have made escape into society almost impossible.

When the prisons became so secure that relief and escape were cut off, the inmates' frustration and agitation turned inward. Prisoners in this "total institution"[28] used disturbances and riots to express their desire for reforms and changes in rules and conditions. Disturbances also served to resolve power struggles between prison gangs[29] and inmate groups. The early disturbances were characterized by disorganization and rapid dispersion; inmates used those methods to settle old grudges, refusing to fall in line behind any kind of leadership. In the 1960s and 1970s, disturbances were commonplace in most large state systems, reflecting the usual grievances: crowded living conditions, harsh rules, poor food, excessive punishment, and guard brutality.[30] Even the highly respected federal prison system was rocked in 1987 by large-scale hostage taking by Cuban inmates who feared deportation. The growing awareness of individual rights on the outside that began in the 1960s led inmates to seek the same rights inside prisons.

Beginning about 1966, the nature of the demands changed from those involving basic conditions to those concerning basic rights. In that year, the Maryland Penitentiary in Baltimore was the scene of a riot involving over 1,000 inmates. The warden claimed the disturbance was caused by heat waves and overcrowding, but "the riot had to have social overtones," said Joseph Bullock, a member of the state house of delegates. "If they don't stop telling these people [blacks] about their rights," Bullock went on, "things will get worse."[31] Rioting and violence spilled over from the streets into the prisons of America. The "political prisoner" label, particularly for blacks and Chicanos, offered a more acceptable way for minority groups to state their feelings of deprivation. They struck out at a system that they perceived gave them an unequal start in life and then jailed them for failing to live up to the rules of that system.[32] Clearly, outside social behavior and conditions do carry over into prison. Little that is new in society starts in prison.

Change, though often temporary, comes about as a result of prison riots. More often today, new voices can help shape prison policies, through an inmate council, grievance procedures, conflict resolution,[33] or inmates serving on regular prison committees, following a collaborative model. Some systems also use an **ombudsman** as a link between the prisoner and the establishment; this official receives and investigates complaints and sees that corrective action is taken. Correctional administrators have learned that the more diverse the correctional staff, the fewer the inmate assaults on other inmates and staff.[34]

The Prison Population Boom

From 1980 to 2008, at the time of this writing, the number of prison inmates in the nation increased more than 365%, from 320,000 to 1,570,815 prisoners. This population boom resulted from fear of crime[35] fueled by politicians, a "get-tough approach to crime," the **War on Drugs**, the media, and special interest groups. Yet crime declined significantly during the past two decades. The level of violence also generally declined during the past few years, but the level of fear has remained steady. Fear of violence, drive-by shootings, juvenile gangs struggling to control the drug trade, drug use, and racism have combined to support a "get-tough" environment.

The results, covered in more detail in later chapters, were rapid prison population expansion (see Figure 2.1) and an unprecedented growth in prison construction, increased prison overcrowding, reduction of early-release mechanisms from prison, and massive jail populations and jail construction. Alternatives to prison—probation, parole, and so-called intermediate punishments—also increased during this time, but did not significantly reduce the pressure to build correctional facilities. Alternatives are needed not only to build-

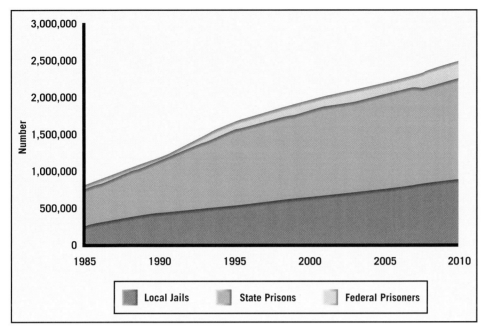

figure 2.1

Number of Inmates in Custody, 1985–2010*

*Data extrapolated to 2010.

From Bureau of Justice Statistics, *Prisoners in 2007* (Washington, DC: BJS, 2008), p. 2.

ing of jails and prisons, but also for policies to buttress and expand corrections in the community. New ideas and programs are badly needed, as the contemporary corrections field appears to be under considerable strain.

Summary

Now, with the first decade of the twenty-first century almost over, corrections in America finds itself at a crossroads, a crisis unparalleled in the past 200 years. The remainder of this textbook will describe in detail current developments and practices in corrections, innovations, proposed solutions, and ways to ease the crisis and improve the effectiveness of the system. To understand those recent developments, we need to explore the correctional ideologies detailed in the next chapter.

Key Words

Pennsylvania system, 21

outside cell, 21

Eastern Penitentiary, 21

inside cell, 25

Auburn system, 25

cell block, 26

congregate system, 26

penitentiary system, 27

disciplinarian, 27

silence, 27

lockstep formation, 27

prison stripes, 27

treadmill, 28

solitary confinement, 28

indeterminate sentence, 29

Irish system, 30

ticket-of-leave, 30

conditional liberty, 30

reformatory, 30

Zebulon Brockway, 30

lease system, 32

industrial prison, 32

Hawes–Cooper Act, 32

Ashurst–Sumners Act, 33

Sanford Bates, 33

Alcatraz, 34

lock psychosis, 34

convict bogey, 34

ombudsman, 36

War on Drugs, 36

Review Questions

1. What effect did the Industrial Revolution have on prisons and prison discipline?
2. Which of the two early nineteenth-century prison systems won out in America? Why?
3. What were the major differences between prisons and reformatories?
4. Why have so many riots occurred in prisons?
5. How were American prison industries reduced in correctional importance?

Endnotes

1. The Philadelphia Society for the Alleviation of the Miseries of Public Prisons was originally formed by a group of concerned citizens in 1787. Because of their continued efforts, the law of 1790 was passed, and the Walnut Street Jail was remodeled to accommodate felons in solitary confinement. The society is now the Pennsylvania Prison Society (245 N. Broad Street, Suite 300, Philadelphia, PA 19107-1518; [215]564-6005; http://www.prisonsociety.org).

2. Outside cells were each about six feet wide, eight feet deep, and nine feet high, with a central corridor extending the length of the building in between. Some of them had individual yards added on the outside, with high walls between them.

3. That system, in modified form, is used to this day in Belgium, France, and West Germany. Additional international correctional material can be found under "Foreign Coverage" in each issue of *American Jails* and in the *International Journal of Comparative and Applied Criminal Justice*. See also Elmer Johnson, "Rule Violation of Japanese Inmates," *International Journal of Comparative and Applied Criminal Justice* 22:1 (1998): 17–30.

4. Inside cells are built back-to-back in tiers within a hollow building. Doors open onto galleries or runs that are eight to ten feet from the outside wall; cells are small and intended only for sleeping. The interior cell block has become characteristic of American prisons.

5. The argument continues. See John Roberts, *Reform and Retribution: An Illustrated History of American Prisons* (Lanham, MD: American Correctional Association, 1997); and Norman Johnston, "The World's Most Influential Prison: Success or Failure?" *The Prison Journal* 84:4(S) (2004): 20S–40S.

6. Walter C. Reckless, *The Crime Problem,* 4th ed. (New York: Appleton-Century-Crofts, 1969), p. 548.

7. Harry Elmer Barnes, *The Story of Punishment,* 2nd ed. (Montclair, NJ: Patterson Smith, 1972), p. 136.

8. Robert G. Caldwell, *Criminology,* 2nd ed. (New York: Ronald Press, 1965), p. 506. See also George Goldman, M. McWilliams, and Vijay Pradhan, *The Economic Impact of Production in California Prison Industries* (Berkeley, CA: Department of Agriculture and Resource Economics, University of California, 1998). But see Corrections and Criminal Justice Coalition, "California Prison Industries Worth in Question," http://www.ccjc.org/id2.htm (accessed January 12, 2005).

9. Barnes, *The Story of Punishment,* p. 140.

10. G. de Beaumont and A. de Tocqueville, *On the Penitentiary System in the United States and Its Application in France* (Philadelphia: Francis Lieber, 1833). See also Marc Mauer, "The Use of Incarceration as a Crime Control Strategy," http://www.sentencingproject.org/Admin/Documents/Publications/OSF-SA_Annual_Report_2006-7%209.pdf (accessed September 3, 2008).

11. Robert Waite, "From Penitentiary to Reformatory: The Road to Prison Reform," in Louis Knafler (ed.), *Criminal Justice History: An International Annual,* Vol. 12 (Westport, CT: Greenwood Press, 1993), pp. 85–106. See also Bob Reece, *The Origins of Irish Convict Transportation to New South Wales* (New York: Palgrave, 2001). A brief biography can be found at ACT Corrective Services, "Biography of Alexander Maconochie," http://www.cs.act.gov.au/amc/home/ambiography (accessed September 3, 2008).

12. Flat sentence refers to a specific period of time (for example, five years, ten years) in confinement for an offense, with no time off for any reason.

13. Harry Elmer Barnes and Negley K. Teeters, *New Horizons in Criminology,* 3rd ed. (Englewood Cliffs, NJ: Prentice Hall, 1959), p. 419. See also Gilbert Geis, "Negley K. Teeters (1896–1971)," *The Prison Journal* 84:4S (2004): 5S–19S.

14. An indeterminate sentence usually has broad beginning and end figures (three to five years, one to ten years, and so on), instead of a certain fixed period. Prisoners are allowed to earn their freedom by means of good conduct. For the Irish experience, see Burke Carroll, *Colonial Discipline: The Making of the Irish Convict System* (Dublin: Four Courts Press, 2001).

15. Progressive penologists of the era met in Cincinnati, Ohio, on October 12, 1870, to plan the ideal prison system. Two earlier attempts to gather had failed, but this meeting of the American Prison Congress developed into the National Prison Association, later the American Correctional Association (4380 Forbes Avenue, Lanham, MD 20706-4322).

16. Barnes and Teeters, *New Horizons in Criminology,* p. 426.

17. Georgia, Florida, Mississippi, Louisiana, and Arkansas, in particular, followed this procedure. See Matthew Mancini, *One Dies, Get Another: Convict Leasing in the American South, 1866–1928* (Columbia, SC: University of South Carolina Press, 1996).

18. Harry E. Allen and Julie C. Abril, "The New Chain Gang: Corrections in the Next Century," *American Journal of Criminal Justice* 22:1 (1997): 1–12. See also Timothy Dodge, "State Convict Road Gangs in Alabama," *The Alabama Review* 53:4 (2000): 243–270.

19. Tom Murton and Joe Hyams, *Accomplices to the Crime: The Arkansas Prison Scandal* (New York: Grove Press, 1967).

20. Margaret Calahan, *Historical Corrections Statistics in the United States: 1850–1984* (Washington, DC: U.S. Department of Justice, 1986), p. 36.

21. Wayne Morse, *The Attorney General's Survey of Release Procedures* (Washington, DC: U.S. Government Printing Office, 1940).

22. Under the piece-price system, a variation of the contract system, the contractor supplied the raw material and paid a price for each delivered finished product. Thailand currently uses this system.

23. In the state-account or public-account system, all employment and activity are under the direction of the state, and products are sold on the open market. The prisoner receives a very small wage, and the profit goes to the state. Usually binder twine, rope, and hemp sacks were produced this way; it provided a lot of work for prisoners, but little training. See American Correctional Association, *A Study of Prison Industry: History, Components, and Goals* (Washington, DC: U.S. Department of Justice, 1986); and Queensland Criminal Justice Consortium, *Queensland Prison Industries 9* (Brisbane, Australia: QCJC, 2000).

24. See Mike Rolland, *Descent into Madness: An Inmate's Experience of the New Mexico State Prison Riot* (Cincinnati, OH: Anderson, 1997). A California prison riot in 2008 sent 22 inmates to local hospitals. See Victorville Daily Press, "Adelanto Prison Riot Sends 22 Inmates to Area Hospitals," http://vvdailypress.com/news/prison_5106_article.html/fire_schramm.html (accessed September 3, 2008).

25. As cited in Barnes and Teeters, *New Horizons in Criminology,* p. 385.

26. Jennifer Harry, "Several Injured in California Prison Riot," *Corrections Today* 63:7 (2001): 12; and Deborah Yetter and Mark Pitsch, "Prison Riot Followed Increase in Inmates," http://www.courier-journal.com/localnews/2004/09/17ky/A1-prison0917-8527.html (accessed January 12, 2005).

27. Brent Staples, "Why Some Politicians Need Their Prisons to Stay Full," http://www.prisonersoffthecensus.org/fact_27-12-2004.shtml (accessed January 12, 2005); and James Inciardi, "The Irrational Policy of American Drug Policy," *Ohio State Journal of Criminal Law* 1:1 (2003): 273–288.

28. Irving Goffman, "On the Characteristics of Total Institutions: Staff–Inmate Relations," in D. R. Cressey (ed.), *The Prison* (New York: Holt, Rinehart & Winston, 1966), pp. 16–22. This concept refers to the sum of conditions created by a large number of people living around the clock within a close space, with tightly scheduled sequences of activity coordinated by a central authority.

29. Reid Montgomery and G. Crews, *A History of Correctional Violence* (Lanham, MD: American Correctional Association, 1998). See also Arjen Boin and William Rattray, "Understanding Prison Riots," *Punishment and Society* 6:1 (2004): 47–65.

30. Ibid. See also John Conrad, "From Barbarism toward Decency: Alabama's Long Road to Prison Reform," *Journal of Research in Crime and Delinquency* 26 (1989): 307–328; and Barbara Belot and J. Marquardt, "The Political Community Model and Prisoner Litigation," *Prison Journal* 78:3 (1998): 299–329.

31. *New York Times* (July 9, 1966): 9. See also Christopher Stone, "Race, Crime and the Administration of Justice," *National Institute of Justice Journal* (April 1999): 26–32.

32. Phillip Kassel, "The Gang Crackdown in Massachusetts Prisons," *New England Journal on Criminal and Civil Confinement* 24:1 (1998): 37–63. See also Kalpana Patel and Alex Lord, "Ethnic Minority Sex Offenders' Experiences of Treatment," *Journal of Sexual Aggression* 7:1 (2001): 40–50.

33. Reginald Wilkinson and Tessa Unwin, "Intolerance in Prison," *Corrections Today* 61:3 (1999): 98–100.

34. Ibid.

35. John Hagan and Juleigh Coleman, "Returning Captives of the American War on Drugs," *Crime and Delinquency* 47:3 (2001): 352–367; and Ronald Weitzer and Charis Kubrin, "Breaking News," *Justice Quarterly* 21:3 (2004): 497–520.

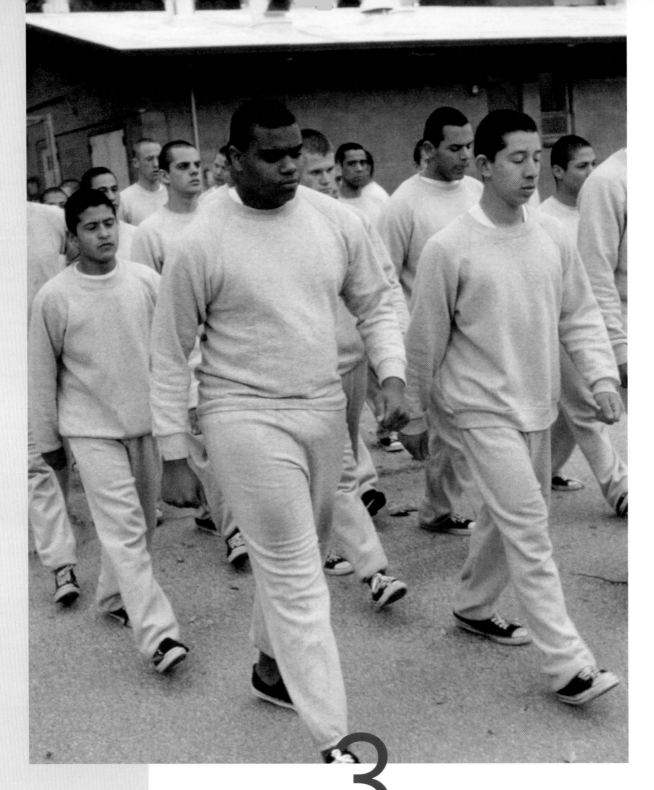

chapter 3

Correctional Ideologies:
The Pendulum Swings

Outline

Overview

So far we have looked at the history and early development of corrections, outlining the major construction of prisons and facilities that reflected the thoughts of those years. An underlying policy question explored in the first two chapters of the textbook concerned the role of criminal law and offenders: Who are offenders and what shall we do with them? The answers identified thus far include the following: They are (1) evil and must be punished, (2) out of touch with God and need to repent, (3) poorly educated and ill trained to function in modern society, and (4) sick and in need of being cured—the punishment, reform, education, and medical models for corrections, respectively. In this chapter, we explore the philosophical underpinnings on which these models were built, and explain the rationales that underlie current correctional developments. We need to understand why the nation has entered into an age of massive change in attitudes and prison construction, what goals are being sought, and what the implications of the new programs and facilities might be. We begin with an understanding of what we refer to as ideologies.

"The massive prison construction represents a commitment by our nation to plan for social failure by spending billions of dollars to lock up hundreds of thousands of people while at the same time cutting billions of dollars from programs that would provide opportunity to young Americans."

–Steven Donziger,
The Real War on Crime

CONFLICTING CORRECTIONAL IDEOLOGIES

To understand the current state of corrections, its problems and issues, and a possible future, we turn first to a discussion of ideologies. An **ideology**, according to *Webster's*, is "a systematic body of concepts, especially about human life or culture." A **correctional ideology**, then, refers to a body of ideas and practices that pertain to the processing of offenders, as determined by the law. Obviously, the actions of various correctional authorities and/or organizational units are shaped in large part by the particular ideologies to which they subscribe or that are the will of the citizens they serve and protect. In the history of treatment and punishment of offenders, the ideologies of different societies have supplied both the basis and the rationalization for the broad range of efforts—draconian to semihumane—aimed at getting criminals off the streets. When a given effort becomes a clear failure, the ideology eventually will shift to justify a different approach.

In modern times, a strong belief in the efficacy of one correctional ideology or another has sometimes led administrators to commit vast sums of public treasure to an unproved approach or theory, thus shackling themselves to a possibly worthless plan for an indefinite period. By the same token, if the correctional administrator's ideology happens to conflict with the approach favored by the society he or she serves, the administrator may try to resolve the conflict in one of two ways: by working out a compromise to make it work better or by trying to sabotage the system to ensure its failure. If the superintendent of a juvenile institution believes society is trying to liberalize rules so rapidly that it threatens personal security, he or she may encourage the use of segregation or restraints by the correctional officers. In corrections, the backgrounds and ideologies of the keepers and the kept often diverge sharply, so it becomes difficult to convince both groups they can work toward a mutual goal.

Most of the ideologies applied to correctional actions over the years fall into one of three categories: **punishment**, **rehabilitation**, or **prevention**. They often overlap, of course—punishment and rehabilitation are usually justified as means to prevention, rather than as ends in themselves—but the division is useful for the purpose of this analysis.

THE PUNISHMENT IDEOLOGY

The idea that punishment can result in the offense being "paid" for and that its effect can be expanded from the specific criminal to the general public has been around from the earliest times. Most of the basic reasons for punishment can be placed in three general categories: retribution, deterrence, and incapacitation.

Retribution

Since the first system of laws was developed, punishment has been officially sanctioned as a means of regulating criminal behavior. The punishment ideology holds that the criminal is an enemy of society who deserves severe punishment, including banishment or death, for willfully breaking its rules. This philosophy has its roots in a societal need for retribution. As noted in Chapter 1, punishment once was administered in the form of immediate and personal retribution, by either the victim or the victim's family. Society's authorization of punishment can be traced to that individual need for retaliation and vengeance. Many theories try to explain the reason for the transfer of the vengeance motive from the individual to the state.

Philosophically, **retribution** generally means getting even with the perpetrator. The term *social revenge* suggests that individuals cannot exact punishment, but that the state will do so in their name. Retribution assumes that the offenders willfully chose to commit the evil acts, are responsible for their own behavior, are likely to commit similar acts again, and should receive the punishment they richly deserve. The "just deserts" movement in sentencing reflects the retribution philosophy. For many, it provides a justifiable rationale for support of the death penalty.

Many students of corrections, and penologists, have considerable difficulty with the concept of retribution, because it requires the state to make an offender suffer for the sake of suffering. To many, that idea runs counter to the Eighth Amendment's prohibition against cruel and unusual punishment. One respected criminologist has proposed that correctional punishments include electroshock in lieu of incarceration, because it can be calibrated, leaves less long-term emotional damage, is cheaper to administer, and would allow the victim the opportunity to witness the retribution. Is it possible that televising the electroshock sessions might act as a deterrent to other potential malefactors?[1]

Philosophers have debated the reasons for this transfer to government of the victim's desire to strike back at the offender. Heinrich Oppenheimer lists several theories in *The Rationale of Punishment* (1913). Three of them are as follows:

1. In the *theological* view, retaliation fulfills a religious mission to punish the criminal.
2. In the *aesthetic* view, punishment resolves the social discord created by the offense and reestablishes a sense of harmony through requital.
3. In the *expiatory* view, guilt must be washed away through suffering.

Ledger Wood advances a fourth explanation, a *utilitarian theory*. Punishment is considered to be a means of achieving beneficial and social consequences through application of a specific form and degree of punishment deemed most appropriate to the particular offender after careful individualized study of the offender.[2]

Deterrence

Yet another reason for punishment of criminals is the belief that such actions have a **deterrent effect**, *specifically* on the offender or *generally* on others who might consider a similar act.[3] With **general deterrence**, it is believed that a sanction deters potential offenders by inflicting suffering on actual ones. For example, when we see the "perp" walk on television, it is hoped that potential criminals will not commit a similar crime in fear of being caught and punished. **Specific deterrence** is when a sanction is imposed on actual offender in the belief that it will stop that individual from committing crimes in the future. It is believed that in order for punishment to serve as a deterrent, it must be swift, visible to others, closely linked to the forbidden action so that it discourages future recurrences of that crime, certain, and categorical (all persons committing a certain crime will receive the same punishment).[4] Furthermore, the state and its representatives must uphold superior values and conforming behavior to serve as irreproachable examples of good citizenship. Finally, after punishment, offenders must be allowed to resume their prior positions in society, without stigma or disability.

Unfortunately, as we know, punishment may continue long after a sentence has been served. For example, even after an offender has successfully completed a punishment-oriented correctional process, the **stigma of conviction** and imprisonment is often carried for the rest of the ex-offender's life.[5] Finding it almost impossible to get a job because of a criminal past, the ex-offender may decide, "If I'm going to have the name, I might as well play the game." At that point, neither the punishment nor the stigma is an effective deterrent, and the offender is likely to return to crime.[6]

Incapacitation

A third reason to punish the offender derives from the concept of **incapacitation**. This theory holds that the best way to limit offenders' ability to break the law is to incapacitate them, usually by locking them up for long periods of time. The solution, therefore, is to

---

key term

Deterrent effect
The extent of crime control by incapacitation, threat of punishment, or announced potential criminal sanction.

key term

General deterrence
Preventing potential criminal behavior by making examples of offenders openly; the message here would be: See what will happen to you if you commit crime.

key term

Specific deterrence
Punishing individual offenders to prevent their further criminal behavior.

key term

Stigma of conviction
Effect of labeling, interference with ordinary social functioning, and resulting diminishing of offender.

key term

Incapacitation
Depriving offenders of the ability to commit additional crime, usually through imprisonment.

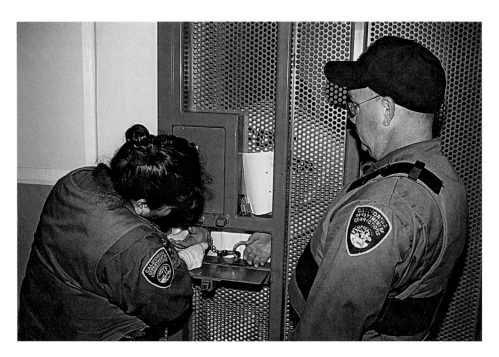

Correctional officers handcuff inmate.
© Adam Tanner/CORBIS All Rights Reserved.

key term

Theory of disablement
Preventing offenders from commission of more crime through isolation, death, banishment, or mutilation.

key term

Selective incapacitation
Incapacitating high-risk offenders believed to pose substantial probability of additional crime, usually through imprisonment.

key term

Recidivism
Continued criminal activity following initial law-violating behavior.

class activity

Ask students to define *retribution* and give three examples of that ideological program. Ask what type of punishment would best fit the crimes of rape, murder, and a gang shooting.

temporarily isolate, remove, or cripple such persons in some way. This approach is sometimes referred to as the **theory of disablement**, a euphemism for death, banishment, or mutilation. Ideally, the disablement should relate to the crime (for example, in some countries castration has been used to punish sex criminals). Incapacitation usually means imprisonment, but it can also include techniques such as house arrest and electronic monitoring. One variation of the isolation rationale of incapacitation is the **selective incapacitation** movement. Greenwood argued that prison overcrowding and the scarcity of beds in prisons require a policy of sending only repetitive or violent offenders to prison; he especially recommended prison for those who commit armed robbery.[7] Selective incapacitation[8] would thus result in better uses of correctional resources and more effective crime prevention, he believed.[9]

Selective Incapacitation

This doctrine of isolating the offender, or causing "social disablement," proposes adopting a policy of incarcerating those whose criminal behavior is so damaging or probable that nothing short of isolation will prevent **recidivism**. This "nothing-else-works" approach would require correctly identifying those offenders who would be eligible for longer-term imprisonment and diverting others into correctional alternatives. Thus we would be able to make maximum effective use of prison cells, a scarce resource, to protect society from the depredations of such dangerous and repetitive offenders.

Current correctional technology, however, does not permit us to correctly identify those who require incapacitation. Rather, the evidence is that we would probably incarcerate numerous noneligibles (a "false-positive" problem) and release to lesser confinement many of those eligible (a "false-negative" problem). Whatever benefits might accrue to this sentencing doctrine have thus far eluded corrections. The difficulty is further spotlighted in the *Report to the Nation on Crime and Justice:*

> Career criminals, though few in number, account for most crime. Even though chronic repeat offenders (those with five or more arrests by age 18) make up a relatively small proportion of all offenders, they commit a very high proportion of all crimes. The evidence

includes data for juveniles and adults, males and females, and for urban and rural areas. In Wolfgang's Philadelphia study, chronic offenders accounted for 23 percent of all male offenders in the study, but they had committed 61 percent of all the crimes. Of all crimes by all members of the group studied, chronic offenders committed:

- *61 percent of all homicides*
- *76 percent of all rapes*
- *73 percent of all robberies*
- *65 percent of all aggravated assaults.*[10]

The Effect of Punishment

It is recognized that some punishment can be effective when applied in the right amounts and at the right time; and punishment may, in some cases, be a necessary predecessor to rehabilitation. Few serious offenders readily seek or are amenable to rehabilitation without some form of coercion or threat. When the ideology of punishment is applied in a correctional institution, however, the result is often negative for both the punished and the punisher. Correctional personnel tend to watch for minor rule infringements or nonconformism (horseplay, abusive language, skipping classes, etc.) so the punishment can be administered, and they overlook any positive actions by offenders.[11] Often the rules that are prepared for a punishment-oriented environment surround the offender with a wall of "do nots," leaving almost no leeway to "do" anything.

As evidenced by a high crime rate, punishment by the law does not seem to create much respect for the law, even in jurisdictions where punishment may actually be swift, harsh, and certain. Overuse of punishment in a society that claims to be open and free creates a situation in which the punished can characterize their punishers as persecutors of the poor and helpless. The accusation turns attention away from the crimes that put them there, and gives rise to the concept of the "political prisoner." Thus, minority-group members are likely to blame their incarcerations on repression by the rich, on political persecution, or on attempted genocide. Punishments are then made more and more severe, in a desperate but hopeless effort to compensate for their ineffectiveness. Often such punishments motivate offenders to become more sophisticated criminals (rather than noncriminals) in the belief (no doubt valid) that the more skilled one is at a trade, the less likely one is to be caught. The offenders become hardened to the punishment, and the administrators learn to dole it out automatically as their only means of control.[12] Both parties are degraded in the process.

Both history and science refute the argument that the use of punishment can halt crime. For example, those people for whom punishment is least effective are:

1. Psychopathic risk takers
2. Those under the influence of drugs or alcohol
3. Those with a history of being punished.

Unfortunately, these are the attributes of an offender population. Punishment does not work with those whom we need it to work most with: criminals.[13]

It must be understood that the significance of punishment as an ideology in correctional practice lies in the viewpoint of the punished offenders. If they see the punishment as an unjust imposition of the will and power of the establishment, and are reinforced in that belief by their peers

A prisoner uses a small mirror to see outside of his cell.
© Shepard Sherbell/CORBIS All Rights Reserved.

(other offenders), their punishment will only encourage them to maintain negative attitudes and behavior patterns. By contrast, if offenders believe their punishment is both deserved and just, and their social group agrees, the punishment may have a startlingly different and more positive result. If a prosocial criminal (one who is not totally committed to a life of crime) is justly treated, that offender may abandon crime; but excessive punishment may push the offender over the edge and destroy every chance of reform. The punished and stigmatized offenders turn to those who are most like them for support and values. If they are embittered by the punishment they have received, they are likely to reject the very values the punishment was intended to reinforce.[14]

James Austin and Aaron McVey[15] examined the effects of recent political policies designed to increase punishment by increasing the probability of an offender's being arrested, convicted, and imprisoned, and serving longer sentences. We extend their predictions by noting that, if current punishment trends continue, the nation will:

- have 2.8 million prison inmates by the year 2010.
- need to open a new 600-bed prison every other week for the next five years just to keep even with and accommodate prison growth.
- need to hire 4,000 new correctional officers for each of the next five years.
- have 200,000 elderly prisoners ("geriatric inmates") in prison by 2020.
- remain number one in the world in rate of incarceration per 100,000 residents.
- have almost 10 million persons under correctional supervision.

Finally, the change in attitude has led to a painful search for alternatives to probation (regarded as too little punishment) and imprisonment (regarded as too expensive a form of punishment). The emerging alternatives—known as intermediate punishments—promise relief from the pressures of prison overcrowding. In addition, the new wave of punitiveness has contributed to selective incapacitation, an important and effective tool for correctional administrators, but only if it is designed to suit an individual offender and an individual situation (see Chapter 6). General and uniform punishment is still the rule rather than the exception, however, and the movement toward a **rehabilitation model** is slow.

THE REHABILITATION IDEOLOGY

A major trend in corrections is to approach the offender much as one would the mentally ill, the neglected, or the underprivileged. This more humane ideology, reflected in the rehabilitation model, sees the change in behavior of the offender produced by treatment and services. With the rehabilitation ideology, the offender chooses to refrain from new crimes rather than being unable to. Although some refer to the criminal as "sick," the rehabilitation ideology is not analogous to a medical approach. The closest comparison with physical illness lies in the need for offenders to recognize the danger and undesirability of their criminal behavior and then to make significant efforts to rid themselves of that behavior. The rehabilitation model does not "remove" criminal behavior, as one might remove an infected limb; rather, the "patient" (inmate) is made to see the rewards of positive behavior and is encouraged and equipped to adopt it as a model.

Treatment, of course, begins with a diagnosis of an offender's needs, the design of a program plan to address that person's needs, the application of the intended program with periodic monitoring, and updating and modification of the plan to maximize effectiveness. Treatment is designed to correct behavior instead of some underlying defect or disease.

The rehabilitation ideology does not encourage inmates to be coddled and allowed to do as they please within the institution. It is a fairly common belief among many elements of the criminal justice system that any program that is not punitive or restrictive is being "soft" or akin to "running a country club." In fact, some form of rehabilitation can be applied in even the most restrictive and security-oriented institutions. The main difference between the rehabilitation and punishment ideologies is that in the former, offenders are assigned to the institution for a correctional program intended to prepare them for readjustment to or reintegration into the community, not just for punishment and confinement. There is room for punishment and security in the rehabilitation approach, but little room for rehabilitation in the punitive approach. The more humane treatment methods are intended to be used in conjunction with the employment of authority in a constructive and positive manner, but inmates must be allowed to try, even if they fail. Authoritarian procedures, used alone, only give the offender more ammunition to support a self-image as an oppressed and impotent pawn of the power structure.

The student should recall that the field of corrections, especially in its early history in America, underwent significant change as innovators again sought the answers to the question mentioned earlier: "Who are the offenders and what should we do with them?" The rehabilitation ideology contains four separate answers to the question, commonly referred to as treatment doctrines.

The Quaker reform movement, arising in 1790, held that offenders were out of touch with God. The corresponding treatment approach was isolation. Prisoners were supplied with a Bible for reading and doing penitence. The doctrine for the Quakers was to help offenders find their way back to God; it was believed that once God was found, crime would cease. The Quakers are a religious group that has a strong pacifist and nonviolent ideology as part of their faith. Probably the best-known Quaker in America was William Penn, after whom Pennsylvania was named.

The **reformatory movement** solutions, after 1890, provided somewhat different answers. Offenders were seen as disadvantaged, "unfortunate" persons whose education, training, and discipline had been inadequate. The **educational doctrine** answer was to provide education at a functional level, emphasis on vocational and occupational skills, and a regime of discipline that was aimed at the internalization of controls to prevent recurrence of criminal behavior when the prisoner was released.

The **medical model** that developed in the late 1920s and early 1930s, under the leadership of Sanford Bates and the U.S. Bureau of Prisons, saw the answers as lying within the individual. It then became necessary to diagnose the individual problem, develop a treatment program that might remedy it, and then apply treatment. When the "patient" was found to be well, he or she would be released to a program of aftercare in the community under the supervision of therapeutic parole officers who would continue casework therapy until the offender was "rehabilitated." The medical model offered hope of rehabilitation. It was the responsibility of corrections to "make the ill well." The "ill" would thus be passive recipients of beneficent therapy like patients in a hospital.

Underlying the treatment model is the indeterminate sentence and its assumptions of rehabilitation and early release, if the offender is treated and is reformed. The minimum and maximum periods (such as a one- to five-year sentence) reflect the inability of the sentencing judge to know exactly when the prisoner would be reformed.

The indeterminate sentence is thus a sentence to incarceration pronounced by a judge that sets minimum and maximum periods of confinement for the offender (such as "from one to five years"). The minimum term would establish the earliest release date (adjusted for certain time credits for, as an example, jail time during pretrial detention) or the date of the first parole consideration to determine if the inmate should be released. At the maximum term, the inmate would have to be released.

Before 1975, the federal system and all of the state systems had sentencing codes that were indeterminate, and boards of prison terms and parole, commonly called parole boards, were given broad discretion in determining when an inmate was ready for release under parole supervision. Since 1976, almost two-thirds of the states as well as the federal system have

key term

Reformatory movement
Offenders are unfortunate persons whose education, training, and discipline are inadequate; offenders should be sent to an educational penal institution for reform.

key term

Educational doctrine
Correctional approach seeking to provide crime prevention by education, emphasizing vocational and educational skills, and teaching inmates to discipline themselves.

key term

Medical model
Model that sees the causes of crime as lying within the individual, and stresses providing treatment and therapy until the offender is well. Leaders in the medical model were Sanford Bates and the Federal Bureau of Prisons.

limited parole board discretion or abolished discretionary parole completely. In addition, the percentage of inmates released through parole board discretion declined from 72% to 35% at the beginning of 2007. Twenty-three states now use guidelines to structure their release decisions.

The fourth doctrine emerged in the late 1960s. It is acceptable to use either 1965 or 1969 as the date of origin, but whichever date is used, this form of treatment was a significant trend throughout the 1980s. Known as the **reintegration model**, this form of treatment made differing assumptions about the cause and solutions to crime and the criminal. The community was seen as the basic etiological factor, and the offender was considered to be the product of a local community that excluded, failed to provide for, or discriminated against the offender. Because the basic cause is regarded as community related, proponents thought it best to address the problem by using community resources that correctional agencies would be able to marshal or develop. These would include reducing poverty rates, investing in children, urban revitalization, Head Start programs, and job training. The offender's role requires active participation in the effort to resolve the difficulty; correctional agencies then serve as brokers for services. Ideally, a community management approach is used, wherein several officers can specialize to maximize the delivery of opportunities to the offender, who is eager to reintegrate and become part of the community. The four doctrines require treatment and coexist in the correctional ideology called *treatment* which we discuss in Chapter 8.

THE PREVENTION IDEOLOGY

As mentioned, the problem of crime cannot be separated from the individual offender. In a sense, the problem can be temporarily removed from the community whenever the offender is sent off to prison. Almost all offenders are eventually released, however, and the problem returns unless it has been effectively treated while the offender was in the prison. Because of the perceived minimal success of present correctional programs (recidivism rates range from 40% to 70%),[16] many communities and governmental agencies are turning to crime prevention as a possible solution. Prevention methods have a dual focus: on the individual and on the environment in which he or she lives.[17] Much crime-prevention activity is designed to steer potential delinquents away from a life of trouble. Such programs generally begin at the school level, where truancy and dropping out are often the precursors of criminal activity. Those early programs, for the most part, attempt to identify the first signs of criminal behavior.

As Pogo Possum, the 1950s cartoon character of Walt Kelly, said: "Prediction is difficult, 'specially when it's about the future." Prediction is a complex process, even when it is carefully controlled.[18] The famous studies by Harvard sociologists Sheldon and Eleanor Glueck illustrate the problems inherent in most prediction efforts.[19] Prevention programs in schools today aim to treat problem children by providing specialized classes, alternative schools, vocational education, and counseling;[20] they do not aim to force juveniles out of the picture by expulsion from school. The prevention ideology recognizes that problem children must have supportive help, or they are very likely to use crime as an outlet for unhappiness and insecurity.

Those who advocate the prevention ideology are well aware that total prevention of crime is probably impossible. One of the early sociological giants, **Emile Durkheim** (1853–1917) believed crime in some form was an inevitable accompaniment to human society and that if serious crime were prevented, authorities would focus their attention on minor offenses.[21] Essentially, the prevention ideology holds that crime may at least be reduced through an attack on the social and emotional problems that encourage a child's criminal inclinations.

The individual's environment is recognized as a crucial focus in the prevention of crime; the prevention ideology emphasizes the need to structure the environment so criminal opportunity is minimized. As an example, it has been said that the greatest crime-prevention device ever invented was the streetlight. The movement toward crime prevention through environmental design has great promise for the future. The object of such an approach is not only to provide barriers to crime (such as window bars, fences, locks, airport electronic search and security checks),[22] but also to enhance the existing features that tend to discourage crime (for example, more lighting around homes and apartment buildings, more windows in dark hallways, and community projects aimed at getting people to know their neighbors). The conditions that produce a high or low crime rate in a given area are not all physical; however, the environment includes the people, activities, pressures, and ideas to which an individual is exposed every day. The prevention ideology advocates the maximum use of resources in areas that have special problems such as poverty and overcrowding—funds should be allocated for crime prevention rather than for prison construction.[23]

In **community corrections**, the prevention ideology is combined with treatment. The emphasis is on the identification and treatment of the problems that have caused past criminal behavior, to prevent its recurrence. Eventually, the emphasis may lead to a closer, more interdependent relationship between the agencies now involved in crime prevention and those that provide community services. As they presently operate, criminal justice agencies actually tend to create more problems for minor offenders, instead of treating the problems that got those people into trouble.[24] If schools, churches, service agencies, and similar organizations could become more involved, before persons become entangled in the criminal justice system, many criminal careers could be prevented before they start. **Diversion** and nonjudicial approaches to offenders are seen as potentially valuable alternatives to a more formal punishment-oriented reaction to the problem of crime. A combination of prevention and treatment ideologies would be the most promising and humane organization of correctional beliefs and practices.

THE PENDULUM SWINGS

From the late 1970s to 1990, high crime rates caused the forces of society to turn again to the punishment ideology.[25] As the populations of the country's jails and prisons have grown to almost unmanageable proportions, administrators and legislatures become more willing to accept the turn backward in order to have at least some way to cope with the growing and more violent criminal populations. The following chapters discuss the problems faced by harried and chronically underfunded correctional administrators trying to deal with institutions that are so overcrowded that they are bursting at the seams. Budgets are stripped of so-called frills such as treatment and must be used to add beds, food, and custody staff to house and feed inmates while trying to protect society. The trend toward determinate sentences and **"get-tough" laws** at all levels exacerbates the situation. At best, treatment is difficult to carry out in a security institution. At worst, treatment is all but impossible to find. That pessimistic situation formed a trend that began in the 1980s. The correctional "nonsystem" entered the first decade of the new century in a continuing state of indecision as to what to embrace as its core ideology.[26] The results were clear, however, and the hope for treatment that dominated in the 1960s and 1970s seems lost in the cry for "hard time" for offenders. Poor economic conditions in inner-city blighted areas and continued overcrowding exist at levels unprecedented in the short history of corrections in America.

Despite the increased reliance on punishment and the conservative backlash that has so negatively impacted corrections during the last two decades, there is growing support

lecture note

Point out that *prevention* emerges from the assumption that one can predict future behavior. Suggest the lack of accuracy in prevention for high-rate (such as theft) and low-rate offenders (such as exhibitionism). Focus on "false positive" and "false negative" issues.

key term

Community corrections
A model of corrections based on the assumption that the offender should be reintegrated into the community through existing and potential community services.

key term

Diversion
Minimizing offender processing through the justice system by imposing treatment, supervision, and referral of offenders to service providers outside of the justice system.

key term

"Get-tough laws"
Belief that offenders should be punished to prevent criminal recidivism; such laws would lengthen the term of incarceration and minimize use of community resources; two important law programs are using the determinate sentence and compelling the inmate to serve a large percentage of the imposed sentence.

for both rehabilitation and prevention among legislators[27] as well as the general public.[28] Indeed there is some evidence that the pendulum is again swinging toward a less punitive approach. For example, some states are reexamining the age at which juveniles can be turned over to the adult system, and draconian drug laws are being repealed. Perhaps that is why the best analogy is of the pendulum and its continuous path as it begins to swing from right to left. It will take major changes in the future for the pendulum of justice to begin a swing back toward the center, but there are signs that this may be happening. The task ahead for today's students will be both important and difficult as they track the path of the pendulum.

RESTORATIVE JUSTICE

The debate over the future of the criminal justice system has historically been between proponents of a retributive, punitive philosophy and advocates of the traditional individual treatment mission. All of these approaches have failed to satisfy basic needs of individual crime victims, the community, and offenders. A new ideology is now being tried, mostly in the juvenile justice system, which seems to have some merit for consideration. The balanced and restorative justice (BARJ) model outlines an alternative philosophy, **restorative justice,**[29] and a new mission, "the balanced approach."

The BARJ model requires criminal justice professionals to devote attention to enabling offenders to make amends to their victims and communities, increasing offender competencies, and presumably protecting the public through processes in which individual victims, the community, and offenders are all active participants.

The BARJ model responds to many issues raised by the victims' movement, including concerns that victims have had little opportunity for input into the resolution of their own cases, rarely feel heard, and often receive no restitution or expression of remorse from the offender. The balanced approach is based on an understanding of crime as an act against the victim and the community, which is an ancient idea common to tribal and religious traditions of many cultures. Practitioners have used techniques consistent with this approach for years; however, they have lacked a coherent philosophical framework that supports restorative practice and provides direction to guide all aspects of juvenile justice practice. The BARJ model provides an overarching vision and guidance for daily decisions.

Criminal justice professionals, including probation and parole officers, prosecutors, judges, case managers, and victim advocates, recognize the need for justice system reform. People who work on the front lines of the system are faced daily with the frustration of seeing growing numbers of young people and adults involved in criminal behavior. These offenders often leave the system with little hope for real change; and, unfortunately, countless crime victims and community members are left out of the process. That frustration has inspired many of these professionals to work toward changing organizational culture, values, and programs to reflect a more balanced and restorative approach to juvenile justice.[30]

The BARJ model is a vision for the future of corrections and criminal justice that builds on current innovative practices and is based on core values that have been part of most communities for centuries. It provides a framework for systemic reform and offers hope for preserving and revitalizing the juvenile justice system. Implementation must begin with consensus building among key stakeholders and testing with small pilot projects to develop the model. This evolutionary process can build on existing programs and practices that reflect restorative justice principles, such as victim–offender mediation,[31] victim–offender panels, family group conferencing, community service, restitution, and work experience.

Balanced and Restorative Justice Philosophy

The foundation of restorative justice practice is a coherent set of values and principles, a guiding vision, and an action-oriented mission. The guiding principles of restorative justice are that crime is injury and crime hurts not only individual victims but also communities and offenders, and creates an obligation to make things right. All parties should be a part of the response to the crime, including the victim if he or she wishes, the community, and the offender. However, the victim's perspective is central to deciding how to repair (restore) the harm caused by the crime. Accountability for the offender means some acceptance of responsibly to repair the harm done.

The community is ultimately responsible for the well-being of all its members, including both victim and offender, and all human beings have dignity and worth. Restoration means repairing the harm and rebuilding relationships in the community. It is the primary goal of restorative justice. Results are measured by how much repair was done rather than by how much punishment was inflicted. This ideology accepts that crime control cannot be achieved without the active involvement of the community.

The justice process is respectful of age, abilities, sexual orientation, family status, and diverse cultures and backgrounds (for example, racial, ethnic, geographic, religious, and economic backgrounds), and all are given equal protection and due process. The restorative justice vision needs to have support from the community, opportunity to define the harm experienced, and participation in decision making about steps for repair that result in increased victim recovery from the trauma of crime. It accepts that community involvement in preventing and controlling crime, improving neighborhoods, and strengthening the bonds among community members results in community protection.

Through understanding the human impact of their behavior, accepting responsibility, expressing remorse, taking action to repair the damage, and developing their own capacities, offenders become fully integrated and respected members of the community. Justice professionals, as community justice facilitators, organize and support processes in which individual crime victims, other community members, and juvenile offenders are involved in finding constructive resolutions to delinquency.

The Balanced Approach and Its Application

Transforming the current justice system into a more restorative model will and must require that professionals have the power to transform justice into a more balanced and restorative system. By developing new roles, setting new priorities, and redirecting resources, justice professionals can:

1. Make needed services available for victims of crime.
2. Give victims opportunities for involvement and input.
3. Actively involve community members, including individual crime victims and offenders, in making decisions and carrying out plans for resolving issues and restoring the community.
4. Build connections among community members.
5. Give offenders the opportunity and encouragement to take responsibility for their behavior.
6. Actively involve offenders in repairing the harm they caused.

Although this approach is relatively new and requires additional research and application before it can be considered viable, it may help turn the tide on the punishment and retribution ideologies that are now so much in favor of politicians and the public.

thematic question

On what philosophical basis could one reasonably argue that "get-tough laws" will impact on the volume of crime?

class activity

Have the class identify how restorative justice reintroduces the victim into the correctional scene.

lecture note

Define *restorative justice* and give three examples of existing programs, identifying their objectives.

thematic question

What elements need to be present for an effective restorative justice program to be developed on the local level?

class activity

Have the class debate the validity of this statement: Restorative justice does not punish the offender enough for the criminal act committed.

class activity

Have the class debate the validity of this statement: Restorative justice programs widen the net of the juvenile and criminal justice system.

CONTEMPORARY CORRECTIONS

The need for correctional reforms and structured plans to achieve them was documented by the President's Crime Commission, appointed by President Lyndon Johnson in the 1960s, by the President's Commission on Criminal Justice Standards and Goals, and by task forces in many states. The early 1960s emerged as a period of research that sought alternative methods, programs, treatment procedures, and designs for facilities. The most astonishing and significant findings included the following:

1. Long sentences are self-defeating with regard to rehabilitation.
2. Most offenders—perhaps as many as 85%—do not need to be incarcerated and could function better back in the community under supervision.
3. Most inmates derive maximum benefit from incarceration during their first two years; after that period, it becomes less and less likely that they could function as productive citizens if returned to society.
4. Community-based corrections are more realistic, less expensive, and at least as effective as incarceration.
5. Corrections, as a system, must encompass all aspects of rehabilitative service, including mental health services, employment services, education, and social services.
6. Some offenders, because of their dangerousness, will require extensive incarceration and treatment programs especially designed and implemented in secure institutions. The staff in those institutions must be extensive and of high quality.
7. Most inmates are not mentally ill but suffer from a variety of educational, medical, psychological, maturational, economic, and interpersonal handicaps that are seldom reduced or resolved in contemporary correctional systems.
8. Inmates must be given the opportunity and capability to earn a living wage so as to compensate their victims and support their own families, keeping them off public assistance rolls.
9. The pay for currently incarcerated inmates is too low to be regarded as wages. Thus the rates of pay must be increased to at least the minimum wage on the outside for similar labor.
10. The private economic sector must be sought out and used to provide both training and work programs that will produce employable workers at the end of the corrections cycle.

key term
_____

Determinate sentencing
Judge-imposed fixed term of incarceration with the expectation the inmate will serve that amount of time.

key term
_____

Indeterminate sentencing
Judge imposes a minimum and maximum period of incarceration time under the assumption that a parole board will identify the maximum benefit from imprisonment and subsequently release the inmate.

Despite the evidence, five important developments in corrections have occurred during the last three decades of the twentieth century: (1) the abandonment of the medical model; (2) the shift to **determinate sentencing**, which places limits on the judge's power to determine how long the offender might serve in prison; (3) a search for punishments that would be more effective than court-ordered probation and less severe than long-term incarceration, the so-called intermediate punishment; (4) renewed emphasis on rehabilitation and effective programming for offenders, and (5) restorative justice.

By 2008, the majority of the states embraced determinate sentencing, abolishing discretionary parole release mechanisms in at least 16 states and imposing mandatory add-on time for use of a gun in crimes, sale of narcotics, and some especially brutal crimes. At least 29 states and the District of Columbia have adopted the federal truth-in-sentencing standard that requires Part I violent crime offenders to serve not less than 85% of their sentence in prison before becoming eligible for release. The reemergence of retribution in contemporary corrections has led in part to seriously overcrowded prisons, a deluge of lawsuits by prisoners seeking better conditions while incarcerated, and an intense search for new alternatives to imprisonment[32] that would still provide public safety and constitutionally viable conditions for prisoners.[33] As Latessa and Allen noted in 1999, "Ironically, for a movement begun by fiscal conservatives, the new get-tough policy has turned out to be the most costly approach to corrections yet attempted."[34] Recent figures

Prisoner training dogs for disabled veterans.
© Brian Snyder/Reuters/CORBIS All Rights Reserved.

compiled by the PEW Charitable Trusts show that total state expenditures have risen 315% in the past 20 years.[35]

By 2007, Americans under some form of correctional supervision swelled to previously unparalleled numbers: 8,060,000 adults. There were 2,258,983 adult men and women in the custody of state and federal prisons, another 766,010 were in local jails on a given day, 4,237,023 were on probation, and some 798,000 were on parole. In addition, 110,000 were in juvenile correctional facilities. Figure 3.1 provides a graphic of the

lecture note

Identify the conclusions of the President's Crime Commission regarding crime and criminals, and the recommended policies in that report.

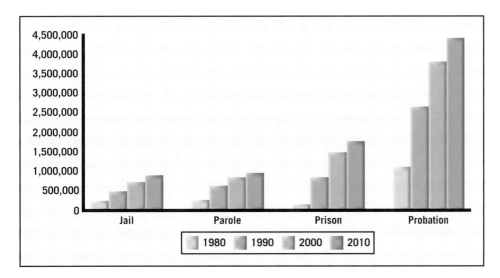

figure 3.1

Adults Under Correctional Control: 1980–2010

SOURCE: Data gathered from: Bureau of Justice Statistics (2007). Correctional Populations, 1980-2010 (*http://www.ojp.usdoj.gov/bjs/pub/pdf/ppus06.pdf*, accessed July 15, 2008). *Data for 2010 are estimated.

growth curves, extended to 2010. There are now 1 in 100 adults behind bars in America. The punishment ideology has contributed heavily to this growth, and has fueled the development of both the intermediate sanction and accreditation programs in the last four decades. These are explored in detail in Chapters 6 and 8.

Almost two-thirds of federal prison inmates are incarcerated for drug law violations; the national average for state systems is about 20%. One in fifteen African American men ages 18 or older are incarcerated on any day, and for black men ages 20 to 34 the number is one in nine.

The War on Drugs has diverted attention from the causes of drug use and social problems, contributed to the abandonment of the lower class in terms of new services, expanded the power of the state in light of the rights of the individual, legitimized intrusion of American politics into Latin and South American governments, and not reduced the volume of crime or drug use. William Weir, an expert on gun control and drugs, argues that cynical politicians have manipulated the public to attain their own agenda and goals and, in so doing, created a "dope fiend" stereotype to generate votes. The "war" has increased violence and enhanced gangster roles for minority inner-city youth.[36]

Summary

In this first decade of the new millennium, corrections in America stands at a crossroads, experiencing a major crisis unparalleled during the past 200 years. The remainder of this textbook describes current developments and practices in corrections, innovations, proposed solutions, and ways to ease the crisis and improve the effectiveness of the system. To understand those recent developments, we needed to explore the correctional ideologies detailed in this chapter.

It appears now that some of our attempts to relieve the problems in the overcrowded fortress prisons have in fact failed. The fortress prisons are still here and they are even more overcrowded, and their maximum-security clients are now the "bottom of the barrel" regarding behavioral problems.[37] This has made it more difficult to offer effective rehabilitation in prisons, and has resulted in a steady movement toward a model emphasizing custody and control over everything else in a futile effort to keep peace in the institutions and "protect society." The problem of selecting a philosophy or ideology that is effective yet also reflective of society's mood is a problem correctional administrators will have to continue to confront in the years to come.

Only when American society decides which ideology or combination of ideologies most deserves its support will the problems facing the correctional administrator be properly addressed. It may be that some combination or blend will be the only practical or possible answer, given the vast variety of problems and offenders. Some offenders may respond only to a punitive ideology, at least until we are able to develop treatment techniques that offer greater potential for success and are constitutionally acceptable. The offender who can respond to treatment, however, must be given a chance to receive it, but without being totally free of some kind of control, because the protection of society remains the primary mission of corrections. The prevention ideology offers great promise, but it seems too idealistic to suffice in and of itself. As prison populations become increasingly large and unmanageable, the challenges facing correctional officials will only multiply. The overcrowding problem, coupled with the high cost of incarceration, will continue the quest to develop other alternatives to imprisonment, and many of these options are outlined in later chapters. To comprehend the current issues in corrections, we must examine the decision process and options available to the judiciary and releasing authorities. That process and its options are described in the next chapter.

Key Words

ideology, 42	stigma of conviction, 43	Emile Durkheim, 48
correctional ideology, 42	incapacitation, 43	reintegration model, 48
punishment ideology, 42	theory of disablement, 44	community corrections, 49
rehabilitation ideology, 42	selective incapacitation, 44	diversion, 49
prevention ideology, 42	recidivism, 44	"get-tough" laws, 49
retribution, 42	rehabilitation model, 46	restorative justice, 50
deterrent effect, 43	reformatory movement, 47	determinate sentencing, 52
general deterrence, 43	educational doctrine, 47	indeterminate sentencing, 52
specific deterrence, 43	medical model, 47	

Review Questions

1. What basic ideologies have determined the handling of offenders over the years? Which is the oldest?
2. What criteria must be met if punishment is to act as a deterrent?
3. How does the rehabilitation ideology differ from punishment? Are they necessarily exclusive of each other?
4. What are some of the changes currently taking place in the clientele of the correctional system?
5. What effect has the punishment ideology recently had on corrections?
6. What is restorative justice?
7. Explain the impact of drugs on the race/ethnicity of prisoners.

Endnotes

1. Graeme Newman, *Just and Painful: The Case for the Corporal Punishment of Criminals* (New York: Free Press, 1983).
2. As cited by Elmer H. Johnson, *Crime, Correction, and Society* (Homewood, IL: Dorsey Press, 1974), p. 173. See also Roger Hood, "Capital Punishment: A Global Perspective," *Punishment and Society* 3:3 (2001): 331–334; and Christopher Hartney (2007), "The Nation's Most Punitive States for Women," *http://www.nccd-crc.org/nccd/pubs/2007_MPS_factsheet.pdf.*
3. Norman Carlson, "A More Balanced Correctional Philosophy," *FBI Law Enforcement Bulletin* 46 (January 1977): 22–25. See also John Cochran and Mitchell Chamblin, "Deterrence and Brutalization," *Justice Quarterly* 17:4 (2000): 685–706.
4. K. Blackman, R. Voas, R. Gullberg, et al., "Enforcement of Zero-Tolerance in the State of Washington," *Forensic Science Review* 13:2 (2001): 77–86.
5. John Irwin and James Austin, *It's About Time* (San Francisco: National Council on Crime and Delinquency, 1987), pp. 12–14. See also Hung Sung, "Rehabilitating Felony Drug Offenders through Job Development," *Prison Journal* 81:2 (2001): 271–286.
6. Bradley Wright, A. Caspi, and T. Moffitt, "Does the Perceived Risk of Punishment Deter Criminally Prone Individuals?" *Journal of Research in Crime and Delinquency* 41:2 (2004): 180–213.
7. Peter B. Greenwood, *Selective Incapacitation* (Santa Monica, CA: Rand Corporation, 1983). But also see Simon Cole, "From the Sexual Psychopath to 'Megan's Law,'" *Journal of the History of Medicine and Allied Science* 55:3 (2000): 292–314.
8. Incapacitation remains a hotly debated topic in corrections. See Daniel Nagin, David Farrington, and Terrie Moffit, "Life Course Trajectories of Different Types of Offenders," *Criminology* 33:1 (1995): 111–139; and Mark Warr, "Life Course Trajectories and Desistance from Crime," *Criminology* 36:2 (1998): 183–216.

9. Hennessey Hayes and M. Geerken argue that it is possible to identify low-rate offenders for early release. See H. Hayes and M. Geerken, "The Idea of Selective Release," *Justice Quarterly* 14:2 (1997): 353–370; and eds., Correctional News, "BI, Inc. Signs Day Report Center Contracts with Calif., Kansas," *Correctional News* 14:3 (2008): 38.

10. Marianne Zowitz (ed.), *Report to the Nation on Crime and Justice* (Washington, DC: Bureau of Justice Statistics, 1983).

11. More than half of prison inmates will be charged with prison rule violations during their current sentences. See James Stephan, *Prison Rule Violations* (Washington, DC: Bureau of Justice Statistics, 1989). See also Stephen Schoenthaler, Stephen Amos, W. Doraz, et al., "The Effect of Randomized Vitamin-Mineral Supplementation on Violent and Non-Violent Antisocial Behavior Among Incarcerated Juveniles," *Journal of Nutritional and Environmental Medicine* 7:1 (1997): 343–352; and eds., Correctional News, "Report: Childhood Lead Exposure Linked to Criminal Behavior in Adulthood," *Correctional News 14:5* (2008): 10–12.

12. See the comments on the Alabama "dog house" by John Conrad, "From Barbarism toward Decency: Alabama's Long Road to Prison Reform," *Journal of Research in Crime and Delinquency* 26 (November 1989): 307–328; Human Rights Watch, "No Escape: Male Rape in U.S. Prisons," http://www.hrw.org/reports/2001/prison (accessed November 30, 2008).

13. Johnson, *Crime, Correction and Society*, pp. 361–365. A European view of punishment can be found in Pieter Spirenburg, *Man and Violence: Gender, Honor and Rituals in Modern Europe and America* (Columbus: Ohio State University Press, 1998).

14. There is a current rebirth of the punishment ideology, described in detail by Donald E. J. MacNamara, "The Medical Model in Corrections: Requiescat in Pace," *Criminology* 14 (February 1977): 439–448. See also Victor Hassine, *A Life Without Parole: Living in Prison Today*, 4th ed. (New York: Oxford University Press, 2008).

15. James Austin and Aaron McVey, *The 1989 NCCD Prison Population Forecast: The Impact of the War on Drugs* (San Francisco: National Council on Crime and Delinquency, 1989), p. 13. See also Lauren Glaze and Thomas Bonczar, *Probation and Parole in the United States, 2006* (Washington, DC: Bureau of Justice Statistics, 2007); William Sabol and Heather Couture, *Prison Inmates and Midyear 2007* (Washington, DC: Bureau of Justice Statistics, 2008); and William Sabol and Todd Minton, *Jail Inmates at Midyear 2007* (Washington, DC: Bureau of Justice Statistics, 2008).

16. Patrick Langan and David Levin, *Recidivism of Prisoners Released in 1994* (Washington, DC: Bureau of Justice Statistics, 2002). But see David Hartmann, J. Wolk, J. Johnston, et al., "Recidivism and Substance Abuse Outcomes in a Prison-Based Therapeutic Community," *Federal Probation* 61:4 (1997): 18–25; and Michael Pendergast, Elizabeth Hall, Harry Wexler, et al., "Amity Prison Based Therapeutic Community," *The Prison Journal* 84:1 (2004): 36–60.

17. James Unnever, "Two Worlds Far Apart: Black-White Differences in Beliefs about Why African-American Men Are Disproportionately Imprisoned," *Criminology 46:2* (2008): 301–359.

18. For a discussion of prediction, see Anthony Petrosino and Caroline Petrosino, "The Public Safety Potential of Megan's Law in Massachusetts," *Crime and Delinquency* 45:1 (1999): 140–158.

19. See the discussion of the Gluecks' arguments in Melissa Johnson, "Youth, Violent Behavior and Exposure to Violence in Childhood," *Aggression and Violent Behavior* 3:2 (1998): 159–179.

20. See Linda Dahlberg, "Youth Violence in the United States: Major Trends, Risk Factors and Prevention Approaches," *American Journal of Preventive Medicine* 14:4 (1998): 259–272. See also American Academy of Child and Adolescent Psychiatry, "Children with Oppositional Defiant Disorder," http://www.aacap.org/publications/factsfam/72.htm (accessed January 20, 2005).

21. Emile Durkheim, *Division of Labor in Society*, trans. George Simpson (Glencoe, IL: Free Press, 1947). See also Dario Melossi, *The Sociology of Punishment* (Aldershot, UK: Dartmouth, 1998).

22. Carri Casteel, "Effectiveness of Crime Prevention through Environmental Design in Reducing Robberies," *American Journal of Preventive Medicine* 18:4 (2000): 99–115; and City of Mesa, Arizona, "Crime Prevention Through Environmental Design," http://www.cityofmesa.org/police/literature/cpted.asp (accessed January 19, 2005).

23. Eric Fritsch, T. Caeti, and R. Taylor, "Gang Suppression through Saturation Patrol, Aggressive Curfew and Truancy Enforcement," *Crime and Delinquency* 45:1 (1999): 122–139.

24. Daniel Nagin and J. Waldfogel, "The Effects of Conviction on Income through Life," *International Review of Law and Economics* 18:1 (1998): 25–40.

25. That trend has stopped. The percentage of U.S. households victimized by violent crime or theft during 2006 remained at the lowest levels since 1994. Since 1994, property crimes have dropped from 320 per 100,000 persons to 150 in 2006. Victimization through violent crime dropped 78% in the same time period. Bureau of Justice Statistics, *Criminal Victimization, 2006* (Washington, DC: BJS, 2007).

26. Harry E. Allen, Edward Latessa, and Gennaro Vito, "Corrections in the Year 2000," *Corrections Today* 49:2 (1987): 73–78.

27. T. Flanagan, E. McGarrell, and A. Lizotte, "Ideology and Crime Control Policy Positions in a State Legislature," *Journal of Criminal Justice* 17 (1989): 87–101; Marla Sandys and Edmund McGarrell, "Attitudes toward Capital Punishment among Indiana Legislators," *Justice Quarterly* 11:4 (1994): 651–677.

28. Francis Cullen, Bonnie Fisher, and Brandon Applegate, "Public Opinion about Punishment and Corrections," in Michael Tonry (ed.), *Crime and Justice* (Chicago: University of Chicago Press, 2000), pp. 1–79.

29. See Prison Fellowship International, "Restorative Justice Online," *http://www.restorativejustice.org/intro* (accessed July 15, 2008).

30. Prison Fellowship International, "Lesson 4: Programmes–Restorative Justice Processes," *http://www.restorativejustice.org/intro/tutorial/processes* (accessed July 15, 2008).

31. The Restorative-Justice Resource Center, "Victim-Offender Mediation or Dialogues," *http://www.restorativejustice.org/victim_offender-mediation.htm* (accessed July 15, 2008).

32. See William Spellman, "What Recent Studies Do (and Don't) Tell Us about Imprisonment and Crime," in Tonry, *Crime and Justice*, pp. 419–494.

33. Craig Hainey, "Mental Health Issues in Long-Term Solitary and 'Supermax' Confinement," *Crime and Delinquency* 49:1 (2003): 124–156; Michael Vaughn and Sue Collins, "Medical Malpractice in Correctional Facilities," *The Prison Journal* 84:4 (2004): 505–534; and Margaret Severson, "Mental Health Needs and Mental Health Care in Jails," *American Jails* 18:3 (2004): 9–18.

34. Edward Latessa and Harry Allen, *Corrections in the Community* (Cincinnati, OH: Anderson Publishing, 2004), p. 43. See also Ryan King, "Disparity by Geography: The War on Drugs in American Cities" (Washington, DC: The Sentencing Project, 2008).

35. PEW Charitable Trusts, "One in 100: Behind Bars in America 2008," *http://www.pewcenteronthestates.org/report_detail.aspx?id=35904* (accessed August 19, 2008).

36. See Daniel Mears et al., "Social Ecology and Recidivism: Implications for Prisoner Reentry," *Criminology* 46:2 (2008): 301–359.

37. Simon Fass and Chung-Ron Pi, "Getting Tough on Juvenile Crime: An Analysis of Costs and Benefits," *Journal of Research in Crime and Delinquency* 39:4 (2002): 363–399; Jesenia Pizarro and Vanja Stenius, "Supermax Prisons," *The Prison Journal* 84:2 (2004): 248–264; Daniel Mears, *Evaluating the Effectiveness of Supermax Prisons* (Washington, DC: Urban Institute, 2006); and Jeffrey Ian Ross, "Supermax Prisons," *Society* 44:3 (2007).

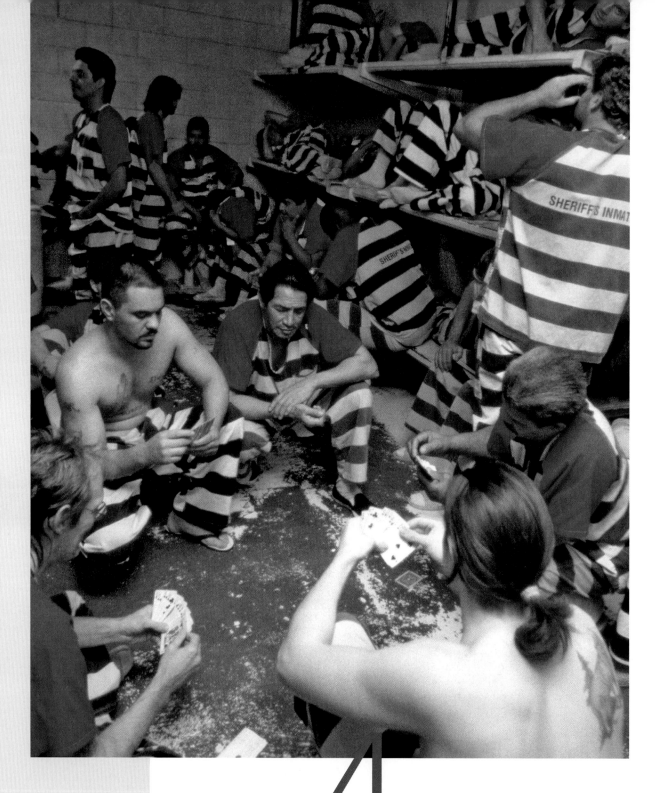

chapter 4

The Sentencing and Appeals Process

Outline

The Correctional Filter
- The Prosecutor's Decision

The Sentencing Decision
- Rapid Change in Sentencing Processes
- New Goals
- Reform Options
- Reform Effects
- Predicting Behavior
- The Presentence Investigation
- Judicial versus Administrative Sentencing
- Practical Problems in Sentencing
- Problems in Setting Prison Terms

Felony Sentences in State Court

Deterrence by Sentencing
- Appellate Review

The Issue of Due Process

The Mechanics of an Appeal
- The Courts of Appeal

Appeals from Behind the Walls

Reform by Judicial Decree

Appeals Flood the Courts
- Types of Prisoner Petitions
- Legislative Initiatives to Reduce Prisoner Litigation

> *"My object all sublime*
> *I shall achieve in time—*
> *To let the punishment fit the crime,*
> *The punishment fit the crime."*
>
> —William S. Gilbert, *The Mikado*

Overview

In this chapter we examine issues that deal with sentencing criminal offenders and some of the processes used to challenge those sentences. Students will also become acquainted with those processes by which offenders are placed in the major components of corrections and how sentencing practices influence correctional practices, programs, and facilities. We will also briefly look at appellate review of convictions and sentencing.

Perhaps no part of the criminal justice system has had more criticism or controversy than the nation's courts as they struggle to make, as noted above, "the punishment fit the crime." This chapter will examine that critical decision and acquaint the student with the impact these decisions have on soaring prison populations and their impact in regard to the "correctional filter," as discussed next. Many criticize the court's efforts to apply "justice" while dealing with public opinion, jail and prison overcrowding, budget shortages, and legislative restrictions on the judge's discretion. Students also need an understanding of the appeals process, which is discussed later in the chapter. The student must keep in mind the incidences of crime and the sheer volume of cases when discussing the sentencing process and decisions made in America's courts. This issue will have a vital relationship to the material already covered and chapters yet to come. It will also prepare the student for understanding the complexities of the appellate process. We begin our examination of sentencing practices and the correctional filter.

key term

Misdemeanor
A relatively minor violation of the criminal law, usually punishable by no more than one year in confinement.

key term

Felony
Serious criminal violation, sometimes punished by death or sentence of at least one year in prison.

key term

Plea bargaining
Process by which the defendant agrees to plead guilty for prosecutorial consideration.

lecture note

Using your computer, play the brief videotape by Harry Allen on "Sentencing and Appeals" (about 5 minutes).

lecture note

Using your computer, play the brief videotape of Francis Cullen on "Youth: Binding over to Adult Court" (5 minutes).

class activity

Ask the class to define *correctional filter* and identify the phases at which offenders are diverted to alternative outcomes in the sentencing process.

THE CORRECTIONAL FILTER

In our examination of the myriad dimensions and trends of corrections in America, we now come to the concept we call the *correctional filter*, representing the various sentencing options that sometimes confuse observers as to what is actually occurring in the criminal justice system. At every point of this filter, certain types of offenders and cases are shunted into alternative dispositions, the great bulk of which involve some type of correctional supervision other than jail or prison. Generally, criminal offenses are divided into one of two types: misdemeanor or felony. A **misdemeanor** is a less serious offense and is usually punishable by up to one year in a local jail or detention facility. A **felony** is a more serious offense, and someone convicted of such a charge can be punished by imprisonment or even death, in the case of a capital crime such as first-degree murder. Those offenders who are finally placed under custody and supervision in prisons are, for the most part, the most serious offenders. We now examine the processes, flows, and rationales of the correctional filter, as illustrated in Figure 4.1.

The Prosecutor's Decision

A major player in the correctional filter process is the prosecutor's office. It is here that prosecutors implement their broad discretionary power to dismiss charges or reduce them to charges for which the defendant will be more likely to plead guilty.[1] Recent studies indicate that as many as 50% to 90% of the felony cases initiated by the police are bargained away by prosecutors; in 2002, this figure was 95% in large urban counties. A high percentage of charges not dismissed are reduced through **plea bargaining** to a less seri-

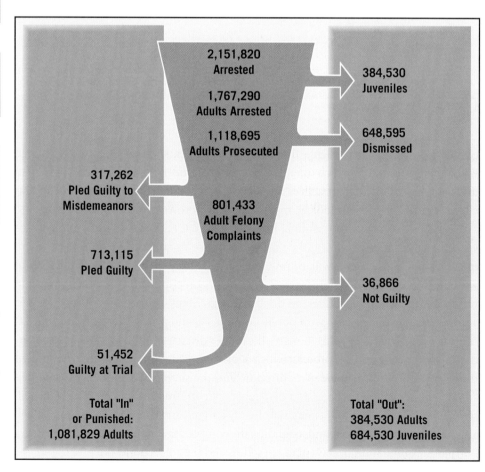

figure 4.1

Outcomes for Arrest for Type I Felony Crimes, 2006

SOURCE: Data gathered from Federal Bureau of Investigation, *Crime in the United States 2006* (http://www.fbi.gov/ucr/cius2006/data/table_01.html, accessed September 11, 2008). Figure adapted from S. Silberman, *Criminal Violence, Criminal Justice* (New York: Random House, 1978): 257–261.

correctional **brief**

Disparate Sentencing for Crack and Cocaine Use

In 1986, Congress created sentencing disparity for two of the most popular types of cocaine: powdered and crack (crystal). The sale of five grams of crack cocaine—barely a teaspoon full—results in a minimum of five years in federal prison for the violator. Sale of 100 times that amount of powdered cocaine—the type preferred by whites—is required to result in a comparable sentence. About 90% of those convicted of selling crack cocaine are black, and only 30% of those convicted of selling powdered cocaine are

black. When the U.S. Sentencing Commission recommended changing the sentencing guidelines to equalize sentencing, both the U.S. House and Senate voted to block any change in the 100-to-1 ratio.

SOURCE: Michael Isikoff, "Crack, Coke, and Race," *Newsweek* (November 6, 1995): 77; and Traci Schlesinger, "Racial and Ethnic Disparity in Pretrial Criminal Processing," *Justice Quarterly 22*:2 (2006): 170–192.

ous charge to which the defendant agrees to plead guilty. Plea bargaining refers to the prosecutor's practice of permitting the defendant to plead to a lesser charge than the one he or she was arrested for, usually because the prosecutor does not feel the case is strong enough on the more serious charge or because the prosecutor hopes to persuade the defendant to provide information about other crimes or offenders. Plea bargaining may lead to the prosecutor agreeing to dismiss multiple charges, reduce charges, or recommend a light sentence. The most common explanation for this action of the correctional filter stems from high caseloads and limited resources, forcing harried prosecutors to dispense with much of their caseload as quickly as possible to avoid overwhelming their own offices, the courts, and overcrowded jails and prisons. The time factor does not explain, however, why some cases are prosecuted and others dismissed. Here, the wide discretionary power given to prosecutors becomes a crucial issue, and prosecutors consider such factors as the case's strength, evenhandedness, harm done to the victim, ethnicity, and the attorneys' personal attributes.[2]

class activity

Have the class identify and explain those factors that influence the prosecutor's decisions in the sentencing process.

lecture note

Explain the authority of the prosecutor to manage the administration of justice, including powers and outcomes.

thematic question

Can the prosecutor achieve a just society by limiting the panoply of rights and protections guaranteed under the U.S. Constitution?

thematic question

How can plea bargaining result in the loss of guaranteed rights?

thematic question

How does plea bargaining decrease the ability of the offender to appeal the sentencing outcome?

THE SENTENCING DECISION

As suggested, defendants who reach the sentencing stage of criminal proceedings are those who have not yet completely evaded the correctional filter. They have either pled guilty to, or been found guilty of, a crime, either by a jury or bench trial.[3] The court must then decide in what fashion it will dispose of them. Making a sentencing decision is often the most complicated and difficult task for any judge. High rates of violent street crime, along with a large number of drug offenders and lengthier determinate sentences, make the sentencing decision more complex than it has ever been. Of course, deciding the sentence involves a great many factors, such as alternative dispositions allowed by statute, the criminal intent of the offender, the amount of harm or loss to the victim, the remorse expressed by the offender, and other mitigating or aggravating factors.

Rapid Change in Sentencing Processes

In 1930, most states and federal courts were operating under the **indeterminate sentencing** structure: The judge would impose a prison sentence with both a minimum and a maximum term in years, such as 2 years minimum to 5 years maximum, or 5 years minimum to 20 years maximum. The wide ranges of sentence lengths reflected the dominant rehabilitation goal of the correctional system and its belief that once the offender had been rehabilitated, the parole board would detect the change and then order the inmate's release. Parole boards would actually determine the length of the sentence served, using their authority of discretionary

key term

Indeterminate sentencing
Punishment imposed by a judge that has both a minimum and maximum period (usually of confinement).

release. Following a long period of relative inactivity (1930 to 1974), American sentencing laws and practices began to undergo a rapid, fundamental restructuring of the sentencing process. The causes have been identified as follows:[4]

1. Prison uprisings (such as at Attica in New York, and others in New Mexico, Oklahoma, California, and Florida) indicated that inmates were particularly discontented with the rhetoric of rehabilitation and the reality of the prison environment.
2. The abuse of discretion caused concerns about individual rights, because prosecutors, judges, and parole boards were immune from review and some practiced arbitrary uses of discretion.
3. Court orders and decisions led to a movement that demanded accountability in official decision making and outcomes.
4. The rehabilitation ideal was challenged, both empirically and ideologically, which undermined the rationale of the indeterminate sentence's "parole after rehabilitation" corollary.
5. Experimental and statistical studies of judicial sentencing found substantial disparity and both racial and class discrimination.[5] Such inconsistencies and disparities fostered the conclusion that sentencing practices were unfair. (**Sentencing disparity** means that offenders committing the same crimes under the same circumstances are given different sentences by the same judge.)
6. Crime control and corrections became a political football,[6] useful for those seeking election to public office.

New Goals

Corrections by the 1970s generally functioned under the utilitarian goal of rehabilitation being possible. Dialogue and arguments from "hard-liners" brought other primary goals to the forefront in the 1980s. These included incapacitation of persons likely to commit future crimes and its variant of selective incapacitation, in which the highest-risk offenders would receive much longer sentences to prevent any more criminal activity.[7] From the mid-1990s on, such concepts as "three strikes and you're out" laws have become popular with the public and legislators. A dramatic rash of "headline crimes," especially heinous, combined with the perception of a growing level of violent crimes, has spurred on such movements since the early 1970s. The specific deterrence of sentenced offenders and the general deterrence of those contemplating committing a crime were legitimized as social policy goals. In addition, the retribution goal became attractive, inasmuch as it would impose deserved punishment. (Such a **just deserts** goal looks backward to the offender's personal culpability, focuses on the nature of the act, and considers the harm done.[8])

In total, 25 states and the federal government have enacted three-strikes legislation, increasing the length of sentences by a multiple of two, or setting minimum time to be served at 25, 30, or even 40 years. Despite claims of prosecutors and legislators that such legislation was an essential crime-fighting tool, both for deterrence and incapacitation, it has not been applied extensively. There is little creditable evidence from investigations that enacting such laws has reduced crime. Instead, the evidence is that criminals are rarely concerned about being apprehended, that the laws target offenders beyond their peak ages of reoffending, that identifying high-rate offenders early on before they perpetrate a high number of crimes is difficult and fraught with "false-positive" errors, and that other criminals simply replace any who would be incarcerated. Finally, eligible offenders have mostly experienced enhanced penalties prior to the imposition of such laws, and the increased incarceration does not sufficiently increase the severity of punishment. There is some reason to suspect that such ineffective crime-control measures serve to increase the geriatric populations in prison, creating a demand for prison nursing homes and other expensive medical treatments.[9]

key term
_____

Sentencing disparity
Difference between both the types and length of sentences imposed for the same crime or seriousness of crimes when there is no legal basis that can be identified to explain this difference.

key term
_____

Just deserts
Sentencing ideology that stresses that any punishment to be applied must be dependent on the culpability of the offender and the seriousness of the offense.

Reform Options

As a result of the reform movement, sentencing practices were changed in the belief that the new practices would limit disparity and discretion and establish more detailed criteria for sentencing or new sentencing institutions. The resulting contradictory options include the following:

1. Abolishing plea bargaining
2. Establishing plea-bargaining rules and guidelines
3. Setting mandatory minimum sentences
4. Establishing statutory determinate sentencing
5. Setting voluntary or descriptive sentencing guidelines or presumptive or prescriptive sentencing guidelines
6. Creating sentencing councils
7. Requiring judges to provide reasons for their sentences
8. Setting parole guidelines to limit parole board discretion
9. Abolishing parole[10]
10. Adopting or modifying good-time procedures
11. Routinizing appellate review of sentences[11]

These options represent only the principal steps designed to limit unbridled discretion, reduce discrimination, make sentencing fairer, and enhance justice.

Reform Effects

In just a few decades, dramatic changes in sentencing structures and practices became evident. Release by a parole board was abolished in a large number of states, and mandatory sentencing guidelines were established in many others. In 1987, the U.S. Federal Sentencing Guidelines were enacted. More than 20 states were using determinate sentencing (a sentence with a specific release date), and at least 48 states had established mandatory minimum sentences for at least one crime. Several states adopted statewide sentencing councils, and at least 50 jurisdictions drew up local sentencing guidelines. It is against that background of concern and change that we will look at the sentencing decision.

Predicting Behavior

If the sentencing procedure had no purpose but to punish the offender, as was the case until fairly recently, the judge's decision could be easily prescribed by statute. In modern times, however, the sentence is also expected to serve other purposes, such as rehabilitation and reintegration of the offender and restoration of the victim and community. Those broadly divergent objectives create a paradox that may force judges to choose between alternatives based on the offense, the offender, the victim, and the community. The choice is often further complicated by subtle pressures from police, prosecutors, and the general public to incarcerate certain offenders for longer periods of time.

One of the main problems with the sentencing decision is that it requires judges to predict human behavior. As judges ask themselves if specific offenders will respond to prison positively or perhaps benefit more from help while on probation, they have little factual information to guide them. In the final analysis, most judges must rely on a presentence investigation and their own intuition, experience, and imagination to produce the best decision.

The Presentence Investigation

Most of the states make a **presentence report** mandatory for offenses for which imprisonment can be more than one year. It is estimated that more than 85% of the states do prepare some kind of presentence report on felony cases, although there may be extreme variation in

---

class activity

Have the class explain why the sentencing decision is the most difficult task for the sentencing judge.

class activity

Ask students to debate the disparity in sentencing for crack and cocaine use. If they do not have concerns about racial disparity in sentencing at this level, ask them to explain the concentration of drug-law violators in state and in federal prisons.

class activity

Ask students to identify five new goals in sentencing from 1965 until the present.

lecture note

Explain the major changes that have occurred in the sentencing process in the last quarter-century, focusing on indeterminate sentencing.

lecture note

Briefly describe the major reform effects in sentencing over the last quarter-century.

lecture note

Using your computer, play the brief videotape of Angela West on "Disparate Sentencing of Crack Users versus Cocaine Users" (about 4 minutes).

lecture note

Using your computer, play the brief videotape of George Higgins on "Changing Views on Sentencing"(about 3 minutes).

key term

Presentence report
Document prepared by agent of the court that investigates the offender's background for judicial determination of punishment.

correctional **brief**

Presumptive Sentencing

One alternative to limit sentencing disparity is the presumptive sentencing system, in which the state legislature sets minimum, average, and maximum terms, allowing the judge to select a term based on the characteristics of the offender and aggravating circumstances. The sentence imposed will be the time served, less any credits against the sentence that the offender earns (such as credit for time served in jail, good behavior in prison, program participation, and so on). California has a presumptive sentencing structure that provides three options to the sentencing judge, as seen here for the crime of burglary:

1. Aggravating circumstances—seven years

2. Presumptive (average) sentence—five years

3. Mitigating circumstances—three years

Ordinarily, the judge would decide if the offender were to be placed on probation or sentenced to prison (the "in–out" decision). Assuming imprisonment to be the answer, the judge would impose the average sentence of five years, unless mitigating circumstances were present at the time of the offense (for example, if the offender were under the influence of a controlled substance or had a weak personality and was easily led into committing a crime for peer approval). If mitigating circumstances were proven, the judge would impose the least sentence (three years). However, if aggravating circumstances were proven, the judge must impose the highest sentence (seven years). Some examples of aggravating circumstances are gross bodily harm to victim, prior incarceration in prison, and vulnerability of victim (older than 60 years of age, blind, paraplegic, etc.).

the report's usefulness and quality. The presentence report, if properly researched and prepared, can be an extremely valuable document for trial judges who are making sentencing decisions.

The presentence investigation report is usually prepared by the court's probation officer. The defense attorney usually reviews, and may challenge, points in the presentence report to help the judge make a sentencing decision based on information from all of the sources. Walter C. Reckless pointed out the essential elements of a workable presentence investigation report. He said that, when written up and presented to the judge, this report should include in summary form the following information:[12]

A court-appointed attorney argues for probation for his client.
Photo by Bob Daemmrich, courtesy of Stock Boston.

1. Present offense (including the person's attitudes toward it and his or her role in it)
2. Previous criminal record, family situation (including tensions and discord and the factors affecting his or her happiness)
3. Neighborhood environment, school, and educational history
4. Employment history (especially skills and efficiency and stability as a worker)
5. Associates and participation
6. Habits (including alcohol, gambling, promiscuity, and so forth)
7. Physical and mental health (as reported by various sources and by special examinations)
8. Summary and recommendations

Most presentence investigations will emphasize such objective facts in a case as number of prior offenses, employment status, age, grade reached in school, number of children, and so on. It is also important that the investigating officer capture additional information such as the defendants' attitudes toward the charges, acceptance of responsibility, and willingness to change their behavior.

The presentence investigation report gives the judge a comprehensive and factual overview of the offender, the actual crime, and the offender's nature, history, habits, personality, problems, needs, and risks. It also usually contains a recommendation to the court of an appropriate disposition for the case. Judges tend to accept the presentence recommendation at a rate of about 83% for probation and 87% for imprisonment.

The presentence report serves many functions. Not only is it of immediate use in determining an appropriate sentence, but it also is used by correctional agencies or institutions for classification and program activities assignments. It will aid the probation officer in handling the case, should probation be the sentence imposed. It will also follow the offender to parole, at which time the parole officer will use it in planning and supervising the case. Appellate review courts use the document when considering an **appeal** of sentence, and the presentence investigation reports also offer a database from which to conduct research on convicted offenders, case flows, and court management.[13]

Judicial versus Administrative Sentencing

Traditionally, the sentencing process has involved a judicial determination of the appropriate punishment for a specific crime. There have been extensive changes in judicial power in the last century, however, particularly during the last two decades. In the early days, when a judge sentenced an offender to ten years in prison, it was almost a certainty that the offender would serve ten years to the day. As administrative forms of sentence shortening (involving such matters as good time, pardon, parole, and clemency) became more common, the correlation between the judge's sentence and the time the offender served largely disappeared. In practice, courts using indeterminate sentencing can establish minimum and maximum sentences within the sentencing statutes, but the actual length of the sentence is often left up to the administrators of the correctional system, that is, to the executive rather than to the judicial branch of government. Therefore, those involved in **administrative sentencing** ultimately decide an offender's fate.

A comparison of the judicial and administrative styles of decision making in sentencing reveals some similar criteria:

1. A determination of how much time is right for the kind of crime at issue, with the decision maker's own sense of values and expectations usually (but not always) heavily influenced by the pressures of the local environment and perceived norms of colleagues[14]
2. Classification within that crime category of the offender's particular acts as mitigated, average, or aggravated
3. Offender's past criminal record (slight, average, or aggravated)
4. Offender's extent of repentance, attitude toward available treatment, and official prognosis of reformability
5. Anticipated public (usually meaning law enforcement) reaction to a proposed disposition

Not all of these criteria are used or even relevant in every case, and many other variables may be raised because of the existence of particular facts (such as strong middle-class background and allegiance) or the peculiarities or hang-ups of an individual decision maker. Something approximating the given basic list, however, appears to comprise the critical factors in most sentence fixing.[15]

Practical Problems in Sentencing

As we have seen previously, the correctional filter of the criminal justice process reveals at every step an imbalance of input to output (number of arrests versus number of incarcerations). Many cases are winnowed out in the early stages, and it is a highly select group of prisoners who end up in prisons like Attica, Pelican Bay, and San Quentin. In a statistical sense, the negative selection process that admits the offender to prison may be considered more discriminating than the positive one that admits students to Ivy League colleges. But for the practical need to spread limited resources over an overwhelming number of cases, scores of additional offenders would join each of the relatively small proportion of offenders that ends

key term

Appeal
Petition to higher courts to reverse procedures and protect offenders based on due process issues.

class activity

Ask students to define and differentiate between probation and parole.

key term

Administrative sentencing
Process by which the actual length of the sentence is left up to the administrators of the correctional system, as seen in such processes as good-time credit, probation, parole, and program participation; the actual sentence served is set by the executive branch rather than the judicial.

class activity

When an offender convicted of possession with intent to sell marijuana is sentenced, does the sentencing judge choose between the offender or the offense?

class activity

Ask the class to identify five factors external to the offender that could influence the "in–out" sentencing decision the judge might make.

lecture note

Describe the presentence investigation process, and the presentence investigation report's functions.

up in prison. The state and federal correctional systems are finite in size. The sentencing decision may be impacted by the decisions at the other end of the funnel process, which determine release rates. The system can become blocked if sentences do not approximately balance releases, resulting in dangerous overcrowding. At worst, prison overcrowding can contribute to judicial overuse of probation for offenders whose risk level is too high. This can result in overworked probation officers and unacceptably high probation failure rates by offenders who continue to commit serious crimes and whose probation is then revoked, requiring resentencing to imprisonment in state institutions. Sentencing, therefore, sometimes takes into account both the numbers of prisoners in the institutions and the limited resources for handling them.[16] Another source of pressure on the already overloaded correctional and court systems is the seemingly endless number of drug arrests that enter the juvenile and adult courts.

Problems in Setting Prison Terms

In the past, the determination of prison terms has been left largely to the courts. Decisions were made within the broad parameters of plea bargaining and statutory limitations. In the past two decades, however, control over the sentencing process has become more of a concern to state legislatures. Concerns about disparate sentences and other abuses or perceived abuses of the system have resulted in six basic strategies to formalize legislative control over the sentencing process:

1. **Determinate sentencing**—sentencing systems under which parole boards no longer may release prisoners before their sentences (minus good time) have expired
2. Mandatory prison terms—statutes through which legislatures require a prison term always to be imposed for convictions for certain offenses or offenders
3. **Sentencing guidelines**—procedures designed to structure sentencing decisions based on measures of offense severity and criminal history
4. Parole guidelines—procedures designed to structure parole release decisions based on measurable offender criteria
5. **Good-time policies**—statutes that allow for reducing a prison term based on an offender's behavior in prison
6. Emergency crowding provisions—policies that relieve prison crowding by systematically making inmates eligible for release sooner.

Prison populations are increasing in many states. Policies for setting prison terms influence the size of prison populations by both the number of people who are sentenced and the length of time that they stay in prison. As a result, many states have attempted to find ways to **modify** prison terms and reduce population pressures. Those methods include sentencing guidelines, such as those in Minnesota, that use available prison capacity as a consideration in setting the length of terms. Mechanisms also exist for accelerating good time and direct release of certain prisoners, usually those already close to their release date, under administrative provisions (such as emergency crowding laws, the use of commutation, sentence revisions, and early release programs).

The determinate sentencing states of California, Colorado, Connecticut, Illinois, Indiana, Maine, Minnesota, New Mexico, North Carolina, and Washington tend to give sentencing judges the least amount of discretion. Offenders usually receive fixed sentences and they are served in full, minus good-time credits. Generally in those states, parole boards continue to handle revocations and good-time decisions.

Such a sentencing structure limits "judicial imperialism" in sentencing, because the legislature heavily influences the sentence length. Whether there are unforeseen problems in **presumptive sentencing** remains to be proven, but California's prison population problems may well be due to a corollary of presumptive sentencing: abolition of parole board early-release authority that had been used in the past to control prison overcrowding. Mandatory prison-term statutes exist in some form, for some crimes, in 48 states. Those statutes apply to certain

---

key term

Determinate sentencing
A flat sentence of punishment imposed by the sentencing court.

key term

Sentencing guidelines
System of sentencing that imposes a predefined sentence length based on prior criminal history and crime severity, which allows judges to depart from the guidelines if warranted by the circumstances.

key term

Good-time policies
Administrative mechanism reducing sentence length by crediting inmates for good behavior, extra work, or other statutory policies.

key term

Modify
Appeal court order requiring change in the trial court's legal decision on guilt or other rights.

key term

Presumptive sentences
A sentencing mechanism fixed by a sentencing commission or legislature that identifies maximum and minimum sentences for punishment to be imposed by the judge, but permitting adjustment for special circumstances.

correctional **brief**

History of the Sentencing Guidelines

More than ten years ago, Congress dramatically changed the federal sentencing system. The changes followed widespread discontent with the old sentencing system, and they ultimately led to the passage of the Federal Sentencing Guidelines in 1987. In the old system, judges determined criminal sentences. They considered the facts of each particular case—including the circumstances of the offense and the life history of the offender—and chose a sentence they considered fair. The only requirement was that the sentence be within a statutory range, and the ranges were often extremely broad. Statutes typically authorized sentences like "not more than 5 years," "not more than 20 years," or in some cases, "any term of years or life." Judges had authority to impose any sentence within the statutory range.

The imposition of the sentence was only the beginning. Once the person was in prison, the parole board determined the actual date of release. The parole board considered circumstances such as the person's conduct in prison and efforts toward rehabilitation, and it released people to parole supervision when it thought they were ready—often after just half the sentence. If the person misbehaved after release, parole could be revoked and the person could be incarcerated for the remainder of the sentence.

In the 1970s, this practice fell into disfavor because it permitted too much disparity between cases. Different judges sentenced similar offenders differently, and parole boards became too powerful. If two identical offenders were each convicted of a crime carrying a sentence of "not more than 20 years," one might spend 3 years in custody and the other might spend 15. Evidence accumulated that the system led to arbitrary decision making and sometimes discrimination against poor people and minorities.

In 1984 Congress addressed these concerns by creating the United States Sentencing Commission and ordering the promulgation of the Federal Sentencing Guidelines. The new system sharply curtailed parole and confined judicially imposed sentences into narrow ranges. Congress enacted the guidelines into law in 1987, and in 1989 the Supreme Court held that the effort was constitutional. (See *Mistretta* v. *U.S.* [1989], 317–320.)

Guidelines use standardized worksheets to calculate the sentence. In principle, the process is a lot like calculating income taxes with a federal 1040 form. The worksheet is complex and intricate, but in theory it guides everybody to the same conclusions. Guidelines operate by assigning an offense level to every crime—low offense levels for minor crimes and high levels for major crimes. At the same time, the guidelines direct the calculation of the criminal history of each defendant. A person with a clean record starts with zero criminal history points, and points are added for every subsequent offense.

The task of the judge is to look up on a grid the spot where the offense level intersects the criminal history. The grid assigns light sentences to people with low criminal histories who commit lesser crimes, and stiff sentences to people with long criminal histories who commit severe crimes. The judge then imposes a sentence in accordance with the sentencing guidelines grid unless there is a reason to depart.

The concept of the guidelines has been well received because it can lead to less sentencing disparity between judges and a more rational system overall. The federal system and roughly one-third of the states now use guideline sentencing systems. Different jurisdictions use different guidelines and have had different experiences with them. The general experience has been that guidelines represent an improvement over unfettered judicial discretion, but that they must be well structured and carefully conceived in order to succeed.

SOURCE: Coalition for Federal Sentencing Reform, "Guideline History," *http://www.sentencing.org* (revised July 2002).

---

crimes of violence and to habitual criminals, and the court's discretion in such cases (regarding, for example, probation, fines, and suspended sentences) has been eliminated by statute.

Perhaps the best example of sentencing guidelines can be seen in the federal system. The Federal Sentencing Guidelines matrix is shown in Figure 4.2. The matrix system factors in the severity of the offense and the criminal history of the offender to arrive at a sentence range. Among the most vocal critics of the Federal Sentencing Guidelines are federal judges, who believe that this system has taken away too much discretion. In 2005, the U.S. Supreme Court ruled that the federal guidelines violated a defendant's Sixth Amendment right to a jury trial because the guidelines required judges to make decisions that affect prison time by considering factors that had not come before the jury during trial. Later that month, the U.S. Supreme Court ordered lower courts to review hundreds of sentences of defendants then appealing their tainted enhanced sentence.

Good-time policies are another way to control behavior in correctional institutions and to control population pressures as well. The threat of losing up to one-third of their credits

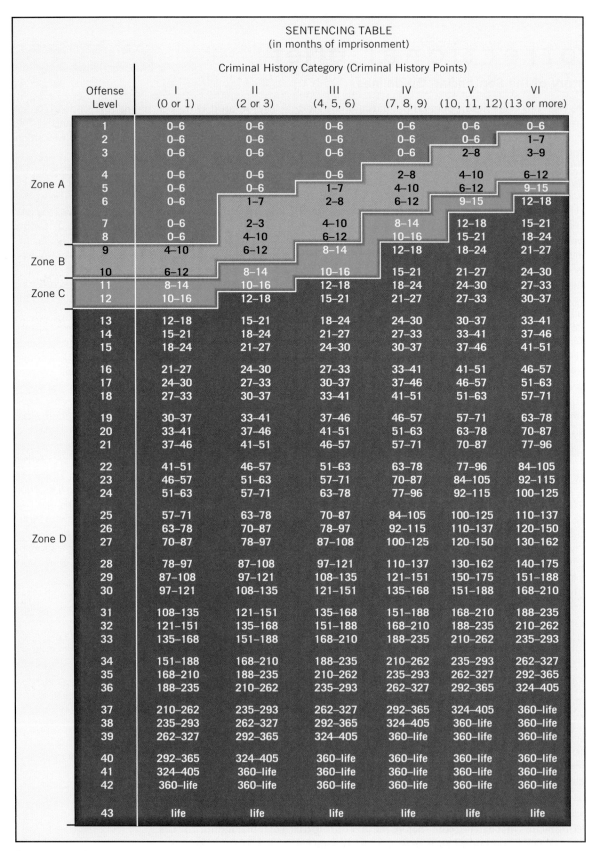

figure 4.2

Federal Sentencing Guidelines

SOURCE: United States Sentencing Commission, "Determining the Sentence," *www.ussc.gov/2007guid/CHAPS.html.*

toward their sentences earned by good conduct serves as a control over some inmates' behavior. Our review of the changes in sentencing practices and their consequences in the last decade clearly shows the shifts that have taken place. Although discretion in determining sentence length has been somewhat removed from the sentencing judge and parole board, it was reduced by legislatures through their enactment of new sentencing structures, for reasons discussed earlier. In turn, in many jurisdictions, the prosecutor's discretion was increased. The prison populations will continue to climb as more and more offenders are committed and serve longer and longer sentences.

FELONY SENTENCES IN STATE COURT

In 2004 (the last year for which there are national data), state courts convicted nearly 1,145,000 adults of a felony. Of convicted felons, 40% were sentenced to a state prison, and 30% were sentenced to a local jail (usually for a year or less). The remaining 30% were sentenced to probation. Of those convicted, some 95% pled guilty; the other 5% were found guilty either by a jury or by the judge in a bench trial.

Felons in state courts were convicted on drug offenses (34%), property offenses (29%), and violent offenses (18%). The rest were convicted of weapons offenses and other nonviolent crime.

The average sentence varied considerably. Those sentenced to local jail received six months, on average. The average probation sentence was three years and two months. The average sentence length to prison was four years and nine months, but offenders are more likely to serve more of that sentence before release than did a comparable group in 1990. Besides being sentenced to incarceration or probation, more than one-third of the convicted felons were ordered to pay a fine, pay victim restitution, receive treatment, perform community service, or comply with some other additional penalty, such as undergoing house arrest or appearing periodically for drug testing. A fine was imposed on at least 25% of convicted felons.[17]

DETERRENCE BY SENTENCING

A discussion of sentencing would be incomplete without mentioning the policy implications of the increasing demand for deterrence. Some writers now argue that those states that imprison more of the offender population (rather than use community corrections) would have lower crime rates if the proportion of persons sentenced to prison were to increase even more. Though **deterrence by sentencing** may appeal to conservatives who believe that the criminal justice system can affect the rates of crime and serve as a deterrent, the data on the effects of higher imprisonment rates do not bear out the presumed effects. In both the United States and Canada, the rates of crime do not go down with increased imprisonment.[18] Instead, the rates of crime go up when the proportion of offenders per 100,000 who are sentenced to prison is raised. Therefore, we may need to reevaluate our thinking about the continued use of imprisonment to deter others from committing crime, when studies show that it has just the opposite effect.[19]

Appellate Review

Our examination of sentencing and legal issues surrounding corrections for offenders and law violators would not be complete without a discussion of the path of appeals from convictions, penalties imposed, conditions of imprisonment, and questions about civil rights violations. The prison walls can no more be a "concrete curtain" between offenders and prisoners under correctional control and those living in the free society. In the twenty-first century, offenders are still granted many of the same rights guaranteed by the U.S. Constitution. Prisoner rights are discussed in detail in Chapter 15. This chapter examines such items as motions to vacate sentences, habeas corpus, and civil rights. We begin with some of the basic tenets that apply to the justice system in America. The many types of legal cases involved with corrections are presented here in their most basic forms. Serious students of corrections, whether future academicians or practitioners, should become familiar with those key cases.

THE ISSUE OF DUE PROCESS

A basic tenet of the criminal justice process in America is that every defendant is presumed to be innocent until proven guilty. Not only does our system demand proof of guilt, it also requires that the proof be obtained fairly and legally. The process of appellate review helps ensure that these conditions will be met. In effect, the appellate review acts as a shield for the defendant caught up in the processes of criminal trial, incarceration, or supervision in the community. The state has considerable resources to prosecute those it considers offenders, and the Constitution protects us from the kind of government **railroading** that could deprive us of life, liberty, or property without the benefit of the due process of law.

Due process has been a constitutional right for all Americans under federal law since the passage of the Fourteenth Amendment in 1868. It was not until the "criminal law revolution" of the 1960s, however, that the due process clause of the Fourteenth Amendment was also made binding on all of the states through a series of Supreme Court decisions. In the field of corrections, like every other segment of criminal justice, those decisions created a climate of great challenge and rapid change. This chapter includes a brief examination of the appeal process and procedure, a glance at several significant cases, and an analysis of trends that appear to be emerging in appeals.[20]

One of the problems with "due process of law" is not that it is *due*—that is, something to which we are entitled—but rather the process of determining how *much* of it is due. Only a few decades ago, very few criminal cases were appealed. Since the U.S. Supreme Court case of *Gideon* v. *Wainwright* (1963), however, the picture has radically changed. The securing of the right to counsel for all defendants, stemming from that landmark decision, has opened the floodgates in the appellate courts across America. In some jurisdictions the rate of appeals is as high as 90% of all convictions.[21] **Collateral attack,**[22] or the filing of an appeal in the federal system while the state case is still undecided (almost unknown before the 1960s), is now routine in most state courts. The result of this massive overload in the appellate system was a monumental increase in the workload for state and federal judges. It has also created extended periods of litigation, often stretched out over several years, that have eroded any lingering belief that a conviction for a criminal offense must be considered final. The review procedure has as many as 11 steps in some state systems, and it is not unusual for a defendant to explore at least four or five. The 11 steps are as follows:

1. New trial motion filed in court where conviction was imposed
2. Appeal to state intermediate appellate court (in states where there is no intermediate appellate court, this step would not be available)
3. Appeal to state supreme court
4. Petition to U.S. Supreme Court to review state court decision in appeal
5. Postconviction proceeding in state trial court
6. Appeal of postconviction proceeding to state intermediate appellate court
7. Appeal to state supreme court
8. Petition to U.S. Supreme Court to review state court decision on appeal from postconviction proceeding
9. Habeas corpus petition in federal district court
10. Appeal to U.S. Court of Appeals
11. Petition to U.S. Supreme Court to review court of appeals decision on habeas corpus petition[23]

The United States Supreme Court.
SOURCE: *Jeff Greenberg/Omni-Photo Communications Inc.*

It is easy to see why the review process can take so long, especially when some steps may be used several times in a single appeal, with reviews of the same case taking place simultaneously in different court systems. Thus, due process may be a long and complicated procedure and, when appeal is part of the scheme, it can become a seemingly endless cycle.

correctional **brief**

The "Landmark Cases" of the 1960s and 1970s

Mapp **v. Ohio**   The case of *Mapp* v. *Ohio* (exclusionary rule), 367 U.S. 643 (1960), opened a Pandora's box of Fourteenth Amendment rulings. A crack in the armor of state proceedings, it paved the way for the flood of cases heard by the Court during the next decade, in reference not only to illegally obtained evidence but also to all areas of individual rights.

Robinson **v. California**   In the California case of *Robinson* v. *California* (cruel and unusual punishment), 370 U.S. 660 (1961), the Eighth Amendment's clause forbidding cruel and unusual punishment was made binding on state proceedings.

Gideon **v. Wainwright**   In the crucial decision of *Gideon* v. *Wainwright* (right to counsel), 372 U.S. 335 (1963), the Court held that defendants in noncapital cases are entitled to assistance of counsel at trial as a matter of right. This right was extended to state proceedings, again under the provisions of the Fourteenth Amendment.

Miranda **v. Arizona**   The application of the Fifth Amendment protections against self-incrimination was influenced by *Gideon* v. *Wainwright*, 372 U.S. 335 (1963). For the first time, in the 1966 decision of *Miranda* v. *Arizona*, 384 U.S. 436, a set of specific and detailed police warnings to the arrested person (and now the prison inmate) was required, through the due process clause, at specific and distinct points in the criminal process.

Johnson **v. Avery**   A significant 1969 decision provided prisoners in state penal institutions with legal assistance in preparing habeas corpus proceedings. In *Johnson* v. *Avery*, 393 U.S. 483, the Court held that states not providing adequate legal assistance would have to put up with "jailhouse lawyers," prisoners determined to research and conduct their own and others' appeals.

Furman **v. Georgia**   In *Furman* v. *Georgia*, 408 U.S. 238 (1972), the issue of cruel and unusual punishment as applied to the death penalty was raised in a petition by several states for clarification of that long-standing dilemma. In June 1972, the U.S. Supreme Court held that any statute that permits a jury to demand the death penalty is unconstitutional.

THE MECHANICS OF AN APPEAL

Throughout the legal proceedings there are points at which appealable errors can occur. Following the effects of some of the major cases, and the potential of future appeals, it is important to know how one makes an appeal following a criminal conviction. The process is highly fragmented and cumbersome, but a basic scheme applies to most jurisdictions. Although there are many alternatives to this basic model, it covers most of the avenues for appeals.

The entire process stems, of course, from a conviction of guilt by some court system at the municipal, county, state, or federal level. In each case, the procedure for appeal is determined by the court of record for that case. Those appeals, known as postconviction remedies, are usually made by the defendant. The state is less likely to appeal a decision, regardless of the outcome. If the accused is convicted, that is the result the state was after, and if the accused is declared innocent, the state cannot appeal because the Constitution guarantees that someone who is found innocent cannot be placed in **double jeopardy**[24] (which is being subjected to a second trial, by the same jurisdiction, on the same facts). The effect of an appropriately introduced appeal is to grant a stay (delay) in the execution of the original sentence until the appeal has been decided. As soon as possible, if not immediately after the sentence is pronounced, the defendant's counsel must either move for a new trial or make an appeal on some reasonable grounds, because appellate courts usually dislike and make short work of "frivolous" appeals. But as long ago as 1933, the significance of the appeal process was firmly established:

> Appellate courts do not reverse decisions simply because they disagree with them. Reversal must proceed from error of law and such error must be substantial. But if this account is to be veracious I must call attention to a fact familiar to every experienced lawyer, yet not apparent in the classical literature of the law, and probably not consciously admitted even to themselves by most appellate judges. Practically every decision of a lower court can be reversed. By that I mean practically every record contains some erroneous rulings [and] they can nearly always find some error if they want grounds for reversal.[25]

Each state has an appellate tribunal that serves as the **court of last resort.** The titles vary, but no matter what the title, a pathway for appeal is open to all in the American judicial system.

The Courts of Appeal

The court level immediately above the trial court is usually called the **court of appeals.** In some states, and in the federal system, there is more than one level of appeal. In those cases, the highest level of appellate court is generally called the Supreme Court. The Supreme Court of the United States is the court of last resort; cases decided there are considered final. The U.S. Supreme Court will usually hear cases from the state systems only after the defendant has exhausted all state remedies and the case has been finally adjudicated.[26]

In most state systems, the court of appeals reviews the trial court's decisions for judicial error. The facts in the case are not in question, and the trial court's decisions on that aspect of the case are generally binding on the appellate court. Because of that aspect of appellate review, evidence on the facts of the case is not presented to the court of appeals. Rather, the review is based only on the trial record. An appellate court cannot **reverse** the factual findings of the trial court unless they are totally erroneous. In states that have a second level of review, the trial record and the intermediary court's decision are examined. Usually, the refusal to hear an appeal over a lower appellate court's ruling is the same as upholding the decision, and the case stops there, unless an appeal is filed separately in a federal court of appeals on some constitutional issue.

The federal court system currently includes 94 trial courts (federal district courts) and 13 intermediary review courts (courts of appeal) between the federal trial courts and the

U.S. Supreme Court. The federal courts of appeal are spread across the country in "circuits" to facilitate servicing the 94 trial courts. Federal courts are restricted in their powers to cases arising under the Constitution, federal laws, or treaties; all cases affecting ambassadors, public ministers, and consuls; admiralty and maritime cases; and controversies where the United States is a party, controversies between states, between a state and a citizen of another state, between citizens of the same state claiming lands under grants from different states, and in cases between a state or citizens of a state and foreign states, citizens, or subjects.[27]

The federal courts of appeal are similar to the state courts of appeal in that they review for error the cases tried by the federal district courts. The Supreme Court is the ultimate interpreter of the Constitution and federal statutes. It reviews the decisions of the courts of appeal, and some direct appeals from district courts. The Supreme Court also reviews the decisions of state courts involving matters of federal constitutional rights where the case has been finally adjudicated in the state court system. Besides its appellate function, the Court has original jurisdiction in suits where a state is a party and in controversies involving ambassadors, ministers, and consuls.[28]

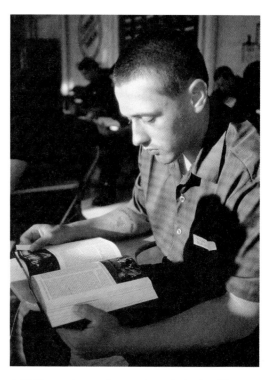

A "jailhouse lawyer" goes through the law library trying to find an appeal route.
Photo by J. Chiasson

APPEALS FROM BEHIND THE WALLS

In the early twentieth century, most appeals were based on the specific issues in the trial. In the 1960s, appeals began to move toward issues related to individual rights as stated and interpreted under the U.S. Constitution. Using the Fourteenth Amendment as a lever, the Supreme Court **affirmed** those rights to individuals in the separate states on a piecemeal basis. Under the "hands-off" doctrine established by chief justice Felix Frankfurter, the court had restricted its early decisions to the actions of judges. Later, abandoning the Frankfurter policy, the court began to impose procedural guidelines on law enforcement, corrections, and every other element of the criminal justice system. See Figure 4.3 for a description of the extent of Court involvement in corrections. Constitutional rights of prisoners (discussed in Part 6) were more sharply defined by the appellate courts' decisions. Many of these appeals came from desperate people behind prison walls,[29] and those appeals continued to increase (civil rights appeals increased *389%* between 1977 and 1994, for example).[30]

key term

Affirm

Appeal court's decision that due processes have not been violated by the government.

lecture note

Explain the system of appeal courts in your state, including the *court of last resort*.

REFORM BY JUDICIAL DECREE

Corrections, as a social system, is above all a political unit established by an authorizing mandate, supported by tax revenues, and subject to political influences. It reflects both the system of justice and the overall sociocultural environment. The latter is the source of externally induced reform. In externally induced reform, individuals or groups outside the correctional system effect changes.[31]

At the state and local levels, correctional reform is usually accomplished through legislative or executive action. Examples of reform by legislation range from the complete revision of a state's criminal code to passage of simple amendments to bills, allowing such benefits as educational and home furloughs. The executive branch of government can also exert a direct effect on correctional reform through executive orders. Those orders can accomplish small but important changes, such as the abolition of mail censorship, the

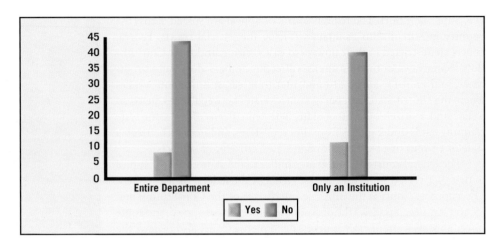

figure 4.3

Departments and Institutions Under Court Order/Consent Decree (September 30, 2003)

SOURCE: American Correctional Association, *2007 Directory* (Lanham, MD: ACA, 2008), p. 15.

appointment of a task force of involved citizens to seek correctional reform, and the with-holding of support for clearly unsound correctional programs.[32]

Between 1960 and 1972, American criminal law passed from a state of *evolution* to a state of *revolution*.[33] The step-by-step extension to the states of the various federal constitutional guarantees of individual rights was clearly the goal of the courts' quiet but effective revolution. The decisions of the much maligned—or revered—Warren Court are more readily understood when viewed from that perspective. During the 1960s, nearly all of the guarantees of the Fourth, Fifth, Sixth, and Eighth Amendments to the Constitution were made binding on the states, although the Rehnquist Court attempted to undo some of these advances. As previously mentioned, the Fourteenth Amendment (due process clause) provided the primary leverage in the landmark decisions that impacted corrections. The extension of constitutional guarantees to all persons accused in state proceedings has produced dramatic and significant changes in criminal law and criminal procedures and important effects on corrections through appeals related to major landmark decisions.

It should be pointed out that in addition to these cases, from the 1960s and 1970s the Supreme Court also entertained cases concerning the civil rights of inmates, through interpretation of the Civil Rights Act of 1871. In the first decade of the twenty-first century, many prisons are under court orders or are facing constitutional challenges under Chapter 42, U.S. Code Section 1983.[34] See Figure 4.3. Many states are being sued, and federal masters have been appointed to oversee the conditions in state prisons.

Two major results of inmate litigation were the development of new mindsets by correctional administrators and the development of nationwide standards to demonstrate to the courts that the level of practice in the institutions being sued was the best the industry could provide.[35] Although litigation is always a trying situation, it may well be the best way to effect change in correctional settings. The threat of federal court suits has brought about significant changes in practices, policies, and procedures.

lecture note

Explain the tendency of inmates to resort to appeals from "behind the walls."

thematic question

Ask how the constitutional bases of democracy require court intervention in corrections management.

APPEALS FLOOD THE COURTS

A flood of appeals made with the help of court-appointed lawyers and jailhouse lawyers filled the dockets of the appeals courts beginning in the 1960s and accelerating through the mid-1990s. As rights were established in the obvious areas outside prison walls (arrest, search and seizure, privacy and intrusion, cruel and unusual punishment), they were eventually tested with regard to events inside the walls as well. The autonomous and discretionary control over inmates was finally lifted, as the right to counsel moved into the prison as well as the courtroom. A milestone case was decided in the 1967–1968 Supreme Court term, when *Mempa* v. *Rhay* extended the right to counsel to state probation revocation hearings, previously considered an essentially administrative action. The Court held that the application of a deferred sentence was a "critical point" in the proceeding.

Types of Prisoner Petitions

The three types of suits filed by prison inmates in federal district court are habeas corpus, civil rights, and mandamus. In brief, habeas corpus suits by prisoners challenge the constitutionality of their imprisonment, civil rights suits seek redress of civil rights violations by government officials, and mandamus suits seek to compel a government official to perform a duty owed.[36]

The basic principle of the **writ of habeas corpus** is that the government is accountable to the courts for a person's imprisonment. If the government cannot show that the person's imprisonment conforms to the fundamental principles of law, that person is entitled to immediate release. The most frequently cited reason for habeas corpus petitions by state inmates is "ineffective assistance of counsel" (25%). Other commonly cited reasons include errors by the trial court (15%), due process violations (14%), and self-incrimination (12%). For federal inmates, habeas corpus petitions generally challenge the constitutionality of imprisonment or constitute motions to vacate a sentence.

The foundation for **civil rights** petitions originates in the Fourteenth Amendment of the U.S. Constitution. It prohibits the states from "depriving any person of life, liberty, or property without due process of law." Petitions by state prisoners most frequently challenge physical security (21%), inadequate medical treatment (17%), and due process (13%).

The **writ of mandamus** ("we command") is an extraordinary remedy based on common law that is used when the plaintiff has no other adequate means to attain the desired relief. The mandamus petition is filed when the inmate seeks to compel a government official to perform a duty owed to the inmate (ministerial or nondiscretionary duties). The petitions are infrequent, varied in nature, and more typically specific to individual circumstances.

Legislative Initiatives to Reduce Prisoner Litigation

In 1980, the Civil Rights of Institutionalized Persons Act (CRIPA) was enacted by Congress to reduce the number of civil rights petitions filed in the federal courts. This act requires inmates to exhaust state-level administrative remedies before filing their petitions in the federal courts. Congress obviously intended to reserve the federal courts for more serious civil rights violations or other significant constitutional issues.

Despite the intent of Congress, the number of civil rights cases filed in federal court has increased more than threefold from the 1980s and 1990s. This increase was primarily caused by the huge increase in the number of state prisoners. The rate of petitions per 1,000 inmates remained stable.

During 1996, two additional legislative enactments sought to further limit prisoners' ability to file petitions in the federal courts. One was the Prison Litigation Reform Act (PLRA), seeking to reduce the number of petitions filed by inmates claiming civil rights violations. The three major changes were requiring inmates to exhaust all administrative remedies before filing in federal court, requiring inmates to pay applicable filing fees and court costs even if filing in *forma pauperis* ("I am a pauper"), and forbidding inmates from filing in *forma pauperis* if they have had prior petitions dismissed as being frivolous or malicious.

The second act (Antiterrorism and Effective Death Penalty Act, or AEDPA) requires inmates to exhaust direct appeals at the state level before filing a petition in federal court, establishes a one-year statute of limitations from the time their conviction becomes final (after all direct appeals of the conviction and/or the sentence have been exhausted), and requires that a panel of the appeals court approve successive petitions being filed in district court.

After the PLRA was enacted, both the rate and number of civil rights petitions decreased dramatically, as was the intent of Congress. After AEDPA, both the filing rate and the number of habeas corpus petitions by state inmates increased, primarily as a consequence of the increasing size of the prison population.

By either measure (the rate per 1,000 prisoners or volume of petitions filed), prisoner petitions filed in U.S. district courts (1980 to 2003) decreased. This pattern is graphically displayed in Figure 4.4.

Some state appellate courts have responded to caseload growth in a variety of other ways. Those coping strategies include adding judgeships, creating new or expanding existing appellate courts, deciding cases without published opinions or writing memo opinions, temporarily assigning judges from the retired ranks or from lower courts, and reducing panel sizes. Expediting hearings, limiting oral arguments, and setting time limits on arguments and briefs are other mechanisms. The reduction of protections of cherished constitutional rights in the name of expediency to meet a crisis or facilitate vague political goals in the name of the War on Drugs (regardless of the nobility of the espoused goals) poses some serious and unacceptable threats to every citizen, convicted criminal or not.

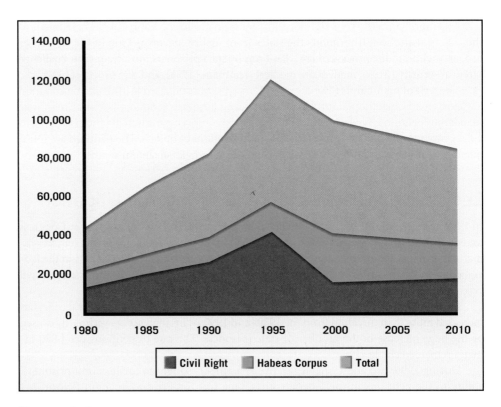

figure 4.4

Petitions Filed in U.S. District Courts by State and Federal Prisoners.

Data from: Sourcebook of Criminal Justice Statistics Online, "Petitions Filed in U.S. District Courts by Federal and State Prisoners," *www.albany.edu/sourcebook/pdf/t565.pfd* (accessed February 13, 2005).

Summary

The past several decades represent a revolution in sentencing in the United States. Its many causes are discussed in this chapter. Among the changes imposed are the abolition of the parole board's authority to release offenders at its discretion and the adoption of sentencing guidelines for judges. Changes also include shifting to mandatory prison sentences for specified crimes, adoption of presumptive sentences, and other efforts to limit discretion and disparity in sentencing and length of time served in prison. So widespread have the changes been that only three states (North Dakota, Virginia, and Wyoming) have left their sentencing laws unchanged.

In addition to the sentencing law changes, sharp increases have occurred in the number of persons incarcerated. Never in the history of the United States have we had so many and such a large percentage per 100,000 of the population incarcerated in prisons. Reasons for the sudden increase are not exactly understood; it is obvious, however, that corrections is once again in crisis. How local, state, and federal jurisdictions will resolve that crisis remains unclear.

Key Words

misdemeanor, 60

felony, 60

plea bargaining, 60

indeterminate sentencing, 61

sentencing disparity, 62

just deserts, 62

presentence report, 63

appeal, 65

administrative sentencing, 65

determinate sentencing, 66

sentencing guidelines, 66

good-time policies, 66

modify, 66

presumptive sentencing, 66

deterrence by sentencing, 69

railroading, 70

due process, 70

collateral attack, 70

double jeopardy, 72

court of last resort, 72

court of appeals, 72

remand, 72

reverse, 72

affirm, 73

writ of habeas corpus, 75

civil rights, 75

writ of mandamus, 75

Review Questions

1. What is the principal reason for the judge's diminished sentencing power?
2. What aids are available to help the judge decide what sentence to impose?
3. What factors have led to the rapid changes in the sentencing structures in the United States?
4. Identify the basic policy goals of sentencing, and define each.
5. What roles can the presentence investigation report play in corrections?
6. Explain sentencing disparity.
7. In what ways can a prosecutor influence sentence length?
8. Why are prison populations increasing?
9. Cite the advantages and disadvantages of the indeterminate sentence. Explain the difference between a court of appeals and a supreme court.
10. Why is there such a logjam in the appellate system? What are some suggestions for easing the pressure?
11. What rights does an inmate have? What rights does an inmate not have?
12. Explain why the rights of inmates began to be extensively defined in the 1960s.
13. What are appeals, and what options are available to appeal courts when a decision is made?
14. What might be done to cut down on frivolous appeals?
15. How can appeal courts manage caseloads more efficiently?
16. What steps has Congress taken to reduce the number of appeals in federal courts?
17. What innovations have states taken to reduce the backlog of appeals in state courts?
18. What are the areas of civil rights violations state prisoners are raising in federal courts?

Endnotes

1. Alaska abolished plea bargaining in 1975. In 1986, approximately 56% of all felony arrests were not prosecuted, and 7% of the felony arrests were reduced to misdemeanors. Alan Barnes, *Disparities between Felony Charges at Time of Arrest and Those at Time of Prosecution* (Anchorage: Alaska Statistical Analysis Unit, 1988). California abolished plea bargaining at the superior (trial) court level in 1988, but numerous strategies were devised to avoid this restriction.

2. John Wooldredge, "The Impact of Jurisdiction Size on Guilty Pleas in 569 State Courts," *Sociology and Social Research* 74:1(1989): 26–33; and David Baldus, George Woodworth, G. Young, et al., *The Disposition of Nebraska Capital and Non-Capital Homicide Cases: 1973–1999* (Lincoln: Nebraska Commission on Law Enforcement and Criminal Justice, 2001).

3. Matthew Durose and Patrick Langan, *Felony Sentencing in State Courts, 2004* (Washington, DC: U.S. Department of Justice, 2007), http://www.ojp.usdoj.gov/bjs/pub/pdf/fssc04.pdf. See also Tracey Kyckelhahn and Thomas Cohen, *Felony Defendants in Large Urban Courts, 2004* (Washington, DC: Bureau of Justice Statistics, 2008).

4. David Kopel, *Prison Blues: How America's Foolish Sentencing Policies Endanger Public Safety* (Washington, DC: Cato Institute, 1994); Michael Tonry, "Parochialism in United States Sentencing Policy," *Crime and Delinquency* 45:1 (1999): 48–65; and The Sentencing Project, "The Sentencing Project Submits Letter to the U.S. Sentencing Commission Recommending Future Priorities," *http://www.sentencingproject.org/NewsDetails.aspx? NewsID=680* (accessed September 12, 2008).

5. Nelson James, *Disparities in Processing Felony Arrests in New York State* (Albany: New York State Division of Criminal Justice, 1995). See also Robert Weidner and Richard Frase, "Legal and Extralegal Determinants of Intercounty Differences in Prison Use," *Criminal Justice Policy Review* 14:3 (2004): 173–195.

6. Steven Donziger, *The Real War on Crime* (New York: HarperCollins, 1996). See also Ted Gest, *Crime and Politics* (Oxford, UK: University of Oxford Press, 2001).

7. Franklin Zimring and Gordon Hawkins, *Incapacitation: Penal Confinement and the Restraint of Crime* (Oxford, UK: Oxford University Press, Studies in Crime and Public Policy, 1995). See also Alex Piquero and Paul Mazerolle, *Life-Course Criminology* (Belmont, CA: Wadsworth, 2001).

8. Michael Tony, *Sentencing Matters* (New York: Oxford University Press, 1996). See also Nancy Marion and Rick Farmer, "A Preliminary Examination of Presidential Anticrime Promises," *Criminal Justice Review* 29:1 (2004): 173–195.

9. Tomislav Kovandzic, John Sloan, and Lynne Vieraitis, "'Striking Out' as Crime Reduction Policy," *Justice Quarterly* 21:1 (2004): 207–239; and New York Times Editorial, "Crime and Punishment in Connecticut," *http://www.nytimes.com/2008/04/22/opinion/22tue3.html?_r=/&ref=opinion&oref=slogin* (accessed September 9, 2008).

10. P. Martinez, B. Bryan, E. Benson, W. L. Cawthon, S. Dhir, and R. Fuessel, *Abolishing Parole for Offenders Sentenced to Prison for Violent Offenses* (Austin: Texas Criminal Justice Policy Council, 1998).

11. Sandra Shane-Dubow, Alice Brown, and Erik Olsen, *Sentencing Reform in the United States: History, Content, and Effect* (Washington, DC: U.S. Department of Justice, 1985). See also Barry Krisberg, A. Breed, M. Wolfgang, et al., "Special Issue: NCCD 90th Anniversary," *Crime and Delinquency* 44:1 (1998): 5–177.

12. Walter C. Reckless, *The Crime Problem*, 4th ed. (New York: Appleton-Century-Crofts, 1967), pp. 673–674. See also Jeanne Stinchcomb and Daryl Hippensteel, "Presentence Investigation Reports," *Criminal Justice Policy Review* 12:2 (2001): 164–177.

13. Paul Wice, "Leadership," *Justice System Journal* 17:2 (1995): 271–372. See also Michael Cavadino, "Pre-Sentence Reports: The Effects of Legislation and National Standards," *British Journal of Criminology* 37:4 (1997): 529–548; and Lauren Glaze and Thomas Bonczar, *Probation and Parole in the United States, 2006* (Washington, DC: Bureau of Justice Statistics, 2007).

14. Peter Brimelow, "Judicial Imperialism," *Forbes* (June 1, 1987): 109–112. See in particular Gordon Bazemore and L. Feder, "Rehabilitation in the New Juvenile Court," *American Journal of Criminal Justice* 21:2 (1997): 181–212. See also Department of Justice Canada, "The Changing Face of Conditional Sentencing," *http://www.justice.gc.ca/eng/pi/rs/rep_rap/2000/op00_3/toc-tdm.html* (accessed September 12, 2008).

15. Mike McCorville and Chester Mirday, "Guilty Plea Courts: A Social Disciplinary Model of Criminal Justice," *Social Problems* 42:2 (1995): 216–234. But see Jon'a Meyer and Tara Gray, "Drunk Drivers in the Courts: Legal and Extra-Legal Factors Affecting Pleas and Sentences," *Journal of Criminal Justice* 25:2 (1997): 155–163.

16. Lisa Stolzenberg and S. D'Alessio, "The Impact of Prison Crowding on Male and Female Imprisonment

Rates in Minnesota," *Justice Quarterly* 14:4 (1997): 793–809. See also Sean Nicholson-Crotty, "The Impact of Sentencing Guidelines on State-Level Sanctions," *Crime and Delinquency* 50:3 (2004): 395–411.

17. Walter Durose and Patrick Langan, *Felony Sentences in State Courts, 2004* (Washington, DC: Bureau of Justice Statistics, 2007).

18. Conservatives are likely to argue that the decline in crime volume and rates that began in 1990 is a direct result of harsher punishment. Yet crime, as measured by the National Crime Victimization Survey, began to drop in 1971 and dropped about 27% since that time. The cause of a phenomenon has to precede the effect. The crime rates began to drop long before increases in sentence length and harsher laws began.

19. Charles Murray, Malcolm Davies, Andrew Rutherford, et al., *Does Prison Work?* (London: Institute of Economic Affairs, Health and Welfare, 1997).

20. Editors, "Supreme Court Review," *Journal of Criminal Law and Criminology* 83:4 (1993): 693–717. But see John Capone, "Facilitating Fairness: The Judge's Role in the Sixth Amendment Right to Effective Counsel," *Journal of Criminal Law and Criminology* 93:4 (2004): 881–912.

21. Because plea bargaining reduces the offender's ability to appeal, it is not surprising that most appeals arise from trials. Trials typically involve crimes against the person and sentences of five years or less. Defendants are not particularly successful; offenders win about 20% of the time and have their convictions overturned in only about 10% of their appeals. See Jimmy Williams, "Role of Appellants, Sentencing Guidelines, Decision Making in Criminal Appeals," *Journal of Criminal Justice* 23:1 (1995): 83–91. Some 16% of offenders convicted in federal courts appealed in 1999. Bureau of Justice Statistics, *Federal Criminal Case Processing, 2004* (Washington, DC: BJS, 2008).

22. For an excellent review of legal trends and issues in corrections, see Rolando del Carmen, S. Ritter, and B. Witt, *Briefs of Leading Cases in Corrections* (Cincinnati, OH: Anderson Publishing, 2005).

23. National Advisory Commission on Criminal Justice Standards and Goals, *Corrections* (Washington, DC: U.S. Government Printing Office, 1973), p. 113.

24. David Chu, "The Substitution of Words for Analysis and Other Judicial Pitfalls: Why David Sattazahn Should Have Received Double Jeopardy Protection," *Journal of Criminal Law and Criminology* 94:3 (2004): 587–623. Also see Tina Bay, "Court: Double Jeopardy Bars Appeal of Enhancement," Metropolitan News-

Enterprise, *http://www.metnews.com/articles/2007/blan021307.htm* (accessed September 12, 2008). This case is U.S. Court of Appeals for the Ninth Circuit, *U.S. v. Blanton, No. 05-5032.*

25. Joseph N. Ulman, *The Judge Takes the Stand* (New York: Knopf, 1933), pp. 265–266.

26. Appeals in federal courts have been reduced in number by congressional initiatives to reduce prisoner litigation.

27. U.S. Constitution, Article III, Section 2. See Singer Hausser, *The State of Corrections: Tennessee's Prisons before and after Court Intervention* (Nashville, TN: The Comptroller of the Treasury, 1998).

28. John Palmer, *Constitutional Rights of Prisoners* (Cincinnati, OH: Anderson, 1999), p. 12.

29. Prison jailhouse lawyers can resist controls and conditions placed on them by correctional institutions by assisting in filing lawsuits, and have been described as "primitive rebels." See Hawkeye Gross, *Tales from the Joint* (Boulder, CO: Palladin Press, 1995); and Dragan Milovanovic, "Jailhouse Lawyers and Jailhouse Lawyering," *International Journal of the Sociology of the Law* 16:4 (1998): 455–475.

30. Gross, *Tales from the Joint.* See also Michael Vaughn and Linda Smith, "Questioning Authorized Truth," *Justice Quarterly* 16:4 (1999): 907–918.

31. John Conrad, "The Rights of Wrongdoers," *Criminal Justice Research Bulletin* 3:1 (1987): 18–24. See also Christopher Smith, "The Prison Reform Litigation Era," *The Prison Journal* 83:3 (2003): 337–358; and Roibin O hE' ochaidh, "Fault Lines: California Prisons in Crisis," *Correctional News* 14:3 (2008): 20–22.

32. Such as prison farming.

33. Editors of *Criminal Law Reporter, The Criminal Law Revolution and Its Aftermath, 1960–71* (Washington, DC: BNA Books, 1972).

34. Richard Ball, "Prison Conditions at the Extreme," *Journal of Contemporary Criminal Justice* 13:1 (1997): 55–72.

35. Malcolm Feeley and E. Rubin, *Judicial Policy Making and the Modern State* (New York: Cambridge University Press, 1998); John Fliter, *Prisoners' Rights: The Supreme Court and Evolving Standards of Decency* (Westport, CT: Greenwood Press, 2001).

36. This section was drawn primarily from the Bureau of Justice Statistics, *Prisoner Petitions Filed in U.S. District Courts, 2000, with Trends 1980–2000* (Washington, DC: BJS, 2002). See also Bureau of Justice Statistics, *Federal Criminal Cases Processing 2004, with Trends 1982–2002* (Washington, DC: BJS, 2005).

Suggested Readings: Part 1

Austin, James. *It's About Time: America's Imprisonment Binge.* Belmont, CA: Thomson Learning, 2009 (4th edition).

Barnes, Harry Elmer. *The Story of Punishment*, 2nd ed. Montclair, NJ: Patterson Smith, 1972.

Barnes, Harry Elmer, and Negley K. Teeters. *New Horizons in Criminology*, 2nd ed. Englewood Cliffs, NJ: Prentice Hall, 1959.

Brockway, Zebulon Reed. *Fifty Years of Prison Service.* Montclair, NJ: Patterson Smith, 1969.

Bureau of Justice Statistics. *Felony Sentences in State Courts, 2004.* Washington, DC: BJS, 2005.

Bureau of Justice Statistics. *Prisoners Inmates at Midyear 2007.* Washington, DC: BJS, 2008.

Clear, Todd, Dina Rose, and J. Ryder. "Incarceration and the Community: The Problem of Removing and Returning Offenders." *Crime and Delinquency* 47:3 (2001): 335–351.

Currie, Elliott. *Crime and Punishment in America; Why the Solutions to America's Most Stubborn Social Crises Have Not Worked–And What Will.* New York: Metropolitan Books, 1998.

Donziger, Steven. *The Real War on Crime.* New York: HarperCollins, 1996.

Edwards, Todd. *The Aging Inmate Population.* Atlanta: Council on State Governments, 1998.

Gest, Ted. *Crime and Politics.* Oxford, UK: Oxford University Press, 2001.

Hassine, Victor. *Life without Parole: Living in Prison Today.* New York: Oxford University Press, 2008.

Irwin, John, and James Austin. *It's about Time.* Florence, KY: Cenage, 2001.

King, Ryan. *Disparity by Geography: The War on Drugs in American Cities.* Washington, DC: The Sentencing Project, 2008.

Latessa, Edward, and Alex Holsinger. *Correctional Contexts: Contemporary and Classical Readings*, 3rd edition. Los Angeles, Roxbury Publishing, 2007.

Latessa, Edward, and Paula Smith. *Corrections in the Community*, 4th edition. Cincinnati, OH: Anderson, 2007.

Love, Margaret. *Relief from the Collateral Consequences of a Criminal Conviction.* Washington, DC: The Sentencing Project, 2008.

Mauer, Marc, and Ryan King. *Schools and Prisons: Fifty Years after* Brown v. Board of Education. Washington, DC: The Sentencing Project, 2005.

Nagel, William. *The New Red Barn.* New York: Walker, 1973.

PEW Charitable Trusts. One in 100: Behind Bars in America 2008 (*http://www.pewcenteronthestates.org/report _detail.aspx?id=35904*).

Roberts, John. *Reform and Retribution: An Illustrated History of American Prisons.* Lanham, MD: American Correctional Association, 1997.

Ross, Jeffrey. "Supermax Prisons," *Society* 44:3 (2007): 60–64.

Ross, Jeffrey, and Stephen Richards. *Behind Bars: Surviving Prisons.* Indianapolis, IN: Alpha, 2002.

Rothman, David J. *The Discovery of the Asylum.* Boston: Little, Brown, 1971.

Stith, Kate, and J. Cabranes. *Fear of Judging: Sentencing Guidelines in Federal Courts.* Chicago: University of Chicago Press, 1998.

part 2

Alternatives to Imprisonment

Overview

Part 2 is concerned with those processes and programs that deal with clients on the "front end" of the corrections system, before offenders are committed to jail or prison for their law-violating behavior. We examine probation and other court sanctions for controlling offenders that fall short of imprisonment: intermediate sanctions. Corrections handles more offenders on the front end than can be found at any other portion of the system, and Part 2 identifies the strengths, challenges, and outcomes of alternatives to imprisonment.

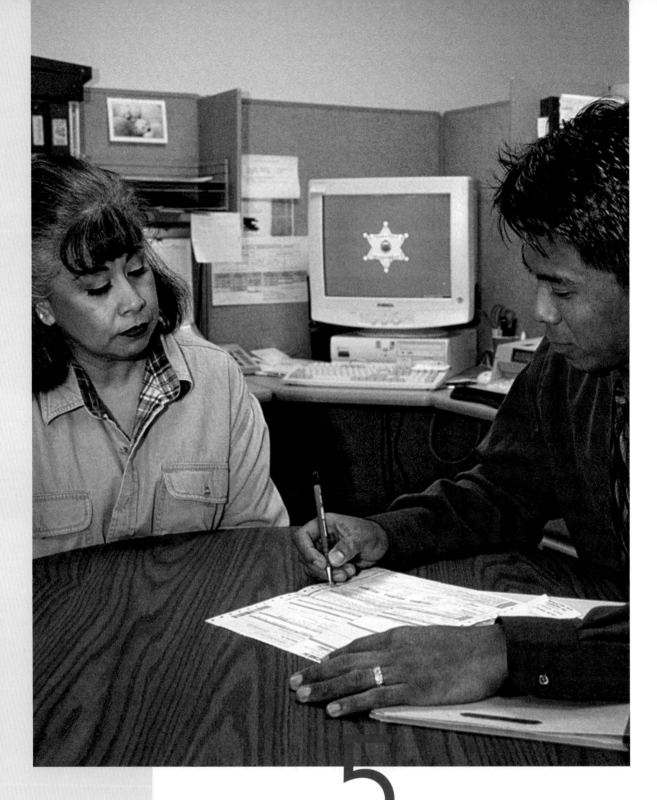

chapter 5

Probation

Outline

"I can forgive, but I cannot forget, is only another way of saying, I will not forgive. Forgiveness ought to be like a cancelled note—torn in two, and burned up, so that it never can be shown against me."

–Henry Ward Beecher

Overview

Our examination of the correctional process now turns to probation and probation supervision, the major alternative to incarceration as used by sentencing judges across America. Although it is the most commonly used correctional sentence, probation is also one of the most maligned and underappreciated aspects of the correctional system. Often seen as a "letting off" of the offender, probation has struggled to gain respect and support from the media, the public and, perhaps most important, those officials who make funding decisions.

Probation is a sentence that does not include confinement and imposes conditions governing the release of the offender into the community, based on good behavior. The sentencing court retains authority to supervise, modify conditions, and cancel the status and resentence if the probation client violates the terms of probation. Increasingly, across the nation, courts are using recent developments in technology to better monitor the behavior of the probationer. This chapter presents a brief history of probation and its developments into the twenty-first century.

key term

Probation

A court sentence to release the offender to the community under supervision, with possible revocation of sentence if conditions warrant.

key term

Suspended sentence

Court determination to stop some formal processing of an offender, primarily stopping prosecution, not pronouncing a determination of guilt, or court not requiring a sentence.

key term

Right of sanctuary

Privilege to avoid punishment by the offender's relocation to a sacred city or location.

key term

Benefit of clergy

The exclusion of offenders from the death penalty if able to read particular segments of ancient texts.

key term

Stigma

A mark of shame and disgrace attached to the offender by virtue of his or her having committed an offense.

key term

Sursis

A suspended sentence in European countries requiring no future punishment provided the offender remains crime-free during a specified time period.

lecture note

Using your computer, play the brief chapter overview videotape by Edward J. Latessa on "Probation" that introduces Chapter 5 (approximately 3 minutes).

SUSPENDED SENTENCE AND SANCTUARY

Probation is a derivative of the suspended sentence, handed down to us somewhat indirectly by way of past judicial procedures. Both the **suspended sentence** and probation mitigate the punishment for an offender through a judicial procedure, and their earliest antecedent is found in the right of sanctuary,[1] frequently cited in the Bible. In many cultures, holy places and certain cities were traditionally set aside as places for sanctuary.

The **right of sanctuary** was written into Mosaic law.[2] To escape the blood vengeance of a victim's family, a killer could go to certain specified cities and find refuge. During the Middle Ages, many churches offered sanctuary for those hiding from harsh secular law. The practice of sanctuary disappeared in England in the seventeenth century and was replaced with **benefit of clergy**. This practice, originally reserved for clerics, was eventually extended to those who could pass the Psalm 51 test—a test of the offender's ability to read the verse that begins "Have mercy upon me." Since anyone who could read (such as the clergy) was eligible to be tried under Church law and thus escape the death penalty, this became known as the "neck verse," meaning they could not be hung by the neck until dead. The result was a form of suspended sentence that allowed the offender to move about in society.

The suspended sentence differs from probation, though the terms are sometimes used interchangeably. The suspended sentence does not require supervision and usually does not prescribe a specified set of goals for the offender to work toward. It is merely a form of quasi-freedom that can be revoked, with a prison sentence imposed at the instruction of the court. Sentence can be suspended in two ways:

1. The sentence is imposed, but its execution is suspended.
2. Both the imposition and execution of the sentence are suspended.

Of the two, the second is the more desirable because of the reduced **stigma**; however, the practice of suspending sentences, like sanctuary, has generally been replaced in America with supervised probation. Sentences may be vacated by the sentencing judge, and the offender may be placed at liberty in the community, but that is a relatively infrequent occurrence.

Under the European model of suspended sentence, or **sursis** (surcease), the offender has satisfactorily fulfilled the conditions if no further offense is committed during the established period. Little control or supervision is provided, with the result that most offenders with suspended sentences are denied the specialized or therapeutic services needed to prevent further criminal involvement.[3]

THE HISTORY OF PROBATION

Probation has undergone a number of changes since its informal beginnings in the nineteenth century. Let us take a brief look at how the concept was born. **John Augustus** (1785–1859),[4] a Boston shoemaker, is credited with being the father of probation. As a member of the Washington Total Abstinence Society, he worked at getting men to give up alcohol. He liked to spend his spare moments observing what took place in the courts, and he was disturbed that minor offenders and common drunks were often forced to remain in jail because they had no money to pay their fines. He convinced the authorities to allow him to pay their fines and offered them friendly supervision. Between 1841 and 1858, Augustus bailed out almost 2,000 men, women, and children.

His method was to bail the offender after conviction, to utilize this favor as an entering wedge into the convict's confidence and friendship, and through such evidence of friendliness as helping the offender to obtain a job and aiding his or her family in various ways, to drive the wedge home. When the defendant was later brought into court for sentencing,

Augustus would report on his progress toward reformation, and the judge would usually fine the convict one cent and costs, instead of committing him or her to an institution.[5]

Augustus's efforts encouraged his home state of Massachusetts to pass the first probation statute in 1878. Four more states had followed suit by 1900.[6] Probation was thus established as a legitimate alternative to incarceration, and a strong impetus to employ it—the need to supervise young offenders and keep them out of adult prisons—came with the creation of the first juvenile court[7] in Cook County, Illinois, in 1899.

THE SPREAD OF PROBATION

Juvenile probation service developed with the growing movement for creation of juvenile courts. By 1910, 37 states and the District of Columbia had passed a children's court act, and 40 had established some kind of probation service for juveniles. Every state had enacted juvenile probation service in some measure by 1927, as the practice became firmly entrenched.

Not until 1956, however, was probation available for adult offenders in every state. The variations in the organization and operation of probation services make it difficult to compare them by state, but the growth in the number of registered probation officers attests to the rapid acceptance of this area of corrections. In 1907, the first directory of probation officers identified 795 volunteers, welfare workers, court personnel, and part-time personnel serving as officers. Most of them were in the juvenile system. By 1937, the figure had grown to more than 3,800, of which 80% were in full-time service. By 2002, it was estimated that probation officers numbered over 88,000.[8] See Figure 5.1.

The enabling legislation eventually passed at state and federal levels not only enacted statutes that permitted probation, but eventually defined specific categories of offenses for which probation could not be granted. The latter could include crimes of violence, assaultive behavior that inflicted gross bodily harm on the victim, rape or other sex offenses, capital offenses, train robbing, livestock rustling, certain habitual offenders, and related offenses. Despite these restrictions imposed by legislatures, granting probation is a highly personalized process that focuses not only on the offender but also on the victim. Restorative justice, which will be discussed in more detail later in the book, is an example of a contemporary thrust that maximizes focus on the offender, victim, and community.[9]

It is clear that the legislators enacting probation statutes intended juvenile offenders and misdemeanants to be its beneficiaries, not hard-core criminal offenders. This was in keeping with the child-saving and progressive agenda that intended to reclaim offenders

A juvenile court judge counsels a probationer.
SOURCE: *Photo by Billy Barnes, courtesy of PhotoEdit Inc.*

before they became antisocial and professional offenders committed to criminal careers. As we shall see later, probation is also a sentencing option for adult felons and, depending on the criminal circumstances, an occasional violent offender. Table 5.1 provides an overview of the frequency with which probation is imposed, by crime category of conviction. As these figures illustrate, probation is used for a wide range of offenses, but property crimes and drug offenses are the most dominant.

The American Probation and Parole Association policy statement given in the accompanying Correctional Brief identifies the purpose and mission of probation. Judges and corrections and justice advocates have identified the advantages of probation, which can be summarized as follows:

- Uses existing community resources to assist offenders to address their personal and individual problems.
- Saves fiscal resources over the cost of imprisonment.
- Avoids prisonization, a process that tends to exacerbate the underlying causes of criminal behavior in an artificial setting that lessens the ability of the prisoner to function when released to society.

table **5.1** | **Imposition of Probation by Crime of Conviction**

Crime of Conviction	Percent of Convicted Felons Receiving Probation Sentences
All Offenses	28
Violent Offenses	20
Property Offenses	30
Drug Offenses	30
Weapons Offenses	27
Other Offenses	29

SOURCE: Matthew Durose and Patrick Langan, *Felony Sentences in State Courts, 2004* (Washington, DC: Bureau of Justice Statistics, 2007), p. 3.

correctional **brief**

Position Statement on Probation

Purpose   The purpose of probation is to assist in reducing the incidence and impact of crime by probationers in the community. The core services of probation are to provide investigation and reports to the court, to help develop appropriate court dispositions for adult offenders and juvenile delinquents, and to supervise those persons placed on probation. Probation departments in fulfilling their purpose may also provide a broad range of services including, but not limited to, crime and delinquency prevention, victim restitution programs, and intern/volunteer programs.

Position   The mission of probation is to protect the public interest and safety by reducing the incidence and impact of crime by probationers. This role is accomplished by:

- Assisting the courts in decision making through the probation report and in the enforcement of court orders;

- Providing services and programs that afford opportunities for offenders to become more law-abiding;

- Providing and cooperating in programs and activities for the prevention of crime and delinquency; and

- Furthering the administration of fair and individualized justice.

Probation is premised upon the following beliefs:

- Society has a right to be protected from persons who cause its members harm, regardless of the reasons for such harm.

- Offenders have rights deserving of protection.

- Victims of crime have rights deserving of protection.

- Human beings are capable of change.

- Not all offenders have the same capacity or willingness to benefit from measures designed to produce law-abiding citizens.

- Intervention in an offender's life should be the minimal amount needed to protect society and promote law-abiding behavior.

- Probation does not recognize the concept of retributive justice.

- Incarceration may be destructive and should be imposed only when necessary.

- When public safety is not compromised, society and offenders are best served through community correctional programs.

SOURCE: American Probation and Parole Association, *APPA Position Statement on Probation*, APPA website, *http://www. appa-net.org/*, accessed September 14, 2008.

- Keeps offenders' families and dependents off local welfare rolls.
- Provides restitution for and reconciliation with victims.
- Allows selective incapacitation, permitting the use of scarce prison cells to isolate and control aggressive and assaultive offenders.[10]

Thus, it should be of little surprise that the majority of offenders are under sentence to probation (see Figure 5.1).

ORGANIZATION AND ADMINISTRATION OF PROBATION

The problems associated with a lack of organization in the criminal justice system are exemplified in probation services. Under the original concept, the judges themselves were to administer the probation services. For many jurisdictions this is still the way in which probation is managed, whereas in other states probation is administered through state or district offices. Unfortunately, the various organizational and operational systems found in probation are often unresponsive to one another's goals or efforts. The most common plan offers probation service at the state level. Even in those states that have attempted to form a state-administered probation system, county participation has sometimes been maintained at the discretion of local officials. This concept of local autonomy is an American tradition, but it has hampered efforts to develop integrated probation services on a statewide basis.

class activity

Ask students to identify crimes that are categorical exclusions from granting probation, and explain why such crimes should be excluded. Then ask them to explain the imposition of probation for those persons convicted of homicide and nonnegligent manslaughter.

lecture note

Describe the progressive movement in corrections in light of probation services.

The means of administering probation programs also vary. In some states, private service contractors, such as the Salvation Army, provide presentence investigation services, as well as probation case supervision for select offenders. It is not uncommon to have misdemeanant probationers supervised by contracted providers.

The Role of the Probation Agency

The role of the probation department has traditionally been viewed as a dichotomy. The supervision role involves maintaining surveillance (societal protection) as well as helping and treating the offender (counseling and rehabilitation). Supervising officers are often left to their own devices with regard to which role would be most appropriate in supervising their caseloads. This dilemma is likely to remain with us even though calls from several quarters of the criminal justice system point toward coming changes in the role of the supervising officer.[11]

To begin, it is necessary to examine the duties and responsibilities of probation agencies. First and foremost, they provide supervision of offenders in the community. The basic question remains: What is the purpose of supervision? To some, the function of supervision, drawn from the social work field, is based on the casework model. Supervision is the basis of a treatment program. The officer uses all information available about the offender to diagnose that person's needs and to design a treatment plan. Yet, providing treatment is only one aspect of supervision. In addition, the probation officer is expected to maintain surveillance of those offenders who make up the caseload. Surveillance can take many forms, ranging from office and field contacts, to drug testing, to electronic monitoring. Although some believe that the treatment and surveillance responsibilities of the probation department are almost diametrically opposed, the reality is that probation has two missions: to rehabilitate the offenders who are amenable to treatment while simultaneously protecting society from those who prove to be dangerous. The agency that can adequately balance these goals can best meet the challenges of probation in the twenty-first century.

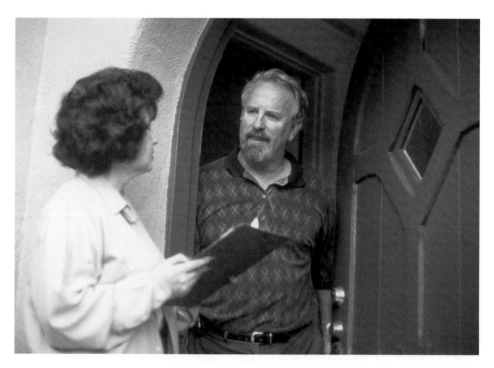

Probation officers often visit probationers at home.
SOURCE: *Photo by M. K. Denny, courtesy of PhotoEdit Inc.*

The Decision to Grant Probation

The decision to grant probation is a complicated process, one further impacted by the plea-bargaining process. Recall that plea bargaining is usually undertaken by the prosecutor and defense counsel and can include a reduction in the severity of the charge, the number of counts to which the offender would plead guilty, probation versus incarceration, the length of sentence to be imposed, and whether sentences are to be served concurrently or consecutively. More recently, with the passage of sentence enhancement, habitual offender, and third-strike statutes, defendants might also negotiate on pleading to a misdemeanor versus a felony charge to avoid the first strike necessary for the imposition of sentence enhancement, particularly third-strike sentences. In California, for example, an offender with two previous felony convictions who is facing conviction for a third felony could receive a sentence of 25 years to life, whichever is higher, and must serve a minimum of 25 years.[12] Often a judge will combine some jail time with probation. This is called a split sentence. Other variations include combining probation with weekend confinement, boot camps, and residential programming.

The judiciary tends to acquiesce to the negotiated plea outcomes but, in many cases, can decide the sentencing outcome or refuse to accept the proposed agreement ("bust the deal"). This is a crucial point, inasmuch as some 90% of felony arrestees may have pled guilty for preferential consideration. Such a plea usually means that the offender cannot appeal, sharply reducing the legal bases for initiating appellate court review.

When the crime for which someone is convicted falls within the legally permissible range of offenses for which probation may be imposed, or where mandated by state law, a presentence investigation will be ordered, although some states permit the offender to waive the presentence investigation. The basic function of the presentence report is to provide information permitting the most appropriate sentence to be imposed. It can also serve as a background document for the supervising probation officer and the prison classification committee, as well as any later parole supervision officer, should the offender be imprisoned. The presentence report also provides a wealth of information permitting process and outcome evaluations, as well as developing sentencing

A public defender works with a jail inmate on getting him probation.
SOURCE: *Photo by Michael Newman, courtesy of PhotoEdit Inc.*

guidelines, probation supervision strategies, and specific programs designed to meet emerging challenges for probation agencies (such as identifying offenders with high drug relapse potential and instituting drug treatment programs particularly designed for high-risk cases).

The Presentence Investigation Report

key term

Presentence investigation (PSI) report
Document that results from an investigation undertaken by a court-authorized officer or agency, designed to provide information on the defendant so the judge can make an informed sentencing decision.

One of the primary responsibilities of the probation agency is investigation. Other responsibilities include supervision, program advocacy, restitution management, victim–offender reconciliation, brokerage, enforcement of probation conditions, and community safety. Investigation includes gathering facts and information about the offense and arrest, offender background, technical violations, and, more immediately, preparing the presentence investigation report.

The **presentence investigation (PSI) report** is the document that results from an investigation undertaken by a court-authorized officer or agency. Under the direction of the criminal court, it evaluates the background, past criminal behavior, offense situation, personal and family circumstances, personality, need, and level of risk of the offender convicted of the crime, in order to assist the court in making an informed disposition decision and, hence, determining the most appropriate sentence.

In addition to such facts about the offender as educational and employment histories, residential stability, financial circumstances, marital and parental responsibilities, and military history, the report also must provide certain subjective data that are useful to the court. These data would include an assessment of the offender's personality and character, needs and risks, and attitude of remorse and contrition. Most reports conclude with a sound recommendation for sentence disposition and relevant conditions to be imposed if the disposition were to be probation. Both reliability and accuracy are essential, because the court tends to closely follow the recommendation of the investigator. The latter needs are so crucial that the PSI report (minus any specific details that might permit identification of sources who might fear retribution) is generally shared with defense counsel and can be challenged or refuted in a sentencing hearing.

A final note about the PSI report: No report is complete without a plan of supervision developed by the investigator and presented to the court. Not only would the report include such traditional supervision options as fines, restitution, community service orders, day reporting, and probation, but increasingly it also gives attention to the victim by allowing a victim impact statement and, on occasion, the victim's recommendation for sentence outcome. Surprisingly, some victims are willing to propose constructive responses and solutions in addition to the self-serving request for restitution and compensation.[13]

class activity

Ask students how private service organizations, such as the Salvation Army, can provide presentence investigation reports.

class activity

Ask students to identify those qualities that are believed to characterize an effective probation officer.

class activity

Have students debate the point: "Probation officers should concentrate on surveillance of rather than service to probationers."

class activity

Have the class identify the major categories of elements that would be included in a presentence investigation report.

The Sentencing Hearing

Most criminal courts conduct sentencing hearings independent of the determination of guilt. At such a hearing, the court would consider the PSI report's contents and recommendations, statements by prosecution and defense counsel, statements from victims, and other evidence that might be germane and relevant to the deliberations.

There are no clear-cut factors that heavily influence the outcome of the sentencing hearing, although it is clear that the presentence investigation report plays a central role. If the offender has prior convictions, has inflicted bodily harm, used a weapon in the commission of the crime, is unknown to the victim or has committed a stranger-to-stranger crime, has previously been imprisoned in a correctional institution, has indicators of mental illness, or appears to be engaged in a career of crime, the more likely recommendation would be incarceration in an institution for adult offenders (prison). Judges tend to concur with such recommendations about 85% of the time.

A probation officer works with a probationer on his plan.
SOURCE: *Courtesy of State of California Department of Corrections.*

If the bulk of the evidence before the court is that the offender displays most of the following, then the sentencing judge is more likely to impose probation:

- Basically a prosocial offender who has committed a first crime
- Good education and work histories
- Married with dependents
- Underlying need to address a personal problem such as drug or alcohol abuse
- Low-risk score

Offenders, of course, seldom fall into the two extreme examples. For this reason, probation departments have adopted **risk and needs assessment** instruments that provide good to excellent prediction of future offender behavior. Such instruments tend to classify clients into risk level (high, medium, low) and need level (high, medium, and low).

Risk Assessment

The latest generation of classification instruments has successfully combined risk and needs and is relatively easy to use. For example, the Level of Service Inventory—Revised (LSI-R)[14] assesses offender risk by examining ten domains:

- Criminal history
- Financial situation
- Companions
- Accommodations
- Alcohol and drug problems
- Education and employment
- Leisure and recreation activities
- Family/marital status
- Emotional problems
- Attitudes and orientation

key term

Risk and needs assessments
Instruments used to determine the probability of recidivism or future criminal behavior.

class activity

Challenge the class to provide a rationale for the private presentence investigation report. If the consensus is that it is constructive, ask if this is generally available to low-income offenders.

lecture note

Point out how probation can reinforce selective incapacitation.

figure 5.2

The Level of Services-Revised and Recidivism

Data from: Don Andrews and James Bonta, "LSI-R": The Level of Service Inventory–Revised (Toronto: Multi-Health Systems, Inc., 1995).

Figure 5.2 shows recidivism rates as they correspond to LSI-R scores; in general, the higher the LSI-R score, the more likely the offender group to reoffend. Assessments such as the LSI-R help judges and probation departments make better decisions about whom to place on probation, whether to increase conditions and supervision levels, and what range and type of services are needed.

TARGETING RISK FACTORS: CHALLENGE FOR PROBATION

Before addressing the conditions of probation that could be imposed by the sentencing court, it is necessary to explore some of the dimensions and problems that probationers face and that cause offenders many additional problems and contribute to the commission of crime. These figures will help you understand the serious and complicated issues with which sentencing courts and supervising probation officers must deal in the corrections process. Although recent national figures are not available, a 2005 study of community corrections in Ohio examined more than 17,000 offenders under community control. This study found that 84% of offenders in the community had a history of drug use, 69% had prior alcohol abuse, 70% had not completed high school, 62% were unemployed at the time of arrest, and the vast majority had a prior criminal record.[15] There is no reason to believe that these rates are not similar across the country. In addition to substance abuse problems and a lack of employment and education, probationers also have a number of other problems and risk factors that must be addressed. These include a lack of self-control, bad companions, antisocial attitudes, emotional problems, family conflict, and mental illness.

Fortunately, studies have demonstrated that recidivism can be significantly diminished if offenders on probation or in detention receive treatment and services specific to their risk and need factors, and if they complete the treatment program.[16] Posttreatment reductions of criminal activities are especially pronounced when certain principles are adhered to. Known as the principles of effective correctional intervention, they form the basis of what has become referred to as the "what works" research.[17] The accompanying Correctional Brief provides more information on the "what works" research.

It should be evident that probationers as a group tend to have a wide range of risk and need factors, and that treatment and services should play a large part in supervision. It also requires the sentencing court to impose specific treatment conditions, and for supervising officers to direct the implementation of that treatment.

CONDITIONS OF PROBATION

Offenders call being on probation being on "paper." Being on "wet paper" means that they are not allowed to drink while under supervision. As we will learn, courts may impose any reasonable condition on the offender, as long as the condition is related to some identifiable correctional objective. The probation officer is expected to monitor the probationer's adherence to these conditions. General conditions imposed on all offenders would include reporting regularly to the supervising officer, obeying laws, submitting to searches, not being in possession of firearms or using drugs, avoiding excessive use of alcohol, not associating with known criminals, not leaving the jurisdiction of the court without prior approval, notifying the officer of any change of job or residence, paying probation fees, and so on.

Specific conditions, not capriciously imposed, can be required of the probationer, such as participating in methadone maintenance, taking Antibuse, attending Alcoholics Anonymous meetings, urine testing, obtaining psychological or psychiatric treatment, attending a day attendance center or halfway house, restitution or victim compensation, house arrest, electronic monitoring, weekend confinement in jail or residential center, vocational training, or other court-ordered requirements. Such specific conditions are individually designed to assist the probationer in successful completion of court requirements and expectations, as well as reintegration. The proportion of probationers who successfully complete probation ranges from about 60% to some 85%. Specific conditions are frequently imposed as part of the original court order for probation, but could also be imposed by the court later if the probation client is not abiding by the conditions of probation or poses a danger for failure of probation (see Table 5.2). Probation officers sometimes ask the court to impose more than one special condition after probation begins, especially if the client ignores the orders or deliberately refuses to participate in a program. Urine tests that reveal continued drug abuse or excessive use of alcohol, or irregular employment attendance, may result in tourniquet sentencing, which happens when the court increases the conditions of supervision to enforce participation in programs until the client agrees to conform his or her behavior to expectations.

The most frequently imposed **special conditions of probation** include intermediate sanctions, which are discussed in more detail in Chapter 6. Some of these are house arrest, day attendance centers, electronic monitoring, intensive supervision, halfway house residency, boot camp programs, and split sentences (jail time followed by probation or by weekend jail time). The point here is that probation supervision can be strengthened by a variety of alternative sanctions that can be imposed to maximize the benefits of probation, avoid criminal reoffending, protect the local community, and assist clients to address their basic and underlying crime-causative needs. The alternative programs are explored in more detail in the following chapter. See Table 5.2 and Correctional Brief (p. 94).

PROBATION REVOCATION

Once placed on probation, clients are supervised and assisted by probation officers who increasingly use community resources and programs to assist in the reintegration effort to meet the individual's needs. If the probationer addresses these, secures assistance from community resources, and resolves underlying problems, the probation officer may request the court to dismiss the offender from supervision by closing the case. Some jurisdictions permit the issuance of "certificates of rehabilitation" for offenders who have been successful on probation. Other offenders do not pursue official recognition, and are never seen in the criminal justice system again.

lecture note

Using your computer, play the brief videotape of Paula Smith on "Treatment Effectiveness" (approximately 3 minutes).

class activity

Ask students to identify special conditions imposed on probationers, and justify their use.

lecture note

Distribute a probation contract used in your local court, and justify the conditions ordinarily imposed.

lecture note

Explain tourniquet sentencing and explain its role in probation.

key term

Special conditions of probation
Additional punishments ordered by the courts to probationers, such as fines, electronic monitoring, and house arrest.

c o r r e c t i o n a l **brief**

What Works in Reducing Recidivism?

"What works" is not a program or an intervention, but a body of knowledge based on more than 30 years of research that has been conducted by numerous scholars in North America and Europe. Also referred to as evidence-based practice, the "what works" movement demonstrates empirically that theoretically sound, well-designed programs that meet certain conditions can appreciably reduce recidivism rates for offenders. Through the review and analysis of hundreds of studies, researchers have identified a set of principles that should guide correctional programs.

The first is the risk principle, or the "whom" to target—those offenders who pose the higher risk of continued criminal conduct. This principle states that our most intensive correctional treatment and intervention programs should be reserved for higher-risk offenders. *Risk* in this context refers to those offenders with a higher probability of recidivating. Why waste our programs on offenders who do not need them? This is a waste of resources, and, more important, research has clearly demonstrated that when we place lower-risk offenders in our more structured programs, we often increase their failure rates (and thus reduce the overall effectiveness of the program). This occurs for several reasons.

First, placing low-risk offenders in with higher-risk offenders only serves to increase the chances of failure for the low-risk offender. For example, let's say that your teenage son or daughter did not use drugs, but got into some trouble with the law. Would you want them in a program or group with heavy drug users? Of course you wouldn't, since it is more likely that the higher-risk youth would influence your child more than the other way around.

Second, placing low-risk offenders in these programs also tends to disrupt their prosocial networks; in other words, the very attributes that make them low risk become interrupted, such as school, employment, family, and so forth. Remember, if they do not have these attributes it is unlikely they are low risk to begin with. The risk principle can best be seen from a recent study of offenders in Ohio who were placed in a halfway house or community-based correctional facility (CBCF). The study found that the recidivism rate for higher-risk offenders who were placed in a halfway house or CBCF was reduced, while the recidivism rates for the low-risk offenders who were placed in the programs actually increased.

The second principle is referred to as the need principle, or the "what" to target—criminogenic factors that are highly correlated with criminal conduct. The need principle states that programs should target crime-producing needs, such as antisocial attitudes, values, and beliefs, antisocial peer associations, substance abuse, lack of problem-solving and self-control skills, and other factors that are highly correlated with criminal conduct. Furthermore, programs need to ensure that the vast majority of their interventions are focused on these factors. Noncriminogenic factors such as self-esteem, physical conditioning, understanding one's culture or history, and creative abilities will not have much effect on recidivism rates. An example of a program that tends to target noncrim-

inogenic factors can be seen in offender-based military-style boot camps. These programs tend to focus on noncriminogenic factors, such as drill and ceremony, physical conditioning, discipline, self-esteem, and bonding offenders together. Because they tend to focus on non-crime-producing needs, most studies show that boot camps have little impact on future criminal behavior.

The third principle is the treatment principle, or the "how"—the ways in which correctional programs should target risk and need factors. This principle states that the most effective programs are behavioral in nature. Behavioral programs have several attributes. First, they are centered on the *present* circumstances and risk factors that are responsible for the offender's behavior. Second, they are *action* oriented rather than talk oriented. In other words, offenders do something about their difficulties rather than just talk about them. Third, they teach offenders new, prosocial skills to replace the antisocial ones (e.g., stealing, cheating, lying) through modeling, practice, and reinforcement. Examples of behavioral programs include structured social learning programs where new skills are taught and behaviors and attitudes are consistently reinforced; cognitive behavioral programs that target attitudes, values, peers, substance abuse, anger, and so on; and family-based interventions that train family on appropriate behavioral techniques. Interventions based on these approaches are very structured and emphasize the importance of modeling and behavioral rehearsal techniques that engender self-efficacy, challenge of cognitive distortions, and assist offenders in developing good problem-solving and self-control skills. These strategies have been demonstrated to be effective in reducing recidivism. Nonbehavioral interventions that are often used in programs include drug and alcohol education, fear tactics and other emotional appeals, talk therapy, nondirective client-centered approaches, having them read books, lectures, milieu therapy, and self-help. There is little empirical evidence that these approaches will lead to long-term reductions in recidivism.

Finally, a host of other considerations will increase correctional program effectiveness. These include targeting responsivity factors such as a lack of motivation or other barriers that can influence someone's participation in a program; making sure that you have well-trained and interpersonally sensitive staff; providing close monitoring of offenders' whereabouts and associates; assisting with other needs that offenders might have; ensuring the program is delivered as designed through quality assurance processes; and providing structured aftercare. These program attributes all enhance correctional program effectiveness.

If we put it all together we have the "who, what, and how" of correctional intervention, also known as "what works."

SOURCE: Edward J. Latessa, "From Theory to Practice: What Works in Reducing Recidivism?" In *State of Crime and Justice in Ohio* (Columbus, OH: Ohio Office of Criminal Justice Services, 2004).

c o r r e c t i o n a l **brief**

Federal Offenders on Probation

The number of federal offenders on probation declined since 1995 (−31%), and at the beginning of 2007 included 24,491 offenders. This decline has been attributed to the use of the Federal Sentencing Guidelines, as discussed in Chapter 4. Offenders required to comply with at least one special condition of supervision increased from 67% to 92% from 1996 to 2007. Between 1987 and 1996 the success rates (offenders terminating supervision successfully) were high:

- 85% of those on probation were successes.

- 66% of supervised releases were successes.

SOURCES: Lauren Glaze and Thomas P. Bonczar, *Probation and Parole in the United States, 2006* (Washington, DC: U.S. Department of Justice, 2007); and William Adams and Jeffrey Roth, *Federal Offenders under Community Supervision, 1987–96* (Washington, DC: U.S. Department of Justice, 1998), p. 5.

Offenders vary in their ability to conform their behavior to expectations. Some are indifferent or hostile, being unwilling or unable to cooperate with their supervising officer or the court. Some are too immature emotionally to comply with directions. A few face unrealistic conditions with which compliance is not possible, such as extensive victim restitution or employment in an economically depressed period or area. Still others drift toward further criminal behavior by violating the conditions of their probation (particularly the alcohol and drug abuse requirements) that might not be illegal per se, but are interpreted as indicators of future illegal behavior. In these circumstances, the supervising probation officer must deal with **technical probation violations**.

In such circumstances, supervising officers must act to issue stern warnings or arrest their clients. Probationers are taken back to court with requests that court-ordered conditions be tightened (or relaxed, if they are inappropriate). The judge typically warns the probationer, and may increase conditions or frequency of supervision. The conditions often imposed on probationers can be found in Table 5.2. Frequently these warnings and official actions are sufficient to coerce client conformity but, if not, or if the client repetitively violates conditions of probation or is arrested by law enforcement officers for an alleged new crime, a hearing may be held to determine if probation should be revoked (a process called **probation revocation**) and a different sentencing alternative may be imposed (such as a jail sentence or imprisonment). If the probationer is not in jail, a warrant may be issued for the arrest of the probationer.

key term

Technical probation violation
Probation sentence change due to charges that the offender violated the rules imposed by the court, but not by committing a new crime.

key term

Probation revocation
Change of sentence from probation to another correctional control status, due to violation of the conditions of probation.

table **5.2**   **Special Conditions Imposed on Probationers**

Condition of Sentence	Percentage of Probationers
Supervision fees	61%
Fines	56
Court costs	55
Employment	35
Mandatory drug testing	33
Restitution to victim	30
Alcohol abuse treatment	29
Community service	26
Drug abuse treatment	23
At least one condition	99

SOURCE: Thomas Bonczar, *Characteristics of Adults on Probation* (Washington, DC: Bureau of Justice Statistics, 1997), p. 7.

key term

Gagnon v. Scarpelli
U.S. Supreme Court decision that held probation is a privilege, not a right, but, once granted, the probationer has an interest in remaining on probation.

| **class** activity

Ask students to identify *technical probation violations* and the role of *tourniquet sentencing.*

| **class** activity

Present a case study of a probationer and the violation of conditions for which a probation revocation hearing is scheduled. Ask students what the judge should do.

| **lecture** note

Explain *Gagnon v. Scarpelli* and its constitutional guarantees.

| **class** activity

Ask students to explain the expansion of felony probation.

| **class** activity

Ask students if a spousal batterer would be a suitable candidate for probation. If the consensus is "yes," ask what special conditions or program participation should be required.

key term

Felony probation
The offender is placed on probation for committing a felony.

The probation hearing is a serious event, because it poses a potential for "grievous loss of liberty" for the offender. The hearing is governed by the U.S. Supreme Court decision known as ***Gagnon v. Scarpelli***. In brief, this case held that probation is a privilege not a right, but, once granted, the probationer has an interest in remaining on probation (an "entitlement"). The Court ruled that probation cannot be withdrawn or be revoked without observing the following elements of due process:

- The probationer must be informed in writing of the charge against him or her.
- The written notice must be given to the probationer in advance of the revocation hearing.
- The probationer has the right to attend the hearing and to present evidence on his or her own behalf.
- The probationer has the right to challenge those testifying against him or her.
- The probationer has the right to confront and cross-examine witnesses.
- The probationer has the right to have legal counsel present if the charges are sufficiently complicated or the case is so complex that an ordinary person would not be able to comprehend the legal issues.

States may provide more rights than those just listed, but cannot provide less.

The revocation hearing can lead to several outcomes:

- The supervision level of the case may be increased.
- The offender is warned and admonished, then returned to probation supervision.
- The court can impose additional conditions, then return the offender to community supervision.
- The court can revoke probation and resentence the offender to an incarceration setting, such as jail or prison.
- The court can consider the legal competence of the offender and order a mental health examination, the outcome of which could be commitment to a mental health service or transfer of the case to a probate court for proceedings under the jurisdiction's health and welfare code, or commitment to a state mental facility.
- A bench warrant can be issued for offenders who cannot be found or who have left the jurisdiction of the court.

Of those probationers who experienced a disciplinary hearing, the most frequent reason for the hearing was absconding or failure to contact a probation officer. This was followed by arrest or conviction on a new offense (38%). Among persons under probation supervision who had experienced one or more disciplinary hearings, 42% were permitted to continue their sentence but only with the imposition of additional conditions. Almost three in ten were incarcerated in jail or prison; and 29% had their supervision reinstated without any new conditions.

FELONY PROBATION

The rapid growth of serious and violent crime in America during the 1980s contributed to prison overcrowding and spurred a movement toward the increase in the use of **felony probation.** Probation, as we have seen, had traditionally been for misdemeanors and low-level nonviolent crime. But prison overcrowding and bulging jails forced the correctional administrators to take a close look at some other categories of felons for relief of an overtaxed system. Because incarceration costs (see Table 5.3) and building costs have become so high, and the institutions so crowded, felony probation has become quite common. We need only look at the dismal results from incarceration to agree that it may be possible to increase this option when combined with a thorough and complete presentencing investigation report and consideration of risk. Programs combined with probation services to protect the community are explored in more detail in the next chapter.

table **5.3**	Daily Cost of Correctional Programs per Client	
Program		Cost
Probation		$ 4.18
Prison		$62.22
Parole		$ 6.94

SOURCE: C. Camp and G. Camp, *The Corrections Yearbook 2002* (Middletown, CT: Criminal Justice Institute, 2003).

THE BROKEN WINDOWS APPROACH

Recently, some leaders of the probation and parole approaches have called for a dramatic change in the way in which community supervision achieves public safety.[18] This new model is called the "broken windows" approach. Borrowing heavily from community policing, the application of **broken windows probation** in probation and parole calls for a new partnership with the community. With this approach, the probation officer is asked to collaborate with the community and victim, hold the offender accountable, and improve and expand the leadership of probation. The key strategies outlined with this model include the following:[19]

- Placing public safety first
- Working in the community
- Developing partners in the community
- Rationally allocating scarce resources
- Enforcing conditions and penalizing violations
- Emphasizing performance-based initiatives
- Encouraging strong and steady leadership

Although the goals of the broken windows approach are lofty, the model is not without its critics. Taxman and Bryne[20] argue that the model is filled with rhetoric, is unrealistic, and is based on a flawed approach. Furthermore, they contend that it ignores the significant body of research indicating that the most effective way to achieve public safety is through well-designed and implemented treatment. Table 5.4 illustrates the differences between what Taxman and Bryne call the **proactive supervision** model and the broken windows model.[21] The Maryland Department of Public Safety and Correctional Services recently initiated the proactive approach to community supervision. Moving away from traditional supervision, this approach advocates a much more prescriptive strategy that includes more fieldwork combined with evidenced-based practices. The accompanying Correctional Brief describes this strategy. The debate about how to make probation more effective will continue, and it remains to be seen if the broken windows model can live up to its promises.

PROBATION AND ITS ROLE IN CORRECTIONS

Because of the prison population crisis across the nation, states are exploring many strategies to reduce the overcrowding. The basic strategies can be described as front-end solutions and back-end solutions. Probation (a front-end solution) is the mostly widely used alternative.

table **5.4**   **Fixing Broken Windows Probation: A Comparison of Two Strategies**

	The Broken Windows Model	The Proactive Supervision Model
Definition of the Public Safety Problem	Probation should be held responsible for the level of public safety in each community, including crime rates, fear of crime, school safety, and quality of life.	Probation should be held responsible for the supervision and control of all offenders under their direct supervision.
The Duties of Probation Officers	Probation officers should be involved not only in offender surveillance and control, but also in crime-prevention efforts and various forms of advocacy and community change.	Probation officers should focus their efforts on the direct supervision of offenders while the responsibility for resource development and coordination should be completed by creating a new "resource specialist" position within probation.
The Location of Probation Officers	Probation officers should supervise offenders exclusively in the community rather than in the office. Supervision should be place-based rather than offender-based.	Probation officers should utilize a combination of office and field visits, but the purpose of the contact is always the supervision of the offender, not the place.
The Role of the Probation Officers	The probation officer should be a "generalist" with the ability to supervise a wide range of offenders (e.g., drug offenders, alcohol offenders, nonviolent offenders, sex offenders, mentally ill offenders), utilizing a classic brokerage model.	Probation officers should be hired and trained with the skills to handle a specialized caseload (e.g., drug offenders, alcohol offenders, nonviolent offenders, sex offenders, mentally ill offenders), including assessment procedures, counseling techniques, and a comprehensive knowledge of the treatment network (inpatient and outpatient).
The Acquisition and Allocation of Probation Resources	Probation departments need to develop improved strategies for the rational allocation of existing resources, focusing on two primary agency needs: (1) better assessment of offender "risk" to public safety (e.g., sex offenders, gang members, drug dealers), and (2) the assignment of field staff to areas with the greatest public safety needs.	Probation departments need to "make the case" for increased resources for offender treatment and supervision, by proposing legislation that mandates minimum levels of probation (e.g., caseload size services) and allows agents to use sanctions as a tool to improve public safety.
Enforcement of Probation Conditions	Probation officers utilize a range of field surveillance techniques to identify offender noncompliance and quickly respond to violations. A structured hierarchy of sanctions will be used for initial violations with revocation and (return to) prison/jail for repeat "offenders."	Probation departments develop strategies (in conjunction with local judiciary) to reduce the number of conditions established and to enforce the conditions set, using a structured hierarchy of nonincarcerative sanctions.
Location of Absconders	Probation departments establish separate probation absconder location and apprehension units to better protect the community.	Probation departments develop a task force to better understand the nature (and impact) of the absconder problem. Utilizing a problem-oriented probation strategy, probation officers will be required directly to focus on addressing the cause(s) of the problem, rather than the consequences.
Partnerships in the Community	A wide range of probation–community partnerships will be developed, including both crime-prevention and community-betterment activities.	Probation departments will focus on improving the treatment networks in their community and on those related activities that will enhance the supervision function.

Data from: Faye Taxman and James Bryne, "Fixing Broken Windows Probation," *Perspectives* 25:2 (2001): 23–29.

correctional **brief**

Being Proactive with Offenders in the Community

Proactive community supervision (PCS) improves community supervision by improving offenders' lives and fully restoring them as productive participants to the community. To accomplish this task, agents are active in the communities in which they serve. The PCS model emphasizes offender management tools such as motivational interviewing, risk and needs assessment, quality contact standards, and implementation of "what works" principles that improve an offender's ability to succeed in the community. By using these tools, the role of the agent is changed: Agents become role models of helpful and prosocial behavior for the offenders and the community.

By working with the community, supervision can accomplish the following:

- Protect public safety,

- Hold offenders accountable to victims and the community, and

- Help offenders become responsible and productive.

Under the PCS model:

- Agents' caseloads are reduced to appropriate levels so that agents can spend more time in neighborhoods working one-on-one with offenders;

- Agents and supervisors receive training on how to motivate offenders, identify critical risk factors, and create practical supervision plans; and

- Agents and supervisors receive suitable technological tools such as laptop computers to help them perform their jobs while working outside the office in the community.

The community can expect agents to:

- Spend their days near where parolees and probationers call home;

- Work with parolees and probationers to help them beat the drug and alcohol addictions that can lead them back to crime and violence;

- Help parolees and probationers get basic education and job skills so they can become contributing citizens;

- Build relationships with offenders' families, friends, and neighbors—people who can alert agents before trouble arises;

- Intervene before an offender commits a new crime; and

- Respond quickly when an offender's behavior necessitates removal from the community.

SOURCE: Maryland Department of Public Safety and Correctional Services, *http://www.dpscs.state.md.us/rehabservs/* (accessed March 8, 2005).

Front-end solutions are alternative sentences such as probation and intermediate punishments that include house arrest, deferred prosecution, electronic monitoring, shock probation, intensive supervised probation, intermittent jail incarceration, and other programs (see Chapter 6).

Back-end solutions refer to ways used to reduce prison populations after the offender arrives in prison. They can be viewed as "early-out" or "extended limits" options: parole, shock parole, emergency release (usually court ordered), expanded good-time credits to count against the minimum sentence, work and educational furlough, prerelease to halfway houses (used extensively by the U.S. Bureau of Prisons, the federal prison system), and other programs. These are explained in Chapter 10.

Probation has established itself as a major component of corrections. It appears the emphasis on probation as the preferred disposition will keep it in the forefront of correctional reform. If the costs of probation and prison are compared, as shown earlier in Table 5.3, daily costs of $4.18 per day as opposed to an average of $62.22 per day in prison, the taxpayer will rule in favor of probation. As the population grows, the number of offenders and variations on probation strategies will surely increase as well. Students of probation concur that the practice is approximately 60% effective on a national basis. An alternative to imprisonment that is about one-eighth as costly (and at least as effective) has great appeal and clearly answers the need for a sound and economical approach to corrections.

key term

Front-end solutions
Options for controlling the number of inmates being sent to prison.

key term

Back-end solutions
Strategies for reducing prison population overcrowding by early release programs, such as parole, shock parole, and expanded good-time credits.

homework

Assign students to locate and read an online report on electronic monitoring of offenders, and submit a one-paragraph statement of the objectives of that program.

Summary

Across the nation, probation is administered by hundreds of separate agencies, with a wide variety of rules and structures seen among the states. Whereas one agency may be required to serve juvenile, misdemeanant, and felony offenders, another agency may handle only one type of offender. The term *probation* has various meanings within the multiple areas of corrections. More than 4.2 millions of the nation's adults are on probation on a given day. African Americans, who comprise about 13% of the nation's population, represented 29% of the probationers in 2006; Hispanic or Latino comprised another 13%.[22]

The set of functions, activities, and services that probation performs for its administrative agency and the offender is the probation *process*. The process model for probation service is usually seen as a series of interlinking activities among the courts, the offender, and the offender's community and its resources. The process includes the offender's *reporting* regularly to a probation officer; the *servicing* of the offender's needs through treatment, counseling, and so on; and the officer's *supervision* of the probationer to ensure that the rules of the probation order are observed. Hence, probation today is a process that gives the judge an alternative disposition, which results in an improved status for the offender within a subsystem of the criminal justice system.

Key Words

probation, 84

suspended sentence, 84

right of sanctuary, 84

benefit of clergy, 84

stigma, 84

sursis, 84

John Augustus, 85

presentence investigation (PSI) report, 90

risk and needs assessment, 91

special conditions of probation, 93

technical probation violations, 95

probation revocation, 95

Gagnon v. *Scarpelli*, 96

felony probation, 96

broken windows probation, 97

proactive supervision, 97

front-end solutions, 99

back-end solutions, 99

Review Questions

1. Explain the purpose of probation, and describe the methods by which it is usually administered.
2. How do probation officers enforce the conditions ordered by the court?
3. What are some of the restrictions often applied to probation? What kinds of offenders are usually denied probation?
4. Do you think a conflict exists between surveillance and treatment?
5. Identify and define five front-end solutions to prison overcrowding.
6. What are the national trends in probation?
7. Why should probation be the sentence of choice?
8. What are special conditions of probation? Give three examples and explain why they might be imposed.
9. Who is credited as the "father of probation," and why was his work so important?
10. Does drug abuse treatment work? Under what circumstances?
11. Explain the general process of probation revocation.
12. Why would an LSI-R be useful in probation supervision?

Endnotes

1. Norman Johnston, *Forms of Constraints: A History of Prison Architecture* (Urbana, IL: University of Illinois Press, 2007). See also Herman Bianchi, *Justice as Sanctuary* (Bloomington: Indiana University Press, 1994).

2. See Numbers 35:6 and Joshua 20:2–6.

3. David Fogel, "Nordic Approaches to Crime and Justice," *CJ International* 3:1 (1987): 8–21. See also D. Farabee, M. Pendergast, and D. Anglin, "The Effectiveness of Coerced Treatment for Drug-Abusing Offenders," *Federal Probation* 62:1 (1998): 3–10; and James Clare, "Methamphetamine Use and Health Implications in Corrections," *American Jails* 21:3 (2007): 40–44.

4. Alexander Smith and Louis Berlin, *Introduction to Probation and Parole* (St. Paul, MN: West, 1976), pp. 76–78. See also Edward Latessa and Paula Smith, *Corrections in the Community* (Cincinnati, OH: Anderson Publishing, 2007), pp. 48–50.

5. Harry Elmer Barnes and Negley K. Teeters, *New Horizons in Criminology*, 3rd ed. (Englewood Cliffs, NJ: Prentice Hall, 1959), p. 554.

6. Missouri (1897), Rhode Island (1899), New Jersey (1900), and Vermont (1900).

7. Cook County (Chicago), Illinois.

8. Extrapolated from Camille Camp and George Camp, *The Corrections Yearbook 2002* (South Salem, NY: Criminal Justice Institute, 2003), p. 7. For an examination of probationer work groups, see G. Bayens, M. Manske, and J. Smykla, "The Attitudes of Criminal Justice Workgroups Toward Intensive Supervised Probation," *American Journal of Criminal Justice* 22:2 (1998): 189–206; and Bill Conlon et al., "Education: Don't Do Prisons without It," *Corrections Today* 70:1 (2008): 48–52.

9. Dennis Sullivan, L. Tifft, and P. Cordella (eds.), "Special Issue: The Phenomenon of Restorative Justice," *Contemporary Justice Review* 1:1 (1998): 1–166. See also Restorative Justice Online, "Introduction to Restorative Justice," *http://www.restorativejustice.org/intro* (accessed September 14, 2008).

10. Latessa and Smith, *Corrections in the Community*, p. 57.

11. See F. Taxman and J. Bryne, "Fixing Broken Windows Probation," *Perspectives* 25:2 (2001): 23–29.

12. Harry E. Allen and Julie C. Abril, "Fanning the Flames of Fear Revisited: Three Strikes in California." Paper presented at the Annual Meeting of the American Society of Criminology, Washington, DC, November 11, 1998. See also Eric Lotke, Jason Coburn, and Vincent Schiraldi, "Three Strikes and You're Out," *http://www.justicepolicy.org/* (accessed September 14, 2008). For a sobering discussion, see Michael Tonry, "Crime and Human Rights—How Political Paranoia, Protestant Fundamentalism, and Constitutional Obsolescence Combined to Devastate Black America," *Criminology* 46:1 (2008), pp. 1–33.

13. See also Mark Umbreit and W. Bradshaw, "Victim Experience of Meeting Adult and Juvenile Offenders," *Federal Probation* 61:4 (1998): 33–39; and David Karp, Gordon Bazemore, and J. D. Chesire, "The Role and Attitudes of Restorative Board Members," *Crime and Delinquency* 50:4 (2004): 487–515.

14. D. Andrews and J. Bonta, *LSI-R, The Level of Service Inventory—Revised* (Toronto: Multi-Health Systems, Inc., 1995).

15. Lia Gormsen, "Judge Uses His Legal Knowledge to Empower Reentering Offenders," *Correctional Today* 70:3 (2008): 33.

16. Christopher Lowenkamp and Edward J. Latessa, *Evaluation of Ohio's CCA Funded Programs* (Cincinnati, OH: Division of Criminal Justice, University of Cincinnati, 2005).

17. Annette Jolin and Brian Stipak, "Drug Treatment and Electronically Monitored Home Confinement," *Crime and Delinquency* 38:2 (1992): 158–170.

18. Paul Gendreau, "The Principles of Effective Interventions with Offenders," in A. T. Harland (ed.), *Choosing Correctional Options That Work: Defining Demand and Evaluating the Supply* (Thousand Oaks, CA: Sage, 1996), pp. 117–130.

19. T. Arola and R. Lawrence, "Broken Windows Probation," *Perspectives* 24:1 (2000): 27–33.

20. The Reinventing Probation Council that drafted the initial report on broken windows and probation included Ronald Corbett, Dan Beto, John DiIulio, J. Richard Faulkner, Bernard Fitzgerald, Irwin Gregg, Norman Helber, Gerald Hinzman, Robert Malvestuto, Mario Paparozzi, Rocco Pozzi, and Edward Rhine. See Reinventing Probation Council, *Transforming Probation through Leadership: The Broken Windows Model*, *http://www.manhattaninstitute.org/html/broken_windows.htm* (accessed September 14, 2008).

21. Taxman and Bryne, "Fixing Broken Windows Probation."

22. Lauren Glaze and Seri Palla, *Probation and Parole in the United States, 2006* (Washington, DC: U.S. Department of Justice, 2007).

chapter 6

Diversion and Intermediate Sanctions

Outline

Diversion: Keeping the Offender out of the System
- Police-Based Diversion Programs
- Community-Based Diversion Programs
- Court-Based Diversion Programs

Between Probation and Prison

Overcrowding

Intermediate Sanctions
- Restitution Programs
- Intensive Supervised Probation
- Drug and Other Problem-Solving Courts
- Community Service Programs
- Home Detention
- Electronic Monitoring
- Community Residential Treatment Centers (Halfway Houses)
- Day Reporting Centers
- Shock Incarceration
- Boot Camp Programs

Overview

Our investigation of the alternatives to imprisonment has focused on probation as the major nonincarceration sanction arrow in the quiver of the sentencing judges. Although probation is by far the most widely used correctional sanction, it is but one aspect of community corrections. In this chapter we explore some diversion options along with the growing use of intermediate sanctions, which are the various new correctional options used as adjuncts to and part of probation. Note, however, that some jurisdictions use these sanctions not as part of probation but as stand-alone programs.

"The manifold implications of the concept of community corrections pivot around a profound idea: official reactions to the convicted offender should be related to the community forces which contribute to criminality, which are involved in the definition of crime as a social problem, and which largely determine whether or not rehabilitation programs will produce his integration within the control system regulating the behavior of non-criminals."

—Elmer H. Johnson

correctional **brief**

Intermediate Sanctions

Intermediate sanctions, ranging in severity from day fines to so-called boot camps, are interventions that are beginning to fill the sentencing gap between prison at one extreme and probation at the other. Lengthy prison terms may be inappropriate for some offenders; for others, probation may be too inconsequential and may not provide the degree of public supervision necessary to ensure public safety.

By expanding sentencing options, intermediate sanctions enable the criminal justice system to tailor punishment more closely to the nature of the crime and the criminal. An appropriate range of punishments makes it possible for the system to hold offenders strictly accountable for their actions.

Intermediate sanctions provide economic disincentives for criminal behavior, permit effective and efficient use of limited criminal justice resources, strengthen the credibility of the court, and provide revenue to offset not only program cost but also victim loss.

SOURCE: Voncile Gowdy, *Intermediate Sanctions* (Washington, DC: U.S. Department of Justice, 1993), p. 1.

DIVERSION: KEEPING THE OFFENDER OUT OF THE SYSTEM

key term

Diversion
Minimizing penetration into the criminal justice system through police, community, or court programs.

Some jurisdictions have established policies to minimize assignment of certain nondangerous or problematic offenders to the justice system, particularly the mentally disordered,[1] drug abusers,[2] and alcohol abusers.[3] **Diversion** from the criminal justice system has taken place in one form or another since social controls were first established. In most cases, informal diversions merely indicate an official's exercise of discretion at some point in the criminal process.

More formal diversions include suspension of the criminal process in favor of some noncriminal disposition. Fewer than 25% of reported offenses in America result in an arrest, and only about one-third of those arrests result in a criminal conviction. This is the correctional funnel at work and an indication that preconviction diversion is not uncommon.

Diversion may occur at a number of points in the criminal justice system. The primary points are prior to police contact, prior to official police processing, and prior to official court processing. Three basic models emerge to determine which agency might be responsible for diversion: police-based diversion programs, community-based diversion programs, and court-based diversion programs. Although each of the models usually involves more than one agency or group, programs will generally be grouped according to who initiates the action and what agency will have primary responsibility for its implementation.

Most diversion programs now in effect constitute informal responses to the ambiguities of existing legislation. The value of such programs is difficult if not impossible to estimate. Again, one must try to measure an event that was prevented: What did not happen as a result of diversion? Their goals and procedures must be clearly articulated and integrated into the rest of the criminal justice system.

lecture note

Using your computer, play the brief chapter overview videotape by Edward J. Latessa that introduces Chapter 6 (about 3 minutes).

Police-Based Diversion Programs

Police agencies have practiced diversion, informally, by using their power of discretion at the time of an offender's arrest. Several programs have been established to encourage more diversions on a formal basis. Police have been reluctant in the past to formalize their practice of discretion because of public opinion criticizing their actions as being too soft. Most formalized programs are aimed at youthful offenders in an effort to keep them from beginning a career of crime.

Another example of diversionary tactics at the police level is the family crisis intervention approach. This approach, which has been used in several large cities, is especially important as domestic violence laws across the country become more tough and are enforced more often.[4] Laws often now result in the arrest of both parties until the question as to who initiated the violence is resolved. There are indications that the police, by identifying conflict situations at an early stage of development, can prevent the escalation of violence. A general model involves the use of officers specially trained for effective family crisis intervention to respond to family disturbances. The officers attempt to resolve the conflict on the scene. If they cannot, the antagonists are arrested and, in some jurisdictions, referred to a community agency instead of jail.

Community-Based Diversion Programs

Diversion projects are most effective when integrated into a community-based correctional system with many levels of supervision and custody. The currently informal options on an accountable basis must be formalized without making the process too rigid. If community-based programs are too restricted, they will become mere institutions without walls. Diversion is seen as the first threshold of the community corrections system, designed to remove as many offenders as possible from the process before their conviction and labeling as a criminal.

Although programs that aim toward a total or partial alternative to incarceration are improvements, they do not always eliminate the stigma of a criminal record. Diversion programs tied to treatment and services in the community, however, both avoid the problems of incarceration and remove the criminal label. Those programs are seen not as a substitute for probation services but as a method of filling the gap between offenders eligible for probation and cases in which the charges can be dropped. Diversion should be accompanied by a formalized agreement with offenders as to what they are to do in return for the elimination of their arrest records. A set of alternative treatment services and residential reinforcements may be needed to help diverted individuals handle their problems. The diverted individuals should have the advantages available to all other categories of offenders and ex-inmates who are being treated in the local network.

Court-Based Diversion Programs

The courts are involved with diversion in several ways. One method is to use civil commitment for individuals who presumably can be treated more efficiently in a hospital situation. A more common and reasonable use of diversion by the courts is found in **pretrial intervention programs,** which have been funded extensively by the U.S. Department of Labor. The general pattern of such actions, at the end of the prescribed period of the continuance, is to allow:

key term

Pretrial intervention programs
Requiring defendants awaiting trial to report to a supervision officer.

1. Dismissal of pending charges based on satisfactory project participation and demonstrated self-improvement
2. Extension of the continuance to allow the program staff more time to work with the person (usually for an additional 30 to 90 days)
3. Return of the defendant to normal court processing, without prejudice, because of unsatisfactory performance in the program.

Diversion is especially appropriate for the public drunk, low-level misdemeanant offenders, and the first-time drug abuser, a major thrust behind the drug-court movement. The current alternative to incarceration for public drunks is to send them to a detoxification center. Voluntary attendance at detoxification centers demonstrates the willingness of many problem drinkers to accept treatment, if only for free room and board.

key term

Treatment in lieu of conviction
Diversion offered to offenders in which successful completion of probation allows the prosecutor or judge to cease prosecution if treatment program results in no conviction.

key term

Community corrections acts (CCAs)
Legislation that funds local community correctional programs designed to divert offenders from prison.

The severity of criminal sanctions and public reaction to most drug offenses makes the diversion of drug-abuse cases a sensitive area. With the country awash in illegal drugs, and drug use by the general population quite high, the wave of enforcement activity has made it difficult to divert all but the least violent of users, leaving the hard cases to sweat it out in institutions that seldom provide meaningful programs. One example of a diversion program is found in Ohio and is called **treatment in lieu of conviction;** it is designed for first-time substance abusers. Successful completion of treatment and no new charges can result in a clean record for these offenders. Most diversion programs for drug users are concentrated on juveniles and are aimed at first-time arrestees, although drug courts address all age groups.

The spectrum of diversionary programs is geared toward the same goal: provision of a reasonable alternative to incarceration in large, overcrowded, and punitive prisons.[5] Again, as in the development of many other aspects of correctional services, such programs often begin as independent actions by concerned professionals and community groups. As a result of earlier efforts, **community corrections acts (CCAs)** have been authorized as a statutory medium for including citizens and bringing funding to local governments and county agencies to plan, develop, and deliver correctional services and sanctions at the local level.[6] At least 22 states have passed such enabling legislation, encouraging intermediate sanctions, advocacy for juveniles, local community organization involvement, victim–offender reconciliation, victim restitution, employment services, and county residential facilities, among many others. Some states contract with private agencies for county programs, whereas others fund local programs run by local officials. Either way, the goal is to offer community correctional programs with control at the local level. The best-implemented CCAs are in Colorado, Ohio, Indiana, and Florida, and offer model programs that could be copied by other jurisdictions.

BETWEEN PROBATION AND PRISON

The dominant characteristic of intermediate sanctions is the use of increased surveillance and tighter controls over nonincarcerated offenders. In this context intermediate sanctions are referred to as "punishing smarter," since the sanction is thought to be tough enough to impress upon the offender the seriousness of the act, without the costs associated with longer-term incarceration. Advocates for the offender object on the basis that these efforts use increased punishment as a rationale and tighter controls are not needed. Others argue that prison construction is too expensive for most jurisdictions and intermediate sanctions save the costs of constructing, staffing, and maintaining incarceration facilities. Still other proponents see intermediate sanctions as a way to push for more treatment and services, which are thought to be more readily available (and more effective) in the community. These advocates note the reintegrative aspects of intermediate sanctions and point to reduced recidivism among offenders assigned to such programs. Some intermediate sanctions are less expensive and more effective than incarceration, while others are clearly intended to "get tough" with offenders. Although not yet fully integrated into the coordinated system of community corrections, these intermediate sanctions are rapidly being adopted across the nation into a wide system of local, county, state, and federal correctional systems. We first review the use of intermediate sanctions as an adjunct to probation.

As we saw in the previous chapter, probation has become the backbone of contemporary corrections and is used to treat offenders and provide protection to the community through supervising probationers. In the last two decades, prompted by crowding of jails and prisons as well as a shift in the philosophical assumptions about controlling offenders,[7] a broad range of different treatments and innovative technologies has been developed. These innovative programs and control schemes are generally called **intermediate sanctions.**[8] A study of intermediate sanctions must start with a look at the overcrowding issue.

key term

Intermediate sanctions
Correctional programs that fall somewhere between probation and prison.

OVERCROWDING

The impetus for the development and expansion of community corrections and intermediate sanctions has been the overcrowding of our jails and prisons. Most repeat offenders receive increasingly severe punishments,[9] including sentences to jail and prison. In the United States, the lag between onset of offending and eventual confinement as an adult is approximately ten years. In other words, *persistent* offenders are more likely to have been subject to other correctional control (fines, **day reporting centers**, community service, **restitution orders**, **house arrest**, and even **electronic monitoring**) while in the community prior to their first incarceration.

The processing of offenders in the justice system has become a **risk-management** strategy, and persistent offenders are usually given increasingly restrictive alternatives while corrections tries to stop their criminal behavior (that is, encourage **desistance**). Many offenders are given a number of such opportunities and assistance before a sentencing judge resorts to incarceration, the most punitive weapon in the armory of corrections.

Before the 1970s, many if not most offenders were placed on probation, to achieve the ideal of rehabilitation.[10] Individualized treatment during that relatively progressive era became subject to strong attack by conservatives, researchers, and liberals of many stripes. The arguments were that prison and parole officials were abusing their discretion, rehabilitation did not work, strict law and order should be used to capture the streets, and offenders richly deserved punishment. This was seen as the only way to protect law-abiding citizens as well as to retain the social fabric. This philosophy was particularly evident in the nation's War on Drugs program, a war that has clearly not been won.[11]

Coupled with the demise of the medical model, politicians at both local and national levels used the issue of crime as a vehicle to demonstrate how getting tough would solve the problem.[12] Seeking reelection on the hard-line bandwagon may have served narrow political ends. However, it also led to the enactment of a series of stringent policies ranging from a shift to determinate punishment, to mandatory minimum sentences to prison, and to the building of more supermax prisons.[13]

These events coincided with the 1945 to 1976 "baby-boom" population bulge, whose members entered the "high-commitment" years of ages 29 to 39 between 1975 and 1985. These four major forces—a larger number of persons at risk to commit crime and be incarcerated, the shift to conservative beliefs about how to deal with offenders and crime, the War on Drugs,[14] and enactment of more stringent punishments—contributed to an ever-increasing stream of offenders being committed to prison (up from 448,264 in 1975 to over 1.5 million in 2007).[15] By 1998, the combined number of prisoners in the nation and in jails exceeded any previous total. "America the Free" has become the free world's leader in rate of incarceration, exceeding even the Russian Republic of the former Soviet Union. Prisons

key term

Day reporting center
Facility to which offenders are sent for scheduling and monitoring of their activities.

key term

Restitution order
Requirement that offender repay the victim.

key term

House arrest
Being confined to one's home except when permission is granted to leave.

key term

Electronic monitoring
Tracking of offender whereabouts electronically.

key term

Risk management
Strategies designed to provide increased supervision and surveillance for higher-risk offenders and less-restrictive options for those of lower risk.

key term

Desistance
Ceasing of criminal behavior by the offender. Can also imply lessening of the severity of criminal offenses.

correctional **brief**

Federal Pretrial Services

While federal pretrial services officers are charged with supervising each defendant released to their custody, not every offender is actively supervised. Some defendants—primarily those the court has determined pose no flight risk or danger to the community—are released only under the condition that they do not commit any offense. Other defendants are released under more restrictive release conditions. These defendants are typically required to report to a pretrial services officer on a predetermined reporting schedule or to reside in a community treatment facility or halfway house. During the release period, the pretrial services officer monitors the defendant's compliance with the release conditions and reports any violations to the court and to the U.S. attorney. Additionally, pretrial services officers might assist released individuals with securing employment and medical, legal, or social services.

SOURCE: John Scalia, *Federal Pretrial Release and Detention, 1996* (Washington, DC: U.S. Department of Justice, 1999), p. 8.

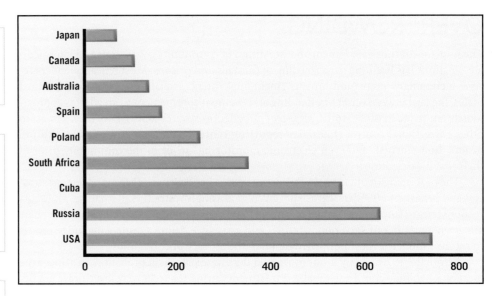

figure 6.1

Rates per 100,000 of Incarceration in Selected Counties

Data from: International Centre of Prison Studies: University of London.
http://www.kcl.ac.uk/depsta/law/research/icps/worldbrief/wpb_stats.php?area=all&category=wb_poprate

bulge, and the nation continues its building binge, trying to construct sufficient numbers of jail and prison cells to accommodate the massive increase of incarcerated offenders. When it earlier became evident that the bricks-and-mortar approach could not be met, correctional innovators turned to developing alternative punishment programs, variously known as intermediate sanctions or intermediate punishments. Data from 2008 shows comparisons of rates of incarceration among the United States, Cuba, South Africa, the Russian Republic, and other nations[16] (see Figure 6.1). What is interesting in these data is the comparison with the rest of the world and the fact that we are far ahead of all other counties.

INTERMEDIATE SANCTIONS

Intermediate sanctions provide midrange dispositions that better reflect the severity of the offense than do probation or imprisonment. While many if not most offenders can best be served by reintegration programming, some are thought to be too dangerous to be released to traditional probation supervision with infrequent face-to-face contacts. Thus, a continuum of sanctions ranging from probation to imprisonment has been developed: restitution, fines, day fines, community service, intensive supervised probation, house arrest, electronic monitoring, and shock incarceration. The latter includes shock probation and shock parole, as well as boot camps. Figure 6.2 depicts the range of sentencing options. James Byrne has identified the major sanction options that sentencing might impose, and ranked them by levels of punishment inherent in each. Restitution, for example, is seen as less punitive than community service; house arrest is a lower level of punishment than jail incarceration.[17] You should remember that judges can and frequently do impose several sanctions simultaneously and retain authority to initiate tourniquet sentencing, a process that increases and tightens the numbers and conditions of punishments until the probationer is brought under the most effective control.

Intermediate sanctions are attractive for the following five reasons:

1. Channeling offenders into community-based corrections is believed to be able to reduce or delay prison overcrowding.

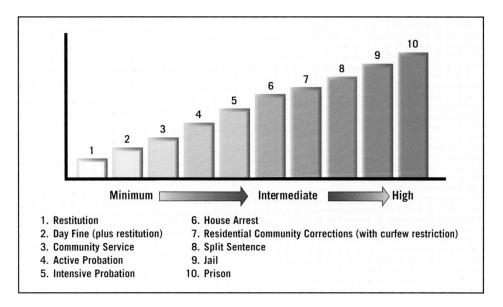

1. Restitution
2. Day Fine (plus restitution)
3. Community Service
4. Active Probation
5. Intensive Probation
6. House Arrest
7. Residential Community Corrections (with curfew restriction)
8. Split Sentence
9. Jail
10. Prison

figure 6.2

A Range of Sentencing Options, Ranked by the Level of Punishment

Data from: James Byrne, "The Future of Intensive Probation Supervision," *Crime and Delinquency* 36:1 (1990): 3–34.

2. Intermediate punishments are designed for offenders believed to pose too much risk for probation services but not enough risk to be sent to prison.
3. They are generally less expensive than incarceration in either jail or prison.
4. They are believed to offer more rehabilitation and reintegration potential than does incarceration.
5. It is believed that expansion and fine-tuning of alternative sanctions will eventually lead to a valid continuum of sentencing alternatives.[18]

We begin our more detailed examination of these programs with restitution.

Restitution Programs

A common condition for probation is the requirement that victims be compensated for their losses or injury as a form of **restitution**. The emphasis given to the study of victimology in the last few years has resulted in some state compensation of crime victims by payment of medical costs and other financial reimbursement. Through the system of probation, however, the offender often repays the victim. It is important that probation authorities link the amount of payment to the offender's ability to pay. Paying through installments is usually the most realistic approach. In some cases a partial restitution may be all that is reasonably possible (for example, in the case of an arsonist who burns down a multimillion-dollar building).

Many reasons are offered to support restitution programs. Obviously, restitution offsets the victim's loss when property is stolen; restitution can even be ordered for the deductible amount an insurance company might require an insured victim to pay before the insurance coverage would become effective. Time lost from work while being a witness in court and being hospitalized is subject to offender restitution. It appears that restitution may be ordered for any injury caused by the offense for which the offender was convicted. Other rationales are that restitution forces the offender to accept personal responsibility for the crime; restitution can lead to reconciliation of offender and victim;[19] and, finally, it provides one way the victim can overcome the otherwise impersonal processing of victims within the justice system. Although more than 30% of all adults on probation in 1995 and 12% of offenders on felony probation

key term

Restitution order
Requirement that offender repay the victim.

in 2002 were ordered to make restitution,[20] it appears that restitution programs are more numerous in the juvenile justice systems than they are in the adult system.[21] Although almost every state has restitution programs in operation, Georgia, Texas, Florida, Minnesota, and Michigan appear to be leaders in program development. (Restitution programs also have been extensively implemented and evaluated in Great Britain, Austria, Germany, and Australia.) In Minnesota, parolees may also be required to reside in a residential restitution center and pay part of their wages to victims. Other jurisdictions require victim–offender conferences to establish the amount of financial compensation due to the victim.

Intensive Supervised Probation

Another alternative sanction program is **intensive supervised probation (ISP),** which is designed to provide increased surveillance of offenders deemed to be too serious for "routine" probation. The program is a management strategy for probation services that need to increase the level of surveillance for individuals who do not adjust to regular probation requirements. ISP is a program frequently found in **tourniquet sentencing.**

Georgia is believed to have been the first jurisdiction to impose a statewide system of ISP (starting in 1974) and, by 1990, every state had at least one jurisdiction—city, county, or state—with the program. There is no generic ISP. It is a form of release that emphasizes close monitoring of convicted offenders and requires rigorous conditions on that release. Most ISP programs call for the following:[22]

- Some combination of multiple weekly contacts with a supervising officer
- Random and unannounced drug testing
- Stringent enforcement of probation or parole conditions
- Required participation in relevant treatment programs, employment, and perhaps community service

Current issues largely revolve around the effectiveness of intensive supervision. Yet, measures of success vary depending on the stated goals and objectives each program sets out to address.[23] For instance, the goals of a treatment-oriented program differ from the goals of a program that places emphasis on offender punishment and control. However, it is possible to isolate two overriding themes of recent intensive supervision programs that raise several issues. First, "intensive probation supervision is expected to divert offenders from incarceration in order to alleviate prison overcrowding, avoid the exorbitant costs of building and sustaining prisons, and prevent the stultifying and stigmatizing effects of imprisonment." Second, ISP is expected to promote public safety through surveillance strategies, while promoting a sense of responsibility and accountability through probation fees, restitution, and community service activities.[24] These goals generate issues regarding the ability of ISP programs to reduce recidivism, divert offenders from prison, and ensure public safety.

In a study summarizing the state of ISP, Fulton, Latessa, Stichman, and Travis[25] summarize the findings concerning ISP:

- ISPs have failed to alleviate prison crowding.
- Most ISP studies have found no significant differences between recidivism rates of ISP offenders and offenders of comparison groups.
- There appears to be a relationship between greater participation in treatment and employment programs and lower recidivism rates.
- ISPs appear to be more effective than regular supervision or prison in meeting offenders' needs.
- ISPs that reflect certain principles of effective intervention are associated with lower rates of recidivism.
- ISP does provide an intermediate punishment.
- Although ISPs are less expensive than prison, they are more expensive than originally thought.

The debate over control versus treatment has raged for many years. Recently, there has been a new movement, initiated by the American Probation and Parole Association, to develop a more balanced approach to ISP supervision.[26] This approach continues to support strict conditions and supervision practices, but within the context of more services and higher-quality treatment.

Drug and Other Problem-Solving Courts

In recent years, many judges have become disillusioned with the revolving door of jail and prison for offenders who suffer from addictions and mental disorders. As a result, there has been an explosion of so-called therapeutic courts, ranging from mental health to domestic violence. Figure 6.3 shows the number of drug problem-solving courts throughout the United States. **Drug courts** divert drug-abusing offenders to intensively monitored treatment instead of incarceration. The main purpose of drug-court programs is to use the authority of the court to reduce crime by changing defendants' drug-using behavior. Under this concept, in exchange for the possibility of dismissed charges or reduced sentences, defendants are diverted to drug-court programs in various ways and at various stages of the judicial process, depending on the circumstances. Judges preside over drug-court proceedings; monitor the progress of defendants through frequent status hearings; and prescribe sanctions and rewards as appropriate in collaboration with prosecutors, defense attorneys, treatment providers, and others. Basic elements of a drug court include the following:[27]

- A single drug-court judge and staff who provide both focus and leadership
- Expedited adjudication through early identification and referral of appropriate program participants, initiating treatment as soon as possible after arrest
- Both intensive treatment and aftercare for drug-abusing defendants
- Comprehensive, in-depth, and coordinated supervision of drug defendants in regular (sometimes daily) status hearings that monitor both treatment progress and offender compliance
- Enhanced and increasing defendant accountability under a graduated series of rewards and punishments appropriate to conforming or volative behavior
- Mandatory and frequent drug (and alcohol) testing
- Supervised and individual case monitoring

class activity

Challenge students to define *intensive supervised probation* and identify how such programs would work. Then ask them if intensive supervised probation is effective.

key term

Drug court
Problem-solving courts that require drug offenders to participate in court-mandated treatment programs.

class activity

Ask students to define *community service programs, community work orders,* and *restitution programs,* and identify their advantages for corrections.

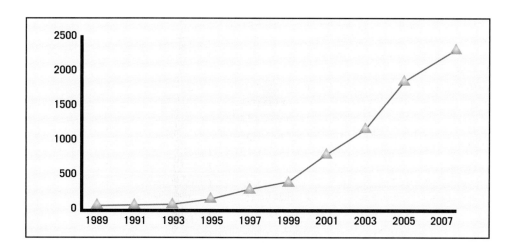

figure 6.3

Operational Drug Court Programs in the United States

SOURCE: C. West Huddleston, Douglas Marlowe, and Rachel Casebolt, 2008. Painting the Current Picture: A National Report Card on Drug Courts and Other Problem-Solving Court Programs in the United States. Bureau of Justice Assistance, U.S. Department of Justice.

Drug-court programs are highly diverse in approach, characteristics, and completion and retention rates, as discussed later. Some programs report that they deferred prosecuting offenders who would enter the program; others allowed offenders to enter the program after their cases had been adjudicated; and still others allowed offenders to enter their programs on a trial basis after entering a plea. Yet all programs have a treatment component as part of their overall approach, although there is wide variation in the type and extent of treatment provided to offenders. Both adults and juvenile offenders are served by drug courts, as well as nonviolent and violent offenders, and first-time or repeat offenders. Overall, most courts treat offenders with a substance addiction.

The growth in drug-court programs has been nothing short of phenomenal. Starting with one program in Miami in 1989, there were 2,147 programs in operation in 2008, with over 70,000 clients processed or in treatment at any given time. Of these, over 756 juvenile and family drug courts were operating with another 104 more in the planning stage, with more than 9,000 juveniles in treatment.[28] The threat of immediate sanctions (jail time, return for prosecution, probation revocation, commitment to prison) is a powerful tool to ensure client compliance and retention in the treatment program.

correctional **brief**

Community Correctional Centers

In a recent study of nonresidential community correctional programs in Ohio involving over 13,000 offenders, Lowenkamp and Latessa found four factors significantly related to outcome. Programs with the following characteristics were more effective:

- Those programs having a greater proportion of higher-risk offenders (at least 75%) were more effective.

- The level of supervision for higher-risk offenders averaged longer periods of supervision than the level for low-risk offenders.

- Higher-risk offenders spent at least 50% more time in treatment than lower-risk offenders.

- Higher-risk offenders received at least three referrals for every referral received by low-risk offenders.

The following chart shows the difference in impact between programs that met these conditions and those that did not.

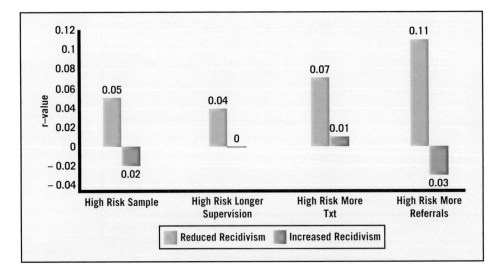

Changes in Recidivism by Program Factors for Community Correctional Programs
SOURCE: Christopher T. Lowenkamp, Jennifer Pealer, Paula Smith, and Edward Latessa, "Adhering to the Risk and Need Principles: Does It Matter for Supervision-Based Programs?" *Federal Probation*, 70:3 (2006), 3–8.

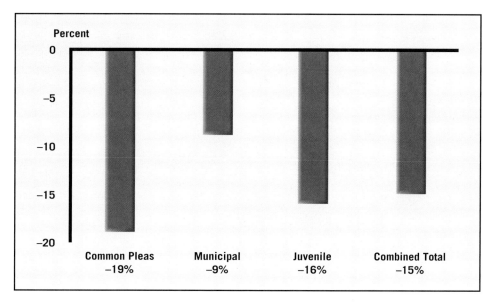

figure 6.4

Reductions in Rearrest Rates Between Drug Courts and Comparison Groups Across All Drug Court Groups

Data from: Edward Latessa, D. Shaffer, and C. Lowenkamp, *Outcome Evaluation of Ohio's Drug Court Efforts* (Cincinnati, OH; Center for Criminal Justice Research, University of Cincinnati, 2002), p. 7.

While findings from drug-court studies have generally been favorable, most have been limited to local drug-court programs. The largest statewide study on drug courts to date was recently conducted in New York. The study found that, on average, the reconviction rate was 29% lower for drug-court participants than for nonparticipants.[29] In another recent statewide study of drug courts in Ohio, Latessa, Shaffer, and Lowenkamp examined outcome data from both adult (felony and misdemeanants) and juvenile drug-court programs.[30] The results from this study are illustrated in the Correctional Brief on the previous page. The data show some variation in the results across drug courts, but overall participants in drug courts reported 15% lower rearrest rates than those drug offenders who did not participate in a drug-court program. See Figure 6.4. Finally, a national study of drug-court programs conducted by Shaffer in 2006 found that across all types of drugs courts the average reduction in recidivism was 9%.[31]

In addition to reducing recidivism, drug courts have been found to be cost effective. A study done by the Washington State Institute for Public Policy estimated that the average drug-court participant produces $6,779 in benefits.[32] In New York, researchers estimate that $254 million in incarceration costs were saved by diverting 18,000 offenders to drug court. Finally, California researchers concluded that drug courts in that state save $18 million per year.[33] See Figure 6.4.

Compared to jail and prison, drug courts appear to be cost effective and to reduce criminal conduct. The success of drug courts has led to the development of other problem-solving courts, including reentry (designed to assist those released from prison), DWI, mentally ill, gun, and gambling courts. While similar data are not yet available on mental-health courts and other problem-solving court programs, drug courts are galvanizing if not revolutionizing the criminal justice system response to drug abuse.[34]

Community Service Programs

Community service or work-order programs represent court-ordered unpaid work for a specific number of hours that offenders must perform, usually in the form of free labor to some charitable organization or in public service such as serving as a volunteer hospital

Community service is a
major option to
incarceration.
*Courtesy of AP Wide World
Photos.*

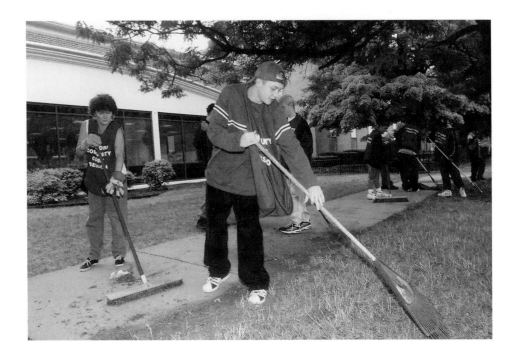

key term
_____

Community work order
Requiring offenders to provide
service to the community to
help repair the harm they have
committed.

orderly, doing street cleaning, performing maintenance or repair of public housing, or providing service to indigent groups. Some examples of the latter would be sentencing a dentist to perform 100 hours of free dental service for welfare recipients or a physician to
provide 50 hours of free medical attention to jail inmates on Saturdays.

Both **community work orders** and restitution programs have their critics.[35] Some argue that offenders committing crimes of violence should not be allowed a penalty less than
incarceration for their offenses, and that the physical and psychological costs to victims of
crimes of violence are almost impossible to calculate. There also seems to be some uncertainty over whether an offender sentenced to perform community work or restitution ought
to be resentenced to incarceration for noncompliance. Despite the criticism, there appears
to be consensus that offenders should repay their victims for losses, even if the repayment
is as symbolic as community work. A recent study of a community service program
designed as an alternative to incarceration for adult misdemeanor offenders found a
66% completion rate.[36]

Home Detention

key term
_____

Home detention
Sentence whereby offenders
serve at least some of their
sentence in their own
domicile.

In the United States, house arrest usually conjures up images of political control and fascist
repression,[37] but it is actually court-ordered **home detention,** the confining of offenders to
their households for the duration of their sentence. Introduced in 1984 in Florida, home detention rapidly spread throughout a nation searching for punitive, safe, and secure alternatives to incarceration.[38] The sentence is usually imposed in conjunction with probation but
may be imposed by the court as a separate punishment (as it is in Florida). Florida's Community Control Program (FCCP) was designed to provide a safe diversion alternative and
to help address the problem of prison population escalation and associated high costs.[39]

Participants may be required to make victim compensation, perform community work
service, pay probation fees, undergo drug and alcohol testing, and, in some instances, wear
electronic monitoring equipment to verify their presence in the residence. (In some jurisdictions, house arrest is used on a pretrial basis, as an isolated sentence, in conjunction with
probation or parole, or with a prerelease status such as education or work furlough.) House
arrest allows the offender to leave his or her residence only for specific purposes and hours

c o r r e c t i o n a l **brief**

Sex Offenders Tracked by GPS

Although it sounds like something out of a science-fiction movie, the reality of GPS tracking is much more down to earth. Recently, a number of states have enacted legislation to require convicted sex offenders to wear a electronic tracking device for the rest of their lives that monitors their whereabouts.

As noted by Koch (2006), "as of January 2006, 13 states had laws requiring or allowing GPS tracking." For example, Wisconsin estimated that over 400 offenders were tracked in 2008. California allocated funds to follow 2,500 offenders in 2009, and Michigan has begun tracking over 1,000 sex offenders.

The increase in GPS is attributed to dramatic advancements in the technology. Not only have the devices become smaller and less expensive, but accuracy has increased, allowing systems to pinpoint a person's location to within 30 feet.

Despite these advancements, GPS tracking is not without its critics. "It is not an effective way to prevent sexual assaults," says Richard Wright, Professor of Criminal Justice at Bridgewater State College. He believes that many serious sex offenders evade police by failing to register, and that others may reoffend regardless of tracking systems. Others believe that GPS tracking is best used as an augmentation of good supervision, not a replacement for it. Despite these concerns, it appears that GPS tracking is here to stay.

SOURCE: Adapted from: Wendy Koch, "More Sex Offenders Tracked by Satellite," *USA TODAY* (June 6, 2006).

approved by the court or supervising officer. Being absent without leave is a technical violation of conditions that may result in resentencing to jail or prison.[40] Home detention is a punitive sentence and was designed in most cases to relieve institutional overcrowding. For many offenders it is their last chance to escape from being committed to prison. In addition to surveillance of the offender, home detention is viewed as a cost-avoidance program, a front-end solution to prison overcrowding, and a flexible alternative for certain offenders (such as a pregnant offender until time of delivery). The use of telemonitoring devices, discussed later, can significantly increase the correctional surveillance of offenders.

The most significant critical argument against home detention is that, by making a nonincarcerative control mechanism available to corrections, many petty offenders who would best be handled by diversion, fines, or mental health services are brought under correctional control. In general, such inclusive actions are viewed as "net widening," which occurs when offenders who might otherwise have received a lesser or even no sentence are sentenced to community control.[41]

The National Council on Crime and Delinquency conducted an evaluation of the Florida CCP and concluded that the impact on prison crowding, offender behavior, and state correctional costs has been positive. With an estimated prison diversion rate of 54%, community control is cost effective despite the combined effect of net widening and the punishments imposed on almost 10% of FCCP participants for technical violations. Furthermore, the new offense rate for community control offenders is lower than that for similar offenders sentenced to prison and released without supervision. For every 100 cases diverted from prison, Florida saved more than $250,000.[42] Home detention is expected to receive increased endorsement in this millennium and may become the sentence of choice for many nonviolent offenders in lieu of jail, prison, or even formal probation.[43]

Electronic Monitoring

Home detention has a long history as a criminal penalty, but its new popularity with correctional authorities is due to the advent of electronic monitoring, a technological link that is thought to make the sanction both practical and affordable. The concept of electronic monitoring is not new, and was proposed in 1964 by Schwitzgebel as **electronic parole.** It was initially used to monitor the location of mental patients.[44] One of the first studies of home detention enforced by electronic monitoring began in 1986, and by 2003, it was estimated that there were 1,500 electronic programs and nearly 140,000 monitoring units in use.[45]

key term

Electronic parole
Community supervision technique that uses electronic devices to maintain surveillance on parolees. Can also include GPS surveillance.

Most electronic monitoring systems use a transmitter attached to the offender's wrist or ankle that sends signals to the supervising office during the hours the offender is required to be at home. The goals and objectives of electronic monitoring include:

- Provide a cost-effective community supervision tool for offenders selected according to specific program criteria;
- Administer sanctions appropriate to the seriousness of the offense;
- Promote public safety by providing surveillance and risk-control strategies indicated by the risk and needs of the offenders; and
- Increase the confidence of legislative, judicial, and releasing authorities that electronic monitoring is a viable sentencing option.[46]

National surveys indicate that electronic monitoring was initially (1987) used for property offenders on probation, but a much broader range of offenders is being monitored now than in the past. Monitoring has been expanded to include probationers but also to follow up on persons after incarceration, to control those sentenced to community corrections, and to monitor persons before trial or sentencing. Studies of telemonitoring of offenders noted certain findings:

- Most jurisdictions using electronic monitoring tested some offenders for drug use, and many routinely tested all. Some sites charged for the testing; more than 66% charged offenders for at least part of the cost of leasing the monitoring equipment.
- The average monitoring term is about 80 days. The longer the period of monitoring, the higher the odds of success. The chances of termination do not vary by type of offense, except that those committing major traffic violations committed fewer technical violations and new offenses.
- There were no significant differences in successful terminations among probationers, offenders on parole, or those in community corrections. All had successful termination rates ranging between 74% and 86%.
- Rule violations resulted in reincarceration, brief confinement at a residential facility, intensified office reporting requirements, stricter curfews, or additional community service.[47]
- The experience of other countries using electronic monitoring indicates an uneven value as a reintegration program.[48]

The latest trend in electronic monitoring is global position systems (GPS) that are increasingly being used with high-risk sex offenders. A number of states have passed legislation that requires selected offenders to wear a device that tracks their whereabouts 24-7 (see Correctional Brief on p. 115).

A recent evaluation in Florida of offenders placed on electronic monitoring or GPS found significantly reduced likelihood of technical violations, reoffending, and absconding.[49] Other studies in Los Angeles, Lake County, Illinois, Oklahoma, Florida, Texas, England, and Wales[50] have shown mixed results. While the technology no doubt will be improved and expanded in the coming decade, many unanswered questions remain about the effectiveness of electronic monitoring.

Community Residential Treatment Centers (Halfway Houses)

Formerly known as halfway houses, **community residential treatment centers** are a valuable adjunct to community control and treatment services. Originally designed as residences for homeless men, they are now seen as the possible nuclei of community-based correctional networks of residential centers, drug-free and alcohol-free living spaces, prerelease guidance centers, and private-sector involvement with multiple-problem offenders in

correctional **brief**

Effectiveness of Community Corrections

"What works" is not a program or an intervention, but a body of knowledge based on more than thirty years of research that has been conducted by numerous scholars in North America and Europe. Also referred to as evidence-based practice, the "what works" movement demonstrates empirically that theoretically sound, well-designed programs that meet certain conditions can appreciably reduce recidivism rates for offenders. Through the review and analysis of hundreds of studies, researchers have identified a set of principles that should guide correctional programs.

The first is the risk principle, or the "who" to target—those offenders who pose the higher risk of continued criminal conduct. This principle states that our most intensive correctional treatment and intervention programs should be reserved for higher-risk offenders. *Risk* in this context refers to those offenders with a higher probability of recidivating. Why waste our programs on offenders who do not need them? This is a waste of resources and, more importantly, research has clearly demonstrated that when we place lower-risk offenders in our more structured programs, we often increase their failure rates (and thus reduce the overall effectiveness of the program). This occurs for several reasons.

First, placing low-risk offenders in with higher-risk offenders only serves to increase the chances of failure for the low-risk offender. For example, let's say that your teenage son or daughter did not use drugs, but got into some trouble with the law. Would you want them in a program or group with heavy drug users? Of course you wouldn't, since it is more likely that the higher-risk youth would influence your child more than the other way around.

Second, placing low-risk offenders in these programs also tends to disrupt their prosocial networks; in other words, the very attributes that make them low risk become interrupted, such as school, employment, family, and so forth. Remember, if they do not have these attributes it is unlikely they are low risk to begin with. The risk principle can best be seen from a recent study of offenders in Ohio who were placed in a halfway house or community-based correctional facility (CBCF). The study found that the recidivism rate for higher risk offenders who were placed in a halfway house or CBCF was reduced, while the recidivism rates for the low-risk offenders who were placed in the programs actually increased.

The second principle is referred to as the need principle, or the "what" to target—criminogenic factors that are highly correlated with criminal conduct. The need principle states that programs should target crime-producing needs, such as antisocial attitudes, values, and beliefs, antisocial peer associations, substance abuse, lack of problem-solving and self-control skills, and other factors that are highly correlated with criminal conduct. Furthermore, programs need to ensure that the vast majority of their interventions are focused on these factors. Noncriminogenic factors such as self-esteem, physical conditioning, understanding one's culture or history, and creative abilities will not have much effect on recidivism rates. An example of a program that tends to target noncriminogenic factors can be seen in offender-based military-style boot camps. These programs tend to focus on noncriminogenic factors, such as drill and ceremony, physical conditioning, discipline, self-esteem, and bonding offenders together. Because they tend to focus on non-crime-producing needs, most studies show that boot camps have little impact on future criminal behavior.

The third principle is the treatment principle, or the "how"—the ways in which correctional programs should target risk and need factors. This principle states that the most effective programs are behavioral in nature. Behavioral programs have several attributes. First, they are centered on the *present* circumstances and risk factors that are responsible for the offender's behavior. Second, they are *action* oriented rather than talk oriented. In other words, offenders do something about their difficulties rather than just talk about them. Third, they teach offenders new, prosocial skills to replace the antisocial ones (e.g., stealing, cheating, lying) through modeling, practice, and reinforcement. Examples of behavioral programs would include structured social learning programs where new skills are taught and behaviors and attitudes are consistently reinforced; cognitive behavioral programs that target attitudes, values, peers, substance abuse, anger, and so on; and family-based interventions that train family on appropriate behavioral techniques. Interventions based on these approaches are very structured and emphasize the importance of modeling and behavioral rehearsal techniques that engender self-efficacy, challenge of cognitive distortions, and assist offenders in developing good problem-solving and self-control skills. These strategies have been demonstrated to be effective in reducing recidivism. Nonbehavioral interventions that are often used in programs would include drug and alcohol education, fear tactics and other emotional appeals, talk therapy, nondirective client-centered approaches, having them read books, lectures, milieu therapy, and self-help. There is little empirical evidence that these approaches will lead to long-term reductions in recidivism.

Finally, a host of other considerations will increase correctional program effectiveness. These include targeting responsivity factors such as a lack of motivation or other barriers that can influence someone's participation in a program; making sure that you have well-trained and interpersonally sensitive staff; providing close monitoring of offenders' whereabouts and associates; assisting with other needs that offenders might have; ensuring the program is delivered as designed through quality assurance processes; and providing structured aftercare. These program attributes all enhance correctional program effectiveness.

If we put it all together we have the "who, what, and how" of correctional intervention, also known as "what works."

SOURCE: Edward J. Latessa, "From Theory to Practice: What Works in Reducing Recidivism?" *In State of Crime and Justice in Ohio* (Columbus, OH: Ohio Office of Criminal Justice Services, 2004).

need of intensive services. They also serve as noninstitutional residence facilities for a number of different classes of offenders, most of whom are high-need offenders and pose a medium to high risk to community corrections.

University of Cincinnati investigators headed by Edward Latessa have conducted much of the contemporary evaluative work in the area of community residential centers. A synopsis of a program evaluation will suffice to suggest how community residential centers fit into intermediate sanctions. In evaluating a treatment program for adult offenders sentenced to probation, Latessa and Travis found that, in comparison with other similarly situated offenders, members of their study group had less formal education and were far less likely to have married. They exhibited more prior involvement in alcohol and drug treatment, and suffered from more psychiatric problems. Hence, the study group was higher need, higher risk, and more likely to recidivate. The center's clients received more services and treatment in almost every area examined. Even though prior criminal histories would have predicted higher failure rates, the center's clients did as well as the comparison group in terms of reoffending. Employment services and enrolling in an educational program reduced recidivism.[51]

In one of the largest studies of residential correctional programs ever conducted, University of Cincinnati researchers examined nearly 14,000 offenders served by over 45 residential programs in Ohio. Overall figures indicated that the residential programs resulted in slightly reduced recidivism rates. However, when the risk level of the offenders was factored in, the results showed that most of the programs had a significant impact with high-risk offenders, but actually increased the failure rates for lower-risk offenders.[52] This finding was not unexpected, since other studies have also shown detrimental effects with low-risk offenders.[53] Figures 6.5 and 6.6 show the results from this study.

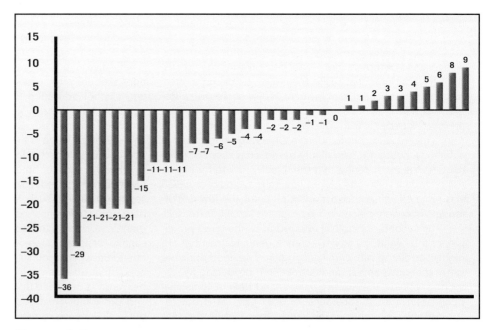

figure 6.5

Treatment Effects for Low-Risk Offenders

- Numbers represent difference in predicted recidivism rates between the comparison and treatment groups.
- Negative numbers indicate a difference favoring the comparison group.
- Each column represents a different program in the study.

Data from: C. Lowenkamp and E. Latessa, *Evaluation of Ohio's Halfway House and Community Based Correctional Facilities* (Cincinnati, OH: University of Cincinnati, 2002).

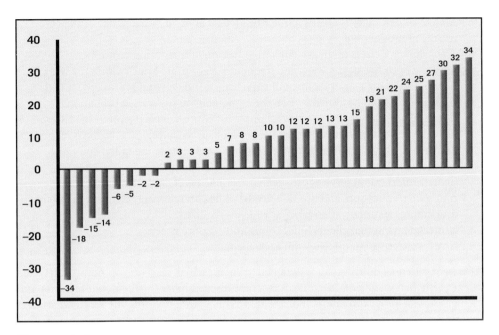

figure 6.6

Treatment Effects for High-Risk Offenders

- Numbers represent difference in predicted recidivism rates between the comparison and treatment groups.
- Negative numbers indicate a difference favoring the comparison group.
- Each column represents a different program in the study.

Data from: C. Lowenkamp and E. Latessa, *Evaluation of Ohio's Halfway House and Community Based Correctional Facilities* (Cincinnati, OH: University of Cincinnati, 2002).

Clearly, for high-risk offenders, residential centers that provide specific client-needed services can be valuable assets in offender control and outcome,[54] particularly for community-control clients whose technical violations are a result of high needs otherwise unaddressed within the community.

Day Reporting Centers

The day reporting center (called the *attendance center* in Australia) is an intermediate punishment option usually associated with probation but that also can accept parolees, parole violators, furloughees from prison, and persons on pretrial release or early release from jail. The center provides a variety of treatment and referral programs, along with extensive supervision and surveillance.

Most centers operate in late afternoon and evening hours and are staffed by probation officers, treatment specialists, vocational counselors, and volunteers; the primary focus is treatment. Participants are usually required to attend every day the center is open, to schedule their next day's activities, and to abide by the schedule. Not only do participants have to call the center at least twice a day, the center may call them at their appointed rounds on a frequent basis to verify their whereabouts and activities. While there are significant differences across centers, Parent and others[55] found certain characteristics to be typical of most:

- Centers accept those on probation, those ordered to attend as a special condition of probation, or those who have violated probation; drug- and alcohol-abusing offenders; and some clients who pose low risk to their communities of residence.

- Almost all participants return to their residences at night, because day centers are usually nonresidential.
- The primary focus is on treatment and reduction of institution crowding.
- Most are open five days a week and frequently 50 or more hours within the week.
- Centers maintain a strict regimen of surveillance and demand more contact with clients than would be available even through intensive supervised probation.
- Centers direct clients through several phases of control, tapering off in the latter phase by providing about 70 hours per week of surveillance.
- Centers test clients for drug use at least once a week during the initial and most intensive phases.
- Centers offer several services on-site that can address clients' unemployment, counseling, education, and life-skill needs, while also referring offenders to off-site drug-abuse treatment, attendance at which is required.
- Centers demand that clients fulfill community service orders.
- Centers collect program fees from each client.

This nonresidential punishment is designed to ensure a high level of community safety and client participation. Clients are forced to accept responsibility for their own behavior and change. Service provision audits indicate that centers are providing the required services and referrals.[56] Such centers have a definite role to play in intermediate punishments.

Shock Incarceration

The intermediate sanctions already discussed assume the offender can be contained and treated within existing community programs and technologies, and that tourniquet sentencing will serve to control behavior and prevent new crime. Intermediate punishments, however, also include two major alternatives for nonpredatory offenders who are, in addition, not career criminals. We discuss two here: **shock probation** and **boot camps.** We begin with shock probation.

Shock Probation

In 1965, the Ohio legislature passed a law permitting sentencing judges to incarcerate offenders in state prisons for short periods of time, and then recall the inmate to probation within the community. The assumption was that a short period of incarceration (90 to 130 days), followed by a period of probation, would "shock" the offender into abandoning criminal activity and into pursuit of law-abiding behavior. Clearly, this program was based on a specific deterrence model, and was designed for a segment of the offender population for whom probation was insufficient punishment but long-term imprisonment was not necessary. The method would not be used for first-time offenders but for persons not yet committed to giving up predatory behavior.

This option, rapidly adopted by at least 14 states,[57] puts decision making squarely in the hands of the judiciary. The sentencing judge is allowed to reconsider the original sentence to prison and, upon motion, to recall the inmate and place him or her on probation, under conditions deemed appropriate.

Evaluations of the effectiveness of shock probation in preventing recidivism and cost avoidance have focused on Ohio, Texas, and Kentucky. Vito has conducted the most sophisticated evaluations and concluded the following:[58]

1. The shock experience should not be limited to first-time offenders; eligibility should properly include those with prior records, as deemed eligible by the judge.
2. The length of incarceration necessary to secure the deterrent effect could be much shorter, probably 30 days or less.
3. Reincarceration rates have never exceeded 26% and, in Ohio, have been as low as 10%. The level of these rates clearly indicates that the program has potential for reintegration.

correctional **brief**

Probationers in Programs

At some time since entering probation supervision, more than 60% of all 4.2 million probationers had participated in some type of special supervision or other program. The most common was alcohol or drug treatment/counseling: 33% of felons and 42% of misdemeanants had received such treatment while under their current sentence of probation.

Nearly one-third had been tested for drugs at least once since entering probation. Some 1% of felony probationers had participated in intensive probation supervision, and another 10% received psychiatric or psychological counseling.

Participation in other programs:

Day reporting program	5.3% (132,500 probationers)
Residential program	4.9
Electronic monitoring	3.5
Sex offender program	2.7

SOURCE: Thomas Bonczar, *Characteristics of Adults on Probation, 1995* (Washington, DC: U.S. Department of Justice, 1997), p. 9.

4. Shock probation has considerable potential to reduce the institutional overcrowding characteristic of contemporary corrections.[59]

Shock probation can be seen as an alternative disposition for sentencing judges who wish to control probationer behavior through deterrence and tourniquet sentencing. It is one of the last-ditch programs of prison avoidance available to judges faced with the difficult decision of how best to protect the public while maximizing offender reintegration.

Boot Camp Programs

Boot camps first appeared in Georgia (1983) and Oklahoma (1984). The concept spread quickly, and it is now estimated that there are 52 boot camp prisons in 39 state correctional jurisdictions, in addition to 15 jail programs and 32 probation and parole camps. It is estimated that in 2001, over 16,150 offenders were placed in adult boot camps.[60]

While labeled a recent innovation, the basic elements of boot camp were present in the Elmira Reformatory in 1876, designed by Zebulon Reed Brockway. In its form, boot camp combines elements of basic military training and traditional correctional philosophy, particularly rehabilitation. Although there is no generic boot camp because individual programs vary in form and objectives, the typical boot camp is targeted at young, nonviolent offenders.[61] Once in the camp, the participant is subjected to a regimen of the following:

- Military drills and discipline
- Physical exercise
- Hard physical labor
- Specialized education and training
- Counseling and treatment for substance abuse and addiction

Most boot camp programs require the inmates to enter as volunteers,[62] offering as an incentive an incarceration period of a few months, compared to the much longer periods they would have spent in prison or on probation. Generally, a state boot camp graduate is released to parole, intensive supervision, home confinement, or some type of community corrections.

The philosophy behind the prison boot camps is simple. Offenders who can be turned around before they commit a major crime should be able to improve their opportunities for living a successful life free of incarceration. Traditional prisons generally have not been viewed as successful in rehabilitating offenders. According to boot camp advocates, the populations at greatest risk of entering prison are the poorly educated, young adult offenders.

lecture note

Define *shock incarceration* and then *shock probation*. Explain "shock" as a psychological concept (specific deterrence). Is shock probation effective?

class activity

Select three intermediate sanctions and ask how these serve the function of protecting society.

lecture note

Explain boot camp programs and the philosophy under which most of them operate. On what theoretical basis would students expect boot camp programs to work? If students cite the New York State studies, ask what elements of treatment might be present in that type of program that probably are not present in others.

lecture note

Using your computer, play the brief videotape of Francis Cullen on "Correctional Quackery" (approximately 5 minutes).

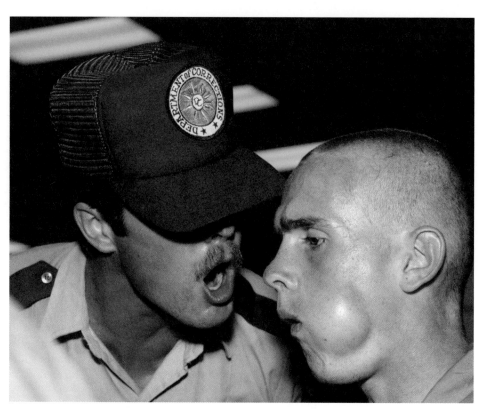

Correctional officer shouting at inmate.
SOURCE: *Bettmann/CORBIS-NY.*

They come from a low-income background, have not had proper role models or discipline, have few or no work skills, and are subjected to an environment where drug use and trafficking are common. Because many misdirected young persons have become productive citizens after exposure to military training, the boot camp endeavors to provide this same discipline and direction to persons who still have a chance of being diverted from a life of crime and incarceration. See Figure 6.7.

Although boot camps are popular with judges, the public, and politicians, results from studies of the effectiveness of boot camp programs in reducing recidivism have not been

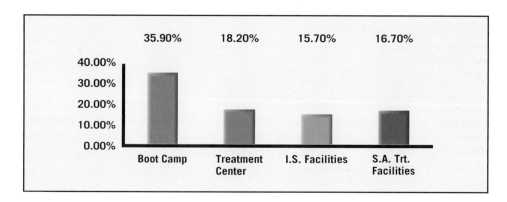

figure 6.7

Rearrest Rates for Residents Discharged from Community Correctional Facilities in Texas: Two-Year Follow-up (in percent)

Data from: *Community Corrections Facilities Outcome Study*, Texas Department of Criminal Justice, January 1999.

positive. An outcome study conducted in Texas[63] compared the rearrest rates of four different types of community facilities for adult offenders: boot camps, treatment centers, intermediate sanction facilities (used for probation violators), and substance-abuse treatment facilities. The boot camp reported rearrest rates nearly double those of the other programs. Note also that when risk and need scores from a standardized assessment tool were compared for offenders in all four programs, the only difference was in the need scores, with the boot camp residents reporting fewer higher-need offenders than the other options. Finally, a study conducted by researchers in Washington State found that, on average, juvenile boot camps increased recidivism rates about 11%.[64] Findings from boot camp evaluations make the following conclusions:

- Low- or moderate-risk juvenile and adult offenders who are subjected to a high level of supervision (boot camps) actually do worse than those left on traditional probation.[65]
- High percentages of minority youth are served by boot camps. The conclusion is that the boot camp model fails to connect with this population.
- Some evidence shows that the rate of recidivism declined in boot camp programs for adults where offenders spent three hours or more per day in therapeutic activity and had some type of aftercare.[66]
- In general, studies have found similar recidivism rates for those who completed boot camps and comparable offenders who spent long periods of time in prison.

There are several reasons why boot camps are not producing the desired reductions in recidivism.[67] Boot camps tend to:

- Bond delinquent and criminal groups together.
- Target non-crime-producing needs such as physical conditioning, drill and ceremony, and self-esteem.
- Mix low-, medium-, and high-risk offenders together.
- Model aggressive behavior.

Despite these findings, the boot camp concept still appeals to diverse elements of the justice system. Offenders generally will be returned to the community in a much shorter period without the stigma of having been in prison. For the judge, it is a sentencing option that provides sanctions more restrictive than probation but less restrictive than a conventional prison. For the correctional system, it allows the placement of individuals outside the traditional prison environment and reduces costs and crowding by moving the persons through the system in less time.

As a result of the research, some boot camp programs have abandoned the military-style training and incorporated education, substance abuse treatment, aftercare, job corps, and industrial components. Only future research will tell if these efforts have been successful.

Summary

Corrections is undergoing rapid change as innovators search for programs, technologies, strategies, and policies for coping with the increasing number and diversity of jail and prison populations, as well as the crush of overcrowding. Not only are institutions crowded, but probation, parole, and community corrections are also impacted by the waves of offenders caught in the arms of the law.

Our review of diversion and intermediate sanctions provides insight into the reasons for the volume of clients and also describes promising programs and strategies for managing the risks posed by different types of offenders who need differing treatments and supervision. Change will continue. This is an exciting time for corrections as a field and for students wishing to have an impact on the futures of clients and the safety of communities.

In the next chapters we examine the use of incarceration, as those who make it through the correctional filter finally end up in the prisons of the nation. Well over 1 million people have been placed into incarceration, and the number grows every day. What is imprisonment and what is it like? The next chapter will seek some answers to these questions.

Key Words

Review Questions

1. Explain several ways in which offenders can be diverted from the correctional system.
2. Differentiate between shock probation and boot camp shock incarceration.
3. What roles do community residential treatment centers play in corrections?
4. Did Florida's Community Control Program achieve its objectives?
5. Describe a boot camp program.
6. Describe the day reporting center and its purposes.
7. Define a drug court and describe its operations.
8. Explain the effectiveness of drug courts and of day reporting centers.
9. What are some other types of specialty courts that are emerging in the United States?
10. Why haven't boot camps been effective in reducing recidivism?
11. What types of offenders should be placed in residential correctional facilities?

Endnotes

1. Maryland Governor's Office, *Administration Report to the State/Local Criminal Justice/Mental Health Task Force* (Baltimore, MD: MGO, 1995); James Byrne and F. Taxman, "Crime Control Policy and Community Corrections Practice," *Evaluation and Program Planning* 17:2 (1994): 221–233; Richard Lamb and L. Weinberger, "Persons with Severe Mental Illnesses in Jails and Prisons," *Psychiatric Services* 49:4 (1998): 483–492; and the special focus issue "Mental Health Issues in Corrections" *Corrections Today* 67:1 (2005).

2. A. Barthwell, P. Bokos, and J. Bailey, "Interventions/Wilmer: A Continuum of Care for Substance Abusers in the Criminal Justice System," *Journal of Psychoactive Drugs* 27:1 (1995): 39–47; and Michael Finigan, *An Outcome Program Evaluation of the Multnomah County S.T.O.P. Drug Diversion Program* (West Linn, OR: Northwest Professional Consortium, 1998). Note that stereotypes of drug users are generally erroneous, particularly the ideas that most drug users are burned out and disconnected from mainstream society. Some seven in ten drug users work full time and are not poor. Laura Meckler, "7 in 10 Drug Users Work Full-Time," America Online, September 8, 1999.

3. Robert Langworthy and E. Latessa, "Treatment of Chronic Drunk Drivers," *Journal of Criminal Justice* 24:3 (1996): 273–281. See also K. Blackmun, R. Voas, R. Gulberg, et al., "Enforcement of Zero Tolerance in the State of Washington," *Forensic Science Review* 13:2 (2001): 77–86; and Michael Tonry, "Crime and Human Rights," *Criminology 46:1 (2008)*: 1–33.

4. Richard Tolman and A. Weisz, "Coordinated Community Incarceration for Domestic Violence: The Effects of Arrests and Prosecutions on Recidivism of Women Abuser Perspectives," *Crime and Delinquency* 41:4 (1995): 401–495; Christopher Calson and F. Nidey, "Mandatory Penalties, Victim Compensation, and the Judicial Processing of Domestic Abuse Assault Cases," *Crime and Delinquency* 41:1 (1995): 132–149; and Carole Chancy and G. Saltzstein, "Democratic Control and Bureaucratic Responsiveness: The Police and Domestic Violence," *American Journal of Political Science* 42:3 (1998): 745–768.

5. Harry E. Allen, R. Seiter, E. Carlson, et al., *Halfway House: Program Models* (Washington, DC: U.S. Department of Justice, 1979). See also Bobbie Huskey, "Community Residential Centers," *Corrections Today* 54:8 (1992): 70–73; and Rhonda Reeves, "Future Forecast: Examining Community Corrections' Role in the Justice System," *Corrections Today* 54:8 (1992): 74–79.

6. Edward Latessa, L. Travis, and A. Holsinger, *Evaluation of Ohio's Community Corrections Acts Programs in Community-Based Correctional Facilities* (Cincinnati, OH: Division of Criminal Justice, University of Cincinnati, 1997).

7. Malcolm M. Feeley and Jonathan Simon, "The New Penology: Notes on the Emerging Strategy of Corrections and Its Implications," *Criminology* 30:4 (1992): 449–474. See also Steven Donziger, *The Real War on Crime* (New York: HarperCollins, 1996), pp. 55–62; and Michael Tonry, "Parochialism in U.S. Sentencing Policy," *Crime and Delinquency* 45:1 (1999): 48–65.

8. Voncile Gowdy, *Intermediate Sanctions* (Washington, DC: U.S. Department of Justice, 1993). See also the theme issue of *Corrections Today* 57:1 (1995); and Jeffrey Ulmer, "Intermediate Sanctions," *Sociological Inquiry* 71:2 (2001): 164–193.

9. Daniel Nagin and David Farrington, "The Onset and Persistence of Offending," *Criminology* 30:4 (1992): 501–524; Mark Cohen, "The Monetary Value of Saving a High-Risk Youth," *Journal of Quantitative Criminology* 14:1 (1998): 5–33; and Shadd Maruna, *Making Good: How Ex-Convicts Reform and Rebuild Their Lives* (Washington, DC: American Psychological Association, 2001).

10. Francis Cullen, Edward Latessa, Velmer Burton, and Lucien Lombardo, "The Correctional Orientation of Prison Wardens: Is the Rehabilitative Ideal Supported?" *Criminology* 31:1 (1993): 69–92; and Jody Sundt and F. Cullen, "The Role of the Contemporary Prison Chaplain," *Prison Journal* 78:3 (1998): 271–298.

11. John Hagan and Juleigh Coleman, "Returning Captives of the American War on Drugs," *Crime and Delinquency* 47:3 (2001): 352–367.

12. Editors, "Alternatives to Prison: Cheaper Is Better," *The Economist* (November 19, 1994): 33; Steven Barkan and S. Cohn, "Racial Prejudice and Support by Whites for Police Use of Force," *Justice Quarterly* 15:4 (1998): 743–753.

13. Michael Tonry, "Racial Politics, Racial Disparities, and the War on Crime," *Crime and Delinquency* 40:4 (1994): 475–494. See also Christiana DeLong and K. Jackson, "Putting Race into Context: Race, Juvenile Justice Processing, and Urbanization," *Justice Quarterly* 15:3 (1998): 448–504.

14. Bruce Benson, D. Rasmussen, and I. Kim, "Deterrence and Public Policy," *International Review of Law and Economics* 18:1 (1998): 77–100.

15. William J. Sabol, Heather Coutour, and Paige M. Harrison, *Prisoners in 2006* (Washington, DC: U.S. Department of Justice, 2007), p. 1.

16. International Centre for Prison Studies: University of London.

17. James Bryne, "The Future of Intensive Probation Supervision," *Crime and Delinquency* 36:1 (1990): 3–34.

18. Peter Wood and H. Grasmick, "Toward the Development of Punishment Equivalencies," *Justice Quarterly* 16:1 (1999):19–50.

19. William Bradshaw and M. Umbreit, "Crime Victims Meet Juvenile Offenders," *Juvenile and Family Court Journal* 49:3 (1998): 17–25; and Audrey Evje and Robert Cushman, *A Summary of the Reconciliation Programs* (Sacramento, CA: Judicial Council of California, 2000).

20. Thomas Bonczar, *Characteristics of Adults on Probation, 1995* (Washington, DC: U.S. Department of Justice, 1997), p. 7; and Matthew DuRose and Patrick Langan, *Felony Sentences in State Courts, 2004* (Washington, DC: Bureau of Justice Statistics, 2007), p. 10.

21. Roy Sudipto, "Juvenile Restitution and Recidivism in a Midwestern County," *Federal Probation* 59:1 (1995): 55–62. See also Karen Suter, *Delinquency Prevention in Texas* (Austin, TX: Texas Juvenile Probation Commission, 1997).

22. Joan Petersilia and Susan Turner, *Evaluating Intensive Supervised Probation/Parole: Results of a Nationwide Experiment* (Washington, DC: U.S. Department of Justice, 1993). See also Angela Robertson, P. Grimes, and K. Rogers, "A Short-Run Cost Benefit Analysis of Community-Based Interventions for Juvenile Offenders," *Crime and Delinquency* 47:2 (2001): 265–284.

23. B. Fulton, S. Stone, and P. Gendreau, *Restructuring Intensive Supervision Programs: Applying "What Works"* (Lexington, KY: American Probation and Parole Association, 1994). See also F. Cullen and P. Gendreau, "From Nothing Works to What Works," *The Prison Journal* 81:3 (2000): 313–338.

24. J. Byrne, A. Lurigio, and C. Baird, "The Effectiveness of the New Intensive Supervision Programs," *Research in Corrections* 2:1 (1989): 1–48.

25. B. Fulton, E. Latessa, A. Stichman, and L. F. Travis, "The State of ISP: Research and Policy Implications," *Federal Probation* 61:4 (1997): 65–75.

26. B. Fulton, P. Gendreau, and M. Paparozzi, "APPA's Prototypical Intensive Supervision Program: ISP as It Was Meant to Be," *Perspectives* 19:2 (1996): 25–41. See

also B. Fulton et al., *Restructuring Intensive Supervision Programs.*

27. C. West Huddleston, "Drug Court and Jail-Based Treatment," *Corrections Today* 60:6 (1998): 98. See also Paul Stageberg, B. Wilson, and R. Moore, *Final Report of the Polk County Adult Drug Court* (Des Moines, IA: Iowa Division of Criminal Justice Policy, 2001).

28. C. West Huddleston, Douglas Marlowe, and Rachel Casebolt, *Painting the Current Picture: A National Report Card on Drug Courts and Other Problem-Solving Court Programs in the United States* (Bureau of Justice Assistance, U.S. Department of Justice, 2008).

29. M. Rempel, D. Fox-Kralstein, A. Cissner, et al., *The New York State Adult Drug Court Evaluation: Policies, Participants and Impacts* (New York: Center for Court Innovation, 2003).

30. Deborah Shaffer, Shelley Listan, Edward Latessa, and Christopher Lowenkamp, "Examining the Differential Impact of Drug Court Services by Court Type: Findings from Ohio." *Drug Court Institute* VI:1(2007): 33–66.

31. Shaffer, D. Reconsidering Drug Court Effectiveness: A Meta-Analytic Review. Doctoral Dissertation, University of Cincinnati, 2006.

32. Washington State Institute for Public Policy, *Drug Courts for Adult Defendants: Outcome Evaluation and Cost Benefit Analysis* (Olympia, WA: WSIPP, 2003).

33. NPC Research, Inc., and Administrative Office of the Courts, Judicial Council of California, *California Drug Courts: A Methodology for Determining Costs and Avoided Costs: Phase I: Building the Methodology: Final Report* (Portland, OR: Authors, October 2002).

34. James Brown, "Drug Courts: Are They Needed and Will They Succeed in Breaking the Cycle of Drug-Related Crime? *New England Journal on Civil and Criminal Confinement* 23:1 (1997): 63–99.

35. Julie Martin, "Community Services: Are the Goals of This Alternative Sentencing Tool Being Met?" *Court Review* 28:4 (1991): 5–11. But see Wade Myers, P. Burton, Paula Sanders, et al., "Project 'Back-on-Track' at One Year," *Journal of the American Academy of Clinical and Adolescent Psychiatry* 39:9 (2000): 1127–1134.

36. Gail Caputo, D. Young, and R. Porter, *Community Services for Repeat Misdemeanants in New York City* (New York: Vera Institute, 1998).

37. Michael Maxfield and Terry Baumer, "Home Detention with Electronic Monitoring: Comparing Pretrial and Postconviction Programs," *Crime and Delinquency* 36:4 (1990): 521–536; and Ann Farrell, "Mothers Offending against Their Role: An Australian Experience," *Women and Criminal Justice* 9:4 (1998): 47–67.

38. Leonard Flynn, "House Arrest," *Corrections Today* 48:5 (1986): 64–68.

39. K. Courtright, B. Berg, and R. Mutchnick, "The Cost Effectiveness of Using House Arrest with Electronic Monitoring for Drunk Drivers," *Federal Probation* 61:3 (1997): 19–22.

40. Government Accounting Office, *Intermediate Sanctions* (Washington, DC: GAO, 1990). Evaluations of the home detention program in Great Britain found a 5% "recall to prison" rate for prison inmates released to home detention. Kath Dodgson, P. Goodwin, H. Philip, et al., *Electronic Monitoring of Released Prisoners* (London: U.K. Home Office, 2001).

41. James Kammer, K. Minor, and J. Wells, "An Outcome Study of the Diversion Plus Program for Juvenile Offenders," *Federal Probation* 61:2 (1997): 51–56; and M. Cusson, "Intermediate Punishments, Electronic Monitoring and Abolitionism," *Revue Internationale de Criminologie et de Police Technique Scientifique* 51:1 (1998): 34–45.

42. Dennis Wagner and Christopher Baird, *Evaluation of the Florida Community Control Program* (Washington, DC: U.S. Department of Justice, 1993), p. 5. It is possible to have cost savings and similar outcomes. See Elizabeth Deschenes and P. Greenwood, "Alternative Placements for Juvenile Offenders," *Journal of Research in Crime and Delinquency* 35:3 (1998): 267–294.

43. See Alison Church and S. Dunston, *Home Detention: The Evaluation of the Home Detention Pilot Programme, 1995–1997* (Wellington: New Zealand Ministry of Justice, 1997).

44. R. K. Schwitzgebel, R. L. Schwitzgebel, W. N. Pahnke, and W. S. Hurd, "A Program of Research in Behavioral Electronics," *Behavioral Scientist* 9:3 (1964): 233–238. See also Michael Vitello, "Three Strikes: Can We Return to Rationality?" *Journal of Criminal Law and Criminology* 87:2 (1997): 395–481.

45. Scott Vollum and Chris Hale, "Electronic Monitoring: Research Review," *Corrections Compendium* (July 2002): 1.

46. Bureau of Justice Assistance, *Electronic Monitoring in Intensive Probation and Parole Programs* (Washington, DC: U.S. Department of Justice, 1989).

47. Joan Petersilia, *Expanding Options for Criminal Sentencing* (Santa Monica, CA: Rand, 1987), p. 37; C. Camp and G. Camp, *The Corrections Yearbook 1998* (Middletown, CT: Criminal Justice Institute, 1998), p. 124. See also Editors, "Florida to Mandate GP

[Global Positioning] Devices for Sex Offenders" *Correctional News* 11:3 (2005), p. 1.

48. Government Accounting Office, *Intermediate Sanctions,* pp. 6–7.

49. Church and Dunston, *Home Detention;* and Mike Nellis, "The Electronic Monitoring of Offenders in England and Wales," *British Journal of Criminology* 31:2 (1991): 165–185.

50. J. R. Lilly, "Tagging Revisited," *The Howard Journal* 29:4 (1990): 229–245; National Association for the Care of Offenders and the Prevention of Crime, *The Electronic Monitoring of Offenders* (London: NACOPC, 1989); and Michael Brown and Preston Elrod, "Electronic House Arrest: An Examination of Citizen Attitudes," *Crime and Delinquency* 41:3 (1995): 332–346.

51. Edward J. Latessa and Lawrence F. Travis, "Halfway Houses or Probation: A Comparison of Alternative Dispositions," *Journal of Crime and Justice* 14:1 (1991): 53–75; and Edward Latessa, L. Travis, and A. Holsinger, *Evaluation of Ohio's Community-Based Correctional Facilities: Final Report* (Cincinnati, OH: Division of Criminal Justice, University of Cincinnati, 1997).

52. Christopher Lowenkamp and Edward J. Latessa, *Evaluation of Ohio's Residential Correctional Programs* (Cincinnati, OH: Center for Criminal Justice Research, University of Cincinnati, 2002). See also Christopher Lowenkamp and Edward Latessa, "Increasing the Effectiveness of Correctional Programming Through the Risk Principle: Identifying Offenders for Residential Placement," *Criminology and Public Policy* 4:2 (2005): 501–528.

53. J. Stephen Wormith and Mark E. Oliver, "Offender Treatment Attrition and Its Relationship with Risk, Responsivity, and Recidivism," *Criminal Justice and Behavior* 29:4 (2002): 447–471.

54. Edward J. Latessa and Lawrence F. Travis, "Halfway Houses or Probation"; and Joseph Callahan and K. Koenning, "The Comprehensive Sanctions Center in the Northern District of Ohio," *Federal Probation* 59:3 (1995): 52–57.

55. Dale Parent, J. Byrne, V. Tsarfaty, et al., *Day Reporting Center* (Washington, DC: U.S. Department of Justice, 1995). See also Editors, "BI Inc. Signs Day Report Center Contracts with California, Kansas," *Correctional News* 14:3 (2008): 38.

56. Stan Orchowsky, L. Jodie, and T. Bogle, *Evaluation of the Richmond Day Reporting Center* (Richmond, VA: Virginia Criminal Justice Research Center, 1995); and Jack McDevitt, M. Domino, and K. Baum, *Metropolitan*

Day Reporting Center: An Evaluation (Boston: Center for Criminal Justice Policy Research, Northeastern University, 1997).

57. Gennaro Vito and Harry Allen, "Shock Probation in Ohio: A Comparison of Outcomes," *International Journal of Offender Therapy and Comparative Criminology* 25:1 (1981): 7.

58. Gennaro Vito, "Developments in Shock Probation: A Review of Research Findings and Policy Implications," *Federal Probation* 50:1 (1985): 22–27.

59. See also Michael Vaughn, "Listening to the Experts: A National Study of Correctional Administrators' Responses to Prison Overcrowding," *Criminal Justice Review* 18:1 (1993): 12–25.

60. *Ibid.,* pp. 23–25. But also see Bruce Mendelsohn, *The Challenge of Prison Crowding* (Frederick, MD: Aspen, 1996). See also Camp and Camp, *The Corrections Yearbook Adult Corrections 2002.*

61. See also Blair Bourque et al., *Boot Camps for Juvenile Offenders* (Washington, DC: U.S. Department of Justice, 1996).

62. The bulk of the following section is drawn from the U.S. Government Accounting Office, *Prison Boot Camps* (Washington, DC: U.S. Department of Justice, 1993).

63. Texas Department of Criminal Justice, *Community Corrections Facilities Outcome Study* (Austin, TX: Texas Department of Criminal Justice, 1999).

64. Steve Aos, P. Phipps, R. Barnoski, and R. Lieb, *The Comparative Costs and Benefits of Programs to Reduce Crime: A Review of the National Research Findings with Implications for Washington State* (Olympia, WA: Washington State Institute for Public Policy, 1999).

65. David Altschuler and Troy Armstrong, *Intensive Aftercare for High-Risk Juveniles: A Community Care Model: Program Summary* (Washington, DC: Office of Juvenile Justice and Delinquency Prevention, Office of Justice Programs, U.S. Department of Justice, 1994).

66. Doris MacKenzie and Sam Souryal, *Multisite Evaluation of Shock Incarceration* (Washington, DC: National Institute of Justice, Office of Justice Programs, U.S. Department of Justice, 1994).

67. Dale Colledge and J. Gerber, "Rethinking the Assumption about Boot Camps," *Journal of Offender Rehabilitation* 28:1 (1998): 71–87. See Kay Harris, "Key Differences among Community Corrections Acts in the United States: An Overview," *Prison Journal* 76:2 (1996): 192–238.

Suggested Readings: Part 2

Bonta, James, S. Wallace-Capretta, and J. Rooney. "Can Electronic Monitoring Make a Difference?" *Crime and Delinquency* 46:1 (2000): 61–75.

Gendreau, Paul, Shelia A. French, and Angela Taylor. *What Works (What Doesn't Work)—Revised 2002: The Principles of Effective Correctional Treatment.* Monograph Series. LaCrosse, WI: International Community Corrections Association, 2002.

Latessa, Edward, Francis T. Cullen, and Paul Gendreau. "Beyond Correctional Quackery: Professionalism and the Possibility of Effective Treatment," *Federal Probation* 66:1 (2002): 43–44.

Latessa, Edward, and Paula Smith. *Corrections in the Community,* 4th ed. Cincinnati, OH: Anderson Publishing, 2007.

Lowenkamp, Christopher, and Edward Latessa. "Increasing the Effectiveness of Correctional Programming through the Risk Principle: Identifying Offenders for Residential Placement." *Criminology and Public Policy* 4:2 (2005): 501–528.

Lowenkamp, Christopher T., Edward J. Latessa, and Alex Holsinger. "The Risk Principle in Action: What We Have Learned from 13,676 Offenders and 97 Correctional Programs." *Crime and Delinquency* 52:1 (2006): 1–17.

Lutze, Faith, and D. Brody. "Mental Abuse as Cruel and Unusual Punishment: Do Boot Camp Prisons Violate the Eighth Amendment?" *Crime and Delinquency* 45:2 (1999): 242–255.

Marciniak, Liz. "The Use of Day Reporting as an Intermediate Sanction," *The Prison Journal* 79:2 (1999): 205–225.

Taxman, Faye, D. Soule, and A. Gelb. "Graduated Sanctions," *The Prison Journal* 79:2 (1999): 182–204.

Tonry, Michael, "Crime and Human Rights," *Criminology* 46:1 (2008): 1–33.

part 3

Institutional Corrections

Overview

Every correctional facility for adults, whether called a jail, prison, reformatory facility, institution, or correctional hospital, has basic minimal functions that must be performed. These fall into two broad categories: custody and treatment. Both functions are defined as correctional organization components and explained in Part 3, identifying the major problems, challenges, pitfalls, and current solutions, as well as the routine of the institution. We also explore correctional institutions such as jails, the federal system of corrections, and private-sector corrections, focusing particularly on parole and reentry, and the death penalty.

chapter 7

Custody Functions

Outline

Overview

The primary mission for any confinement facility, prison, or jail is to "protect the public." That prime directive sometimes has been, and still is, carried to the extreme. Whether from fear, ignorance, apathy, or poor training, custody staffs are defensive of their role and tactics. Emotions in a high-security cellblock can run high, with tensions spawning inappropriate behaviors on both sides of the bars. The custody staffs are the front lines of corrections and deserve utmost respect and appreciation for what they do. If the entire staff of an institution cannot work together, they will fail separately.

> "Our endeavors to control violence, in whatever setting, should be shared similarly by what we know about treating violent behavior. . . . Criminal behavior is learned behavior and ignoring its origin is wrong."
>
> —Joseph D. Lehman

Custody over another person came into being when the first tribal member was asked to guard a thief until punishment was meted out. The long history of custody far outstrips the short time that "treatment" has been on the correctional scene. Treatment has only been on the agenda of correctional management since the early 1930s in any seriously organized fashion. The long-standing battles between custody and treatment started at the beginning and have continued, sometimes subdued, since that time. Outwardly, although the basic arguments seem to be over one or the other philosophy of corrections, the differences are more often seen in conflict over budgets, manpower, and turf. This chapter and the next examine and compare the various organizational components of corrections to see what they do and how they might do it better. Because custody comprises the largest part of that organizational system, we start with it.

INSTITUTIONS: BUREAUCRATIC CONTROL

Despite technological and educational advances, the prevailing management climate for correctional institutions seems to be one of **bureaucratic control,** especially in long-term adult felony institutions. In most major correctional facilities, the inmate population is usually controlled by a combination of coercive rules that are intended to prohibit certain kinds of behavior and punishments that are imposed when the rules are broken. Bureaucratic organizations are insulated by all kinds of documented rules, regulations, and procedures, and violations are quickly punished in the name of equity and control.

In institutions that house thousands of prisoners, each with his or her own personal problems, the bureaucratic style seems to be the only functional way to maintain order and control; the processes take precedence over the individual, and prisoners become faceless commodities to be housed, moved, worked, fed, secured, and released. This nineteenth-century model stressed warehousing and subjugation of offenders. Any rehabilitation was incidental, a welcome but low-priority by-product, because the bureaucratic style clearly conflicted with any emphasis on rehabilitation. The separate functions of the rigid and formalized organizations create an impoverished climate for behavioral change.[1]

Administration's Problem: Punish, Control, or Rehabilitate?

The lack of coordination articulated for both intersystem and intrasystem activity on corrections, outlined in the previous chapters, suggests some of the reasons correctional administrators are often harried and hampered in their efforts to secure, control, and rehabilitate inmates. Although the public is willing to espouse reformatory goals for corrections, it is seldom willing to provide the support and funding that would make such reform

correctional **brief**

Correctional Managers

Adult correctional agency directors and institutional managers have not been extensively researched in corrections. Some basic facts are described here.

In 2008, the average length of time an agency director had been in office was more than four years, and a director's average salary was over $98,700 a year. Both the average length of time in office and salary varied by region of the country. The longest term (33 years) was found for a direc-

tor in the Northeast, but the director of the Federal Bureau of Prisons earned the highest (over $125,000).

Most wardens express moderate to strong support for the rehabilitation model, and also strong support for treatment. Most would approve of conjugal visits. While wardens vary in background and orientation, there is evidence that such correctional managers have similar attitudes and values, particularly on the death penalty and sexual assault in prisons.

a legislative priority. That inconsistency places dedicated correctional administrators in an awkward position: They can implement only the most meager of programs, and even then they must maintain an overall emphasis on control and punishment. Regardless of the approach to the problem, some aspect of operations will suffer.[2] If improvement requires an increase in the number of security guards, the administrator must obtain the necessary funds by decreasing the support for a treatment or other type of program; and if the administrator tries to amplify the treatment programs, it must usually be done at the expense of the custody staff.

lecture note

Discuss the nature of bureaucratic control in institutions, focusing on the need for order and safety.

ADX Supermax Prison in Colorado.
© *Lizzie Himmel/Sygma/CORBIS All Rights Reserved.*

CUSTODY: A 24-HOUR IMPACT

Impacts on institutional behavior and the attitudes of incarcerated persons are usually learned by observing and responding to those staff that have direct and continuous contact with them. Administrative and treatment staffs have limited interaction with inmates on a daily basis. Custody staffs, however, are with them 24 hours a day. It has been found that, if the whole institutional staff is not working as a team, months of discipline can fall by the wayside as a result of one serious event. Conversely, months of professional counseling can be destroyed by a single custody officer's words or actions. The term **custody** refers to the level of immediate control exercised over offenders within correctional institutions. The levels can range from supermax, to maximum or close, to medium and minimum.

Supermax, maximum, or close custody usually means the inmate is seen as a security risk and cannot be trusted to move from one area to another, in the general prison or in the cell blocks, without being escorted by a correctional officer. It also implies that inmates will not be allowed to have contact visits or to associate with other prisoners freely without supervision. They are also limited in their contacts with other persons in general. The ratio of correctional officers to inmates in most facilities designated as supermax, maximum, or close is usually quite high, as many as one for every three or four inmates. (Death row inmates are usually considered to be in close custody and therefore are expensive to house, especially with their time from conviction to execution running sometimes to 20 years, and 12 years on the average. See Chapter 14.)

Medium and minimum custody levels generally accommodate less risky or dangerous offenders or those closer to the end of their sentences. Generally speaking, the difference between medium and minimum custody is the presence of a high wall or fence and armed guard towers surrounding the former, with reasonably free movement within the facility for both categories. The inmates classified as medium security in an enclosed institution are allowed in what is referred to as **general population** (all prisoners not under special custody control). Staff-to-inmate ratios generally decrease at this level, with 1 custody staff to every 8 or 12 inmates being a common range.

Inmates classified as minimum in a fenced or walled prison are often used on institutional jobs with very little supervision or observation (i.e., groundskeeping, sweeping, and cleanup). Minimum-custody offenders are often placed in honor camps or farms, with low levels of supervision for a period of time prior to release, usually three to six months. This is a system that can reimpose a higher level of security, which often serves as both a carrot and a stick—a reward for good behavior and a loss of privileges for misbehavior. Most custody staff see this as a control mechanism and a pathway to **graduated release.** Generally speaking, custody administrators will err on the "side of the angels" and assign a higher level of custody when there is any level of doubt, especially until the inmate becomes established in the institution.

key term

Custody
Term referring to the level of immediate control exercised over offenders within correctional institutions.

key term

General population
Prisoners not restricted to tighter controls than other inmates.

key term

Graduated release
Programs bridging inmate status from imprisonment to community control.

Even though much better trained and educated **correctional officers** have now replaced the old-time prison guards in almost all prisons, many institutions still follow the same oppressive custodial procedures, especially in times of unrest. Until the cause-and-effect relationship between autocratic organizational styles and institutional disturbance is openly acknowledged, the advocates of rigid custodial control will retain their influential role.

WARDENS AND SUPERINTENDENTS

Wardens (sometimes called superintendents) are the chief executive officers of prisons and have management responsibility for attaining mission goals. The warden's primary responsibility is to manage the operations, supervisory staff, support staff, and inmates. To do this, the warden is usually assisted by several deputy wardens, typically one each for management, custody, industry, and treatment programs. Most wardens are male, although recent growth in the number of managers and new appointments has primarily been females (see Figure 7.1). Most wardens are believed to "earn their way up" by serving in subordinate positions in the chain of command within a prison, assuming higher ranks and authority with experience and proven abilities. For many correctional workers, the post of warden is the capstone of a lengthy career, occasionally served within only one institution.

Wardens tend to "face outward" in their daily duties, dealing with politicians, administrators in the central office of corrections, the media, and interest groups. Running the daily affairs of the prison facility is usually delegated to a deputy warden, usually the custody deputy. Few have the time and luxury of overseeing the affairs of the inside of the facility. As former Warden Benjamin Cooper said: "The warden's job is made much easier if he follows the MBWA ("Management By Walking Around") principle. You have to tour the facility every day." Information on race/ethnicity of wardens is found in Figure 7.2.

Contemporary wardens are less powerful and exercise less authority than those in office before the period of massive prison litigation began, usually identified as 1970. They defend rehabilitation and reform, face judicial intervention through court orders, deal with inmate grievances, serve as the management representative with unionized correctional officers, deal with the media, and negotiate with directors of corrections as well as the governor. Most go to work each day, leaving behind a partially packed suitcase on the ready in case they trigger a notorious administrative failure.[3]

figure 7.1

Gender of Managing Officers, 2012 (in percent)

SOURCE: American Correctional Association, *2007 Directory* (Alexandria, VA: ACA, 2007), pp. 40–41. Data from 2008–2012 are estimated.

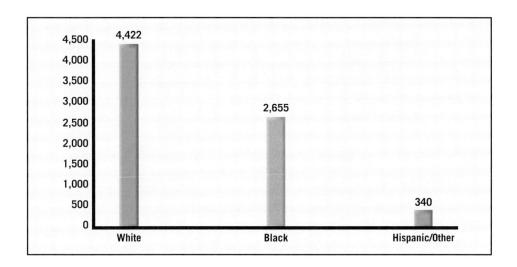

figure 7.2

Wardens and
Superintendents: 2012

SOURCE: American Correctional
Association, *2006 Directory*
(Alexandria, VA: ACA, 2007),
pp. 40–41. Data from 2006 to
2012 are estimated.

CORRECTIONAL OFFICERS AND JAILERS: ON THE FRONT LINES

Although custody staff members have been called guards, jailers, prison guards, turnkeys, "**screws**," hacks, detention officers, correctional officers, or security staff, for purposes of this text we choose to use the term *correctional officer*. Regardless of the title used, it refers to those women and men charged with control, movement management, and observation of the inmates in the jails and prisons of America. By 2007, well more than 250,000 uniformed custody staff members were working in state, federal, and local adult prisons in America.[4] Also, more than 118,000 line officers worked in jails and local detention facilities in 2007, over 70% of the total staffing. The proportion of female officers in the prison systems was about 27%, with more than 33% in local jails and detention facilities. Some 28% of prison correctional officers[5] and some 29% of jail and local detention officers were nonwhite (see Figures 7.3 and 7.4).

key term

"Screws"
Inmate term for correctional
officers.

Correctional Officer Attitudes

The last century saw the "get-tough-on-crime" advocates place new and greater demands on correctional officers to do more with less, with little or no recognition. Moreover, prisons can be antagonistic and stressful working environments, as evidenced by the increasing

class activity

Ask students to identify ten
functions performed by
correctional officers.

class activity

Challenge students to describe
the social characteristics of
correctional officers.

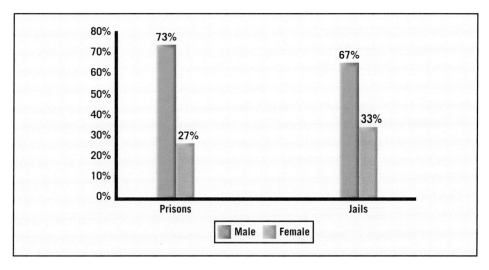

figure 7.3

Gender of Correctional Officers

Data from: American Correctional
Association, *2007 Directory*
(Alexandria, VA, 2007), pp. 44–45; and
Camille Camp and George Camp, *The
2000 Corrections Yearbook: Jails*
(Middleton, CT: The Criminal Justice
Institute, 2000), p. 62.

figure 7.4

Uniformed Correctional Staff

Data from: American Correctional
Association, *2007 Directory*
(Alexandria, VA: ACA, 2007),
pp. 44–45; and Camille Camp and
George Camp, *The 2000 Corrections
Yearbook: Jails* (Middleton, CT: The
Criminal Justice Institute, 2000), p. 57.

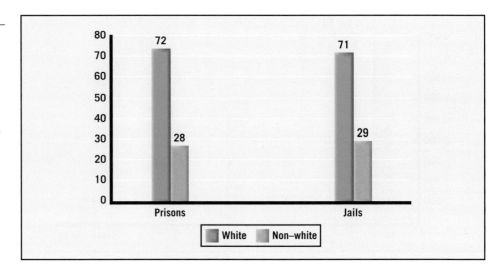

number of assaults on correctional officers by inmates, and by the number of disciplinary actions taken by administrators against correctional officers.

Diminished Control

Correctional officer degradation is a recent phenomenon that has emerged largely as a result of court rulings and an increase in violence and gang (institutional threat group) membership among inmates. Specifically, some administrators are seen to have adopted a "hands-off" doctrine concerning inmate behavior. Some researchers argue that this doctrine has exposed prison regimes to outside accountability, limited an institution's recourse to coercive sanctions, and provided inmates with a legitimate means of expression with which to challenge the system of social control.

The impact of recent court decisions has been to establish a perceived link between the administrative and inmate control systems. The prison system's typical response to court decisions has been to develop administrative structures to maintain order consistent with the procedural and substantive rights of inmates. However, it appears that the rights of correctional officers might have been neglected while correctional administrators conformed to litigation. For instance, a latent result of court compliance by prison administrators is increased bureaucratic regulations and obligations for corrections personnel. This can be accomplished in a variety of ways, including a drastic increase in the direction and length of a correctional officer's training program. Also, when custody personnel arrive at basic or in-service training classes, correctional instructors should explain the mission of the training, which is to protect the state from further inmate litigation, and they should inform their students that future responsibility for courtroom resolutions rests with corrections personnel.

New legal standards have emerged, burying correctional officers in bureaucratic responsibilities. For instance, when correctional officers use force, they now must complete an official report, with videotapes and other corroborating evidence. This new "bureaucratic-legal order" also forces officers to conform to the letter of the law in the application of force. Some researchers suggest that several prison riots, including the Attica riot of 1971, can be traced to excessive inmate freedoms and the responses of prison systems to court decisions. Thus, inmate rights have produced a variety of bureaucratic regulations that have taken the authority and structure of custody away from the corrections professional.

An increase of violence, due in part to a rise in prison gangs, puts many officers in the trenches of our nation's prisons. Prison violence, crime, and drug trafficking are ways of life for most inmates in high-custody prisons. In fact, some experts say that as gangs and violence increase in high-custody penitentiaries, the less likely an officer is to want to deal directly with inmates; instead, he or she will want to transfer into administrative work.

If the primary concern is to render humane and quality custody service, it appears highly unlikely that alienated officers are motivated toward those ends. A second concern is the need to enhance in-service training at a professional level conducted outside the prison facility. Other recommendations from this study included the idea that administrations should manage through encouraging positive values instead of regulations, and that raises and promotions should be linked to merit, education, and experience.[6]

Unionization and the Correctional Officer

Unionization, found in almost every sector of business and industry, has in recent decades spread to the ranks of state and federal employees. The union movement has extended to the "sworn" officers charged with the police, fire, and correctional protection of the public. Police officers and firefighters have established collective bargaining agencies in most urban departments, with improved working conditions and better pay as a result.

Because many jurisdictions forbid government employees from striking, other tactics are employed to create power negotiation in collective bargaining. Correctional officers have resorted to "**blue flu,**" the practice by uniformed personnel of taking sick leave en masse to back up their demands for improved working conditions, salary increments, and other items on their agenda. This method permits negotiating leverage without forcing the employees to strike, an illegal act.

As agents of public protection became more successful in their demands, their counterparts in the correctional institutions took notice. The great move in the late 1960s toward more professionalism and the sharp increases in prisoner populations, community corrections, and other programs pointed up some of the needs of the long-neglected correctional officer. Initial efforts to organize met with disapproval from administrators, often because of limited budgets and already overtaxed custody forces in the crowded prisons. Most administrators wanted the few available funds to be used for new personnel, not pay raises for the officers they already had. In some cases the correctional officers did go on strike, and their duties were assumed by administrative and office personnel.[7]

key term

Unionization
Organization of correctional officers for purposes of improved work conditions or salaries.

key term

"Blue flu"
Ploy used by correctional officers to strengthen their hands in negotiations with command officers.

INMATE ORGANIZATION: THE SOCIAL SYSTEM

Prisons are **total institutions**[8] in which the residents' every moment, activity, movement, and option are carefully regulated by the correctional administrators. Inmates are given little individual responsibility and autonomy, important characteristics of everyday life in a modern achievement-oriented society. The tight regime compounds their personal inadequacies rather than correcting them. Cut off from ordinary social intercourse and their families and friends, then isolated in bastion-like prisons, inmates are quickly taught by the other residents how to exist in that environment. As we described earlier, the process of learning how to exist in prison—the appropriate attitudes and behaviors, the norms of prison life—is called **prisonization.** This process leads to the adoption of the folkways, mores, customs, and general culture of the prison.[9]

Former inmates can import prisonization into prisons if they are reincarcerated. It also occurs spontaneously even in newly opened institutions. The process is handed down from prisoner to prisoner, remaining a strong force that is later transmitted between prisons, working against the rehabilitation goals of even the most enlightened administrator. It impedes rather than facilitates treatment efforts, preventing inmates from acquiring the skills, talents, attitudes, and behavior necessary for successful adjustment in free society. Indeed, the opposite tends to occur: Inmates become more like infants[10] than mature adults.

As part of the process of prisonization, inmates learn codes and roles, and they are subjected to a reward and punishment system that encourages them to act like "good cons." Prison codes emphasize a number of specific behaviors: loyalty to other inmates ("never rat on a con"), maintenance of calm ("keep cool," "don't start feuds"), avoidance of trickery or fraud ("always share with your cellmates," "sell hoarded goods at the going rate"), manliness ("don't complain," "never cry"), and quick-wittedness in prison dealings ("don't be a sucker," "guards are screws, never to be confided in or trusted").

Leg irons are used in prison.
Courtesy of Smith and Wesson.

Inmates who conform to those expectations become "right guys," "home boys," or "stand-up guys" who can be trusted and are looked up to by other inmates. They share in the privileges available in prisons, and they can count on support if another inmate attacks them physically. Those who violate the normative structure become outcasts and are referred to by various descriptive and unpleasant names such as rat, snitch, fag, merchant, fink, and punk.

Two recent developments in America's jails and prisons have exacerbated those problems. The first is the rise of gangs in prisons. Most of these gangs have street-gang origins and are racial or ethnic in nature, grouping together for power and protection. For example, the four major gangs in California's prisons are two Chicano gangs (ghetto Chicanos or "Nostra Familia" and the Mexican Mafia or "EME"), the Black Brotherhood (often based on gang affiliation such as "Crips" or "Bloods"), and the Aryan Brotherhood (includes most bikers, white supremacists, and others such as the skinheads). Gangs with many variations on these themes are found in jails and prisons nationwide (see the Correctional Brief on p. 140 for an example from Texas).

Conflicts between the gangs have led to stabbings, murder outside prison, rape, blackmail, and exploitation of nonaligned prisoners. All prison gangs are organized strictly to take part in antisocial and criminal behavior. Many administrators have ordered **lockdowns** that confine prisoners to their cells to avoid bloodshed and violence. Such lockdowns have been criticized by legislators and other staff.[11] Jail and prison overcrowding has made matters worse, and many an administrator has resigned because of a sense of hopelessness. Due in large part to institutional threat groups, correctional managers have developed Special Housing Units (SHUs) to isolate and control violent and aggressive gang members and operations.

Most gang members were involved with street-level gangs as continuing criminal enterprises, subsequently being sentenced to imprisonment. Almost all will be released and will return to their free-world gangs, where they will continue their drug-trafficking, murdering, protection extortion, and more violent crime. Law enforcement agencies will eventually rearrest paroled gang members who will be recommitted to prison on their second or third strike. They will serve longer and enhanced sentences. Such recommitments increase prison overcrowding, institutional violence, assaults on staff, and the level of tension in the prison.

To cope with gangs, gang members and crimes, and both staff and inmate intimidation, correctional managers have formed intelligence units. These units are expected to gather information on street-level crimes by gang members, their prison activities, security breaches, institutional crimes being planned, drug-trafficking, communications, and directives to lower-level members ("soldiers") who are directed to "hit" other inmates and staff (and their families). The list of such activities could profitably be expanded.

The intelligence unit will typically employ a wide variety of data-gathering procedures designed to turn data into intelligence through such strategies as:

- developing confidential sources
- turning a gang member
- infiltrating a gang
- conducting mail scans
- monitoring telephone conversations
- identifying current and incoming street-gang members, and
- plugging security breaches.

The value of the intelligence unit will no doubt increase as it becomes more proficient.

Three white male Aryan Supremacist inmates stand together in a recreation room, Maricopa County Jail, Arizona.
Photo by A. Ramey, courtesy of PhotoEdit Inc.

Lockdowns
Control of prison and inmates by not permitting inmates to leave their cells or rooms.

Tattooed Prison Inmate.
© *Andrew Lichtenstein/CORBIS All Rights Reserved*

correctional **brief**

Profiles of Texas: Seven Major Gangs

Texas prisons contend with seven major gangs. Each insists on a lifetime commitment: Once committed to one of these organizations, death is the only way out. Each prison gang is highly structured and operates under a specific "constitution" or set of rules. What follows is a brief description of these gangs and their histories.

- **Texas Syndicate** The Texas Syndicate began in the California Department of Corrections in the mid-1970s. It is mostly comprised of Hispanic inmates who migrated to California from Texas, although a few white inmates have been accepted. Through violent acts, the gang made a reputation for itself as a group to be feared and respected among general-population inmates.

  On release from the California Department of Corrections, gang members returned to Texas and continued their illegal activities. Many were subsequently incarcerated in Texas. Since their arrival [arriving in our agency], gangs have been involved in more than 48 inmate and many correctional officers and other prison staff homicides, and numerous other nonfatal assaults on staff and inmates.

  The Texas Syndicate is structured along paramilitary lines and has a set of strictly enforced rules; violations may result in death. The group's members are known to have been incarcerated in California, New Mexico, Arizona, Florida, Illinois, and the Federal Bureau of Prisons.

- **Mexikanemi** Mexikanemi, or MM, is the largest and fastest-growing prison gang in the Texas Department of Criminal Justice (TDCJ). Mexikanemi is an Aztec term meaning "free or liberated Mexican." The group originated in Texas prisons in the early 1980s. It initially started as a group of inmates interested in their cultural background, but it rapidly transformed into a prison gang involved in extortion, narcotics trafficking, and assaults on inmates and staff.

  The gang is structured along hierarchical lines, with a president (its founder), a vice president, and three generals, each of whom is responsible for a specific region in the state. Generals can appoint members under them to run activities in specific facilities.

  The gang's constitution states that "in being a criminal organization, we will function in any aspects or criminal interest for the benefit or advancement of the gang. We will traffic in drugs, contracts of assassinations, prostitution, robbery of high magnitude and anything we can imagine."

- **Aryan Brotherhood of Texas** This group, comprised of white racist inmates, originated in the TDCJ in the early 1980s and should not be mistaken

with other groups with similar names found across the country.

  The Aryan Brotherhood of Texas has been involved in assaults and murders of inmates in our agency and also conspired to have a state judge assassinated. Operating under a structure resembling a steering committee or a commission, this group has extended its illegal activities to the outside.

- **Texas Mafia** The Texas Mafia is mostly comprised of white inmates, but a few Hispanics have been accepted. The gang has an extensive background in narcotics; many of its members are involved in producing crystal methedrine and have ties with motorcycle gangs. The group is very violent and has been involved in inmate homicides and staff assaults. It has a close working relationship with the Texas Syndicate.

- **Nuestro Carnales** This group has fewer than 100 members. However, they have established a reputation for violence by being involved in several inmate assaults, including one homicide. Formed along a hierarchy structure with one recognized leader, this group is attempting to gain a foothold in the community as well as maintaining its status inside the prison walls. This gang appears to have strong ties with the Texas Syndicate.

- **Hermanos de Pistoleros Latinos** Composed of 174 members within TDCJ, this group has posed security problems for the agency by being involved in numerous illegal activities, including inmate assaults and inmate homicides. An additional 104 members have been released to the community and will have an impact for outside law enforcement agencies. This group appears to have ties with the Texas Syndicate and has been known to discuss joint illegal activities with that group.

- **Raza Unida** This group is the most recent to be identified as a disruptive group within the TDCJ. With a membership of only 64 members, this group has yet to achieve the status and respect afforded the other prison gangs by the inmate population. However, they are rapidly gaining notoriety due to their recent assaults on inmates at various facilities within the agency. Classification of inmates from one specific region has assisted the group in forming and evolving into a prison gang.

SOURCES: Salvador Buentello, "Texas Turnaround: New Strategies Combat State's Prison Gangs," *Corrections Today* 54:5 (May 1992): 59. See also Gary Klivans, "Gang Codes: Gang Identity Theft," *American Jails* 22:4 (2008): 70–77; and Gary Klivans, "Gang Codes: Not Hiding in Plain Sight," *American Jails* 22:3 (2008): 57–59.

We stress again that the importance of prisonization lies in its negative impact on attempts to provide rehabilitative programs that encourage inmates to engage in legitimate noncriminal activities.

CUSTODY AS A WAY OF LIFE

The *assistant superintendent for custody* or *security programs,* also known as the *deputy warden for custody* or the *captain of custody* in jails, is one of the most important figures in any correctional facility. His or her main responsibility is to develop ways of accounting for the whereabouts of all prisoners at all times. Techniques have become more humane and permissive in recent years, but in most institutions the **count** is still the principal method of determining the prisoners' whereabouts, and counts are sometimes conducted as often as every two hours. Preoccupation with counting and recounting prisoners makes it difficult to conduct meaningful programs or permit individualized operations. To some extent, however, outside work details and opportunities for educational and vocational training and furloughs have been included in more streamlined counting methods. Today, counts are often called in to a central office in the prison's control room and tabulated against the daily tally of inmates, in some cases using bar-coded wristbands, access cards with magnetic data stripes, and computers.[12] Although the count is more sensibly administered nowadays, it still remains the most important task for which the custody staff is responsible.

Another function of the custody staff is to establish and maintain security procedures. Security procedures, at a minimum, include the inspection of persons and vehicles passing in and out of the institution, usually at a **sally port** at entry and exit points. The sally port is an area enclosed by a double gate. A vehicle or individual enters through the first gate, which is then closed. Before the second gate is opened, the search for forbidden articles (contraband) is made. After the search is completed, the second gate is opened and the individual or vehicle passes through that gate. At no time may both gates be open, and many gate systems are mechanically adjusted so it is impossible to open them both at the same

The control room, from which all doors may be opened and closed. In the event of a riot, officers could oversee all movements from this super-secure room.
Photo by Tony Savino, courtesy of The Image Works.

correctional **brief**

Nonlethal Weapons in Prison

As correctional facilities become more crowded, administrators are searching for nonlethal weaponry to run smarter and safer jails and prisons. One approach uses computerized inmate tracking and alarm systems to update the location of every inmate every two seconds. Inmates wear wristwatch-size devices that emit wireless signals that are collected by receivers and fed back along a cable system to display on a control-room computer the exact location of inmates. Lurking inmates are easily detected. Other facilities provide officers with pager-size wireless systems worn on their belts that automatically sound an alarm if the officer falls or is forced into a horizontal position. Assistance can immediately be dispatched.

In addition, various pepper spray devices can be carried on belts, sprayed from fire extinguishers, deployed from water pistols, or used with hoses to douse inmates up to 150 feet away. Pepper spray canisters in inmate dining rooms can be used to quell uprisings, riots, and gang disturbances. Some of these devices are marketed as nonlethal weapons filled with "food-grade pepper with water."

Guns that fire rubber bullets, hard rubber rounds, hard sponge devices, and bean bags are also being adopted as nonlethal armature for prisoner control in close environments, although lawsuits have been filed and are pending that allege excessive force, cruel and unusual punishment, and wanton infliction of unnecessary pain. Does the U.S. Constitution reach behind prison walls?

---

class activity

Ask students to define *lockdowns,* the *count, sally port,* and *shakedowns.* Identify the need for each.

class activity

Ask students how correctional staff can control/limit drug use in prisons.

class activity

Ask students how to best control *contraband,* and what techniques they would use to do so.

lecture note

Discuss the prison *riot* as a breakdown in the custody procedures in prison.

thematic question

Describe the major mechanisms for importation of drugs into a prison, and discuss strategies for interdicting drugs, including intelligence and technological measures.

key term

Prison rules

Written documents designed to control inmate behaviors.

time. Sometimes a visitor feels it is as hard to get into the institution as it is to get out. The fear that inmates and visitors will try to smuggle in contraband or other items to assist escape pervades the maximum-security prison. Searches of vehicles and the requiring of visitors to pass through electronic metal detectors have become standard practices and procedures at major institutions.

Unfortunately, under the assumption that all inmates are alike, medium- and minimum-security prisons have also adopted similar security practices. It took over a century before America was prepared to build a prison without massive walls; it may take even longer to convince old-guard custody personnel that less stringent security measures may serve as well to ensure control.[13]

Discipline and Inmate Traffic Control

Rules and regulations for inmates are usually aimed at strict traffic control. Prisoners' movements are carefully planned and controlled in every detail. In the past, all prisoners were awakened, moved to work, and fed at the same time, always under the eye of custody personnel. That degree of planning has slackened in many institutions; the trend is toward more reasonable controls over inmate traffic within the walls.

The suggestion that when inmates are treated as if they are dangerous, they will become dangerous is generally considered valid. One way to avoid that problem is for staff and inmates to maintain meaningful communications. If the custody staff loses contact with inmates, the latter responds only to the inmate subculture. All too often, such limited interaction results in violence among the inmates. The most effective controls over inmate traffic and movement may well be those that guide our behavior in the free community.

The most recently available report on prison rule violators analyzed the characteristics of state prison inmates charged with infractions of institutional rules. Despite an increase of 64% in state prison populations from the previous study conducted ten years earlier, some 54% of prisoners had infractions charged to them in both studies. Other important aspects of this study are as follows:

- Younger inmates and those with more extensive criminal careers or drug histories were the most likely to have violated **prison rules.**
- Inmates housed in larger prisons or maximum-security prisons had higher percentages of rule violations than prisoners in other types of facilities.

A correctional officer searches an inmate at California State Prison, Sacramento, in Folsom, California. Guards throughout state prisons are being ordered to limit use of deadly force in breaking up inmate fistfights. *Photo by AP Wide World Photos.*

- More than 90% of the inmates charged with violating prison rules were found guilty in prison administrative proceedings.
- The 90%-and-above rate of guilty decisions occurred for different racial/ethnic, age, and sex categories and did not vary by size or security level of the prison.
- Inmates serving their first sentence in prison had a lower average annual rate of infraction (1.0) than did recidivists (1.6), regardless of how long they had served on their current sentence. A higher percentage of male inmates (53%) than female inmates (47%) was charged with rule breaking. On an average annual basis, however, women had a higher prison infraction rate than men (2.0 average violations per year versus 1.4 for men).
- Inmates who used drugs prior to admission were more likely to violate prison rules than were nonusers of drugs, 57% compared to 37%.
- Whites and blacks committed infractions at the same rate—approximately 1.5 violations per inmate per year. White and black rule violators reported nearly identical distributions of punishments received for rule violations. The most common penalties were solitary confinement or segregation and loss of good-time credit.

More recent studies of rule-violation behaviors found that the pattern and types of misconduct were the same for males and females in a state prison, although levels of infractions were lower for women. Younger prisoners began their "misconduct careers" sooner.

A second study focused on major and minor ("serious" and "regular") infractions in a medium-security prison and found the ratio to be about 1:3, respectively. Minor infractions include theft of food, horseplay, lying, and use of abusive language to a correctional officer. More serious offenses include homicide, assault, possession of a weapon, and threatening to set a fire. The average processing cost of an infraction is estimated to be about $70 for each infraction charged that results in a finding of guilty. The figures tend to show that the problems with inmate infractions do not seem to have increased any faster than the growing population and that disciplinary actions may deter many other rule infractions. Institutional rules were designed to regulate inmate behavior.

class activity

Ask students what technologies might be used to prevent escape, and what institutional procedures limit inmate flight.

class activity

Structure a debate on the following: Electrified fences that surround a prison are tantamount to executing an escaping inmate.

class activity

Ask students to describe those inmates most likely to violate institutional rules.

class activity

Ask students to identify and then rank various nonlethal approaches to inmate control in prison.

lecture note

Define *escape* and identify the major categories of inmates who attempt flight.

thematic question

Why is the military model the most dominant practice in prison custody?

Note, however, that most correctional officers are dedicated and humane persons, and maximizing their potential is an important challenge to concerned administrators. The situation with regard to educating those officers is improving. Prison guards were once hired off the street and trained on the job. Most states now offer extensive preservice training to ensure a minimal level of competence in the officers before they are placed on the job; all states require at least minimal preservice training. The basic course ranges from 40 to 640 hours of preservice training. In-service training is generally 56 hours annually, but many states provide 80 hours.[14] As this trend continues, salaries, the quality of personnel, and working conditions will improve. The tendency to use outdated and counterproductive forms of discipline should decrease accordingly, and the correctional officer, long recognized as the single most important agent for change in institutions, will be able to realize his or her[15] potential contribution to the rehabilitation approach.

Contraband and Shakedowns

key term

Contraband

Any object forbidden in prison.

In early years of corrections in America's jails and prisons, **contraband** was officially defined as any item that could be used to break an institution's rule or to assist in escape. In practice, the term usually ended up referring to anything the custody staff designated as undesirable for possession by the inmates. Such banning power is unrestricted. It can start with a particular object, such as a knife, and extend to anything that might conceivably be made into a knife—a policy that has placed some relatively innocuous items on contraband lists.

Any item that is not issued or not authorized in the institution is contraband. Control of contraband is necessary for several reasons:

- To control the introduction of articles that can be used for trading and gambling,
- To control the collecting of junk and the accumulation of items that make housekeeping difficult, and
- To identify medications and drugs and items that can be used as weapons and escape implements.

Controlling contraband requires a clear understanding of what contraband is, of regulations that are designed to limit its entry into the institution, and of effective search procedures. The definition of contraband just given is simple and clear. However, this definition can become useless if the facility attempts to supplement it with a long list of approved items. If the institution permits prisoners to have packages, the problem of contraband control will be made difficult, since the list of authorized items may grow long.

Long lists of approved and forbidden items often complicate what appears to be a relatively simple definition. A broad and clear definition, followed by the use of common sense by trained correctional officers, will usually result in better control and less conflict over what is or is not contraband. Prison administrators often see an excessively long contraband list as a challenge to the inmate and an indication of suppression. Such items as guns, however, are clearly dangerous contraband, and prison administrators must continually check packages, visitors, and correctional officers to detect such material. This is usually accomplished using modern metal detecting and X-ray equipment.

The generally accepted way of defining contraband was to use the affirmative approach. For example, "contraband is any item, or quantity of an item, that is not specifically authorized by the institution rules." This clearly defines what is not contraband and leaves the decision as to what is contraband to the inmate. Contraband is more often found to be the acquisition of excess items that are authorized (e.g., extra blankets, extra books, hoarded food), rather than those items that are dangerous per se. Amassing contraband in this sense is seen as an expression of an inmate's power, plus a way to beat the system and show fellow inmates that the forbidden can be done. That power is used to trade favors or show favoritism to more powerful inmates. Contraband is often used in bartering and as currency (cigarettes and matches, for example) just as we use barter on the outside.

Because the loss of contraband is the loss of power, searches and shakedowns are another source of potential conflict with inmates in security institutions. The most common type of search to prevent contraband entry into and movement within institutions is the **frisk search.** This type of search is used when prisoners enter or leave the institution and when institutional personnel suspect a prisoner may be hiding contraband on his or her person. Figure 7.5 shows the proper procedures for a frisk.

key term

Frisk search
Process of detecting inmate contraband by manual search of the bodies of inmates.

figure 7.5
The Frisk Search

SOURCE: Nick Pappas, *The Jail: Its Operation and Management* (Lompoc, CA: Federal Prison Industries, 1971), p. 23.

key term

Strip search
Process of detecting inmate contraband by visual inspection of the bodies of inmates.

key term

"Keester"
To hide contraband objects within the rectum or vagina of prison inmates.

key term

Shakedown
Cell search to detect and control contraband.

When a prisoner is suspected of having access to drugs, weapons, or other items that can be secreted on the body or in a body cavity, and a frisk reveals nothing, a **strip search** may be conducted. The strip search is ordinarily made in a location where the prisoner will not be observed by other inmates and subjected to ridicule. The basic strip search requires only the visual observation of the entire body and orifices. If a more extensive body cavity search is merited, it must be conducted with the knowledge and permission of the chief administrator of the facility (superintendent, sheriff, etc.). Qualified medical personnel must conduct a body cavity search. Failure to follow those procedures can result in serious lawsuits against the institution.

Plastic capsules or vials inserted in the inmate's rectum are one way to hide ("**keester**" or "keestering") drugs and other small items of contraband, so when there is probable cause, body cavities may need to be examined. The strip search frequently follows visits, usually for every inmate or on a random sample basis. In the past, frequent strips were used to debase and abuse prisoners, a practice that greatly increased prison tension and resulted in many legal actions against offending staff. Frisks are a necessary part of institutional security, but if strip searches become part of an everyday routine, the procedure soon degrades not only the searched but also the searcher.

As rules prohibiting contraband grow more detailed, inmates seek ways to secret those items in the living area and throughout the institution. There is virtually no limitation to the ingenuity employed in hiding contraband in prisons. Ironically, the older—and presumably more "secure"—institutions and plants lend themselves best to secret hiding places. The process can almost be seen as a game, with correctional officers periodically searching the same old spots. The need for **shakedowns** (searching of an entire cell or cell block) is reduced when contraband rules are made realistic and humane; prohibiting such items as family pictures and toothpicks creates a needless irritant. The shakedown also has greater effect if used only to locate items that represent a clear and present danger to the institution, not just for the sake of what inmates call "Mickey Mouse" harassment.

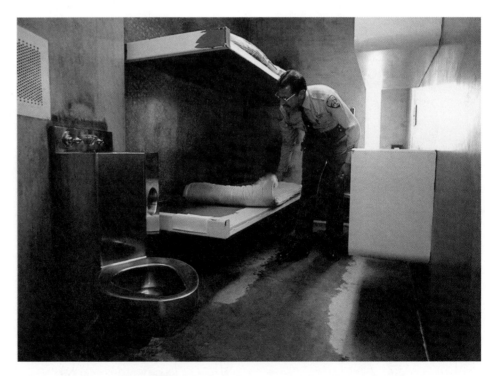

Correctional officer Michael Melo searches a high-security cell at Corcoran State Prison in Corcoran, California. Corcoran has earned a reputation as a repository for the worst prisoners in the state.
Photo by AP Wide World Photos.

PREVENTION OF ESCAPE

Maximum-security jails and adult prisons were built as though they had to contain the most dangerous creature imaginable. "A jail or prison is designed to be as strong as the strongest inmate" is an old correctional chestnut. The high walls, corner towers, and armed guards are external signs of preoccupation with escape. The nature of most jail and prison populations, although changing to harder types, does not seem to justify that model. **Escape** (flight of a confined person from an institution) and riots are serious concerns for administrators, however, and although in 2003 there were about 2,200 escapes and almost 4,000 returned escapees, most escapees were recaptured quickly.[16] They were mostly walkaways from minimum-security or community programs and represented only a miniscule percentage of the average daily population. When we consider the increasingly dangerous nature of some of the incarcerated inmates, this is actually a very good record (but bad news when they commit serious crimes while on escape status).

The conception of inmates as highly dangerous, when coupled with the extreme overcrowding of institutions, increases the concern of many correctional officers about the possibility of escape.[17] The issue is complex but revolves around two problems. The first is the philosophy of mass treatment, firmly established since the time when lockstep and silence were required for all prisoner movements. The second reason is political. Seasoned superintendents know that frequent escapes will be extremely damaging to their records, and so their extreme measures to prevent them are directed toward all prisoners, rather than toward the few who might actually try to escape. In a few prisons, however, administrators have begun to realize that a tax evader and an ax murderer do not have the same potential for escape attempts.

key term

Escape
Flight from prison facilities and illegal absences from institutions.

Technology to Prevent Escapes: Electric Fences

The move to replace continuously staffed guard towers with lethal electrified perimeter fences could very well become a national trend because of state governments' urgent need to reduce operating costs. In November 1993, the California Department of Corrections

Sign at roadside warns motorists not to pick up hitchhikers near North Kern State Prison vicinity, Delano, California.
Photo by Michael Newman, courtesy of PhotoEdit Inc.

The state of California uses electric fences in high-security facilities.
Photo courtesy of State of California Department of Corrections.

Electrified fence
Barrier to prevent inmate escape through electronic punishment or death.

(DOC) activated an electrified fence model at Calipatria State Prison in Imperial County. Since then, another 23 have been installed, one is under construction, and more new prisons with electrified fences are being planned. **Electrified fences** have been installed at adult facilities for men and women throughout California's agricultural areas, foothills, deserts, coastal and urban areas, and a few at higher elevations.

At most of the facilities included in the California Statewide Electrified Fence Project, traditional perimeter guard towers are spaced at distances that allow correctional officers to use deadly force to prevent escapes. At newer facilities, as many as ten towers (or 48.3 staff positions over three watches) can be deactivated. Using lethal fences greatly reduces the need for armed tower staff, for they can stop escapes by killing the inmates.[18]

A SWAT team stands watch outside the cafeteria where inmates were holding prison guards hostage at the Broad River Correctional Institution near Columbia, South Carolina. The inmates released the hostages and then surrendered.
Photo by AP Wide World Photos.

Project Costs and Operational Savings

The construction cost of electrified fences varies depending on the perimeter length and site-specific conditions at each prison. The construction cost typically is within the range of $1 million to $2 million for an individual electrified fence of approximately 8,000 lineal feet. The average cost is approximately $1.5 million. The operational cost savings of the electrified fence project result from the reduced staffing of the prison's guard towers and berm positions, minus the operations and maintenance costs of the fence and the additional roving patrol vehicle. Generally, the cost savings range between $400,000 and $2.1 million per year per prison, with an average operational cost savings of $1.38 million per year each. Therefore, the cost of each fence is recouped within the first or second year. For the fences completed or now under construction, the California DOC expects a system-wide reduction of more than 750 positions for a savings of approximately $40 million per year.

The Military Model

The need for an organized and effective custody and control force in jails and prisons has instilled a paramilitary flavor in most security staffs. The adoption of militaristic organizational structures and procedures early in corrections history made it easier to train a force with limited background to do a specific job. The **paramilitary model** is seen in the uniforms, titles, and procedures of custody personnel. Training is directed to the mission of security, and there is little emphasis on interaction with inmates. The model of the aloof but efficient guard has emerged, and the hiring of custody personnel until very recently was rarely based on the applicant's ability to work with people. The shift to unit management and new-generation prisons (see following discussion) has shifted prehire qualifications, and potential officers are increasingly being hired for their "human-skills" qualifications. To a great extent, correctional hiring practices have inhibited those people who can best fulfill the newer mission of rehabilitation. The seniority system and the growing power of correctional officer unions still often discourage the infusion of custody personnel with higher education in the behavioral sciences.

To provide the best entry-level personnel, and to maintain a level of quality and growth in their staff, many jurisdictions have established rigid training standards along the lines recommended by the American Correctional Association. Such requirements will ensure that all staff are eventually exposed to methods that are not simply "more of the same." To reflect the population in institutions, personnel should actively recruit from minority groups, women, young persons, and prospective indigenous workers and see that employment announcements reach those groups and the general public.

It is useful to conduct a task analysis of each correctional position (to be updated periodically) to determine the tasks, skills, and qualities needed. Hands-on testing based solely on relevant features, to ensure that proper qualifications are considered for each position, helps the administrator determine what is needed and can be provided by training. Those procedures will lead to an open system of selection in which any testing device is related to a specific job and is a practical test of a person's ability to perform, at an acceptable standard, the tasks identified for that job. Professionalization of corrections will continue well into this century, in part because it lowers the potential for a successful lawsuit.

These are a few of the steps that might help span the currently large communication gap between keepers and the kept. Correctional officers and custody staff spend more time with the inmate population than does anyone else in the institution. They should relate well to others because they can be the most positive agents of change in that corrections subsystem. They can also destroy any efforts toward change attempted by a treatment staff that tries to bypass them. A further move away from the military/police image to the correctional image is critical to effective change in the institutional setting.

key term

Paramilitary model
Organization of custody staff into ranks of armed forces.

class activity

Ask students what is meant by *compartmentalization*, and how its occurrence can be minimized.

class activity

Describe an unsuccessful inmate assault on a correctional officer and then ask students to develop an ideal process for responding to the assault.

Glass-Topped Cells for Violent Inmates

Surveillance of violent inmates in jails and prisons can be both dangerous and dirty. Even local jails using direct supervision experience frequent officer assault by violent inmates. When confined to their cells, these inmates routinely throw feces, urine, and other bodily fluids at officers.

Some incarceration facilities are considering glass ceilings over special management unit cells for violent offenders, allowing the officers to walk on the glass ceiling, where they can observe and check on every movement of violent inmates, yet not come into direct contact with them.

UNIT TEAM AND OTHER METHODS TO AVOID COMPARTMENTALIZATION

With regard to ongoing conflicts between custody and security, a few final comments seem appropriate to show the student the situation is not hopeless. Many institutions already adhere to these concepts, and only the overcrowding, prison gangs, and violence are keeping progress in the slow lane.

First, policies should be developed jointly to define the relationships between critical custody and security functions. All staff must be involved in meeting rehabilitative program goals and custody needs for their institutions. The obvious dichotomy between custody and treatment must be erased and greater recognition given to the fact that each is supportive of the other. This kind of activity has been instituted in many institutions as **unit team management,** in which all members of the team of a given cell block, tank, pod, or wing work as a team to provide custody, support, and rehabilitative services in a single coordinated package.

Second, policies and guidelines for institutional rules and regulations should be developed and all present rules and regulations revised to ensure that the demands of security do not negate the objectives of treatment. In policy formation and in specific rules, the principle of clear and present danger should apply; if the regulation is required for the safety of the institutional community, it should be kept. If not, it should be abolished.

Third, in cases where force has been used on an inmate, videotaping of the extraction or other safety procedures should be conducted. When possible, a command officer should be present, and a medical examination of the inmate undertaken. In addition, an investigation by the institution and/or an outside agency, resulting in a written report, should routinely be conducted, and that report should include information from the prison physician and by the inmate. Finally, the correctional authority should respond to requests from families that they be permitted to visit and see inmates if they believe excessive force has been used against them. If they desire an outside physician to examine prisoners, their request should be granted without delay, in accordance with rules to be promulgated by the correctional authority. Copies of all "Use of Force" reports should be filed with the correctional authority and be made available for inspection by the inmate's family, attorney, and, with the inmate's written permission, other appropriate people.

UPGRADING CORRECTIONAL PERSONNEL

The most important rehabilitative tool is the impact of one person on another. Thus, a primary goal for the correctional system is the recruitment, training, and retention of employees who are able—physically, emotionally, educationally, and motivationally—to work as a team. In the correctional system, including the nation's prisons and jails, it is hard to hire or keep qualified personnel. There are few reasons for the correctional officer and jailer to complain about salaries in the field. The national average entry-level starting pay of about $25,000 is not bad when one considers that the current minimum qualifications for applicants is usually only a high school diploma or equivalent (GED) and no criminal record.

But even now, in the twenty-first century, some jail and prison jobs go begging. This will make young people interested in possibly seeking jail and prison custody jobs more difficult to hire as they compete in a growing economy. Because of the persistent problem of unfilled slots on most shifts, supervisors ask officers on duty to work another shift (work "doubles"). That situation leads to overtired staff and high overtime budgets, but legislators are seldom willing to increase expenditures for staff. They fear that correctional officers are just padding the rolls, or perhaps are trying to avoid the costs of providing fringe benefits to more employees. Yet the fact is that prisons need a certain number of officers on duty at all times: "minimum critical staffing." Many administrators have tried to implement this concept, but budget needs still seem to override attempts at rationalizing staffing patterns.[19]

Perhaps more important than salary is the custody employees' sense of public rejection, reinforced in some institutions by the belief (whether true or false) that the administrators and professional staff do not consult them, treat them fairly, or care what they think.[20] New channels of communication must be opened between administrators and employees, as well as between employees and inmates. Administrators should meet with staff to discuss employee problems; custodial and treatment staff should also meet together. Those meetings should be regularly scheduled and formally integrated into institutional procedures.

Summary

Even though the official policy of the institution may be humane, the people who are in direct contact with the inmates may have an entirely different view of their role, which sometimes leads to degrading and even brutal treatment of inmates. Recruitment and hiring standards, practices, and procedures have not established sufficiently high educational or personality standards for the position of corrections officer in every state. Salaries authorized by most legislatures for custodial personnel, while improving, are not yet high enough to attract and retain treatment-minded persons with high levels of education. It speaks well for today's correctional personnel that relatively few have been identified as brutal persons and excessive force litigation is rare. The nature of the situation, however, lends itself to individual expressions of punitiveness.

All involved in corrections recognize that custody and security are necessary but are not the only correctional goals. The next chapter deals with management and treatment functions as the other essential components of prison and jail operations.

Key Words

bureaucratic control, 132

custody, 133

general population, 133

graduated release, 133

correctional officers, 134

"screws," 135

unionization, 137

"blue flu," 137

total institution, 138

prisonization, 138

lockdowns, 139

count, 141

sally port, 141

prison rules, 142

contraband, 144

frisk search, 145

strip search, 146

"keester," 146

shakedown, 146

escape, 147

electrified fence, 148

paramilitary model, 149

unit team management, 150

Review Questions

1. What is the primary focus of the bureaucratic style of prison management?
2. Where have prison guards been obtained from in the past? How does this situation create problems?
3. Why has the military model been so popular in the prisons?
4. Why do disciplinary and security considerations so greatly affect treatment programs? How can that issue be resolved?
5. What are the effects of imprisonment on inmates? Staff?
6. In what ways have the roles and positions of correctional officers improved during the last two decades?
7. What are the problems with prison gangs? What is their makeup?
8. What have been the effects of institutional threat gangs on the operations of corrections facilities?
9. Give a description of unit team management. How does it work?
10. Discuss the effects of a prison escape.
11. How can management and staff work toward making prison work more rewarding?
12. Does the use of the electric fence around the prison perimeter equate to the death penalty for attempting to escape from prison?

Endnotes

1. Clifford English, "The Impact of the Indeterminate Sentence on an Institutional Social System," *Journal of Offender Counseling, Services and Rehabilitation* 8:1/2 (1983): 69–82; and Victor Hassine, *Life without Parole* (New York: Cambridge University Press, 2008).
2. Michael Vaughn and C. Morrissey, "Violence in Confinement," *Journal of Offender Rehabilitation* 25:1/2 (1997): 21–42; Rosemary Gido (ed.), "Evaluation of the Concepts of Correctional Organization and Organizational Change," *Criminal Justice Policy Review* 9:1 (1998): 1–139; and Frank Marcell, "Security Threat Groups' Effect on Corrections during the Past Decade," *Corrections Today* 68:2 (2006): 56–59.
3. Research on prison wardens and superintendents is minimal. The major professional organization is the North American Association of Wardens and Superintendents, C/O Arthur Leonardo, P.O. Box 11037, Albany, NY 12211-0037). See also Christopher Hensley and Richard Tewksbury, "Wardens' Perception of Prison Sex" *The Prison Journal 85:2* (2005): 186–197.
4. Extrapolated from Camille Camp and George Camp, *The Correctional Yearbook 2000: Adult Corrections* (Middletown, CT: Criminal Justice Institute, 2000), p. 140.
5. Camp and Camp, *The Correctional Yearbook 2000,* p. 134.
6. Dennis J. Stevens, "Correctional Officer Attitudes: Job Satisfaction Levels Linked to Length of Employment," *Corrections Compendium* 23:7 (1998): 19–20.
7. Correctional officers have gone on strike in Washington State and in institutions in the Ohio State system. When that happens, administrative personnel or state police are required temporarily to fill the correctional officers' posts. Although police strikes have been found to have a limited impact on the rates of reported crime, little is known about institutional disturbances and rule violations in prison when correctional officers strike.
8. Donald Clemmer, *The Prison Community* (New York: Rinehart, 1940); Anthony Scacco, *Rape in Prison* (Springfield, IL: Chas. C Thomas, 1975); and Hassine, *Life without Parole.* For a depiction of girls in gangs, see Mars Eghigian and Katherine Kirby, "Girls in Gangs: On the Rise in America," *Corrections Today* 68:2 (2006): 48–53.
9. See David Shichor and Harry Allen, "Correctional Efforts in the Educated Society: The Case of Study Release," *Lambda Alpha Epsilon* 39 (June 1976): 18–24. See also Jon Sorenson, R. Wrinkle, and A. Gutierrez, "Patterns of Rule Violating Behaviors and Adjustments to Incarceration among Murderers," *Prison Journal* 78:3 (1998): 222–231; and South Carolina Senate, Budget Proviso Codification Act [educational furlough], http://www.scstatehouse.net/sess117_2007-2008/prever/530_20080605.htm (accessed October 30, 2008).
10. Shichor and Allen, "Correctional Efforts," p. 21. See also Judith Clark, "The Impact of Prison Environment on Mothers," *Prison Journal* 75:3 (1995): 306–329.
11. Peter Nacci and Thomas Kane, "Sex and Sexual Aggression in Federal Prisons: Inmate Involvement and Employee Impact," *Federal Probation* 47:4 (1983): 31–36; Florida House of Representatives Committee on Corrections, "Corrections Officers: Turnover, Security and Safety" (Tallahassee, FL: FHRCC, 1996); "A Lockdown Is in Effect at the Pueblo County Jail," http://certops.com/certops/news/May060501.html (accessed May 8, 2005); and Allen Beck and Paige Harrison, *Sexual Victimization in State and Federal*

Prisons Reported by Inmates, 2007 (Washington, DC: Bureau of Justice Statistics, 2008).

12. Peter Nacci, Kevin Jackson, and Karry Cothorn (eds.), "The Future of Automation and Technology," *Corrections Today* 57:4 (1995): 66–120 (theme issue); and Kevin Jackson, F. Roesel, T. Roy, et al., "Technology and Society," *Corrections Today* 60:4 (1998): 58–96 (theme issue).

13. Michael Reisig, "Rates of Disorder in Higher-Custody State Prisons," *Crime and Delinquency* 44:2 (1998): 229–244.

14. Camp and Camp, *The Corrections Yearbook 2000,* p. 148.

15. Stephen Walters, "Changing the Guard," *Journal of Rehabilitation* 20:1/2 (1993): 46–60; and Mark Pogrebin and E. Poole, "Sex, Gender and Work," in Jeffrey Ulmer (ed.), *Sociology of Crime, Law and Society* (Stamford, CT: JAI Press, 1998), pp. 105–126.

16. American Correctional Association, *2007 Directory* (Lanham, MD: ACA, 2007), p. 58–61.

17. James Lyons, *Inmate Escape Incidents 1992–1996* (Albany, NY: Department of Correctional Services, 1997); and Centre for Research Evaluation and Social Assessment, *Escape Prisoners: Inside Views of the Reasons for Prison Escapes* (Wellington: New Zealand Ministry of Justice, 1996).

18. Brian Hoffman, Gary Straughn, Jack Richardson, and Allen Randall, "California Electrified Fences: A New Concept in Prison Security," *Corrections Today* 58:4 (1996): 66–68.

19. John Shuiteman, "Playing the Numbers Game: Analysis Can Help Determine Manpower Requirements," *Corrections Today* 49:1 (1987): 40–42. See also Henry Steadman, S. Steadman, and D. Dennis, "A National Survey of Jail Diversion Programs for Mentally Ill Inmates," *Hospital and Community Psychiatry* 45:11 (1994): 1109–1113; and Marcus Nieto, *Health Care for California State Prisoners* (Sacramento: California Research Bureau, California State Library, 1998).

20. Frances Cheek and Marie De Stefano Miller, "Reducing Staff and Inmate Stress," *Corrections Today* 44:5 (1982): 72–76, 78. See also John T. Super, T. H. Blau, B. Charles, et al., "Using Psychological Tests to Discriminate Between 'Best' and 'Least Best' Correctional Officers," *Journal of Criminal Justice* 21:2 (1993): 143–150; and Stevens, "Correctional Officer Attitudes."

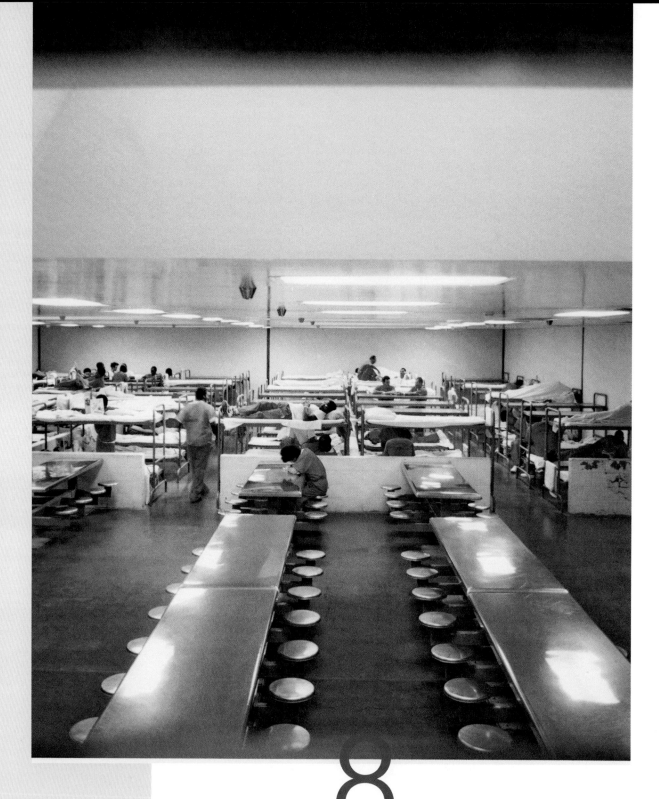

chapter 8

Management and Treatment Functions

Outline

The Treatment Model

Perceptions and Correctional Management

Classification for Security and Treatment

Treatment in Prison
- Health and Medical Services
- Smoking
- Religious Assistance and Services
- Educational and Training Programs for Inmates

The Vocational-Rehabilitation Model

The Reintegration Model

Overview

In the last chapter, we focused attention on such custody issues as contraband, security, personnel, custody, and discipline. These issues are, understandably, the dominant concerns of correctional administrators and their management staff, and they consume great amounts of administrative time as well as large fiscal allocations by state or local correctional institutions. That led us to explore the development of management styles in corrections and the application of those styles to the major strategic processes of corrections—custody and treatment. Custody was seen as having a long history of a bureaucratic style of management.

Above all, corrections and correctional institutions are a product of the people's will and legislative action to resolve a perceived problem in society. The early prisons and penitentiaries had no problem with the "lock 'em up" wishes of society. In the twentieth century, however, we have been struggling to determine just what we really want to do with, to, or for our offenders. As noted in Chapter 3, this "model muddle" continues to be a problem for the correctional administrator. As a manager, the correctional leader must contend with staff members who are typically bifurcated into those who are mainly concerned with security and custody and those who are concerned with programs and treatment. As we progress through the second decade of the twenty-first century, we need to understand the problems faced by administrators who are required to accomplish both goals while dealing with overcrowding, budget cuts, a changing clientele, and various other issues. As discussed in Chapter 7, custody's primary role is to protect society. Treatment efforts attempt to return inmates to society prepared to serve it in a humane fashion. Treatment leads to lowered recidivism and thus enhanced public safety.

Living within the prisons but seldom part of the management and administrative components are the inmates, who are involuntarily sentenced to prison facilities and, for the most part, eager to be released. In the better prison systems, inmates receive humane treatment and handling designed to prepare them for their eventual return to society. For most inmates, however, the demands of custody and the philosophical orientations of administrators and staff will mean restriction or denial of treatment opportunities. This chapter deals with the current status of treatment programs and policies designed to reduce criminal inclinations and tendencies while strengthening motivations to adopt law-abiding behavior.

"Recently published evaluative studies [of prison-based therapeutic communities involving drug-abusing inmates] show remarkably consistent reductions in recidivism for offenders who complete the programs."

—Douglas S. Lipton

THE TREATMENT MODEL

Treatment services generally include vocational training, education, counseling, teaching, casework, religious activities, therapeutic communities, peer counseling, and clinical activity, and are believed to play a significant role in offender rehabilitation.[1] In the past, especially in the larger institutions, the allocation of resources and personnel for treatment bore little, if any, relation to that assumed significance. As a national average, the resources allocated for **treatment services** amounted to only about 10% of the expenditures of the institutional staffs.

Part of the disproportionate allocation of resources results from a basic difference in nature between treatment and custody operations. Staff on the custody side must work 24 hours a day, 7 days a week, 365 days a year. Prisons do not close in observation of national or religious holidays. Furthermore, some inmates are mobile within the correctional facility at all hours of the day or night; inmate-to-inmate violence occurs hourly; and there is never silence in the general population, regardless of the hour.

Treatment staff members, on the other hand, usually work only eight hours a day, five days a week, and have holidays, vacations, and weekends off. When a custody officer is sick or takes vacation, he or she must be replaced (the common term is **backfilled**) by another corrections officer. This often requires someone working overtime, but will be done because minimum critical staffing must be maintained to protect the public. That protection is still the primary mission of corrections. When treatment staff members are sick or take vacation, their position usually goes unfilled until they return to work. Because each 24-hour post requires 5.4 to 5.6 full-time staff, the ratio will always seem heavily weighted toward custody staff.

In the entire corrections system, a very small percentage of institutional personnel are employed in social work or psychological services, and the number of psychiatrists in corrections is infinitesimal. Diagnostic workups and testing processes tend to consume the workday of those involved in these services. Also, some treatment personnel must often spend long hours sitting on disciplinary hearing courts, classification and reclassification committees, and honor placement committees, leaving little time to spend on ongoing treatment with inmates. For example, group psychotherapists in the nation's prisons for men spend about one-third of their time providing individual psychotherapy and less than 30% of their time providing group therapy.[2] In addition, correctional administrators and the treatment staff frequently have to contend with the deeply ingrained antagonism of the staff members who are primarily oriented toward custody, security, and maintenance of calm.[3]

Only in recent times has the associate superintendent or deputy warden for treatment been selected from candidates with training in the social sciences, rather than through the promotion of a faithful custody supervisor. This is important, because the typical rank-and-file custody person was usually not someone who had earned the job through training and education, but through experience and staying out of trouble. Thus, a person with a high school education (or less) was often placed over psychiatrists, psychologists, medical doctors and nurses, social workers, and educators who possessed far more academic credentials. Understandably, those roles created many problems as treatment became more important.

PERCEPTIONS AND CORRECTIONAL MANAGEMENT

Three pervasive themes have run through correctional management. First, the goals of restraint and reformation have helped reinforce correctional administrators' perceptions of offenders as morally, psychologically, physically, and educationally inferior human beings who must be upgraded and, in the meantime, controlled. As a result of that perception, correctional administrators focused the resources at their command primarily on the individual offender. Because the offender was the principal target of organizational activity, little effort was made to mobilize and co-opt community resources, a function that is the very essence of the reintegration model of correctional intervention. That management posture has many consequences, such as the division of offenders into caseloads for purposes of treatment and supervision; recruitment of varied specialists (therapists) whose efforts are seldom coordinated; and, as we mentioned earlier, the scarcity of well-conceived efforts to work cooperatively with such community institutions as the schools, employment services, and neighborhood centers.

A second persistent attribute of correctional management has been a **gradualism approach** to program development and change. This approach has been characterized by a somewhat frivolous subscription to "new" ideas (such as boot camps) and generally nonrigorous, nonscientific rules of thumb for determining what to delete from the old system and what to add to it. The predominant conservatism of system managers has militated against deviations from familiar ways, has encouraged the avoidance of risk, and has led to tokenism in the launching of new measures.

Correctional administrators are not so much responsible for that condition as they are victims of two realities: society's uncertainty about the causes of and solutions to the crime problem and, until recently, the inability of social science and research to provide a solid frame of reference for considering alternative courses of action and estimating their consequences.[4] Nevertheless, in any effort to understand how correctional executives might be effective innovators, it is necessary to confront the difficulties and frustration that currently surround the process of change.

It is important to note the numerous examples of change in correctional organization and programming that run counter to the general pattern we have described.[5] Some experimental programs have been firmly supported by theoretical premises and have been evaluated objectively. The use of meta-analysis, a recent development in detecting the effectiveness of programs in reducing recidivism, has provided substantial evidence that demonstrates how certain programs (such as education, anger management, vocational training, and cognitive therapies) reduce criminal reoffending after parole. It is that growing edge of innovation, of improved dissemination of knowledge, and of close connection between discovery and implementation of technique that offers hope for more treatment gains in the near future.

The third and final theme, which has its roots in the prison culture of the past and still runs through correctional management today, is the syndrome of **isolationism and withdrawal.** That condition has helped conceal from the public the realities of life in institutions and probation and parole agencies, and has thus acted to perpetuate stereotypes and myths. Prisons, after all, were designed and located to keep criminals out of the sight and mind of the larger populace. Prison administrators found it expedient to honor that mandate. When community-based correctional programs gingerly sought to gain a foothold, their managers seemed intuitively to avoid exposure to public scrutiny and judgment. Whereas the police tend to publicize aggressively their views of crime and punishment, the leaders of corrections tend to avoid public debate, particularly debate centering on controversial issues,[6] although former (and even current) prisoners have been more active in this area.

That tendency has had serious consequences. The correctional field has had little success in developing public understanding and support for needed changes. Simplistic or erroneous conceptions of the nature of crime and its treatment have flourished, partly because of the lack of effective spokespeople for more sophisticated interpretations, especially at times of "opportunity" when conflict or crisis have awakened the interest of an otherwise apathetic public.[7]

Unionized correctional staffs have, in some states, developed effective political action groups whose financial contributions have often influenced politicians into adopting a "hard line" in sentencing and construction of more prisons.

key term

Gradualism approach
A "go-slow" approach to design and implementation of new programs.

class activity
Ask students what implications the treatment model has for the assumptions about the nature of offenders in prison.

class activity
Ask students how management's traditional conservatism has discouraged innovation in treatment programs.

key term

Isolationism and withdrawal
Implementing programs without a systematic, rational scheme.

lecture note
Discuss the tendency of institutional corrections to drift from fad to fad with inadequate indicators of the effectiveness of such programs.

CLASSIFICATION FOR SECURITY AND TREATMENT

key term
Classification
The process of dividing and assigning incoming inmates into meaningful categories for assignment to institutions and programs.

key term
External classification
Process leading managers to assign inmates to an institution.

key term
Internal classification
Process of assigning inmates to types of programs and work and cell locations.

key term
Reclassification
The process by which inmate control and programming are changed.

lecture note
Describe the intake/ classification process in your state or jurisdiction.

class activity
Describe a particular inmate's case and characteristics, and ask students to describe that inmate using both external and internal classification. If the inmate is "low risk" and "high need," ask students to identify a treatment plan that would address those needs.

class activity
Challenge students to reclassify the inmate from the previous Class Activity in an annual inmate review and, assuming the inmate has successfully completed some program(s), what next steps should be undertaken to reduce the "high needs."

Classification is the process of dividing an inmate population into manageable groups for custody and treatment purposes. One major goal is to aggregate persons roughly similar on such characteristics as danger, escape potential, need for treatments, gang affiliation, and so on. The similar groups can then be assigned to custody level and treatment programs. Dividing inmates into groups to be assigned to various prison facilities is known as **external classification.** Inmates can then be assigned to various housing or cell units, work assignments, and programming based on an inmate's perceived level of risk (aggressiveness, violence, escape potential), treatment needs, and time to be served. This latter process is called **internal classification.** Both classification processes typically occur at the receiving institution, such as a reception and classification center, or prison intake unit. Over the passage of time and based on the inmate's record, inmate assignments may be (and most routinely are) reviewed and **reclassification** may be undertaken. Most state prisoner reclassification occurs at regularly scheduled intervals, such as every 12 months during the inmate's annual review.

Classification is a relatively recent management innovation in corrections and can be found more often in probation and parole supervision situations than in jail and prison facilities. The classification process can frequently intensify the conflict between treatment and custody staff if it is not carefully handled. In most correctional classification processes (either at the individual institution or at a central classification facility), concern lies more with the danger the new inmates might present to the institution than with the possibility that they might respond to treatment. As a result, new inmates are often assigned to higher custody grades than their backgrounds warrant, until they can prove themselves. This security-oriented concept of classification often excludes inmates from participation in programs that could lead to their rehabilitation. Their early treatment, in fact, may be restricted to health care, an essential program because most offenders are in poor physical condition when they enter the institution.

There are advantages to classification. First, classification will assign dangerous or aggressive inmates to a high-security institution, thus increasing prison security by lessening tensions in prison. It will also avoid misclassification of most inmates, as correctional staff members have a tendency to classify inmates into higher custody facilities than might be necessary, ineffectively expending valuable resources and creating inmate resentment. Finally, a good classification system (such as the Adult Internal Management System or AIMS, and behavior-based systems or BBSs) more likely correctly places inmates and contributes significantly to the deployment of staff.

TREATMENT IN PRISON

The treatment model for corrections is seen in the three basic services first offered to prisoners: religious, medical, and educational. We now examine the development of those services, along with an analysis of some more recent treatment innovations. Much of the public still views any "special programs" for inmates as a form of coddling, and many administrators have responded to this view by rejecting new and promising rehabilitation techniques created by behavioral scientists. Instead, they chose to favor "wars"—against crime, criminals, drugs, ad infinitum—as the easiest way to garner votes from the uninformed and often uncaring public. In fact, the protection of society, not the pampering of offenders, is also the basic reason for treatment and specialized programs in corrections. If at least some of the sources of an individual's criminality can be dealt with before he or she is referred back to the community, or released from aftercare back to the community, corrections should achieve that.

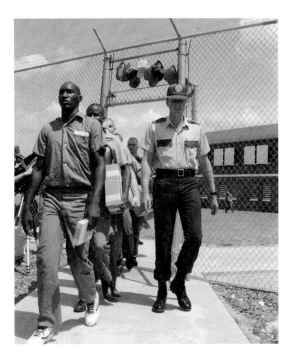

Prison guard walking with inmates at Sumter Correctional Institution, Florida.
Courtesy of Bettmann/Corbis-NY.

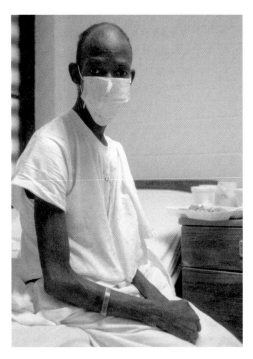

Prisoner with AIDS in isolation room, Hamilton Prison, Alabama.
Photo by A. Ramey, courtesy of PhotoEdit Inc.

The basic services provided by the treatment side of corrections can be combined as health and medical services, religious services, and educational and training programs for inmates. Descriptions of these services and programs follow.

Health and Medical Services

Even in the earliest days of American prisons, certain times were set aside for **sick call.** Of course, the treatment provided was less than one would expect to receive at a clinic in the community. Prisoners often use sick call merely to obtain a brief respite from prison labor or from the dull routine. Time wasted on **goldbrickers** is time the medical staff cannot give to those who really need care. Because the correctional funnel selects out all but the most serious and manipulative offenders, the cream of society does not often end up in prisons; therefore, those who are imprisoned usually have numerous medical and dental needs.

Medical services are often a source of inmates' complaints and frequently become a real headache for administrators. In many areas throughout the country, qualified medical personnel are generally in short supply, and that shortage is felt even more acutely in correctional institutions. To supply the total medical care for which an institution is responsible, it is often necessary to combine the services of full-time medical employees, contractual consultants, and available community resources. Even with all those efforts, inmates and the public often tend to look down on any medically trained person who is willing to become involved with a correctional institution. Any doctor who accepts the prison physician's relatively low income and standard of living, it is thought, must have been a failure in the community. Proper medical care is important to the overall rehabilitation effort. Poor diet, drug abuse, a history of inadequate medical attention, and other debilitating conditions are not uncommon among inmates. Once they have been restored to reasonable health, it is often easier to work on the causes behind their problems.[8]

key term

Hepatitis A and B
Viral infections resistant to medical treatments.

key term

Comorbidity
Two or more occurring medical treatment needs for one inmate.

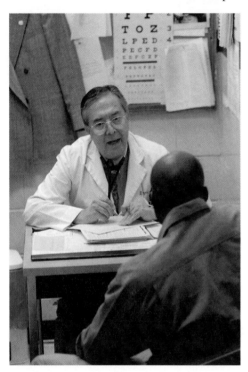

Dr. Fernando Hoyas talks with an inmate at the New Jersey State Correctional Facility in Trenton, New Jersey, about a medical problem.
Photo by AP Wide World Photos.

figure 8.1

Correctional Expenditures in Texas, 2008

Data from: Texas Department of Criminal Justice, 2010–2011, *Goals* (http://www.tdcj.state.tx.us/publications/finance/2010-2011_LAR_Summary_Document.pdf, accessed November 1, 2008).

Major medical problems now commonly faced by jail and prison inmates are **hepatitis A and B,** HIV infection, mental illness, geriatric issues, prenatal care, rubella (measles), and drug-resistant tuberculosis. Drug-dependent inmates,[9] frequent transfers of inmates among facilities, and overcrowded living conditions are conducive to rapid transmission of diseases that could result in epidemics, especially multidrug-resistant tuberculosis. Tuberculosis is easily airborne transmitted, and even dormant carriers can transmit the bacillus. Tuberculosis transmission from inmates to staff has already been documented. And staff could spread the infection to family and friends (tertiary infection), bringing this serious disease into the outside community. Inmates and staff should have tuberculin skin tests on a routine basis,[10] because the incidence of the disease has increased dramatically.[11] Treatment of prisoner health problems is expensive; $1 of every $8 spent on prisoners in Texas is for medical care (see Figure 8.1).

As early as 1988, it was recognized that about 80% of all state prison inmates had been serious alcohol and drug abusers. More than three in four state inmates and almost 70% of federal prisoners and jail inmates had used drugs regularly in the month preceding arrest. Furthermore, substance-abusing inmates were more likely to be repeatedly reimprisoned. From 1980 until 2006, drug-law violators accounted for at least 30% of the growth in the number of imprisoned felons, two-thirds of the increase in federal prisoners, and more than 40% of the jail populations.

In addition to drug and alcohol problems, inmates also have a number of other problems and risk factors that must be addressed. These include lack of employment, bad companions, antisocial attitudes, emotional problems, mental illness, and lack of education.

Drug use has been found to predict subsequent violent behavior among both females and males. When substance abuse occurs among persons with psychopathological problems (**comorbidity**), there is a stronger correlation with subsequent violent behavior among females. One study of probationers undergoing mandatory substance abuse treatment in a residential facility found that 80% of the sample had psychopathological problems, more than 70% had drug-abuse problems, and almost six in ten had concurrent drug abuse and psychopathological problems (comorbidity). Furthermore, prison inmates with both drug abuse and psychopathological problems engaged in more frequent preadmission illegal behaviors,

AIDS prisoners conducting their own AIDS-awareness course, Limestone Correctional Facility, Alabama.
Photo courtesy of AP Wide World Photos.

had more extensive social impairments, and were found to have *higher* motivation for treatment. Female inmates are even more impacted by co-occurring conditions and higher needs (see Chapter 17).

In 2007, an estimated one-third of state and federal prison inmates reported having a physical impairment or mental condition. More than three in ten state inmates and one in four federal inmates reported having a learning or speech disability, a hearing or vision problem, or a mental or physical condition. About one in five of all inmates said they had been injured in an accident since admission. The longer the period of incarceration, the more likely the inmate was to report an injury.

About one in five inmates reported a medical condition that limits their ability to work. On the federal level, the medical conditions of record were high blood pressure (8%), poor mental health (5%), asthma and diabetes (4% each), heart problems (3%), and HIV/AIDS (1%). Medical problems were more common among inmates who had used a needle to inject drugs (one in three inmates) and those who were alcohol dependent (38% of inmates). Much time and resources are needed to meet the minimal health needs and mandatory medical care.[12] Information on participation in educational programs can be found in Figure 8.2.

Another major service for the offender is found in the dental clinic, because most prisoners have very bad teeth. Even in an institution fortunate enough to have good dental care facilities, dental service can take many months because prisoners' teeth have often suffered from long neglect and need extensive work. The effects of dental treatment are similar to those of plastic surgery: Improved appearance enhances the offender's feelings of confidence and well-being, and he or she may be relieved of chronic pain and irritation as well.

Smoking

Smoking in confinement facilities has become a major issue in corrections, primarily due to related medical treatment, lawsuits, and service costs. Prisoners in the United States are twice as likely to smoke than other residents. In Canada, the estimate is 50% more (three times more likely). Secondhand smoke is described as almost as dangerous to the nonsmoker as smoking is to the smoker. The rates of nicotine addiction are high, yet tobacco is and has been an important part of prison culture.[13]

class activity

Ask students to determine what *quality* of medical treatment must be provided and inmate avenues for redress when the quality is inadequate.

class activity

Ask students what inmate medical history problems pose challenges to prison administrators.

class activity

Ask students to develop a policy for handling HIV-infected inmates in prison.

class activity

Ask students to describe five common medical needs of prison inmates.

lecture note

Point out that inmates have a constitutional right to receive medical attention, as they cannot secure it on the outside. The state thus has a *ministerial duty* to provide adequate medical treatment.

lecture note

Explain the *costs* associated with delivery of medical services, and the implications of an aging population on costs in the future.

class activity

Organize a class debate on this statement: No one should be allowed to receive discretionary parole until demonstrating they are functionally literate.

class activity

Ask students to identify prison industries and products, and show how prison industries can lead to lowered recidivism.

class activity

Ask students to identify those forces and elements that reduce the potential for prison industries to ease the inmate's reentry.

Correctional systems also face significant danger of class-action and constitutional-issue lawsuits. Inmates have been suing over the degree of risk they face when others smoke. Prison staff members are also vulnerable to secondhand smoke, and both lawsuits and union pressures for better working conditions are frequent. Prisoners, inmates, and visitors must be protected from the dangers of secondhand smoke.

Across the nation, most states have restricted smoking to designated open-air spaces, or have implemented total institutional bans. West Virginia, Iowa, and Canada have recently banned smoking outright. Canada forbids both tobacco within the institution and staff smoking anywhere on the prison grounds while at work. The Federal Bureau of Prisons has been smoke-free since 2004.

Nicotine withdrawal leads to significant psychological and physical symptoms. Administrators have implemented a wide variety of strategies to enforce a smoking ban while not letting inmates withdraw "cold-turkey." Both inmates and staff have been given large lead times so they can prepare for the ban, mostly through reducing cigarettes over a year.[14] Also provided across the nation are:

- Gradually increasing the number of the facility's areas with smoking bans
- Smoking cessation classes
- Reprimanding or sanctioning staff for smuggling tobacco into a facility
- Offering counseling therapies
- Providing nonsmoking tools such as nicotine patches and gum[15]
- Transferring repeat inmates to higher-custody facilities

Smuggling of tobacco into facilities (by some visitors and staff) is highly lucrative. One pencil-lead-thin self-rolled cigarette can sell for $12 to $15, perhaps ever higher in certain institutions. Inmates receiving a 6-ounce bag of tobacco can easily earn $3,000 per bag. Staff in many institutions can sell cigarettes to inmates, at comparable profit margins.

Resistance to smoking bans can be stiff, and lawsuits should be expected. Issues are "cruel and unusual punishment" and violation of rights, although inmates can become quite innovative in protest actions (including riots and attacks on staff). Thus far, state supreme courts (and circuit courts) have generally backed prison administrators in their banning efforts.

Perhaps the clearest policy can be found in Canadian prisons, where inmate smoking is banned at all institutions. Staff may not smoke while on duty, cannot bring cigarettes into prisons, cannot smoke on campus, and must keep all personal tobacco products in a locked container (such as a glove compartment) in their vehicles while at work.[16]

Religious Assistance and Services

From 1790 until today, one service that has traditionally been available to the incarcerated felon is religious assistance and guidance. Solitary meditation in the Walnut Street Jail was intended to make offenders realize the error of their sinful ways and make them penitent. Penitence was often encouraged by visits from local ministers and priests. Later, the large institutions of the early 1800s created the need for a full-time chaplain on the premises.

key term

Correctional chaplaincy
A program of recruiting clergy who minister to the religious needs of inmates.

The **correctional chaplaincy** has been and is currently the least-sought-after position among ministers, who evidently prefer to serve more conventional congregations. Part of the problem, too, is the remote location of most prisons and a widespread public belief (shared by many administrators) that religion in prisons should be confined to the chaplain's traditional duties. Not well known by the public is the range of services, types of counseling, guidance, and innovation offered by chaplains within prisons.[17] A movement has sprung up to establish a core of clinically oriented clerics, but the correctional field is less attractive to them than are other kinds of institutions. There is a definite need to upgrade the role of the correctional chaplain to attract the best into the institutions. The role of the chief chaplain can be enhanced if it becomes accredited by the Association for Clinical Pastoral Education. With that background, the chaplain can develop programs, recruit and train chaplaincy candidates, and even use seminary students to augment his or her resources.

prevented from attending classes for disciplinary reasons may miss enough to be required to forgo the rest of the term. Denying education as part of disciplinary action devalues its effectiveness as a treatment component and doubles the punishment factor.

The classes held in some institutions are conventional and relatively old fashioned, in contrast with those that use the new learning technologies and innovations available to students at all levels on the outside. Yet educators are making considerable headway with computer technology and rapid change is under way. Most prisoners have had little formal education and probably resisted whatever teaching they were exposed to. Material that bored them as children or truant teenagers is not likely to hold them enthralled as adults. What mature felons neither want nor need are "Dick and Jane" readers or other textbooks designed for children. Inmates may be actually or functionally illiterate, but they are adults in the main, and are in possession of a lot of street smarts. To be given such materials is embarrassing and difficult for them. But because of the low priority and minimal funds assigned to education in most institutions, useless texts are often provided to prisoners, usually by public schools that no longer use them—small wonder that most prison programs are neither accredited nor enthusiastically supported by inmates. Inmates prefer listening and reading modes for learning.[22] Those with learning disabilities (from 7% to 25% of institutional populations) may respond best to tape recorders, television, and computers.[23]

The surprising fact is that some educational services thrive and contribute to the inmates' rehabilitation.[24] Texas has an education district that covers the entire prison system. In Ohio, the Department of Rehabilitation and Correction also established a complete school district composed entirely of the educational programs within the state prison system. In the states of New York and Washington, education programs are contracted with local community colleges and they provide excellent programs, from adult basic education[25] to degree programs in the institutions. **Project Newgate,** a program bringing the first years of college into the prisons, along with instructors and a complete curriculum, was the model for such programs in the 1970s.

Two other education-related programs that have been attempted, with varying results, are work/training release and educational release (sometimes called **furlough**). Furloughs are release from custody for a discrete and prescribed amount of time for specific reasons, with prior formal authorization by prison authorities. Of the 8,964 furloughs granted in

Inmates ask the teacher a question as they study for the GED examination.
Photo by A. Ramey, courtesy of Photo Edit Inc.

<u>key term</u>

Project Newgate
Prison treatment program stressing full-time college work, group counseling, and aftercare following parole.

<u>key term</u>

Furlough
Program of temporary leave from a prison for educational, work, or emergency purposes.

Inmates at the Hutchins State Jail pray during an Islamic education program.
Jerry Hoefer, AP Wide World Photos

George Trabing, director of the University of Houston-Clear Lake program at the Ramsey I Unit of the Texas Department of Corrections, speaks to inmates taking courses leading to a master's degree.
Photo by AP Wide World Photos.

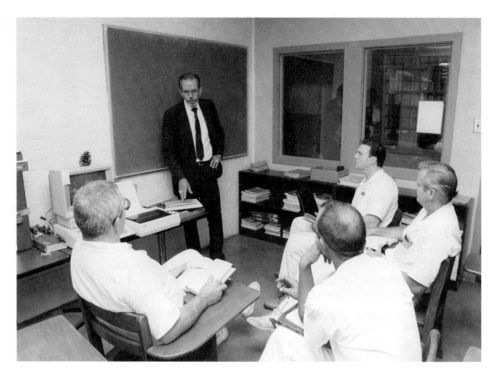

1999, only 44 inmates failed to return or committed another crime, a 0.005% failure rate.[26] In educational release, inmates are allowed to leave the institution to attend college, high school, or vocational-technical schools during the day, though they must return to the institution or an approved site when not at school or at night. The use of educational release became quite widespread in the United States before 1990, but the programs have been somewhat curtailed due to highly visible failures or budget cuts. In the work/training release program, an inmate may be allowed to leave the limits of confinement to secure education and a job; this enables offenders to develop a work history, learn a trade, support dependents, or even make restitution to the victim of their crimes. Forty-two of the fifty states, and both the Federal Bureau of Prisons and the District of Columbia, have work and education release programs. Of the 44,000 participating prisoners in 1999, few were arrested and reconvicted, although a small number were recalled to prison. This high success rate is partially a function of the process by which eligible inmates are selected, and in part a result of the legal status of the participant who remains an inmate, easily returned to prison for nonconformity to rules and regulations.

Education, medical care, and religious practice have served as the basic treatment programs in America's prisons since the days of the Walnut Street Jail. In recent years, this limited three-sided approach to treatment has expanded to include a wide variety of programs aimed at the rehabilitation of incarcerated offenders.

THE VOCATIONAL-REHABILITATION MODEL

Vocational and technical training in prisons has been available to prisoners ever since the industrial prison was established in the early 1800s. That early training, however, was aimed not at prisoner rehabilitation but at institutional profit. Later, at the Elmira Reformatory, the concept of training for the purpose of teaching a trade to ex-offenders was introduced, and it has slowly taken root over the years. A major setback to adequate **vocational training** came with the passage of restrictive federal laws on the interstate transport of prison industry goods. Those laws, passed during the Depression Era, sounded the death knell for many work programs in state prisons. Only in the past 30 years have institutions begun to reemphasize vocational training programs.

Prison industry has continued on a somewhat smaller scope since the restrictive laws were enacted. Prison industry went through several phases, starting at the contract labor level through increasingly more restricted systems. In contract labor, part, if not the whole, of the prison population was rented to private contractors who used their labor for private gain. Next came the piece-price scheme, in which private contractors provided raw materials and paid a set price to the prison for produced items (such as soccer balls). The next phase was the public account system in which the prison became the manufacturer of a product to be sold on the open market, such as twine, bailing wire, bags ("croaker sacks"), and airplane chocks. These efforts failed for a variety of reasons, including prison corruption, union resistance, excessive cruelty, padded budgets, and inordinate up-front costs. The current prison industry system is the state-use system in which prison labor produces items that do not enter the open market and are instead sold to state-run institutions, facilities, and agencies. This includes the ubiquitous license plate manufacture, tables and chairs used in educational institutions, clothing for inmates and mental patients, soap and eggs, and so on. Critics have raised the question of the usefulness of the limited skills learned in prison industry, and have labeled the work by inmates as exploitation of prisoners.

A common problem with prison industries is their multiple goals, for they sometimes shift and are always ambiguous. The prison administrator may believe the goal of prison industries to be generation of profits; shop managers are convinced it is to train inmates; and inmates believe it is "make work" and that they will receive some wage unrelated to productivity.[27] Leadership in resolving those conflicting goals was exerted by Congress in 1979, when it passed the Prison-Industries Enhancement Act, selectively repealing portions of the federal laws limiting prison industries. Since then, more than 20 states (such as Arizona, Minnesota,

key term

Vocational training
Any training program designed to increase job readiness and skills for inmates.

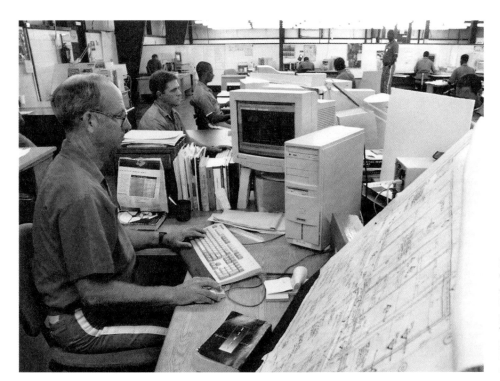

Prisoners at Liberty Correctional Institution work at digitally mapping records of a European utility company as part of PRIDE enterprise's workforce within the state's prison system shown in Bristol, Florida.
Photo by AP Wide World Photos.

correctional **brief**

Literacy and its Impact on Reoffending

The federal prison system established a mandatory literacy program in 1982, requiring sixth-grade reading as the minimum literacy standard. This was changed to eighth-grade reading in 1986, and to a General Education Development (GED) certificate in 1991. The adult basic education program has been very successful when completion rates are compared from 1981 to 1990, which saw an encouraging 724% increase in the number of inmates achieving basic literacy.

Twelve studies on the effects of education on reoffending are also encouraging. One investigator reported on three studies by David Fairchild. On the first, there was only a 15% reoffending rate for New Mexico inmates who had completed at least one year of college, compared to 68% for the general population. Fairchild found zero recidivism for college graduates versus a reoffending rate of 55% for the general prison population studied at a California prison. Finally, Fairchild reported that none of the first 200 Indiana reformatory inmates earning a college degree offered by a university extension program returned to the reformatory.

Consistently favorable outcomes have been linked to education in Canada, where three of four prisoner-students remained free of subsequent incarceration for at least three years. Significantly lower relapse and recidivism rates have been found for education and work release in Delaware, and college education in North Carolina and Georgia.

Adult basic education programs show promise for decreasing recidivism, even for inmates with learning disabilities. Technology education (particularly computers) provides inmates with marketable skills. Studies have concluded that the recidivism rate can be as low as 11% for inmates who successfully complete training, and as high as 70% for those who do not. The National Literacy Trust of the United Kingdom reported a statistically significant connection between repeated offending and poor literacy.

SOURCE: Robert Hall and Mark Bannatyne, "Technology Education and the Convicted Felon," *Journal of Correctional Education* 51:4 (2000): 320–323; and National Literacy Trust, "Links between Reoffending and Literacy, http://www.literacytrust.org.uk/Database/ prisonarchive.html#Young (accessed November 2, 2008).

Washington, and Kansas) have authorized some form of private-sector involvement with state penal industries, such as in the areas of data processing, hotel chain reservations, and manufacturing. Many of those private-industry efforts must deal with insurance, initial plant investment costs, and quality control problems. It remains to be seen how effective private industry will be in collaborating with prisons,[28] but such efforts are welcome signs in times of prison overcrowding.

Inmates take a computer class.
*© John Zich/CORBIS All Rights
Reserved*

Exciting programs working with companies in South Carolina, California, and Connecticut have formed successful projects with state and local correctional agencies. Some positive features of these collaborations include the following:[29]

1. A cost-competitive, motivated workforce that can continue to work after release from prison
2. The proximity of a prison-based feeder plant to the company's regular facility
3. Financial incentives, including low-cost industrial space and an equipment purchase subsidy, that are offered by correctional officials
4. Safe work environment due to the presence of security personnel and a metal detector that keeps weapons out of the shop area
5. The partial return to society of inmate earnings to pay state and federal taxes, offset incarceration costs, contribute to the support of the inmate's families, and compensate victims.

THE REINTEGRATION MODEL

The movement toward treatment and corrections in the community has highlighted the need to make programs inside the walls relate to circumstances in the outside world. Crime cannot be controlled by the reformation of prisoners alone. Efforts at reformation and reintegration into the community must continue.

Toward that end, many of the barriers shutting off prisons from their communities have come down in the last decade. The treatment concept has been expanded to include a variety of inmate treatment programs and models usually discussed in correctional treatment courses. We mention five major offender-based institutional models to illustrate the entry of treatment professionals into the prison system.

Perhaps the most effective of therapies is **cognitive intervention,** an approach that focuses on the ways in which offenders think. Thinking includes a wide array of skills and processes, such as problem-solving skills, the ability to empathize with others and victims, the ability to formulate and then achieve plans for the future, and the ability to foresee the consequences of one's own behavior. For example, hitting a correctional officer on the head with a battery wrapped in a sock ("sucker punch") would be perceived by most inmates as a portent of concerted forcible effort to arrest, possibly punish, but certainly isolate the offender in a punitive segregation cell. **Cognitive** also refers to the beliefs, values, attitudes, and stability we impose on our conception of the world around us. (See Chapter 7). Flowing from this approach are techniques that attempt to influence and change the cognitions of offenders. This is done through role-playing, psychodramas, modeling, and changing of irrational beliefs.

One example of program application to prisoners is **anger management.** Without belaboring the theory, it should be noted that many prisoners are clinically depressed, and depression can generate anger expression (assault, verbal abuse, spousal abuse, and even rape). Anger management focuses on preventing the negative behavior that arises from impulsive hostile aggression by teaching self-awareness, self-control, and alternate thinking and behavior. The therapist may intend to reduce aggressive behavior through activating the offender's self-intervention and management skills. The key is to teach the inmate how to lower arousal levels, use relaxation techniques and thinking controls, communicate feelings, recognize anger, and use coping mechanisms (to "cage the rage").

Other interventional programs in use include guided group interaction, therapeutic communities, and reality therapy. Although these programs have major differences, the primary focus (even in therapeutic communities) is on helping the offender change those thoughts, beliefs, attitudes, and actions that create the potential for and actual criminal behavior. These are almost always preparatory to release back into the community, although therapeutic communities increasingly extend from the institution to the community.

correctional **brief**

Prison Release Programs

Work, occupational training, and education are three major objectives for which inmates are allowed to leave the prison. In most states, the legal mechanism for allowing an inmate to leave prison is the furlough program: The legislature extends the limits of confinement to include placement in the community while the prisoner pursues some common and identifiable correctional goal.

Furlough candidates are usually screened carefully and supervised by an agency. Although the extent of recidivism among furlough users is unknown, it is generally believed to be low. One reason for the low recidivism probably is that furloughees in most jurisdictions remain inmates and can be returned to prison easily if they show overt signs of being unable to conform their behavior to community expectations.

Oklahoma has used home furlough (house arrest of inmates) as a mechanism to reduce prison overcrowding, and the recidivism rate is markedly low. In Massachusetts, furlough participation had a pronounced and consistently positive impact on recidivism. More states are exploring the opportunities of increasing furlough programs to extend the limits of confinement for low-risk inmates, and plan to couple house arrest with electronic monitoring, unscheduled drug and alcohol testing, and supervision fees. This approach may become a major prison-release mechanism in the next decade.

Prison treatment also encompasses the efforts of community-based professionals, and community volunteers have begun to give offenders the support and guidance needed to ensure successful reintegration.[30] The main objective of the **reintegration model** is to return the offender to the community as a responsible and productive citizen, rather than as a feared and shunned "ex-con" with little hope for success. Institutions dedicated to that objective have learned to overcome deficits in funding and personnel by using the ingenuity of prison staff and the resources available in the community. Teachers and graduate students are encouraged to offer courses on topics that will help reintegrate the inmate, including such subjects as social problems, mental health, and the use of community resources.[31]

In many institutions, the barriers are coming down for traffic in both directions ("the door swings both ways"). Outside activity by inmates and prison personnel ranges from touring lecture programs to work and educational furloughs. The latter programs serve as a method of graduated release back to the community.[31] The rationale for graduated release has its roots in the problems faced by the newly released inmate. Release is a very stressful time for inmates, especially when they emerge directly from an institution. Inmates know they have failed in the past and fear they will fail again. Without a chance to ease back into society in stages, as is possible with graduated release, the inmate feels vulnerable if he or she has been inside the walls for a long time. The released prisoner needs new social skills and a chance to catch up with a rapidly moving society.

Summary

Corrections has undergone great change in the years since the emphasis shifted from custody to rehabilitation. Public safety demands that the convicted offender emerge from our correctional system a better person, certainly no worse, than when he or she entered it. That high expectation has stimulated the search for more effective ways to handle offenders. One reason for the pressure to create community-based corrections has been the recognition that prisonization can actually aggravate an offender's criminality.

The future of corrections clearly lies in community-based programs. A major obstacle, however, is the prominence of the institutional model, with its physical plants and other programs already in operation, whereas organized community programs have not yet gained widespread acceptance. While most community programs emerged as demonstration projects or individual experiments, rather than as the products of systematic interaction among police, courts, and conventional correctional services, basic changes are under way. The drug court, discussed in Chapter 6, is just one example of integration of formerly separate components of the justice system.

Incarceration clearly is a series of destructive situations for the offender: The custody model intensifies the likelihood of physical danger, deprivation of human values, and loss of self-esteem. It is a basic humanitarian concept that only offenders who pose a threat to society should be subjected to the trauma of incarceration. This last issue demands, of course, a valid system of diagnosis, classification, and evaluation.

The correctional treatment process has many elements. The key to treatment is an organized program designed to prepare the inmate for successful reintegration within the free society. It is obvious how important the cooperation and understanding of the security and custody staff can be in the success of any of the efforts described as "treatment." As the single most influential agent of change, the correctional officer is the keystone to the success or failure of any kind of treatment program. A cooperative effort by custody and treatment staffs, including the blurring of roles, is the essence of an effective institutional program. But treatment cannot end at the prison gate. To ensure maximum success, the treatment must be continued and reinforced in the community. Community programs are discussed in Chapter 19. Chapters 16 through 19 discuss the variety of clients in corrections, and the challenges each poses for the criminal justice system.

Key Words

treatment services, 156

backfilled, 156

gradualism approach, 157

isolationism and withdrawal, 157

classification, 158

external classification, 158

internal classification, 158

reclassification, 158

sick call, 159

goldbrickers, 159

medical services, 159

hepatitis A and B, 160

comorbidity, 160

correctional chaplaincy, 162

functionally illiterate, 163

GED, 163

Project Newgate, 165

furlough, 165

vocational training, 167

cognitive intervention, 169

cognitive, 169

anger management, 169

reintegration model, 170

Review Questions

1. Why are there more correctional officers than treatment staff?
2. Is classification more properly a security or a treatment function? Why?
3. Define: classification, internal classification, external classification, and reclassification.
4. Explain why corrections in general has so few spokespersons.
5. Describe the roles of the chaplain in prison.
6. What motivates inmates to participate in prison treatment programs?
7. What are five common health problems found in prisons?
8. How are religious services delivered inside prisons?
9. Does education lower recidivism when inmates are paroled?
10. What kinds of inmates are given furloughs?
11. What jobs are available in prisons for staff? Inmates?
12. What can be done to prepare inmates for community reintegration?

Endnotes

1. See Don Gibbons, "Review Essay—Changing Lawbreakers: What Have We Learned Since the 1950s?" *Crime and Delinquency* 45:2 (1999): 272–293; Rolf Loeber and D. Farrington (eds.), *Serious and Violent Juvenile Offenders* (Thousand Oaks, CA: Sage, 1998); Michael Prendergast et al., "Amity Prison-Based Therapeutic Community," *The Prison Journal* 84:1 (2004): 36–60; and Amity Foundation, Amity Experience and Expertise, http://www.amityfdn.org/About%20Amity/ (accessed November 6, 2008).

2. Robert Morgan, C. Winterowd, and S. Ferrell, "A National Survey of Group Psychotherapy Services in Correctional Facilities," *Professional Psychology Research and Practice* 30:6 (1999): 600–606.

3. See Rob Wilson, "Who Will Care for the 'Mad' and the 'Bad'?" *Corrections Magazine* 6:1 (1980): 5–17. See also Joan Petersilia, "Justice for All? Offenders with Mental Retardation and the California Corrections System," *Prison Journal* 77:4 (1998): 358–380; and Glenroy Sinclair, "Prison Sex Scandal," *Jamaica Gleaner,* http://www.jamaica-gleaner.com/gleaner/20060415/lead/lead1.html (accessed November 6, 2008).

4. But see the excellent evaluation of Joan Petersilia, *The Influence of Criminal Justice Research* (Santa Monica, CA: RAND Corporation, 1987); Jeffrey Fagan and M. Forst, "Risk Fixers and Zeal: Implementing Experimental Treatment for Violent Juvenile Offenders," *Prison Journal* 76:1 (1996): 22–59; and Loeber and Farrington, *Serious and Violent Juvenile Offenders.*

5. Francis Cullen and B. Applegate (eds.), *Offender Rehabilitation: Effective Treatment Intervention* (Aldershot, UK: Ashgate, 1997); U.S. Office of Justice Programs Drug Courts Program Office, *Looking at a Decade of Drug Courts* (Washington, DC: U.S. Department of Justice, 1997); and Lorraine Reitzel, "Best Practices in Corrections," *Corrections Today* 67:1 (2005): 42–45, 70.

6. Francis Cullen and K. Gilbert, *Reaffirming Rehabilitation* (Cincinnati, OH: Anderson Publishing, 1982). But see American Correctional Association, *Corrections Issues: Point–Counterpoint* (Lanham, MD: ACA, 1997).

7. See Steve Donziger, *The Real War on Crime* (New York: HarperCollins, 1996), pp. 194–219: John Irwin and J. Austin, *It's about Time,* 2nd ed. (Belmont, CA: Wadsworth, 1997); and Charles Terry, "Managing Prisoners as Problem Populations: The Evolving Nature of Imprisonment: A Convict's Perspective," *Critical Criminology* 12:1 (2003): 43–66.

8. The relationship between ingestion of drugs and crime appears quite strong. See in particular Christopher Mumola, *Substance Abuse and Treatment: State and Federal Prisoners, 1997* (Washington, DC: U.S. Department of Justice, 1999); John Potterat, R. Rothenberg, S. Muth, et al., "Pathways to Prostitution: The Chronology of Sexual and Drug Abuse Milestones," *Journal of Sex Research* 35:4 (998): 330–340; and Craig Rosen, Paige Ouiette, Javaid Sheikh, et al., "Physical and Sexual Abuse History and Addiction Treatment Outcomes," *Journal of Studies on Alcohol* 63:6 (2002): 683–687.

9. Drug abuse is widespread among prison inmates but treatment programs are in short supply. See Donald Dowd, S. Dalzell, and M. Spencer (eds.), "The Sentencing Controversy: Punishment and Policy in the War against Drugs," *Villanova Law Review* 40:2 (1995): 301–427; and James Marquart, V. Brewer, J. Mullings, et al., "The Implications of Crime Control Policy on HIV/AIDS-Related Risk among Women Prisoners," *Crime and Delinquency* 45:1 (1999): 82–98.

10. Theodore Hammett, *Public Health and Corrections Collaboration: Prevention and Treatment of HIV/AIDS, STDs, and TB* (Washington, DC: Office of Justice Programs, 1998).

11. U.S. Department of Health and Human Services, *Control of Tuberculosis in Correctional Facilities: A Guide for Health Care Workers* (Washington, DC: USDHHS, 1992). See also Marcus Nieto, *Health Care in California State Prisons* (Sacramento, CA: California Research Bureau, California State Libraries, 1998); and Kenneth Faiver (ed.), *Health Care Management Issues in Corrections* (Lanham, MD: American Correctional Association, 1998).

12. Bureau of Justice Statistics, *Medical Problems of Inmates, 1997* (Washington, DC: BJS, 2001), p. 1, 12; Sophie Davidson and P. Taylor, "Psychological Distress and Severity of Personality Disorder Symptomatology in Prisoners Convicted of Violent and Sexual Offenses," *Psychology, Crime and the Law* 7:3 (2001): 263–272; Kristen Rasmussen, R. Almvik, and S. Levander, "Attention Deficit Hyperactivity Disorder, Reading Disability, and Personality Disorders in a Prison Population," *Journal of the American Academy of Psychology and the Law* 29:2 (2001): 186–193; and Jack Baillergeon, Sandra Black, Charles Leach, et al., "The Infectious Disease Profile of Texas Prison Inmates," *Preventive Medicine* 38:5 (2004): 607–612.

13. Mannix Porterfield, "Smoking Has Its Problems in W. VA. Prisons," *The Register-Herald* (June 16, 2008), http://www.register-herald.com/archivesearch/local_story_168222359.html (accessed November 1, 2008).

14. William Petroski, "Despite Exemption, Prisons to Ban Smoking," http://m.desmoinesregister.com/news.jsp?key=252368&rc=In&p=2 (accessed November 1, 2008).

15. Editors, *Correctional News,* "Michigan Prisons Prepare for Total Smoking Ban" *Correctional News* 14:3 (2008): p. 18.

16. *CBC New,* "'Tempers Will Flare' as Prison Smoking Ban Takes Effect, Inmate Says," http://www.cbc.ca/health/story/2008/05/05/prison-smoke.html (accessed November 1, 2008).

17. But see Jody Spertzel, "Rev. Henry Bouma: Chaplain's Ministry Links Facility with Community," *Corrections Today* 55:3 (1993): 91; and Jody Sundt and F. Cullen, "The Contemporary Prison Chaplain," *The Prison Journal* 78:3 (1998): 271–298.

18. Robert Marsh and V. Cox, "The Practice of Native-American Spirituality in Prison: A Survey," *Justice Professional* 8:2 (1994): 79–95.

19. Dennis Stephens and C. Ward, "College Education and Recidivism: Educating Criminals Is Meritorious," *Journal of Correctional Education* 48:3 (1997): 106–111.

20. Richard Lawrence, "Classroom v. Prison Cells: Funding Priorities for Education and Corrections," *Journal of Crime and Justice* 18:2 (1995): 113–126; and Elliott Currie, *Crime and Punishment in America: Why the Solutions to America's Most Stubborn Social Crisis Have Not Worked—And What Will* (New York: Metropolitan Books, 1998).

21. James Anderson, J. Burns, and L. Dyson, "Could an Increase in AIDS Cases among Incarcerated Populations Mean More Legal Liabilities for Correctional Administrators?" *Journal of Criminal Justice* 21:1 (1998): 41–52.

22. T. L. Felton, "The Learning Modes of the Incarcerated Population," *Journal of Correctional Education* 4:3 (1994): 118–121; and Theodore Hammett, P. Harmon, and L. Marushak, *1996–1997 Update: HIV/AIDS, STDs, and TB in Correctional Facilities* (Washington, DC: U.S. Department of Justice, 1999), pp. 25–45.

23. Eva Fisher-Bloom, "The Import of Learning Disabilities in Correctional Treatment," *Forum* 7:3 (1995): 20–26; and Barbara Belot and J. Marquart, "The Political Community Model and Prisoner Litigation," *Prison Journal* 78:3 (1998): 299–329.

24. Arnie Nielsen, F. Scarpitti, and J. Inciardi, "Integrating the Therapeutic Community and Work Release for Drug-Abusing Offenders," *Journal of Substance Abuse and Treatment* 13:4 (1996): 349–358. See also Roger Boe, A. Thurber, L. Montiuk, et al. (eds.), "Offender Reintegration," *Forum on Corrections Research* 10:1 (1998): 3–47.

25. See Rick Linden and L. Perry, "The Effectiveness of Prison Educational Programs," *Journal of Offender Counseling, Services and Rehabilitation* 6:1 (1982): 43–57; and Lisa Allen, G. Rondeau, N. Harms, et al. (eds.), "Current Research and Clinical Practice," *Journal of Offender Rehabilitation* 24:3/4 (1997): 101–181.

26. C. Camp and G. Camp, *The Corrections Yearbook 2000: Adult Corrections* (Middletown, CT: Criminal Justice Institute, 2000), pp. 126–129.

27. Neil Singer, *The Value of Inmate Manpower* (Washington, DC: American Bar Association Commission on Correctional Facilities and Manpower, 1973). See also David Scharf, "Are Day Reporting and Reentry Programs the Future of Corrections in Our Country?" *American Jails* 12:3 (2008): 25–27. But see Rose Burton, D. Pens, P. Wright, et al., *The Celling of America: An Inside Look at the U.S. Prison Industry* (Monroe, ME: Common Courage Press, 1998).

28. Betty Fortuin, "Maine's Female Offenders Are Reentering—and Succeeding," *Corrections Today* 69:2 (2007): 34–37; and Bonnie Johnson, "First Book and Hope House: Bridging the Gap for Families from Behind Bars," *Corrections Today* 22:3 (2008): 88–90.

28. Larry Mays and T. Gray (eds.), *Privatization and the Provision of Correctional Services* (Cincinnati, OH: Anderson Publishing, 1996).

29. George Sexton, *Work in American Prisons: Joint Ventures with the Private Sector* (Washington, DC: U.S. Department of Justice, 1995), p. 2.

30. Edward Latessa, L. Travis, and H. Allen, "Volunteers and Paraprofessionals in Parole: Current Practices," *Journal of Offender Counseling, Services and Rehabilitation* 8:1/2 (1983): 91–106; and American Probation and Parole Association, *Restoring Hope through Community Partnerships* (Lexington, KY: APPA, 1996).

31. David Onek, *Pairing College Students with Delinquents: The Minnesota Intensive Case Monitoring Program* (San Francisco: National Council on Crime and Delinquency, 1994); and Pamela Hewitt, E. Moore, and B. Gaulier, "Winning the Battles and the War," *Juvenile and Family Court Journal* 49:1 (1998): 39–49.

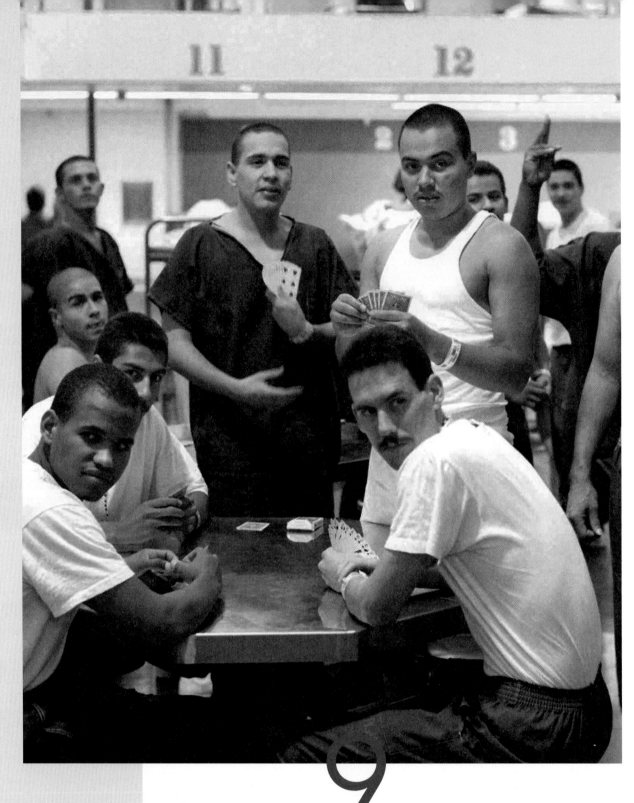

chapter 9

Jails and Detention
Facilities

Outline

". . .more than 11 million people a year are booked into local jails and another 11 million are released from the jails, which is almost comparable to the entire population of Ohio and Illinois."

—Ken Kerle

Overview

Now that we have explored the alternatives and programs designed with offenders at the "front end" of the corrections system, it is time to examine the major forms of imprisonment, starting with jails. The vast majority of offenders begin their journey through the correctional system in a **jail** or detention facility. For some, this is the last stop, whereas for others, it is only the beginning.

This chapter provides an overview of one of the most overused sanctions in the correctional system: the local jail. Clearly our nation has developed many different processes and institutions to meet the primary mission of corrections, that is, to protect society. This chapter takes an in-depth look at local jails and detention centers as the very first step in an often long and winding road, taken in the name of justice. That path will eventually result in most of the offenders returning to society, having paid a debt for crimes committed, large or small. The "scales of justice" attempt to balance the crime and the appropriate punishment, and this process starts with apprehension by the police and booking at a local facility.

As the student will discover, of all the institutions through which offenders pass on their way through the correctional funnel, none has a more diverse population (or a more sordid past) than the jails. Jails are confinement facilities usually operated by a local law enforcement agency, for holding detained persons pending adjudication and/or persons committed after adjudication for less than one year (although there are some exceptions to this practice). The jail is the first institutional contact within the criminal justice system that most accused adult males and females (and many juveniles) experience. Most jails are small, although some are huge. See Figure 9.1. Whether large or small, however, jails are predominantly city, county, or regional facilities, funding for which can be erratic and unpredictable.

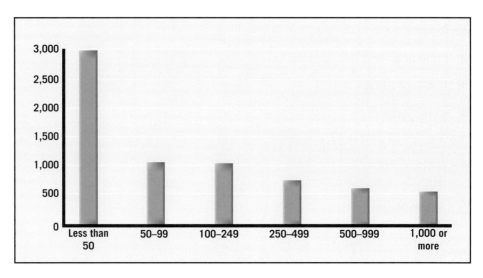

figure 9.1

Number of Jails by Their Rated Capacity, 2007

SOURCE: William Sabol and Todd D. Minton. *Jail Inmates at Midyear 2007* (Bureau of Justice Statistics, Washington, DC: US Dept. of Justice, 2008).

key term

Jail
A local secure facility designed to house offenders, usually for one year or less

JAILS: A GRIM HISTORY

The housing of offenders and suspected criminals in local detention facilities is a practice as old as the definition of crime. The processes and practices at the local gaol, lockup, workhouse, stockade, hulk,[1] or detention center changed little over the centuries, until about the mid-1900s. Only recently has any serious attempt been made to provide programs or treatment for jail inmates, and even those efforts must be carefully monitored or officials are likely to abandon them.[2] Originally devised as a place to lock up and restrain all classes of misfits, the jail has a long and sordid history. As discussed in Chapter 1, John Howard was made keenly aware of the appalling gaol conditions in eighteenth-century England when he found himself the proprietor of one of its worst. His effort to reform the practices and improve the conditions in the gaols and prisons of England and the rest of Europe parallels the periodic attempts by American reformers to clean up our jails. As recently as the early 1970s, little had changed with regard to the jails of America, some of which were almost a century old.

The early jails in America were similar to those in Europe. Most were composed of small rooms in which as many as 20 to 30 prisoners were jammed together. The purpose of jails, as originally conceived by Henry II of England when he ordered the construction of the first official English jail at the Assize of Clarendon in 1166, was to detain suspected or accused offenders until they could be brought before a court. Seldom were the jails adequately heated or ventilated, and food was either sold by the jailer or brought in by family or friends. Conditions within the early jails defy description, and the problems of overcrowding and poor sanitation continue to plague some jails today. Many are exemplary, but at best a few are warehouses for the misdemeanant, vagrant, petty offender, and common drunk. At worst, they are overcrowded, understaffed, underfunded "festering sores," as described by a former director of the Law Enforcement Assistance Administration. The jail, perhaps more than any other segment of the correctional system, has been difficult to change and tends to deterio-

Police officer booking man at jail takes his palm print.
Photo by Spencer Grant, courtesy of PhotoEdit Inc.

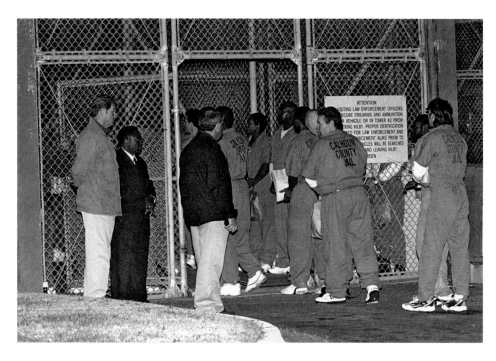

Inmates from Calhoun County Jail who have been dumped at a state prison door, due to overcrowding at that jail.
AP Wide World Photos/Jamie Martin.

rate more quickly than it can be improved. Undoubtedly, some of this is because jails are funded through local taxes. Traditionally jails have not been high on the priority list for support from local politicians. Thus, jails have been called the "cloacal region of corrections."[3]

Felons, misdemeanants, and those awaiting trial make up the major population of jails. However, additional categories of **jail inmates** include persons with mental illnesses for whom there are no other facilities, parolees and probationers awaiting hearings, federal prisoners awaiting pickup by marshals, and offenders sentenced to departments of corrections for whom there is not yet space but who cannot be released. In some states, felons serving relatively short sentences can also be housed in local jails to complete their sentences (for example, in Texas, offenders serving two-year sentences or less can be housed in jail).

The jail has been at the end of the line for receiving public and governmental support since the days when John Howard inherited the abomination of a gaol at Bedfordshire, England, in 1773. Though public attention turns to jails from time to time when politicians or the media expose a particularly appalling situation, the jails seem to revert quickly back to their original deplorable state. In the last few years, a number of new facilities based on new management concepts have been constructed to provide better conditions and programs for the misdemeanant prisoners and felony detainees, but these new facilities are still too few, and many jurisdictions still operate antiquated facilities from another era. While community programs and facilities are sometimes used to provide work and educational programs for short-term sentenced prisoners, there are too few of these programs to alleviate the boredom and poor conditions of many jails.

Of all the problems that plague the criminal justice system, none is more confused and irrational than the question of what should be done with the offender in the period before trial (see Figure 9.2). In the United States, the concept of "innocent until proven guilty" creates many problems for the local jail. Pretrial detention and procedures for pretrial liberty have been the subject of hot debate among personnel in the criminal justice system for many decades.[4] The **presumption of innocence** is difficult to maintain once the defendant has been arrested and detained in jail. The police find that presumption difficult to accept if they have acted on probable cause (high probability of guilt) in first making the arrest or have caught the individual in the act. Several projects studying the effects of pretrial decisions on sentencing offer evidence that this period is critical to later correctional efforts.[5] It is even

key term

Jail inmates
Offenders housed in a local facility, including those waiting for trial, those awaiting transport to a state or federal prison, and those convicted of a crime, usually punishable by less than one year.

key term

Presumption of innocence
Under the U.S. Constitution, those charged with a crime are presumed innocent until convicted in a court of law.

more difficult for the public to realize that "not guilty" does not necessarily mean that the offender is "innocent." Not guilty simply means that it was not possible to establish guilt "beyond a reasonable doubt" for the offense for which the defendant was charged and tried.

The problem of pretrial release is clear when we consider that the Sixth Amendment to the Constitution guarantees a "speedy and public trial." This presents a problem for the innocent person being held, because he or she looks guiltier with each passing day in confinement. A 2002 study found that the median time from arrest to adjudication for felony defendants was about six months. In 2004, 72% of all convicted offenders received sentences to incarceration.[6]

JAILS TODAY

Urban-dwellers in America have responded to the need for local lockups and correctional facilities in a number of ways. The most common confinement facility is the lockup, but the size and quality of those facilities vary greatly. There is quite a difference between the one-cell lockup of a small town and the gigantic facilities of New York City and Los Angeles, which have capacity ratings of 19,686 and 21,364, respectively. The counterpart of the city lockup is the county jail, but jails, lockups, detention facilities, workhouses, and a number of other units are all commonly referred to as jails. (We refer to all of these facilities as city or county jails, except when it is more relevant to refer to them by another designation.) Policies and programs vary greatly among cities and counties, but some general descriptions and suggestions can be made for small, medium, and large systems. About 80% of U.S. jails hold fewer than 50 up to 249 inmates, yet the 50 largest jail systems hold almost one in every three jail inmates. See Figure 9.1.

JAIL POPULATIONS AND CHARACTERISTICS

The felon and the misdemeanant, the first-time and the repeat offender, the adult (male and female), and the accused and the convicted, not to mention the guilty and the innocent, are housed in America's jails. Jails house individuals pending arraignment as well as those awaiting trial, conviction, and sentencing; probation, parole, and bail-bond violators and absconders; persons with mental illnesses awaiting transfer to appropriate facilities in the mental health system; chronic alcoholics; and drug abusers.[7] Individuals in jail also include

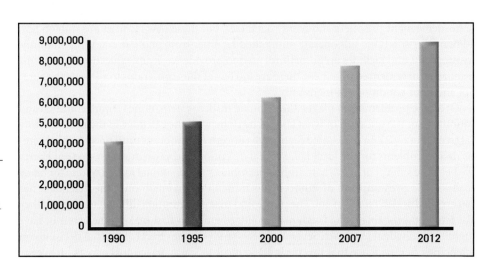

figure 9.2

Number of Jail Inmates: 1990–2012

SOURCE: William Sabol and Todd D. Minton. *Jail Inmates at Midyear 2007.* Bureau of Justice Statistics, Washington, DC: US Dept. of Justice, 2008. Data for 2012 are extrapolated.

persons being held for the military or in protective custody; material witnesses; persons found in contempt of court; persons awaiting transfer to state, federal, or other local authorities; and temporarily detained persons. More than one-half of the persons jailed are there pretrial, about 10% have been found guilty but are as yet not sentenced, and the remainder are actually serving sentences. (This latter category is rising as local jurisdictions crack down on those who drive while intoxicated[8] and on domestic disturbance[9] crimes.) Each of these categories represents a challenge to jail administrators and managers.

Because jails are so scattered and varied in operations and record keeping, it is always difficult to develop accurate data regarding jails and jail populations. However, the most recent study of jail inmates available from the U.S. Department of Justice provides reasonably current and reliable information.[10]

Data sources available for analysis indicated an average daily population of 780,581 locally operated jails in mid-2007, an increase of nearly 12% over the 2003 total, and nearly double that of 1990 (see Figure 9.3). It is estimated that about 13 million persons were admitted to jail during 2007. The latest profile of jail inmates reflected the traditional twofold function of a jail: a place for the temporary detention of pretrial defendants and a confinement facility where many convicted persons, predominantly misdemeanants, serve out their sentences, usually for less than one year. To further complicate the situation, many pretrial inmates may be kept in a jail for several months or longer before they can get a trial date. Slightly more than half of all jail inmates have not been convicted of a crime.

In 2007, 62% of the jail inmates were pretrial, accused but not convicted of a crime. Court-appointed lawyers, public defenders, or legal aid attorneys were representing most of those who had counsel. A large percentage of all pretrial inmates remained in jail, even though the authorities had set bail for them.

For those persons held in the nation's jails in midyear 2007, there were 4% more whites than blacks, but blacks were still disproportionately represented. Relative to the number of black U.S. residents, blacks were some five times more likely than whites to have been held in a local jail in midyear 2007. Hispanics were the fastest growing segment of the jail population, which is consistent with their rising number in the U.S. population (see Figure 9.4).[11]

The 2007 adult jail population consisted predominantly of males at 87%, and the number of women reached over 100,000 up from about 70,000 in 2000 and will increase to almost 125,000 by 2012 (see Figure 9.3). Most jail inmates were young men in their 20s. The overall number of jails declined between 1999 and 2005, but this was due to the closing of small jails, many of which were consolidated with other facilities to form larger jails. In 2005 there were 2,876 jail facilities of every size and description.[12]

In addition to the pretrial and convicted offenders who are serving short sentences (usually less than a year) that typify city and county jails, some states (such as Texas) operate state

class activity
Ask the class to explain why only 25 jails in the nation hold one in three jail inmates.

class activity
Ask students to characterize the jail population along social dimensions.

class activity
Challenge students to explain the forced inactivity of jail inmates.

class activity
After examining extramural supervision of jail inmates, ask how decision makers can identify which inmates should participate in such programs.

lecture note
Describe the growth of the jail population and why the concept of *capacity* is important.

lecture note
Point out the disproportionate concentration of African Americans in jails and challenge the class to explain the representation. If the consensus is "racism in action," or "result of the War on Drugs," ask students to explain the high proportion of African Americans arrested for crimes of violence. If the consensus is "high rate of criminal activity," ask students to explain the high proportion of arrests for drug possession.

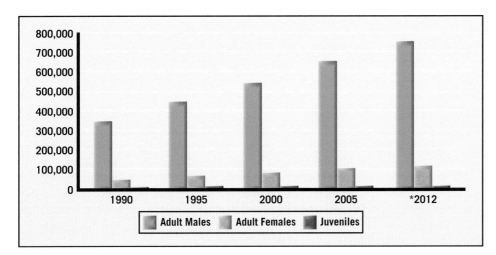

figure 9.3
Demographic Trends in Jail Populations 2000–2012*
*Data extrapolated for 2012
SOURCE: Bureau of Justice Statistics, *Demographic Trends in Jail Populations* (www.ojp.usdoj.gov/bjs/glance/tables/jailagtab.htm), accessed October 4, 2008.

figure 9.4
Demographics of U.S. Jail
Population: 2007

SOURCE: William Sabol and Todd D.
Minton. *Jail Inmates at Midyear 2007*
(Bureau of Justice Statistics,
Washington, DC: U.S. Dept.
of Justice, 2008).

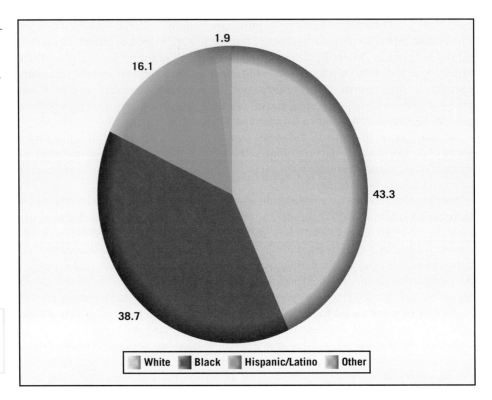

key term

New-generation jail
Developed in the 1970s, a
new-generation jail is a facility
designed for maximum
interaction between the staff
and inmates.

jails. Texas has 16 adult detention facilities (jails) housing nonviolent third-degree felony of-fenders or Class A misdemeanants. Punishment for this group of offenders could be up to two years of incarceration in a state jail facility and a fine not to exceed $10,000, with possible com-munity supervision following release from the state jail. In 2008, the state jail facilities in Texas housed more than 70,000 offenders.[13]

The most effective way to deal with nondangerous persons or to protect the inno-cent is either to keep them out of jail or to release them as soon as possible. Pretrial di-version, electronic monitoring, weekend confinement, community work orders, increased use of bail and personal recognizance, more extensive use of fines (including day fines and time payments), and various forms of work and study release all are viable alterna-tives to the destructive and expensive enforced idleness of most jails.[14] In many jurisdic-tions, jail crowding has forced many public officials to seek creative ways to handle offenders. Figure 9.5 illustrates programs that jails are using to supervise offenders out-side of the jail facility.

THE NEW-GENERATION JAIL

Jail design was essentially unchanged until the 1970s when we began to see a new type of jail facility now referred to as the **new-generation jail.** This jail is a radical departure from the tra-ditional jail in its architecture, interior design, and design philosophy. The new-generation jail is a facility designed for maximum interaction between the staff and inmates. In traditional jails, inmates were only occasionally observed by correctional officers ("intermittent supervi-sion"). In the new-generation jails, inmates are under continuous and direct supervision.

In the third-generation new jails, cells continue to be laid out in a line, but inmates can spend most of their waking hours in a communal dayroom area (instead of in their cells). The fourth-generation jail contains a podular cell block, a central control and observation room, and a dayroom corridor for circulation to and from services. Ken Kerle aptly de-scribes these podular jails:

figure 9.5

Percentage of Persons Supervised Outside Jail Facilities: Midyear 2007

SOURCE: William Sabol and Todd D. Minton, *Jail Inmates at Midyear 2007* (Washington, DC: Bureau of Justice Statistics, 2008).

Simply stated, direct supervision in a jail means an officer is constantly present to supervise the inmates. Jail architecture historians follow how this history of jail architecture evolved through three different phases. The first phase, called linear/intermittent surveillance, spawned institutions with corridors often at right angles, where an officer walked by a series of identical cells to monitor inmate activities. This was usually done on an hourly basis in most institutions and the rest of the time the inmates were left to their own devices. This architectural approach dominated the incarceration industry from the nineteenth century to the latter part of the twentieth century.

During the 1970s, architects submitted improved correctional designs, and more sophisticated construction techniques were introduced whereby a single dayroom was surrounded by either single cells or multi-occupancy cells, or dorms. This area was eventually called a "pod." A vandal resistant control booth, to protect the officer in charge of the pod, gave him improved surveillance and the opportunity to monitor inmate activities on a constant basis. This second development was called podular/remote surveillance.

Note that the word supervision does not appear in either of these concepts. In the first instance, an officer walking by a cell block has little time to actively supervise unless something untoward occurs. In the second instance, the officer is locked in the control booth to keep the inmates out. While the officer has communication with the inmates through a speaker system, he is not in the position to actively supervise them. A jail administrator summarized the problems with this approach:

- If a problem occurred in a pod, the officer had to call "out front" for assistance. Inmates did not recognize the officer as the authority; rather, he appeared to them as a "puppet master" inside the booth, which they referred to as a "fishbowl."

- From a staff point of view, the flow of information between officers and inmates was drastically reduced.

- When an incident occurred, staff frequently didn't know to what they were responding.

- If there was violence and many staff members responded, the inmates often ended up going through the disciplinary process. Chances of working out compromises were minimized.
- Staff on duty in the "fishbowl" would frequently overlook minor infractions. They believed it just wasn't worth the trouble to operations elsewhere by calling for assistance.
- Staff lacked knowledge of individual inmates and could not give accurate information on inmate behavior. They had to second guess stress levels when trouble emanated in the pod. In both the linear/intermittent and the podular/remote designs, the vandal-proof furnishings graced the inside of the cells and dayrooms. Architects and contractors, jail and staff all assumed from past experience that the inmates would try to tear the place up, and so the stainless steel picnic tables were bolted to the floor, stainless steel combination toilets/washbasins were installed in the cells, and all doors were solid steel with maximum security locking devices.

key term
_____

Podular/direct supervision
With podular/direct-supervision housing units, inmates have interaction with staff and other inmates through day rooms or common areas.

The **podular/direct supervision** model began in 1974 in the Federal Bureau of Prisons' three metropolitan correctional centers in New York City, San Diego, and Chicago. Instead of the vandal-proof fixtures, this jail had commercial grade chairs, tables, and vitreous china toilets and sinks. Soft furnishings and carpeting helped to reduce the noise caused by steel and concrete. Much to the surprise of everyone, the more normalized physical environment survived and the predicted destruction did not occur. The twenty-two beds in segregation units did not fill up and there was no locking down of any of the housing units.

Classification and counseling can be done right inside the pod in new facilities.
Photo by Clifford E. Simonsen, courtesy of King County Department of Adult Detention.

Local jails were slow to emulate this new approach, whereby a correctional officer stayed inside the pod with the inmates for the entire shift. It was not until 1981 that the first local facility opened as a direct supervision jail in Contra Costa County, California. Still, many people who worked in jails could not believe that this new approach would work. Some assumed erroneously that federal inmates weren't as tough as local inmates. These local inmates, they believed, would tear up the jail and assault the single officer controlling a pod that held up to fifty inmates. Of course, some resented the idea of commercial grade furnishings that produced a more humanized environment and made it more livable. These inconsiderate individuals conveniently forget that the staffs who manage and supervise the inmates spend their working days in the jail environment. Pleasant surroundings and reduced noise levels can help inhibit stress. Despite the initial reluctance at the local government level, there was a substantial increase in the number of new jails adopting the direct supervision model. By the time AJA had published its 2nd edition of *Who's Who in Jail Management 1994,* it listed 114 jails that had switched to direct supervision (pp. 401–405). The following year, the NIC Jails Division published *Podular Direct Supervision 1995,* which showed a considerable increase in direct supervision jails. The direct supervision strategy is believed to reduce inmate violation of and formal processing for contraband possession, destruction of property, escapes, insolence, suicides, and violence problems.[15]

THE JAIL IN CONTEXT
The Problem with Overcrowding

Mandatory sentences, get-tough polices, and increased pressure from state correctional systems to reduce institutional populations is rapidly changing the makeup of America's jails, with serious offenders being housed together with local drunks and misdemeanants. Already overcrowded and difficult to control, many jails have become dumping grounds where little is accomplished other than locking up and feeding the population.

Although there have been improvements, in many physical facilities these have been set back by overcrowding and by the more violent populations.[16] Many of our largest jails are under court order to limit population and to improve specific conditions of confinement (food service, medical services, fire hazards, inmate classification, segregation policies, etc.).

Who are the "rabble" that the jail accepts at entry to the justice system and will probably discharge after a brief stay? Are they dangerous predators? Or are they just marginal people who pose some threat to the community and must be controlled? The answer may be both. We turn first to an examination of the makeup of these residents of the nation's jails. About one in every eight jail inmates is being held for other correctional authorities, about 12% of the total inmates, a consistent pattern for the past several years. They are being held back for state and federal prison systems, as well as other local correctional agencies. Almost all of the **"holdback" jail inmates** were being delayed due to overcrowding in adult prisons for felony offenders. A small percentage was federal prisoners being held for transfer to U.S. Bureau of Prisons institutions. The Bureau of Prisons has recently developed jail facilities in its own system and therefore reduced its population of holdbacks drastically. Holdbacks are found at about half of all jails. Most jails charge fees for holding inmates for other jurisdictions. Those holdbacks, while helpful to the jail's budget, can contribute to jail overcrowding in many local jail jurisdictions.

A large percentage of jail inmates has used alcohol and drugs sometime in their lives, and more than four of ten had been drinking just before their offense, almost half being drunk or very drunk at the time of their offense. This pattern of substance abuse is even more pronounced among convicted jail inmates. More than half were under the influence of drugs or alcohol (or both) at the time of their current offense. About a quarter of the jail inmates had participated in a drug treatment program and nearly a sixth in an alcohol-abuse treatment program.

As noted earlier, the 25 largest jails in the United States house 31% of the nation's total jail inmates, with 36% exceeding their capacity. Most jail administrators acknowledge that all flexibility in a jail, with regard to classification and housing, is lost when the jail is at 90% of capacity. The local jails in 2007 were at 96% of capacity. [17] A major cause of overcrowding in facilities is the pressure to close other facilities that do not meet acceptable

key term

"Holdback" jail inmates
Inmates held in jail awaiting transportation to a federal or state prison.

Growing populations have made vast and varied jails—including tents.
Photo by Clifford E. Simonsen, courtesy of Maricopa County Sheriff's Department.

Jail overcrowding can lead to using corridors as dormitories in jails.
Photo by Mark Richards, courtesy of PhotoEdit Inc.

standards.[18] Between 1999 and 2005, the number of jails available to house adult prisoners dropped from 2,999 to 2,876. That number of jail facilities will most likely continue to decline. Rated capacities (total beds) for jails have risen sharply to 813,502, indicating that while there were fewer jails, the size was increasing. The explanation for this trend is due largely to the fact that most new jails that replace the older, smaller facilities are built to hold many more beds. Although most of the old, decrepit jails probably deserved to be closed, the expanding jail populations and related problems have created management and control problems within the system. Overcrowding and idleness have thus become typical of those jails that have not expanded programs along with the "brick-and-mortar" approach to jail crowding.

Some efforts to find solutions to reduce overcrowding include conversion of an abandoned motel to a jail annex, purchase of manufactured housing units (modular units that can be interconnected), construction of a canvas-tent-based housing community, leasing bed space from other jurisdictions, house arrest for work-release prisoners, electronic monitoring of defendants not otherwise eligible for pretrial release, double-bunking at an existing facility, and contracting with community residential programs for alcohol- and drug-dependent inmates in need of such services.[19]

Problems with Personnel

The structures used to house our jails reflect the multitude of problems connected with those facilities. Certainly, the lack of adequate personnel is a crucial factor. Most jails are operated by the law enforcement agency that has jurisdiction in the particular area, although in at least one state, Kentucky, "jailers" are elected by the public. Many sheriff's deputies begin their service with a mandatory two-year tour of duty as a jailer, which many feel is not the role for which they were hired and trained. Because many of the full-time jail personnel are county police officers, dedicated to putting offenders into jail, the primary emphasis is on custodial convenience rather than correctional services. The philosophy behind that includes an almost fanatical concern with security, leaving the responsibility for the jails' internal operation to the inmates themselves. It is that situation which has produced the most reprehensible conditions in many of the large municipal jails. When jail personnel are not

c o r r e c t i o n a l **brief**

Rape in a County Lockup

This story began on February 14, 2003 (Valentine's Day). An unidentified 18-year-old boy was caught and arrested after trying to flee from a state trooper. The teen was clocked doing 35 mph over the speed limit on a narrow, two-lane road. He was taken to the local detention center to be booked on traffic violations.

While being processed at the jail, a number of guards began to tease the teen about his appearance. He was about 5' 10" and weighed 125 lbs. They said he would make a "good girlfriend" for inmates locked up in Cell 101, part of a 300-bed facility housing some very dangerous inmates, located in a far-flung corner of the jail. Jail protocol called for the teen to be locked up in a holding cell just off the booking room.

However, the shift supervisor decided that the teen needed to be scared and taught a lesson, so he ordered two of the guards to tell the group of 14 inmates in Cell 101 to expect some fresh meat.

As the teen was being escorted to the cell in the 300-bed jail, inmates screamed, "He's such a cutie" and "Bring him to me." As the guards pushed the scared teen youth into the cell, yet another inmate yelled "Happy Valentine's Day."

In civil litigation, the teen says he was carried overhead by a mob of inmates and led to the showers. The teen was stripped naked, beaten with jail slippers, forced to perform sexual acts, and raped. The brutal attack was carried out right through the night with multiple inmates participating in raping the youth. "This is a case of a 10th-grader's worst nightmare," said the Federal Civil Rights prosecutor.

After the victim told his father he was raped, the supervisor began organizing a cover up, according to court papers. He lied to investigators when he said the victim was locked up with felons because the floor drain was clogged in the drunk tank. He also fabricated shift logs to make it appear that guards under his watch were checking on the victim's welfare, but the victim wasn't let out of the cell until the first shift came on duty the next morning. He also threatened a female guard who was considering telling the truth.

Two prison guards pleaded guilty in the case and two other guards stood trial. . . . and were found guilty of conspiring to violate the teen's civil rights by allowing other inmates to sexually assault him. They were also found guilty of obstruction of justice because the jury also found there was aggravated sexual abuse.

The teen survived the ordeal and reached a $1.4 million settlement with the county in 2005. The traffic violations against the teen were ultimately dropped. A total of three inmates were also convicted in the sexual assault.

The victim, who is now 23, leads a very nonsocial life, said his lawyer, who sued the jail on behalf of the teen. "It is a day-by-day thing for him," he said. "He stays to himself. He doesn't go out in public."

---

sworn officers but lower-paid custodial individuals, the conditions can become still worse. The need for preservice and in-service training of jailers and other jail personnel has been clearly perceived by jail inspectors. The immediate requirement is not an influx of professional staff, but extensive training aimed at breaking the habitual work patterns of uninterested, politically appointed, and unqualified jail personnel. Low pay, high turnover, and poor working conditions contribute significantly to the personnel problems faced by many jail facilities.

One problem with upgrading personnel and facilities has its roots in the long history of the jail's separate **fee system,** which stems from a practice in early England. The office of sheriff in those days was an important political position of pomp and prestige (the sheriff was the king's executive officer at the local government level), but the sheriff did very little work in the jail. The distasteful duty of caring for the jail and its inmates was usually sold as a concession to a keeper, or gaoler. Fees for maintaining the inmates were extracted from their families, friends, or estates. Under that system, the greater the number of inmates and the longer they were kept, the more income would accrue to the jailer. To increase his profit, the jailer cut his expenses to a minimum and operated the jail as cheaply as possible.

The fee system was used in America for many years, until it was largely replaced by a variation. The inmates themselves are no longer required to pay the fees for their upkeep (although in some jurisdictions inmates housed in jail are now being required to pay for their keep, or at a minimum an "intake fee"). In many states, a per diem fee for each prisoner's upkeep is paid by the state or by federal agencies with which the jail has a contract. Leasing bed space from other jurisdictions is a more current example. Some

key term

Fee system
Fees charged to state and federal prison systems to house inmates in local jails.

Male inmates talk on phones in the recreation room at Maricopa County Jail, Arizona.
Photo by A. Ramey, courtesy of PhotoEdit Inc.

states (such as California) pay their counties to incarcerate state-sentenced offenders with short sentences. Not surprisingly, sheriffs will often exploit a system that pays the sheriff to arrest and jail as many persons as possible. In other states it is the local county that pays for the keep of offenders housed in jail. In rural counties it is not unheard of for a judge to send someone to prison to save the county the cost of housing the offender.

Jail Standards

The standards for jails have been a matter of concern for many years. Many argue that given the diversity of size and function, not to mention funding disparity, it is difficult to implement standard criteria. However, at least 21 states report having some jail standards, with all but 4 being mandatory. Maine was the first to report the establishment of some standards in 1951, followed by Michigan in 1953 and California with full standards in 1963.[20] In addition, professional organizations, such as the American Jail Association and the American Correctional Association, have developed standards and accreditation processes, and the National Institute of Corrections has provided technical assistance to numerous jails across the country. Despite the challenges, there has been an increasing movement to upgrade and improve the jails operating in America. Making jails more humane is a worthy goal; however, for many public officials, the most persuasive reason for adopting jail standards is to avoid costly litigation and lawsuits. It is clear that upgrading jails is as critical a need as any other in the criminal justice system.[21]

Health Care in Jails

No discussion of jail conditions would be adequate without addressing health conditions. During the last two decades, the health care of jail inmates has been the subject of endless litigation,[22] included in civil rights mandates, addressed through court orders, and mandated through state regulation. It is clear that provision of adequate inmate health and mental health care[23] is no longer an option but is compulsory. Across the nation, jail managers are taking steps to meet these mandates, including the following:

1. Determining the real costs of and identifying existing community medical service providers; adopting health maintenance organization (HMO) models

2. Resolving security issues for transporting inmates to hospitals and medical care appointments
3. Innovating scheduling for medical staff
4. Providing special housing (for geriatrics, tuberculosis patients, early-stage HIV inmates, pregnant inmates, etc.)
5. Seeking accreditation (sometimes as a defense against litigation and claims of deliberate indifference)
6. Planning for future problems[24]

Demands of this nature will require jail managers to find ways to creatively adopt proven techniques and implement innovations that would permit continued quality health care while curtailing costs of services.[25]

It is estimated that about 44% of jail inmates have a mental health problem, which is defined as: a recent history of symptoms within the past 12 months, including a clinical diagnosis or treatment by a mental health professional. Findings from this recent study included:[26]

-   Female inmates in jails had higher rates of mental health problems than males (75% versus 63%).
-   About 76% of local jail inmates who had a mental health problem met criteria for substance dependency or abuse.
-   Jail inmates who had a mental health problem (24%) were three times as likely as jail inmates without (8%) to report being physically or sexually abused in the past.
-   Only 1 in 6 jail inmates with a mental health problem had received treatment since admission.

These findings help illustrate some of the difficulties local officials face in managing the jail population. Some believe that jails have become a dumping ground for the mentally ill, especially since many states have closed mental health hospitals. Clearly, many of these inmates require treatment that often becomes difficult to provide in a jail setting.

ALTERNATIVES TO JAIL

Extended confinement of presumed innocent persons, as with pretrial detention of the nonadjudicated felon later found not guilty, is a serious problem. The defendant who is truly innocent, but is exposed through long pretrial confinement to the conditions of even the finest jail, will soon build up considerable resentment and animosity toward the criminal justice system and to corrections in particular. The convicted offender eventually sent to a correctional institution also will have negative feelings about the inequities of a system that appears to choose arbitrarily to confine some defendants before trial while releasing others.

Fines

The confusion in defining and enforcing misdemeanor statutes is reflected in the absence of uniform techniques and systems for dealing with misdemeanants. Although different states vary greatly in their approaches, and jurisdictions within states may also be inconsistent, some patterns are fairly constant. As mentioned, the bulk of the misdemeanor cases are disposed of through confinement or probation, but alternatives for disposition exist, the most prevalent being the use of fines.

Cynical inmates often refer to fines as **price-tag justice.** In the case of misdemeanor offenses, the fine is in many cases offered as an alternative to a period of confinement, meaning the offender who cannot pay is confined, in effect, for being "poor" rather than

Outside work crews must be carefully searched upon return to their cells.
Photo by Clifford E. Simonsen, courtesy of King County Department of Adult Detention.

for being "guilty." The sheer number of misdemeanor cases the lower courts must hear forces the judges to be able to provide only the most cursory kind of justice. Some lower courts may hear more than 100 misdemeanor cases in a single morning. It is difficult, under such circumstances, to conduct any kind of in-depth diagnosis of the offender, the offense, or the offender's ability to pay a fine. The amount of fine for a particular crime is virtually standardized, and paying it is like paying forfeited bail or a parking ticket. For the individual unable to pay, a term in the lockup is often seen as the only alternative. In some cases, however, fines can be paid on the installment plan. That procedure gives offenders a chance to keep their jobs or seek work to pay the fine. Combined with weekend confinement and community work orders, the installment plan has greatly improved misdemeanor justice.

As part of the increased enthusiasm for intermediate punishments and search for a graduated progression of intermediate sanctions (see Chapter 6), courts have increasingly begun to use fines and day fines (a sliding dollar amount determined by the offender's daily wages). The Vera Institute of Justice implemented a project to demonstrate and then evaluate the efficacy of using day fines in Staten Island, New York. The project demonstrated the following:

1. The day-fine concept could be implemented in a typical American court of limited jurisdiction.
2. Day fines could substitute for fixed fines ("the same or similar amount to be imposed on all defendants convicted of similar offenses").
3. Fine amounts were higher for more affluent offenders under the day-fine system.
4. Overall revenues increased.
5. High rates of collection could be sustained despite the higher average day-fine amounts.
6. The deep skepticism among criminal justice professionals about the court's ability to enforce and collect such fines was unfounded.[27]

Both fines and day fines are likely to be used more extensively by courts to achieve a graduated progression of penalties for less serious crimes as well as enhancing the programs and efforts aimed at reducing jail overcrowding.

Weekend Confinement

To lessen the negative impacts of short-term incarceration and allow offenders to retain current employment, some jurisdictions permit sentences to be served during nonworking weekends. Many refer to it as "doing time on the installment plan." Such weekend confinement generally requires a guilty misdemeanant to check into the jail on Friday after work and leave Sunday morning, sometimes early enough to permit church attendance. A **weekender** serving his or her sentence over a number of months would generally be credited with three days of confinement per weekend. Minimum-security facilities (not the maximum-security jails) are appropriate for such offenders.

Community Work Orders

Sentencing judges sometimes order misdemeanants to perform a period of service to the community as a substitute for, or in partial satisfaction of, a fine. This disposition is generally a condition of a suspended (or partially suspended) sentence or of probation. It can be used in a variety of ways: a sentence in itself, work in lieu of cash fine, a condition of suspended sentence, or a condition of probation.[28]

The offender "volunteers" his or her services to a community agency for a certain number of hours per week over a specified period of time. The total number of hours, often assessed as the legal minimum wage, is often determined by the amount of the fine that would have been imposed or by the portion of the fine that is suspended.

Other alternatives for the misdemeanant are probation without adjudication and the suspended sentence. Both are variations on the same theme: holding formal disposition over the head of the offender for a period of time, often under specified conditions, and then nullifying the conviction. In probation without adjudication (also known as deferred prosecution), offenders can forego prosecution as long as they meet certain established conditions, usually for a specific period of time. The suspended sentence is used whenever offenders obviously do not require supervision to ensure their good behavior. This alternative is primarily used for first offenders considered to be so impressed with their arrest and conviction that further sanctions against them would be of little positive value.

The extent to which these alternatives are employed is not really known, because little research has been conducted in this area; at midyear 2007, at least 8% of jail inmates were outside the facility on confinement alternatives.[29] It is apparent that the misdemeanants, like adult felons, often fall out of the correctional funnel before it narrows. If they did not, the jails of the country simply could not hold them.

ALTERNATIVES TO JAIL AT THE PRETRIAL STAGE

Incarceration is one of the most severe punishments meted out by the American criminal justice system. Yet more than one-half of all persons in local jails are awaiting trial. In effect, we are using our most severe sanction against many individuals who have not yet been convicted of a crime. If detention were necessary and if there were no reasonable

key term

Weekender
A jail inmate who is allowed to live at home during the week (usually to work) and who must report to jail to serve his or her sentence on weekends.

class activity

Ask students to list ten misdemeanor and low-level felony offenses, and have them establish fine amounts for each offense, including both the first and second offense.

class activity

Ask students if they know anyone who was sentenced to a community work order, and if that offender completed the work. How does the individual feel about that experience?

lecture note

Describe the major alternatives to jail confinement, noting the advantages and disadvantages of each.

class activity

Ask students to identify pretrial alternatives and arrange them along a continuum of increasing controls or sanctions.

class activity

Ask students whether jail incarceration is more painful for male or female offenders. If the class stratifies offenders by criminal history, ask who should take custody of any children if the mother is incarcerated in jail.

lecture note

Point out that jail incarceration disables offenders but also can rupture community ties. In the case of dependents, jail incarceration may also punish the offender's family.

key term

Pretrial alternatives
Programs and sanctions designed to release those jail inmates who are awaiting trial; alternatives can include electronic monitoring, supervision, treatment programs, house arrest, and other creative options designed to reduce jail populations.

key term

Pretrial jail incarceration
Holding someone accused of a crime who cannot make bail.

homework

Assign students to read "Drug Court" (http://www.ocgov.com/ Probation/eArrested/ 9ianw_drugc.asp) and write a one-paragraph statement of the requirements imposed by the court.

alternatives to the jailing of suspects, that situation would be understandable; but experience with alternatives to jail has indicated that many (but not all) people now incarcerated could probably be released safely and economically, pending disposition of the charges against them. Most of them would appear in court as required without being held in jail.

Some tentative conclusions can be drawn from the experience of existing programs:

1. Pretrial alternatives generally cost much less than jail incarceration.
2. Persons released before trial seem to fare better in court than do those who are incarcerated.
3. Pretrial release alternatives appear to be as effective as jail in preventing recidivism and can reduce the size of criminal justice agency workloads.
4. Alternative programs can reduce jail populations and eliminate the need for expansion or new construction.

Pretrial alternatives to detention run along a continuum of increasing controls or sanctions. Any community wishing to maximize the use of alternatives will provide a series of options that offer varying levels of supervision and services. Such a process will permit the release of more persons with less waste of expensive resources. The least interventionary and least costly options are used for low-risk cases. More expensive options and options involving greater interference in the life of the individual, such as house arrest and electronic monitoring, are reserved for cases in which those are the only alternatives to the even more costly option of jail incarceration.

Although jails keep alleged offenders off the streets, they also keep those same individuals away from their work, family, friends, and business (even if crime might be their business). Already tenuous ties to the community may be further strained by the jail experience. Moreover, other disreputable members of society (derelicts, drug abusers, hustlers, drunks, etc.) may vandalize and/or burglarize their residence, which may have been left unattended and unguarded for even the brief time of jail detention. The average length of stay in jails nationwide (both pretrial and sentenced) is a combined average of almost 90 days. Finally, jails are important because of what happens to the inmates there. The shock of incarceration, loss of control over their environment, danger from violent inmates, absence of meaningful activity, and dead time weigh heavily on the minds of new inmates. Psychological problems already affecting behavior may be exacerbated; self-mutilation[30] and suicide[31] occasionally occur. Sometimes it is difficult to rebut those who argue that the purpose of **pretrial jail incarceration** is punishment.

Less than one-half of all jail inmates grew up in a household with both parents present; almost four in ten have lived in a single-parent household. More than a third have family members (usually a brother or sister) who have also been incarcerated. More than a fourth have a parent or guardian who abused alcohol while the inmate was growing up. One in six male inmates reported sexual or physical abuse (or both) by an adult before the current incarceration, and one in eight had taken medication prescribed by a psychiatrist or other doctor for an emotional or mental problem.

Characteristics of female jail inmates are explored in greater detail in Chapter 17, and the patterns just described are generally more egregious for female than male jail inmates. Self-reports on drug abuse by jail inmates, sometimes known for their self-serving and deceptive purposes, are in part verified through urinalysis testing conducted at jail sites across the nation. Results for arrestees and across different charges at arrest indicate even more extensive drug use than previously self-reported, particularly by robbery and burglary arrestees.

As for their criminal activities, usually almost one in four has been arrested for a crime of violence and another three of four have been arrested for crimes against property. A large percentage of criminals is charged with drug violations. A bit less than one-half have been

correctional **brief**

The Purpose of Correctional Sanctions?

Two important issues have been given a great deal of attention in the media: the need for new jails and the reentry of offenders back in the community. These issues are obviously related and lead us to the question of "What is the purpose of correctional sanctions?" While most would agree that public protection is the primary goal of corrections, disagreements arise as to the best methods to achieve this goal. On one side are advocates for more punitive policies such as increased use of incarceration or simply increasing control and monitoring if the offender is supervised in the community. Those advocating such strategies of crime control do so on the basis of the often-interrelated goals of punishment: retribution, deterrence, and incapacitation. On the other side are those who argue that we must address the underlying causes of crime and criminal behavior, and provide programs and services to address the needs of the offender, especially for those returning to the community. So can we achieve the goal of public protection and meet the dual needs for punishment *and* rehabilitation? I believe that we have to consider both sides if we want to reduce the revolving door that has become our penal system.

Punishment is an inherent part of the correctional system, and is often justified simply because a person has broken the law. Society demands that certain offenders be punished, and expect our elected officials to see that offenders be held accountable. The problem is the belief that somehow punishment alone will deter offenders from continuing to break the law in the future. The underlying assumptions of deterrence is that the offenders are aware of the sanction, they perceive it as unpleasant, they weigh the cost and benefits of their criminal conduct, and they assess the risk and, in turn, make a rational choice to break the law (or not). The problem is that most street-level criminals act impulsively; have a short-term perspective; are often disorganized and have failed in school, jobs, and relationships; have distorted thinking; hang around with others like themselves; use drugs and alcohol; and are not rational actors. In short, deterrence theory collapses. Incapacitation, which attempts to limit offenders' ability to commit another crime (usually by locking them up), can have some effect, but as many have found out, simply locking up offenders and "throwing away the key" has proven to be a very expensive approach to crime control. This strategy is also limited, since the vast majority of offenders returns to society. Without treatment, many will return unchanged at best and, at worst, with many more problems and intensified needs for services. Even if one supports incapacitation, one must ask, "What should be done with offenders while incarcerated?" This leads us to rehabilitation. With this approach, the offender chooses to refrain from new crimes rather than being unable to. So what works in changing offender behavior?

Most researchers who study correctional interventions have concluded that without some form of human intervention or services, there is unlikely to be much effect on recidivism from punishment alone. If you don't believe that, just look at the number of offenders who have been incarcerated in our jails over and over again. As Einstein once said, "The sign of insanity is doing something over and over again and expecting a different outcome." Unfortunately, not all correctional treatment programs are equally effective; however, considerable research has demonstrated that well-designed programs that meet certain conditions can appreciably reduce recidivism rates for offenders. Effective programs have many characteristics, and space does not allow me to elaborate; however, two are particularly noteworthy. First, it is important to target crime-producing needs that are highly correlated with criminal conduct. The most effective programs are centered on the *present* circumstances and risk factors that are contributing to the offender's behavior. Antisocial attitudes, values, beliefs, and peer associations; substance abuse; lack of problem-solving skills; and poor self-control are some of the more important targets for change for offenders. Second, effective programs are *action* oriented rather than talk oriented. In other words, offenders do something about their difficulties rather than just talk about them. These types of programs teach offenders new prosocial skills to replace the antisocial ones (e.g., stealing, cheating, lying, etc.). Interventions based on these approaches are very structured and emphasize the importance of modeling and behavioral rehearsal techniques that engender self-efficacy, challenge cognitive distortions, and assist offenders in developing new prosocial skills. So, should we hold offenders accountable for their behavior? Absolutely. But punishment and treatment need not be incompatible, and doing one without the other is not likely to achieve long-term public safety.

Edward Latessa

key term

Criminal history data
Information related to an offender's prior arrests and convictions.

key term

Mental health issues
A range of diagnosed mental illnesses that often afflict jail inmates.

previously sentenced to incarceration or probation prior to their current offense. As you have already learned, the proportion of inmates with mental illness is high.

Those sociodemographic and **criminal history data** suggest a marginal group of mostly male offenders who have had a lengthy but not necessarily serious involvement in criminal activity. They could best be seen as a group of high-need disadvantaged urban-dwellers whose needs have not been adequately addressed by the social services agencies in their local communities. The number of inmates of the largest jails who died further describes their needs. Of the 919 inmates who died in jails at the beginning of 2000, more than one in three died at their own hands (suicide). Almost 42% died of natural causes (excluding AIDS). The fact that 1 of 11 inmate deaths in jails was attributed to causes related to AIDS suggests that compassionate release of the fatally ill is a concept that has still to be fully embraced by local correctional facilities.

Summary

We have covered the somewhat disconnected jail system and its operational problems, innovations, and future directions. This chapter provides a snapshot and characteristics overview of the kinds of people and their behaviors who make up the clients of the nation's jails. The data, as difficult as they are to gather, suggest that these "clients" are a group of the American society's so-called losers. The best way to solve the long-term problems of the millions of residents who rotate through America's jails is to address the underlying problems faced by jail inmates. The jail system, which deals with problems ranging from drunk drivers and petty theft to aggravated murder, evokes terror in some involuntary residents of these facilities and a "business-as-usual" attitude in others who have experienced it before. These residents are trying to cope with drug and alcohol abuse, unemployment, domestic problems, medical and **mental health issues** and needs, inadequate education and illiteracy, and failure to adapt to an urban environment. Students interested in making an impact on corrections and finding creative solutions to persistent problems can fulfill that desire by beginning their career with the local jails and community corrections.

What becomes of this varied population of offenders passing through the jails of America? Most are convicted and become labeled as "offenders," then move on to the many options discussed in later chapters. The four categories of persons who move on to other venues of the correctional system are male offenders, female offenders, juvenile offenders, and a particular set of clients known as "special-category offenders." In later chapters, we examine each of these categories and discuss their impact and special characteristics as applied to corrections. As mentioned at the beginning of this chapter, these discussions deal with developing a better understanding of the people in the system and using such knowledge to improve the ways to deal with them in the various systems of corrections.

Although improving jail facilities and upgrading jail personnel takes a great deal of time and money, many other helpful procedures can be initiated more simply. The National Jail Committee of the American Correctional Association recommended some in 1937. The fact that so many of those suggestions would still benefit jails today, almost 70 years later, reflects most of local jail systems' general resistance to change. The accreditation process has significantly improved jail practices in many jurisdictions, as have standards, both developed by the American Correctional Association in the 1990s. Jail administrators have an obligation to society to seek methods that can work in their own communities. Administrators are the practitioners who, with community involvement, must break the tradition of neglect and indifference that is the jail's legacy. Unless vigorous and imaginative leadership is exhibited, even revitalized jails will soon regress to their squalid past.

The best policy is to search for ways to keep people out of jail, yet still protect the citizenry. Providing security and staff training and meeting the standards suggested by the professional associations that oversee the staff can meet both goals.

The student must be constantly aware that it is the fine people who keep the jails of America moving ahead, against tremendous problems that keep them from slipping back into the horrors of the past. We now move on to a look at one of the major alternatives for going from jail to a prison after conviction—probation. In times of overcrowding, probation has become a major player in correctional supervision and will probably expand further in the coming decade.

Key Words

jail, 176

jail inmates, 177

presumption of innocence, 177

new-generation jail, 180

podular/direct supervision, 182

"holdback" jail inmates, 183

fee system, 185

price-tag justice, 187

weekender, 189

pretrial alternatives, 190

pretrial jail incarceration, 190

criminal history data, 192

mental health issues, 192

Review Questions

1. Why has the fee system been such a detriment to jail progress?

2. Do you think offenders housed in jail should be made to pay for their upkeep? Their medical care?

3. What is the area of greatest weakness in the jails? Would more personnel be the answer? Why or why not?

4. What are the major alternatives to pretrial confinement?

5. Describe the operation of a new-generation jail.

6. What medical problems must jails address?

7. Draft a plan for reducing jail overcrowding.

8. Why is the jail so important to the correctional system?

9. What is meant when we describe the jail population as "rabble"?

10. Identify five major problems that jail inmates bring to the institution.

11. Why are so many prison-bound inmates held back in jails?

12. Describe the diversity of the jail inmate population.

13. What special problems do inmates bring to the jail setting?

14. Identify three trends in jail facilities.

Endnotes

1. Norval Morris and David Rothman (eds.), *The Oxford Dictionary of the Prison: The Practice of Punishment in Western Society* (Oxford, UK: Oxford University Press, 1995).

2. For an excellent overview of involving the community in jail administration, see William Wood, "A Practical Guide to Community Relations," *American Jails* 6:5 (1992): 14–17; and Taylor Dueker, "Visitation Boom in Omaha," *American Jails* 18:5 (2004): 65–67.

3. Hans Mattick and Alexander Aidman, "The Cloacal Region of Corrections," *The Annals* 381:1 (January 1969): 109–118. See also Karol Lucken, "The Dynamics of Penal Reform," *Crime, Law and Social Change* 26:4 (1997): 367–384. Yet jails are deluged with mentally ill people. See Lois Ventura, C. Cassel, J. Jacoby, et al., "Case Management and Recidivism of Mentally Ill Persons Released from Jail," *Psychiatric Services* 49:10 (1998): 1330–1337.

4. Thomas Bak, *Defendants Who Avoid Detention: A Good Risk?* (Washington, DC: Administrative Office of the U.S. Courts, 1994).

5. Marian Williams, "The Effect of Pretrial Detention on Imprisonment Decisions," *Criminal Justice Review* 28:2 (2003): 299–316.

6. William Durose and Patrick Langan, *State Court Sentencing of Convicted Felons, 2002* (Washington, DC: Bureau of Justice Statistics, 2004), p. 1; *State Court Sentencing of Convicted Felons, 2004* (Washington, DC: Bureau of Justice Statistics, 2007), p. 1; and Bureau of Justice Statistics, *Felony Defendants in Large Urban Counties, 2004,* http://www.ojp.usdoj.gov/bjs/pub/html/fdluc/2004/tables/fdluc04st25.htm (accessed October 4, 2008).

7. William Sabol and Todd Minton, *Jail Inmates at Midyear 2007* (Bureau of Justice Statistics, Washington, DC: U.S. Department of Justice, 2008).

8. David DeYoung, "An Evaluation of the Effectiveness of Alcohol Treatment Driver License Actions and Jail Terms in Reducing Drunk Driving in California," *Addiction* 92:8 (1997): 989–997; and Arthur Pratt, "The Results of Substance Abuse Treatment Programs in Five County Jails," *American Jails* 12:5 (1998): 59–61. See

also Allen Rodgers, "Effect of Minnesota's License Plate Impoundment on Recidivism of Multiple DWI Violators," *Alcohol, Drugs and Driving* 10:2 (1995): 127–134; and Robert Langworthy and Edward Latessa, "Treatment of Chronic Drunk Drivers: The Turning Point Project Five Years Later," *Journal of Criminal Justice* 24:3 (1996): 273–281.

9. Amy Thistlewaite, J. Wooldredge, and D. Gibbs, "Severity of Dispositions and Domestic Violence Recidivism," *Crime and Delinquency* 44:3 (1998): 388–398; Edward Gondolf, *The Impact of Mandatory Court Review on Batterer Program Compliance* (Harrisburg, PA: Pennsylvania Commission on Crime and Delinquency, 1997); and Eric Smith, Matthew Durose and Patrick Langan, *State Court Processing of Domestic Violence Cases* (Washington, DC: Bureau of Justice Statistics, 2008).

10. Sabol and Minton, *Jail Inmates at Midyear 2007.*

11. Although blacks are disproportionately involved in the criminal justice system, a long-standing criminological taboo exists against discussing the relationship between crime and race. There is no "black criminology" to tease out the data or theoretically interpret the observed overinvolvement. The three basic arguments are that there are more black offenders per 100,000 population, or that certain black offenders tend to commit very large numbers of crime, or that criminal justice system personnel decision makers are biased against blacks in decision making. See the excellent critique by Kathleen Russell, "Development of a Black Criminology and the Role of the Black Criminologist," *Justice Quarterly* 9:4 (1992): 667–683; Shawn Gabiddon, Helen Greene, and Kideste Wilder, "Still Excluded?" *Journal of Research in Crime and Delinquency* 41:4 (2004): 384–406; and Editors, "Racial Inequality and Drug Arrests," *New York Times* (May 10, 2008), p. 18. For an examination of the juvenile justice system issues, see Christina DeJong and K. Jackson, "Putting Race into Context: Race, Juvenile Justice Processing, and Urbanization," *Justice Quarterly* 15:3 (1998): 487–504.

12. Sabol and Minton, *Jail Inmates at Midyear 2007.*

13. Doris J. James and Lauren E. Glaze, *Mental Health Problems of Prison and Jail Inmates* (Washington, DC: Bureau of Justice Statistics, 2006).

14. John Clark and H. Alan, *The Pretrial Release Decision Making Process* (Washington, DC: Pretrial Services Resource Center, 1996); and Brian Paine and Randy Gainey, "The Electronic Monitoring of Offenders Released from Jail or Prison," *The Prison Journal* 84:4 (2004): 413–435.

15. Ken Kerle, *American Jails* (New York: Butterworth-Heinemann, 1998), pp. 190–191. See also Jeffrey Senese, Joe Wilson, Arthur Evans, et al., "Evaluating Jail Reform: Inmate Infraction and Disciplinary Response in a Traditional and a Podular/Direct Supervision Jail," *American Jails* 6:4 (1992): 14–24. See also James Skidmore, "Tarrant County Sheriff's Metropolitan Confinement Bureau," *American Jails* 13:5 (1998): 80–81.

16. Virginia Hutchinson, K. Teller, and T. Reid, "Inmate Behavior Management," *American Jails* 19:2 (2005): 9–14.

17. Sabol and Minton, *Jail Inmates at Midyear 2007,* p. 818; and Wayne Welsh, *Counties in Court: Jail Overcrowding and Court-Ordered Reform* (Philadelphia: Temple University Press, 1995). See also Ernest Cowles, R. Schmitz, and B. Bass, *An Implementation Evaluation of the Pretrial and Drug Intervention Programs in Illinois' Macon and Peoria Counties* (Chicago: Illinois Criminal Justice Information Agency, 1998).

18. Ken Kerl, "Jail Crowding and Increasing Jail Populations," *American Jails* 23:5 (2008): 5, 95.

19. National Center of Addiction and Substance Abuse at Columbia University, *Behind Bars: Substance Abuse and American Prison Population* (New York: NCASACU, 1998). See also Michael Havens, "ACLU Sues Nevada DOC over Inmate Care," *Correctional News* 14:3 (2008), p. 28.

20. Mike Howerton, "Jail Standards in 2001: Results of a 21-State Survey," *American Jails* 15:5 (2001): 9–11.

21. A review of the first two decades of new-generation jails can be found in Raymond Harris and David Russell, "Podular Direct Supervision: The First Twenty Years," *American Jails* 9:3 (1995): 11–12. See also Gerald Bayens, J. Williams, and J. Ortiz, "Jail Type and Inmate Behavior," *Federal Probation* 61:3 (1997): 54–62; and Detention Bureau Center, City of Alexandria, Virginia, "A New Generational Jail," http://www.alexandriava.gov/sheriff/info/default.aspx?id=8460 (accessed October 4, 2008).

22. Frederick Bennett, "After the Litigation: Part I," *American Jails* 6:3 (1992): 81–84; "After the Litigation: Part II," *American Jails* 6:4 (1992): 30–36; Matthew Lopes, "The Role of the Masters in Correctional Litigation," *American Jails* 6:4 (1993): 27–29; Daniel Pollack, "How to Find a Good Lawyer," *Corrections Today* 54:8 (1992): 114–118; and Heidi M. Murphy, "Supreme Court Ruling Changes the Standard on Inmate Abuse," *Corrections Today* 54:1 (1992): 195.

23. Patrick Kinkade, M. Leone, and S. Semond, "The Consequences of Jail Crowding," *Crime and Delinquency* 41:1 (1995): 150–161. See also the special issue "Mental Health Issues in Corrections," *Corrections Today* 67:1 (2005): 22–53; and Editors, "Cal Prison Health Czar Heads to Court," *Correctional News* 14:6 (2008), p. 8. (sic).

24. James Tesoriero and Malcom McCullough, "Correctional Health Care Now and into the Twenty-First Century," in *Vision for Change* (New York: Prentice Hall, 1996), pp. 215–236.

25. Patricia Satterfield, "Creating Strategies for Controlling Health Care Costs," *Corrections Today* 54:2 (1992): 190–194. See also Frank Cousins, "The Business Side of Health Care in the Corrections Industry," *American Jails* 18:3 (2004): 56–60.

26. For information about Texas jails, go to: http://www.tcjs.state.tx.us/index.php?linkID=320.

27. Linda Winterfield and Sally Hillsman, *The Staten Island Day-Fine Project* (Washington, DC: US Department of Justice, 1993). See also the policy statement of the National Council on Crime and Delinquency, *Criminal Justice Policy Statement* (San Francisco: NCCD, 1992); Judith Greene, *The Maricopa County FARE Probation Experiment* (New York: Vera Institute of Justice, 1996);

and Cambridge Encyclopedia, "Day Fines," http://encyclopediastateuniversity/pages/7501/fine/html (accessed October 4, 2008).

28. Paul Hudson, *The State Jail System Today* (Austin: Texas Criminal Justice Policy Council, 1998).

29. Harrison and Karberg, *Prison and Jail Inmates at Midyear 2003*, p. 8.

30. Janet Haines et al., "The Psycho-Physiology of Self-Mutilation," *Journal of Abnormal Psychology* 104:3 (1995): 471–489; and Human Rights Watch, "Suicide and Self-Mutilation," http://www.hrw.org/reports/2003/usa1003/22.htm (accessed October 4, 2008).

31. Lindsay Haines and Eric Blauw (eds.), "Prison Suicide," *Crises* 18:4 (1997): 146–189; and Alan Felthouse and A. Tomkins (eds.), "Mental Health Issues in Correctional Settings," *Behavior Sciences and the Law* 15:4 (1997): 379–523.

chapter 10

State and Local Prison Systems

Outline

Overview

In past chapters, we have examined the philosophies, the clients, and the functions and tasks of the operators of jails, probation, and America's prisons. We have seen the male–female and racial allocations to the facilities that make up systems that cost the taxpayers almost $50 billion to operate each year. (See Figure 10.1 for a breakdown of these system costs.) This chapter takes you into the basic functions and characteristics of the state prisons, using male adult offenders, who constitute 93% of the population, as our vehicle.[1] Female inmates are discussed in Chapter 17. Because they are not an insignificant part of daily state and local adult prison activity, the male inmate and institution are used here as a demonstration of how most of the systems operate.

> "The endurance of these monolithic structures is surpassed only by the tenacity of the assumptions and attitudes on which they were founded: the cause of crime is located in the individual offender; he should be punished for his acts; behavior is modifiable; and isolated institutions are appropriate settings in which to modify an individual's behavior. America had created a theory, reformation by confinement, and the system has been unwilling to abandon it although it has proved unworkable."
>
> —William G. Nagel,
> *The New Red Barn*

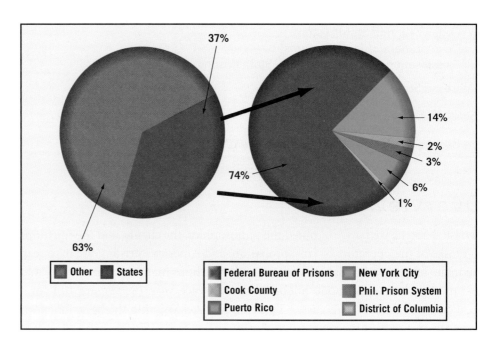

figure 10.1

Annual Costs of Prisons: $49,251,273,843.00

SOURCE: American Correctional Association, *2007 Directory* (Alexandria, VA: ACA, 2007). p. 18.

STATE CORRECTIONAL INSTITUTIONS: THE CORE OF THE SYSTEM

This chapter explores the state systems for housing the well over 1,767,000 adult sentenced male and female offenders in more than 1,600 adult state and local prisons in America[2] as of 2012. Juvenile institutions, detention centers, jails, workhouses, and other facilities for misdemeanants and minor offenders are not included. The major correctional institutions contained in the state systems are supermaximum prisons, maximum/close prisons, medium-security prisons, and minimum-security prisons (see Figure 10.2), many of which are modeled after the nineteenth-century concepts in the Auburn penitentiary.

Those institutions form the core of most state correctional programs charged with the simultaneous, and often conflicting, functions of punishment and reform. Most are short on money and personnel, but they are still expected to prevent their graduates from returning to crime. Security and custody are the primary emphases in these prisons, and their environments are isolated both physically and philosophically from the mainstream of life. James V. Bennett, a former director of the Federal Bureau of Prisons, described the ironic situation 30 years ago:

> Even our modern prison system is proceeding on a rather uncertain course because its administration is necessarily a series of compromises. On the one hand, prisons are expected to punish; on the other, they are supposed to reform. They are expected to discipline rigorously at the same time that they teach self-reliance. They are built to be operated like vast impersonal machines, yet they are expected to fit men to live normal community lives. They operate in accordance with a fixed autocratic routine, yet they are expected to develop individual initiative. All too frequently restrictive laws force prisoners into idleness despite the fact that one of their primary objectives is to teach men how to earn an honest living. They refuse a prisoner a voice in self-government, but they expect him to become a thinking citi-

lecture note

Using your computer, play the brief chapter overview videotape of Harry Allen on "State and Local Prison Systems" that introduces Chapter 10 (about 4 minutes).

class activity

Ask students to define the various levels of male inmates by security level.

class activity

Challenge students to draft a timeline for major correctional programs and innovations in corrections, from the Walnut Street Jail to the day reporting systems.

class activity

Ask students on what variables incoming prisoners are classified in your jurisdiction, and when they might expect to be reclassified.

lecture note

Address the conflicting expectations of correctional administrators, and then ask students to prioritize those expectations.

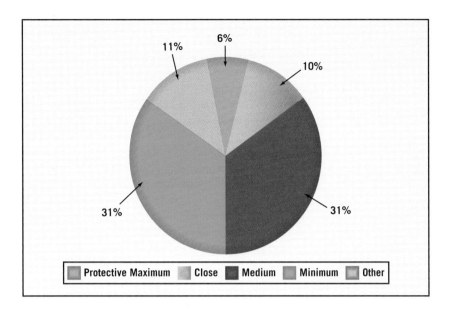

figure 10.2
Percentage of Male Inmates by Security Level, 2012

SOURCE: American Correctional Association, Directory 2006 (Alexandria, VA: ACA, 2007), p. 57.

key term

Alternative to death and flogging
Any correctional punishment less than the death penalty, such as imprisonment, probation, diversion, and so on.

zen in a democratic society. To some, prisons are nothing but "country clubs" catering to the whims and fancies of the inmates. To others the prison atmosphere seems charged only with bitterness, rancor, and an all-pervading sense of defeat. And so the whole paradoxical scheme continues, because our ideas and views regarding the function of correctional institutions in our society are confused, fuzzy, and nebulous.[3]

Correctional institutions are both a blessing and a curse. Reflecting a positive and humane movement away from the cruel punishments of the eighteenth century, they provided an **alternative to death and flogging;** but in terms of reforming inmates so they can lead a noncriminal life in the free world, prisons have mostly failed. Still, the public's perceived need to feel safe and secure and the prison's effectiveness in isolating offenders from society have unfortunately made this system the primary response to criminal behavior. The 1,470,000 male and female inmates confined in state correctional institutions for adults in 2012 were distributed among maximum-security, close-medium-security, and minimum-security institutions, along with institutions of other security levels.[4] We project that by the year 2012, prison population (state, federal, and local city systems) will have grown to approximately 1.8 million Americans (see Figure 10.3).

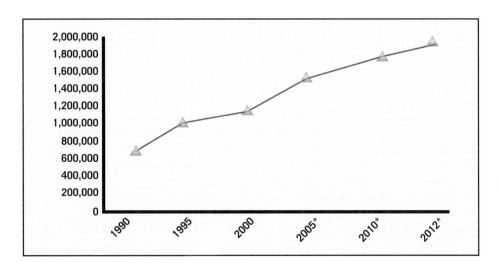

figure 10.3
Population Growth: 1990–2012*

SOURCE: William Sabol and Heather Couture, *Prison Inmates at Midyear 2007* (Washington, DC: Bureau of Justice Statistics, 2008), p. 1.

Raol Leon, who is serving a life sentence for an execution-style murder, in a holding cell, is photographed through a slot in the cell door at Pelican Bay Prison in California.

Organization of State Systems

Of all the thousands of various types of correctional facilities in America—public and private, adult and juvenile, community and city, and others—only 16% of them are under the control of state agencies. It is not surprising that the correctional "system" in most states is not really systematized at all. Organizational rigidity and huge investments in "bricks-and-mortar" responses have handicapped meaningful revision and modernization of corrections. Rehabilitation and reintegration require that organizational structures be concerned with more than just institutional programs. In at least six states, that organizational need has been met by exercising control over all correctional activities at the state level. Hawaii, for example, has a unified jail and prison system. In Canada, all offenders sentenced to two years or less of imprisonment are incarcerated at a provincial ("state-level") prison, whereas those serving longer sentences are committed to the federal prison system.

Corrections at the state level generally is organized into a separate department of corrections (with a cabinet-level secretary or director appointed by the governor) or a division within a larger state department. Most correctional administrators consider the separate department to be more effective, and having the director at the cabinet level adds great flexibility and prestige to the correctional operation. Without an intermediate level of organization, the director of a separate department has the ability to move more freely at the policy-making level. An autonomous department is able to control the allocation of personnel and fiscal resources, using economy-of-scale purchasing and operating with minimum competition from other divisions within the same department. Centralized control also has the advantage of providing effective administrative functions that are unique to correctional problems.

The corrections process must include a system of multilevel programs and facilities to provide the spectrum of services required to make a statewide program work. Most state correctional systems are concerned only with the principal institutions and parole services, leaving the majority of correctional problems in the state to units of local government.

Development of State Systems

Each type of state correctional system has developed as a matter of historical accident as much as in response to a state's particular needs. As might be expected, the large industrial prisons of the northeast United States are more in evidence in the major industrial states, generally in the area between Illinois and New York. Most of those institutions were built early in the prison movement and were designed to take advantage of the cheap labor force inmates represented. They were the hardest hit by the restrictions the government later placed on prison industries in the 1930s.

At present, the industry allowed in the giant institutions does not provide full employment for large inmate populations.[5] In an effort to spread the few jobs among the many inmates, supervisors try to slow production and make the work last as long as possible. Those procedures are not likely to provide the inmate with a very good model for job success on the outside. The general picture of activity in the one-time industrial prisons is one of idleness and boredom. Despite even the most dedicated attempts by the staff inside and outside the institutions, there are just not enough meaningful jobs or other programs to help the thousands crowded into the likes of the Raifords (Florida), Atticas (New York), and San Quentins (California) of the country, although some exceptional programs exist.

Dozens of aging prisoners resting and relaxing.
© Shepard Sherbell/SABA/CORBIS All Rights Reserved.

The **agricultural prison** was begun in the southern states. Prison farms became very profitable ventures for those states and thus have been slow to change. Prisoners who served on public works and state farms replaced the pre–Civil War slave labor in many states, not only in the South.[6] Here again, authorities may have rationalized that the training received from farm work and mines[7] helped prepare offenders for return to a basically agrarian southern economy, but the real intent was to use free labor to produce farm products. Cheap prison labor was often leased out to farm owners at a great profit to both the farmer and the state that collected the fee. The use of prison farms has become less profitable, however, with the advent of highly mechanized farming methods in most agricultural states.

Other regions of the country have designated certain institutions as farm oriented. The food produced in those institutions has been used to feed the rest of the institutions in the state. Many states have now begun to abandon that practice as the realization has hit that farming experience is of little value to the primarily urban inmate found to be a large majority in most contemporary prisons. Another problem with prison farms has been the negative reaction from farm organizations, whose members argue that competition from the state is unfair, much the same argument as union workers protested about prison manufacturing industries in the early part of the twentieth century.[8]

Many states have chosen to set up **work camps** and other forms of prisoner activity appropriate to their particular needs. Lumber camps have been used, as have road prisons or camps to construct and maintain roads. Recent versions of the work camp have been geared to provide a combination of hard work in the outdoors and programmed treatment aimed at preparing the offender for release. It is considered more beneficial for offenders to do time in the relatively healthful atmosphere of a small work camp than to languish in the idleness and boredom of the large prisons.

Classification and Assignment in State Prisons

Most state codes provide for the separation or classification of prisoners,[9] their division into different grades with promotion or demotion according to merit or demerit, their employment and instruction in industrial pursuits, and their education. Most also stipulate that reformation of prisoners is a primary goal, although certain exceptions apply. California, for example, still stresses punishment.

In most systems, the **initial classification** determines the institution to which an inmate will be assigned. The receiving institution then determines whether the individual shall remain in maximum security or be transferred to a medium- or minimum-security penitentiary. (Each state in the United States has at least one maximum-security institution.) Most states base their transfer decisions on a perception of the individual's ability to handle the next-lowest-level of security. Also important is an evaluation of the individual's ability to adjust to a program geared primarily to work, to academic or vocational training, or to the needs of the growing number of older offenders. A classification committee usually participates in making those decisions.

The **classification process** continues at the institutional level. Although each receiving institution emphasizes different programs, each has some version of education, counseling, and the other ingredients of a total program. Theoretically, individuals are assigned according to their needs but, realistically, assignments are too often made to conform to **institutional needs.** For example, an inmate may genuinely want to learn welding. If the welding class is filled, as it often might be, but there is a vacancy in the furniture shop, the inmate may be assigned to the furniture shop, and no effort would be made to offer additional welding instruction. Also, inmates will often be assigned to a maintenance operation, such as food service or janitorial work, which is unlikely to conform to their own vocational plans or ambitions. An essential element of effective classification is a periodic review of the inmate's progress through the recommended program. All institutions allow for this reevaluation, usually called *reclassification*. The purpose is to adjust the program in accordance with the inmate's progress and needs. Realistically, however, decisions are all too frequently made on the basis of the available vacancies and institutional needs.

In 2005, the U.S. Supreme Court determined that new or recently transferred inmates may not be segregated by race in the classification process. Prison administrators would argue that such segregation serves institutional interests and has legitimate correctional functions, lowering the volume of conflicts between security threat groups ("gangs") and staff and inmates who bear grudges against other inmates or groups.[10]

Institution personnel may genuinely wish to provide the recommended program for an inmate. However, the need to keep the institution going smoothly inevitably shapes these decisions. Personnel may rationalize maintenance assignments on the basis that many, if not most, inmates need the experience of accepting supervision, developing regular work habits, learning to relate to coworkers, and other such skills. All of that may be true, but the treatment staff members are no less frustrated than the inmates when their recommended and prescribed programs are ignored. The classification and assignment process just described is only a composite of what the more effective programs provide.

INMATES IN STATE PRISONS

In 1983, the U.S. Department of Justice conducted a national survey of inmates in state correctional facilities in the United States and found an estimated 381,955 offenders under the jurisdiction of state government.[11] Since that study was conducted, the population of state prisons has skyrocketed to almost 1.8 million, an increase of over 471% (see Table 10.1).

An overwhelming majority of the inmates (93%) are males, and relative to the numbers of men and women in the U.S. resident population, their incarceration rate is about ten times higher (1,406 males to 136 females) per 100,000 populations. The number of white male to black male inmates has been increasing at the state level, and is now 37% and 41%, respectively.[12] All other minority males (Hispanics and others) now total 22% of the state prison populations. Hispanics are the fastest growing group in state prisons.[13] The average age is about 32 years; and almost 10% of the total population was at least age 50, reflecting the graying of America's general population as well as populations of inmates. Imprisonment rates for adult males by race, age, and ethnicity can be found in Figure 10.4. Minorities, particularly African American males, are incarcerated at a much higher rate than are white males.[14]

table **10.1** | Number of Sentenced Male Prisoners under State or Federal Jurisdiction, 2007, by Race and Age

Age	Total	White	Black	Hispanic
18–19	86,600	27,100	36,500	17,700
20–24	353,300	108,200	145,600	80,100
25–29	354,100	106,200	143,400	83,900
30–34	328,600	109,500	125,600	73,800
35–39	303,100	113,700	118,200	55,000
40–44	273,600	114,200	103,300	41,900
45–54	184,200	77,500	71,200	27,800
55 or older	89,900	60,700	24,700	13,000
Total	2,090,800	755,500	814,700	410,900

SOURCE: William Sabol and Heather Couture, *Prison Inmates at Mid-year 2007* (Washington, DC: Bureau of Justice Statistics, 2008). p. 7.

The offenses for which the state prisoners were currently incarcerated are shown in Figure 10.5. In sum, six in ten inmates in state prisons were convicted of crimes of violence, including murder, manslaughter, rape, sexual assault, robbery, and assault. About one in six was incarcerated for a drug offense, usually drug trafficking. Less than one in four were in prison for property and all other crimes (see Figure 10.5).

As a group, state prison inmates were much less educated than their counterparts in the civilian population. At least 70% of the inmates had not received a high school diploma or GED, in contrast with 36% of the general population 18 years of age or older who had not.

In terms of their criminal offenses, almost 60% were classified as violent in 2012. The average sentence length imposed was more than eight years,[15] although 9% of the prisoners were incarcerated under life sentences. One in three had incurred at least one other sentence, in addition to the instant offense, and one in four had previously served time as a juvenile offender.

In 2012, the 1,800,000 adult male inmates will be in state facilities with an average capacity of nearly 100% (full). Twenty-two states (and the federal prison system) will be

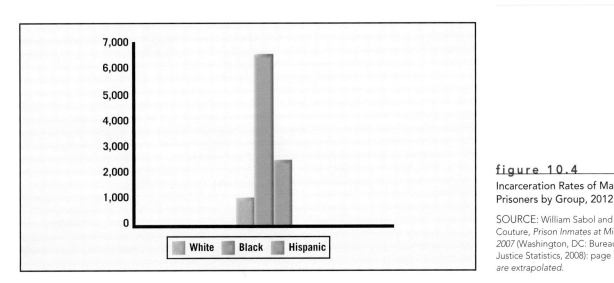

figure 10.4

Incarceration Rates of Male Prisoners by Group, 2012

SOURCE: William Sabol and Heather Couture, *Prison Inmates at Midyear 2007* (Washington, DC: Bureau of Justice Statistics, 2008): page 7. *Data are extrapolated.*

figure 10.5

Current Offenses of State
Inmates: 2012

SOURCE: William Sabol, Heather
Couture and Paige Harrison, *Prisoners
in 2006* (Washington, DC: Bureau of
Justice Statistics, 2007), p. 25. Data for
2010 and 2012 are extrapolated.

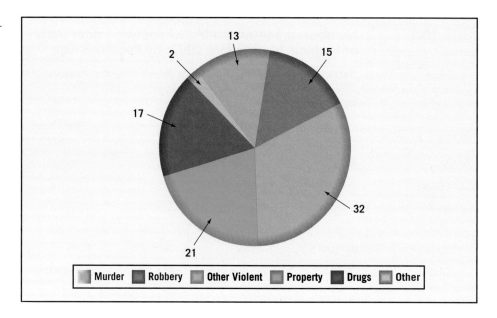

operating at or above their highest capacity. California has the largest number of inmates, but Louisiana has more inmates per 100,000 residents than any other state (814 inmates).

To keep abreast of the crush of new commitments, states have been forced to resort to a bricks-and-mortar construction binge. The number of prison beds constructed each year is astounding. Prison beds are expensive to build, averaging $74,000 per bed in 2000 (excluding interest to be paid on any construction bonds).[16] If the state borrows funds ("floats a bond") to construct a prison and pays the loan off over 30 years at 4% interest, the cost of a maximum-security bed could be as much as $160,000.

In general, the lower the security level, the less the cost per bed; minimum-security beds cost an average of $29,311 versus $80,000 or even more for maximum-security beds. The prison-bed construction costs for 2003 alone were over $6.7 billion. The per diem cost of incarceration for adults averages $62.05 per inmate, or $88 million a day to house, feed, control,

Vocational training helps build
a new facility.
*Photo by Spencer Tirey, courtesy of
Getty Images, Inc.-Liaison.*

and care for the nation's adult male state inmates. Despite the construction, remodeling, re-designing, and renovations, American prisons generally remain overcrowded. The U.S. Supreme Court may have to examine again the realities of imprisonment in the first decades of the 2000s and the Eighth Amendment, thus forcing change in corrections. Clearly the escalating problems for harried correctional administrators are only beginning. Fortunately, some of those problems are being addressed in actions in the U.S. Supreme Court.

LOCAL ADULT CITY-OPERATED PRISONS

In calculating the numbers of inmates in adult prisons, one must not forget the "Big Four," a group of local institutions that are even larger than most states' prison systems:

1. Cook County Department of Corrections
2. New York City Department of Corrections
3. Washington, D.C., Department of Corrections
4. Philadelphia Prison System

These four large systems consist of 110 adult prisons and a large number of other institutions and programs, and could well hold over 30,000 adult offenders by 2012. One seldom thinks of cities as needing their own correctional systems, but these four cities have chosen to do so. Their operations are similar to the state prisons, but they allow inmates to be housed nearer to home. It may be that some of the other large U.S. cities may get into their own corrections game as well, but most have shown little interest. Many local jail systems are already so overcrowded that most do not have the time to plan that far ahead. The trends of the Big Four should be followed carefully.

Two other groups of jurisdictions that operate prison systems are the five U.S. military branches and correctional authorities in the U.S. territories and commonwealths. Information on these correctional authorities is detailed in the accompanying Correctional Brief and in Figure 10.6.

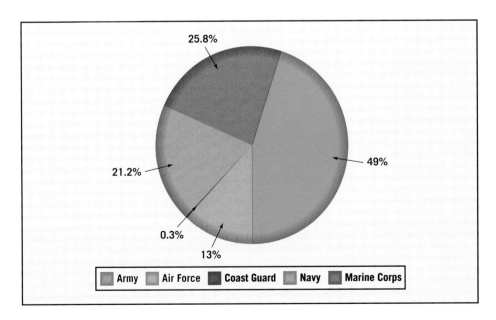

<u>**figure 10.6**</u>

Prisoners Under Military Jurisdiction and Branch of Service, 2012 (Approximately 1500 Total)

SOURCE: William Sabol and Heather Couture, *Prison Inmates at Midyear 2007* (Washington, DC: Bureau of Justice Statistics, 2008), p. 26.

correctional **brief**

Prisoners in Custody of Correctional Authorities in the U.S. Territories, 2012

The U.S. territories and commonwealths—American Samoa, Guam, Northern Mariana Islands, Puerto Rico, and Virgin Islands—will have 13,654 inmates under the jurisdiction of their prison systems at yearend 2012, somewhat less than yearend 2006.

Puerto Rico, the largest of the territories, will have the most sentenced prisoners (12,278 at yearend 2012. Twenty-

five states and the District of Columbia will have fewer inmates than Puerto Rico.

SOURCE: William Sabol and Heather Couture, *Prison Inmates at Midyear 2006* (Washington, DC: Bureau of Justice Statistics, 2007), p. 25.

Prisoners in Custody, Yearend 2012

Territory	Number
American Samoa	253
Guam	394
Mariana Islands	116
Puerto Rico	12,278
U.S. Virgin Islands	613

class activity

Ask students what a "court master" is, and have them describe the role a master might play in bringing about change.

ARE PRISONS "CRUEL AND UNUSUAL PUNISHMENT"?

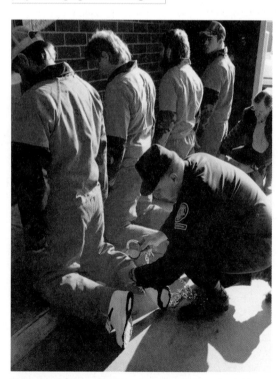

Prisoners are shackled to do volunteer work picking up trash on the highway.
Photo by AP Wide World Photos.

Whether prisons are state or local, or house males or females, the problems of institutionalization are ever present in our prisons. Understaffing, underbudgeting, and lack of citizen interest or involvement often become excuses for allowing conditions to deteriorate and sink to the lowest levels. Beginning in the 1970s, both state and federal courts were asked to examine the operations and policies of correctional facilities and personnel to ensure compliance with the Eighth Amendment's prohibition against cruel and unusual punishment. By February 1983, the courts had declared unconstitutional the entire prison systems of Alabama, Florida, Louisiana, Mississippi, Oklahoma, Rhode Island, Tennessee, Texas, and all the male penal institutions of Michigan. In addition, at least one or more facilities in another 21 states were operating under either a court order or a consent decree (permission to continue to operate until a fix has been completed within a specific timeframe) as a result of inmate crowding and/or the conditions of confinement. Yet another seven states were involved in ongoing litigation relating to overcrowding and/or the conditions of release from prison. Finally, in eight states, the courts had appointed receivers or masters to operate the state prison system or facility, had ordered the emergency release of inmates because of crowding, or had designated specific prisons to be closed.[17] The courts took those actions only as a last resort and when it was clear the impacted states had relinquished their responsibility to protect the constitutional rights of the inmates under their custody and care. Correctional construction began in earnest as a response to prison overcrowding. Between 1987 and 2012, more than 800 new prisons will have been built and added to correctional systems.[18]

The states, understandably, have reacted with great indignation over the Supreme Court's intruding into the domain of the executive branch at the state level. Where does the Court get the right to intervene in such matters? The Civil Rights Law of 1871 provides for the principal method of allowing such inmate complaints into the federal courts. That statute provides that citizens denied constitutional rights by the state may sue in the federal court. Originally designed to protect the newly freed slaves in the post–Civil War era, the statute was generally forgotten until a landmark case in 1964 (*Cooper* v. *Pate*). In that case, the Court finally ruled in favor of a prisoner's seeking relief in federal court by way of the 1871 act.

The procedure has been tentative and careful, each step breaking new ground for prisoners' rights:

> These decisions provided almost all of the legal groundwork necessary for "conditions suits." They all came while Earl Warren was chief justice. But under Warren Burger, the Supreme Court has shown even more interest in prison cases. In some areas, it has extended prisoners' rights; in others it has held the line. But it has held fast to one principle: no one must interfere with the right of inmates to take their complaints to federal courts.
>
> With these sketchy guidelines, federal district judges have been feeling their way. In the first cases dealing with specific prison practices, the judges would balance the constitutional rights of the prisoners against the prison officials' legitimate interests in security, rehabilitation, and order. If the officials' defense were not sufficient, then the practice would be ordered changed. If such a ruling was upheld on appeal by one of the eleven U.S. Circuit Courts of Appeal, then it became a binding precedent within that circuit and was available to guide judges in other circuits. Only if the U.S. Supreme Court issues a ruling on a case is the precedent binding across the nation, although approval can be implied when the Court declines to hear an appeal. The Supreme Court has declined appeals on all the broad conditions suits that have been brought before it. District court judges have generally built upon each other's decisions in these areas. This judicial activism has not taken place in a vacuum, of course. In most areas of constitutional law inmates have ridden on the coattails of more popular causes such as school desegregation and voting rights for minorities. The extension of the class-action suit has made broad-based challenges to prison conditions possible. Increased activism among lawyers and the growth of legal aid programs was an important factor.[19]

The states are not giving up easily, however, and have appealed these decisions. Each case is different, of course, but they have all been slowed in their immediate impact by the issuance of a decision of the Fifth Circuit Court of Appeals, written in regard to the Alabama order:

> This seemingly inexorable march toward greater judicial activism was slowed when the Fifth Circuit Court of Appeals issued its ruling on the state's appeal of the Alabama order. In an opinion by a three-judge panel, written by Judge J. P. Coleman, a former governor of Mississippi, the appeals court affirmed the basic finding of unconstitutionality, but it reduced the scope of Johnson's original order. The court ordered a new hearing on the judge's requirement of 60 square feet of space per inmate in new construction. It dissolved the Human Rights Committee and dismissed the hired consultant, although it said the judge could appoint a single monitor for each prison "to observe, and to report his observations to the court, with no authority to intervene in daily prison operations" [emphasis in original]. The court also overturned Judge Johnson's order forbidding the state to require women visitors to prisons to stand over a mirror and drop their underwear as part of a routine search for contraband.
>
> The most significant part of Judge Johnson's order, that dealing with idleness, was also cut back. Rehabilitation programs, the court said, could not be required. Because the order that each inmate be assigned to a job "should not impose any real burden" on prison officials, it let that part stand. But it ruled that

Jail inmates stand in the doorway of their dorm in the Los Angeles County Jail, part of the 20,000 inmates in a system built for half that number.
Courtesy of AP Wide World Photos.

correctional **brief**

The Supermax Prison

Violent, seriously disruptive, assaultive, and escape-prone inmates, including gang activists, pose immense challenges to prison security and custody. Challenges include threats to the safety of staff and other inmates, danger to the security of the institution, and inmates who require protective custody. The supermaximum prison ("**supermax**") is a response to the need to manage and securely control inmates exhibiting violent or seriously disruptive behavior while incarcerated.

A supermax prison is a free-standing facility (or distinct unit within a facility) that provides for the management and secure control of inmates who have been officially designated as exhibiting violent or seriously disruptive behavior while incarcerated.

The first supermaximum prison was Alcatraz; the earliest supermax housing opened in 1954 in Mississippi. At present there are at least 57 supermax facilities or units nationwide, providing about 20,000 beds, or about 2% of those serving sentences of at least a year.

Within the supermax can usually be found a special housing unit (SHU) for the most difficult-to-handle offenders, sometimes called the "worst of the worst." The SHU enforces the strictest discipline and isolation, reinforced by physical means. There, inmates are typically held in their cells 23 hours a day and eat in their cells. There are few interactions between staff and inmates, and almost none between inmates.

When a SHU inmate leaves the cell, that prisoner is typically cuffed and leg-shackled; two or three officers escort each unit inmate. Recreation is solitary, typically for 30 minutes, perhaps three times a week, in a bare cell with no equipment.

Controversy abounds over the operations of a SHU. First is the question of how inmates are selected for SHU isolation; one sufficient criterion is gang membership. How does a gang member earn release from an SHU? By renouncing the gang and providing intelligence to correctional officers? What are the implications of this snitch behavior for a "blood-in, blood-out" prison gang, and would this lead to shortened life expectancy?

Second is the cost penalty, because SHUs are labor intensive; multiple escorts are required for each inmate leaving the cell. Third is the surge of litigation over sensory deprivation, classification, access to law libraries and attorneys, quality of mental health services, and excessive use of force (*Madrid* v. *Gomez*, 889 F. Supp. 1146, 1995). This Pelican Bay, California, lawsuit determined that holding mentally ill inmates in an SHU where there was extremely limited mental health services and in isolation (which can accelerate mental health deterioration) was cruel and unusual punishment, a violation of the Eighth Amendment. (The current practices and effects of supermax prisons are discussed by Jesenia Pizarro and Vanja Stenius, "The Supermax Prison," *The Prison Journal* 84:1 [2004]: 248–264.)

On the other hand, using the supermax prison can dramatically cut down on prison violence, assaults, and murders of prison officers and other inmates. What would you do if you were managing an institution operating at 83% over its maximum capacity, with several gangs and a high concentration of severely violent and aggressive inmates present?

SOURCE: LIS, Inc., *Supermax Housing: A Survey of Current Practice* (Langmont, CO: National Institute of Corrections, 1997), pp. 1–6.

Key Term

Supermax prison
A free-standing prison or designated area within a prison that functions to control and contain dangerous, violent, disruptive, and other serious behavior in a prison facility.

lecture note

Describe the transition from the pre-1980 prison culture to the gang-dominated contemporary scene. Identify how staff members have been empowered to deal with security-threat groups.

it could not be used as a precedent in future cases. "If the state furnishes its prisoners with reasonably adequate food, clothing, shelter, sanitation, medical care, and personal safety, so as to avoid the imposition of cruel and unusual punishment, that ends its obligations under Amendment Eight," the decision stated.[20]

Eighth Amendment lawsuits over prison conditions continue (*Madrid* v. *Gomez*, for example).[21]

Realistically, we must acknowledge that the prison has little control over who will be committed. Nor does it exercise much control over sentence length, parole eligibility, minimal sentence proportion to be served, or legislative allocations. The current prison situation is a result in part of the high-risk age category (age 16 to 29) that the baby boom has brought about, the more conservative response to crime, the public's fear of crime and criminals, increased sentence lengths, and the higher failure rates of parolees who must then be returned to prison. Yet the cruel and unusual punishment conditions continue.

Prior to the mid-1970s, the inmate social system was controlled internally by "old-hand" inmates whose exemplary behavior had won them the grudging respect of the inmate body. Challenges to their status and the prison routine desired by the old hands would be met with the necessary force to remove the challenger through murder or, where necessary, institutional riot. When the War on Drugs began, members of street gangs and "crazies"

c o r r e c t i o n a l **brief**

Security-Threat Groups ("Prison Gangs")

The prison security-threat group (STG) was defined by the American Correctional Association as "two or more inmates, acting together, who pose a threat to the security or safety of staff/inmates, and/or are disruptive to programs and/or to the orderly management of the facility/system." Members engage in such activities as planning, organizing, and committing unlawful acts (selling drugs, murder) and threatening, soliciting, or financing unlawful acts or other acts that would violate the institution's or department's policies, rules, or regulations. Unlike street gangs, with which many are affiliated, STGs are more sophisticated, organized, and calculating. They seek to control their environment by threats and intimidation of staff and other inmates.

Frequently organized along racial and ethnic lines, members adhere to a strict code of behavior, silence, and lifelong membership. They have a hierarchical order and are frequently organized along such clearly defined goals and objectives as contract murder, homosexual prostitution, drug trafficking, and gambling. Group cohesion and behavior are enforced by brutal and violent means that include beatings, maiming, and murder. Most STGs are not only anti-authority, they are also characterized by both racist hate and distrust of other gangs. Vendettas between gangs within an institution can wreak havoc with order and create inmate fear, staff anxiety, and avalanches of requests from inmates for administrative segregation.

Dealing with the escalating growth of STGs requires intelligence, the systematic gathering of information on individuals and groups, and the marshalling of that information into useful data that can be used to combat prison gangs. Prison administrators can sensitize staff to be vigilant for gang signs (colors, tattoos, interactions between individuals, hand signs, etc.). After gangs and their members have been identified, gang isolation inside and between institutions can reduce the threat potential and STG activities. In the long run, combating gang activities by attacking a gang's line of authority and internal organization are not enough. Facilities must also provide programs and activities for nongang inmates. Small STG prisons that isolate members of a specific gang and that have both low inmate-to-staff ratios and direct supervision are a start. Supermax prisons are mandatory for control of the gang leaders, once STGs are entrenched.

These proactive strategies and efforts are not sufficient to manage this set of problems. Nonaffiliated inmates must be protected from the unlawful activities and enforced recruitment into gangs. Institutional programs must be developed and emphasized that range from educational and vocational training through industrial and recreational programs. Options include developing a continuum of lessened security levels to which nongang members might aspire, and this must be developed as part of the modern correctional system. While this discussion does not exhaust the list of possible policies that can be used to contain gang threat, it serves as an exploration of the challenges of corrections in the current century.

SOURCES: American Correctional Association, *Gangs in Correctional Facilities* (Laurel, MD: ACA, 1993). See also Reginald Wilkinson, M. Meyer, and T. Unwin, *Ohio Prison Gangs: A Counterfeit Family* (Columbus, OH: Ohio Department of Rehabilitation and Correction, 1996); and Security Threat Group Intelligence Unit, Florida Department of Corrections, "Major Prison Gangs," http://www.dc.state.fl.us/ security_reports_gangs_prison/html (accessed April 20, 2005).

were committed to prison, where they challenged the former social system. The old hands lost control of the institutions and prison gangs emerged as a segment of the social structure in institutions, in part as a defense mechanism against the superviolent and aggressive acts of the crazies and other gangs.[22] Correctional administrators, faced with violent acts and correctional officer casualties, began to create supermaximum prisons to isolate the most dangerous and violent, as well as gangs (**security-threat groups** or **STGs**). Supermax prisons were greeted with an explosion of lawsuits that continue today.[23] Corrections administrators thus face many emerging challenges.

One other response by corrections was to add more correctional personnel. More than 510,000 persons will be employed in state correctional facilities in 2012, an increase of 163% over the number in 1985. The staff-to-inmate ratio will be one officer for each almost 6 overall. On September 30, 2003, there were more than 248,000 custodial staff employees, 23% of whom were female.[24] The number of custodial staff will continue to increase during the second decade of the twenty-first century.

Correctional opportunities will continue to increase, and recruits will be sought who have the skills and willingness to work in the prisons of tomorrow. There is clearly a need for active citizen support for corrections, especially at the state level, and for active monitoring of our prison conditions.

key term

Security-threat group (STG)
Prison gangs; a criminal enterprise having an organizational structure and internal leadership, acting as an ongoing criminal conspiracy that uses violence and other criminal activity to continue.

Summary

The state and local adult correctional systems in America are as diverse as the states and cities themselves. We have provided only an overview of the problems facing correctional administrators when they try to model a unified and coordinated system of corrections within the framework of fragmented and antiquated institutions, poorly trained and low-paid officers, and often antiquated procedures. The prison remains the core of most state correctional systems, despite its clear failure as a means of rehabilitation and reintegration of offenders (currently the two major goals of corrections). Classification of inmates and subsequent assignment and reassignment are still based more on the institution's needs and security than on individual needs.

Movements to absorb all correctional programs under the state's supervision and control encounter almost insurmountable political and practical obstacles at every step. The massive overcrowding in state institutions, causing funding to go for bricks-and-mortar responses rather than for managerial or administrative improvements, also hampers new concepts. Capacities of institutions also reflect the continuing problems created by overcrowding and growth. Obviously all of the major systems are extremely and critically overcrowded.

Longer sentences and stiffer enforcement measures have filled existing beds faster than they can be built. Alternatives to confinement have been used for all but the very few, and those few are not generally the individuals the public wants out on the streets. Although the new institutions are being constructed, in the majority of cases, to constitutional standards in regard to square footage and other considerations, there seems to be little doubt that the single cells will soon become double-bunked. Taxpayers are beginning to rethink the allocation of funds to build more and more prisons, often at a total cost of up to $200,000 per bed.

State correctional systems have inherited the legacy of a sometimes well-intentioned but often inhumane past. The purposes for which many of the crumbling old institutions were built and the procedures for operating those facilities are no longer in tune with society or behavioral science. The cry to tear down the monuments is a valid one, but practicalities dictate that the flood of inmates must be kept somewhere, and public safety takes precedence over innovative solutions. Many new programs outside the prisons are being constructed, including intermediate sanctions. Much progress is being made, sometimes at the prodding of citizens' groups. In the next chapter we examine a truly centralized and integrated correctional system: the Federal Bureau of Prisons.

Key Words

Review Questions

1. Characterize the current state inmate population in the nation.
2. How much time does a state inmate generally spend in prison?
3. How would you decide that a prison was "cruel and unusual" punishment?
4. Why are alternatives to incarceration beginning to be so necessary for correctional administrators?
5. What impact does overcrowding have on the reform of institutional programs in state systems?
6. How are inmates classified?
7. Has the institutional inmate-to-staff ratio gone up or down? Why?
8. What are three likely trends in state correctional facilities over the next ten years?
9. Why did the supermax prison arise?
10. What can be done to reduce the challenge of prison gangs?

Endnotes

1. American Correctional Association, *2007 Directory* (Alexandria, VA: ACA, 2007), p. 18.

2. American Correctional Association, *2007 Directory*, pp. 52–53.

3. Quoted in Harry Elmer Barnes and Negley J. Teeters, *New Horizons in Criminology*, 3rd ed. (Englewood Cliffs, NJ: Prentice Hall, 1959), pp. 461–462.

4. William Sabol and Heather Couture, *Prison Inmates at Midyear 2007* (Washington, DC: Bureau of Justice Statistics, 2008), p. 1.

5. Steven Garvey, "Freeing Prisoners' Labor," *Stanford Law Review* 50:2 (1998): 339–398. Camp and Camp report that 64% of adults in prison were employed in a prison industry, on a prison farm, or in other prison work in 2000. Camille Camp and George Camp, *The Corrections Yearbook 2000: Adult Corrections* (Middletown, CT: Criminal Justice Institute, 2000), pp. 96–97.

6. Harry E. Allen and Julie C. Abril, "The New Chain Gang: Corrections in the Next Century," *American Journal of Criminal Justice* 22:1 (1997): 1–12. See also David Oshinsky, *Worse Than Slavery: Parchman Farms and the Ordeal of Jim Crow Justice* (New York: Free Press, 1996); and Rebukah Chu, Craig Rivera, and Colin Loftin, "Herding and Homicide," *Social Forces* 78:3 (2000): 971–978.

7. Karen Shapiro, *The New South Rebellion: Tennessee Coalfields, 1971–1986* (Chapel Hill: University of North Carolina, 1998); and Mary Curtin, *Black Prisoners and Their World* (Charlottesville, VA: University Press of Virginia, 2000).

8. James Vardalis and Fred Becker, "Legislative Opinions Concerning the Private Operations of State Prisons," *Criminal Justice Policy Review* 11:2 (2000): 136–148.

9. Editors, "California Prisons End Housing Segregation," *Correctional News* 14:5 (2008), p. 18.

10. Bureau of Justice Statistics, *Prisoners in 2003* (Washington, DC: Bureau of Justice Statistics, 1985).

11. Bureau of Justice Statistics, *Prisoners in 1983* (Washington, DC: Bureau of Justice Statistics, 1984).

12. William Sabol and Heather Couture, *Prisoners in 2006*, p. 7.

13. Ibid, p. 9. See also Karen Garrison, "Home for the Holidays," *Crack the Disparities Newsletter* 1:2 (2008).

14. Disproportionate minority confinement is a heated controversy in corrections, particularly in secure juvenile facilities. See Patricia Devine, K. Coolbaugh, and S. Jenkins, *Disproportionate Minority Confinement: Lessons Learned from Five States* (Washington, DC: Office of Justice Programs, 1998). See also Leadership Conference on Civil Rights, *Justice on Trial: Racial Disparities in the American Criminal Justice System* (Washington, DC: LCCR, 2000).

15. Bureau of Justice Statistics, *Trends in State Parole, 1990–2000* (Washington, DC: Bureau of Justice Statistics, 2001), p. 6; and Bureau of Justice Statistics, "Criminal Sentencing Findings," http://www.ojp.usdoj.gov/bjs/sent.htm (accessed September 24, 2008).

16. Extrapolated from Camille Camp and George Camp, *The 2000 Corrections Yearbook: Adult Corrections*, p. 73. See the annual costs for individual prison facilities published in the American Correctional Association, *2007 Directory*.

17. Bureau of Justice Statistics, *Report to the Nation on Crime and Justice* (Washington, DC: US Department of Justice, 1983), p. 80.

18. American Correctional Association, *2004 Directory*, p. 22.

19. S. Gettinger, "Cruel and Unusual Prisons," *Corrections Magazine* 3 (December 1977): 3–16.

20. *Ibid*, p. 10.

21. 889 F. Supp. 1146 (1995). See also Nadine Curran, "Blue Hair in the Bighouse," *New England Journal on Criminal and Civil Confinement* 26:2 (2000): 225–264.

22. Victor Hassine, *Life without Parole: Living in Prison Today* (Los Angeles, CA: Roxbury, 2002).

23. To learn more about supermax prisons, see also David Ward, "A Corrections Dilemma: How to Evaluate Super-Max Regimes," *Corrections Today* 57:5 (1997): 108; Rodney Henningsen, W. Johnson, and T. Wells, "Supermax Prisons: Panacea or Desperation?" *Corrections Management Quarterly* 3:2 (1999): 53–59; and Jeffrey Ross, "Supermax Prisons," *Society* 44:3 (2007), pp. 60–64.

24. American Correctional Association, *2007 Directory*, pp. 36–37.

The Federal System

Outline

"That there is hereby established in the Department of Justice a Bureau of Prisons ... responsible for the safekeeping, care, protection, instruction, and discipline of all persons charged with or convicted of offenses against the United States."

—Public Law No. 218, approved by President Herbert Hoover, May 14, 1930

Overview

With this proclamation, the federal government went into the business of corrections in a big way. The history of incarcerating offenders for violations of federal law is long and interesting. With the power of the federal government (and the federal purse) behind it, the Federal Bureau of Prisons has become an innovator and leader in correctional management and operations. The Bureau of Prisons (BOP) is a system entirely separate from state and local correctional agencies. It is designed and intended to deal primarily with adults and juveniles who have violated federal laws. Based on a 1997 federal law, the BOP is also responsible for incarcerating the District of Columbia's sentenced felon inmate population. Because the federal system, like the juvenile system discussed in Chapter 18, slowly developed as an independent entity, a review of its background and history is necessary and useful for understanding where this system originated, what it is doing, and where it might be going.[1]

THE USE OF STATE FACILITIES

In the late 1700s and for most of the 1800s, federal prisoners were sent to state and local institutions to serve their sentences. One of the first acts of Congress was to pass a bill (An Act to Establish the Judicial Courts of the United States) encouraging the states to pass laws providing for the incarceration of federal law violators in state institutions. Most of the states did pass such laws, and all federal offenders sentenced to one year or more served their sentences in state facilities. Offenders who were sentenced to terms of less than one year or those being held in detention awaiting trial were usually confined in local jails, a practice that continues today on a limited scale.

In 1870, Congress established the **Justice Department.** A general agent was established in the Department of Justice and was placed in charge of all federal prisoners in state and local institutions. Later, the "general agent" became the superintendent of prisons, responsible to an assistant attorney general for the care and custody of all federal prisoners.

State prisons became seriously overcrowded in the period that followed the Civil War. With increased numbers of both state and federal prisoners, many states became reluctant to take federal prisoners when they could not even care properly for their own. Consequently, in some states only federal prisoners from that specific state were accepted. In states where neither suitable nor adequate facilities were available, transporting federal inmates to appropriate facilities involved lengthy travel and high costs. In 1885, there were 1,027 federal prisoners in state prisons and approximately 10,000 in county jails. By 1895, those numbers had risen to 2,516 federal prisoners in state prisons and approximately 15,000 in county jails.

On March 3, 1891, the U.S. Congress passed a bill (An Act for the Erection of United States Prisons and for the Imprisonment of United States Prisoners, and for Other Purposes) authorizing the construction of three penitentiaries, although their funding was not approved until later. The establishment of federal prison facilities was considered necessary because of the rapidly increasing number of federal inmates, the states' growing reluctance to house federal prisoners, and the exclusion of federal prisoners from contract labor.

Aerial view of former Federal Prison, Fort Jefferson.
© Tony Arruza/CORBIS All Rights Reserved.

EARLY FEDERAL PRISON FACILITIES

Until 1895, all military prisoners not in state prisons were confined at Fort Leavenworth in eastern Kansas. But the War Department then decided to house its prisoners in several different military installations. Consequently, the Department of Justice acquired the surplus military prison at Fort Leavenworth. For the first time, federal prisoners, including those transferred from state institutions as well as new commitments, were confined in a federal facility. In short order the Department of Justice realized the prison, adapted from former quartermaster warehouses, was inadequate. Therefore, on July 10, 1896, Congress appropriated funds for the construction of one of the previously authorized penitentiaries. It would be capable of holding 1,200 inmates and was to be built on the Fort Leavenworth military reservation three miles from the existing prison. Because the penitentiary was built by convict labor, construction took many years. The Leavenworth Penitentiary opened in 1906, but was not finally completed until 1928.

A second penitentiary at McNeil Island, Washington, was constructed between 1872 and 1875. The federal government designated it as a **U.S. penitentiary** in 1909.[2] Construction on a third penitentiary at Atlanta, Georgia, began in 1899 and it opened in 1902. The Auburn style of architecture, characterized by multitiered cellblocks and a fortress-like appearance, was adopted for all three penitentiaries.

Between 1900 and 1935, American prisons, including federal institutions, were primarily custodial, punitive, and industrial. Overcrowding at the federal prisons during this period left few resources for anything but custodial care. Nevertheless, significant developments during the early 1900s affected the operation of federal institutions, including passage of the following acts:

- White Slave Act in 1910 (interstate commerce of prostitution)
- Harrison Narcotic Act in 1914 (records must be kept and taxes paid on controlled substances)
- Volsteadt Act in 1918 (prohibit the sale and consumption of alcohol)
- Dyer Act of 1919 (interstate transportation of stolen vehicles)

Together, these acts brought a large number of people under federal criminal jurisdiction. The number of offenders incarcerated under those statutes swelled the federal prison population beyond the available physical capacity. Largely because of the population increase in federal prisons, Congress authorized in 1925 a reformatory for "male persons between the ages of seventeen and thirty," which was constructed in Chillicothe, Ohio.[3]

By the 1920s, growth in the number of female prisoners being housed in state facilities warranted the building of special federal facilities for women. In 1927, a new 500-bed female institution opened at **Alderson,** West Virginia. In 1929, when overcrowding reached a critical stage in the New York City area, the state and local authorities ordered all federal prisoners removed from the Tombs and the Raymond Street Jail. Responding to this crisis, a federal detention center was built in a newly constructed three-story garage and called the Federal Detention Headquarters (also known as the West Street Jail).

THE BUREAU OF PRISONS IS BORN

In 1929, Congress created the House Special Committee on Federal Penal and Reformatory Institutions. After extensive deliberations it offered the following recommendations:

- Establishment of a centralized administration of federal prisons at the bureau level
- Increased expenditure for federal probation officers, to be appointed by federal judges and exempt from civil service regulations
- Establishment of a full-time parole board
- Provision of facilities by the District of Columbia for its prisoners

- Transfer of all military prisoners held in civil prisons to Fort Leavenworth military barracks
- Removal of the minimum age of prisoners at the U.S. Industrial Reformatory at Chillicothe, Ohio
- Expeditious establishment of the two narcotic treatment farms previously authorized
- Passage of H.R. 11285 authorizing road camps for federal offenders
- Provision of additional employment opportunities for federal offenders
- Employment of an adequate number of nonfederal jail inspectors and linking payments for those facilities to conditions and programs found in them
- Construction of institutions to include two additional penitentiaries, a hospital for the care of the criminally insane, and a system of federal jails and workhouses in the more congested parts of the country

Legislation was drafted, passed, and signed into law by President Herbert Hoover on May 14, 1930, creating the **Federal Bureau of Prisons** within the Department of Justice. **Sanford Bates,** an experienced warden, was appointed by President Hoover to be the first director of the Bureau of Prisons. The selection of Bates signified that the attitude toward penal administration in the federal government had shifted from political patronage to professional qualifications.

Early Growth of the Federal Bureau of Prisons

It was soon obvious that three penitentiaries, a reformatory for young men and one for women, a jail, and eight camps did not meet the growing needs of the federal prison system. Federal prisoners with sentences of a year or less could not be legally confined in the penitentiaries, and many were unsuitable for open camps. The Department of Justice decided to build new structures or remodel existing structures to serve as regional jails.

Sanford Bates.
Courtesy of Federal Bureau of Prisons.

In the early 1930s, the old New Orleans Mint was modified for use as a jail. A new regional jail was opened in La Tuna, Texas, primarily to house the influx of immigration violators. A similar institution was opened in Milan, Michigan (near Detroit). Another penitentiary was added in Lewisburg, Pennsylvania, and a men's reformatory was constructed west of the Mississippi River in El Reno, Oklahoma. A hospital for mentally ill prisoners (and for those with chronic medical ailments) was opened in Springfield, Missouri. The crime wave of the 1930s, combined with the expanding role of the federal government in crime control, brought the old military prison on Alcatraz Island in California under the control of the Department of Justice in 1934.

Recent Developments

Public attitudes toward criminals and the appropriate societal response to them were influenced by many factors during the 1980s. Chief among those were increasing crime rates and the growing problems in administering prisons. Inmate disruptions at Attica and other institutions provided opportunities for the public to reexamine the goals of prisons.[4]

In the early 1970s, the courts began to intervene more often in prison issues. Then-director Norman A. Carlson realized the direction the court system was taking. He saw to it that some significant changes were made in inmate management in the BOP, including (1) enhancements to due process in disciplinary procedures, (2) an administrative remedy process (allowing inmates to express concerns and gain relief from prison administrators before burdening the courts), and (3) an enhanced equal employment opportunity program that increased recruitment of minorities for staff positions.

Director Carlson (who served from 1970 to 1987) believed that the bureau should cooperate with and assist state and local correctional systems. In 1972, the National Institute of Corrections was established within the bureau as an entity to provide assistance and training to state and local correctional and detention facilities. In 1974, the bureau was divided into five regions, each region being managed by a regional director. Also that year, Mr. Carlson formed an executive staff of the agency's assistant directors and regional directors. In the mid-1970s, bureau institutions began to seek accreditation from the American Correctional Association, the country's premier professional organization for corrections.

Mr. Carlson's insistence on the importance of staff training resulted in the establishment of several small staff training facilities and later the consolidation of training at the Federal Law Enforcement Training Center (FLETC) in Glynco, Georgia, in 1982. The mainstay of the bureau's Staff Training Academy at FLETC is a three-week introduction to basic correctional techniques course for all new employees.

A significant development during the 1970s and 1980s was the assignment of responsibility for the planning and management of inmate programs to treatment teams under the concept of unit management. Although the staff makeup of the teams varied among institutions, they usually included a caseworker and a correctional counselor. Unit management gives inmates direct daily contact with the staff members who make most of the decisions about their daily lives. Most of these staff members have offices in inmate living units. This results in improved inmate access to staff and greater staff access to inmates, providing staff with an awareness of significant inmate concerns and potential problems. The unit staff is directly responsible for the program involvement of inmates in the unit. Unit staff receive input from other employees involved in an inmate's progress (such as work supervisors, teachers, and psychologists) and meet with the inmate on a regular basis to develop, review, and discuss the work assignment and programs in which the inmate should be involved, as well as any other needs or concerns. These regularly scheduled meetings do not preclude inmates from approaching a member of the unit team or any other appropriate staff member at any time to discuss their particular issues. The BOP considers its staff to be the most important part of inmate management. Constructive interaction and frequent communication between staff and inmates help to ensure accountability, security, and positive inmate

homework

Assign students to locate at least two articles or reports that deal with Sanford Bates, and submit a one-page summary on his accomplishments.

lecture note

Explain the causes underlying the establishment of the Federal Bureau of Prisons.

The federal penitentiary at Atlanta burns as a result of a Cuban prisoner uprising in 1987.
Photo by AP Wide World Photos.

behavior. The BOP encourages staff to talk with and be available to inmates and to be receptive to inmate concerns.

The bureau's rehabilitation programs and their increasing sophistication were challenged in the mid-1970s by academicians, researchers, and practitioners who pointed out that little documentation supported the existing traditional rehabilitation programming.[5] The bureau had relied on the medical model, which viewed crime as a "sickness" and inmates as "treatable." In 1976, the bureau formally de-emphasized the medical model and adopted a more balanced approach, recognizing that rehabilitation, retribution, incapacitation, and deterrence were legitimate objectives of corrections. Within the balanced model, the bureau continued to provide a variety of work and literacy programs, as well as educational, vocational training, counseling, and self-improvement programs.

The 1970s found the Bureau of Prisons with more new facilities than it had at any time since the 1930s. A steady increase in inmate population during the first five years of the decade dictated the acquisition of additional and modernized facilities to reduce overcrowding, create more humane and safe living conditions, and possibly close the first three old penitentiaries at McNeil Island, Washington; Atlanta, Georgia; and Leavenworth, Kansas.[6]

The Bureau of Prisons experienced as much change in the 1970s as it did at any other time in its history, yet many of the bureau's fundamental activities remained unchanged. This apparent contradiction can be explained as the result of contradictory input from Congress, public professional corrections personnel, and others who, on the one hand, wish prisons to be secure and protective of the public and, on the other, wish in some way to reform or change the individual. Contradictory demands and confused mission-based programs impede the BOP.

ORGANIZATION AND ADMINISTRATION

The federal Bureau of Prisons provides administration at the central office in Washington, D.C., and from six **regional offices.** The central office consists of the director's office and eight divisions that are responsible for establishing national policy, developing and reviewing programs, providing training and technical assistance to the field, and coordinating agency operations in the various disciplines. The bureau has divided responsibility for overseeing day-to-day operations of federal prisons in six regions. An assistant director heads each division; an Office of General Counsel and an Office of Inspections report to the director. The six regions are headed by regional directors and are located in Atlanta, Dallas, Philadelphia, Kansas City, Dublin (near San Francisco), and Annapolis Junction (in Maryland).

The regional offices and the central office provide administrative oversight and support to federal prisons and community corrections offices. Institution wardens are responsible for managing the prisons, and report to a regional director. Community corrections offices oversee community-based programs such as halfway houses and home confinement.

INMATE POPULATIONS EXPLODE

Hedge fund manager Samuel Israel, sentenced to a federal prison term of 240 months.
© US Department of Justice/Handout/Reuters/CORBIS
All Rights Reserved.

The inmate population of the Bureau of Prisons numbered more than 200,000 in mid-2008 (approximately 167,000 of these inmates were confined in one of the 114 BOP-operated correctional institutions or detention centers). This is 137% of highest capacity.[7] The rest were confined through agreements with state and local governments and through contracts with privately operated community corrections centers, detention centers, prisons, and juvenile facilities. Inmate prison population increases are due to federal court sentencing of offenders to longer terms of confinement for serious crimes and the effort to combat organized crime, drug trafficking, and illegal immigration. As of March 2007, the percentage of inmates serving sentences for drug-law violations was 54%. The Bureau of Prisons has opened at least 21 new correctional facilities since the year 2000.

COMMUNITY-BASED PROGRAMS AND CONTRACT FACILITIES

Prison space is a scarce and costly resource, to be used in situations when the interests of society must be protected. Because of the continuing record-high prison population growth in the federal system, the use of alternatives to incarceration for nonviolent offenders is essential. Some 15% of prisoners are confined in the BOP's contract facilities. Approximately 75% of eligible offenders released to the community are regularly released through community treatment centers. Those centers are used for offenders near release as a transition back to home, job, and community. Time is used to find a job, locate a place to live, and reestablish family ties. Some adult inmates sentenced to less than six months are confined in halfway houses or local jails.

All persons adjudicated under the Juvenile Justice and Delinquency Prevention Act are placed under contract in local and state facilities as well as in such facilities as boys' ranches, group homes, or foster homes. Most adult inmates sentenced to serve less than six months are confined in local jails.

With the rapid growth of the federal inmate population, the BOP has contracted for private corrections beds to complement the facilities constructed and operated by the agency. The BOP's utilization of private sources for secure bed space began in the mid-1980s and has grown significantly in the recent past. The BOP had approximately 25,000 inmates in secure adult correctional and detention facilities being provided by private corrections firms in mid-year 2008. The BOP contracts for housing federal offenders when that

class activity

Ask students if the Bureau of Prisons is a centralized system of corrections. Use the organization of the BOP as an avenue for answering that question.

class activity

Challenge students to use materials in Chapter 11 to explain the sudden growth of the population in the Federal Bureau of Prisons.

lecture note

Explain how the federal prison population has grown so dramatically since 1990.

class activity

Ask students how federal offenders can expect to return to the community. Has any recent change occurred through executive order?

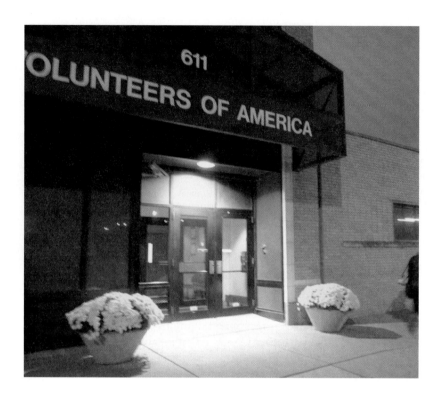

key term

Minimum-security level
A lower level of custody and freedom to interact with other prisoners and programs consistent with the offender's imprisonment.

key term

Low-security level
A correctional assignment of prisoners permitting limited mobility and program participation consistent with their incarceration.

key term

Medium-security level
A correctional classification restricting offenders' movements and privileges while incarcerated.

key term

High-security level
A classification designation reducing inmate movement and treatment participation within the correctional facility; may also refer to "supermax," security housing units, or "close supervision."

arrangement is cost effective, complements its operations and programs, and provides some flexibility to avoid extreme overcrowding. The BOP has had success in contracting with the private sector for the confinement of minimum-security and low-security inmates.

A MODEL INMATE CLASSIFICATION SYSTEM

The BOP's latest formal inmate classification system has been in effect since April 1979. Variables such as severity of offense, history of escapes or violence, expected length of incarceration, and type of prior commitments are used to determine an inmate's security level. The federal system groups the 102 institutions into five security levels: minimum, low, medium, high, and administrative, as follows:

1. **Minimum-security-level** institutions, also known as federal prison camps, have dormitory housing, a relatively low staff-to-inmate ratio, and limited or no perimeter fences. These institutions are work and program oriented, and many are located adjacent to larger institutions or on military bases, where inmates help to serve the labor needs of the institution or base.
2. **Low-security-level** federal correctional institutions (FCIs) have double-fenced perimeters, mostly dormitory housing, and strong work and program components. The staff-to-inmate ratio in these institutions is higher than in minimum-security facilities.
3. **Medium-security-level** FCIs have strengthened perimeters (often double fences with electronic detection systems), mostly cell-type housing, a wide variety of work and treatment programs, and an even higher staff-to-inmate ratio than low-security institutions, providing even greater internal controls.
4. **High-security-level** institutions, also known as U.S. penitentiaries (USPs) have high-security perimeters (either walled or double fenced), multiple- and single-occupant cell housing, close staff supervision, and close control of inmate movement.

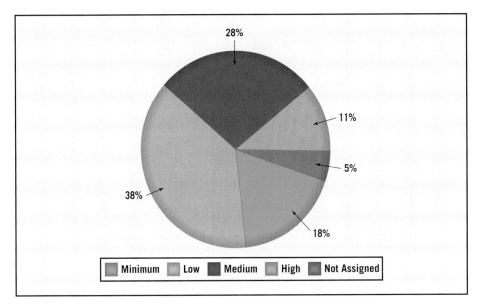

figure 11.1

Inmates by Security
Classification

SOURCE: Federal Bureau of Prisons,
State of the Bureau, 2007
(Washington, DC: FBOP, 2008): 52.

5. **Administrative-security-level** facilities are institutions with special missions, such as the detention of pretrial offenders, the treatment of inmates with serious or chronic medical problems, or the containment of extremely dangerous, violent, or escape-prone inmates. Administrative facilities are capable of holding inmates in all security categories.[8]

Data on inmates of the BOP by inmate security level are presented in Figure 11.1.

The Bureau of Prisons is responsible for carrying out the judgments of federal courts when a period of confinement is ordered. All sentenced offenders who are medically able are required to complete a regular daily work assignment. In addition, all offenders have opportunities to participate in educational, vocational training, work, religious, and counseling programs. In their major institutions, ranging from minimum to high security, more than 34,500 employees were at work in April 2008. They were 72% male and 28% female. Addressing its growth projections, the BOP had 114 facilities online at mid-year 2008, in hopes of providing for continued growth in the federal prison population. The types of offenses committed by BOP inmates are shown in Figure 11.2.

The classification system, designed to place offenders in the least restrictive institution possible that is closest to their homes, has been effective. Moving as many inmates as possible

key term

Administrative-security level
Facilities with special missions
that might contain inmates
from all custody levels.

class activity

Ask students to explain the
security levels of the Bureau
of Prisons, and the relative
concentration of inmates
by security level.

thematic question

Point out the increase in the
number of drug-law violators
in the Bureau of Prisons, and
demonstrate its contribution
to the sudden growth of the
system.

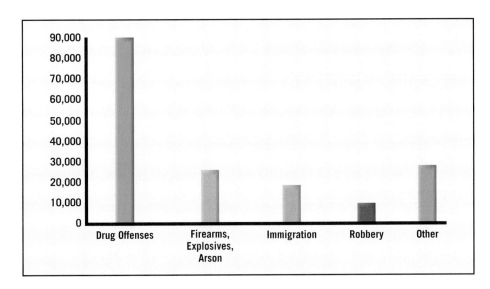

figure 11.2

Types of Offenses Committed by
BOP Inmates: 2007

SOURCE: Federal Bureau of Prisons,
State of the Bureau, 2007
(Washington, DC: FBOP, 2008): 52.

figure 11.3

Length of Sentences Imposed

SOURCE: Federal Bureau of Prisons, *State of the Bureau, 2007* (Washington, DC: FBOP, 2008): 52.

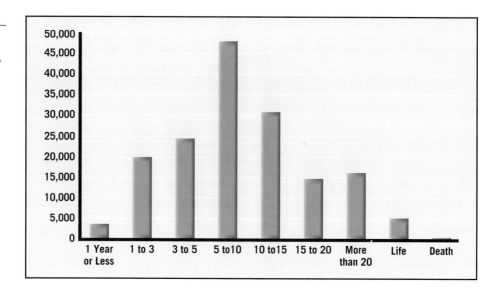

figure 11.4

Citizenship of Inmates in 2007

SOURCE: Federal Bureau of Prisons, *State of the Bureau, 2007* (Washington, DC: FBOP, 2008): 52.

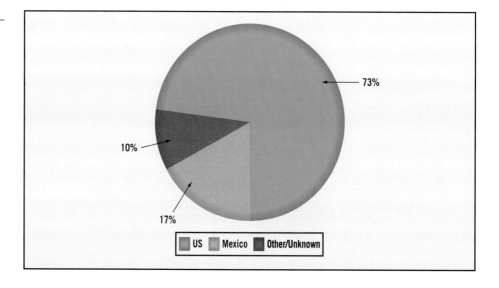

into such open institutions as prison camps results in higher-security-level institutions becoming more humane through reduced crowding. Characteristics of federal prisoners in 2007 are shown in the Figures 11.3 and 11.4.

UNICOR: FEDERAL PRISON INDUSTRIES, INC.

Federal Prison Industries, Inc., with the corporate trade name **UNICOR,** is a wholly owned government corporation that sells its products and services to other federal agencies. UNICOR's mission is to support the Bureau of Prisons through the gainful employment of inmates in diversified work programs.

Approximately 25% of eligible inmates confined in the federal prison system are employed by UNICOR. The industrial operations located in most federal institutions constructively employ inmates and assist in preparing them for employment opportunities upon release. Occupational training is also offered through UNICOR (as well as through institutional education programs) and includes on-the-job training, vocational education,

key term

UNICOR

A wholly-owned federal subsidiary that supports the Federal Bureau of Prisons through the gainful employment of inmates across a variety of work programs.

and apprenticeship programs. Federal institutions offer hundreds of formal training programs in various trades. Vocational training, apprenticeship programs, and occupational education programs exist in at least 90% of the federal institutions. An active program of plant modernization and expansion of industries was begun in 1983 and continues apace in hopes of providing meaningful activity for the expected increases in population. As it continues, the program will ensure modern production capacity far into the future.

EDUCATION AND TRAINING: INMATES AND STAFF

The BOP provides academic and occupational training programs to prepare inmates for employment upon release. Enrollment is voluntary, but program options are extensive, ranging from adult basic education (ABE) through college courses. Occupational training programs include accredited vocational training, apprenticeship programs, and preindustrial training.

A mandatory literacy program was implemented for inmates in 1983. It originally required all federal inmates to function at least at a sixth-grade educational level. Those who could not were required to enroll in the adult basic education (ABE) program for a minimum of 90 days. In 1986, the standard was raised to an eighth-grade literacy level, the nationally accepted functional literacy level. In 1991, the Crime Control Act of 1990 (P.L. 101-647) directed the Federal Bureau of Prisons to have a mandatory functional literacy program for all mentally capable inmates in place. The BOP voluntarily raised the standard to 12th grade and required participation for a minimum of 240 hours or until participants obtain the GED. All promotions in federal prison industries and in institution work assignments were made contingent on the inmate's achieving literacy. The Violent Crime Control and Law Enforcement Act of 1994 and the Prison Litigation Reform Act of 1995 link good-time credits to participation in the GED program.

The ABE program has been quite successful. Certificates for completion of the GED program have been awarded to tens of thousands of inmates (at least 6,000 a year). English as a second language (ESL) is also provided for all who need it. Other vocational training programs provide job training in such fields as computer sciences, business, diesel mechanics, construction and building trades, drafting and blueprints, and culinary arts.

Staff training provides every BOP employee with the knowledge, skills, and abilities required to ensure high standards of employee performance and conduct. The staff-training network consists of the Staff Training Academy at the Federal Law Enforcement Training Center in Glynco, Georgia, and the Management and Specialty Training Center in Denver, Colorado. Administrators in the Human Resource Management Division in Washington, D.C., oversee the program. All new employees are required to undergo three weeks of formal training during their first 60 days with the Bureau of Prisons, as well as an institution familiarization program at their worksite.

FEDERAL FEMALE OFFENDERS

The Bureau of Prisons continues to focus on improving programs and services for female offenders. It operates a number of all-female facilities and at least 21 co-gender facilities.

Dialysis nurse provides kidney dialysis in prison infirmary.
Courtesy of Federal Bureau of Prisons, Springfield.

ADX Supermax Prison in Colorado.
Lizzie Himmel/Sygma/CORBIS
All Rights Reserved.

These facilities include stand-alone secure institutions and many prison camps adjacent to secure institutions.

The number of female offenders in the BOP's inmate population continues to increase. Recognizing that female offenders have different social, psychological, educational, family, and health-care needs, the BOP continues to design and implement special programs for female offenders. Programs include teaching women how to reduce stress; how to prevent, identify, obtain, and manage treatment for medical problems; and how to improve their personal relationships, how to be a better parent, and how to grieve over lost relationships. Several facilities also operate intensive treatment programs that focus on helping women who have histories of chronic sexual, emotional, or physical abuse by teaching them how to handle their victimization and learn ways to seek positive relationships. Federal facilities housed over 11,300 female offenders in 2007, about 7% of the total population of federal inmates.[9]

COMMUNITY CORRECTIONS IN THE FEDERAL SYSTEM

Community corrections is an integral component of the BOP's correctional programs. The BOP contracts with community corrections centers (also known as halfway houses) to provide assistance to inmates who are nearing release from prison. Community corrections centers provide a structured, supervised environment and support in job placement, counseling, and other services. Community corrections centers allow prerelease inmates to gradually rebuild their ties to the community, and they allow correctional staff to supervise offenders' activities during this readjustment phase. An important component of the community corrections center program is transitional drug-abuse treatment for inmates who have completed residential substance-abuse treatment while confined in a BOP institution.[10]

Some federal inmates are placed on home confinement for a brief period at the end of their prison terms. They serve this portion of their sentences at home under strict schedules and curfew requirements. Some community corrections centers enhance the accountability of inmates on home confinement through electronic monitoring.

Approximately 45% of federal offenders in community-based programs are housed in comprehensive sanctions centers. Comprehensive sanctions centers are similar to community corrections centers, but they have a more structured system for granting offenders gradual access to the community. They also require inmates to participate in more programs and they formally involve the U.S. Probation Office in the release-planning process.

Through the community corrections program, the BOP has developed agreements with state and local governments and contracts with privately operated facilities for the confinement of juvenile offenders and for the detention or secure confinement of some federal inmates.

The BOP's community corrections program is administered by the staff in its central office, community corrections regional administrators, regional management teams in each of the bureau's six regional offices, and the employees of 29 community corrections management field offices throughout the United States.

CHANGING POPULATION OF FEDERAL INSTITUTIONS

A former governor of Georgia, Lester Maddox, is credited with saying (when asked how to improve that state's correctional system) "What we need here is a better class of prisoner." The Bureau of Prisons was looked on for years as dealing with just the "cream of criminals." Whether true or apocryphal, times have changed, and the federal system has to deal with some real problem inmates today. The BOP is now experiencing some of the challenges associated with crowding and management of inmates with significant histories of violence and gang-related activities. In 1984, Congress passed a law that abolished federal parole, limited good time, established a number of determinate sentences, and created the U.S. Sentencing Commission as an independent body, located in the judicial branch of the government. The commission began its work in 1985 and submitted new guidelines that have dramatically altered sentencing practices in the federal criminal justice system. Federal prison populations grew markedly by 2007, more as a result of the Anti-Drug Abuse Act of 1986 and the career offender provision of the Comprehensive Crime Control Act of 1984 than as a result of the guidelines. A summary of their impacts follows:[11]

1. "Straight" probationary sentences (i.e., sentences that require no form of confinement) were reduced significantly.
2. For especially serious crimes, such as drug offenses and crimes against persons, probationary sentences were no longer available.
3. For other crimes, such as property offenses, the proportion of sentences involving some form of probation did not change appreciably, although probation with a condition of confinement may have been substituted for straight probation.
4. Average time served for violent offenses increased substantially. For most property crimes, average time served remained largely unchanged. Exceptions include burglary and income tax fraud, for which average time served went up.

The changes have had a major impact on the correctional administrators in the Bureau of Prisons, in the form of a massive increase in the numbers and types of inmates confined in federal institutions, which are already quite overcrowded.

Summary

The Bureau of Prisons is a major correctional system that helps to meet society's goals of ensuring public safety and providing appropriate, efficient, safe, and humane correctional services and programs to federal offenders. The BOP has attacked some of the major issues head-on and has made notable progress; but there are no simple solutions to the long-festering problems of corrections, whether state or federal. Much hard work lies ahead for the BOP and for all other correctional agencies in the United States.

One of the bright spots on the horizon is the increasing use by the courts and corrections of community-based treatment as a less-structured alternative to incarceration for selected offenders. Substantial numbers of offenders, however, are not suitable for treatment in the relative freedom of community-based programs. Into that category fall many multiple offenders who have long histories of serious, often violent, crimes.

To achieve maximum correctional benefits for all offenders, the Bureau of Prisons has sought to develop a balanced approach, recognizing that no single, all-purpose treatment method can be expected to produce effective results. One main challenge of the future undoubtedly will be to sustain the present level of public and legislative interest, which demands a concerted effort by the correctional community and by concerned citizens.

Key Words

Justice Department, 214

U.S. penitentiary, 215

Alderson, 215

Federal Bureau of Prisons, 216

Sanford Bates, 216

regional offices, 218

minimum-security level, 220

low-security level, 220

medium-security level, 220

high-security level, 220

administrative-security level, 221

UNICOR, 222

Review Questions

1. Explain the various kinds of institutions in the federal prison system.
2. What forces led to the shift in philosophy of the Federal Bureau of Prisons in the 1970s?
3. Outline the institutional security classification system.
4. Why does the BOP have such an advantage over state systems in generating programs?
5. Why has the prison population of the BOP increased during the last few years?
6. Characterize inmates in the BOP institutions.

Endnotes

1. This chapter has drawn heavily from BOP annual reports and various other BOP publications. The authors appreciate the cooperation and assistance and especially the provision of historical and other photographs. For critical views, see Jim Coyne, *The Repugnant Warehouse: An Exposé of the Federal Prison System* (Clifton Park, NY: Elysium Publishing, 1995); Daniel Rose Burton, D. Pens, P. Wright, et al., *The Celling of America: An Inside Look at the U.S. Prison Industry* (Monroe, ME: Common Courage Press, 1998); and Michael Santos, *Life behind Bars in America* (New York, NY: St. Martine's Press, 2006).
2. The facility is now part of the prison system of the state of Washington.
3. This facility is currently an Ohio correctional institution.
4. Between November 21 and 23, 1987, 89 federal prison staff were seized as hostages at the Atlanta Penitentiary and at the Alien Detention Center at Oakdale, Louisiana. The uprisings have been described as the most disruptive episodes in the history of the Bureau of Prisons. Hostages were eventually released after the attorney general agreed to review each case of the Marielitos, Cubans who arrived in the nation during the Mariel boatlift. See "After Atlanta and Oakdale," *Corrections Today* 50 (1988): 26, 64–65; Bert Useem, C. Camp, and G. Camp, *Resolution of Prison Riots* (South Salem, NY: Criminal Justice Institute, 1993);

and Mike Rolland, *Descent into Madness* (Cincinnati, OH: Anderson Publishing, 1997). Coverage of smaller but more lethal riots in federal prisons has been increasing, particularly in 2008. See The Colorado Independent, "Bureau of Prisons," http://www .coloradoindependent.com/tag/bureau-of-prisons (accessed November 11, 2008).

5. See Harry Allen and Nick Gatz, "Abandoning the Medical Model in Corrections: Some Implications and Alternatives," *Prison Journal* 54 (Autumn 1974): 4–14; and Simon Dinitz, "Nothing Fails Like a Little Success," in Edward Sagarin (ed.), *Criminology: New Concerns* (Beverly Hills, CA: Sage, 1979), pp. 105–118. But see C. T. Lowenkamp and E. L. Latessa, "Developing Successful Reentry Programs," *Corrections Today* 76:2 (2005), 72–77; and Pamela Lattimore, "The Challenges of Reentry," *Corrections Today* 69:2 (2007): 88–91.

6. Only McNeil Island has been closed, and has since been sold to the state of Washington to help solve some of that state's prison overcrowding. The institutions at Atlanta and Leavenworth still serve the overcrowded system.

7. William Sabol, Heather Couture, and Paige Harrison, *Prisoners in 2006* (Washington, DC: Bureau of Justice Statistics, 2007), p. 20; and the Federal Bureau of Prisons, *State of the Bureau 2007* (Washington, DC: FBOP, 2008).

8. Federal Bureau of Prisons, "Quick Facts," http://www .bop.gov/about/facts.jsp (accessed April 26, 2005).

9. Federal Bureau of Prisons, *State of the Bureau 2007* (Washington, DC: FBOP, 2008), p. 52.

10. Federal Bureau of Prisons, "Release Preparation," http://www.bop.gov/inmate_programs/release_emp .jsp (accessed November 11, 2008).

11. National Institute of Justice, "The Impact of Federal Sentencing Guidelines," in *NIJ Reports: Research in Action* (Washington, DC: U.S. Department of Justice, 1987), p. 52. But see The Sentencing Project, "Smart on Crime: Recommendations for the Next Administration," http://www.sentencingproject.org/ tmp/File/DrugPolicy/dp_transitiondocument.pdf (accessed November 11, 2008).

chapter 12

Private-Sector Systems

Outline

Overview

The words quoted above, written a decade ago, foretold the continuing overcrowding problem that the student has seen as a constant issue throughout this text. The state, city, and federal correctional administrators wrestled with this issue when the population of their combined institutions was approximately one-third of what it is now. This chapter deals with what has become another major factor in trying to keep up with the tidal wave of populations under the supervision of criminal justice agencies: privatization of correctional services and facilities.

As will be shown, privatization of institutions is not a new idea. The major challenge for privatization is to provide for the incarceration of convicted felons in long-term, secure facilities by a private, for-profit company. The state of Tennessee was the first to consider the privatization of its entire adult prison system. One of the first and largest of the providers of privately operated adult correctional facilities made an offer to take over the complete management and operation of the beleaguered Tennessee system. For a number of reasons, that proposal was not accepted and Tennessee decided instead to pour millions into upgrading what it had. This chapter discusses the pros and cons of privatization and its vast growth in the last two decades. See Figure 12.1 for more detail. We have seen this issue grow from a single paragraph to an entire chapter in the past few editions of this text. It seems fitting that this chapter is the sixth in your overview of institutional corrections, because it relates to almost every other topic in the text. Bear in mind that private-sector *prisons* remain the fourth largest correctional system in the nation.

"Prison supply, especially at current prices, is unable to meet demand. The resultant overcrowding, combined with taxpayer reluctance to bear the costs of new construction and added operational expenses, creates a dilemma for penology. Commercial prisons, privately owned and operated under government contract, may offer at least a partial solution."

–Charles Logan and Christine Rausch

lecture note

Using your computer, play the brief chapter overview videotape by Harry Allen on "Private-Sector Systems" that introduces Chapter 12 (approximately 3 minutes).

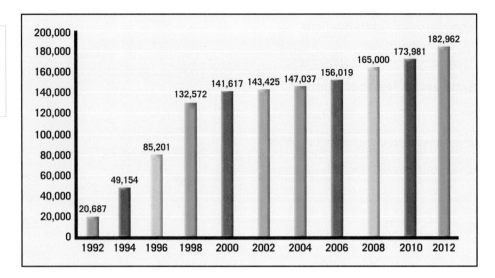

figure 12.1

Growth of Private Sector Capacity (beds)

Data from: Charles Thomas, Rated Capacities of Private Facilities by Geographical Location (http://web.crime .efl.edu/pep/cendus/2002/Chart1.html; and Richard Seiter, Private Corrections: A Review of the Issues (www.correctionscorp.com/STATIC/ASSETS/Private_Corr_Review_of_Issues.pdf, accessed November 14, 2008). Data from 2008 to 2012 are extrapolated.

class activity

Ask students why private-sector involvement in corrections has been so extensive. What are its main advantages?

class activity

What types of services do private-sector systems provide to correctional clients?

class activity

Challenge students to explain the reluctance of many correctional administrators to accept the involvement of private-sector systems with maximum-security institutions.

class activity

Ask the class if public-sector correctional administrators can contract away their liability for private-sector violations of constitutional rights of offenders and public safety issues. If the consensus is "no," ask if the public sector can require private-sector providers to underwrite insurance to cover such public safety issues.

THE PRIVATE SECTOR IN COMMUNITY CORRECTIONS

The idea of involving the private sector in providing management and operation of correctional facilities may come as a shock to many students, but the concept of having government services provided by contracting with the private sector was actually the primary method of obtaining those services for the first hundred or so years of the United States' existence. Transportation, fire protection, police, and even armies were often provided on contract. It was only in America's second century that services began to be provided through governmental bureaucratic agencies. In recent years, however, the cost of government-provided services has risen so high that many services are now moving "back to the future" to obtain correctional services being provided through the private sector.

The correctional field has experienced a number of privatization precedents: health care, food service, education, mental health, transportation, and training have been provided by private contractors to many systems. From the time of John Augustus, most juvenile and adult halfway houses and other services have been provided by private for-profit, private nonprofit, or charitable organizations. As the need for more community corrections has grown, primarily due to overcrowded jails and prisons, many entrepreneurs in the private and private nonprofit sectors have become involved in the "boom" industry of community-oriented corrections. Almost 7% of confined adults are in privately owned or operated facilities.[1] Many of those entrepreneurs are now expanding across state borders and operating prisons, jails, and community services almost like a franchise. Only 19 states do not contract with private-sector prisons for adult prison systems. Such agencies tend to ease the correctional problems by providing (1) alternatives to incarceration in the community, (2) meaningful programs inside the prisons to help prepare inmates for a better life when they are released, and (3) a bridge from incarceration to the free society that will assist in that difficult transition.

The main advantage of private service providers is their ability to expand and contract quickly when needs change. When a government invests in the operation of a community-based program or the building of a major correctional facility, it is often obliged to continue to staff them and operate them even if it is not cost effective to do so.[2] The entrepreneurs of community corrections can choose to modify an existing facility instead of building from the ground up, provide staff on a contract basis, utilize existing community resources for professional services, and close the facility when it is no longer needed and use it for another purpose. The private-sector community corrections programs and agencies of the federal courts and prisons house over 3,600 adult inmates in 391 contracted community correctional centers, as well as 1,141 facilities for juveniles. Most states also contract for at least some of their community corrections, so this sector of business has continued to burgeon.[3]

One of the major issues for the contractor concerns liability for potential public safety issues. Most government agencies are **self-insured.** This insurance protects them with the resources of the entire government entity—federal, state, county, or municipality. The private-sector operator, however, must have some type of liability insurance to cover the same problems. With the incredible growth of litigation in the United States, government agencies have become targets for opportunistic attorneys looking for new markets.[4] This feeding frenzy of litigation has caused insurance rates to skyrocket and has impacted operations in the private sector. The small operators have been put in a squeeze, and the large ones could be hurt as well.

In sum, the private sector is extensively involved in such correctional services as providing food, medical care, and training to facilities and agencies; filling gaps in services governmental agencies cannot or will not address (halfway houses, secure juvenile residential programs); and managing such correctional systems as high-security jails and prisons. Only the latter is the center of heated controversy, not only in light of liability issues, but also over program inadequacies and potential use-of-force situations for which employees might not be adequately trained and competent.

key term

Self-insured
Government unit whose operations are not covered by external insurers.

lecture note
Explain the lengthy history of private-sector involvement with corrections, beginning with the Quakers and continuing through the International Community Corrections Association.

The Privately-run T. Don Hutto Residential Center is one of only two federal Immigration and Customer Enforcement (ICE) detention centers for families with children in the United States. This prison, run by the CCA, has come under fire for alleged lack of education for children in the facility.
© Bob Daemmrich/CORBIS All Rights Reserved.

SOME HISTORICAL CONSIDERATIONS
Early History

From a historical perspective, private involvement in corrections during the period from 1870 to 1930 was neither notable nor distinguished. Before this era, some states would lease out their entire prison populations to private bidders who would contract to provide food, custody, and clothing to inmates for a flat fee per inmate annually, in return for the labor of the inmates. Contractors would use the inmates basically to farm or harvest crops, much like the **slaves of the master.** The state would make a profit and could avoid the cost of building additional and adequate facilities, hiring correctional staff, feeding and clothing inmates, and otherwise assuming such care, custody, and provisioning as would have been required. In brief, prisons became attractive "profit centers" for those states willing to lease out their convict populations. Costs incurred by contractors were significantly below those that would have been incurred if free-world labor had been hired or if, in the pre–Civil War era, more slaves had to be bought who would have had to be fed, clothed, housed, and disciplined more attentively than mere criminals.

During the period from 1870 to 1930, when industrialization was running under full steam in this nation, leasing out inmates continued. Inmates were put to work building roads, railroads, and trestles or manufacturing wagons, shoes, boots, and many other consumables easily sold on the open markets. To protect profit margins, contractors often would transport inmates in rolling cages, where they lived without sanitary and bathing facilities and were worked from dawn to dusk under the watchful eye of heavily armed guards ("overseers") who were not afraid to use brute force to achieve production quotas. Inmates attempting to escape were killed or beaten, placed in leg irons, forced to wear ball-and-chain restraints, dressed in distinctive garb, and had shortened life expectancies. Food was abysmal and in short supply, and health care was nonexistent. Seeking redress in court was impossible, and avenues of appeal and protest were closed.[5]

key term

Slaves of the master
Inmates who are compelled to obey correctional managers and their staff.

class activity

Ask students to explain the contract labor system from 1870 through 1930, and describe some of the most egregious instances of exploitation.

class activity

Ask students in what areas and programs private-sector systems assist corrections.

class activity

Some private-sector system contractors argue that they can do a better job in providing services than the unit of government can, and can provide those services at less cost. Ask students how this might be so.

lecture note

Go online to locate photographs of chain gangs in such states as Georgia and Florida, and arrange those into a PowerPoint presentation to accompany your historical overview of chain-gang portions of private-sector involvement in corrections (such as www.Yahoo.com, "Chain gangs" with "Georgia"). Be careful not to violate copyrights.

Chain gang working on street.
Photo courtesy of Brown Brothers.

The suffering of inmates under these "chain-gang" conditions is common knowledge. What is not as well known is the large percentage of inmates leased out who died under contract arrangements, a figure frequently exceeding 50% in a given year. Loss of workers through death, however, had little consequence. Prison administrators were neither criticized nor condemned, and the media rarely covered those events. If a shortage of laborers occurred, prison administrators would lease out newly arrived prisoners who were quickly placed into harnesses and assigned to labor gangs. Not all states, of course, were this brutal in their approach to prisoners, and perhaps this description best fits only some states in the Deep South after the Civil War, when their prisons were filled with former slaves confined for law-violating behavior.[6] This was one of the most odious chapters in the early history of American corrections, and the residue of feelings and sentiments about leasing inmates through private-sector involvement even now colors, even if unfairly, the arguments about privatization of corrections.

More Recent Developments

As noted, **privatization** is by no means a new concept in the field of corrections. Many services provided to state, federal, and local correctional facilities have come from the private sector almost from the beginning, and they have persevered. The criminal justice system often appears to be stumbling around like a clumsy giant. It can impose lengthy prison terms, and even execute a few criminals. It can slap offenders on the wrist with fines and suspended sentences. It seems able to do little in between, however, although this condition is changing; but government moves very slowly. In the twentieth century, probation and parole were used as the most frequent options to incarceration. The ability of these two types of sanctions to supervise and control offenders became the standard for the community. We have seen, however, that both of these options came under fire in the 1990s for charges of ineffectiveness.

As discussed in Chapter 8, the development of intermediate sanctions has provided three major options for direct private-sector involvement in corrections: (1) treatment programs, (2) supervised release and low-security custody, and (3) **technologies for surveillance** of offenders not incarcerated. These three options provide the greatest area of potential growth opportunity for private contractors, as opposed to the operation of high-security correctional facilities.

key term

Privatization
The provision of correctional services by private-sector purveyors.

key term

Technologies for surveillance
Application of electronic and other programs designed to allow for the identification of locations of offenders.

PRIVATE-SECTOR TREATMENT PROGRAMS

Supervised treatment programs, usually imposed as a condition of probation, include drug and alcohol abuse treatment and job training programs. Virtually nonexistent 30 years ago, such programs are now commonplace components of the criminal justice system. Almost all are private and many are run for profit, deriving both their clients and their incomes from contracts with local governments. Some are designed as long-term residential facilities and others as outpatient clinics. Program philosophies vary widely:

- Some are organized with strict, military-like discipline.
- Others are based on religious beliefs.
- Some are devoted to group therapy.
- Others stress rugged individualism and self-reliance.

The growing problem and critical need to respond to the widespread use of drugs creates a demand to treat drug abusers and has rekindled interest in these types of programs, and we can expect their numbers to increase.

Prisoners at the Kyle New Vision Chemical Dependency Treatment Center receive awards.
Photo courtesy of Wackenhut Corrections Corp.

Private-sector programs handle a large number of criminal offenders. For every offender housed in a privately managed jail or prison, there are hundreds in privately operated noncustodial programs operating under contract with state and local governments. Despite their numbers and importance, these private programs are largely ignored in discussions of the privatization of corrections. This may be because such programs are regarded as merely service providers rather than penal programs, or because their roles as agents of state control are obscured because client participation is primarily voluntary.

Most private operators of prison facilities are for-profit corporations, and are generally listed on stock exchanges as investments. As such, they can be seen as a **growth industry.** Some of the major private operators include Corrections Corporation of America (CCA), The GEO Group, Inc. (formerly Wackenhut Corrections), Cornell Companies, Inc., and Management and Training Corporation. Arguably, the largest is CCA (http://www.correctionscorp.com/aboutcca.html).

LOW-SECURITY CUSTODY PROGRAMS

Another important development in corrections in recent years has been the growth of low-security custodial facilities.[7] Many of the most innovative types of low-security facilities have been designed and implemented by advocates of privatization and, as such, are operated by private contractors. Today, this form of custody constitutes one of the fastest growing areas of corrections and the most important segment in the business of private, for-profit corrections contractors. See Figure 12.2.

The juvenile justice system, in particular, has come to rely on private contractors to provide such low-security custodial facilities. This in turn has both increased the

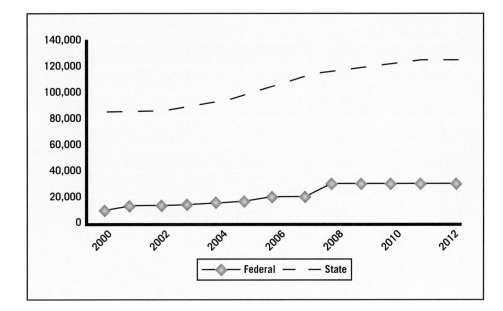

figure 12.2

Growth in the Number of
Prisoners in Federal and State
Facilities: 2000–2012

SOURCE: William Sabol, Heather
Couture and Paige Harrison, *Prisoners
in 2006* (Washington, DC: Bureau of
Justice Statistics, 2007): 4. Data for
2007–2012 are extrapolated.

government's flexibility in dealing with juveniles and expanded its capacity to commit them into custody. California, Florida, Massachusetts, Michigan, Pennsylvania, Rhode Island, and Washington, among others, rely heavily on private contractors to care for their wards. In a number of states, placement in out-of-home settings constitutes a major component of the state's juvenile corrections policy; in some, private placements outnumber placements in public facilities. We should stress that these private custodial placements are not simply more efficient versions of state-run programs. Although these programs have diverted some and provided services to other juveniles who would otherwise have been placed in secure public institutions, they also target groups that once would not have been placed in custody at all. In short, such programs add a new intermediate level of sanctioning to the state's repertoire. See Figure 12.3.

class activity

Ask students how the private
sector can be usefully involved
in low-security custody
programs and in medium-
security programs.

class activity

Challenge students to decide if
private prison contractors can
provide safe maximum-security
jail operations.

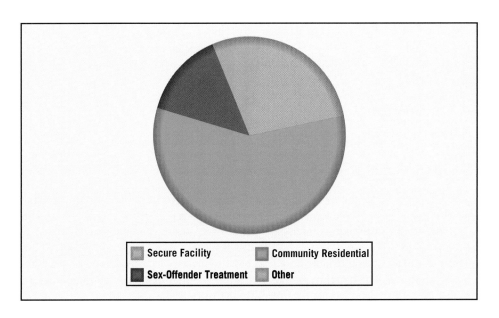

figure 12.3

Number of Privatized Adult
Facilities: 2006

SOURCE: American Correctional
Association, *2007 Directory*
(Alexandria, VA: ACA, 2007): 30-31.

Inmates at a privately-run SANTA FE jail of California use the outdoor gym to take in some sun during their recreation time.
© *Ed Kashi/CORBIS All Rights Reserved.*

Private contractors have also played a similar role in developing low-security facilities for adult offenders, and there is a growing differentiation between what the private- and public-sector facilities have to offer. The private sector is developing more facilities at the low end of the spectrum, such as residential treatment facilities, community work release centers, prerelease centers, short-term detention facilities, restitution centers, return-to-custody facilities, and the like. Nonetheless, private-sector providers also manage and provide services for secure jail and prison institutions.

Private-sector involvement in community corrections is increasing, and there are indications that it will continue to grow, especially if prison populations continue to exceed capacity and pressures mount to increase alternatives that are more flexible and less costly. See Figure 12.4. Time will tell if this "net-widening" effect of such expanded services will actually reach enough of the problem clients in the community who would not normally have been served.

SURVEILLANCE AND CONTROL TECHNOLOGIES

New technologies represent yet another area that has emerged in response to the growing concern with crime. Only a few years ago, state laboratories performed chemical testing in a costly and time-consuming manner. Now private drug-testing companies across the nation can offer fast, cheap, and reliable tests to detect a large variety of illegal substances. But expanded use of cheap and reliable drug tests has also increased the likelihood of detection of illegal substances, which in turn has raised the number of probation and parole violators, helping to transform probation and parole officers from social workers to law enforcement

The lounge area of a privately operated work release facility in Seattle.
Photo by Clifford E. Simonsen, courtesy of Pioneer Human Services.

officers. The upsurge in the numbers returned to custody has in turn generated demands for specialized low-security custodial facilities and new forms of confinement (such as in Texas and California). In short, new technology has placed burdens on the correctional system and affected its more traditional roles.

Private contractors have also introduced a variety of high-tech electronic devices that monitor the movement of people. These devices can be used for surveillance and offer the possibility of confinement without custody, as was also noted in Chapter 6. Developed by specialized security firms and now ubiquitous in application, **electronic monitoring** has vast potential as an effective and inexpensive intermediate form of punishment. For instance, it can supplement if not replace work-release facilities and be used to confine drunk drivers to their homes and places of work.

CORRECTIONAL PRIVATIZATION: ISSUES AND EVIDENCE

It is now widely understood that, first, privatization arrangements cast the government and not a private firm as the entity which establishes public priorities and that, second, they involve the efforts to achieve public goals by reliance on private rather than public means. Importantly, one really cannot appreciate the significance of the privatization trends today without having a basic understanding of what is so different today from as little as 25 years ago. In 1980, there was not a single privatized jail or prison here or abroad.

The precise moment when this concept of privatization of secure adult facilities was born is the subject of much debate. The foundation was probably laid on or near the date in 1983 when **Corrections Corporation of America (CCA)** was formed in Nashville, Tennessee. The first local contract for a secure county facility was awarded to CCA in 1984.

key term

Electronic monitoring
Any system or telemetry program that allows correctional staff to know the location of offenders.

lecture note

Briefly describe some other countries that now have private-sector prisons for adult or juvenile offenders.

key term

Corrections Corporation of America (CCA)
A private business seeking to provide correctional services to units of government; also known as the "parent of private-sector prison facilities."

key term

U.S. Corrections Corporation (USCC)
A private-sector correctional provider.

key term

The GEO Group
A private-sector correctional provider formerly known as the Wackenhut group.

lecture note

Point out to students that the national average cost for incarceration of adult inmates was about $26,700 in 2007. Explain what fringe benefits (and salaries) raise this average cost. Then point out what lesser benefits and costs private-sector prisons can save. How can private-sector prisons earn a profit?

class activity

Ask students if private-sector prison providers have reduced overpopulation in select states, and how this was accomplished.

class activity

Ask students if the agency managing your local jail or detention facility employs sworn law enforcement officers, and how those officers were trained for their jobs.

Kentucky awarded the first state-level contract to **U.S. Corrections Corporation (USCC)** in 1985. The first federal-level contract of any size went to CCA from the Immigration and Naturalization Service in 1984. Soon there was a rush of private companies to get into this new field and the number of beds and companies grew apace. The Texas Department of Corrections awarded contracts for four 500-bed facilities, to include their design, construction, and management. Two were awarded to CCA and two to the new Wackenhut Corrections Corporation (WCC), the forerunner of the **GEO Group.** This moved the private corrections industry into a much larger arena for privatization of correctional facilities. The first overseas venture involved a joint venture with the CCA and the Corrections Corporation of Australia. The industry appeared to move from a novel idea to a viable alternative to publicly provided services. Resistance to privatization by correctional agencies has varied from experimentation to outright rejection, especially when privatization efforts were seen as an attack on job security.[8]

The result was rapid growth in this new niche of the private-services sector. In just the decade between 1992 and midyear 2006, the contract capacity for private secure adult correctional facilities across the nation grew from 15,300 to an estimated 183,000, an increase of over 1,000%. See Figure 12.4.

Privately managed adult facilities now house diverse prisoner populations in both small and large facilities. The number of jurisdictions electing to hold their prisoners in privately managed facilities has grown nationally at a substantial rate. Critics predicted that no maximum-security facility could be privatized, but CCA opened a privately managed maximum-security facility in Leavenworth, Kansas, in 1992. Numerous other privately managed facilities house significant numbers of maximum-security classified prisoners. The evidence is mixed regarding control problems such as inmate-on-inmate assaults, inmate-on-staff assaults, minor disturbances, riots, and escapes.[9]

At least three of the companies that manage adult correctional facilities (CCA, the GEO Group, and others) have also contracted for youthful offender programs. These programs deal primarily with older juveniles and put less emphasis on treatment, a focus in the typical residential programs that Children Comprehensive Services and Youth Services both

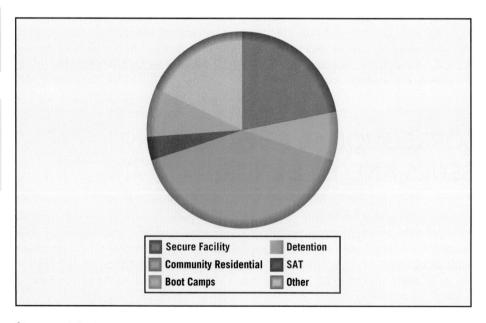

figure 12.4

Number of Privatized Juvenile Facilities: 2006

SOURCE: American Correctional Association, *2007 Directory* (Alexandria, VA: ACA, 2007): 34-35. SAT is Substance Abuse Treatment.

operate. The youthful offender programs that are managed by adult corrections companies have lower per-diem charges on average (approximately $65 to $80 per day), when compared to residential programs run by primarily juvenile service providers ($85 to $180 per day). To date, private corrections companies concentrating on the adult market have chosen not to compete with the companies that concentrate entirely on juvenile programs.

At year-end 2006, privately operated prisons held more than 108,000 state and federal inmates, over 20,263 on the federal level and almost 74,000 on the state level. These represent almost 13% and 7% of their prison populations, respectively.

Correctional systems using private prison providers include 32 states, the District of Columbia, and the federal system. Among states, Texas (with 17,500 state inmates housed in private facilities) and Florida (with 6,200) reported the largest number in 2006. Four states had at least 25% of their prison population housed in private facilities: New Mexico (44%), Montana (27%), Alaska (33%), and Wyoming and Oklahoma (at 37% and 22%, respectively). The use of private facilities was concentrated among southern and western states. See Figure 12.5 for information on the largest states with private facilities.

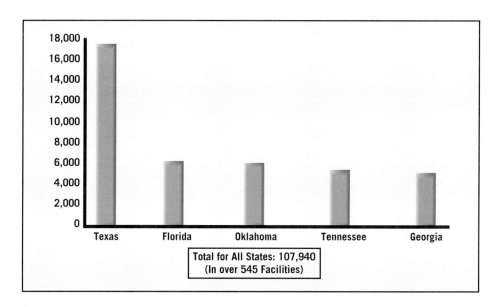

figure 12.5

Number of Inmates in Private Facilities: 2007

SOURCE: Bureau of Justice Statistics, *Prisoners in 2006* (Washington, DC: BJS, 2007): 4; and American Correctional Association, *2007 Directory* (Alexandria, VA: ACA, 2007): 31.

Summary

It is difficult at this time to determine if private-sector correctional providers, especially of prison facilities, are more effective than public-sector providers, if they are cost effective, if they have comparable or better recidivism rates, and if they provide adequate services, particularly in the realm of medical services. The data are just beginning to be amassed and organized, allowing us to see some patterns and directions. This is the first time we have been able to gather enough information to put together a comprehensive chapter on this important topic. The future of privatization seems to be very promising.[10]

Growth in contracting for the management of secure correctional facilities happened far more rapidly in the last decade than virtually everyone expected. Still, it is also true that almost 7% of all prisoners in the United States are presently being housed in private facilities. Although private facilities are now in operation, under contract, or under construction for speculation in many states, and although private facilities presently house prisoners in at least 33 states, it is important to note that not all American jurisdictions have awarded local or state-level contracts. Those that have refrained from contracting include numerous states that have both a large prisoner population and significant problems caused by the prisoner populations being above 100% of the highest design capacity of their systems (for example, Massachusetts, New York, and Washington).

Most privatization initiatives have involved contract awards that were intended to expand the capacity of correctional systems. Although potential cost savings and performance improvements that could flow from decisions to privatize existing facilities are arguably possible, obvious political considerations reduce the appeal of this kind of contracting. In fact, the Tennessee proposal, mentioned at the beginning of this chapter, was at least in part rejected because the chairperson of the Criminal Justice Committee asked the question of his colleagues: "If these people can do this job cheaper and better, why can't we?" This is an obstacle for privatization proponents. The obstacle could become troublesome as the current general population growth trends continue.

The appeal of many types of privatization is considerable beyond the boundaries of the United States. However, it remains true that facility management contracts have been awarded in few countries (Australia and the United Kingdom are the largest exceptions). Opposition both to the enactment of legislation authorizing privatization and to exercising existing statutory authority remains strong in many jurisdictions. Corrections managers and administrators, as well as correctional unions, are generally opposed to private-sector prison providers.

The arguments have been given here to stimulate the student's interest in this battle during the first decade of the twenty-first century. Perhaps the next decade will see the reinvention of corrections into a model of public and private cooperation to achieve new goals and objectives for the beleaguered system of corrections.

Key Words

self-insured, 231

slaves of the master, 232

privatization, 233

technologies for surveillance, 233

growth industry, 234

electronic monitoring, 237

Corrections Corporation of America (CCA), 237

U.S. Corrections Corporation (USCC), 238

The GEO Group, 238

Review Questions

1. What are the primary reasons for the private sector to become involved in prisons and jails?
2. How many beds are being supplied by the private sector in adult prisons?
3. What are the major arguments against privatization of adult jails and prisons?
4. What are the major arguments in favor of privatization of correctional services?
5. What vested interests are evident in the controversy over privatization of correctional facilities?

Endnotes

1. William Sabol, Heather Couture, and Paige Harrison, *Prisoners in 2006* (Washington, DC: Bureau of Justice Statistics, 2007), p. 1.
2. Joseph Jacoby, "The Endurance of Failing Correctional Institutions," *The Prison Journal* 82:2 (2002): 168–188.
3. Richard P. Seiter, "Private Corrections: A Review of the Issues," http://www.correctionscorp.com/STATIC/ ASSETS/Private_Corr_Review_of_Issues_.pdf (accessed November 16, 2008).
4. Douglas McDonald, E. Fournier, E. Russell, et al., *Private Prisons in the United States* (Cambridge, MA: Abt Associates, 1998).
5. Harry E. Allen and J. Abril, "The New Chain Gang: Corrections in the Next Century," *American Journal of Criminal Justice* 22:1 (1997): 1–12; and Matthew Mancini, *One Dies, Get Another: Convict Leasing in the American South* (Columbia, SC: University of South Carolina Press, 1999). See also Major W. Cox, "Chain

Gang's Newest Wedge," http://www.majorcox.com/columns/chains.htm (accessed November 16, 2008).

6. James Anderson, L. Dyson, and W. Brooks, "Alabama Prison Chain Gangs," *Western Journal of Black Studies* 24:1 (2000): 9–1; and Timothy Dodge, "State Convict Road Gangs in Alabama," *The Alabama Review* 53:4 (2000): 243–270. See also Scott Henry, "How Do You Say 'Chain Gang' in Arabic?," http://blogs.creativeloafing.com/freshloaf/2008/02/14/how-do-you-say-chain-gang-in-Arabic?/ (accessed November 16, 2008).

7. For example, California has 13 contract correctional facilities providing minimum security and treatment. In 2007, nine of these ten units housed more than 5,500 offenders. American Correctional Association, *2007 Directory* (Lanham, MD: ACA, 2007), pp. 129–129.

8. Richard P. Seiter, *Private Corrections,* supra note 3.

9. A series of evaluation studies can be found at http://www.correctionscorp.com/researchfindings.html. None of the authors has any financial interest in any private-sector correctional group.

10. Large portions of this chapter were extracted and paraphrased from materials provided by Charles Thomas, former director of the Center for Studies in Criminology and the Law, University of Florida. We are grateful to him for sharing these earlier data and reports.

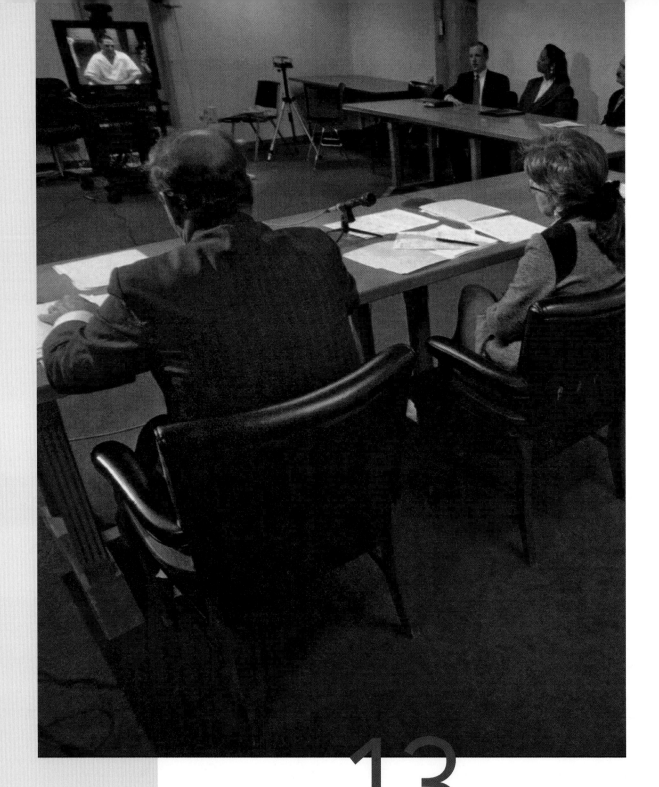

Parole and Reentry

Outline

> "We must develop and maintain the capacity to forgive. He who is devoid of the power to forgive is devoid of the power to love."
>
> –Martin Luther King, Jr.

Overview

The correctional process as described so far has followed offenders as they were filtered through the correctional system. We have seen how those who wind up in prison face both challenges and opportunities as they serve out their sentences and descend the classification ladder until they reach their minimum status and ultimate release date. This chapter now brings our focus to parole, traditionally the most common method for leaving prison and reentering society in a graduated manner. Parole (or earned early release) is a correctional process that has often found itself under attack as a method for inmates to easily gain early release from their stated sentence. The attitude that has swept the nation in the past couple of decades, as prison populations continued to soar, is to make sentencing even harsher and to make the inmates serve as much of their sentence in a prison as possible.[1] The student needs to understand the fact that many other issues underlie the process of parole in today's environment and to reexamine the use of this time-tested tool. We begin with a brief history of parole.

THE DEVELOPMENT OF PAROLE

Parole is a correctional option that often evokes strong feelings. Some people argue that it should be abolished entirely, whereas others believe it provides men and women with an opportunity to demonstrate that they can reenter society and lead law-abiding and productive lives. Regardless of one's position, parole is an important part of the American correctional scene. Because more than 600,000 inmates were released to the community in 2008, many of whom were under some form of correctional supervision, it is important that we understand the roots of parole and how it is granted.

The Roots of American Parole

Parole from prison, like the prison itself, is primarily an American innovation.[2] It emerged from a philosophical revolution and a resulting tradition of penal reform established in the late eighteenth century in the newly formed United States. As with many other new ideas that emerged in early America, parole had its roots in the practices of English and European penal systems.

In England, orders of transportation were thought to be a severe punishment. In the eighteenth century, banishment, a common penalty for the aristocracy or nobility for centuries, was imposed on the common offender for the first time. The judge would order the common offender transported to the colonies rather than to the gallows or pillory. The criminal would be allowed to go at liberty in the new land, sometimes for a period of indenture,[3] on the condition of not returning to England for a specified time period (such as ten years), if at all.[4]

Criminologists commonly accept punishment by transportation as the principal forerunner of parole.[5] They argue that transportation was an organized, uniform process by which thousands of convicts were punished in a manner short of execution or corporal punishment, because it was a system wherein offenders eventually obtained their freedom.

profile

Alexander Maconochie

The "father" of parole who developed the concept while overseeing the penal colony at Norfolk Island, off the east coast of Australia.

key term

Irish system

Developed in Ireland, one of the first parole systems that permitted inmates to work their way into lower security settings.

profile

Sir Walter Crofton

Director of the Irish penal system in 1946, he improved on the "ticket-of-leave" system developed by Maconochie; his system also had provisions for supervision by police, the first parole officers.

Early Practices in Other Nations

The governor of a prison in Spain started the first operational system of conditional release in 1835. Up to one-third of a prison sentence could be reduced by good behavior and a demonstrated desire to do better. A similar system was enacted in Bavaria in 1837, and many prison reformers in France in the 1840s advocated the adoption of similar conditional release systems. In fact, the term *parole* comes from the French *parole d'honneur*, or "word of honor," which characterized the French efforts to establish parole release. Prisoners would be released after showing good behavior and industry in the prison,[6] and on their word of honor that they would obey the law.

Despite the fact that these efforts predate those of **Alexander Maconochie,** it is he who is usually given credit as being the father of parole. In 1840, Captain Maconochie was put in charge of the English penal colony in New South Wales at Norfolk Island, about 1,000 miles off the coast of Australia. To this colony were sent the criminals who were "twice condemned." They had been shipped from England to Australia, and then from Australia to Norfolk. Conditions were allegedly so bad at Norfolk Island that men reprieved from the death penalty wept and those who were to die thanked God.[7]

It was under these conditions that Maconochie devised an elaborate method of granted conditional release.[8] Under his plan, prisoners were awarded marks and moved through stages of custody until finally earning release. Although Maconochie was soon removed from his position, the ideas he had formulated spread to Ireland, and eventually the United States. The **Irish system** as designed by **Sir Walter Crofton** permitted inmates to work their way into lower security settings, earn a ticket-of-leave, and work and live outside the prison.

c o r r e c t i o n a l **brief**

Good-Time Laws

The term **good time** does not refer to having fun within prison walls. Instead, it involves taking days off an offender's sentence as a result of conduct and behavior in accordance with the institutional rules. In 1817, New York was the first state to pass a good-time statute. The rules throughout the nation were firm and fairly straightforward, even though they varied from state to state. New York's statute enabled the correctional administrator to reduce by one-fourth the

time of any prisoner sentenced to imprisonment for not less than five years, upon certificate of the principal keeper and other satisfactory evidence that such prisoner had behaved well and had acquired, on the whole, the net sum of $15 or more per annum. Every state in the Union and the District of Columbia had passed some kind of good-time law by 1916. California began awarding good time in 1990 at a "1 for 2" ratio: one day of reduction for every two days of good time.

Parole Comes to the United States

In 1870, the first meeting of the American Prison Association was held in Cincinnati, Ohio. Reform was the battle cry of the day, and the meeting took on an almost evangelical fervor.[9] Both Sir Walter Crofton and American warden F. B. Sanborn advocated the Irish system.[10]

Armed with the success of the meeting, the focus of prison reformers shifted from incarceration as the answer to crime to a concentrated movement to return offenders to society. Prisons remained central, but they were now seen almost as a necessary evil, not as an end. Prison reformers everywhere began to advocate adoption and expansion of good-time laws, assistance to released prisoners, the adoption of the ticket-of-leave system, and parole. In 1869, the New York State legislature passed an act creating the Elmira Reformatory and an indeterminate sentence ". . . until reformation, not exceeding five years."

With the passage of this law, parole in the United States became a reality. It soon spread to other jurisdictions, and by 1944, every jurisdiction in the nation had a parole authority.[11]

PARDON AND PAROLE:
TWO OF THE WAYS OUT OF PRISON

Most offenders who enter the prisons of America eventually end up back on the streets of the old neighborhoods. Unless prisoners die in prison (from natural or other causes), almost all will be released back into society someday. The cruelly long sentences of the nineteenth century usually meant that the few offenders who did leave the prisons were bitter, broken, or both. Today, many offenders leave prison on parole, sometimes long before the expiration of their maximum sentences. In recent years, the number and percentage of prisoners **released on parole** have declined steadily. In 1966, prisoners released on discretionary parole numbered 61% of the total, but that figure declined to 39% in 1990. Since the **truth-in-sentencing movement**[12] (explained in Chapter 4), the percentage has declined even more, down to an estimated 35% in 2006. Although the use of discretionary parole release before sentence expiration has declined, many offenders whose sentences expire are now required to have a period of parole supervision (sometimes called *postrelease control*). As a result, the U.S. total of persons under parole supervision increased from about 531,000 in 1990 to more than 774,000 by the beginning of 2004, over 11% of the total of those placed under correctional supervision.[13] The significance of parole is clear when we recognize that the only alternatives are clemency, commutation, completion of sentence, death, escape, or some form of shock probation. Information on avenues by which inmates leave prison is given in Figure 13.1. As can be seen in these data, conditional **discretionary release,** which is traditional parole release with supervision, has declined steadily since 1992. Conditional **mandatory release** is when an offender is released prior to expiration of sentence (usually

key term

Good time
Taking days off an inmate's sentence for good behavior while incarcerated.

key term

Released on parole
Release of an inmate from confinement to expiration of sentence on condition of good behavior and supervision in the community.

key term

Truth-in-sentencing movement
Begun the 1990s, this movement required inmates to serve a significant portion of their sentence before consideration for release.

key term

Discretionary release
Parole of an inmate from prison prior to expiration of maximum sentence according to the boundaries set by the sentencing body or legislature.

key term

Mandatory release
The required release of an inmate from incarceration because the statutes mandate the release of any inmate who has served his or her maximum sentence.

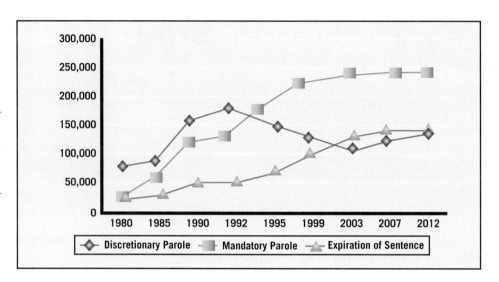

figure 13.1

Releases from State Prison by Method of Release: 1980–2012

SOURCE: Timothy Hughes, Doris Wilson, and Allen Beck, *Trends in State Parole, 1990–2000* (Washington, DC: Bureau of Justice Statistics, 2001), p.4. Data for 2012 are extrapolated.

key term

"Max out"
Release after serving the entire sentence.

key term

Executive clemency
A pardon, reduction of sentence, or release of an inmate by the governor or pardoning authority.

key term

Pardon
Exoneration of blame for the offense by the governor or paroling authority.

key term

Amnesty
A form of pardon for a class of offenders, such as draft dodgers.

key term

Reprieve
A reduction in sentencing severity; sometimes used in death penalty cases, when execution of the offender is at least temporarily stopped.

key term

Commutation
A reduction of the severity of the sentence by the executive branch of government.

key term

Parole
Release of the inmate from confinement after he or she has served a portion of the sentence, under the continued custody of the state and under conditions that permit reincarceration in the event of misbehavior.

triggered after a set portion of the sentence has been served), with supervision in the community. This mechanism for release has steadily increased due primarily to determinate sentencing. Unconditional release is when the sentence has expired ("expiration of sentence") and the offender is released without conditions or supervision.

In the days of frequent capital punishment and life sentences, death in prison was always a strong possibility. The prisoner might die as a result of natural causes, an accident, suicide, or homicide inside the walls. Another way out, sometimes not much better from the offender's viewpoint, is to be forced to serve the entire maximum sentence before release (to **"max out"** a sentence). Infinitely better, but rare, is **executive clemency,** in the form of a pardon or similar action by the governor. A full **pardon** usually means complete exoneration of blame for the offense and relieves the prisoner of the stigma of guilt. One version of the pardon is **amnesty,** which may be granted to a group or class of offenders. For example, the United States has a long tradition of granting amnesty to soldiers who deserted or avoided service in major wars. In countries where it is customary to imprison political dissidents, the government also may use mass amnesty to gain public favor. Executive power can also be used to grant a **reprieve,** usually in the case of the death penalty (a well-used plot line in grade B movies of the 1930s and 1940s, in which the star is granted a last-minute reprieve while being strapped into the electric chair). A reprieve does not usually result in a release, but merely a reduction in the severity of the punishment or a delay in its imposition. Punishment can also be lessened by **commutation,** shortening of the sentence by executive order. Usually the commutation is based on time already spent in jail and prison and results in almost immediate release of the petitioner. Another form of release, discussed in Chapter 4, results from some sort of appellate review action. These procedures, along with parole (and, of course, escape or natural death), cover the major ways a prisoner can expect to leave prison.

WHAT IS PAROLE?

The classic definition of **parole** is "release of an offender from a penal or correctional institution, after he has served a portion of his sentence, under the continued custody of the state and under conditions that permit his reincarceration in the event of misbehavior."[14]

correctional **brief**

APPA Position Statement on Parole

The purpose of parole is to improve public safety by reducing the incidence and impact of crime committed by parolees. Parole is not leniency or clemency but a logical extension of the sentence to provide the opportunity to return offenders to society as productive and law-abiding citizens after a reasonable period of incarceration and at a time when they are assessed to have the capability and desire to succeed and live up to the responsibilities inherent in such a release. Conditions of parole and supervision services provided to conditionally released offenders are means by which the parole authority can assist the offender to successfully reintegrate into the community while providing a continuing measure of protection to society. The core services of parole are to provide investigation and reports to the paroling authority, to help offenders develop appropriate release plans and to supervise these persons released on

parole. Parole authorities and supporting correctional agencies, in addition to fulfilling these responsibilities, may provide a wide variety of supporting pre-release and post-release programs and services, such as employment and life skills counseling, halfway house accommodation, counseling services, specialized community work programs and family services.

Parole is premised on the following beliefs:

- The majority of incarcerated offenders can benefit from a period of transition into the community prior to completion of their sentence.

- The protection of society is a primary objective of conditional release.

The definition by the American Probation and Parole Association (APPA) can be found in the accompanying Correctional Brief. Parole has two major elements: the release of an offender from prison under some guidelines, and the supervision of the offender in the community.

Today, all but 2 states have some system of parole supervision for released offenders, even though some 16 states and the federal government have eliminated parole-board release ("discretionary parole"), and another 4 have abolished parole-board authority for releasing certain violent offenders. In 1999, Wisconsin became the most recent state to abolish parole-board release.[15]

lecture note

Define *executive clemency, pardon,* and *parole.* Briefly trace the history of each.

lecture note

Explain the *truth-in-sentencing movement* and its effects on prison populations and parole.

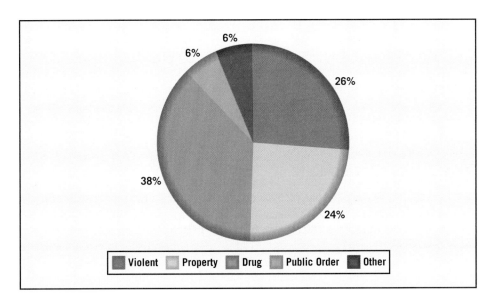

figure 13.2

Types of Crimes of Parolees, 2007

SOURCE: Lauren Glaze and Thomas Bonczar, Probation and Parole in the United States, 2007 (Washington, DC: Bureau of Justice Statistices, 2008).

PAROLE ADMINISTRATION

If prisoners want to be released on parole, they must be recommended for it and their records reviewed by some procedure that will select them for that option. For this reason, how parole is administered and by whom is of vital concern to the prison population, as well as to the rest of society.

Parole is a complex procedure and has many functions and processes that differ from one jurisdiction to another. Traditionally, parole includes five basic functions:

1. Selecting and placing prisoners on parole
2. Establishing conditions of supervision
3. Aiding, supervising, assisting, and controlling parolees in the community
4. Returning parolees to prison if the conditions of parole are not met
5. Discharging parolees when supervision is no longer necessary or when sentence is completed

The executive branch of government administers parole, unlike probation, which is a judicial function. As such, its form and operation vary from state to state.

THE PAROLE BOARD

Just who are the people who make so many inmate release decisions?

When parole selection procedures were first instituted, many states had a single commissioner of parole, appointed by the governor. That kind of political patronage soon led to corruption and controversy and was generally abandoned after World War II. Today most states have a **parole board** that serves the function formerly held by one person. Today, parole boards across the country vary greatly by size, operating procedures, independence, and selection. For example, New York has 19 members on the board, whereas three states have only 3 members.[16] In some states, parole-board members are closely linked to, or actually part of, the correctional system staff; in other states, parole-board members are appointed by the governor and are independent of correctional institutions and the administrators of the system. It is important to remember that even states that have abolished parole release will operate parole boards long into the future in order to hear cases that were sentenced under previous sentencing laws.

Although an independent board may well be more objective than the correctional bureaucracy in making parole recommendations, it does not provide the perfect system. The argument is sometimes made that independent systems tend to place on parole boards persons who have little training or experience in corrections, which in turn causes unnecessary conflict between prison authorities and the boards.

PAROLE RELEASE

How is an offender selected for parole? This question is important, not only for the inmate being considered, but also for the public.

Parole selection guidelines differ widely from state to state. The U.S. Supreme Court has consistently held parole to be a privilege, and consequently held that a full complement of due process rights does not need to be afforded at parole-granting hearings.[17] As a result, the states have been given the opportunity to establish whatever inmate privileges they believe appropriate at parole-granting hearings.

Most states have established regulations as to the amount of time an inmate is required to serve prior to parole eligibility. In 16 states, eligibility is obtained on completion of the minimum sentence. In ten states, eligibility is achieved on completion of one-third of the maximum sentence. Other states use the number of prior felony convictions and length of prior sentences to calculate eligibility rules. Even in the states that use the same eligibility guidelines, wide variation exists in the length of the minimum and maximum prison terms handed down for the same offense. In reality, there are literally as many variations in eligibility as there are parole jurisdictions.[18] In addition to time factors, some states restrict the use of parole for those convicted of various serious personal offenses, such as first-degree murder, kidnapping, and aggravated rape.[19] Many states now advise victims of pending parole hearings, especially if the inmate has been convicted of a violent crime. Victims are permitted to submit written commentary and attend (or send a representative to) the parole board hearing. Videoconferencing allows victims to participate without being threatened by their assailant. Evidence suggests that parole boards are heavily influenced by such communications.[20]

If inmates do not meet the standards the board has established for parole, their sentences are continued and they are **"flopped."** But if accepted, they are prepared for turnover to the parole authority for a period of supervision determined by the parole board.

Our discussion about parole has concerned the adult system; however, it should be noted that several states also operate parole boards for juveniles. For example, in Ohio, youth committed to the Ohio Department of Youth Services go before a Release Authority, which then decides the release date and conditions. The Release Authority acts very similarly to an adult parole board.

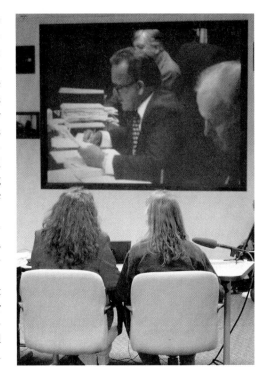

Victims participate in a parole board meeting in California via videoconferencing for the first time. *Courtesy of AP Wide World Photos.*

PAROLE RELEASE GUIDELINES

Critics of the parole process have commented on the release decision, characterizing it as arbitrary, capricious, prejudiced, lawless, and offering no meaningful future directions for inmates who have not been released. One response to those criticisms has been the development of parole guidelines. Today, 30 states have structured parole guidelines.[21]

The most common guideline system will factor in the seriousness of the crime, and the traits and previous criminal behaviors the inmate brings to the current offense (that is, substance-abuse history, prior record, work history), to construct a matrix that specifies the amount of time (within narrow bounds) an inmate would have to serve before release.

key term

"Flopped"
Inmate term for denial of parole.

correctional **brief**

Shock Incarceration and Parole

Shock incarceration facilities, or boot camp prisons for young female adults, have been developed in city, county, and state jurisdictions. These include the New York State Program for youthful female offenders. A typical case is discussed below. Rita is an example of the type of offender who often ends up in a boot camp program. Her case is described to indicate how boot camps interface with parole.

Women in Shock Incarceration   Rita finishes 50 sit-ups and springs to her feet. At 6 A.M. her platoon begins a five-mile run, the last portion of this morning's physical training. After five months in New York's Lakeview Shock Incarceration Correctional Facility, the morning workout is easy. Rita even enjoys it, taking pride in her physical conditioning.

When Rita graduates and returns to New York City, she will face six months of intensive supervision before moving to regular parole. More than two-fifths of Rita's platoon did not make it this far; some withdrew voluntarily, and the rest were removed for misconduct or failure to participate satisfactorily. By completing shock incarceration, she will enter parole 11 months before her minimum release date. The requirements for completing shock incarceration are the same for male and female inmates. The women live in a separate housing area of Lakeview. Otherwise, men and women participate in the same education, physical training, drill and ceremony, drug education, and counseling programs. Men and women are assigned to separate work details and attend "Network" group meetings held in inmates' living units.

Good-time and earned-time credits can reduce the anticipated prison sentence. Such an approach permits the offender to know immediately how long the sentence will be and what must be done to shorten it. This approach also reduces the anxiety and hostility of the on-the-spot decision-making process frequently found in other jurisdictions. Generally, guidelines attempt to structure discretion, not eliminate it, and while parole boards can deviate from the recommendations of the guidelines, they usually have to provide a rationale in writing.

PAROLE CONDITIONS

Parole is in essence a contract between the state and the offender. If the offender is able to abide by the terms of the contract, freedom is maintained. If a violation of these conditions occurs, or if a parolee is charged with a new crime, the parole board may revoke parole and return the offender to prison. The offender must abide by the contract, and stay under parole supervision for the period of time outlined by the parole board. Although every state has its own policies and procedures, parole usually lasts more than two but usually less than seven years. Some states may permit discharge from parole after a very short time, as long as the offender has diligently adhered to the prerelease contract. Although the exact content of the contracts varies among states and individuals, the Correctional Brief below shows a simple and commonsense **parole agreement.**

PAROLE REVOCATION

Parolees who violate the conditions of their release can be returned to prison for a **technical violation.** Because of arbitrary procedures used in earlier parole revocation hearings, the

correctional **brief**

Statement of Parole Agreement

The Members of the Parole Board have agreed that you have earned the opportunity of parole and eventually a final release from your present conviction. The Parole Board is therefore ordering a Parole Release in your case.

Parole Status has a two-fold meaning: One is a trust status in which the Parole Board accepts your word you will do your best to abide by the Conditions of Parole that are set down in your case; the other, by state law, means the Adult Parole Authority has the legal duty to enforce the Conditions of Parole even to the extent of arrest and return to the institution should that become necessary.

1. Upon release from the institution, report as instructed to your Parole Officer (or any other person designated) and thereafter report as often as directed.

2. Secure written permission of the Adult Parole Authority before leaving the [said] state.

3. Obey all municipal ordinances, state and federal laws, and at all times conduct yourself as a responsible law-abiding citizen.

4. Never purchase, own, possess, use or have under your control, a deadly weapon or firearm.

5. Follow all instructions given you by your Parole Officer or other officials of the Adult Parole Authority and abide by any special conditions imposed by the Adult Authority.

6. If you feel any of the Conditions or instructions are causing problems, you may request a meeting with your Parole Officer's supervisor. The request stating your reasons for the conference should be in writing when possible.

7. Special Conditions: (as determined). I have read, or have had read to me, the foregoing Conditions of my Parole. I fully understand them and I agree to observe and abide by my Parole Conditions.

Witness _____
Parole Candidate _____
Date _____

SOURCE: State of Ohio, Department of Rehabilitation and Correction, Adult Parole Authority, *Statement of Parole Agreement APA. 271* (Columbus: State of Ohio).

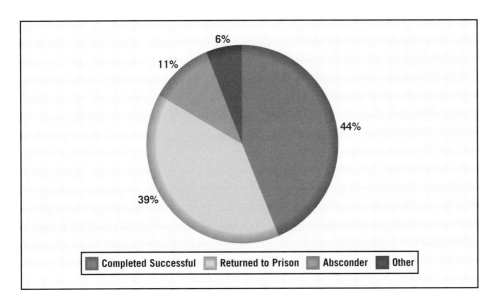

figure 13.3
Outcomes of Adults Exiting Parole, 2006

SOURCE: Glaze, Lauren and Thomas P. Bonczar, *Probation and Parole in the United States, 2006.* (Washington, DC: Bureau of Justice Statistics, 2007).

lecture note

Discuss the impact of parole-board rejection of the inmate's petition for parole. What special steps are taken to minimize institutional damage by inmates denied parole?

U.S. Supreme Court in 1971 defined the basic rights of parolees at a parole revocation hearing in **Morrissey v. Brewer,** 408 U.S. 271. Parolees must be notified in writing of the charges they face, at least 24 hours before the preliminary hearing ("probable cause"). Revocation candidates have a right to hear the evidence against them, to cross-examine, and to refute the testimony. Furthermore, they can present their own evidence, and they have the right to a written report from the hearing that must be held before a neutral third party. Some states mandate legal counsel at this stage. At the second hearing, usually before a representative or member(s) of a parole board, the same rights are continued. Figure 13.3 shows the outcome

key term

Morrissey v. Brewer
The U.S. Supreme Court decision that spells out the rights of an offender at a parole revocation hearing.

class activity

Present students with two case summaries, and ask them to decide on whether to release the inmates. If the consensus is "no," ask them what qualities of the cases led them to this decision.

lecture note

Explain *parole release guidelines* and their strengths and weaknesses.

class activity

Distribute a fictitious case description to the class and ask what special conditions they might think necessary for that particular offender. Ask students to indicate if they concur on the first three special conditions mentioned.

lecture note

Distribute a blank form used by your parole board on the standard and special conditions of parole supervision. Explain the rationale for the standard conditions.

If necessary, parole agents can arrest parolees who violate their parole conditions.
Courtesy of State of California Department of Corrections.

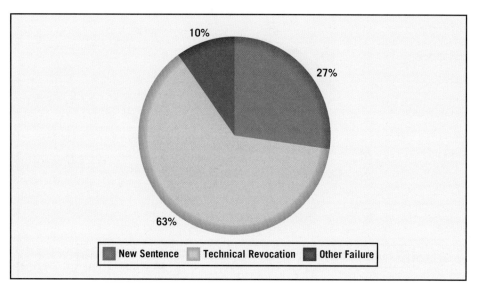

figure 13.4

Type of Failure for Parolees in 2006

SOURCE: Glaze, Lauren and Thomas P. Bonczar, *Probation and Parole in the United States, 2006.* Washington, DC: Bureau of Justice Statistics, 2007.

of state parole discharges in 2003. As shown, parole revocations are major issues facing corrections. See Figure 13.4 for information on types of failure of parolees.

PAROLE REMAINS A MAJOR SEGMENT OF CORRECTIONS

Despite growing pressures for the determinate sentence and the elimination of supervision on release, parole is still a growing segment of community corrections and a critical element in the correctional system. Although many prisoners are now released unconditionally back to the community, many are still released to community supervision. In some states, the title of *parole officer* has been changed to *community control officer,* to reflect a custodial leaning, but the inmates remain under essentially the same controls as before.

Both parole and probation have a similar history and, even though they occur at opposite ends of the correctional process, their clients are supervised in much the same way. Thirty-four states have combined the administration of probation and parole into a single agency. Even probation, which had traditionally been a preincarceration option, now takes place in many cases after a brief period of jail or prison time. The main difference remains the method by which the offender is placed under either option. Probation remains a direct sentence by the court, whereas parole is a function of the executive branch, with discretionary parole being granted by the parole board and mandatory parole by corrections agencies under the governor. These parole agencies provide a variety of services.

PARDONS

Across the nation, parole boards are often directly involved in the consideration for a pardon, recommending this act of clemency to the state's governor. Although pardons are relatively rare, they can lessen social stigma and restore rights.[22] No mention of parole boards

correctional **brief**

Pardon

An act of executive clemency that absolves the party in part or in full from the legal consequences of the crime and conviction. For the accused, pardon stops further criminal justice proceedings. Pardons can be full or conditional; the former generally applies to both the punishment and the guilt of the offender and blots out the existence of guilt in the eyes of the law. It also removes an offender's disabilities and restores civil rights. The conditional pardon usually falls short of the remedies available in the full pardon, is an expression of guilt, may restrict some freedoms, and does not obliterate the conviction but may restore civil rights.

Perhaps the most famous pardon was granted to former President Richard Nixon by President Gerald Ford. Many believe that this decision cost Ford the 1976 election. More recently, President Bill Clinton was widely criticized for his end-of-term pardons.

would be complete without mentioning their role in pardons. Some states restore civil rights when parole is granted; others do the same when the offender is released from parole. In still others, it is necessary for a governor to restore all rights, usually through a pardon. Some parole boards (such as those in Alabama) exercise pardon authority.

California's **procedures for pardon** illustrate the latter. What is required for a pardon in California? Generally, the offender must have led a crime-free existence for ten years following release from parole. The offender must initiate a petition for pardon in a superior court (also called a court of common pleas in other jurisdictions). A formal hearing is held, and the presiding judge solicits opinions from the local district attorney and chief law enforcement officer in the jurisdiction. A computer search is made for any arrests and convictions. The local probation department prepares a pre-pardon hearing report. If the preponderance of evidence were favorable and no arrest or conviction record were found, the petition would be approved by the superior court and forwarded to the governor's office. The governor may then order the equivalent of a parole board (Board of Prison Terms) to prepare an investigation that would contain a recommendation for pardon. If the report is favorable, the governor may pardon the petitioner, thereby restoring to him or her all of the rights and immunities of an ordinary citizen. It is evident that most ex-offenders, though no doubt preferring a pardon, may favor even more having the crime and conviction put as far behind them as possible. They may also not have the perseverance to endure such an involved and expensive procedure. Finally, statistics show that most ex-offenders are rearrested within the ten-year time period, even without further action by criminal justice system officials. No wonder so few ex-offenders seek and receive pardons.

key term

Procedures for pardon
Legal steps for a pardon, such as being crime free and meeting other conditions set by the state.

lecture note

How are civil rights generally restored to parolees?

lecture note

Explain the pardon procedure in your state, pointing to the steps that must be taken to restore civil rights.

REENTRY: THE NEW CHALLENGE

The large number of incarcerated offenders in the United States has led to the inevitable result—numerous offenders will reenter society each year. In fact, reentry has become the new buzzword used by policy makers to describe the process by which offenders come back into the community. Some have argued that parole is essential to this process,[23] while others[24] believe that since a high percentage of offenders pose minimal risk to public safety, parole supervision should be eliminated or shortened to about six months. Given estimates that a significant percentage of offenders who will be returning to the community have a number of important needs,[25] little doubt remains that services and treatment in the community should be an important part of the reentry process. Indeed, several states have already created reentry programs designed to coordinate efforts and services between the institution, parole, and community correctional programs and treatment providers. Recently, the federal government committed funds to states to assist with the reentry process and to help ensure that offenders receive the services and treatment necessary to help them remain crime free. Discussed next are some of the programs that have been traditionally used for offender reentry into the community from the institution.

Work-Release Programs

One of the earliest programs for releasing prisoners before their full sentences expired was the result of the first **work-release** legislation. The use of offenders for community work programs had its origins in ancient Rome, where prisoners aided in the construction of massive public works. Those workers, however, had no hope for release; their work was just another form of slave labor, but with a new label. This has been the fate of many new efforts by penologists over the history of correctional efforts. The work-release philosophy, which permits inmates to work on their own in the free community, dates back to a 1913 Wisconsin statute that allowed misdemeanants to continue to work at their jobs while serving short sentences in jail. North Carolina applied the principles of the Wisconsin statute to felony offenders in 1957, under limited conditions; Michigan and Maryland soon followed suit with similar acts. In 1965, Congress passed the Federal Prisoner Rehabilitation Act, which provided for work release, furloughs, and community treatment centers for federal prisoners. This act served as a model for many states.

Institutional work release is not intended to be a substitute for parole, but it can be a valuable tool for the correctional administrator and the parole officer who must eventually supervise an individual who has participated in work release. The work-release program is not really an alternative to incarceration. Rather, it is a chance for offenders to develop and test their work skills, job discipline, and personal control over their behavior in the community—and it allows them to spend the major part of the day away from the institution. Because offenders must still return to the institution, the work-release program may be considered only a partial alternative that gives limited relief from the negative pressures of incarceration.

Work release has other benefits besides allowing inmates to be outside the walls for a period of time each day. The income derived from the work can be used in a number of ways: If the inmates have families, the earnings can be used to keep them off welfare rolls or to augment the assistance they might be receiving; inmates can reimburse victims for their

Work release facilities provide a place to grow, and even have a meaningful job on parole.
Courtesy of Ohio Department of Rehabilitation and Correction.

loss, if the judge has required it;[26] or they may be able to build a nest egg for the time when they will be released. In many cases, the inmates can contribute toward their cost of housing and sustenance as well. This teaches them valuable budgeting and money-management skills. One of the main fringe benefits is that their community becomes aware of their ability to maintain a job without creating problems for themselves or others. Also, their association with stable coworkers in the free world may give them support and guidance[27] that they could not find inside the walls. In the American tradition, the ability to do a good day's work both heightens the offenders' self-esteem and commands respect from others. Scandinavian prisons have some kind of work facility attached to them, allowing inmates to work at real-world jobs for pay equal to that earned by a similarly skilled outside worker.

Furlough Programs

Another form of partial incarceration is the **furlough.** Both work release and furlough extend the limits of confinement to include unsupervised absences from the institution. Furloughs and home visits have been allowed for many years on an informal basis. The death of a family member or some other crisis situation at home ("emergency furlough") was the most common reason for the home furlough. As states have passed legislation making furloughs a legal correctional tool, furloughs have been used for a number of purposes, including a home visit during holidays or just before release ("meritorious furlough"), so the return to the free world is a graduated process and includes **reintegration.** Education has been another reason for extensive use of the furlough; it often allows the inmate to be in residence at the school during the week; he or she then returns to the correctional institution on the weekend. One benefit of home furloughs, obviously, is decreased sexual tension in institutions. More uses for furloughs are being explored as correctional administrators gain experience with them.[28] A major roadblock to progress in such programs has been a few highly publicized and sensational failures. Those failures,[29] combined with the generally increasing numbers of violent and dangerous inmates coming out of the prisons, have made it difficult to promote any kind of furlough program.[30]

Halfway Houses

The search for ways to assist offenders transitioning from prison has pumped new life into an old option: the **halfway house.**[31] The interest in the halfway house as an important part of the reentry process has grown in the past few decades. Although earlier halfway houses served as residences for homeless men and women released from prison, they have since been used for a variety of purposes. Small residences offering shelter have been managed by prison aid societies since the early 1800s. In recent years, more attention has been given to halfway houses as the possible nuclei of community-based networks of residential treatment centers, drug-free and alcohol-free living spaces, or as prerelease guidance centers.[32]

There are different patterns of referral to halfway house programs, the most frequent of which occurs when an inmate is granted a conditional release (such as parole, shock parole, or shock probation) and is required to enter a halfway house during at least the initial period following release. This provides services to and surveillance of parolees who need support during this period. Time of residency may be specified before referral, but usually is a shared decision to be made collaboratively by the supervision officer, client, and house

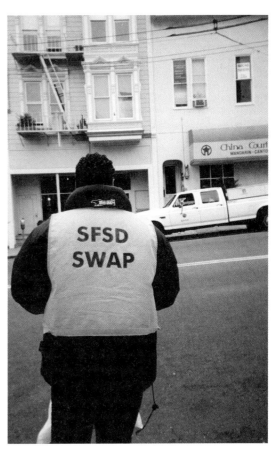

Participant in the San Francisco Sheriff Department's SWAP program, released from jail to perform community service.
Photo by Harry E. Allen, Ph.D.

key term

Furlough
A prison-release program permitting the inmate to pursue education, vocational training, or employment in the community.

key term

Reintegration
The planned transition of an inmate from prison to the community.

key term

Halfway house
A residential house or facility for offenders in the community; often used for inmates prior to final release to parole.

PMI residents talk about their day while eating supper. PMI is a halfway house funded primarily by the Missouri Department of Corrections and has been operating in Columbia since 1983.
Courtesy of AP Wide World Photos.

staff. This decision is frequently based on such factors as resident's readiness to leave the house, employment, fine and restitution payments, savings, and alternative residential plan. The offender generally continues on supervision after leaving the halfway house.

Another source of residents are those inmates whose release plans call for placement in a halfway house as the initial phase of their release procedure. Unlike the first option, however, halfway house residency occurs prior to formal granting of parole and subsequent supervision as a releasee or parolee. These inmates typically have a definite release date before they move from the prison to the halfway house. Note that these clients remain inmates who will serve the remainder of their sentences while residing in a halfway house. For these residents, halfway houses provide needed and significant assistance and direction in the transition from prison to community.[33] Additional benefits include continuation of jurisdiction by the referring correctional agency,[34] ability to return the inmate to incarceration without formal violation of parole, development of a more positive attitude toward the halfway house by the resident, lessening of loneliness and sense of isolation,[35] and less expensive aftercare service that can be more legitimately compared to imprisonment, rather than the

correctional **brief**

Turning Point Program

The Turning Point Program is part of the Talbert House, Inc., a nonprofit multiservice agency that consists of over 40 programs in four areas: victim assistance, chemical dependency, mental health, and criminal corrections. The Turning Point Program consists of a 40-bed, 28-day chemical dependency treatment program for men and women serving sentences for multiple DUI offenses.

After a 30-day jail incarceration, select offenders are relocated to the program site, a community residential confining program that permits visits but not leaves. The program is a comprehensive treatment regimen focused on drug and alcohol addiction and includes individualized alcohol treatment, family counseling, and educational services. AA (Alcoholics Anonymous) and NA (Narcotics Anonymous) are required. Turning Point participants were less likely after treatment to be arrested than comparison groups; the comprehensive treatment reduced DUI behavior.

SOURCE: Pratt, Travis, Alexander Holsinger, and Edward J. Latessa, "Treating the Chronic DUI Offender: 'Turning Point' Ten Years Later," *Journal of Criminal Justice*, 28:4 (2006): 271–281.

A drug lifer offender pleads for parole in the community under a relaxed lifer law in Plymouth, Michigan.
Courtesy of AP Wide World Photos.

costs of parole.[36] The U.S. Bureau of Prisons was a leader in initiating this model for using halfway houses, and continues to use this model on a prerelease basis.

The third avenue for residents to enter a halfway house differs by time of placement into the program; most offenders under probation and parole supervision do not initially reside in a halfway house. However, if such clients revert to criminal behavior or encounter unanticipated problems that could be resolved by program services or by a period of residency in a halfway house, the supervising agency may remand the offender to short-term residency in such a community corrections program. For example, in one study of halfway houses it was found that parole violators who were placed in a halfway house had a 12% lower recidivism rate than those returned to prison.[37]

At the federal level, the U.S. Bureau of Prisons established prerelease guidance centers in major metropolitan areas during 1961. The offender is sent to those centers from a correctional institution several months before he or she is eligible for parole. The offender is allowed to work and attend school in the community without supervision, and he or she participates in a number of programs in the halfway house itself. This approach has been copied by many states and appears to be a viable program when properly staffed and supervised. As possible uses for the halfway house are explored and outcomes are verified,[38] such units will offer not only short-term residency before the prisoner's placement on parole but also noninstitutional residence facilities[39] for a number of different categories of offenders.[40] At that point, **community residential centers** will constitute the first real alternative to institutional incarceration that works well in the community.

Reentry Courts

Following the popularity of drug courts, a new movement has taken root in which local courts have become more involved in the **reentry** of offenders back into the community. Reentry courts are specialized courts that are designed to reduce recidivism and improve public safety through the use of judicial oversight. The responsibilities generally assigned to reentry courts include: (1) review offenders' reentry progress and problems, (2) order offenders to participate in various treatment and reintegration programs, (3) use drug and alcohol testing and other checks to monitor compliance, (4) apply graduated sanctions to offenders who do not comply with treatment requirements, and (5) provide modest incentive rewards for sustained clean drug tests and other positive behaviors.[41]

key term

Community residential center
Any correctional facility existing to provide services and maximize reintegration of the offender back into the community.

key term

Reentry
Process of inmates' return to the community and their adjustment to society ("free world").

key term

Reentry courts
Specialized courts designed to reduce recidivism and improve public safety through judicial oversight of those offenders released from prison.

correctional **brief**

Reentry Courts

Reentry courts represent a new form of jurisprudence that has elevated the partnership between courts and corrections in seeking the common goal of successful offender reintegration. The concept of the reentry court necessitates considerable cooperation between corrections and local judiciaries since it requires the coordination of the work of prisons in preparing offenders for release and actively involving community corrections agencies and various community resources in transitioning offenders back into the community through active judicial oversight.

As with the drug-court concept, active judicial authority is applied to the reentry court to provide graduated sanctions and positive reinforcement, and to marshal resources for offender support. Central to this effort is the development of a three-fold strategy that seeks to improve the supervision of offenders, prepare communities to address public safety concerns, and provide services to aid offenders in reentering society. Despite being in its infancy with pilot sites in California, Colorado, Delaware, Florida, Iowa, Kentucky, New York, Ohio, and West Virginia, several core elements are present in each of these reentry-court initiatives. According to the Office of Justice Programs (1999), these core elements include:

- *Assessment and planning* that involves the offender, corrections department, and judiciary to identify the needs and develop a plan to begin building linkages in the community to support successful reintegration.

- *Active oversight,* whereby the reentry court meets with the offender at a high degree of frequency; meetings also include other relevant supporters or representatives from the supervising agency, family, and community. The underlying premise is for the judge to meet with offenders who are making progress as well as those who have failed to perform.

- *Management of supportive services* marshaled by the court to draw upon community resources. The reentry court must have a broad array of supportive resources, including substance-abuse treatment, job training programs, faith institutions, and housing services.

- *Accountability to community* through the development and involvement of citizen advisory boards, crime victims' organizations, and neighborhood groups. Accountability mechanisms may include ongoing restitution orders and participation in victim impact panels.

- *Graduated and parsimonious sanctions* established by the court that involve a predetermined range of sanctions for violations of the conditions of release. Paralleling drug courts, an array of relatively low-level sanctions that could be swiftly, predictably, and universally applied is developed.

- *Rewards for success* that incorporate positive judicial reinforcement such as negotiating early release from parole after established goals are achieved or by conducting graduation ceremonies similar to those used in drug courts.

SOURCE: Wilkinson, Reginald and Gregory Bucholtz, "Prison Reform Through Offender Reentry: A Partnership between Courts and Corrections." Unpublished Paper submitted to Pace Law School on the "Symposium on Prison Reform Law," October 2003.

class activity

Ask students if they have a friend or relative undergoing reentry and, if so, what assistance that individual is receiving from community programs.

class activity

Ask students to do a report on a reentry court.

lecture note

Discuss reentry courts and why it is unusual to have judicial involvement with inmates returning from prison.

The emergence of reentry courts is a major departure from traditional practice, where the responsibility of the court to an offender ended when the offender was sentenced by a judge. Judges typically have no role in the broad array of activities that carry out the terms of the sentence, the preparation of the offender for release, or the transition of the offender back into the community. The failure of traditional "solo" approaches, in which agency or system operated independently, and the realization that offenders leaving prison are returning to the community, have led to the development of this innovative approach to offender reentry. While research has just begun to examine the effectiveness of this strategy, hopes are high that the approach will produce positive results.

IS PAROLE EFFECTIVE?

The most critical question asked of parole and other postreleases programs is whether or not they are effective. Outcome measures can include cost, humaneness, employment, and family reunification just to name a few; however, the most important measure is public safety. Public safety is usually operationalized in corrections as recidivism, which, while it

figure 13.5

Probabilities of Rearrest within Two Years of Release for Parolees

Data from: C. T. Lowenkamp and E. J. Latessa. *Does Parole Work? A Reanalysis of the Urban Institute Study* (Cincinnati, OH: University of Cincinnati, 2005).

has some inherent limitations, is the ultimate indicator of a correctional program's success. The indicators used to measure recidivism, such as how it is defined (i.e., arrest, conviction, incarceration), the lengths of follow-up, and the source of data (official, self-report), are all factors that can affect reported recidivism rates. Indeed, the best way to ensure a low recidivism rate may be to define it very narrowly (e.g., incarceration in a state penal institution) and to utilize a very short follow-up period. Despite these challenges, recidivism remains the most important outcome of a correctional sanction.

Despite its widespread use, little is actually known about whether parole reduces recidivism. We do know that fewer than half of parole discharges successfully complete parole. Figure 13.5 shows that, among state parole discharges in 1999, over half of discretionary parolees successfully completed their term of supervision compared to a third of mandatory parolees, but this actually tells us little about the effectiveness of parole. In a 2005 study of parole, the Urban Institute concluded that parole supervision has little effect on rearrest rates of released prisoners.[42] However, using the same data, Lowenkamp and Latessa came to very different conclusions.[43] Figure 13.6 shows the adjusted probabilities of rearrest within two years of release. This figure indicates that discretionary parolees outperformed both mandatory parolees and unconditional releasees. Furthermore, overall, parolees had a lower rearrest rate than those who were not supervised. The debate about the effectiveness of parole will certainly continue into the future, and only more research will answer this important question.

lecture note

Discuss the major programs of reentry, addressing the categories of offenders that might best be served through each.

lecture note

Using your computer, play the brief videotape by Angela West on the topic of "Female Reentry" (approximately 3 minutes).

figure 13.6

Successful State Parolees by Method of Release, 1990–2005 (in percent)

SOURCE: Timothy Hughes, Doris Wilson, and Allen Beck, *Trends in State Parole, 1999–2000* (Washington, DC: Bureau of Justice Statistics, 2001), p. 11. Data for 2005 are extrapolated.

correctional **brief**

Effective Correctional Reentry

The development of services for those reentering society varies widely across the nation. While some jurisdictions or even states have spent considerable time and money developing services for parolees as they are released back into their communities, others are forced to rely on a more fragmented approach to service delivery. We still know relatively little about the overall effectiveness of parole, and even less about the effectiveness of the "newer" reentry programs.

According to Taxman and her colleagues, in an ideal model, reentry programs should include three or more phases designed to transition the inmate into the community. The first phase would begin in the institution, with service delivery congruent with the inmate's needs. The second phase would begin as the inmate is released from the institution. The inmates' risks and needs may change significantly as they enter the community context. Ideally, the individuals would continue in their treatment services and case plans would be updated as needed. The final phase is an aftercare or relapse-prevention phase where clients would receive ongoing support and services to address their needs. While this model may provide the overall structure necessary to implement an effective reentry program, the processes and services offered by these programs are key to their success.

SOURCE: Excerpted from Listwan, Shelley, Francis Cullen, and Edward J. Latessa, "How to Prevent Prisoner Re-Entry Programs from Failing: Insights from Evidence-Based Corrections," *Federal Probation* 70:3 (2006): 19–25.

In a recent study of parole violators in Pennsylvania, researchers found a number of factors related to failure. Those parolees who had their parole violated:

- Were more likely to hang around with individuals with criminal backgrounds
- Were less likely to live with a spouse
- Were less likely to be in a stable supportive relationship
- Were less likely to identify someone in their life who served in a mentoring capacity
- Were less likely to have job stability
- Were less likely to be satisfied with employment
- Were less likely to take low-end jobs and work up
- Were more likely to have negative attitudes toward employment and unrealistic job expectations
- Were less likely to have a bank account
- Were more likely to report that they are "barely making it" (yet success group reported over double median debt)
- Were more likely to report use of alcohol or drugs while on parole (but no difference in prior assessment of dependency problem)
- Had poor stress-management skills, a primary contributing factor to relapse
- Had unrealistic expectations about what life would be like outside of prison
- Had poor problem-solving or coping skills
- Did not anticipate long-term consequences of behavior
- Failed to utilize resources to help themselves
- Acted impulsively to immediate situations
- Felt they were not in control
- Were more likely to maintain antisocial attitudes
- Viewed violations as an exceptional option to situation
- Maintained general lack of empathy
- Shifted blame or denied responsibility

In addition, success and failure groups did not differ in difficulty of finding a place to live after release, and both groups were equally likely to report eventually obtaining a job.

These findings are consistent with other research that has shown that criminogenic factors are the most important indicators of recidivism. Only by adequately addressing these factors will correctional professionals improve the outcomes of offenders.

Summary

We have seen that nearly every offender who enters prison is eventually released in some fashion. The question is not when the offender will be released, but how; and although the number of offenders released through discretionary parole has dropped, the number released to some other type of supervision continues to grow. Two functions are involved in parole: the surveillance function, ensuring adequate supervision and control (in the form of a parole officer) to prevent future criminal activity; and the helping function, marshaling community resources to support the parolee in establishing noncriminal behavior patterns.

The parole process is a series of steps that frequently includes an appearance before a parole authority, establishment of a set of conditions to be met by the parolee, the assignment to a parole officer followed by regular meetings with the officer, appearance at a revocation hearing if parole is violated, and the eventual release from conditional supervision. That process has sometimes been changed or modified by the heat of public opinion and court decisions.

Although the parole process is a valuable aid to the corrections system, it is far from perfect, and the research on its effectiveness is not conclusive. The issue of how to improve offender reentry has recently become a hot topic, especially since the number of offenders being released is at an all-time high. Halfway houses, furloughs, and work release are three of the major ways in which offenders are reintegrated back into society. In the last chapter we will consider some of these issues as we discuss the future for corrections.

Key Words

Alexander Maconochie, 244

Irish system, 244

Sir Walter Crofton, 244

good time, 245

released on parole, 245

truth-in-sentencing movement, 245

discretionary release, 245

mandatory release, 245

"max out," 246

executive clemency, 246

pardon, 246

amnesty, 246

reprieve, 246

commutation, 246

parole, 246

parole board, 248

"flopped," 249

parole agreement, 250

technical violation, 250

Morrissey v. *Brewer,* 251

procedures for pardon, 253

work release, 254

furlough, 255

reintegration, 255

halfway house, 255

community residential center, 257

reentry, 257

reentry courts, 257

Review Questions

1. What are the main models of parole boards?
2. What are the main differences between parole and probation?
3. Why should parole boards be independent of institutions? Why not?
4. How much time do offenders spend in prison? For how long are they under correctional control? How do you feel about this?
5. What are parole guidelines and how do they structure discretion?
6. Should parole supervision be abolished?
7. Why has the number of offenders released on discretionary parole declined?
8. What is your evaluation of the qualifications for parole-board members?
9. Why is graduated release so beneficial to both the community and the offender?
10. What are reentry courts?
11. How can the effectiveness of a correctional program be measured?

Endnotes

1. Restrictions on early release from prison and other reforms to reduce the discrepancy between sentence imposed and actual sentence served in prison have come to be known as "truth in sentencing." See Thomas Bonczar and L. Glaze, *Probation and Parole in the United States, 1998* (Washington, DC: U.S. Department of Justice, 1999), p. 6.

2. Various forms of conditional release from incarceration were developed in other countries before an American state adopted a parole system; however, the core elements of a parole-system administrative board making release decisions and granting conditional, supervised release with the authority to revoke it were first created by legislation in New York State (1869).

3. A. Pisciotta, "Saving the Children: The Promise and Practice of Parens Patria, 1838–1898," *Crime and Delinquency,* 28:3 (1982): 410–425.

4. K. O. Hawkins, "Parole Selection: The American Experience," unpublished doctoral dissertation (Cambridge, England: University of Cambridge, 1971).

5. Ibid.

6. R. M. Carter, R. A. McGee, and K. E. Nelson, *Corrections in America* (Philadelphia: J. B. Lippincott, 1975).

7. See Ellen Chayet, "Correctional Good Time as a Means of Early Release," *Criminal Justice Abstracts,* 26:3 (1994): 521–538.

8. J. V. Barry, "Captain Alexander Maconochie," *Victorian Historical Magazine* 27:1 (June 1957): 1–18. For a history of the American Correctional Association, see A. Travisono and M. Hawkes, *Building a Voice: The American Correctional Association, 125 Years of History* (Landham, MD: ACA, 1995), available online at http://www.corrections.com/aca/history/html.

9. D. Fogel, *We Are the Living Proof…* (Cincinnati, OH: Anderson Publishing Co., 1975).

10. John Langbein, "The Historical Origins of the Sanction of Imprisonment for Serious Crime," *Journal of Legal Studies* 5 (1976): 35–60.

11. Hawkins, "Parole Selection: The American Experience."

12. Probation and Parole Statistics, *Summary Findings* (Washington, DC: Bureau of Justice Statistics, U.S. Department of Justice, 2002).

13. *Probation and Parole in the United States, 2003* (Washington, DC: U.S. Department of Justice, 2004), available online at http://www.ojp.usdoj.gov/bjs/pardp.htm.

14. Wayne Morse, *The Attorney General's Survey of Release Procedures* (Washington, DC: U.S. Government Printing Office, 1939), p. 23.

15. Paula Ditton and Doris Wilson, *Truth in Sentencing in State Prisons* (Washington, DC: Bureau of Justice Statistics, 2004), p. 3.

16. Camille Camp and G. Camp, *The Corrections Yearbook, Adult Corrections 2002* (South Salem, NY: Criminal Justice Institute, 2002).

17. *Greenholtz* v. *Inmates of the Nebraska Penal and Correctional Complex,* 99 S. Ct. 2100, 1979.

18. No presidential pardon was awarded from 1994 to 1998, but 12 conditional pardons were awarded in 1999.

19. U.S. Office of the Pardon Attorney, *Civil Disabilities of Convicted Felons: A State-by-State Survey* (Washington, DC: USOPA, 1996).

20. Brent Smith, E. Watkins, and K. Morgan, "The Effect of Victim Participation on Parole Decisions," *Criminal Justice Policy Review* 8:1 (1997): 57–74.

21. J. Runda, E. Rhine, and R. Wetter, *The Practice of Parole Boards* (Lexington, KY: Council of State Governments, 1994).

22. U.S. Office of the Pardon Attorney, *Civil Disabilities.*

23. J. Travis and J. Petersilia, "Reentry Reconsidered: A New Look at an Old Problem," *Crime and Delinquency* 47 (2001): 291–313. See also Shelly Listwan, F. Cullen, and E. Latessa, "How to Prevent Prisoner Re-Entry Programs from Failing: Insights from Evidence-Based Corrections," *Federal Probation* 70:3 (2006): 19–25.

24. J. Austin, "Prisoner Reentry: Current Trends, Practices, and Issues," *Crime and Delinquency* 47 (2001): 314–334.

25. A. J. Lurigio, "Effective Services for Parolees with Mental Illnesses," *Crime and Delinquency* 47 (2001): 446–461.

26. Cece Hill, "Inmate Fee-for-Service Programs," *Corrections Compendium* 23:8 (1998): 7–16. See also Editors, "Rising Medical Costs Encourage States to Release Sick, Dying Inmates," *Correctional News* 14:6 (2008): 16.

27. The longer a work-release participant remains employed in the same work-release job after earning parole status, the greater the potential for parole success. Kyu Man Lee, *The Wichita Work Release Center: An Evaluative Study* (Ann Arbor, MI: University Microfilms International, 1983). See also Richard Jones (ed.), "Conditions of Confinement," *Journal of Contemporary Criminal Justice* 13:1 (1997): 3–72.

28. James Ryan, "Who Gets Revoked? A Comparison of Intensive Supervision Successes and Failures in Vermont," *Crime and Delinquency* 43:1 (1997): 104–118.

29. David Anderson, *Crime and the Politics of Hysteria: How the Willie Horton Story Changed American Justice* (New York: Random House, 1995); and Tali Mendelberg, "Executing Horizons: Racial Crime in the 1988 Presidential Campaign," *Public Opinion Quarterly* 61:1 (1997): 134–157.

30. The failure rate (both new crimes and failure to return) in furlough programs is remarkably low: about 1%. Camp and Camp, *The Corrections Yearbook, Adult Corrections 2000,* p. 148.

31. James Bonta and L. Motiuk, "The Diversion of Incarcerated Offenders to Correctional Halfway Houses," *Journal of Research in Crime and Delinquency*

24:3 (1987): 302–323; Edward Latessa and L. Travis, "Residential Community Correctional Programs," in James Byrne and A. Lurigio (eds.), *Smart Sentencing? An Examination of the Emergence of Intermediate Sanctions* (Beverly Hills, CA: Sage, 1991); and Sarah Twill, L. Nackerud, E. Risler, et al., "Changes in Measured Loneliness, Control and Social Support Among Parolees in a Halfway House," *Journal of Offender Rehabilitation* 27:3/4 (1998): 77–92.

32. Additional information may be obtained from the International Community Corrections Association, P.O. Box 1987, La Crosse, Wisconsin 54602; (608) 785-0200 (http://www.iccaweb.org, accessed October 21, 2009).

33. Carolyn Tucker, K. Herman, B. Brady, et al., "Operation Positive Expression: A Behavioral Change Program for Adolescent Halfway House Residents," *Residential Treatment for Children and Youth* 13:2 (1995): 67–80.

34. Brian Grant, L. Montiuk, L. Brunet, et al., *Day Parole Program Review* (Ottawa: Correctional Service of Canada, 1996).

35. Twill et al., "Changes in Measured Loneliness."

36. Camp and Camp report that the cost per resident for private halfway house providers is 14% less than that provided by state departments of corrections. Camp and Camp, *The Corrections Yearbook 1998* (Middletown, CT: Criminal Justice Institute), p. 123.

37. C. T. Lowenkamp and E. J. Latessa, *Evaluation of Ohio's Halfway Houses and Community-Based Correctional Facilities* (Cincinnati, OH: University of Cincinnati, 2002).

38. Marc Levinson, "In South Carolina, Community Corrections Means the Alston Wilkes Society," *Corrections Magazine* 9:1 (1983): 41–46. See also Bobbie Huskey and A. Lurigio, "An Examination of Privately-Operated Intermediate Punishments in the United States," *Corrections Compendium* 17:12 (1992): 1, 3–8; and Joseph Callahan and K. Koenning, "The Comprehensive Sanctions Center in the Northern District of Ohio," *Federal Probation* 59:3 (1995): 52–57.

39. Daniel Glaser, "Supervising Offenders outside Prisons," in James Wilson (ed.), *Crime and Public Policy* (San Francisco: Institute for Contemporary Studies, 1983), p. 212.

40. James Beck, "An Evaluation of Federal Community Treatment Centers," *Federal Probation* 43:5 (1979): 36–41; and Paul Gendreau, M. Shilton, and P. Clark, "Intermediate Sanctions: Making the Right Move," *Corrections Today* 57:1 (1995): 28–65.

41. For more information of reentry courts, see http://www.dsgonline.com/mpg_non_flash/reentry_court.htm. (accessed October 20, 2008).

42. A. L. Solomon, V. Kachnowski, and B. Avinash, *Does Parole Work?* (Washington, DC: Urban Institute, 2005). See also C. T. Lowenkamp, and E. J. Latessa, *Does Parole Work? A Reanalysis of the Urban Institute Study* (Cincinnati, OH: University of Cincinnati, 2005).

43. See Pennsylvania Department of Correction, Department of Corrections Parole Violator Study (Phase 2), 2007 (http://www.cor.state.pa.us/stats/lib/stats/RIRV9N4.pdf, accessed October 20, 2008).

chapter 14

The Death Penalty

Outline

> "I am not convinced that capital punishment, in and of itself, is a deterrent to crime because most people do not think about the death penalty before they commit a violent or capital crime."
>
> —Willie L. Williams

Overview

Perhaps no subject in the field of corrections has had as much controversy at the individual, judge, church, or the administrator levels than **capital punishment.** The arguments rage on, ranging from the aspects of morality, through to the fringes of justice, to the core of retribution and revenge. Is it right to kill someone in the name of the state for killing someone? We change the methods of execution to somehow make the act more acceptable to the general public. Popular films such as *Dead Man Walking*[1] attempt to show both sides of this controversial ultimate punishment.

This chapter explores the history, methods, nature of crimes, application, and operation of the death penalty. Whether a person is for or against capital punishment often depends on who the offender is and who the victim(s) may be. The student must keep an open mind about the death penalty and realize it has been around as long as societies have existed. Is it time to abolish the death penalty—or make it more efficient, less gruesome, and more certain? We cover all the bases in this chapter, exploring a unique facet of American justice and a problem for corrections.

key term

Capital punishment
The imposition of a sentence of death by the state.

key term

Execution
The killing of an offender by the state.

lecture note

Using your computer, play the brief chapter overview videotape by Edward Latessa on "The Death Penalty" that introduces Chapter 14 (approximately 3 minutes).

lecture note

Define *capital punishment* and illustrate its methods of execution over the years.

class activity

Ask students to define *execution* and explain whether execution is the state murdering a murderer. What similarities exist? How are they different?

class activity

Ask students if televising the execution would serve as a *general deterrent* to others from committing death-eligible crimes. If the consensus is "yes," ask what elements of the execution would be the deterrent.

ORIGINS OF THE DEATH PENALTY

In earlier chapters, we made brief references to some of the issues regarding capital punishment, or the death penalty. The frequency with which the topic comes up demonstrates how intertwined it is with the other aspects of criminal justice. The term *capital punishment* generally refers to the **execution,** in the name of the state, of a person convicted of certain crimes. The crimes for which this punishment has been imposed have varied over the centuries, but treason, murder, and rape have been the most common. In some states in the nation, death-eligible offenses also include train wrecking, treason, and perjury causing execution, drug trafficking, aircraft piracy, and contract murder.[2] The U.S. military, the federal government, and most states have the death penalty except Alaska, the District of Columbia, Hawaii, Iowa, Maine, Massachusetts, Michigan, Minnesota, North Dakota, Rhode Island, Vermont, West Virginia, and Wisconsin.

The methods by which the punishment has been carried out have been even more varied, and include being hanged, burned, boiled in oil, impaled, shot, strangled, beheaded, drawn and quartered, electrocuted, gassed, and now injected with lethal drugs. In the United States, contemporary techniques include the firing squad, hanging, the gas chamber, electrocution, and lethal injection. Lethal injection appears to be the most frequent and humane technique, although debate continues as to whether execution should be humane.[3]

In the nation's earliest history, executions were almost always administered as a public spectacle, in the hope they would serve as a warning and a deterrent to others. It could be argued that the human desire to obtain retribution for crimes was transferred from the individual to the state in a way that finally became repugnant to many enlightened societies. Still, long after the elimination of the more bloody forms of capital vengeance, controversy still centers on the possible deterrent value of the death penalty. The arguments for and against the death penalty concern the issues of deterrence, excessive cruelty (Eighth Amendment arguments), equability (Sixth and Fourteenth Amendment considerations), and attitudes toward capital punishment.[4]

BETTER WAYS TO DIE?

Probably America's most innovative contribution to the various methods of execution was the invention of the electric chair. Although this invention was extolled as a more humanitarian way to kill the offender than the then current ways (hanging and firing squad, for example), many considered it merely a promotional scheme of the New York electrical company that developed it. The first electrocution was conducted at the Auburn Penitentiary in New York on August 6, 1890. The first person to die in this highly touted new device was William Kemmler, a convicted murderer from Buffalo, New York.

Opponents of the electric chair, including Thomas Edison, claimed that it must be excessively painful (a claim vehemently denied by prison administrators who used it).[5] The opposition advocated lethal gas as the most humane execution method. The first person to die in America in a prison gas chamber was a Chinese immigrant worker named Gee Jon. The crude system, gaining favor after a series of incredibly gruesome executions by electric chair, used cyanide gas. On February 8, 1924, in Nevada, Gee died in just six minutes.

In an effort to make the execution of condemned criminals easier and cleaner still, lethal injection gained favor in the 1970s and 1980s. It seems that many states thought they could reinstate the death penalty more easily if it was seen to be less cruel and unusual. Charles Brooks, a co-defendant in a murder, was the first prisoner to die in this manner, executed December 6, 1982, in Texas.

It is interesting to note that 35 states (some states authorize more than one method) and the federal government have passed legislation to use a lethal injection of chemicals as the latest, "most humane" form of execution as the primary or secondary option.[6] Since 1976, about

85% of executions have been with lethal injection. Noteworthy is that physicians' associations are expressing concern that their members, whose profession it is to save lives, may be asked by the state to take lives and create a conflict with their Hippocratic Oath. It seems we are still seeking a way to make the process, if not the practice, of execution more humane.

The physical pain of the execution is probably the smallest concern of the offenders during their prolonged wait in the death house, a wait that averages almost 11 years.[7] The longest time from being sentenced to death and execution appears to be 25 years. The mental anguish the condemned must endure, which that long wait can only intensify, has been a primary focus of the recent widespread controversy surrounding the death penalty, as the more industrialized societies have moved to abolish it.[8] The use of the death penalty in the United States peaked in the crime-laden 1930s, when a total of 1,513 prisoners were executed, an average of about 14 per month. The increased number of appeals and rising opposition to the death penalty peaked in the turbulent 1960s, and in 1972 the U.S. Supreme Court placed a moratorium on the death penalty while states considered legislation that could meet strict constitutional guidelines.[9] That moratorium was dissolved by the decision of *Gregg v. Georgia* in 1976, and executions began anew in 1977 with convicted murderer Gary Gilmore's cry of "Let's do it!" before being voluntarily executed before a firing squad in Utah. Today there are 14 states without the death penalty: Alaska, Hawaii, Iowa, Maine, Massachusetts, Michigan, Minnesota, New Jersey, New York, North Dakota, Rhode Island, Vermont, West Virginia, and Wisconsin, as well as the District of Columbia. In 2000, Governor George Ryan of Illinois imposed a moratorium on the state's death penalty. "We have now freed more people than we have put to death under our system—13 people have been exonerated and 12 have been put to death. There is a flaw in the system, without question, and it needs to be studied."[10] In 2003, Governor Ryan commuted the sentences of all 156 death-row inmates to life. Today there are 13 inmates on death row in Illinois.

key term

Gregg v. *Georgia*
The 1977 case that ended the moratorium on the death penalty.

class activity

Organize a debate on the topic of whether or not all executions should be by lethal injection.

lecture note

Using your computer, play the brief videotape of Francis Cullen on "Why the U.S. Is One of Only Five Western Countries with the Death Penalty" (approximately 6 minutes). For a differing view, play the brief videotape of Gennaro Vito on "Why the U.S. Is the Only Major Western Country with the Death Penalty" (approximately 4 minutes).

key term

Capital crimes
Offenses for which an offender can receive the death penalty, usually murder and rape.

ARBITRARY AND INFREQUENT PUNISHMENT

To better understand the magnitude of the death penalty issue, we must examine the somewhat incomplete records on the subject. The total number of executions between 1976 and midyear 2008 was 1,123, with the highest number in 1999 at 98. As mentioned earlier, the death penalty has most often been prescribed for murder and rape. One thus would reasonably expect a fairly high correlation between the number of such offenses and the number of executions. In the 1930s, the earliest period for which relatively reliable statistics are available, the average number of executions was about 165 per year. The number of murders and rapes reported per year during the 1930s averaged 3,500 and 3,800, respectively, a ratio of about 1 execution to every 44 **capital crimes** reported.[11]

Also significant is the number of executions in different states and regions. Most executions have taken place in the South. Two-thirds of the 1,123 executions between 1976 and midyear 2008 took place in the five states of Texas (414), Virginia (102), Oklahoma (88), Missouri (66), and Florida (66). Industrial states that extend from Illinois to New York accounted for only about 4% of the executions. It is worth noting that 34% of those executed between 1976 and midyear 2008 were black, 7% were Hispanic, and 2% were Native Americans and Asians.[12]

The number of executions per year dropped to only 11 in 1988 (see Figure 14.1). The pace since then has fluctuated, with 98 in 1999, down to 42 in 2007. When we consider the thousands of murders and rapes reported during that period, we must consider the comments of Justice William Brennan:

> When a country of over 200 million people inflicts an unusually severe punishment no more than fifty times a year, the inference is strong that the punishment is not being regularly and fairly applied. To dispel it would indeed require a clear showing of non-arbitrary infliction.[13]

figure 14.1

Executions: 1976–2008 (1223)

SOURCE: Death Penalty Information Center (www.deathpenaltyinfo.org, accessed October 15, 2008).

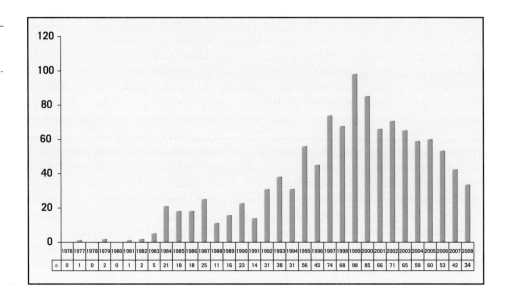

	1976	1977	1978	1979	1980	1981	1982	1983	1984	1985	1986	1987	1988	1989	1990	1991	1992	1993	1994	1995	1996	1997	1998	1999	2000	2001	2002	2003	2004	2005	2006	2007	2008
	0	1	0	2	0	1	2	5	21	18	18	25	11	16	23	14	31	38	31	56	45	74	68	98	85	66	71	65	59	60	53	42	34

Even if one agrees that the number of murders and rapes does not necessarily reflect the number for which the death penalty might have been imposed, the difference is still staggering. As Justice Potter Stewart explained in ***Furman* v. *Georgia,*** the death penalty is "freakishly" or "spectacularly" rare in its occurrence. In an argument in *Furman,* Justice Brennan in 1972 summed up the **arbitrary** nature of the death penalty:

> When the punishment of death is inflicted in a trivial number of cases in which it is legally available, the conclusion is virtually inescapable that it is being inflicted arbitrarily. Indeed, it smacks of little more than a lottery system. The states claim, however, that this rarity is evidence not of arbitrariness, but of informed selectivity: Death is inflicted, they say, only in "extreme" cases.
>
> Informed selectivity, of course, is a value not to be denigrated. Yet presumably the states could make precisely the same claim if there were ten executions per year, or five, or even if there were but one. That there may be as many as fifty per year does not strengthen the claim. When the rate of infliction is at this low level, it is highly implausible that only the worst criminals or the criminals who commit the worst crimes are selected for this punishment. No one has yet suggested a rational basis that could differentiate in those terms the few who die from the many who go to prison. Crimes and criminals simply do not admit of a distinction that can be drawn so finely as to explain, on that ground, the execution of such a tiny sample of those eligible. Certainly the laws that provide for this punishment do not attempt to draw that distinction; all cases to which the laws apply are necessarily "extreme." Nor is the distinction credible in fact. If, for example, petitioner Furman or his crime illustrates the "extreme," then nearly all murderers and their murders are also "extreme." Furthermore, our procedures in death cases, rather than punishment, actually sanction an arbitrary selection. For this Court held [that] juries may, as they do, make the decision whether to impose a death sentence wholly unguided by standards governing that decision, *McGautha* v. *California* 402 U.S. 183, 196–208 (1971). In other words, our procedures are not constructed to guard against the totally capricious selection of criminals for the punishment of death.[14]

This argument is further reinforced by the fact that the two crimes of murder and rape have accounted for nearly 99% of the executions in the United States since 1930, with 87% of the total for murder alone.

It appears that the original practice of *mandating* the death penalty for murder has become repugnant to American society as a whole. This is demonstrated by the reluctance of juries to convict in such cases, despite the earlier efforts of state legislators to pass laws that call for mandatory executions for certain types of murder.

The concept of **intent to kill**, or **malice aforethought,**[15] usually an essential element of proof in the capital murder statutes, provided a rationale for juries to opt for a lesser penalty. Legislatures finally recognized that juries were using this concept to avoid the death penalty and passed statutes that attempted to differentiate between the degrees of various capital crimes (for example, first- and second-degree murder, and first- and second-degree rape), thus trying to restrict mandatory execution to the first offenses. In response, juries simply refused to convict in cases in which they felt—arbitrarily—that the death penalty was inappropriate. The further refinement of the distinction between capital and noncapital cases was abandoned by legislation in many jurisdictions, and juries were given legal discretion to continue the practice they had already established in fact. The sentence of death is now discretionary in every jurisdiction in which it is still used, and it is the jury that must determine to impose death rather than another sentence.

In those states with capital punishment, the prosecutor must decide to seek the **death penalty,** using the vast discretion inherent in that office. If the decision is not to pursue a death-eligible charge, then the jury is usually prevented from imposing the sentence of death. Consistent (but not unchallenged) evidence suggests that race of the victim colors the prosecutor's decisions: Victim-based discrimination has been found to be an important determinant in Texas,[16] the Chattahoochee Judicial District (Georgia),[17] and Kentucky,[18] but not in California.[19] Evaluations of prosecutorial discretion are ongoing.[20] We discuss the role of the prosecutor in more detail later.

THE EIGHTH AMENDMENT AND THE DEATH PENALTY

American jurisprudence has borrowed much from the English law. The ban against **cruel and unusual punishment** embodied in the Eighth Amendment was lifted from the English Bill of Rights of 1689. As Justice Thurgood Marshall indicated in *Furman* v. *Georgia:*

> Perhaps the most important principle in analyzing "cruel and unusual" punishment questions is one that is reiterated again and again in the prior opinions of the Court: i.e., the cruel and unusual language "must draw its meaning from the evolving standards of decency that mark the progress of a maturing society." Thus, a penalty, which was permissible at one time in our nation's history, is not necessarily permissible today. The fact, therefore, that the Court, or individual justices, may have in the past expressed an opinion that the death penalty is constitutional is not now binding on us.[21]

The reference to unusual punishment helps clarify the relationship between this particular amendment and the customs and practices of any given period. The death penalty was surely not an unusual punishment in the early nineteenth century, and there appears to be no national consensus that it is in the second decade of the twenty-first century.[22] In *Furman,* the U.S. Supreme Court found that Georgia's death penalty gave the sentencer (judge or jury) complete and unguided discretion to impose the death penalty, and ruled that the Georgia death penalty had been imposed arbitrarily and discriminatorily against minorities. In the later *Gregg* v. *Georgia* opinion, the U.S. Supreme Court mandated a bifurcated trial, the first part to determine guilt and the second trial to determine the penalty.

Cruelty was examined by the Supreme Court in 1878 in *Wilkerson* v. *Utah.*[23] It was Utah's practice to punish premeditated murderers by shooting them at a public execution. This case examined the concepts of the developing frontier and the execution practices being used in other areas around the world. The Court did not stick to the doctrine of traditional practice, but examined contemporary thought on the matter of cruel punishment. It

key term

Intent to kill
Malice aforethought; having the intent to kill prior to the crime. Planned and premeditated crime.

key term

Malice aforethought
Having the intent to kill prior to the commission of the crime; planned and premeditated.

key term

Death penalty
Execution of the offender by the state.

class activity
Ask students what legal elements must be present to make a criminal case a "death-eligible crime."

key term

Cruel and unusual punishment
Prohibited by the Eighth Amendment to the Constitution.

lecture note
Trace the death penalty from 1960 through current practice, noting the constitutional issues considered by courts.

lecture note
Using your computer, play the brief videotape of Gennaro Vito on "Trends in the Application of the Death Penalty" (about 4 minutes).

lecture note
Using your computer, play the videotape of George Higgins on the "Role of the Prosecutor in Death-Eligible Cases" (about 5 minutes).

Three ways to carry out a
sentence.

a. Lethal injection.
Courtesy of AP Wide World Photos.

c. Gas chamber.
Courtesy of AP Wide World Photos.

b. Electric chair.
Courtesy of AP Wide World Photos.

found that the case against Utah was not cruel in the context of the times, but it left open
the door for future Court examinations of the cruelty issue:

> Difficulty would attend the effort to define with exactness the extent of the constitutional
> provision which provides that cruel and unusual punishments shall not be inflicted: but it
> is safe to affirm that punishments of torture . . . and all others in the same line of unneces-
> sary cruelty, are forbidden by that amendment to the Constitution.[24]

Only with the introduction of the electric chair in New York was the issue of cruel and
unusual punishment raised again. The 1890 case of *In re Kemmler* challenged the use of that
new form of execution as cruel and unusual punishment, but the Court was unanimous in
its decision that electrocution was not unconstitutional just because it was unusual. It also
came very close to employing the due process clause of the Fourteenth Amendment in the
case, giving early warning that it might do so at a later, more substantial hearing. In the 1892
case of *O'Neil* v. *Vermont,* the court again affirmed that the Eighth Amendment did not
apply to the states, but with three strong dissenting opinions. One of the dissenting justices
wrote the following:

> That designation [cruel and unusual], it is true, is usually applied to punishments which in-
> flict torture, such as the rack, the thumbscrew, the iron boot, the stretching of limbs and the
> like, which are attended with acute pain and suffering. . . . The inhibition is directed not only
> against punishments of the character mentioned, but against all punishments which by

their excessive length or severity are greatly disproportionate to the offenses charged. The whole inhibition is against that which is excessive.[25]

This logic, though a minority attitude at the time, prevailed to dominate the 1910 landmark case of *Weems* v. *United States*,[26] the first time the Court invalidated a penalty because they found it excessive. Clearly, excessive punishment had become as objectionable to the Court as what was inherently cruel. Not until 1947 did the Court decide another significant case on the issue of whether the Eighth Amendment applied to the states. In the case of *Louisiana ex rel. Francis* v. *Resweber*,[27] the Court was virtually unanimous in its agreement that the infliction of unnecessary pain is forbidden by traditional Anglo-American legal practice. This unusual case involved a convicted murderer (Francis) who was sentenced to die in the electric chair. The electrical system malfunctioned at the execution, so Francis was not killed the first time the current passed through his body.[28] Pleading that a second attempt at electrocution would be cruel and unusual punishment, Francis took his case to the Supreme Court. Although the case brought out many of the crucial Eighth Amendment issues, the Court stopped short of enforcing that amendment on the states, and Francis lost his appeal on a five-to-four split. He thus was finally executed, but his case paved the way for several that came in the 1960s.

The next significant case we note is the landmark 1972 case on capital punishment, *Furman* v. *Georgia*. The Court's decision was five to four in favor of a ban on using capital punishment as it was currently being practiced. Indeed, the justices were so widely divided on the issue that each wrote a separate opinion. Only two of the justices (Brennan and Marshall) held that the death penalty was cruel and unusual punishment under all circumstances. The due process clause of the Fourteenth Amendment was evoked, leaving the states with the problem of passing legislation that met the Court's requirements, as described in the opinion of Chief Justice Warren Burger:

> The legislatures are free to eliminate capital punishment for specific crimes or to carve out limited exceptions to a general abolition of the penalty, without adherence to the conceptual strictures of the Eighth Amendment. The legislatures can and should make an assessment of the deterrent influence of capital punishment, both generally and as affecting the commission of specific types of crimes. If legislatures come to doubt the efficacy of capital punishment, they can abolish it either completely or on a selective basis. If new evidence persuades them that they acted unwisely, they can reverse their field and reinstate the penalty to the extent it is thought warranted. An Eighth Amendment ruling by judges cannot be made with such flexibility or discriminating precision.[29]

Although the minority opinion seemed to feel the Court had overstepped its jurisdiction, the tenor of the dissenting remarks made it clear they were willing to hear a new appeal when the findings in *Furman* were challenged. The high level of legislative activity in the states, seeking to reinstate the death penalty under the Court's new guidelines, suggested there would be a challenge in the near future. Though *Furman* gave a new lease on life[30] to the 600-plus men who had been sitting on death row,[31] new death sentences continue to be handed down, awaiting final resolution of the issue.

Two recent decisions by the Supreme Court have further limited the use of the death penalty. In *Atkins* v. *Virginia*, the Court held that that is unconstitutional to execute defendants with mental retardation. This was followed in 2005 with *Roper* v. *Simmons*, in which the court struck down the use of the death penalty for juveniles. Since 1976, 22 defendants had been executed for crimes committed as juveniles.

PROSECUTOR'S DISCRETION

As yet unresolved is the controversial role of discretion in the decision to seek the death penalty. The prosecutor must enter a formal charge and may or may not seek the death penalty. One factor that affects the decision to seek the death penalty is the race of the

class activity

Ask students to locate online reports of witnesses to executions, and submit a one-paragraph summary of witness sentiment after the execution.

lecture note

Explain the Eighth Amendment's prohibitions against cruel and unusual punishment. What types of execution methods existing at the time did the framers of the Constitution probably have in mind when this amendment was created?

lecture note

Using your computer, play the brief videotape of George Higgins on "Ratios of African Americans on Death Row" (approximately 5 minutes).

victim. In South Carolina, for example, studies show that if the victim is white and the offender black, then the black offender is eight times as likely to face a death sentence as that same offender would face if the victim were black.[32] Keil and Vito found that, in Kentucky, blacks who killed whites, as compared to other homicide offenders, had more than an average chance of being charged with a death-eligible crime (by the prosecutor) and sentenced to die (by the jury). They also found 13 cases in their study's time frame in which whites murdered blacks and prosecutors failed to seek the death penalty even once. Prosecutors have a **gatekeeper function** in the judicial system: If they choose not to seek the death penalty, then the jury cannot impose it. Keil and Vito suggest the following:

> It may be to the prosecutor's political and career advantage to treat murders in which the black kills a white more seriously than murders involving other racial combinations, even when such murders have the same legal attributes of seriousness. Juries may find it socially expedient to act in the same way in sentencing offenders to death.[33]

Radelet reaches a similar conclusion using status attributes (race, social class, economic status) in his study of executions since 1608.[34]

The effect of offender's race in light of the race of the victim suggested racism at work in the pre-*Furman* years. The death-row population has since shifted from a majority black population to a more diverse population in which blacks are only about one-third of the offenders on death row. Yet the race of the victim continues to play a major role. More than 80% of the murder victims whose cases resulted in an execution were white; nationally, about half of the murder victims generally were white. Does racism jaundice the decisions of law enforcement, prosecutors, judges, and juries? The debate continues.

DETERRENCE OF THE DEATH PENALTY

While there are substantial claims that the death penalty may act as a **deterrent** to others, depending on the ideological position of the debater, one should realize that if the death penalty were a deterrent, no crime would occur. Those who favor the death penalty ("retentionists") point out that a lighthouse sits beside a dangerous rock-strewn coastline to warn ships away. The fact that a few ill-fated ships run afoul of the dangers the lighthouse proclaims is no reason to tear the lighthouse down—or to abolish capital punishment. For those ships the lighthouse warns away, there is no evidence of deterrence, although deterrence has no doubt been in effect. Only the ones that ignore to their peril the lighthouse's warning will show up as "failures" of the deterrent effect.

It is also interesting to note that states without the death penalty have had consistently lower murder rates. Figure 14.2 shows the difference between murder rates in death penalty and non-death-penalty states. Since 1990, states without the death penalty have had lower murder rates.

Public Opinion and the Death Penalty

The American public's attitude toward the death penalty has fluctuated wildly, as reflected in public opinion polls. Although most polls show strong support for the death penalty in the abstract (that is, if no alternative is considered)—with a 69% approval in a 2007 Gallup poll—several opinions are somewhat softened when the public is given viable alternatives. As shown in Figure 14.3, support for the death penalty falls to only 47% when the alternative is life without parole. However, this fact seems to have as little impact on death penalty

figure 14.2

Percentage Gap Between Murder Rates in Death Penalty and Non-death Penalty States

Data from: Death Penalty Information Center (www.deathpenaltyinfo.org, accessed October 15, 2008).

legislation as public opinion has on gun control. Those who advocate the death penalty claim there is no viable alternative that provides equal protection for society. They would also argue that the seriousness of the crime requires the maximum penalty.[35] The 2007 survey shows that many would be supportive of a true life sentence.

Many who oppose the life sentence as a replacement for the death penalty observe that the parole laws in many states make it possible for a "lifer" to get out in a relatively brief time.[36] Usually, those who receive life sentences become eligible for parole in 13 years, but the national average served under a life sentence is currently less than 18 years. The proposed answer to this argument is to remove the hope of parole from a prisoner given a life sentence (**life certain**), but that action would constitute an admission that certain prisoners

key term

Life certain
Judge's sentence that precludes parole eligibility; order to incarcerate the offender until dead.

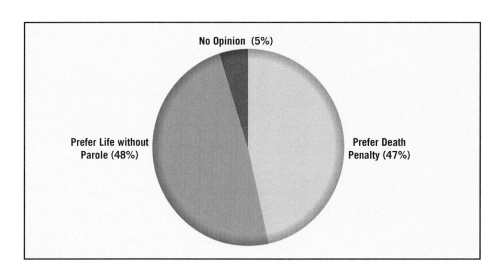

figure 14.3

Support for Life without Parole

Data from: Death Penalty Information Center (www.deathpenaltyinfo.org, accessed October 15, 2008).

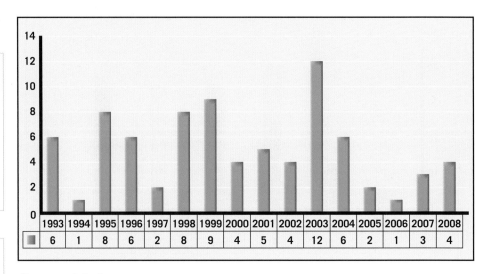

	1993	1994	1995	1996	1997	1998	1999	2000	2001	2002	2003	2004	2005	2006	2007	2008
▪	6	1	8	6	2	8	9	4	5	4	12	6	2	1	3	4

figure 14.4

Number of Death Row Offenders Exonerated Since 1993.

Data from: Death Penalty Information Center (www.deathpenaltyinfo.org, accessed October 15, 2008). From 1973–1999, there was an average of 3.1 exonerations per year, from 2000–2007, the average was 5 exonerations per year.

could not be rehabilitated and would destroy the offenders' possible incentive to change their behavior patterns. The chance that an innocent person might be convicted also detracts from the acceptability of the irreversible death penalty.[37] Since 1974, 130 death-row inmates have been exonerated. See Figure 14.4.

Earl Washington came within nine days of execution before being cleared by DNA tests. He spent almost ten years in prison for a crime he did not commit.
Photo by REUTERS/Alexa Welch Edlund/Richmond Times Dispatch/CORBIS-NY.

The Controversy Continues

Many death-row inmates profess their innocence, and recently developed scientific techniques (such as DNA testing) have established the factual innocence of at least a dozen inmates on death row, some of whom were within days of executions and all of whom have subsequently been released.

In 2002, Justice Jed Rakoff, United States District Judge in the Southern District of New York, addressed the problem of executing the innocent before they might establish their innocence. He concluded that this would deprive them of their opportunity to prove their innocence, and thus would be a violation of rights under the Fifth Amendment. Judge Rakoff then declared the federal death penalty statute unconstitutional.[38] A U.S. court of appeals reversed the decision; the U.S. Supreme Court denied certiorari (124 S. Ct. 807, 2003).

Kerry Duns, on death row in Texas, being escorted to the shower while officer slides Plexiglas shield to prevent attacks on Duns by other inmates.
Photo by David Lesson/Dallas Morning News, courtesy of The Image Works.

key term

Equability
Whether the punishment is applied even-handedly across a jurisdiction.

THE ISSUE OF EQUABILITY

The heart of the question of **equability** is whether the punishment is applied evenhandedly across a jurisdiction. Are judges imposing similar sentences on offenders who have committed similar crimes? Another related question involves the issue of whether the punishment fits the crime. This question arises in the case of a single court staffed by 11 judges, all of whom sentence offenders accused of driving under the influence of alcohol. One judge may routinely impose fines of $100 on all offenders to be sentenced; another sentencing judge may impose 30 days in jail plus 30 hours of community service. The other nine judges may place their offenders on probation, one condition of which may be compulsory attendance at meetings of Alcoholics Anonymous. Which one, if any, of these punishments best fits the crime: a fine, jail time plus community service, or probation with mandatory attendance in an alcohol-avoidance program?

In terms of the death penalty, perhaps the question could best be phrased like this: "Are blacks who kill white victims more likely to receive a death sentence than white killers who murder black victims?" As noted earlier, the answer is most certainly yes. Retentionists might argue that such selectivity is immaterial.

Behavioral science may not provide the most adequate basis for arguments against the equitable application of the death penalty for juveniles or adults, but available evidence suggests that the death penalty is not evenly applied and may be wanton and freakish in its imposition. That conclusion, in more tentative form, can be found in the 1990 report by the General Accounting Office,[39] as well as in the work of Keil and Vito, cited previously.

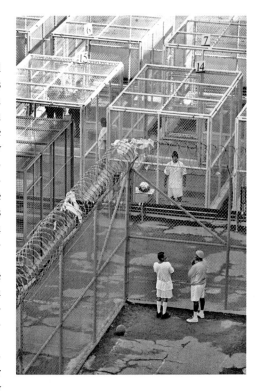

Death row inmates exercising in 8 × 12 cages, to which they must enter and leave in handcuffs.

correctional **brief**

The Execution Process Today

In Florida, when the governor signs a death warrant, the prison superintendent reads the warrant to the condemned inmate. The inmate then is taken from the death row cell to the death watch cell. Final preparation for the execution begins five days prior to the week of the scheduled execution. At this time, the condemned inmate and the administrative staff review the inmate's wishes for disposal of personal property, visits, last meal, and disposition of the body.

Executions are usually scheduled for 7 A.M. so as not to disrupt the institution's routine and to ensure the availability of the [Department of Corrections] secretary and the governor's staff before regular office hours.

The morning of the execution, the inmate is served a final meal and is showered. [Death-row inmates may choose between lethal injection and electrocution. If electrocution is selected,] . . . staff must shave the inmate's head and leg. The inmate is allowed a chaplain visit before being led down the hall to the execution chamber.

The assistant superintendent for operations and the chief correctional officer escort the inmate to the chamber. The superintendent leads the inmate into the chamber, where the maintenance superintendent and an electrician secure the straps around the head, chest, arm, and leg. The inmate is given an opportunity to make a final statement or read a prepared one before having the head gear put on.

The prison superintendent indicates to the executioner that the execution is to proceed. The executioner, an anonymous citizen hired by the Department of Corrections, is paid $150 per execution. He or she pulls a switch to activate the electrical equipment. The electrocution cycle lasts two minutes or less. A physician then verifies the inmate's death.

Twelve volunteer citizen witnesses and twelve media representatives are present in the viewing room at the execution. They are escorted into the room by two correctional officers, and a public information officer is available to assist them. The superintendent and assistant superintendent are also available to respond to reporters' inquiries.

Media representatives are selected from a pool of credentialed reporters and are required to provide information to all media representatives who are not able to attend.

In addition to the media attention, a contingent of supporters and opponents of the death penalty usually gathers across the street to demonstrate and hold vigils before and during the execution. Local law enforcement are on hand to maintain order.

SOURCE: Kerry Flock, "In Florida: Day-to-Day Death Row Operations," *Corrections Today* 55:4 (1993): 78.

Serial killer and prostitute Aileen Wuornos taking oath during a murder trial. She was convicted of killing six men and was executed in 2002.
Photo by Daytona Beach News Journal, courtesy of CORBIS-NY.

WOMEN AND THE DEATH PENALTY

In general, both the sentencing-to-death rate and the death-row population remain very small for women in comparison to that for men. Actual execution of female offenders is quite rare, with only 564 documented instances beginning with the first in 1632. These 564 female executions constitute less than 3% of the total of 19,510 confirmed executions in the United States since 1608. In the past 100 years, 40 women have been executed in the United States, and 11 female offenders have been executed since 1976, the most recent on September 15, 2005 in Texas (Frances Newton).

Death sentences and actual executions for female offenders are also rare in comparison to such events for male offenders. In fact, women are more likely to be dropped out of the system the further the capital punishment system progresses. Following in summary outline form are the data indicating this screening-out effect:

- Women account for about 1 in 10 (10%) murder arrests.
- Women account for only 1 in 50 (2.0%) death sentences imposed at the trial level.
- Women account for only 1 in 67 (1.5%) persons presently on death row.
- Women account for only 1 in 100 (1%) persons actually executed since *Furman*.[40]

Homicides by women are less likely to involve the felony murders and other specific circumstances that are more likely to result in death sentences.

c o r r e c t i o n a l **brief**

Executed Females

Eleven females have been executed since 1976. Here are several of their stories:

- **Velma Barfield** in North Carolina on November 2, 1984. She was in a relationship with Stuart Taylor, who was a widower. She forged checks on Taylor's account to pay for her addiction. Fearing that she had been found out, she mixed an arsenic-based rat poison into his beer and tea. Taylor became very ill. As his condition worsened, she took him to the hospital, where he died a few days later. There was an autopsy that found the cause of Taylor's death was arsenic poisoning, and Velma was arrested and charged with his murder. At the trial, her defense pleaded insanity but this was not accepted and she was convicted. The jury recommended the death sentence. Velma appeared cold and uncaring on the stand and gave the district attorney a round of applause when he made his closing speech.

- **Karla Faye Tucker** in Texas on February 3, 1998. When she was 13, she began traveling with the Allman Brothers Band. In her early 20s she started to hang out with bikers, and on June 13, 1983, she entered the home of another biker with Danny Garrett and James Leibrant to steal a motorcycle. During the robbery, two persons were killed, and Garrett and Tucker were convicted of committing murder with a pickaxe. This case entered the U.S. and international news because she had become a born-again Christian while in prison and George W. Bush, then governor of Texas, had to decide on her request for clemency, which he ultimately denied.

- **Betty Lou Beets** in Texas on February 24, 2000. She was convicted of shooting her fifth husband, Jimmy Don Beets. On August 6, 1983, Beets reported that her husband was missing from their home in Henderson County, Texas. Her son, Robert Branson, would later testify that Beets had said that she intended to kill her husband and told her son to leave the house. On returning two hours later to the house, he found Jimmy Don Beets dead with two gunshot wounds. He helped his mother conceal the body in the front yard of the house, after which Beets telephoned the police. At the time of the execution, she was 62 years old, and had five children, nine grandchildren, and six great-grandchildren.

- **Christina Riggs** in Arkansas on May 2, 2000. Riggs, a licensed nurse, was convicted of murder by smothering her two preschool-aged children in their beds at the family's Sherwood home. She wrote suicide notes saying "I hope one day you will forgive me for taking my life and the life of my children. But I can't live like this any more, and I couldn't bear to leave my children behind to be a burden on you or to be separated and raised apart from their fathers and live knowing their mother killed herself." Riggs then took 28 Elavil tablets, normally a lethal dose, and injected herself with enough undiluted potassium chloride to kill five people. The next day, police officers entered her apartment, and found Riggs and rushed her to the hospital. During the death penalty phase, Riggs would not allow attorneys to put on a defense, saying she wanted a death sentence. The jury obliged, and she was sentenced to death by lethal injection. Riggs said "Thank you" and squeezed her attorney's hand.

- **Wanda Jean Allen** in Oklahoma on January 11, 2001. She was sentenced to death in 1989 for killing her lover, Gloria Leathers, in Oklahoma City in 1988. The two women, who had met in prison, had a turbulent relationship. Leathers's death followed a protracted argument between the couple that began at a local shop, continued at their home, and culminated outside a police station. Allen maintained she had acted in self-defense, claiming that Leathers had struck her in the face with a hand rake during the confrontation at the house, and that outside the police station Leathers had again come at her with the rake. Allen shot Leathers. The wound to Allen's face from the rake was still visible when she was photographed in jail. Later in 1995, a psychologist conducting a comprehensive evaluation of Wanda Jean Allen found "clear and convincing evidence of cognitive and sensory-motor deficits and brain dysfunction," possibly linked to an adolescent head injury.

- **Aileen Wuornos** in Florida on October 9, 2002. Wuornos was a prostitute and convicted serial killer who was sentenced to death by the state of Florida in 1992. She ultimately received five additional death sentences. Wuornos admitted to killing seven men, in separate incidents, all of whom she claimed raped her (or attempted to) while she was working as a prostitute. The 2003 movie *Monster*, starring Charlize Theron and Christina Ricci, tells Wuornos's story from the moment she met Selby Wall (based on Wuornos's lover and four-year companion, Tyria Moore) until her first conviction for murder.

- **Frances Newton** in Texas on September 14, 2005. She was executed for the April 7, 1987, murder of her 23-year-old her husband Adrian; her son Alton, 7, and daughter Farrah, 21 months. The prosecution suggested that the motive for the killings was to collect the U.S. $100,000 life insurance policy. Newton said that a drug dealer killed the three. The Houston police claimed that her husband, Adrian Newton, was a drug dealer and was in debt to his supplier. Newton maintained her innocence from her first interrogation in 1987 until her execution in 2005.

SOURCE: Death Penalty Information Center, "Women and the Death Penalty," http://www.deathpenaltyinfo.org/women-and-death-penalty (**accessed October 21, 2008**).

homework

Ask students to examine the crimes that serial killer Aileen Wuornos committed that led to her execution in 2002, and submit a one-paragraph analysis of those special conditions that would have merited capital punishment.

lecture note

Explain the underrepresentation of females on death row.

key term

Retentionist
Person seeking to retain the death penalty.

key term

Revenge
Seeking retribution for a harm inflicted.

key term

Just deserts argument
Argument that offender should receive severe punishment because of the nature of the crime committed.

key term

Societal protection argument
The argument that once executed, the offender cannot commit another crime, thus protecting society.

Women usually kill friends and relatives, for which they are unlikely to get death. Of the about 3,500 inmates on death row at the start of 2008, only 51 offenders (or 1 of every 71 of the condemned on death row) were women, even though about 1 of 10 arrestees for murder is a woman. This unequal ratio of sentences to death for women who commit murder seems to be a harbinger for a more tough and "equitable" push for the death penalty for women in the future.[41]

JUVENILES AND THE DEATH PENALTY

The United States still endorses capital punishment as a response to crime, particularly homicide. Fluctuating but substantial public support remains for the death penalty, particularly for homicide. In a 2006 Gallup poll, as noted earlier, some 69% of respondents endorsed the death penalty in general. There is apparently less support for the death penalty for juveniles; 79% of the respondents in one 2003 survey opposed capital punishment for juvenile offenders.[42]

The U.S. Supreme Court ruled in 1988 that a death penalty for a person committing a crime while age 15 or under was "cruel and unusual punishment" and thus a violation of the Eighth Amendment.[43] A year later, the Court decided the death penalty was not cruel and unusual if imposed on 16-year-old offenders.[44] In 2004, the Court held that the Eighth and Fourteenth Amendments forbid the execution of offenders who were under the age of 18 when their crime was committed.[45]

Justifications

Nowhere else in the correctional system can the justifications for capital punishment be seen so clearly than in the area of the murderer. Three major justifications for the death penalty are collectively referred to as the **retentionist** position, and include revenge, just deserts, and protection. Those advocating **revenge** as a justification argue that victims, survivors, and the state are entitled to "closure." Only after the execution can psychological, emotional, and social wounds begin to heal. Executing the offender permits that closure. This argument is sometimes referred to as "life for a life."

Other proponents argue that some persons are beyond rehabilitation, and their acts are so grievous an affront to societal standards and humanity that the only adequate response is the penalty of death. This is sometimes referred to as the **just deserts argument.**

Finally is the **societal protection argument.** Once executed, the dead cannot continue their violent and frequently murderous life-course. They can commit no further crime. In this sense, social defense is strengthened when the offender is permanently disabled through execution. Many members of society believe that all three arguments form a sufficient basis for retaining and imposing the death penalty, even on mentally retarded, mentally ill, and (previously) juvenile offenders. (In June 2002, the Supreme Court declared execution of persons with mental retardation unconstitutional.[46])

Other persons favoring the death penalty argue that capital punishment has a deterrent effect, and increasing the probabilities of being executed tends to *reduce* the crime rate.[47] Some retentionists argue that Christian scriptures mandate the death penalty;[48] others argue that society has a *duty* to impose the death penalty for heinous crimes, because any other punishment would denigrate both the values that crime violates and the victim.

Finally, some retentionists argue that there are killers on death row who, if not executed but eventually released, would continue to kill other victims. Case studies of certain offenders whose death sentences were commuted to life in prison and were subsequently paroled only to kill again are used as examples that prove their dangerousness. This position is sometimes called the "*mad dog*" argument in favor of the death penalty.[49] The debate continues.

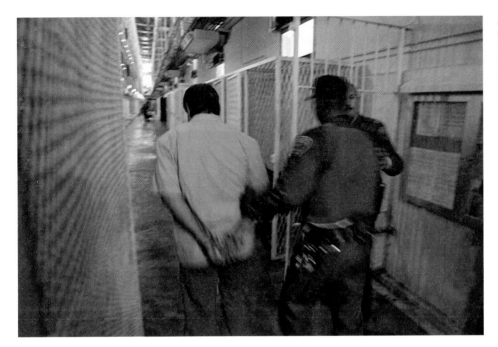

A prisoner on death row at San Quentin Prison California, is led back to his cell in the East Block, holding 520 condemned inmates.
Eric Risberg, Pool/AP Wide World Photos

THE DEATH PENALTY AND TERRORISM

The federal government and the U.S Code of Military Justice have death penalty statutes that permit capital punishment for designated offenses. The accused would be tried in either a federal court or military tribunal, depending on the jurisdiction. If tried in federal court, the panoply of rights, immunities, and protections afforded under the U.S. Constitution would apply, including rules of procedure and evidence. The U.S. Code of Military Justice restricts many of the rights otherwise available to civilians. At the time of this writing, it is unclear which, if either, jurisdiction would be appropriate for terrorists.

By midyear 2005, a number of captured Taliban and al-Qaeda prisoners had been taken to military detention camp "X-ray" at Guantanamo Bay, Cuba. Such detainees are believed to pose a threat to the United States or have intelligence value. Exactly how many detainees have been imprisoned and their identities are unknown, although plans are to build 2,000 cells on this site and a permanent 200-bed military prison. Detainees may face a military trial, a trial in U.S. courts, prosecution in their homelands if returned, or trial in an international court. The first two of those options could result in the death penalty.

The nation's policy toward this special group of offenders challenges national and international law, as the government attempts to redefine criminal actions to avoid Articles of War and rights guaranteed under the Geneva Convention. If defendants were punished with limited or no due process, would there be secret trials? How could the accused call witnesses to offer evidence to refute the prosecutor's evidence? How could exculpatory evidence be offered? Will appeals be permitted? It is challenges such as these that not only sharpen the contrast between a government and citizenry under law, but also validate the necessity of adhering firmly to rights, liberties, and freedom.

THE COST OF THE DEATH PENALTY

While some may argue that it is cheaper to invoke the death penalty than to incarcerate an offender in prison for life, studies do not bear that out. For example, a study in New Jersey estimated that the death penalty has cost taxpayers $253 million dollars since 1983.[50] This

class activity

Have a debate, with one side arguing for the death penalty for juveniles and the other against.

class activity

Present students with the hypothetical arrest and extradition of Osama bin Laden. Should he be tried for capital murder? If convicted, should he be executed?

class activity

Assume a terrorist bombing in a major city and the capture of two of the foreign terrorists. Some 34 Americans were killed. The crime occurred in a state without the death penalty. Should the two terrorists be tried for capital murder and, if sentenced to death, executed?

lecture note

Explain U.S. legal responses to the events of "9/11" and the Afghanistan and Iraq wars. Identify the legal basis of imprisoning suspects without conviction.

figure is over and above what it would have cost that state had it utilized life without parole instead of death. Some findings from various states are as follows:[51]

- Washington: at the trial level, death penalty cases are estimated to generate roughly $470,000 in additional costs to the prosecution and defense over the cost of trying the same case as an aggravated murder without the death penalty.
- On direct appeal, the cost of appellate defense averages $100,000 more in death penalty cases than in non-death-penalty murder cases.
- Tennessee: death penalty cases cost an average of 48% more than the average cost of trials in which prosecutors seek life imprisonment.
- Kansas: the investigation costs for death-sentence cases were about three times greater than for non-death-sentence cases. The appeal costs were 21 times greater.
- Indiana: the cost of the death penalty is 38% greater than the total costs of life-without-parole sentences.
- North Carolina: death penalty cases cost $2.16 million more per execution than the non-death-penalty murder cases with a life sentence.
- Florida: the state would save $51 million each year by punishing all first-degree murderers with life in prison without parole.
- California: the death penalty costs $114 million a year beyond the cost of simply keeping the convicts locked up for life. This figure did not include the millions spent on court costs to prosecute capital cases.

Clearly, there is a high financial cost to the death penalty. While some might argue that it is a cost that is worth bearing, others believe that this is one more reason to abolish the death penalty.

COMMITMENTS TO DEATH ROW CONTINUE

With more than 3,500 prisoners on death rows across the nation (see Figure 14.5) and the number of executions still high, what will be the public's reaction if an unprecedented number of executions occur in the next few years? Administrators, politicians, legislators, and the public wrestle with what to do about the backlog of incarcerated evil.

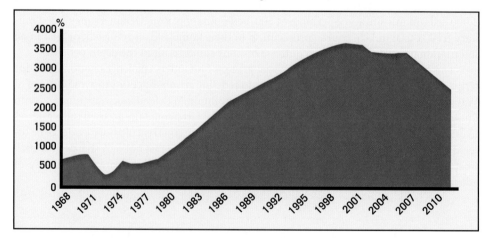

figure 14.5

Size of Death Row, 1968–2012.

SOURCE: Death Penalty Information Center (www.deathpenaltyinfo.org, accessed October 27, 2008). Data to 2012 are extrapolated.

Summary

At midyear 2008, 1,123 men and women had died by state execution since the day Gary Gilmore was shot through the heart in 1977. The U.S. Supreme Court has streamlined and expedited its procedures for appellate review and seems to have tackled the issue of capital punishment head-on. However, the death rows in 36 states are packed, with over 3,500 convicted persons sentenced to die, primarily by lethal injection.

After it showed clearly what provisions it was willing to accept with regard to the death penalty in *Gregg*, the Supreme Court has been relatively supportive of the states' implementing them. It is clear, however, that the limited circumstances acceptable for the ultimate punishment must be administered on a scrupulously equitable basis or the Supreme Court may hold that even such limited application of the sanction of death is unconstitutional. The matter of equity is the one that must be watched during the next few years, as the number of admissions to death row continues.

Finally, while the death penalty is a large chalkboard on which the basic rights of citizens are charted, only a small percentage of imprisoned offenders is on death row. Most will serve their sentences and be released to reenter society. We now turn to parole and inmate reentry.

Key Words

capital punishment, 265

execution, 266

Gregg v. *Georgia*, 267

Capital crimes, 267

Furman v. *Georgia*, 268

arbitrary, 268

intent to kill, 269

malice aforethought, 269

death penalty, 269

cruel and unusual punishment, 269

gatekeeper function, 272

deterrent, 272

life certain, 273

equability, 275

retentionist, 278

revenge, 278

just deserts argument, 278

societal protection argument, 278

Review Questions

1. Explain the guidelines that came out of *Furman* v. *Georgia* and its related decisions.
2. Prepare an argument for the retention of the death penalty, and then prepare an argument against it.
3. How does the race of the victim affect being charged with a capital crime?
4. Why might the number of executions increase sharply in the 2000s?
5. Who were the first to die in America by electrocution, by the gas chamber, and by the use of lethal injection? What are your reactions to each form?
6. Debate: The death penalty should be abolished.
7. Defend the death penalty.

Endnotes

1. Tim Robbins, director, *Dead Man Walking* (Hollywood, CA: Grammercy/Polygram Film Productions, 1995). This film was nominated for a number of Academy Awards. Susan Sarandon played the nun who tried to help save a condemned man's soul by counseling him to admit to the crimes, and she won the best actress Oscar for 1995.
2. Death Penalty Information Center, *Crime Punishable by the Death Penalty,* http://www.deathpenaltyinfo.org/capitaloffenses.html. See also Bureau of Justice Statistics, *Capital Punishment Statistics,* http://www.ojp.usdoj.gov/bjs/cp.htm (accessed October 29, 2008).
3. See Chris Little, "Bible Supports the Death Penalty," http://i2i.org/Publications/Op-Eds/Other/op971029.htm (accessed February 12, 2003). See also "Death Penalty Debate," http://www.lexingtonprosecutor.com/death_penalty_debate.htm; "Seventeen Arguments for the Death Penalty," http://yesdeathpenalty.com/argument_1.htm; and http://www.prodeathpenalty.com (accessed October 28, 2008).

4. The most readable discussion of these issues can be found in P. Lewis, Harry Allen, Henry Mannle, and Harold Vetter, "A Post-*Furman* Profile of Florida's Condemned—A Question of Discrimination in Terms of the Race of the Victim and a Comment on *Spinkellink* v. *Wainwright*," *Stetson Law Review* 9:4 (Fall 1979): 1–45. The general public strongly supports the death penalty. A 2007 Gallup poll reports that 64% of adults nationwide support the death penalty: "Death Penalty," http://www.gallup.com/poll/1606/Death-Penalty.aspx (accessed October 28, 2008). See also John Arthur, "Racial Attitudes about Capital Punishment," *International Journal of Comparative and Applied Criminal Justice* 22:1 (1998): 131–144; and J. D. Unner and F. T. Cullen, "The Racial Divide in Support of the Death Penalty," *Social Forces* 85 (2007): 281–301.

5. Personnel required to participate in an execution are an ignored component of capital punishment. See Robert Johnson, *Death Work: A Study on the Modern Execution Process* (Belmont, CA: Wadsworth, 1998).

6. In February 2008, the Nebraska Supreme Court ruled electrocution, the state's sole execution method, was unconstitutional. Up until then Nebraska was the only state that required electrocution.

7. Harry Barnes and Negley Teeters, *New Horizons in Criminology* (New York: Prentice Hall, 1948), p. 309. In 1988, the average wait from conviction to execution was 6 years and 8 months, but by 2006 it had increased to almost 12 years. John Bonczar and Tracy Snell, *Capital Punishment 2003*, http://www.ojp.usdoj.gov/bjs/pub/pdf/cp03.pdf, p. 12; and Bureau of Justice Statistics, *Capital Punishment 2006* (Washington, DC: Bureau of Justice Statistics, 2007).

8. For a good reference to this controversy, see Ernest van den Haag and J. Conrad, *The Death Penalty: A Debate* (New York: Plenum, 1983). See also Roger Hood, "Capital Punishment—A Global Perspective," *Punishment and Society* 3:3 (2001): 331–354.

9. *Furman* v. *Georgia*, 408 U.S. 238 (1972).

10. http://archives.cnn.com/2000/US/01/31/illinois.executions.02/.

11. J. Edgar Hoover, *Crime in the United States* (Washington, DC: US Government Printing Office, 1931–1939). A rough average of such crimes known to the police is presented.

12. Death Penalty Information Center, "Race of Defendants Executed since 1976," http://www.deathpenaltyinfo.org/dpicrace.html (accessed October 28, 2008).

13. Justice William J. Brennan, *Furman v. Georgia*, 408 U.S. 238 (1976).

14. Brennan, *Furman* v. *Georgia*. See also Susan Cho, "Capital Confusion: The Effect of Jury Instructions on the Decision to Impose Death," *Criminology* 36:3 (1998): 711–733.

15. Malice aforethought means malice in fact or implied malice in the intent of one who has had time to premeditate an act that is unlawful or harmful. This issue is wrapped around the plea of not guilty by reason of insanity. See William Schabas, "International Norms on Execution of the Insane and the Mentally Retarded," *Criminal Law Forum* 4:1 (1993): 95–117; and James Aker, R. Bohm, and S. Lanier (eds.), *America's Experiments with Capital Punishment* (Durham: North Carolina University Press, 1998).

16. Paige Ralph, J. Sorensen, and J. Marquart, "A Comparison of Death-Sentenced and Incarcerated Murderers in Pre-*Furman* Texas," *Justice Quarterly* 9:2 (1992): 185–209.

17. Death Penalty Information Center, *Chattahoochee Judicial District: Buckle on the Death Belt: The Death Penalty in Microcosm* (Washington, DC: DPIC, 1992); see also Death Penalty Information Center, *Killing Justice: Government Misconduct and the Death Penalty* (Washington, DC: DPIC, 1992).

18. Gennaro Vito and T. Keil, "Capital Sentencing in Kentucky: An Analysis of Factors Influencing Decision Making in the Post-*Gregg* Period," *Journal of Criminal Law and Criminology* 79:2 (1988): 483–508. See also Thomas Keil and G. Vito, "The Effects of the *Furman* and *Gregg* Decisions on Black–White Execution Ratios in the South," *Journal of Criminal Justice* 20:3 (1992): 217–226; and Richard Deiter, *The Death Penalty in Black and White* (Washington, DC: DPIC, 1998).

19. Stephen Klein and J. Ralph, "Relationship of Offender and Victim Race to the Death Penalty in California," *Jurimetrics Journal* 32:3 (1991): 33–48. But see Steven Shatz and N. Rivkind, "The California Death Penalty Scheme," *New York University Law Review* 72:6 (1997): 1283–1343.

20. Franklin Zimring, A. Sarat, R. Emerson, et al., "Symposium: Research on the Death Penalty," *Law and Society Review* 27:1 (1993): 9–175; Mark Small, "A Review of Death Penalty Caselaw: Future Directions for Program Evaluation," *Criminal Justice Policy Review* 5:2 (1991): 114–120; Thomas Keil and J. Vito, "Race and the Death Penalty in Kentucky Murder Trials: 1976–1991," *American Journal of Criminal Justice* 20:1 (1995): 17–35; and John Whitehead, " 'Good Ol' Boys' and the Chair," *Crime and Delinquency* 44:2 (1998): 245–256. On the possible impact of racial stereotyping

and death eligibility, see Sara Steen, Rodney Enger, and Randy Gainey, "Images of Danger and Culpability: Racial Stereotyping, Case Processing and Criminal Sentencing," *Criminology* 45:2 (2005): 405–468.

21. Justice Thurgood Marshall, *Furman* v. *Georgia.* Actually, the U.S. Supreme Court shifted from the earlier standard (concerned only with historical techniques for imposing punishment) to the "emerging standards" doctrine in 1910 (*Weems* v. *United States,* 217 U.S. 349). See also Julia Fleming, "The Death Penalty: Another Threat to the Culture of Life," *Journal of Religion and Society* 4:3 (2008): 126–134.

22. *Atkins* v. *Virginia,* 536 U.S. #304 (2002).

23. *Wilkerson* v. *Utah,* 99 U.S. 130 (1878). The State Supreme Court of Utah upheld a lower-court decision sentencing a prisoner convicted of murder in the first degree to be shot publicly. See also Kay Gillespie, *The Unforgiven: Utah's Executed Men* (Salt Lake City, UT: Signature Books, 1991). See also *Baze et al* v. *Rees, 553 U.S. Baze* v. *Rees, 07-5439, U.S.* (2008).

24. Justice Nathan Clifford, *Wilkerson* v. *Utah,* 99 U.S. 130 (1878). See also William Schabas, *The Death Penalty as Cruel and Unusual Torture* (Boston: Northeastern University Press, 1996).

25. Justice Stephen Field, *O'Neil* v. *Vermont,* 1944 U.S. 323 (1892). See also Faith Lutze and D. Brody, "Mental Abuse as Cruel and Unusual Punishment," *Crime and Delinquency* 45:2 (1999): 242–255.

26. *Weems* v. *United States,* 217 U.S. 349 (1910). This decision represented a broad interpretation of the Eighth Amendment, asserting that "cruel and unusual punishment" could apply to prison sentences of a length disproportionate to the offense.

27. *Louisiana ex rel. Francis* v. *Resweber,* 329 U.S. 459 (1947). The Louisiana State Supreme Court denied a writ of habeas corpus against a second attempt to execute a prisoner convicted of murder, the first attempt at electrocution having failed because of mechanical difficulty.

28. See Death Penalty Information Center, "Post-*Furman* Botched Executions," http://www.deathpenaltyinfo. org/botched.html; and http://www.deathpenaltyinfo. org/some-examples-post-furman-botched-executions (accessed October 27, 2008).

29. Burger, *Furman* v. *Georgia.*

30. Gennaro Vito and D. Wilson, "Back from the Dead: Tracking the Progress of Kentucky's *Furman*-Commuted Death Row Populations," *Justice Quarterly* 5:1 (1988): 101–111. Also see: Vito, Gennaro F., Deborah Wilson, and Edward J. Latessa, "Comparison

of the Dead: Attributes and Outcomes of *Furman* Convicted Death Row Inmates in Kentucky and Ohio," in R. Bohm (ed.), *The Death Penalty in America: Current Research* (Cincinnati: Anderson, 1990).

31. They included such notable figures as Sirhan Sirhan, the convicted killer of Senator Robert Kennedy, and Charles Manson, leader of the group of mass killers in California known as the "Family."

32. Raymond Paternoster and A. Kazyaka, "The Administration of the Death Penalty in South Carolina: Experience over the First Few Years," *South Carolina Law Review* 39:2 (1988): 245–411; and Aker et al., *America's Experiments.*

33. Thomas Keil and G. Vito, "Race and the Death Penalty in Kentucky Murder Trials: An Analysis of Post-*Gregg* Outcomes," *Justice Quarterly* 7:1 (1990): 189–207. See also Amy Phillips, "Thou Shalt Not Kill Any Nice People," *American Criminal Law Review* 35:1 (1997): 93–118.

34. Michael Radelet, "Executions of Whites for Crimes against Blacks: Exceptions to the Rule?" *Sociological Quarterly* 30:4 (1989): 529–544. Also see Keil and Vito, "The Effects of the *Furman* and *Gregg* Decisions." But see John DiIulio, "My Black Crime Problem, and Ours," *The City Journal* 6:2 (1996): 14–28.

35. In a telephone survey of respondents in Ohio, Skrovon et al. found disapproval of the death penalty being used on juveniles. Sandra Skovron, J. Scott, and F. Cullen, "The Death Penalty for Juveniles: An Assessment of Public Support," *Crime and Delinquency* 35:4 (1989): 546–561. William Carlsen reports that Californians solidly support the death penalty for adults (63% favor versus 33% opposed), but life in prison without the possibility of parole as an alternative to capital punishment is favored by 67% of the respondents. William Carlsen, "Support for the Death Penalty—Sometimes," *San Francisco Chronicle* (March 28, 1990): A9. The war against drugs has been spread to the death penalty. See Charles Williams, "The Death Penalty for Drug-Related Killings," *Criminal Law Bulletin* 27:5 (1991): 387–415.

36. Richard Deiter (1993), "Sentencing for Life: Americans Embrace Alternatives to the Death Penalty," http://www.deathpenaltyinfo.org/article.php?scid-45&did-481. For the average time to be served, see Paula Dixon, *Truth in Sentencing in State Courts* (Washington, DC: U.S. Department of Justice, 1999), p. 7.

37. H. Bedeau and M. Radelet, "Miscarriages of Justice in Potentially Capital Cases," *Stanford Law Review* 40:1 (1987): 21–179. See also Elizabeth Rapaport, "The Death Penalty and Gender Discrimination," *Law and Society Review* 25:2 (1991): 367–383; Michael Radelet,

H. Bedeau, and C. Putnam, *In Spite of Innocence: The Ordeal of 400 Americans Wrongly Convicted of Crimes Punishable by Death* (Boston: Northeastern University Press, 1992); and Michael Weinstock and G. Schwartz, "Executing the Innocent: Preventing the Ultimate Injustice," *Criminal Law Bulletin* 34:4 (1998): 328–347.

38. *United States of America v. Alan Quinones* (2002 U.S. Dist. Lexis 7320).

39. *Death Penalty Sentencing: Research Indicates Pattern of Racial Disparities* (Washington, DC: General Accounting Office, 1990).

40. Death Penalty Information Center, "Women and the Death Penalty," http:www.deathpenaltyinfo.org/.

41. Darrell Steffensmeier, J. Schwartz, H. Zhong, and J. Ackerman, "An Assessment of Recent Trends in Girls' Violence Using Diverse Longitudinal Sources: Is the Gender Gap Closing?" *Criminology* 43:2 (2005): 255–405. See also Jennifer Schwartz and Brian Rookey, "The Narrowing Gap in Arrests," *Criminology* 46:3 (2008): 637–672.

42. A new poll conducted by ABC News revealed strong opposition to the death penalty for juveniles in general: only 21% were in favor of the death penalty for juveniles, versus the 62% who preferred the sentence of life without parole. The poll was conducted Dec. 10–14 (ABC News, Dec. 19, 2003).

43. *Thompson v. Oklahoma,* 487 U.S. 815 (1988).

44. *Stanford v. Kentucky,* 492 U.S. 361 (1989).

45. *Roper* v. *Simons,* 03-633 (2004). See also *Atkins* v. *Virginia,* 536 U.S. 304 (2002).

46. Hashem Dezhbakhsh, Paul Rubin, and Joanna Mehlhop Shepherd, "Does Capital Punishment Have a Deterrent Effect?" http://www.ipta.net/pubs/emory.edu.

47. Dudley Sharp, "Death Penalty and Sentencing Information," http://www.prodeathpenalty.com/DP.html.

48. Dudley Sharp, "Death Penalty and Sentencing Information," http://www.prodeathpenalty.com/DP .html#F.Christianity.

49. Clark County Prosecutor, "Robert Lee Massie," http:// www.clarkprosecutor.org/html/death/US/massie703. htm. See also "Press Release: New Jerseyans for Alternatives to the Death Penalty, Nov. 21, 2005"; for full report go to http://www.njadp.org.

50. Death Penalty Information Center, "Financial Facts about the Death Penalty," http://www.deathpenaltyinfo .org/costs-death-penalty, accessed May 5, 2009.

51. http://deathpenaltyinfo.org/costs-death-penalty (accessed October 28, 2008).

Suggested Readings: Part 3

American Correctional Association. Special theme issue: Reentry. *Corrections Today* 67:2 (2005).

American Correctional Association. Special theme issue: Reentry. *Corrections Today* 69:2 (2007).

Amnesty International. *Nigeria: Waiting for the Hangman.* New York: Amnesty International, 2008.

Bailey, William. "Deterrence, Brutalization and the Death Penalty: Another Examination of Oklahoma's Return to Capital Punishment." *Criminology* 36:4 (1998): 711–733.

Bureau of Justice Statistics. *Capital Punishment 2006.* Washington, DC: U.S. Department of Justice, 2007. Available online at http://www.ojp.usdoj.gov/bjs/pub/ html/cp/2006/cp06t.htm.

Bureau of Justice Statistics. *Prisoners Executed in the United States: 1930–1999.* Available online at http:// www.ojp.usdoj.gov/bjs.

Burke, Peggy. *Abolishing Parole: Why the Emperor Has No Clothes.* Lexington, KY: American Probation and Parole Association, 1995.

Council of State Governments. *Report of the Re-Entry Policy Committee.* Lexington, KY: Council of State Governments, 2004.

Cullen, Francis T., E. Latessa, and V. Burton, Jr. "The Correctional Orientation of Prison Wardens: Is the Rehabilitative Ideal Supported?" *Criminology* 31:1 (1993): 69–92.

Currie, Elliott. *Crime and Punishment in America: Why the Solutions to America's Most Stubborn Social Crisis Have Not Worked—And What Will.* New York: Metropolitan Books, 1998.

Death Penalty Information Center, http://www .deathpenaltyinfo.org.

Ditton, Paula. *Mental Health and Treatment of Inmates and Probationers.* Washington, DC: Bureau of Justice Statistics, 1999.

Editors, Correctional News. "CCA Completes Initial Phases of 3,600-Bed Arizona Facility," *Corrections News* 14:6 (2008): 19.

Editors, Correctional News. "Marshals Service to House Inmates in GEO Group Facility in Georgia," *Corrections News* 14:2 (2008): 13.

Editors, Corrections Today. *Corrections Today* 69:2 (2007). Special theme issue on "Reentry."

English, Kim, S. Pullen, and L. Jones. *Managing Adult Sex Offenders in the Community: A Containment Approach.* Washington, DC: U.S. Department of Justice, 1997.

Feeley, Malcolm. "The Privatization of Prisons in Historical Perspective." *Criminal Justice Research Bulletin* 6:2 (1991): 6–8.

Finn, Peter. *Chicago's Safer Foundation: A Road Back for Ex-Offenders.* Washington, DC: U.S. Department of Justice, 1998.

Finn, Peter. *Successful Job Placement for Ex-Offenders.* Washington, DC: U.S. Department of Justice, 1998.

Glaze, Lauren, and Thomas Bonczar. *Probation and Parole in the United States 2006.* Washington, DC: Bureau of Justice Statistics, 2008.

Glaze, Lauren, and L. Maruschak, *Parents in Prison and Their Minor Children.* Washington, DC: Bureau of Justice Statistics, 2008.

Hanrahan, Kate, John Gibbs, and Sherwood Zimmerman. "Parole and Revocation." *The Prison Journal* 85:3 (2005): 251–269.

Harris, George A. (ed.). *And Tough Customers: Counseling Unwilling Clients.* Laurel, MD: American Correctional Association, 1991.

Hassine, Victor. *Life without Parole.* New York: Oxford University Press, 2008.

Hughes, Timothy, and Doris Wilson, *Reentry Trends in the United States.* Washington, DC: Bureau of Justice Statistics, 2005. Also available at http://www.ojp.usdoj.gov/bjs/reentry/reentry.htm.

Johnson, Robert. *Death Work: A Study of the Modern Execution Process.* Belmont, CA: Wadsworth, 1998.

Johnson, Robert, and H. Toch. *Crime and Punishment: Inside Views.* Los Angeles: Roxbury, 2000.

Kilpatrick, D., D. Beatty, and S. Howley. *The Rights of Crime Victims.* Washington, DC: U.S. Department of Justice, 1998.

Langan, Patrick, and David Levin. *Recidivism of Prisoners Released in 1994.* Washington, DC: Bureau of Justice Statistics, 2002.

Lanza-Kaduce, Lonn, K. Parker, and C. Thomas. "A Comparative Recidivism Analysis of Releasees from Private and Public Prisons." *Crime and Delinquency* 45:1 (1999): 28–47.

Latessa, Edward, and Harry Allen. *Corrections in the Community.* Cincinnati, OH: Anderson, 2003.

Latessa, E. J., and Paula Smith. *Corrections in the Community.* Cincinnati, OH: Anderson Publishing, 2007.

Lilly, J. Robert, and M. Deflem. "Profit and Penalty: An Analysis of the Corrections-Commercial Complex." *Crime and Delinquency* 42:1 (1996): 3–20.

Love, Margaret. *Relief from Collateral Consequences of a Criminal Conviction.* Washington, DC: The Sentencing Project, 2008.

Lowenkamp, C. T., and Edward Latessa. *Does Parole Work: A Reanalysis of the Urban Institute Study.* Cincinnati, OH: University of Cincinnati, 2005.

Lutze, Faith, and D. Brody, "Mental Abuse as Cruel and Unusual Punishment," *Crime and Delinquency* 45:2 (1999): 242–255.

Maruschak, Laura. *HIV in Prisons and Jails, 2006.* Washington, DC: Bureau of Justice Statistics, 2008.

Maruschak, Laura, and A. Beck. *Medical Problems of Inmates, 2006.* Washington, DC: Bureau of Justice Statistics, 2008.

Mumola, Christopher. *Substance Abuse and Treatment, State and Federal Prisoners, 1997.* Washington, DC: Bureau of Justice Statistics, 1999.

Mumola, Christopher, and J. Karberg. *Drug Use and Dependence, State and Federal Prisoners, 2005.* Washington, DC: Bureau of Justice Statistics, 2006.

Petrosino, Anthony, and C. Petrosino. "The Public Safety Potential of Megan's Law in Massachusetts." *Crime and Delinquency* 45:1 (1999): 122–139.

Scalia, John. *Prisoner Petitions filed in U.S. District Courts, 2000.* Washington, DC: Bureau of Justice Statistics, 2004. Available online at http://www.ojp.usdoj.gov/bjs/pub/pdf/ppfusd00.pdf.

Seiter, Richard P. "Private Corrections: A Review of the Issues." http://www.correctionscorp.com/static/assets/Private_Corr_Review_of_Issues.pdf.

Sexton, George E. *Work in American Prisons: Joint Ventures with the Private Sector.* Washington, DC: U.S. Department of Justice, 1995.

Sorensen, Jon, and D. Wallace, "Prosecutorial Discretion in Seeking Death." *Justice Quarterly* 16:3 (1999): 559–578.

Sundt, Jody, and F. Cullen. "The Role of the Contemporary Prison Chaplain." *Prison Journal* 78:3 (1998): 271–298.

Thomas, Charles W. *Correctional Privatization: The Issues and Evidence.* Toronto: The Fraser Institute, 1996.

Thomas, Charles W. "Prisoner Rights and Correctional Privatization: A Legal and Ethical Analysis." *Business and Professional Ethics Journal* 10:1 (1991): 3–45.

Tonry, Michael. "Crime and Human Rights: How Political Paranoia, Protestant Fundamentalism, and Constitutional Obsolescence Combined to Devastate Black America," *Criminology* 46:1 (2008): 1–34.

Turner, Susan, and J. Petersilia. "Work Release in Washington: Effects on Recidivism and Courtroom Costs." *Prison Journal* 76:2 (1996): 138–164.

Vaughn, Michael, and Sue Carter Collins, "Medical Malpractice in Correctional Facilities: State Tort Remedies for Inappropriate and Inadequate Health Care Administered to Prisoners," *The Prison Journal* 84:4 (2004): 505–534.

Wilkinson, Reginald, and Edward Rhine. "Confronting Recidivism," *Corrections Today* 67:5 (2005): 54–57.

part 4

Correctional Clients

Overview

Part 4 (Chapters 15–19) deals with correctional systems and correctional functions, and the legal environment in which they operate. The last four chapters deal with the human beings incarcerated in institutions. In particular, we deal with male and female offenders, juvenile inmates, and special categories of inmates. Amongst the latter are groups of inmates with more problems than the other offenders in the mainstream of criminal behavior: the mentally disordered offender, the developmentally challenged offender, the sex offender, HIV-infected inmates, and geriatric inmates. Together, these categories represent the spectrum of the individual offenders under the custody and treatment of corrections administrators.

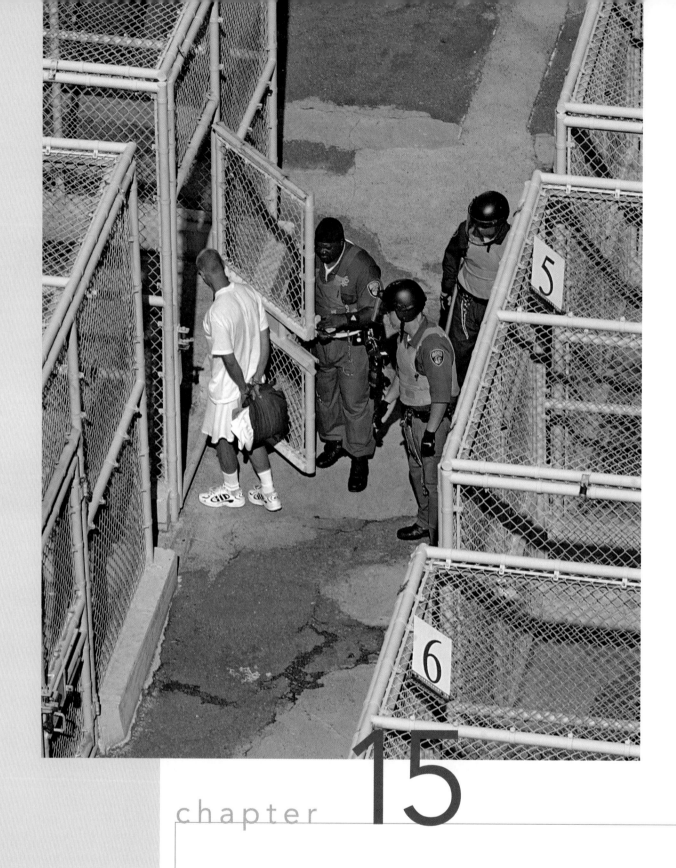

Inmate and Ex-Offender Rights

Outline

Overview

Ask the average person on the street what "rights" prisoners have coming to them when in confinement—or eventually when released after their sentences have been served. After a few seconds of a blank stare, most would answer, "What do you mean rights? They don't have any." In Part 4, Chapter 15, we present in some detail the misunderstood world of those rights that apply to inmates and ex-offenders. The incredible amount of litigation in institutions, the long battles for the lives of what appear to be heinous animals who deserve to die, and the problems with the ex-prisoner trying to deal with society and carrying a heavy record for life cause us to wonder how this all came about.

The rights of inmates and offenders are important, and the courts and rights advocates carefully monitor them. When those persons have finally done their time and now find themselves back in their former neighborhood—burdened by a record and a stigma that are hard to overcome—they still have rights as well. Literally millions of citizens on the streets of America have been convicted of a crime and placed under correctional supervision at some point in their lives. (Well over 7 million inmates and ex-offenders are under active correctional supervision, from probation to incarceration to parole.) This chapter deals with the sometimes gray

"Young, unskilled, poorly educated, the typical offender has few marketable capabilities to offer potential employers. Unable to find or keep a job upon his release from prison, the offender often returns to crime—the only 'business' he knows. Breaking the cycle of recidivism is a difficult task, involving many complex contributing factors. One of these is employment potential. Effective programs for building relevant job skills do ease the offender's reentry into society."

—Gerald M. Caplan,
Former Director, Law
Enforcement Assistance
Administration

correctional **brief**

Individual Rights Guaranteed by the Bill of Rights

A Right against Unreasonable Searches of Person and Place of Residence

A Right against Arrest without Probable Cause

A Right against Unreasonable Seizures of Personal Property

A Right against Self-Incrimination

A Right to Fair Questioning by the Police

A Right to Protection from Physical Harm throughout the Justice Process

A Right to an Attorney

A Right to Trial by Jury

A Right to Know the Charges

A Right to Cross-Examine Prosecution Witnesses

A Right to Speak and Present Witnesses

A Right Not to Be Tried Twice for the Same Crime

A Right against Cruel or Unusual Punishment

A Right to Due Process

A Right to a Speedy Trial

A Right against Excessive Bail

A Right against Excessive Fines

A Right to Be Treated the Same as Others, Regardless of Race, Sex, Religious Preference, and Other Personal Attributes

A Right to Be Assumed Innocent Until Proven Guilty

SOURCE: Frank Schmalleger, *Criminal Justice Today*, 5th ed. (Upper Saddle River, NJ: Prentice Hall, 2001).

key term

Convicted offender

Guilty law violator who has exhausted all appeals of conviction and sentencing.

key term

Court master

Representative of the court ordered to monitor correctional compliance with a court's orders.

area of the offender and the problems offenders face while incarcerated and while trying to reintegrate into society. This task is one that has many bumps in the road back to being a productive and useful citizen, but many more make that trip and succeed than we often acknowledge. This chapter considers the restrictions on inmates and ex-offenders and the current status of efforts to provide additional rights. We start with some of the myths and legends about these efforts.

THE STATUS OF THE CONVICTED OFFENDER

When defendants have gone through the whole criminal justice process, including all appeals, and their sentences have been upheld, they officially acquire the status of **convicted offender**. They may already have spent a long time in jail or prison as their appeals made their tedious way through the courts. But with the final guilty verdict in, the offender's relationship to the correctional system undergoes a significant change. In this section we examine the offender's new status and his or her rights during and after incarceration. Over the years, a body of folklore has grown about the rights of prisoners and ex-prisoners. We hope this chapter will dispel some of those myths and clarify recent developments.

With almost 7 million people[1] subject to the control of some kind of correctional authority in America each day, the status of those convicted offenders poses a significant problem. Correctional officials have been slow to draw up internal policies and procedures to guide their administrators in protecting the offenders' rights. Under the "hands-off" policy mentioned in Chapter 4, the courts were reluctant to criticize decisions and procedures developed by correctional administrators. That policy was abandoned in the mid-1960s, opening the door to case after case regarding prisoners' rights, with no end in sight. There are many state Department of Corrections under judicial review, most with a court-appointed monitor (**court master**) who supervises conformity to the Court's order. Let us start with the basic rights of the confined inmate.

BASIC INMATE RIGHTS

Visiting and Community Ties

You should recall from Chapter 1 that penal punishments included **civil death**, which meant that the offender's property was confiscated in the name of the state and his wife declared a widow, eligible to remarry. To society, the offender was, in effect, dead. The vestiges of civil death are probably most visible in correctional practices that pertain to the privilege of having visitors. Debate continues about whether having visitors is actually a privilege or is in fact a right. The practice of having visitors is not new. Occasional visitors were allowed even as early as 1790 in the Walnut Street Jail. If a prisoner was diligent and good, a visit was allowed from a close family member—but only once every three months, for 15 minutes, through two grills, and under the scrutiny of a keeper.[2] This procedure may seem absurdly strict, but is not too far from the current practice in some high-security correctional institutions. The overriding security focus at most prisons dictates that visits be limited, subject to highly regimented conditions, and likely to discourage close physical or emotional contact. The dehumanizing rules and procedures for visiting do not accord with modern goals of rehabilitation and correction. Although security is important in maximum-security prisons, it could be tempered with humanity in such a personal thing as a visit from a friend or family member.

Limitations on visiting hours, restricted visitor lists,[3] overcrowded visiting rooms, and the overwhelming presence of guards contribute to the inmate's difficulty in maintaining ties with family and the outside world.[4] Most institutions are located far from large urban centers (where most inmates' families live), requiring long hours of travel and expense for visitors. Not only family ties but also friendships wither quickly under such conditions. This alienation creates serious problems for both the inmate and the institution. Typically, an inmate is allowed to receive a visitor once a week (in some places as seldom as once a month), usually a member of his or her immediate family. This is hardly representative of social life in contemporary America.

For the married inmate, family ties are inevitably weakened by long separation. With divorce frequent, the social consequences to the family, community, and institution are incalculable; imprisonment itself is grounds for divorce in some jurisdictions.[5] Institution officials often face severe problems caused by the deterioration of an inmate's family situation. When, for example, a wife does not write, or the inmate hears through the grapevine that she has a lover, violence can and often does result—expressed in attacks against prison personnel,[6] another prisoner,[7] or attempts to escape.

Deprived of even a semblance of normal relations with the outside, the inmate turns to the other inmates and the inmate subculture for solace. It seems ironic that inmates are cut off from both friends and relatives and must depend almost entirely on the company of criminals. Yet when finally released on parole, some parole rules forbid the parolee to associate with known ex-offenders. Such paradoxical situations seem to run counter to the basic premises of American corrections. There is no better way to combat the inmate social system and prepare an inmate for freedom than by strengthening his or her ties with the outside world through visitations, family or conjugal visits,[8] home furloughs, telephone access, and mail.

Use of Mail

The mail system is closely tied to visitation as another way to maintain essential contact with the outside world. As in the case of visits, stated reasons for the limitation and censorship of mail are tied either to security or to the

Couple checking in at a window to visit relatives at juvenile hall annex, Santa Ana, California.
Photo by Spencer Grant, courtesy of PhotoEdit Inc.

correctional **brief**

Family/Conjugal Visiting

During a conjugal visit, or what is most commonly called a "family visit," inmate, spouse, and children are allowed to spend time together on the prison campus, unsupervised and alone in private quarters, trailers, houses, and rooms. During this time, the couple may or may not engage in sexual intercourse. Visits covering three days are not uncommon.

European and Latin American countries have been the leaders in permitting conjugal visiting, but some states (e.g., California and Mississippi) have formal programs of conjugal visiting. Others (such as Montana) permit the program without granting formal approval. In 2007, California began allowing overnight visits for lesbian and gay partners of imprisoned inmates to conform to the state's newly enacted domestic partnership law.

Advantages cited in some studies include lessening forced and voluntary homosexual acts within prison, maintaining a more normal prison environment, lowering tension levels, lessening attacks on correctional officers, reinforcing gender-appropriate roles, helping to preserve marriages, and (from the perspective of the prison administration) encouraging appropriate behavior by inmates hoping to earn a conjugal visitation pass. Opponents argue that it puts too much emphasis on the physical aspects of marriage, is unfair to the unmarried resident, raises welfare costs through increased family size, and decreases the intensity of punishment to offenders.

SOURCE: Don Thompson, "Conjugal Visits for Gays, Lesbians OK in State Prisons," *The Desert Sun* (June 2, 2007): A-3.

Couple visit by telephone in jail, separated by a glass partition.
Photo by Spencer Grant, courtesy of PhotoEdit, Inc.

class activity

Ask students what types of rights extend to inmates. How are these guaranteed?

class activity

Ask students if inmates have a right to family/conjugal visiting. If the consensus is "no," use the Scandinavian examples to give differing views. Are these countries more democratic than the United States is?

class activity

Ask students when institutional staff can read incoming mail for inmates. When can they not?

class activity

What is the standard of free exercise of religious rights in prison?

lecture note

Discuss the reach of the U.S. Constitution to offenders in the community and in confinement.

prison's orderly administration. Although the use of the mail system is a right, case law has established that correctional administrators can place reasonable restrictions on prisoners in the exercise of that right if there is a "clear and present danger" or compelling state need. As with most situations behind the walls, in the past, mail rules were systematically stiffened to facilitate the institutions' smooth operation. If it became too great an administrative burden to read all the incoming and outgoing mail, the number of letters or the list of correspondents was reduced. Eventually, a small maximum of allowed letters and very restrictive lists of correspondents became the standard. As long as the prisoners could not turn to the courts, this practice did not create a stir. When the attorneys appointed to help prisoners began to see the unjustness of restrictions concerning mail and other so-called privileges, they began to question the rules and reestablish those privileges as rights.

How much mail should a prisoner receive? Administrators have usually restricted it to an amount that can readily be censored. During personnel shortages (in wars, for example), the amount of mail was often limited to one letter a month. Outgoing mail was similarly restricted. Communications with an attorney could be opened and read, but not censored unless the correspondence referred to plans for illegal activity[9] or contained contraband. More recently, court decisions have found that most censorship of communications between inmates and their lawyers is unconstitutional;[10] this direction also appears in decisions regarding communications with the news media.[11]

Death-row inmates frequently receive only photocopies of correspondence sent to them from persons other than attorneys. There is a clear and present danger of poisoning from chemicals sprayed on stationery at the inmate's request. Stamps can also be affixed to envelopes with a liquid poison or drugs. Finally, lethal poison can also be suspended in ink. Ironically, death-row inmates cannot be allowed to kill themselves before their execution, although many do commit suicide.[12]

Contraband and Mail

In the past, contraband was commonly described as "any material that might be used for an escape or used to take advantage of other prisoners." Such items as matches, money, pornographic pictures, guns, knives, lubricants, drugs, and tools are generally considered contraband. Any item could have been placed on the contraband list if it was seen as a threat to the prison's orderly operation.

The more recent definition of contraband is any item found on the prisoner or in his or her cell that is not specifically authorized by the administration in written rules. This helps simplify the process and eliminate any controversy as to what is, or is not, contraband. (For example, if written rules state that a prisoner is authorized two blankets, and three are found in a cell inspection, the third blanket is, by definition, contraband and subject to removal.)

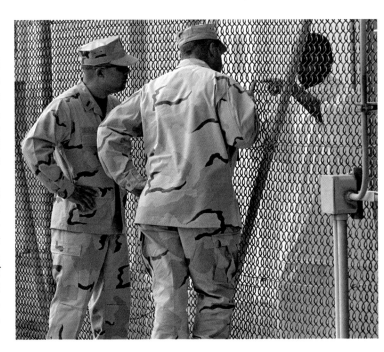

When an inmate wishes to communicate with a second inmate, either a friend or jailhouse lawyer who is incarcerated at another institution, the courts have stuck to a hands-off policy, leaving that problem to the discretion of the correctional administrators. The general policy has been to prohibit the passage of any correspondence between inmates. This policy continues to be under attack, however, and has been rejected by some states.[13] In most court cases, the test for permissibility of mail and literature has been the **clear and present danger** standard:

> We accept the premise that certain literature may pose such a clear and present danger to the security of a prison, or to the rehabilitation of prisoners, that it should be censored. To take an extreme example, if there were mailed to a prisoner a brochure demonstrating in detail how to saw prison bars with utensils used in the mess hall, how to make a bomb, or how to provoke a prison riot, it would properly be screened. A magazine detailing for incarcerated drug addicts how they might obtain a euphoric "high," comparable to that experienced from heroin, by sniffing aerosol or glue available for other purposes within the prison walls, would likewise be censored as restraining effective rehabilitation. Furthermore, it is undoubtedly true that in the volatile atmosphere of a prison, where a large number of men, many with criminal tendencies, live in close proximity to each other, violence can be fomented by the printed word much more easily than in the outside world. Some censorship or prior restraint on inflammatory literature sent into prisons is, therefore, necessary to prevent such literature from being used to cause disruption or violence within the prison. It may well be that in some prisons where the prisoners' flash-point is low, articles regarding bombing, prison riots, or the like, which would be harmless when sold on the corner newsstand, would be too dangerous for release to the prison population. The courts have also upheld restrictions on incoming newspapers and magazines that would permit receipt of such mail if "only the publisher" is the sender.[14]

Ohio took the lead in the reform of mail censorship, eliminating all of it in Ohio's prisons on August 3, 1973.[15] Under the Ohio system, both incoming and outgoing mail is merely inspected for contraband and delivered unread. Each inmate may write and receive an unlimited number of items of mail. The adoption of those standards has caused few if any problems. Most states, however, still inspect, electronically, incoming packages and open letters to look for contraband.

Religious Rights in Prison

The idea underlying the penitentiary was drawn from religious precepts. It thus seems ironic that there would be any conflict in providing freedom of religion in prisons, but this has indeed been the case. The early efforts to restore the criminal through penitence and prayer were conducted in small homogeneous communities. As immigration to America expanded, it became the most heterogeneous nation in the world. Because the United States was founded on a belief that freedom of worship could not be infringed by the government, the First Amendment addressed those issues: "Congress shall make no law respecting an establishment of religion, or prohibiting the free exercise thereof. . . ." It is the conflict between what constitutes an established religion and the individual's right to exercise it that has caused grief in the nation's prisons.

A clear example of this problem was the **Black Muslim** decision, which has dominated case law for more than two decades. After a long string of cases,[16] the courts finally held that the Black Muslim faith did constitute an established religion and that the Black Muslims were therefore entitled to follow the practices the religion prescribed.[17] The resolution of the Black Muslim issue meant the standards applied there could be applied to any duly recognized religion.[18] This puts a strain on the prison administrator, who must allow equal protection for all inmates. The question of whether the state really grants each inmate "free exercise" simply by ensuring access to a minister of his or her particular faith is still unsettled.

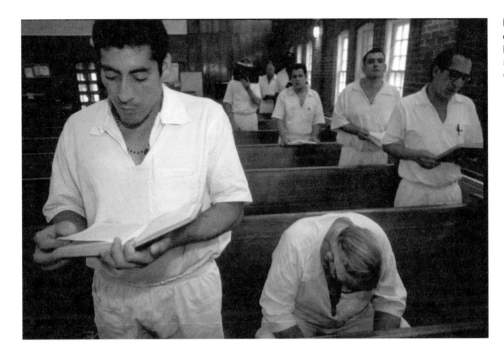

Inmates partake in a prison church service at the Walls, Huntsville, Texas.
Photo by Andrew Lichtenstein, courtesy of Corbis/Sygma.

Access to Court and Counsel

Access to the federal courts was not established as a constitutional right for inmates until 1940, in a case called *Ex parte Hull*. In that decision, the U.S. Supreme Court established that "the state and its officers may not abridge or impair a petitioner's right to apply to a federal court for a writ of habeas corpus." Despite that clear ruling, the courts still maintained a strict hands-off policy in this regard until the 1964 case of *Cooper* v. *Pate*.[19]

Once the prisoners' right to use jailhouse lawyers was established in *Johnson* v. *Avery*,[20] inmates needed to be assured of an adequate supply of legal research materials; in 1971, the case of *Younger* v. *Gilmore*[21] guaranteed the inmate writ writers such assistance. But the extent of provided materials has varied considerably, from complete law libraries[22] in the state prisons to the bare essentials elsewhere.[23] Meanwhile, other states allow law students to run legal clinics inside institutions, under the supervision of a law school faculty member qualified to practice in that jurisdiction. It seems the courts must continue to require that correctional administrations offer adequate legal counsel to inmates, or they will have to live with the continued use of jailhouse lawyers and the problems that result.

The right to consult with counsel has been clearly established.[24] The problem, before *Gideon* and the cases it generated, was that most inmates could not afford a lawyer to defend them or prepare later appeals.[25] Early prison rules restricted the use of **jailhouse lawyers,** those inmates who learn something about the law and use their skills to assist other inmates to file suits against correctional administrators and facilities. Restricting jailhouse lawyers from helping other inmates meant that few prisoners were able to file writs in the federal courts. After the courts established the right to counsel in *Gideon, Johnson* v. *Avery* covered those administrative agencies that could not or would not comply. Though not all jurisdictions have been able to provide counsel for all inmates, the remedies incorporated in the court decisions have helped fill the void—while incidentally creating a flood of writs that have washed over the civil and appeals courts. During the past two decades, the petitions filed in the U.S. district courts by federal prisoners increased 64%, and those by state prisoners increased 238%. The latter's civil rights suits increased by a whopping 389%. As a result of this steep increase, Congress enacted two legislative initiatives that sought to limit prisoners' ability to file petition in federal courts: the Prison Litigation Reform Act and the Antiterrorism and Effective Death Penalty Act. Together, these initiatives have sharply reduced inmate civil rights petitions.[26]

key term

Jailhouse lawyer
An inmate's provision of legal services to another inmate.

The Right to Medical Treatment and Care

The issue of adequate medical care in our prisons has finally prompted a decision from the U.S. Supreme Court. Only when a constitutionally guaranteed right has been violated has the Court become involved in the provision of medical care. Because both medical programs and the backgrounds of prison medical personnel are extremely diversified, the quality of medical aid varies among institutions.[27] Ironically, a nation that demands adequate medical care for all inmates is, at this writing, still struggling with providing adequate medical care for all of its citizens.

The U.S. Supreme Court has taken the position that inmates in state prisons should seek remedy in the state courts. In the 1976 case of **Estelle v. Gamble,**[28] that position was made even clearer. Although suits in the past have shown that prisoners' rights to proper diagnosis and medical treatment of illness have been violated on a grand scale, the courts have moved slowly in that area. In *Estelle,* however, the Court stated, "We therefore conclude that *deliberate indifference* [emphasis added] to serious medical needs of prisoners constitutes the unnecessary and wanton infliction of pain proscribed by the Eighth Amendment. This is true whether the indifference is manifested by prison doctors in their response to the prisoner's needs or by prison guards in intentionally denying or delaying access to medical care or intentionally interfering with the treatment once prescribed."[29] This was a giant step forward in the provision of medical treatment, but it still falls short of the individual remedies provided by decisions in other areas. For example, the U.S. First Circuit Court of Appeals has ruled that inmates must receive "adequate medical care" but do not necessarily deserve "the most sophisticated care that money can buy."[30] Medical care in prison in relationship to the AIDS problem has been described as "a national disgrace."[31]

Estelle stated a position of sympathy for complaints about the system-wide failure to provide adequate and humane medical care. The test of **deliberate indifference,** however, a requirement for evoking the Eighth Amendment, seems to be a major hurdle for most who choose to use *Estelle* as a basis for action. Mere negligence or malpractice leaves the prisoner with remedy only in a state civil case. Total deprivation of medical service seems to be the current standard for application of constitutional prohibitions.

key term

Estelle v. Gamble
First U.S. Supreme Court case dealing with prison medical treatment.

key term

Deliberate indifference
Total deprivation of medical services.

Dentist provides dental care to an inmate as a guard looks on at a San Quentin State prison.
© Adam Tanner/Reuters/CORBIS
All Rights Reserved.

correctional **brief**

Deliberate Indifference Standard, *Farmer* v. *Brennan*

For a claim to be presented, the inmate must show that he or she was incarcerated under conditions posing a substantial risk of serious harm. This is the objective test, the *Rhodes* test: "Was the deprivation sufficiently serious?" If a plaintiff is able to establish a sufficiently serious deprivation, he or she must next satisfy the *Farmer* test, the "deliberate indifference" test: "Did the officials act with a sufficiently culpable state of mind?" *Farmer* v. *Brennan*, 511 U.S. 825, 114 S. Ct. 1970 (1994).

Before the 1994 *Farmer* case, courts looked to an objective standard to determine if a prison official violated a prisoner's rights. The *Farmer* decision of 1994 set entirely different and personally responsible standards: "For a claim . . . based on a failure to prevent harm, [Plaintiff] must show that [the inmate] [was] incarcerated under conditions posing a substantial risk of serious harm. [The objective test] The state of mind requirement follows from the several Supreme Court holdings that only the unnecessary and wanton infliction of pain implicates the Eighth Amendment.

To violate the Cruel and Unusual Punishments Clause, a prison official must have a sufficiently culpable state of mind. [The subjective test] The subjective component is the equivalent of criminal recklessness, much more than negligence or even malice. It is not similar to; it is criminal conduct that is required to be proven.

"'Subjective recklessness' as used in the criminal law is a familiar and workable standard that is consistent with the Cruel and Unusual Punishments Clause as interpreted in our cases, and we adopt it as the test for 'deliberate indifference' under the Eighth Amendment." *Farmer*, 511 U.S. at 838, 114 S. Ct. at 1980.

SOURCES: Personal communications with Deputy Attorney General Martin Basiszla, Office of the Attorney General, State of Hawaii, Honolulu, 1999. See also Mary Sylla, "HIV Treatment in U.S. Jails and Prisons," *BETA*, http:www.sfaf.org/files/site1/asset/beta_2008_win_jails_prisons.pdf (accessed November 18, 2008).

One recent example of state failure to provide adequate health care services is seen in the state of California. In 2002, a federal judge determined that the California Department of Corrections system that provided health care to roughly 164,000 inmates was unconstitutional. He ordered major medical reforms, but the state failed to comply. As many as 64 preventable deaths of inmates a year (and injury to many others) due to medical malfeasance led to the Court's 2005 decision to order a receiver to take control of California's prison health care system.[32]

correctional **brief**

Court Masters in Corrections

Both federal and state courts in which litigation over correctional issues has been filed may appoint a servant of the court, or court master, a functional adjunct whose task is to assist the court in whatever manner the court directs. Typically, the master oversees the day-to-day compliance of the institution or institutional system to the decree of the court or the consent decree. A decree of the court implies that the defendant (correctional unit) lost the case and the court has issued orders that are to be implemented. A consent decree occurs where the complainants (inmates) or defendants agree to a set of actions that both would find acceptable.

Generally, masters monitor the lawsuit, report to the court, investigate complaints by inmates, have access to prisoners and their files, hold hearings, and write reports that inform the appointing judge about progress in the settlement of the orders. They also advise the court (through their special expertise in corrections, in particular) and help arrange compromises between the extremes of the demands of the inmates and the realities of prison administration.

When a master is appointed, correctional administrators tend to resist the intrusion of the master into the routine affairs of the institution. Some masters have their own reform agenda or fail to represent the correctional unit in securing compromise. Finally, the defendant (correctional system) must pay for the master and any staff, and there usually is little disincentive to the master's office running up long hours of work at high rates of compensation. Currently, masters are seen as providing correctional expertise to a court that has no competence in correctional administration. Future correctional administrators will need to develop positive working relationships with the court and negotiate with all parties to define clearly the powers, role, and scope of the master, to minimize any negative fallout from the appointment of an intervention agent.

In 2007, the entire systems of nine states or territories were under consent orders, and another 224 institutions were under consent decrees.

SOURCE: American Correctional Association, *2007 Directory* (Alexandria, VA: ACA, 2007), p. 15.

correctional **brief**

Alternatives to Litigation

Civil litigation abounds over correctional issues such as prison overcrowding, compensation for lost personal property, need for a special diet, and restoration of good-time credits, increasing every year at great expense and time consumed by institutional managers. Further, court litigation is not a speedy technique for resolving inmate needs. Finally, correctional administrators have become increasingly concerned with the impact of lawsuits on the institution, including the reluctance of correctional staff to take actions, decline in staff morale, officer stress, and general reluctance to comply with discretionary duties. In the search for alternatives to litigation, four basic approaches have been proposed: grievance boards, inmate grievance procedures, the ombudsman, and mediators.

The grievance board is usually staffed by institutional employees, or an occasional concerned citizen, to accept and investigate inmate complaints and then propose solutions, as relevant, to correctional administrators.

The inmate grievance procedure is similar to the grievance board, except that inmates are selected to serve as part of the grievance committee, a procedure many correctional managers find unacceptable, because it might strengthen the influence of inmate grievance committee members over staff and other inmates.

The third alternative is the ombudsman, a public official who investigates complaints against correctional personnel, practices, policies, and customs and who is empowered to recommend corrective solutions and measures. Empowered to investigate, the ombudsman has access to files, inmates, records, and staff. The ombudsman (and office staff) tends to be impartial, have special expertise, and be independent of the correctional administrator. Reports are filed not only with the institutional manager, but also with the correctional department director and funding agent for the office of the ombudsman. At least 17 correctional systems in the nation operate with the ombudsman to protect inmates.

Mediators are relatively new on the correctional scene and represent a third party skilled in correctional work who agrees to hear differences and to render a decision to remedy the condition that would be binding on both parties. Maryland, Rhode Island, Arkansas, and South Carolina have experimented with this approach.

An inmate might file a lawsuit in conjunction with any of these alternatives. The methods are seen as promising ways to avoid litigation over correctional issues. Federal prisoners are required to seek administrative remedies before filing a civil rights lawsuit.

SOURCE: Tracey Kychelhahn and Thomas Cohen, *Civil Rights Complaints in U.S. District Courts, 1990–2006* (Washington, DC: Bureau of Justice Statistics), pp. 1, 8.

key term

Section 1983
Legal statute for seeking redress regarding deprivation of legal rights of prisoner.

Because of the relative ineffectiveness of using state and tort courts to remedy inadequate medical services and treatment in institutions, inmates have more recently begun to sue correctional administrators through **Section 1983** of the U.S. Code. This section, passed in 1871 to protect the civil rights of recently freed slaves, allows petitioners to sue in a federal court without having first exhausted all existing state courts' remedies. The federal district and circuit courts are currently deciding a number of important cases, and some of those will eventually come before the U.S. Supreme Court.

CIVIL RIGHTS ACT "1983" SUITS

Title 42, Section 1983, of the U.S. Code, commonly known as the Civil Rights Act, reads as follows:

> Every person who, under color of any statute, ordinance, regulation, custom, or usage, or any state, or territory, subjects or causes to be subjected, any citizen of the United States or other person within the jurisdiction thereof to the deprivation of any rights, privileges, or immunities secured by the Constitution and laws, shall be liable to the party injured in an action at law, suit in equity, or other proper proceedings for redress.

One example of the use of Section 1983 to redress medical malpractice and mistreatment can be seen in *Tucker* v. *Hutto*,[33] a Virginia case in which Tucker's arms and legs became permanently paralyzed as a result of improper use of antipsychotic drugs while he was a patient at the Virginia State Penitentiary Hospital. The suit was initiated by the National

Prison Project[34] and settled out of court for $518,000. Section 1983 suits can be an effective, although usually unwelcome, avenue for defining and improving prisoner rights while under confinement.

Many times the federal courts have been forced to overlook the issue of constitutional rights in order to correct situations involving a flagrant disregard of the need for adequate medical service. That disregard has often produced prison riots in the past, and it will continue to be a factor in right-to-treatment cases during the 2000s. Right to treatment is covered in detail in Chapter 19.

REMEDIES FOR VIOLATIONS OF RIGHTS

The first steps to remedy the almost standard practice of depriving convicted offenders of most rights have been taken, starting with the recognition that the Constitution does entitle those individuals to retain a substantial portion of their rights, even while incarcerated. The push for that recognition has come from the offenders themselves, often with the assistance of jailhouse lawyers, and has resulted in active and sympathetic judicial intervention.[35] The writ of habeas corpus, designed as a tool for prisoners to test the legality of their confinement, has been the main weapon in the battle for prisoner rights.[36] In 2002, the U.S. Supreme Court struck down Alabama's hitching post restraints as cruel and unusual punishment (*Hope* v. *Pelzer,* 536 U.S. 730 [2002]). The battle continues today, especially with regard to increased maintenance of community ties and the abolition of the death penalty.

The role of the federal courts in responding to inmate complaints is significant. The number of complaints filed in state and federal courts over jail and prison conditions, violations of inmate civil rights, due process violations, mistreatment, and lack of treatment of inmates has increased every year for the last two decades. Clearly, the rights of prisoners have become a driving factor in planning by administrators, legislators, and jurists in regard to operations and conditions in America's jails and prisons. Next we examine the plight of the ex-offender and the problems faced with a record that may result in a number of rights either being taken away or restored.

THE LEGEND OF THE EX-CON

The highly stylized version of the **ex-con** presented in the movies and on television usually depicts a tough, streetwise, scar-faced thug who is able to survive on wits and muscle, with a good-looking, submissive, and willing woman not too far in the background. The ex-con is often depicted as a person to be feared and never trusted. With a granite jaw and shifty eyes, he talks out of the corner of his mouth and prefers a life of crime. The real-life ex-offender, of course, is something quite different from our legendary ex-con of movie and mystery novel fame. Newly released ex-offenders found in most cities are young, with little life experience outside prison walls; they are male or female, poor, with only the funds they managed to acquire while in prison; uneducated, generally with less than a high school diploma; former illicit drug users; and frightened, most having spent several years away from a rapidly changing world. After release from prison, these individuals must start a new life and make it in the free world while being watched by the correctional authorities, local police, employers, curious neighbors using computerized offender databanks, friends, and family. They often return to the same social and environmental conditions that gave rise to their trouble in the first place. The wonder is not that so many ex-offenders recidivate—but that more do not do so. If we add to this already heavy burden the legal and administrative restrictions placed on ex-offenders, it becomes evident that the happy-go-lucky ex-con is indeed a legend invented for the reading and viewing public.[37]

lecture note

Define the Civil Rights Act (Title 42, Section 1983, U.S. Code) and identify grievances inmates file under that act. Are they usually successful?

lecture note

What changes in corrections have occurred under Section 1983 lawsuits?

lecture note

What alternatives to litigation exist for inmates? Are they largely successful?

key term

Ex-con
Formerly institutionalized offender who has now given up a life as a criminal.

class activity

Ask students to examine a notorious offender and identify characteristics reflected in coverage by the mass media.

lecture note

What stereotypes of offenders reinforce correctional ideology?

CONSEQUENCES OF A CONVICTION

Conviction for an offense carries with it the punishment imposed by statute. In addition, the convicted offender must carry several other disabilities and disqualifications that result from the conviction per se. Many state and federal statutes restrict some of the rights and privileges ordinarily available to law-abiding citizens in the nation. They include the rights to vote, to hold offices of private and public trust, to assist in parenting, to be on jury duty, to own firearms, to remain married, and to have privacy. Those and other rights may be lost upon conviction. They are collectively called **collateral consequences** of criminal conviction. Just how many citizens face collateral consequences is unknown, but a conservative estimate is that there are at least 50 million persons living in our societies who have been arrested for some offense in the nation, and at least 14 million of them have been convicted of a felony.

Even after offenders have served their sentences,[38] these secondary handicaps continue to plague them in the form of **social stigma**, loss of civil rights, and administrative and legislative restrictions. Each of those areas interacts with the others, and their overall effect is to prevent the successful reintegration of ex-offenders into the free community. The greatest dilemma faced by the ex-offender in search of a job is obvious.

Stigma

The **stigma** of a prison record is to ex-offenders like a millstone to be worn around their necks until death. Though we pride ourselves that we have mostly advanced beyond the eye-for-an-eye mentality of the past, we do not show it in the treatment of our offenders who have allegedly paid their debt to society. Aaron Nussbaum pointed out some of the problems of stigma for the discharged prisoner:

> It is a grim fact that total punishment for crime never ends with the courts or jails. None can deny that a criminal record is a life-long handicap, and its subject a "marked man" in our society. No matter how genuine the reformation, nor how sincere and complete the inner resolution to revert to lawful behavior, the criminal offender is and remains a prisoner of his past record long after the crime is expiated by the punishment fixed under the criminal codes.
>
> This traditional prejudice and distrust stalks him at every turn no matter what crime he may have committed or the nature of the punishment meted out to him. It strikes at the first offender as ruthlessly, and with as deadly effect, as upon the inveterate repeater or the professional criminal. It pursues those alike who have served time in imprisonment, of long or short duration, and those who have been merely cloaked with a criminal record in the form of a suspended sentence, a discharge on probation, or even a fine.[39]

One needs **self-efficacy** to survive in the competitive atmosphere of the free world. Thus, the diminished self-efficacy of the offender makes it difficult to bridge the gap between institutional life and the community.[40] It is the search for self-efficacy and status that leads many ex-offenders back to the circle of acquaintances that first led them afoul of the law. The personal disintegration encouraged by the fortress prisons of America makes many a discharged offender both a social and an economic cripple. We can only hope that the new techniques in corrections, designed to strengthen competencies and produce reasonable readjustment in the community, will help offset that effect, as will increased use of community corrections and intermediate punishments.

The Transition Period

Many ex-inmates, particularly those having served long sentences, face a difficult **transitional period** when released back into the communities of America, regardless of whether they are under parole supervision. Not only do they have breaks in their employ-

key term

Collateral consequences
Disabilities imposed on an offender on the basis of conviction.

key term

Social stigma
Mark of dishonor or shame.

key term

Stigma
Mark of dishonor or shame attached to a person based on how deviant the crime or criminal status and behavior.

key term

Self-efficacy
Ability of offenders to assume direction of their lives.

key term

Transitional period
Period from parole to rehabilitation and restoration of rights.

ment histories that are difficult to explain to potential employers, but also many are taken aback by the cost of food and services on the outside, especially when inflation may have doubled the cost of housing, food, and other basic commodities during a long incarceration. Because of those problems, many ex-offenders need intensive assistance from reintegration services, such as community residential centers and halfway houses.[41] In the Federal Bureau of Prisons and many state systems, large numbers of prerelease inmates in fact spend their last six months in halfway houses, where they receive training in how to fill out employment applications, how to get and hold a job, how to deal with family problems and crises, where to secure services available in their communities, how to manage money, and so on. Such services will be even more important as states decrease or eliminate parole services, while even more inmates are incarcerated and sentences are extended. The concept of charging ex-offenders fees for parole services may even further aggravate the situation.[42] It seems obvious that few will be eager or able to pay for their own parole.[43]

Loss of Civil Rights

Though most people recognize that released prisoners do not automatically regain all of their civil rights that were lost in prison, there is widespread confusion as to which rights are permanently lost and which suspended, and what machinery is available to regain them. Sol Rubin, a lawyer and writer on penology, discussed the offender's loss of the rights to vote and engage in certain kinds of employment:

> [W]hen a convicted defendant is not sentenced to commitment, but is placed on probation, and receives a suspended sentence, he should lose no civil rights. This is a recommendation of the Standard Probation and Parole Act published as long ago as 1955. It is a contradiction of the purposes of probation and parole that this view does not prevail. A California case cites the following instruction to a new parolee: "Your civil rights have been suspended. Therefore, you may not enter into any contract, marry, engage in business, or execute a contract without the restoration of such civil rights by the Adult Authority." A look at the rights restored by the Adult Authority at the time of release on parole is just as sad, hardly more than that on release he may be at large. He may rent a habitation, he is told, buy food, clothing, and transportation, and tools for a job; and he is advised that he has the benefit of rights under Workman's Compensation, Unemployment Insurance, etc.
>
> When the sentence is commitment, the principle of *Coffin* v. *Reichard* ought to apply, that a prisoner retains (or should retain) all rights of an ordinary citizen except those expressly or by necessary implication taken away by law.[44]

The issue of restoring the rights of disenfranchised felony offenders in the nation is hotly debated, led in part by the Sentencing Project.[45]

Legal Consequences of a Felony Conviction

Under federal law and the laws of many states, conviction of a felony has consequences that may continue long after a sentence has been served. For example, convicted felons may lose essential rights of citizenship, such as the rights to vote and to hold public office, and may be restricted in their ability to obtain occupational or professional licenses. Under the federal gun control laws, and under the laws of virtually all states, felons lose their firearms privileges. These and other "collateral" consequences of a felony conviction are burdens that follow from conviction, in addition to any prison sentence, probation, or fine imposed by a court. Restoration of one or more of these rights frequently can be achieved, either automatically by the passage of time or the occurrence of an event, such as completion of sentence, or through some affirmative executive or judicial act, which may be based on evidence of rehabilitation.

class activity

Ask students what collateral consequences are relevant to prevent criminal reoffending. Which are not?

class activity

Ask students if they agree with the federal firearms disability of convicted felons. If the consensus is "necessary," ask how that disability can be overcome.

lecture note

Identify the *collateral consequences* of a conviction in your state.

lecture note

Invite an ex-offender to guest lecture in your class, focusing on difficulties experienced in trying to "go straight." Have students prepare written questions on factors that helped in going straight, and those that hindered. (If you are teaching this course online, use a chat room for discussion purposes.)

lecture note

Discuss employment requirements of probation and parole status, and their relevance to avoiding criminal reoffending. What do correctional supervisors suggest to their clients about informing potential employers of their criminal record?

Although it may come as a surprise to many, state rather than federal law imposes a number of significant disabilities on conviction, even when the conviction is for a federal rather than state offense. The losses of the rights to vote, to hold state office, and to sit on a state jury are chief examples of such disabilities. Just as state law imposes a disability on a federal felon, so too a federal felon may be able to employ a state procedure to remove the disability, instead of employing the only presently available federal restoration mechanism, presidential pardon.

The Office of the Pardon Attorney in the U.S. Department of Justice conducted research on federal statutes and the principal laws of all 50 states and the District of Columbia that deal with the effect of a felony conviction on the rights to vote, to hold office, to sit as a juror, and to possess firearms. It revealed that the laws governing the same rights and privileges vary widely from state to state, making something of a national crazy-quilt of disqualifications and restoration procedures. It also showed that there were disagreements among agencies about how the law in a particular jurisdiction should be interpreted and applied. More important, the uncertain state of the law in various jurisdictions raises questions about a convicted felon's ability to determine his or her legal rights and responsibilities, which obviously can have serious consequences for affected individuals, particularly in connection with some felons' legal ability under federal law to possess firearms.

Not all states have paid consistent attention to the place of federal offenders in the state's scheme for loss and restoration of civil rights. While some state statutes expressly address federal offenses, both as to the loss of rights and as to the availability of restoration procedures, many do not. The disabilities imposed on felons under state law generally are assumed to apply with the same force whether the conviction is a state or federal one; in only a few states have particular disabilities been held not to apply to federal offenders. Similarly, state laws dealing with restoration of rights do not always address how federal felons' rights may be regained, particularly when state-law disabilities for state offenders can be removed only by a state pardon. In at least 16 states, federal offenders cannot avail themselves of the state procedure for restoring one or more of their civil rights, either because state law restores that right to state offenders only through a pardon and federal offenders are ineligible for a state pardon, or because a state procedure to restore rights to state offenders is unavailable to federal offenders.

There is considerable variation among the states as to whether loss or denial of a license or permit based on a conviction is mandatory or discretionary. Under some **occupational disability** statutes, revocation and/or denial of a license or permit are mandatory for certain offenses and/or for certain occupations. For example, revocation and denial of a teaching certificate may be mandatory for someone convicted of a drug offense or of a sex offense involving children. Nearly all states have enacted statutes requiring the registration of sex offenders.

The federal **firearms disability** on convicted felons raises particularly complex issues for state offenders because the applicability of the federal disability turns on the extent to which the state felon's "civil rights have been restored" under state law and the extent to which the restoration "expressly provides that the person may not ship, transport, possess, or receive firearms." Although federal firearms laws seem to assume that restoration of civil rights is a monolithic concept with a specific meaning, that premise is belied by practice. Federal courts have grappled with whether and to what extent the federal firearms disability applies to state felons who lost no civil rights under state law as a result of their conviction, compared to state felons who lost civil rights on conviction but who had them automatically restored by operation of state law. State felons, despite restoration of their political rights and certain firearms privileges, are still prohibited by state law from exercising other firearms privileges.

RIGHT TO WORK VERSUS NEED TO WORK

Ex-offenders are often faced with the cruel paradox that they must have employment to remain free, even though the system denies them employment because they have a record.[46] Many studies have shown that opportunity for employment is one of the most important fac-

key term
_____

Occupational disability
Offender is forbidden to practice designated occupations due to fact of conviction of crime.

key term
_____

Firearms disability
Loss of rights of ex-felons to own, possess, or exercise control over firearms.

tors in the successful reintegration of ex-offenders into the community. In the past, ex-offenders could move on to new territory and establish a new identity, thus escaping the stigmatization that goes with a prison record. On the advancing frontiers of early America, the new settlers asked few questions and judged individuals on their present actions rather than past records. But today, computers record every aspect of our lives, and privacy has become less a right than a very rare privilege. To many people, the informational expansion is a boon. To ex-offenders, it often represents a mystery and potential catastrophe. Even citizens who find themselves involved in an arrest that does not result in conviction may suffer the worst consequences of a record, including the failure to obtain a job—or loss of a current one.

There appear to be two levels where action is necessary to alleviate this crushing burden for the ex-offender. At the community level, barriers to employment that work against the poor and uneducated must be overcome; that is, more realistic educational requirements for jobs must be negotiated. (Degrees and diplomas are often used as screening devices for jobs that do not require them in order to keep out most ex-offenders.) A structural framework must be created in which the community has jobs to fill, training to give, and a willingness to offer both to inmates and ex-offenders. Those conditions can be met only by basic changes in society, not by programs for the individual. The use of ex-offenders as parole officer agents by some states is an example of such a favorable development.

At the individual level, the offender must overcome any personal handicaps. Many recent programs are aimed at the employability of the inmate and the ex-offender, often the young, the unemployed, and the unskilled (frequently also members of minority groups), who comprise the bulk of official U.S. arrest statistics. In community-based programs to help in the employment of inmates and ex-offenders, it must be assumed that the person has the capability for regular employment but is unfamiliar with and inexperienced in certain of the required behavioral skills. In other words, behavioral training, rather than therapy, is needed. It must also be assumed that if inmates learn to handle themselves in the

A skill—the ultimate rehabiliation.
Courtesy of Federal Bureau of Prisons.

Barber training program in jail.
Courtesy of Prince George's Co. Dept. of Corrections

community while under correctional control, they will be able to do so when those controls have been lifted. In planning employment assistance for inmates and ex-offenders who may need it, program planners are faced with the following questions:

- Should supportive services be provided in-house or be contracted?
- How good a job should be sought ("dead end," having job mobility, on a career ladder, etc.)?
- Who should be trained, and what kind of training should be offered?
- What kind of and how much training should be provided in the institutions? When?

To answer these questions, a comprehensive service program should include the following:

- Assessment of the client's skills and abilities
- Training in job hunting and job readiness skills and in acquiring acceptable work attitudes
- Job training and basic education, if necessary
- Job development and job placement
- Follow up with employee and employer after placement
- Other supportive services, as required (medical or legal aid)

class activity

Ask students what trades and occupations are closed to ex-offenders, and why. Do students consider these denials reasonable crime-prevention strategies?

key term

Employment restrictions
Denial of employment opportunities due to being an ex-offender.

RESTRICTED TRADES: BARRIERS TO EMPLOYMENT

Although barriers to employment still exist in general for ex-offenders, today's standards are more likely to apply to the individual and his or her offense. Ex-offenders as an identified class (or minority) are appealing more to the courts. The 1990s continued to work toward improvements in that area, especially in the removal of **employment restrictions** for ex-offenders based simply on their being ex-offenders.[47] It is only the general unemployment picture that most severely affects the ex-offender. When work is scarce for all, the ex-offender finds it more difficult to find any kind of employment. This tends to highlight the overall problem in all aspects of society that results from a criminal record. Slowly decreasing levels of crime and incarceration have brightened the picture for the present.

The National Alliance for Business and the Probation Division of the Administrative Office of the U.S. Courts operate a partnership venture designed to test a delivery system for ex-offender training services and employment. The model is designed to use existing resources, which are coordinated to attain the model's objectives. The alliance provides technical assistance to localities attempting to implement the model, and it is proving to be a promising operation.[48]

class activity

Assign students to locate the state sex offender registration system. Pick a consecutive sample of ten registrants and note the crimes and dates of crimes that resulted in the criminal registration. Submit a one-paragraph summary of those criminal acts.

lecture note

Explain registration of offenders while on community supervision, and after release into the community. What purposes does this serve?

THE PROBLEM WITH A RECORD

As we have seen, the person with a record of conviction is at a major disadvantage when trying to reintegrate into the community. The deprivation of rights and bars to employment are related to that record, and so it is vital to know what having a record means in the age of information. It seems that a record, even a record of mere contact with the criminal justice system, is extremely difficult to shed once it has been acquired. This record becomes the basis for special attention by the police and difficulty with credit agencies. Once the record has been placed in the computers, it can be retrieved when requested by an authorized agency and, inevitably, by some unauthorized agencies.

The problem with having a criminal record in this country is especially critical when an arrest does not result in a conviction. In most foreign countries, an arrest with no conviction cannot be used against the person in later actions. In the United States, in most jurisdictions, employment applications can include questions about an arrest, regardless of whether a conviction followed. Even a pardon, exonerating the suspect from guilt, does not remove the incident from the record. Not surprisingly, current attacks on this perpetual record are based on the cruel and unusual punishment clause of the Eighth Amendment.[49] Another legal approach is reflected in recent suits claiming that prisoners and ex-offenders are being discriminated against as a class, instead of being treated on the basis of individual merit: It is a truism that we find hard to accept that the protections of the Bill of Rights against police and other official abuse are for all of the criminals, the noncriminals, and us. But when we consider that perhaps as many as 50 million people have a record of arrest, it is clear that the civil rights of those who are in conflict with the law are, indeed, in the most pragmatic way, the interest of all. We are in an era of struggle for civil rights—for blacks, for Latinos, for women, for those with mental illnesses, for the young, even the delinquent young. We are well into a period of civil rights for homosexuals and others whose sexual practices are unreasonably subject to legal condemnation.

It is timely, indeed, that we awake to the excesses in punishing those in conflict with the law. It is a field of great discrimination, and must be remedied, just as much as other discriminations must be remedied. Not all people with a criminal record are vicious or degraded to begin with or, if their crime was vicious, doomed to remain as they were—unless, of course, we strive by discrimination and rejection to make them so.[50] Too often the way the public deals with ex-offenders is like driving a car by looking in the rearview mirror—eventually there will be a serious crash.

Registration of Criminals

Registration of criminals has been a practice ever since society started imprisoning individuals. In ancient times, registration was used to identify prisoners in penal servitude: Prisoners were branded or marked to decrease their already minimal chances of escape. Because penal slaves had no hope of ever being free, the markings were a sign of their permanent status. The **"yellow card"** was later used in European countries to identify former prisoners who were lucky enough to have lived through their sentences.[51] The registration of felons has also been a widespread practice in America, especially at the local level. A problem with local registration is that it tends to single out offenders for special attention from authorities to which they would not otherwise be subject. Most of those requirements are obsolete today. As information on offenders and arrested persons is placed into computer data banks, a public official can easily query the computer to check the status of almost anyone.

Registration of Ex-Offenders

The most common form of local registration concerns sex-related offenses. The **sex offender file** is used to check out former offenders in the event of similar crimes. Such a file is no doubt an asset to law enforcement, but it becomes a real problem for the ex-offender who is seriously trying to reform. Such inquiries are legitimate for law enforcement personnel; however, the discretion with which they are conducted can make a great difference to the ex-offender.

This problem was recently highlighted in the state of Washington, where legislation allows for community notification when a predatory sex criminal is about to be released and considered to be still dangerous under the state's **Community Protection Act,** passed and implemented in 1990. The release of Joseph Gallardo, a convicted sex offender, with police notification to the community under the act and the citizen anger it engendered apparently resulted in the arson of the ex-offender's home and his being badgered out of the state and, subsequently, out of a second state. No matter how one might feel about the crimes committed by such offenders, it seems clear that the practices used to notify (and often inflame) communities will almost certainly end up being challenged in the Supreme Court before this kind of behavior is ultimately approved or banned.

lecture note

Explain the tragic circumstances that gave rise to the national movement to require registration of predatory sex offenders ("Megan's law"). Who would be required to register?

lecture note

Invite a law enforcement officer working with sex crimes to guest lecture in your class on the topic of the unclosed case, and what motivations that officer can explain for keeping the cases open. Have the class prepare questions in advance about best cases resolved and worst cases still open. (If you are teaching this class online, use a chat room for discussion purposes.)

key term

Registration of criminals
Requirement imposed by government that all offenders be registered with local law enforcement agencies.

key term

"Yellow card"
European identification card, yellow in color, that signifies the carrier has been convicted of a crime.

key term

Sex offender file
Official documents containing information on a sex-offender and previous crimes.

key term

Community Protection Act
Legislation requiring offenders to register and live under public scrutiny.

The practice of registering felons seems to be matter of interest again, mainly because of the mobility of our present American society, and is now in force in all jurisdictions. The furor around the Washington State law will surely raise the issue to a level of prominence again. Registration may be much more subtle than the practice of branding with a scarlet letter,[52] but it also has the potential to become a permanent stigma.

In 1994, Megan Kanka was killed in New Jersey by a paroled sex offender who had twice been committed to prison for sex offending. His criminal history was unknown to the local community before he killed the child. Her mother led a movement to enact a sex offender and community notification law that, in conjunction with federal statutes, coalesced into a national movement to require registration of predatory sex offenders. All 50 states have now passed such laws (**Megan's Law**, named after the slain girl), and at least 47 of the states have included community notification components. Whether such laws will lead to increased public safety and whether identified offenders will be displaced to other communities are not known, and these assumptions should be continuously assessed.

Expungement as a Response

Clearly the debilitating effect of a criminal conviction is often heightened, rather than reduced, when the ex-offender returns to the free society. Some states have recognized that fact and attempted to develop **expungement** statutes, which erase the history of criminal conviction and completely restore the ex-offender's rights, thus removing the stigma of a criminal record. This idea was first developed in 1956, at the National Conference on Parole:

> The expunging of a criminal record should be authorized on a discretionary basis. The court of disposition should be empowered to expunge the record of conviction and disposition through an order by which the individual shall be deemed not to have been convicted. Such action may be taken at the point of discharge from suspended sentence, probation, or the institution upon expiration of a term of commitment. When such action is taken the civil and political rights of the offender are restored.[53]

Note that not all states restore rights at expungement; in others (such as Louisiana), a pardon remains necessary for full restoration of rights. Almost three decades ago, the American Bar Association Project on Standards for Criminal Justice made the following points regarding the need to remove the record stigma. These statements are still valid, but their general adoption has been agonizingly slow.

> Every jurisdiction should have a method by which the collateral effects of a criminal record can be avoided or mitigated following the successful completion of a term on probation and during its service.

> The Advisory Committee is not as concerned with the form which such attitudes take as it is with the principle that flexibility should be built into the system and that effective ways should be devised to mitigate the scarlet letter effect of a conviction once the offender has satisfactorily adjusted.

> Clearly, there is growing support for the principle that ex-offenders (especially those who have demonstrated they are in fact reformed) should be given a means of eliminating the brand of the felon. Though expungement is not the only answer to the problem of the burden and consequences of a criminal record, a sensible approach to the method is sorely needed.[54]

RESTORING OFFENDER'S RIGHTS

Some states restore civil rights when parole is granted; others do so when the offender is released from parole. In still others, it is necessary for a governor to restore all rights, usually through a **pardon**.[55] California's procedures for pardon illustrate the latter, as explained in the following Correctional Brief. What is required for a pardon in California?

key term

Megan's Law
Legislation requiring sexual offenders to inform local police agencies of their location and nature of their prior conviction.

key term

Expungement
Process by which a record of crime conviction is destroyed or sealed after expiration of a statutorily required period of time; also refers to the act of physically destroying information—including criminal records—in files, computers, or other depositories.

class activity

Ask students to identify five types of executive clemency and what results from those types of executive clemency.

lecture note

Explain your state's pardon procedures to the class, noting the steps the offender must initiate before possibly being pardoned.

key term

Pardon
Executive clemency restoring at least some rights to the offender.

correctional **brief**

California Pardon Procedures

California's procedures illustrate some of the steps required for a pardon. Generally, the offender must have led a crime-free existence for ten years following release from parole. The offender must initiate a petition for pardon in a superior court (also called a court of common pleas in other jurisdictions). A formal hearing is held, and the presiding judge solicits opinions from the local district attorney and chief law enforcement officer in the jurisdiction. A computer search is made for any arrests and convictions. The local probation department prepares a prepardon hearing report.

If the preponderance of evidence is favorable and no arrest or conviction record is found, the petition is approved by the superior court and is forwarded to the governor's office. The governor may then order the equivalent of a parole board (Board of Prison Terms) to prepare an investigation that would contain a recommendation for pardon. If the report is favorable, the governor may pardon the petitioner, thereby restoring to the petitioner all of the rights and immunities of an ordinary citizen. It is evident that most ex-offenders, though no doubt preferring a pardon, may favor even more having the crime and conviction put as far behind them as possible. They may also not have the perseverance to endure such an involved and expensive procedure. Finally, statistics show that almost all ex-offenders are rearrested within the ten-year time period, even if there is no further action by criminal justice system officials. No wonder so few ex-offenders seek and receive pardons!

Pardons can be full or conditional; the former generally applies to both the punishment and the guilt of the offender, and blots out the existence of guilt in the eyes of the law. It also removes an offender's disabilities and restores civil rights. The conditional pardon usually falls short of the remedies available in the full pardon, is an expression of guilt, and does not obliterate the conviction but may restore civil rights.

The U.S. Supreme Court decisions on pardons and their effects are directly contradictory, and thus state laws usually govern pardons. While pardons are not frequent in the nation at this time, it is reasonable to expect they may become more frequent as prison overcrowding becomes more critical. In 2003, Illinois Governor George Ryan pardoned four inmates he was convinced had been tortured into confessing to murder. President George W. Bush pardoned no one in 2006.

homework

Assign students to locate information on a recently executed death-row inmate, and submit a one-paragraph statement on the execution witnesses.

key term

Annulment
Judicial proceeding that nullifies, abolishes, cancels, and abrogates a judgment or former judicial proceeding.

correctional **brief**

Clemency and the President

The U.S. Constitution (Article II, Section 2) authorizes the president to grant executive clemency for federal offenses. Petitions are received and reviewed by a pardons attorney who makes recommendations. Clemency may be a reprieve, revision of a fine or penalty, commutation of a sentence, or a full pardon. A pardon, which is generally considered only after the completion of a sentence, restores all basic civil rights and may aid in the restoration of professional credentials and licenses that were lost due to the conviction. A commutation is a significant reduction in the sentence. Outcomes for clemency applications are listed on the right for the years shown.

SOURCE: Office of the Pardon Attorney, "Presidential Actions," http://www.usdoj.gov/pardon/actions_administration.htm (accessed November 18, 2008).

Executive Clemency Granted/Denied

Year	Pardons	Commutation	Denied
1980	155	11	500
1985	32	3	279
1990	0	0	289
1994	0	0	785
1998	21	0	378
2000	59	3	601
2002	0	0	1,985
2004	12	2	960
2006	39	0	1402
2008	46	2	2,695

Summary

Laws that deprive ex-offenders of civil rights are vestiges from distant times and contradict both the principles of reintegration and the purposes of correction. It seems sensible and fair that all laws depriving ex-offenders of civil rights should be abolished until and unless it is proved that the public's safety and protection require them. Doing so would advance the goals of corrections and reintegration and is more defensible than is the continuing disenfranchisement of current law-abiding persons.

Many organizations contend that when convicted felons have paid their debt to society, they should have a chance to start over with a clean record. This belief has been translated into statutes that provide for the **annulment** and expungement of criminal records in a number of states, but many of them lack adequate mechanisms to implement the provisions. These efforts seem to get derailed today by extremely violent crimes, especially those involving predatory sex offenders, that have frightened the public and inflamed them to press for tougher measures to control those who return to society with this stigma. This group of ex-offenders is small, but has a great impact on the public and the criminal justice system. The vast majority of ex-offenders (living today in almost every community in America) need to have a way to deal with the problems of never-ending stigma. Only when the general public has fully accepted the idea of a fresh start for the ex-offender will our legislators pass the revisions necessary to make the statutes fully effective.

Key Words

convicted offender, 290

court master, 290

civil death, 291

clear and present danger, 294

Black Muslims, 294

jailhouse lawyer, 295

Estelle v. *Gamble*, 296

deliberate indifference, 296

Section 1983, 298

ex-con, 299

collateral consequences, 300

social stigma, 300

stigma, 300

self-efficacy, 300

transitional period, 300

occupational disability, 302

firearms disability, 302

employment restrictions, 304

registration of criminals, 305

"yellow card," 305

sex offender file, 305

Community Protection Act, 305

Megan's Law, 306

expungement, 306

pardon, 306

annulment, 307

Review Questions

1. Discuss the collateral consequences of a conviction.
2. How could expungement improve the reintegration process for ex-offenders?
3. Why does registration of criminals have such a drastic effect on the ex-offender? What are the alternatives?
4. What will be the outcome of registration of predatory sex offenders? How do you feel about this practice?
5. Why is it important for offenders to retain their ties with the community?
6. What are the advantages and disadvantages of having a court master?
7. Explain Megan's Law.
8. What is the name of the writ that tests the legality of confinement?
9. How have the courts developed offender rights?
10. What are four alternatives to litigation that inmates might use to secure their rights?
11. What have been the impacts of the more conservative courts on the definition of inmate rights?

Endnotes

1. Lauren Glazer and Thomas Bonczar, *Probation and Parole in the United States 2006* (Washington, DC: Bureau of Justice Statistics, 2007), p. 1.

2. Harry Barnes and N. Teeters, *New Horizons in Criminology,* 3rd ed. (Englewood Cliffs, NJ: Prentice Hall, 1959), p. 505.

3. Visiting lists may be restricted, and persons who have violated visiting regulations may be removed from the lists. See *Patterson* v. *Walters,* 363 F. Supp. 486 (W.D. Pa. 1973). In addition, any person who previously attempted to help an inmate escape may be required to visit via noncontact means. See *In re Bell,* 168 Cal. Rptr. 100 (App. 1980).

4. But see the evaluation of the New York Family Reunion Program in Bonnie Carlson and Neil Cervera, *Inmates and Their Wives: Incarceration and Family Life* (Westport, CT: Greenwood, 1992); Sara Unnutia, "Words Travel," *Corrections Today* 66:2 (2004): 80–83; Taylor Dueker, "Video Visitation: A Boon at Omaha,"*American Jails* 18:5 (2004): 65–67; and Lauren Glaze and Laura Maruschak, *Parents in Prison and Their Children* (Washington, DC: Bureau of Justice Statistics, 2008).

5. Velmer Burton, Francis Cullen, and Lawrence Travis, "The Collateral Consequences of a Felony Conviction: A National Study of State Statutes,"*Federal Probation* 51 (1987): 52–60.

6. James Stephan, *Prison Rule Violators* (Washington, DC: U.S. Department of Justice, 1989); and Andrea Toepell and L. Greaves, "Experience of Abuse among Women Visiting Incarcerated Partners," *Violence Against Women* 7:1 (2001): 80–109.

7. R. W. Dumond, "The Sexual Assault of Many Inmates in Incarcerated Settings," *International Journal of the Sociology of Law* 20:2 (1992): 135–158; Victor Hassine, *Life without Parole* (New York: Oxford University Press, 2008), pp. 71–76; and Allen Beck and Paige Harrison, *Sexual Victimization in State and Federal Prisons Reported by Inmates, 2007* (Washington, DC: Bureau of Justice Statistics, 2008).

8. George Kiser, "Female Inmates and Their Families," *Federal Probation* 55:3 (1991): 56–63; Peter Breen, "Bridging the Barriers," *Corrections Today* 57:7 (1995): 98–99; and Don Thompson, "Conjugal Visits for Gays, Lesbians OK in State Prisons." *The Desert Sun* (June 2, 2008): A-3.

9. Gary Klivans, "Gang Codes: Gang Identity Theft," *American Jails* 22:4 (2008): 70–77.

10. *Palmigiano* v. *Travisono,* 317 F. Supp. 776 (D.R.I. 1970).

11. William Gilbertson, "Irked by Focus on Inmates, California Bans Interviews," *The New York Times* (December 29, 1995): A-4.

12. See the special death penalty theme issue of *Corrections Today* 55:4 (1993): 56–98; Kevin Correia, "Suicide Assessment in a Prison Environment," *Criminal Justice and Behavior* 27:5 (2000): 581–599; Elizabeth Gillespie, "Suicide Prevention in Jails," *American Jails* 19:1 (2005): 17–21; and Don Thompson, "State Works to Cut Inmate Suicides," *The Desert Sun* (May 26, 2007): A-3.

13. Some courts have upheld the restriction of communications between inmates at different institutions for security reasons. *Schlobohm* v. *U.S. Attorney General,* 479 F. Supp. 401 (M.D. Pa. 1979).

14. *Guajardo* v. *Estelle,* 580 F. 2d 748 (5th Cir. 1978). See also Joseph Bouchard and A. Winnicki, " 'You Found What in a Book? ' Contraband Control in a Prison *Library*," *Library and Archival Security* 17:1 (2002): 9–16.

15. Executive Order Number 814 for incoming mail, 814A for outgoing mail. Office of the Governor, State of Ohio, August 3, 1973.

16. *Sewell* v. *Pegelow,* 304 F. 2d 670 (4th Cir. 1962); *Banks* v. *Havener,* 234 F. Supp. 27 (E.D. Va. 1964); and *Knuckles* v. *Prasse,* 435 F. Supp. 1255 (3rd Cir. 1970). These three cases dealt with the right of Black Muslim inmates to freedom of religion. In *Knuckles* v. *Prasse,* the court of appeals held that prison officials were not required to make available to prisoners Black Muslim publications that urged defiance of prison authorities and thus threatened prison security, unless properly interpreted by a trained Muslim minister. In the *Sewell* decision, a clear instance of discrimination against a Black Muslim prisoner was brought before the court of appeals, which dismissed the case on the grounds that it properly came under the jurisdiction of the district court. In *Banks* v. *Havener,* responding to a petition under the Civil Rights Act by Black Muslim prisoners, the district court held that the antipathy of inmates and staff occasioned by the Black Muslims' belief in black supremacy was alone not sufficient to justify suppression of the practice of the Black Muslim religion. See also *Hasan Jamal Abdul Majid* v. *Henderson,* 533 F. Supp. 1257 (N.D. N.Y., March 11, 1982).

17. Although correctional personnel originally feared them, the Black Muslims are paradoxically now viewed as a source of stability among inmates. See Keith Butler, "The Muslims Are No Longer an Unknown Quality,"*Corrections Magazine* 4 (June 1978): 55–65. But see Elaine Ganley, "Manual Outlines Muslim Radicalization in Prisons," http://www.sfgate.com/cgi-bin/article.cgi?f=/n/a/10/01/international/132258D37.DTL (accessed October 1, 2008).

18. Access to a minister is a constitutional right. See *Cruz* v. *Beto,* 405 U.S. 319 (1972).

19. *Cooper* v. *Pate.* See also Rudolph Alexander, "Slamming the Federal Courthouse Door on Inmates," *Journal of Criminal Justice* 21:2 (1993): 103–116.

20. *Johnson* v. *Avery,* 393 U.S. 483, 484 (1969). Through a writ of *certiorari,* a court of appeals decision was reversed in favor of an inmate who had been disciplined for violating a prison regulation that prohibited inmates from assisting other prisoners in preparing writs. The court of appeals had reversed a

district court decision that voided the regulation because it had the effect of barring illiterate prisoners from access to general habeas corpus.

21. *Younger* v. *Gilmore,* 92 S. Ct. 250 (1971).

22. Alexander Parker and Dana Schwertfeger, "A College Library and Research Center in a Correctional Facility," *Journal of Offender Rehabilitation* 17:1/2 (1991): 167–179.

23. Gene Teirelbaum, *Inspecting a Prison Law Library* (New Albany, IN: W. Homer Press, 1989); and American Association of Law Libraries, *Correctional Facility Law Libraries: An A to Z Resource Guide* (Laurel, MD: American Correctional Association, 1991). See also Craig Hemmens, Barbara Belbot, and Katherine Bennett, *Significant Cases in Corrections* (Los Angeles, CA: Roxbury, 2004).

24. The U.S. Supreme Court has determined that death-row inmates wishing to challenge their convictions and sentences have no constitutional right to a court-appointed counsel. See Michael Mello, "Is There a Federal Constitutional Right to Counsel in Capital Post-Conviction Proceedings?" *Journal of Criminal Law and Criminology* 79 (1990): 1065–1104, for arguments in favor of such a right. The other side is addressed by Donald Zeithaml, "Sixth and Fourteenth Amendments—Constitutional Right to State Capital Collateral Appeal: The Due Process of Executing a Convict without Attorney Representation" *Journal of Criminal Law and Criminology* 80 (Winter 1990): 1123–1144. The case is *Murray* v. *Giarranto*, 109 S. Ct. 2675 (1989). See also "High Court Overturns another Death Penalty Case," *USA Today,* http://www.usatoday.com/news/Washington/2005-06-20-scotus-wrap_x.htm (accessed November 23, 2009).

25. Jennifer Gararda Brown, "Posner, Prisoners and Pragmatism," *Tulane Law Review* 66:5 (1992): 1117–1178.

26. Tracey Kychelhahn and Thomas Cohen, *Civil Rights Complaints in U.S. District Courts, 1999–2006* (Washington, DC: Bureau of Justice Statistics, 2008), p. 8.

27. Editors, "California Prison Health Czar Heads to Court," *Correctional News* 14:6 (2008): 8; and Editors, "Rising Medical Care Costs Encourage States to Release Sick, Dying Inmates," *Correctional News* 14:6 (2008): 16.

28. *Estelle* v. *Gamble,* 97 S. Ct. 285 (1976). The standard for judging the adequacy of medical treatment is the level of care offered to free people in the same locality. The prison must furnish comparable services, and inmates may collect damages for inadequate medical treatment. See *Newman* v. *Alabama,* 559 F. 2d. 283 (1977). Medical treatment in jails is generally less adequate than that in prisons. See also American College of Physicians, National Commission on Correctional Care, "The Crisis in Correctional Health Care: The Impact of the National Drug Control Strategy on Correctional Health Services," *Annals of Internal Medicine* 117:1 (1992): 71–77. Also see Kipnis Kenneth et al., "Correctional Health Care—In Critical Condition," *Corrections Today* 54:7 (1992): 92–120. Also see B. Jayne Anno, *Prison Health Care: Guidelines for the Management of an Adequate Delivery System* (Washington, DC: U.S. National Institute of Corrections, 1991).

29. Ibid. In 1995, the U.S. district court in San Francisco ruled that the California Pelican Bay Prison inflicted unconstitutional cruel and unusual punishment on prisoners. See Bill Wallace, "Pelican Bay Prison Ruled Too Harsh," *San Francisco Chronicle* (January 12, 1995): A7.

30. *United States* v. *DeColegro,* 821 F. 2d, 1st Circ., 1987.

31. Frederick Millen, "AIDS in Prison—A National Disgrace," *San Francisco Sentinel* (March 8, 1990): 7. See also Howard Messing, "AIDS in Jail," *Northern Illinois University Law Review* 11:2/3 (1991): 297–317. Especially useful is John R. Austin and Rebecca S. Trammell, "AIDS and the Criminal Justice System," *Northern Illinois University Law Review* 11:2/3 (1991): 481–527. See also Susan Jacobs, "AIDS in Correctional Facilities: Current Status of Legal Issues Critical to Policy Development," *Journal of Criminal Justice* 23:2 (1995): 209–221 and the special theme issue "Pandemic Disease: Are Jails Prepared?" *American Jails 12:3* (2008).

32. James Sterngold, "Judge Orders Takeover of State's Prison Health Care System," *San Francisco Chronicle* (June 30, 2005), p. 1. See also James Sterngold, "U.S. Seizes State Prison Health Care; Judge Cites Preventable Deaths, 'Depravity of System,'" http://sfgate.com/cgi-bin/article.cgi?f=/c/a/2005/07/01/MNGOCDHPP71.DTL&hw=prison+medicine&sn=001&sc=1000 (accessed July 1, 2005).

33. In *Tucker* v. *Hutto,* entered as a civil case under 78–0161-R, Eastern District of Virginia, the trial judge approved the out-of-court settlement on January 5, 1979, just five days before the trial was to open. See also R. Allinson, "Inmate Receives $518,000 Damage Award," *Criminal Justice Newsletter* 10 (January 15, 1979): 7.

34. The National Prison Project, American Civil Liberties Union Foundation, 1346 Connecticut Avenue, N.W., Washington, DC 20036.

35. Office of Legal Policy, *Report to the Attorney General: Federal Habeas Corpus Review of State Judgments* (Washington, DC: U.S. Department of Justice, 1988).

36. Sue Davis and Donald Songer, "The Changing Role of the United States Court of Appeals: The Flow of Litigation Revisited," *Justice System Journal* 13 (1989): 323–340.

37. Dennis Massey, Doing *Time in American Prisons: A Study of Modern Novels* (Westport, CT: Greenwood Press, 1989). See also Hassine, *Life without Parole.*

38. Gabriel Chin, "Felon Disenfranchisement and Democracy in the Late Jim Crow Era," *Ohio State University Journal of Criminal Law* 5:2 (2007): 329–340. See also Stephen Janis, "Ex-Felons Register for the Right to Vote," http://www.examiner.com/a-810882~Ex_felons_register_for_the_right_to_vote.html (accessed November 23, 2008); and Applied Research Center, "Compact for Racial Justice," http://www.sentencingproject.org/NewsDetails.aspx?NewsID=717.

39. As cited in Barnes and Teeters, *New Horizons in Criminology,* p. 544.

40. Michael Braswell, "Correctional Treatment and the Human Spirit: A Focus on Relationship," *Federal Probation* 53:2 (1989): 49–60. See also Michael T. French and Gary A. Zarkin, "Effects of Drug Abuse on Legal and Illegal Earnings," *Contemporary Policy Issues* 10:2 (1992): 98–110 (compares the impact of length of time in drug treatment and post-treatment legal and illegal earnings).

41. Ann Yurkanin, "Meeting Offenders Halfway: An Interview with J. Brian Riley," *Corrections Today* 51 (April 1989): 16–20.

42. For a parallel discussion of fees in probation, see Christopher Baird, Douglas Holien, and Audrey Bakke, *Fees for Probation Services* (Madison, WI: National Council on Crime and Delinquency, 1986); and Gordon Bazemore, "New Concepts and Alternate Practice in Community Supervision of Juvenile Offenders Rediscovering Work Experience and Competency Development," *Journal of Crime and Justice* 14:1 (1991): 27–52. See also American Probation and Parole Association, "Supervision Fees," http://www.appa-net.org/about%20appa/supervis.htm (accessed November 23, 2008); and Bucks County Adult Probation and Parole, "Supervision Fees," http://www.buckscounty.org/Courts/Criminal/AdultProbation/SupervisionFees.aspx (accessed November 22, 2008).

43. Extra-legal factors that influence parole board decisions are race and ethnicity. Black offenders spend a longer time in prison awaiting parole compared with white offenders. Hispanic men, on the other hand, are released on parole more quickly that either Black or white men. Beth Huebner and Timothy Bynum, "The Role of Race and Ethnicity in Parole Decisions," *Criminology* 46:4 (2008): 907–938.

44. Sol Rubin, "The Man with a Record: A Civil Rights Problem," *Federal Probation* (September 1971): 4. See also A. J. Klick, "Should Ex-Cons Have Their Rights Restored?" http://www.tucsoncitizen.com/daily/local/56389.php (accessed November 22, 2008).

45. The Sentencing Project (see http://www.sentencingproject.org/issues_03.cfm).

46. Kathleen Dean Moore, *Pardons: Justice, Mercy, and the Public Interest* (New York: Oxford University Press, 1989).

47. There is a potential liability in disclosing a parolee's background to a prospective employer if it results in the client not getting the job. See Rolando del Carmen and Eve Trook-White, *Liability Issues in Community Service Sanctions* (Washington, DC: U.S. Department of Justice, 1986), pp. 19–21. See also Davis E. Barlow, Melissa Hickman Barlow, and Theodore G. Chiricos, "Long Economic Cycles and the Criminal Justice System," *Crime, Law, and Social Change* 19:2 (1993): 143–169 (examines the relationship between long cycles of capitalist activity and formation of public policy on criminal justice).

48. For a discouraging note on the impact of fiscal constraints on ex-offender programs, see Danesh Yousef, "Baton Rouge Ex-Offenders' Clearinghouse: A Casualty of Misguided Savings," *International Journal of Offender Therapy and Comparative Criminology* 33 (1989): 207–214. See also Ted Chiricos, Kelle Barrick, William Bales, and Stephani Bontrager, "The Labeling of Convicted Felons and its Consequences for Recidivism," *Criminology* 45:3 (2007): 547–581.

49. "Excessive bail shall not be required, nor excessive fines imposed, nor cruel and unusual punishment inflicted."

50. Rubin, *The Man with a Record,* pp. 6–7.

51. Most European countries have required residents to carry identification cards for population control purposes. A "yellow card" (identification card of yellow color) was, in many countries, a sign of an ex-offender.

52. The scarlet letter was a scarlet "A" that the Puritans required known female adulterers to wear around the neck as a punitive mark. The practice is fully described in Nathaniel Hawthorne's novel *The Scarlet Letter.*

53. Georgetown University Law School, *The Closed Door: The Effect of a Criminal Record on Employment with State and Local Public Agencies* (Springfield, VA: National Technical Information Service, 1972), p. v.

54. American Bar Association, *Laws, Licenses and the Offender's Right to Work* (Washington, DC: ABA, 1973), p. 7.

55. For a discussion of executive clemency, see Center for Policy Research and Analysis, *Guide to Executive Clemency among American States* (Washington, DC: National Governors' Association, 1988).

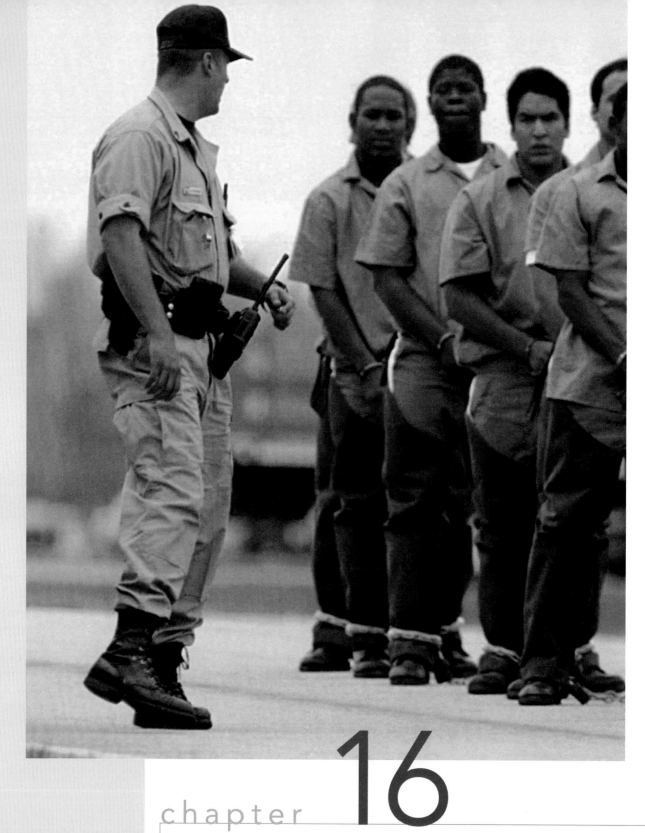

chapter 16

Male Offenders

Outline

"We know how hard it is to help prisoners become better men, and many penal authorities have given up too easily on that task. But whatever prisons do, they must not make men needlessly worse."

—John P. Conrad

Overview

In the next chapter we will acquire an understanding of the variety of female offenders who are dealt with as "clients" of the jail and prison systems of America. As we saw in Part 1, until very recently, earlier incarceration practices were not intended to "correct" the behavior of inmates. Consequently, the young and the old, the sick and the well, the women and the men, and the dangerous and the helpless were housed and placed indiscriminately in a single, all-inclusive facility. As the concepts of penitence and corrections were developed, men and women were segregated into separate institutions. Later, institutions became further specialized, with different kinds of institutions for the younger inmates, who were separated from the more hardened felons (though these groups are still sometimes hard to tell apart), and a separate system was created for juveniles (see Chapter 18).

In this chapter we examine the processes used with and conditions of men who have been convicted and sentenced to the adult prisons of America, and probably placed there following some length of exposure to the conditions of jail life. If corrections and prisons can be considered businesses, we continue our analogy by considering adult male inmate groups as clients with different needs, problems, and demands than other types of clients. Using a business analogy, we can describe corrections in all areas as a growth industry. As this chapter unfolds, you will see the crimes for which inmates are committed, problems inmates pose to staff and correctional officers, the inmate culture into which they settle, the realities of danger and death in prison, and the challenges of the aged prisoner. Inmates face widespread boredom, lack of contact with the outside world, dulling routine, and bland and frequently repetitive food. Most institutions are loud, cheerless, and (sometimes) fraught with dangers that range from sexual assault to unwarranted punishment from correctional officers to gangs, "crazies," and foes. This is the environment into which most inmates step when they are sent to prison.

This chapter deals with several questions. Who are the male prison inmates? What are their needs, and what programs should be devised to address those needs? What should we know about their backgrounds? What happens to the men in the prisons of America?

A lot of "doing time" results in dead time.
Photo by Lew Lause, courtesy of SuperStock, Inc.

PRISON POPULATIONS CONTINUE TO SOAR

Keeping track of the rapidly fluctuating adult male prison population is like trying to paint a moving bus. The number of male offenders housed in America's prisons is rising at an alarming rate, along with the total prison population. The population will rise from 883,500 in 1993 to the staggering figure of 1,500,000 in the middle of 2012. See Figure 16.1. This does not include almost 78,000 males sentenced to state prisons by the courts but who were, at the time, "holdbacks," that is, inmates being held in county jail facilities because of prison overcrowding.

Some 88% of male inmates were incarcerated in state prisons and slightly more than 12% were in federal prisons. Another 51,000 inmates were being held in other adult long-term institutions (for example, the Cook County Department of Corrections, the New York

figure 16.1

Sentenced Male Offenders: 1920–2010

SOURCE: William Sabol and Heather Coutre, *Prison Inmates at Midyear 2007* (Washington, DC: Bureau of Justice Statistics, 2008). Data for 2012 are extrapolated.

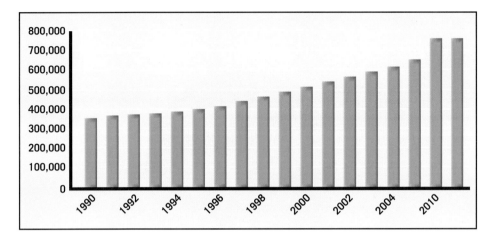

figure 16.2

Male Jail Inmates: 1990–2012

SOURCE: Bureau of Justice Statistics, Jail Populations by Age and Gender *(www.ojp.usdoj.gov/bjs/glance/ tables/jailagtab.htm, accessed October 13, 2008). Data for 2010–2012 are extrapolated.*

City Department of Corrections, and the Philadelphia Prison System). In total, there are approximately 957 male inmates in adult prisons for every 100,000 male residents in the country. Said differently, almost 1% of the adult males in the nation were in prison on a given day in 2007. (Another 529 out of 100,000 adult males are in jail on any given day, and almost nine out of every ten jail inmates are males.) See Figure 16.2.

PRISONER POPULATION

Criminal History

Male prisoners have committed a broad range of criminal acts, and at least eight in ten are recidivists. Violent offenses account for more than half (53%) of the crimes for which males were sentenced to prison, and these include homicide, manslaughter, rape, robbery, aggravated assault, sexual assault, and rape. Drug-law violations (possession, possession for sale, and trafficking) accounted for one in five sentences being served by males in state correctional facilities. All other crimes, ranging from forgery, fraud, embezzlement, theft, and motor vehicle theft to public order offenses, accounted for just one in three male inmates. See Figure 16.3.

We must remember that those sentenced and actually incarcerated in adult prisons are at the bottom of the correctional filter. As a group, men in prisons are undereducated and underemployed, primarily because of their social class and lack of opportunity. Those men are often beset with medical and psychological problems, particularly depression (see the Correctional Brief on page 317, "Characteristics of Jail Inmates"). Two-thirds are from minority **racial and ethnic groupings**, are poor, and have been unable to cope with the complexities of urban life. Almost one-third or more black men were in jails and prison in 2000 than were enrolled in all college and universities.[1] This sharply reverses the pre-1980 pattern in which black men in colleges and universities outnumbered incarcerated black men by a ratio of three to one. The number in confinement in 2000 was 791,600; the number in institutions of higher education was 603,032. Explanations of this vast disparity include law enforcement bias, selective incapacitation, saturation policing of black neighborhoods, lack of social services and employment opportunities, zero tolerance policies, and law enforcement focusing on crack (rather than cocaine) sales. Crack (primarily for cost factors) is the drug

key term

Racial and ethnic groupings Division of prisoners based on racial or ethnic characteristics.

figure 16.3

Offenses of Male Offenders
Sentenced to State Prisons, 2006

SOURCE: William Sabol, Heather
Couture and Paige Harrison, *Prisoners
in 2006* (Washington, DC: Bureau of
Justice Statistics, 2007), p. 24.

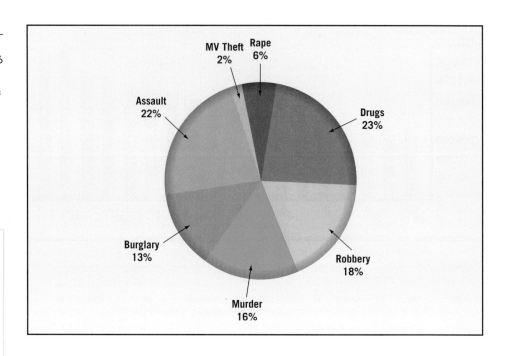

lecture note

Use the correctional filter as a
teaching tool to explain the
question of the high rate of
recidivism among male
prisoners. Note their criminal
history and social backgrounds,
and ask what programs are
designed to address their
criminogenic needs.

Dead time is also a problem
in jail.
*Photo by Dennis MacDonald, courtesy
of PhotoEdit Inc.*

lecture note

Discuss the underrepresentation
of white inmates (and females)
in prisons, and ask what factors
work to reduce the proportion
of imprisoned whites. Are those
factors present when people of
color are processed from arrest
through imprisonment?

of choice for lower-income persons, including blacks; cocaine is most frequently trafficked and used by wealthier whites. But police find that crack
sales occur on the streets and public places, are easy to videotape, and can be
more readily done with marked bills. In addition, surveillance and arresting
officers generally have a clear line of sight necessary for successful prosecution on the evidence. These latter factors contribute to building prosecutable
and convictable offenses. Approximately 17% of black males age 20 to 29
were in prisons in 2007.[2] It is also interesting to note that according to the
Government Accounting Office, in 2004, more than 49,000 foreigners were
incarcerated in state prisons, the majority from Mexico.

Recent arrivals often have limited job skills and do not know how to use
available social services in the community. Many come from broken homes
with low annual incomes, frequently have other family members who have
been convicted and incarcerated in jails and prisons, and a large number are
drug and alcohol abusers. Those characteristics suggest the number of treatment challenges faced by correctional administrators whose mandate is to
provide reasonable and effective reintegration services while protecting society from the offenders. The problems in meeting this mission are exacerbated by a hardening of public attitudes toward the male felon.[3]

Dangerousness

Adult male prisons (and almost all other detention facilities) are overcrowded to the danger
point,[4] and it is obvious that the present systems will be unable to meet the increasing demands.
Some male offenders are extremely dangerous and must be isolated from others. In the 1970s,
it was estimated that only some 15% to 25% of the male population in prison fell into this category. That situation, however, has changed; overcrowding and citizen alarm about violence in
the community have tended to force correctional administrators to find ways to release those
men considered least dangerous back into the community. This has left an increasing percentage of violent offenders smoldering in the potential tinderbox of the maximum-security prison,
as well as the creation of the supermax prison. In some states, the number of violent offenders
in maximum-security prisons who committed crimes against the person is closer to 62% and

correctional **brief**

Characteristics of Jail Inmates

There were more than 780,400 male jail inmates at midyear 2007, a majority of whom were black (39%) or Hispanic (16%), and almost 55% of whom had not been convicted. Almost half of jail inmates in 2007 were under correctional or court supervision at the time of their most recent arrest, almost a third on probation, an eighth on parole, and 7% on bail or bond. More than seven out of ten male inmates had prior sentences to probation or incarceration, over four in ten had served at least three sentences, and almost one in three were violent recidivists.

Almost seven in ten convicted male inmates reported they consumed alcohol (beer, wine, or liquor) regularly, and one in three said they had used alcohol at the time of their instant offense. When drug use and alcohol use are combined, more than half of the convicted male inmates were using drugs or alcohol (or both) at the time of the offense. In 2005, they reported life experiences they had after using alcohol and drugs, and about half said that, through use of alcohol or drugs, they had threatened their own or others' lives, had damaged relationships with other people, or had marred their personal and work histories. Nearly two-thirds confessed to driving a motor vehicle after drinking or drug use, including almost one in five who had been in a subsequent accident. Almost half had been in a physical fight after substance consumption. More than one in five had lost a job because of substance abuse. In 2002, 10% of sampled jail inmates were positive for one or more drugs consumed while in jail. More than one-third of male inmates reported they had a physical, mental, or emotional condition, or difficulty seeing, learning, hearing, or speaking. Over their lifetime, more than four in ten had developed an illness, injury, or medical condition that needed professional medical attention. A third had a medical problem in jail (such as a cold or the flu).

One in twenty had been injured in a fight or assault after admission to jail. Some one in four had at least once received treatment for a mental or emotional problem other than drug or alcohol abuse. In 2002, one in six men was defined as mentally ill, a third of the mentally ill jail inmates were alcohol dependent, and more than one in four received mental health services while in jail. The picture that emerges from the characteristics of men in jail suggests a group of "problemed" men in need of a variety of remedial and interventional programs designed to lessen their criminal activities and proclivities. They appear to be particularly in need of drug and alcohol treatment programs, including self-help groups, drug-resistance training, counseling, residential treatment programs, detoxification, antabuse treatment, or related programming. Despite widespread cynicism about enforced substance-abuse treatment, there is accelerating evidence that such treatment works in lessening recidivism.

Many of these unconvicted defendants will later be committed to prison, where they will receive mostly inadequate or insufficient treatment for their underlying conditions.

SOURCES: Darrell Gilliard, *Prison and Jail Inmates 1998* (Washington, DC: U.S. Department of Justice, 1999); Caroline Wolf Harlow, *Profile of Jail Inmates 1996* (Washington, DC: U.S. Department of Justice, 1998); Paula Ditton, *Mental Health and Treatment of Inmates and Probationers* (Washington, DC: U.S. Department of Justice, 1999); Doris Wilson, *Drug Use, Testing and Treatment in Jails* (Washington, DC: U.S. Department of Justice, 2000); Doris James, *Profile of Jail Inmates, 2002* (Washington, DC: Bureau of Justice Statistics, 2004); and Jennifer Karberg and Doris James, *Substance Dependence, Abuse, and Treatment of Jail Inmates, 2002* (Washington, DC: Bureau of Justice Statistics, 2005).

growing, as property offenders are given alternatives to incarceration. The presence of prison gangs (**institutional threat groups**) heightens anxiety, triggers lawsuits, and poses potential personal threat to other inmates.[5] Deaths of prison inmates are detailed in Figure 16.4.

key term

Institutional threat groups
Prison gangs.

Drugs and Alcohol

As stated earlier, male offenders tend to be heavy users of alcohol and drugs. In 1997, for example, almost one-third of the men in prison had been drinking at the time of their current offense and more than one-third were under the influence of drugs. That pattern has changed only in the acquisition of a broader catalog of ever more powerful **"designer" drugs,** such as methamphetamine and Ecstasy, many of which can induce violent behavior.

Tests of inmates at male adult prisons and correctional facilities continue to find ongoing drug use. Of all inmates tested, at least a percentage tested positive for cocaine and heroin. Another 2% were positive for methamphetamines, and almost 6% were positive for marijuana. These statistics indicate that drug and alcohol abuses are serious problems that continue to contribute negatively to the offenders' behavior, both in the community and in the

key term

"Designer" drugs
Analogues of controlled substances manufactured by underground chemists.

figure 16.4

Deaths of Prisoners in
Correctional Facilities, 2006

Data from: Sourcebook of Criminal
Justice Statistics Online, Deaths of
Prisoners in State Correctional
Facilities (www.albany.edu/source-
book/pdf/t600102006.pdf, accessed
October 13, 2008).

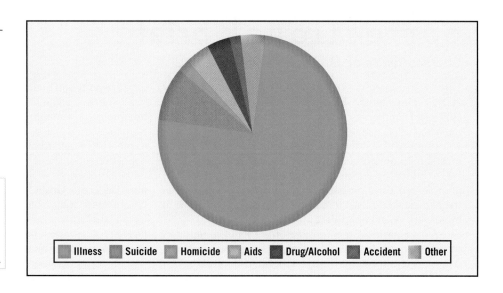

Illness   Suicide   Homicide   Aids   Drug/Alcohol   Accident   Other

lecture note

Call student attention to
Figure 16.3 and ask students to
explain the seriousness of major
crimes among male prisoners.
Then ask if drug-law violations
are as serious as Type 1 offenses.

lecture note

Explain the high rates of
preincarceration drug and
alcohol use among male
inmates, and detail how drug
use continues in confinement
facilities.

class activity

What are the functions of a
prison subculture?

institutions. In California, some 35% of incoming male inmates were convicted of drug-law violations. Drug and alcohol treatment programs both in and out of prison are no longer a luxury—they are a necessity.[6]

Education and Work

Education is an important factor in American society; it is viewed by many as an essential prerequisite for economic stability and success. In a high-tech society such as that of the United States, education is crucial for getting a job and earning an adequate income. De-

correctional **brief**

Suicide in Confinement Facilities

The number of suicides in California's jails increased dramatically in 2001 to a record high of 38, or a rate of 52 per 100,000 jail inmates. Most died of strangulation by using socks, shoelaces, or jail bedding. The California state prison rate was much lower: 21 per 100,000 prisoners. Nationally, the 2002 suicide rate in jails was 47 per 100,000 inmates, over three times the rate in state prisons.

This jail suicide rate was the highest since 1983, before wrongful death and liability suits led to jail reforms and prevention programs for potentially suicidal inmates. This may be a reflection of the number of mentally ill inmates in jail. The number of mentally ill jail inmates receiving treatment has more than doubled in the last five years.

Many first-time prisoners may become unstable in a confinement environment. The public has increasingly become intolerant of quality-of-life crimes such as aggressive panhandling ("unarmed robbery") and public drunkenness. At the same time, the number of community mental health services and treatment facilities has been drastically reduced, leaving no alternative to jail detention and punishment.

Nationally, there are between 400 and 600 jail suicides each year, about nine in ten by hanging. Suicide is the lead-

ing cause of deaths in most jails. The rate (per 100,000 inmates) is four times greater than in the community. There are almost 200 prison suicides each year, a rate that is close to that in the community. Violent offenders in both local jails (192 per 100,000 population) and state prisons (19 per 100,000 prison inmates had suicide rates over twice as high as those of nonviolent offenders. Fortunately, suicide rates in confinement facilities have been steadily decreasing, in part due to liability issues and subsequent training of correctional staff.

SOURCES: "In California's County Jails, Suicides Are up Sharply," *The Bakersfield Californian*, http://www.bakersfield.com/24hour/ healthscience/v-print/story/436652p-3494415c.html (accessed July 16, 2002); Lindsay Hayes, "Scope of a National Public Health Problem," *Preventing Suicide* 2:4 (2002): 3; Bureau of Justice Statistics, "Suicide and Homicide in State Prisons and Local Jails," http://www.ojp.usdoj.gov/bjs/abstract/shsplj.htm; and National Center on Institutions and Alternatives, "Liability for Custodial Suicide: A Look Back," http://www.ncianet.org/suicideprevention/ study.asp (accessed October 18, 2008).

spite this need for education, the most recent national survey found that one in five Americans can be considered **functionally illiterate.**[7] As a group, male state prison inmates are less educated than their counterparts in the civilian population. Sixty-three percent of the inmates have not received a high school diploma, in contrast with 36% of the general population 18 years of age or older. This sad situation may become worse if youths pass through our public school systems without being properly prepared to function with developed problem-solving skills in an urban environment. It is not too surprising that crime is often chosen as one alternative for survival under those circumstances. It is not enough that many inmates are now given a chance to earn a high school education in prison; the nation as a whole must insist that the education provided by our public school systems supplies the skills needed to keep these men out of prison.

Finally, almost one in four imprisoned men are eligible to be furloughed into an early release procedure, but fewer than half of those eligible are given the opportunity to take such a furlough. Most inmates (69%) have some kind of **institutional work assignment,** but the average pay is less than $1 per hour for their work. It is hard to motivate an incarcerated man to make a serious effort to learn a trade while he is working in prison for such low wages, when the same man has made up to $500 a day illegally in his community—and knows it can be done again.

Reasons for the Soaring Prison Populations

As will be noted in Chapter 17, the increase in female inmates in prison has been heavily impacted by the War on Drugs and violence. This is true also of male inmates. This factor was discussed in Chapter 3, in terms of a pendulum swing toward strong enforcement and the opening up of the floodgates into adult male prisons. Violent offenses accounted for 54% of the prison population increase from 1990 to 2004; drug offenses were the second largest category.[8] More than one in five male state prison inmates, and almost six of ten federal prison inmates, are serving time for a drug-law violation or drug-related crime. A decline in the prison release rate (down from 37 to 31 per 100 state prisoners) and an increase in the number of parole violators returned to prison account for most of the rest of the portion of the prison population growth.

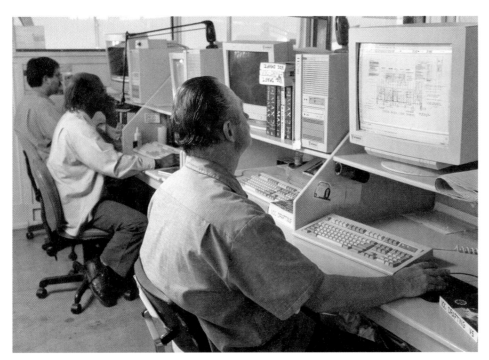

key term

Functionally illiterate
Prisoners with low-level education skills who are unable to read and follow written instructions.

key term

Institutional work assignment
Prison industry jobs based on institutional operational needs, community projects, or prison industry programs.

class activity

Ask students to explain the psychological damage of homosexual attacks on heterosexual males in prison. What do they think will happen when the victims of such attacks are returned to free society?

lecture note

Explain *prisonization* as an adaptive response to the artificial environment of the prison. What values are reinforced in the prisonization process? How can prisonization spring up in new generations of male prisoners?

lecture note

Describe the extent of sexual aggression and homosexual activities in prisons for males, and point out that the majority of the aggressors are heterosexual males who will likely revert to heterosexual behaviors when released. Why are homosexual relationships created?

Inmates learn drafting at Deuel Vocational Institution, California.
Photo by Frank Pedrick, courtesy of the Image Works.

Inmates begin the day in a crowded dormitory at a prison in the Northeast.
Photo by AP Wide World Photos.

As discussed, prison populations have sharply increased, much to the dismay of both prisoner advocates and concerned correctional administrators. There is little agreement on the exact reasons for the population boom, although some correctional personnel are quick to note that the police and courts may have become more efficient more quickly than the correctional subsystem did. Not only did law enforcement increase in efficiency, but expanded use of plea bargaining by prosecutors led to more commitments to prison. Court administration procedures were enhanced by using computers and other technology, further feeding the growth of prison populations.

Others have identified the hardening of public opinion as a factor, pointing out that judges are perceiving considerable local pressure to commit offenders rather than use other alternatives. It could be that the reaction to crime in America has exceeded the threshold of fear[9] and reached panic proportions, with widespread public clamor for commitments contributing to prison overpopulation. This is particularly probable in the drug-abuse area.[10]

It is more likely, however, that one cause is the increase in the **population at risk**,[11] those males in the age range of 18 to 29. Inasmuch as crime is a young person's occupation and considering the fact that the number of persons in the high-crime-rate ages doubled between 1965 and 1985, one would expect the factor of age to contribute heavily to the overpopulation of American prisons. The **age-at-risk** problem was made worse by a population shift over the last 15 years, during which families with young sons moved to urban areas from rural environments. The rural settings had provided more control and more wholesome outlets for young men. Historically, such population shifts—regardless of the population group in motion—meant that the second generation engaged in more frequent criminal behavior. In that case, recent population shifts coincided with an increase in the population at risk, and we can therefore expect the committed population to rise for several more years.

Three other factors have contributed to the growth in male prison populations, although the amount of effect is not yet precisely known. First, sentence enhancements were enacted by many states and include lengthening of prison sentences, enactment of three-strikes legislation (in some states mandating 20 years to be served in prison before possibility of parole release), and "prior imprisonment" statutes, mandating prison terms for any subsequent felony conviction, even if the first disposition was not incarceration.

correctional **brief**

Effect of the Baby Boom

After World War II, returning soldiers tended to marry young and begin families. The result was a large number of offspring born between 1945 and 1964, some 200% larger than would have been expected had the war not created delays in family formation and childbearing.

These large numbers of children worked their way through the school system, and the children matured, creating overcrowding first in grade school and then in high school populations. Many baby boomers entered college, creating another service-delivery crisis.

The significance of the baby boom for corrections lay in the high-crime-rate years of ages 19 to 29, when offend-

ers were most likely to commit crime. Thus, the baby boom struck the correctional system from about 1970 to 1985. Because there is a **commitment lag** (generally ten years) between early onset of criminal behavior and being sent to prison, correctional overcrowding in the late 1980s can be seen as being caused in part by World War II.

Baby boomers have themselves begun families, and there is an "echo boom" in the making that will continue to affect the criminal justice system and corrections in the first decade of the twenty-first century.

Second, Congress enacted a "truth-in-sentencing" program that provides funds for states to construct new prisons, provided the state enacts legislation requiring inmates to serve 85% of the imposed sentence. Male offenders are serving greater portions of their sentences, thus slowing the "turnover" rate.

Finally, prosecutors appear determined to focus on crimes of violence in their communities, seeking imprisonment as a sentencing outcome and stiffening plea negotiations by raising the minimum period of incarceration recommended to sentencing judges. A collateral consequence of such a strategy is that a subsequent second felony conviction, in some states, imposes a mandatory sentence of imprisonment that would be twice as long as if the offender had never been convicted.

America seems determined to resolve its crime problems with a "lock 'em up and throw away the key" philosophy.[12] Although incapacitation may be an effective way to prevent crime temporarily, helping offenders expand their opportunities and enter the mainstream of American society might be a more permanent way of lowering crime rates and the collateral national costs of incarceration.[13]

key term

Commitment lag
Avoidance of sentencing offenders to imprisonment on the first few offenses.

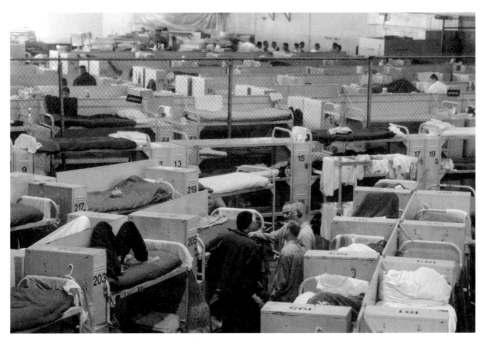

An auditorium converted into a dormitory to house prisoners at Deuel Vocational Institution, California.
Photo by Frank Pedrick, courtesy of The Image Works.

PRISONIZATION PLAYS A ROLE

Every venture intended to elevate humanity (or at least to encourage improvement) has as many unplanned and unwanted effects as it has desired effects. Efforts to give male offenders a setting in which to do penance and be "reformed" have resulted in a number of unwanted side effects, ranging from the mental and physical deterioration caused by extreme solitary confinement at Sing Sing to a more contemporary unwanted phenomenon called **prisonization.** The originator of the term, Donald Clemmer, described this process as "the taking on in greater or less degree of the folkways, mores, customs, and general culture of the penitentiary."[14] Clemmer observed that acculturation into the prison community subjects the inmate to certain influences that either breed or deepen criminal behaviors, causing the prisoner to learn the criminal ideology of the prison, that is, to become "prisonized." Prisonization is a process that includes accepting the subordinate role into which one is thrust as an inmate; developing new habits of sleeping, dressing, eating, and working; undergoing status degradation; adopting a new language; and learning that one is dependent on others (including one's fellow inmates) for the scarce pleasures found in incarceration, including food, work assignment, freedom from assault, and privileges. Students of prisonization believe this process not only leads the inmate to further identify with criminal codes, goals, and behaviors, but also serves to undercut reintegration programs and to lessen the offender's ability to adjust to society after release.[15]

Many inmates have come to develop a set of social beliefs, attitudes, and conception of destiny from experiences in their younger and formative years, as well as hearing such negative comments and orientations from peers and, to some extent, parents. They believe, for example, that a victim of theft has insurance and will not be harmed, thus devaluing and dehumanizing the victim; and that most of the people they assault were about to assault them first or owed them money and the only way to secure it was the use of physical force. Others think life owes them a living, since they never got any "breaks" when growing up. They also learn quickly to deny responsibility for their behavior, assigning responsibility to the "stupid person who tried to jack me up" and who "failed to show respect." Such offenders have poor

key term

Prisonization
The process by which the newly committed inmates (and some prison staff) are introduced into the culture of the society of captives, and learn to live within that inmate culture.

correctional brief

Inmate Slang

Male prisons are a society unto themselves, separated almost totally from the free society. Under these conditions prison slang, a form of dialect, is developed. Slang has emerged partly as an expression of community for the inmates, and also as an effort to confuse the correctional staff. We include some examples of inmate slang terminology, which may or may not be in use in every institution:

- The barn: a large open dorm
- Box: radio
- Brown shirt: correctional officer
- Dead man walking: inmate on way to execution
- Fire in the hole: correctional officer approaching
- Hack: guard
- Duck: a new guard
- Fish: a new inmate

- Home boy: someone from the same city
- One time: stash the drugs, guard on floor
- The man: usually the warden, can be a captain
- Pack the rabbit: hide object in rectum
- Shank: homemade knife
- Snitch: informant
- Stinger: homemade electric apparatus for heating water
- Tailor-mades: factory-made cigarettes
- Thump: to fight
- Keester it: hide object in rectum
- Pruno: homemade alcohol
- Range queen: inmate who takes woman's role

self-control, are often self-centered, and possess distorted perceptions of the world. Most have almost no skills in management of aggression and lack appropriate assertiveness. They have low victim empathy, little impulse control, and undertake behavior that sets themselves up in a high-risk situation. These are cognitive beliefs that assure the offender that criminal behavior makes sense. In some ways, no amount of boot camp programming will remove this socially disruptive behavior or dissolve this negative approach, address cognitive defects, or erase poor parenting. This treatment approach (cognitive skill building) has been repeatedly shown to significantly reduce criminal reoffending. The point here is that prisonization is a ubiquitous process and mechanism of reinforcing antisocial patterns of reasoning.

The phenomenon of prisonization appears to exist in all prisons, not just the large gothic bastions that testify to archaic prison philosophies. Former inmates can bring it into the prison, but even in new prisons that receive first-time offenders, the inmates' pains of imprisonment can generate the prisonization process.

Because prisonization occurs in every institution, although to varying degrees, it is necessary to understand the benefits that accrue to the men who adhere to the inmate codes. The future correctional administrator must also understand the pains of imprisonment that encourage socialization into the inmate subculture. Those pains are status deprivation, sexual deprivation, material deprivation, and enforced intimacy with other and more dangerous offenders.

If the institutional administrator and staff emphasize individual and group treatment rather than custody and discipline, if a pattern of cooperation can be developed between informal inmate leaders and institutional authorities, if a medium or minimum custody level can be achieved, and if violators of rules governing the use of force by the correctional staff are consistently reprimanded, then the prison culture and the prisonization process can be markedly reduced. Some researchers have suggested that shorter prison terms tend to undercut the power of the prison culture, because inmates can and do participate in "anticipatory socialization" as they near the end of their prison sentences and begin to prepare for their participation in the activities of the free world. It thus is reasonable to assume that short, fixed periods of incarceration would help reduce the negative effects of prisonization.

Los Angeles Sheriff's deputies escort mentally ill patients to a new facility.
Photo by AP Wide World Photos.

Rape and Sexual Assault in All-Male Institutions

In 2003, President Bush signed the Prison Rape Elimination Act, the first U.S. government law passed to deal with sexual assault behind bars. The law calls for the gathering of national statistics about the problem, the development of guidelines for states about how to address prisoner rape, the creation of a review panel to hold annual hearings, and the provision of grants to states to combat the problem. Estimates are that one in five men in prison has been sexually abused, often by other inmates. Rates for women, who are most likely to be abused by male staff, reach as high as one in four in some facilities.

In a detailed study of aggression among men behind prison walls, Anthony Scacco boasted that sex is a vehicle for exploitation rather than an expression of pathological personality or situational frustration.[16] The sexual assaults that occur within prisons and jails cannot be categorized solely as **homosexual attacks;**[17] rather they are often assaults made by heterosexually oriented males for political reasons—that is, to show power and dominance over other human beings. It is a depressing fact that victimization, degradation, racism, and humiliation of victims are the foremost reasons that sexual assaults are perpetrated on men in this setting. As Victor Hassine, himself an inmate, notes:

key term

Homosexual attacks
Sexual assaults on potential victim inmates, usually by heterosexual prisoners.

> Gang bangers often rely on rape in prison to generate fear and to maintain power over the general population. While street gangs use gunplay and murder to gain power, prison gangs use the threat of rape to dominate inmates and to ensure the repayment of even small debts. Some prison gangs require new inmates to commit rape as a gang initiation ritual. The act of raping another inmate is viewed as a way for gang members to demonstrate courage, strength, and cunning.[18]

In institutions for only male felons, homosexual behavior between consenting adults has been a recurrent phenomenon, as in other such unisexual settings as naval ships and religious monasteries. It is unreasonable to expect inmates to abandon sexual behavior in prison, particularly when they face increasingly long sentences. As Peter Buffum noted,

> [The present pattern of homosexuality in prisons] means that as long as the prison is an environment, which is largely devoid of situations where legitimate affectional ties can be established, there will be a tendency for the formation of homosexual relationships, especially among those persons serving long sentences who have concomitantly lost contact with meaningful persons in the free community. If in addition the prison does not allow legitimate attempts of the inmates to control their own lives and does not give an opportunity for expressions of masculinity and self-assertion that are meaningful among men at this social level, there will be homosexual relationships created to fulfill this need.[19]

Especially among younger inmates and those who accept passive roles, homosexual behaviors and relationships could impair future commitments to heterosexuality as well as create exploitative situations. When such relationships create jealousy among inmates, the potential for serious violence and administrative problems increases. If a third inmate becomes involved in a dyadic relationship or there is a transfer of affection, extreme violence can occur. The once frequent pattern of transferring the passive partner to another institution is no longer an adequate or constitutional response by prison management. Segregating passive partners may cause the active inmates to coerce others into sexual behavior, as well as to raise legal issues of inmate rights and to create the potential for lawsuits arising from such isolation.

key term

Family (conjugal) visits
Prison program designed to reinforce family ties through unsupervised contact, usually between husband and wife.

Prison administrators will need to consider and implement home visits at known intervals for those under long sentences, as well as provide activities and programs that will attack the real problems. At the beginning of 2005, however, only six states reported permitting inmates to have **family (conjugal) visits.** This allowed inmates to have some control over their own lives and maintain affectionate relationships and stable interpersonal interaction. Encouraging correspondence with and visits from relatives and family helps reduce the pains of imprisonment and help family reunification. Conjugal visits are programs in California, Connecticut, Mississippi, New Mexico, New York, and Washington.

THE GRAYING OF AMERICA'S MALE PRISONERS

The proportion of prisoners in the nation's institutions who are elderly is rapidly increasing, in part due to the tougher long-term sentences inherent in the current "get-tough-on-crime" stance, but also in part due to the aging of the general population in America. It has been estimated that by the year 2012, at least one in ten (about 125,000 inmates) will be age 50 or over. There were more than 76,000 prisoners ages 55 and older in all prison institutions in the nation in 2007.

The growth rate of "geriatric inmates" (age 50 or above) in Florida already exceeds the growth rate of younger offenders; in California, over 8,300 men are serving sentences of 25 years to life for conviction of a "third-strike" felony.[20]

Elderly inmates are *more* likely than other prisoners to have committed crimes such as homicide and manslaughter, as well as sexual offenses. They are *less likely* than other inmates to be imprisoned for robbery and burglary. Because of their significantly longer sentences, elderly inmates may be concentrated in prisons well beyond their proportions in the civilian population, which will pose problems for them as well as prison administrators.

First, they will have health care concerns and need preventive health care programs that, if not provided, could be a source of considerable and, for correctional administrators, substantial litigation costs. At the least, they will suffer from depression and differing nutritional needs (less protein, fewer calories, and more soft food and fiber). Because taste sensations decline with aging, the elderly will request food richer in seasonings and will have a decrease in gastric acid and increase in gas production and constipation.

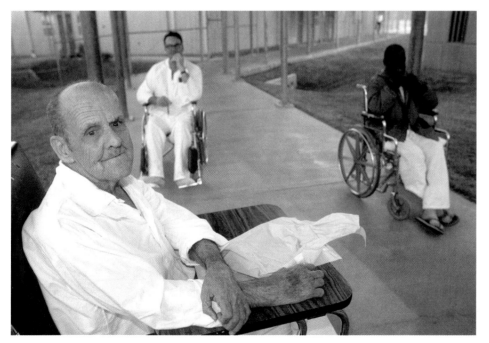

A geriatric unit in Estelle Prison, Texas.
Photo by Andrew Lichtenstein, courtesy of The Image Works.

A psychiatrist begins his day at the Pelican Bay Supermax Prison in northwest California.
Photo by AP Wide World Photos.

In addition, growing old in prison will mean having to avoid exploitation and violence by younger inmates,[21] having to adjust new personal needs to prison life, and not having suitable programs (recreational, educational, or housing). Vulnerability to victimization, frailty, and isolation from outside relatives and friends will take their toll, as will fear of death, hopelessness, and being unable to cope when released.

Health care costs will increase significantly as a result of treatment for hypertension, diabetes, stroke, cancer, and emphysema. Glasses, dentures, kidney dialysis, and heart surgery will be required. In 2001 the medical costs for prisoners exceeded $3.8 billion, and it has been estimated that by the year 2012, health care costs for elderly inmates will increase 14-fold.[22] Many prisons will become **geriatric centers**,[23] and special staff and staff training will be necessary to treat this special problem segment of the nation's offenders. Perhaps a nation that can explore outer space can find the necessary compassion to care for that small but increasing group during this decade of the new century. Executive clemency, including pardons, may once again become a frequent act as government struggles with the problems of elderly inmates.

Summary

Male offenders in prison are increasing in number as well as age. It is evident that such changes will continue to have significant impacts on prison management, programs, and costs. Corrections will be tasked with doing more, but with fewer resources than are needed. This will in turn pose management issues for correctional administrators.

It is likely that the next decade will see efforts to expand custody technology within maximum-security institutions, as well as lower the potential for assault on staff and inmates. Rape of male inmates by other men will continue to be a challenge, probably due to court decisions on liabilities of correctional managers for inattention to sexual aggression.

Another challenge corrections will face is the development of geriatric programs if not centers within a state's correctional facilities. Some states may opt to aggregate elderly inmates into one or more facilities or cellblocks. Others may decide to implement humanitarian release by extending the limits of confinement to include placement of geriatric inmates in community corrections. Many of these policy changes will be driven in part by consideration of expenses associated with incarcerating large numbers of offenders in general, and geriatric offenders in particular.

Male offenders will continue to crowd existing prisons that will be overcrowded to the extreme. Much remains to be done to resolve the underlying issues and problems.

Key Words

Review Questions

1. Why have prison populations increased recently? What short-term effects will result from that increase?
2. What is meant by the "population at risk"? How does it contribute to the population problem in male prisons?
3. Explain the dynamics of rape in a male prison.
4. What factors contribute to prisonization?
5. What can be done to reduce homosexuality in prisons?
6. How should male inmates be sentenced?
7. Why are so many prisoners members of minority groups?
8. What problems do elderly inmates pose or face?
9. How can corrections address the problems of elderly offenders?
10. What impacts do street and prison gangs have on prison management?
11. Debate: Offenders should be released to community control when they reach age 70.

Endnotes

1. Fox Butterfield, "More Black Men Are in Jail than in College," *Cincinnati Inquirer* (August 28, 2002): A4. See also Marc Mauer and Ryan King, *Schools and Prisons Fifty Years after Brown* v. *Board of Education* (Washington, DC: The Sentencing Project, 2004); and Marc Mauer, "Racial Fairness Gaining Ground in the Justice System," http://www.baltimoresun.com/news/opinion/oped/bal-op.racial30jul30,0,4407252 (accessed October 17, 2008).
2. William Sabol and Heather Couture, *Prison Inmates at Midyear 2007* (Washington, DC: Bureau of Justice Statistics, 2008), p. 22.
3. Timothy Hart, "Causes and Consequences of Crime and Violence," *American Journal of Criminal Justice* 23:1 (1998): 131–143; and Tomislav Kovandzic, "The Impact of Florida's Habitual Offender Law on Crime," *Criminology* 39:1 (2001): 179–203.
4. Prison administrators argue that reserve capacity is needed to operate a prison effectively. Prison dormitories and cells need to be repaired and maintained periodically. Additional space may be needed for emergencies. Special housing (such as protective custody and punitive segregation) and administrative units (such as prison recreation, intake, and program space) are required. The federal prison system is running at 137% of capacity, and 21 states are over at least their lowest capacity, some (such as California) by as much as 206% of capacity. (Sabol and Couture, *Prisoners at Midyear 2007*, p. 21).
5. Dan Eckhart, "Civil Actions Related to Prison Gangs," *Corrections Management Quarterly* 5:1 (2001): 9–64. See also Frank Marcell, "Security Threat Group Effect on Corrections during the Past Decade," *Corrections Today* 68:2 (2006): 56–59.
6. Caroline Wolf Beck, *Drug Enforcement and Treatment in Prison, 1990* (Washington, DC: U.S. Department of Justice, 1992). See also Henry Wexler, "The Success of Therapeutic Communities for Substance Abuse in American Prisons," *The Prison Journal* 75:1 (1995): 57–66; Dorothy Lockwood, J. McCorkle, and J. Inciardi, "Developing Comprehensive Prison-Based Therapeutic Community Treatment for Women," *Drugs and Society* 13:1/2 (1998): 193–212; and Michael Pendergast et al., "Reducing Substance Abuse in Prisons," *The Prison Journal* 84:2 (2004): 265–280.
7. Charles Bailey, "Prison Populations Surging, and Not Just Because of the Nation's Economic Slowdown," *Corrections Digest* 7:2 (1976): 9. See also Miriam Williford, *A Contradiction in Terms?* (Phoenix, AZ: Oryx Press, 1994); and Elliott Currie, *Crime and Punishment in America: Why the Solutions to America's Most Stubborn Social Crisis Have Not Worked—And What Will* (New York: Metropolitan Books, 1998).
8. Sobol and Couture, *Prison Inmates at Midyear 2007*, p. 7.

9. Ron Akers et al., "Fear of Crime and Victimization among the Elderly in Different Types of Communities," *Criminology* 25:4 (1987): 487–505. See also Ronet Bachman, *Elderly Victims* (Washington, DC: U.S. Department of Justice, 1992); Steven Donziger, *The Real War on Crime* (New York: HarperCollins, 1996); and Matthew Yeger, "Ideology and Dangerousness: The Case of Lisa Colleen Neve," *Critical Criminology* 9:1/2 (2000): 9–21.

10. Donziger, *The Real War,* pp. 99–129; Richard McCorkle and T. Miethe, "The Political and Organizational Response to Gangs: An Evaluation of a 'Moral Panic' in Nevada," *Justice Quarterly* 15:1 (1998): 41–64; and Scott Paguting, Greg Noble, and Paul Tabar, "Middle Eastern Appearances: Ethnic Group, Moral Panic and Media Framing," *Australian and New Zealand Journal of Criminology* 34:1 (2001): 67–90.

11. Rob Wilson, "U.S. Prison Population Sets Another Record," *Corrections Magazine* 4:2 (1980): 5; Currie, *Crime and Punishment.* But see Grant Stitt, Donia Giascopassi, and Mark Nichols, "The Effect of Casino Gambling on Crime in New Casino Jurisdictions," *Journal of Crime and Justice* 23:1 (2000): 1–23.

12. A term developed in the 1930s. See also Joan Petersilia, "California's Prison Policy: Causes, Costs, and Consequences," *The Prison Journal* 72:1/2 (1992): 8–36; and Theodore Sasson, *Crime Talk: How Citizens Construct a Social Problem* (Hawthorne, NY: Aldine, 1995).

13. See Curie, *Crime and Punishment;* and John Donahue and P. Siegelman, "Allocating Resources among Prisons and Social Programs in the Battle against Crime," *Journal of Legal Studies* 27:1 (1998): 1–43.

14. Donald Clemmer, *The Prison Community* (New York: Rinehart, 1940), p. 8. See also Barbara Peat and T. Winfree, "Reducing the Intra-Institutional Effects of 'Prisonization': A Study of a Therapeutic Community for Drug-Using Inmates," *Criminal Justice Behavior* 19:2 (1992): 206–225; Hans Toch, "Inmate Involvement in Prison Governance," *Federal Probation* 59:2 (1995): 34–39; and Darren Lawson, C. Segrin, and T. Ward, "The Relationship between Prisonization and Social Skills among Prison Inmates," *The Prison Journal* 76:3 (1996): 293–301.

15. Kenneth Adams, "Adjusting to Prison Life," in Michael Tonry (ed.), *Crime and Justice: A Review of Research* (Chicago: University of Chicago Press, 1993), pp. 275–359; and Paula Faulkner and W. Faulkner, "Effects of Organizational Change on Inmate Status and the Inmate Code of Conduct," *Journal of Crime and Justice* 20:1 (1997): 55–72.

16. Anthony Scacco, *Rape in Prison* (Springfield, IL: Chas. C. Thomas, 1975); Michael Scarce, *Male on Male Rape* (New York: Plenum, 1997); Thomas Fagan, D. Wennerstrom, and J. Miller, "Sexual Assault of Male Inmates," *Journal of Correctional Health Care* 3:1 (1996): 49–65; and Christine Saum, H. Surratt, and J. Inciardi, "Sex in Prison: Exploring the Myth and Realities," *The Prison Journal* 75:4 (1995): 413–430. But see Richard Tewksbury, "Measures of Sexual Behavior in an Ohio Prison," *Sociology and Social Research* 74:1 (1989): 34–39; Richard Tewksbury and Elizabeth Mustaine," Lifestyle Factors Associated with the Sexual Assault of Men," *Journal of Men's Studies* 9:2 (2001): 23–42; and Christopher Hensley and Richard Tewksbury, "Wardens' Perceptions of Inmate Fear of Sexual Assault," *The Prison Journal* 85:2 (2005): 198–203.

17. Helen Eigenberg, "Homosexuality in Male Prisons: Demonstrating the Need for a Social Constructionist Approach," *Criminal Justice Review* 17:2 (1992): 219–234. See also Genesis 19: 1–9, in which non-gay men planned to sexually assault angels. The "Sodomites" are heterosexual men with a hatred of outsiders, and who intend to violate cultural mores by attacking the angels. The "sin" is breaking the hospitality rules.

18. Victor Hassine, *Life without Parole* (New York: Oxford University Press, 2008), p. 138.

19. Peter Buffum, *Homosexuality in Prisons* (Washington, DC: U.S. Government Printing Office, 1972), p. 28. See also James Stephan, *Prison Rule Violators* (Washington, DC: Bureau of Justice Statistics, 1989); David Hallpren, "Sexual Assault of New South Wales Prisoners," *Current Issues in Criminal Justice* 6:3 (1995): 327–334; and Saum et al., "Sex in Prison."

20. Harry E. Allen and Bruce S. Ponder, "Three Strikes Legislation and Racial Disparity in California: 1994–2001." Paper presented at the Annual Meeting of the Academy of Criminal Justice Sciences, Anaheim, CA, March 8, 2002; and California Department of Corrections, "Second and Third Strike Felons in the Adult Institution Population," http://www.cdcr.ca.gov/Reports_Research/Offender_Information_Services_Branch/Quarterly/Strike1Archive.html (accessed October 17, 2008).

21. Richard Dagger, "The Graying of America's Prisons," *Corrections Today* 50:3 (1988): 26–34; and Ronald Day, "Golden Years behind Bars," *Federal Probation* 58:2 (1994): 47–54.

22. American Correctional Association, *2005 Directory* (Lanham, MD: ACA, 2005), p. 22. See also Sarah Bradley, "Graying of Inmate Population Spurs Corrections Challenges," *On the Line* 13:2 (March 1990): 5. The average costs for imprisoning elderly inmates is high because they suffer from an average of three chronic illnesses during their incarceration. In New York, these costs range from $50,000 to $75,000 a

year. Rozann Greco, "The Future of Aging in New York State," http://aging.state.ny.us/explore/project2015/briefs04.htm (accessed February 16, 2005).

23. Gennaro Vito and D. Wilson, "Forgotten People: Elderly Inmates," *Federal Probation* 49:2 (1985): 18–24; Deborah Wilson and G. Vito, "Long-Term Inmates: Special Need and Management Considerations," *Federal Probation* 52:3 (1988): 21–26. At least 22 states already have special geriatric prison wings or housing units for their older inmates. See also Todd Edwards, *The Aging Inmate Population* (Atlanta, GA: Council of State Governments, 1998); and Project for Older Prisoners, California Department of Corrections, "A Look at Other States' Program for Older Inmates," http://www.sfgate.com/cgi-bin/article.cgi?file=/news/archive/2003/02/25/state2034EST0156.DTL (accessed December 16, 2004).

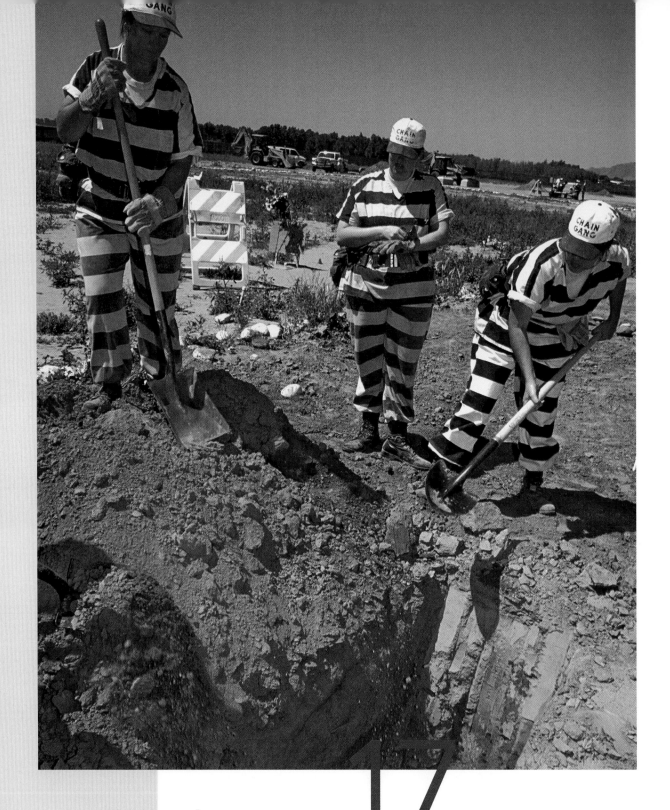

chapter 17

Female Offenders

Outline

"Females tend to commit survival crimes, fed by a drug-dependent life, and escape brutalizing conditions and relationships."

—Barbara Owen

Overview

Although male offenders (Chapter 16) do provide the lion's share of adult prisoners (92%), the female inmate population is increasing at a higher annual rate of growth: 4.8% to 2.7% in 2006. In this chapter we examine that phenomenon, as well as those similar processes and conditions with which females must contend. We look at the kinds of women and the crimes that place them in state, federal, and other adult female prisons and correctional institutions. You will find that many female offenders are moving away from "woman crime" and becoming more mainstream in their criminal behaviors and levels of violence, posing new challenges to old approaches.

To compare the relative levels of incarceration between female and male prisoners, we first examine the crime rates for both categories and look at the differing patterns of conviction and sentencing rates for those crimes. The "steel ceiling" that has traditionally tended to divert females from long-term incarceration in correctional facilities into community mental health and correctional alternatives seems to have cracked somewhat recently; different trends are emerging for female prisoners. The student is presented with information about problems specific to female offenders that may cause them to need special treatment. What happens to female offenders in the prisons of America?

lecture note

Using your computer, play the brief chapter overview videotape by Edward Latessa on "Female Offenders" that introduces Chapter 17 (approximately 4 minutes).

lecture note

Describe the changing patterns of arrest rates for female offenders, and note the frequency of arrests for drug-law violations. What implications do these patterns have for female offenders on the county and state corrections levels?

class activity

Ask students to describe the rate of incarceration of female offenders over the last 20 years, and explain the changes.

key term

Arrests by gender
Comparison of arrest data between male and female offenders.

key term

Preferential treatment
Argument that female offenders receive more lenient treatment at all phases of the criminal justice system.

FEMALE CRIME AND INCARCERATION RATES

As shown by Figure 17.1, the number of female prisoners in adult facilities will continue to grow rapidly, reaching a predictable all-time high of 140,500 in 2012, excluding the approximately 3,600 holdbacks still in jail due to lack of space in state, federal, and other institutions. Although this grand total represents just less than 8% of the U.S. prison population overall, it is a significant and worrisome trend. Although the total number of male prisoners has grown by more than 48% since 1995, the number of female prisoners grew by nearly 64%, continuing a long trend of higher rate of growth for female inmates. They constitute almost 13% of the jail population on a given day.[1] See Figure 17.1. To get a better understanding of just who these prisoners are and why the rate and numbers are increasing, one has to look closer at the kinds of crimes, regionally and nationally, being committed by females.

The period from 1970 through the 1990s included the years when women's equality and civil rights were asserted, if not established, on almost every front.[2] Yet only recently has there been a movement to push for the rights of female prisoners in corrections. In a way, females still receive differential, sometimes even preferential, treatment at almost every station of the criminal justice system, partly in deference to traditional female gender roles (except in the area of drug arrests).[3] We now examine the more common kinds of Crime Index (see Chapter 4) offenses committed by females, and compare some of the dispositions to institutions for females in a rapidly changing environment.

Although the criminal statistics contained in the FBI's Uniform Crime Reports are somewhat limited and "soft," especially for crimes involving females, they are the best available and can at least be accepted as indicators of trends.[4]

A comparison of total **arrests by gender** in 2003 for the eight major (index) crimes can be found in Table 17.1. Two major conclusions are evident from examination of these data. First, females were arrested for 23% of all crimes. Second, they represent a large portion (29%) of persons arrested for larceny-theft, which accounts for a whopping 71% of all index arrests for females. The eight index crimes do not include drug offenses. As Figure 17.2 illustrates, women are arrested almost three times more frequently for drug offenses than for crimes of violence.[5] The most serious crime for which females are arrested can be seen in Figure 17.3.

These figures clearly indicate the growing role of the female offender in the entire criminal justice system. As we note later, **preferential treatment** of females seems to be disappearing for those females arrested for nontraditional crimes (crimes of violence and crimes

figure 17.1

Female Prisoners in State and Federal Prisons, and Local Jails 1983–2012

SOURCE: Bureau of Justice Statistics, Demographic Trends in Jail Populations (www.ojp.usdoj.gov/bjs/glance/tables/jailagtab.htm, accessed February 25, 2008); and William Sabol and Paige Harrison, *Prison and Jail Inmates at Midyear 2006* (Washington, DC: BJS, 2007): 5. Data for 2007 and 2012 are extrapolated.

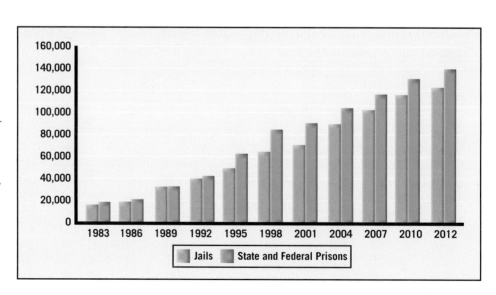

table **17.1**	Arrests of Females by Type of Part I Crime, 2006			
Offense Charged	Total	Female Crimes	Female Percentage	Female Distribution
Total: All Crimes	904,406	355,083	38.2%	100.0%
Murder and nonnegligent manslaughter	6,677	838	12.6	.002
Forcible rape	13,945	182	.013	.001
Robbery	62,687	7,974	12.7	.023
Aggravated assault	207,009	54,031	26.1	16.2
Burglary	204,761	27,327	13.3	7.7
Larceny-theft	817,048	240,312	29.4	70.6
Motor vehicle theft	106,221	12,836	12.1	3.7
Arson	11,330	1,583	14.0	.005
Violent crime	290,318	63,025	21.7	17.7
Property crime	614,088	292,058	47.2	82.3
Crime Index Total	904,406	355,083	22.8	NA

SOURCE: Federal Bureau of Investigation, *Crime in the United States 2006* (Washington, DC: U.S. Department of Justice, 2007), p. 33.

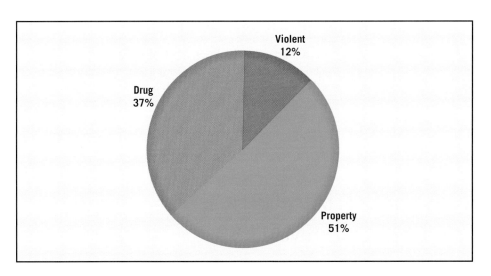

figure 17.2

Arrests of Females by Type of Crime, 2006

SOURCE: Federal Bureau of Investigation, *Crime in the United States 2006* (http://www.fbi.gov/ucr/cius2006/data/table_33.html,) *accessed February 25, 2008).*

committed with one or more other female offenders). We may have to take a new look at the **"traditional" female crimes** as we continue to examine the "new" female offender of the twenty-first century.

The general increase in female criminality may also be seen as reflecting the changing patterns of criminal opportunity for females. It is interesting that arrests for prostitution, the crime Freda Adler calls "the oldest and newest profession,"[6] decreased 22% between 1997 and 2006.[7] Whether this decrease relates to more jobs and better jobs for females, the growth of AIDS awareness, or a changing moral climate we leave for others to determine.[8]

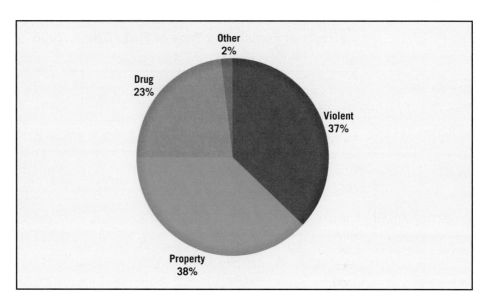

figure 17.3

Most Serious Crime Committed by Female Prisoners, 2012

SOURCE: William Sabol, Heather Couture, and Paige Harrison, *Prisoners in 2006 (Washington, DC: Bureau of Justice Statistics, 2008): 24. Data for 2012 are extrapolated.*

The arrest figures for prostitution, however, are only the tip of the iceberg. Because prostitution is one of the so-called **"victimless" crimes,**[9] and clients seldom complain because they would be implicating themselves, the number of arrests for prostitution usually reflects only cases of flagrant solicitation, rampant disease, or a local cleanup campaign.[10] Considerable folklore surrounds prostitution, most of it with no basis in fact. Those who profit from prostitution (almost never the prostitutes themselves) are not about to compile statistics or seek publicity. It is a business that thrives on sexual appetite, with the ultimate motive being simple profit.

A DIFFERENTIAL JUSTICE SYSTEM FOR FEMALES?

The previous scarcity of research in the area of female equality in general, and the role of females in the criminal justice system in particular, makes this area the current gold mine for researchers and writers.[11] It is unfortunate that much of the earlier literature was a warmed-over version of the old myths and inaccuracies of the 1940s and 1950s.

The first point at which the female offender comes into contact with the criminal justice system is the point of arrest. Although arrest may be a traumatic experience for the male offender, it has special problems for the female. It is estimated that 80% of the female offenders in America have dependent children at home, and that a percentage of those children have no one else to care for them.[12] About 80,000 females in jails and prisons have an estimated 200,000 children under age 18.[13] Concern for the children and a tendency among officers to identify female offenders with their own mothers or sisters may cause arresting officers to use more discretion than they might with a male in the same situation. A recognition of the need to provide more pretrial services for female offenders has prompted many communities to develop volunteer programs to assist with the female problems at home. It is important to remember that the children of female offenders often are placed with relatives or foster parents, or become residents of juvenile institutions as a result of their mothers' actions. To the juveniles who are removed from the community and placed in what they perceive as a facility for other juveniles who have committed offenses, it becomes hard to accept that protection, not punishment, is the state's motivation (see Chapter 18). The incoming pregnant female resident whose child is removed from her care at or immediately following birth may find it hard to believe that her child will grow up without bonding with her.

An officer's reluctance to arrest females for traditional crimes is also the result of age-old customs, mores, and laws that have created great distinctions between men and women under apprehension.[14] Although police officers seldom hesitate to place a male offender "up against the wall" and to respond to force with equal force, they often loathe doing so with a female. Most police departments have strict rules and regulations regarding the apprehension, search, and detention of females. In most cases, a female officer or matron is assigned to detain females and conduct searches of their persons.

The female offender seldom spends much time in detention before trial. Concern for the family and the lack of adequate female detention facilities or female personnel in the police department almost demand pretrial release for females.[15] Until quite recently, female offenders also usually committed less serious offenses and could therefore be released on bail or on their own recognizance. Beginning in the 1980s, however, females have been committing more serious crimes and, perhaps owing to the move to equalize punishments for co-defendants, have been receiving more severe sentences (see Table 17.2). However, as females are arrested in greater numbers for crimes that have been committed primarily by men in the past, they can expect the **paternalistic attitude of judges**—if such an attitude now exists—to diminish rapidly.[16] As Meda Chesney-Lind notes, the male model of prisons is being superimposed on female prisoners in the rush to vengeful equity.[17]

key term

Paternalistic attitudes of judges
Sentiments found in a system under which an authority undertakes to supply needs or regulate conduct of those under its control, particularly for female offenders.

table **17.2**   Types of Sentences Imposed by State Court, Female Felons, 2004

Most Serious Conviction Offense	Percent of Felons Sentenced To:						
		Incarceration			Nonincarceration		
	Total	Total	Prison	Jail	Total	Probation	Other
All Offenses	100%	60%	27%	33%	40%	36%	3%
Violent Offenses	100%	65%	35%	29%	35%	33%	3%
Murder	100	87	84	3	13	13	0
Sexual assault	100	68	44	25	32	27	5
Robbery	100	79	58	21	21	20	1
Aggravated assault	100	59	27	32	41	38	3
Other violent	100	69	33	26	31	28	3
Property Offenses	100%	58%	27%	32%	42%	39%	3%
Burglary	100	72	38	35	28	26	1
Larceny	100	59	29	34	41	37	3
Fraud	100	54	25	29	46	43	3
Drug Offenses	100%	60%	26%	34%	40%	35%	4%
Possession	100	59	25	35	41	35	6
Trafficking	100	61	28	33	39	36	3
Weapons	100%	64%	31%	32%	36%	35%	2%
Other Offenses	100%	63%	24%	38%	37%	35%	3%

SOURCE: Bureau of Justice Statistics, "Distribution of Types of Felony Sentences Imposed in State Courts by Offense and Gender of Felons, 2004," http://www.ojp.usdoj.gov/bjs/pub//html/scscf04/tables/scs04204tab.htm (revised July 25, 2007, accessed February 26, 2008).

The differential treatment accorded to females in many cases does not automatically mean better treatment or consideration. Moreover, as an alternative to differential treatment, the model of the male prison is sometimes copied, even to the point of ignoring the female inmates' obvious physical differences.[18]

For those and other reasons, female offenders had traditionally received discretionary treatment by police and prosecutors. Females brought to court now are still apt to receive consideration for probation, fines, and suspended sentences more often than are men who commit comparable crimes. Of course, female offenders are less likely to have long criminal offense records and to commit violent crimes.

Statistics on the growth of female prisoners in state prisons and their offenses between 1999 and 2012 can be found in Figure 17.4.[19] It appears that the greatest change has been in the area of females committed for violent and property offenses. With regard to violent crime, the numbers are still significantly lower than for males. The War on Drugs has become a war on females and has materially contributed to the exploding growth of female prisoners. Yet they are not the "major players" in the drug trade; at least one-third are jailed for drug possession. In one sense, they can be seen as "prisoners" of the War on Drugs; in the federal prison system, drug offenders approach 60% of the prison population.

Why has the female prison population increased so sharply? No one knows for certain, but some of the reasons given are that females have more opportunities to commit crime than ever before, they are committing more serious crimes, and they are being sentenced more severely by judges. Many state drug statutes mandate imprisonment and restrict the sentencing discretion of the judge. Other theories are that presentence investigators and the judiciary, influenced by the **women's liberation movement,** are less likely to give favorable sentencing considerations than they were in the past, that parole boards are using uniform sentencing guidelines that force female inmates to serve more time, and that females are getting their "just deserts" under the conservative backlash to treat all offenders more severely. Others argue that the War on Drugs has sent many more female drug addicts into prisons than in the past, and that excessively long sentences for possession of controlled substances to which the offender is addicted (a medical problem) may violate the U.S. Constitution

key term
_____

**Women's liberation
movement**
A series of social movements
intended to narrow the gaps
between rights and privileges
accorded to males and to free
females from oppressive
minority status.

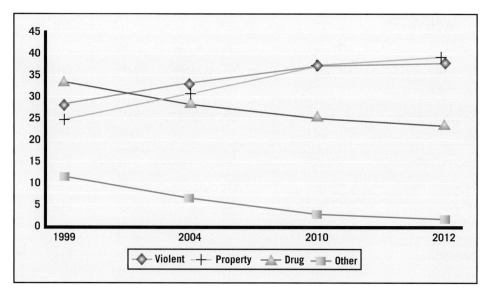

figure 17.4
_____

Crimes of Imprisoned Females: 1999–2012

SOURCES: Allen Beck and Paige Harrison, *Prisoners in 2000* (Washington, DC: Bureau of Justice Statistics 2002): 11; and William Sobol and Heather Couture, *Prisoners in 2006* (Washington, DC: Bureau of Justice Statistics 2007): 24. Data for 2012 are extrapolated.

prohibition against "cruel and unusual punishment." There are many theories, but not much data to support any one theory in particular.

Characteristics of Drug-Abusing Female Offenders

To gain a picture of the special needs of drug-abusing women offenders, information was taken from several sources covering women arrestees, women incarcerated in jails and prisons, women offenders diverted into community-based treatment instead of incarceration or as a condition of probation or parole, and women in publicly supported drug and treatment programs. The following are characteristics of these women:

- **Health problems.** Many drug-abusing women are physically or mentally ill. All drug users, and cocaine users in particular, are at increased risk for extreme weight loss, dehydration, digestive disorders, skin problems, dental problems, gynecological and venereal infections, tuberculosis, hepatitis B, hypertension, seizures, respiratory arrest, and cardiac failure.
- **Educational/vocational background.** Most of the women are unemployed or work at low-paying jobs. Most have not completed high school, have inadequate vocational skills, and lack many of the skills and knowledge needed to function productively in society.
- **Psychosocial problems.** Drug-addicted women tend to come from families with a high incidence of mental illness, suicide, alcohol or drug dependence, or violence, or are victims of incest, rape, or physical or sexual abuse.
- **Responsibility for parenting.** Most drug-abusing women offenders are of childbearing age, already have children, and are single mothers. Many of them receive little or no help from the children's father(s), lack supportive family and social networks, and have limited or no financial resources. Often their children become drug abusers themselves, thereby perpetuating both drug abuse and dysfunctional parenting across generations.
- **Drug use and treatment.** Most drug-abusing women offenders started abusing drugs and alcohol at an early age, and many used drugs, especially cocaine, on a daily basis prior to incarceration. In one survey of women in prison, 46% of respondents reported they had used drugs and/or alcohol at the time of their offense. Approximately 25% of adult women offenders have spent some time in a drug/alcohol treatment program, which, however, has most likely been of limited duration and intensity.
- **Criminal justice and child protective services involvement.** A percentage of drug-abusing women who seek treatment have had some involvement with the criminal justice system or with child protective services. One study reported that an estimated 60% to 80% of child abuse and neglect cases were from substance-abusing families.

Although these characteristics have been found to typify the population of drug-abusing women offenders, they have different implications for programs. Individual women will differ in the manifestations and severity of these characteristics and attendant problems. Such diversity calls for an assessment of specific clients' needs and the provision of services designed to meet those needs. If a program lacks a well-developed assessment procedure, clients are less likely to receive appropriate services, such as treatment in a style matched to cultural identity and cognitive level and of adequate intensity and duration.[20]

The plight of the woman behind jail or prison bars is often a difficult one. In terms of institutions, the male-oriented criminal justice system may totally ignore the special requirements of the female offender.[21] The nature of punishment for female offenders has come a long way from the time when they were thrown into the gaols as diversions for the incarcerated male felons, but more needs to be done before treatment of the female offender can be said to be an integrated part of corrections.[22]

class activity

Ask students to define the characteristics of substance-abusing female offenders. What implications do these characteristics have for treatment programs?

A typical female detention cell.
Photo by Clifford E. Simonsen, courtesy of King County Department of Adult Detention, Washington.

FEMALES IN JAIL

Females have never been a large portion of the inmates of jails in the nation, but the War on Drugs has contributed significantly to the number arrested and placed in jails and detention centers and has also increased the proportion of all inmates who are female. The number of females held in America's jails has increased dramatically during the past 15 years, and is up over 265% since 1990.[23] The characteristics of female jail inmates are generally the same, except for drug-related crime increases, as those found in an earlier survey of jails. More than 80% had used drugs in their lives, and more than half of the convicted inmates had used drugs in the month prior to the current offense that brought them to jail; almost 40% had used drugs daily. Some 24% of the female jail inmates had used cocaine or crack in the month before their current offense. About one in six convicted females in jail reported they had committed their current offense for money to buy drugs. Better than one in three convicted female inmates reported being under the influence of alcohol at the time of their offense.

A profile of jail inmates from 2002 illustrates other important demographic and criminal characteristics of females in jails, including the following:[24]

- About 12% of the female inmates were in jail for a violent offense.
- Female jail inmates were more likely than males to be drug offenders, 29% versus 24%.
- More than 49% of the females were first-time offenders, compared to 37% for men.
- Female jail inmates were less likely to be employed in the month prior to their arrest than males, 40% versus 60%.
- Around 16% of female jail inmates had sustained an injury following an assault.

Female inmates relax on bunk beds in Tent City at Maricopa County Jail in Arizona.
Photo by A. Ramey, courtesy of PhotoEdit Inc.

Part of a group of 21 women waiting for mercy while serving life sentences for killing men who they say abused them.
Photo by AP Wide World Photos.

- More than 55% of females reported they had been sexually abused in their past, up from 47.5% in 1996. Of these, more than 20% reported the abuse had occurred prior to age 18. Women were also more likely to have been abused by an intimate partner (68%) than men (11%), and 26% said they had been abused by a parent or guardian, and 34% by a friend.
- More than 46% were using drugs or alcohol at the time of their offense, and more than 55% admitted to drinking regularly.
- Low income was typical of almost all inmates.

A recent study of women in jail found high rates of lifetime trauma exposure (98%), current mental health disorders (36%), and drug and alcohol problems (almost three out of four). Most were deficient in parenting skills.[25]

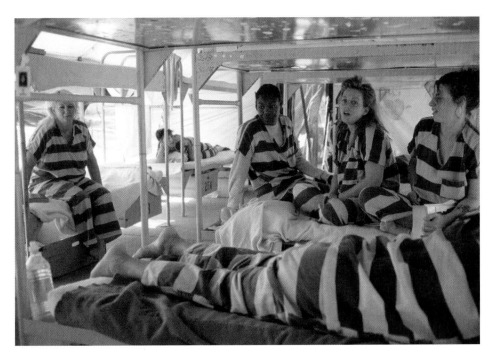

Female prisoners in stripes take a break from work in a tent detention center in Arizona.
Photo by A. Ramey, courtesy of PhotoEdit Inc.

This brief overview of female jail inmates suggests that they generally are not drawn from mainstream America, come from deprived and unstable backgrounds, have been extensively abused over time, and face significant employment, financial, psychological, emotional, and social barriers in their efforts to live in and seek reintegration into their local communities.[26] Most of these jail inmates are not dangerous but need assistance in existence and living. Incarceration in jail or prison may achieve punishment; societal goals would probably be better achieved if these high-problem female offenders were sentenced to community alternatives and received extensive treatment and service delivery. This is particularly true of abused females who enter the correctional system.[27]

FEMALES IN PRISON

As noted earlier, despite the earlier preferential treatment of female offenders, the number of incarcerated females in the United States started to rise sharply in the 1980s. Today, California, Texas, Florida, and the federal system hold four out of every ten female inmates, while Oklahoma leads the country in the incarceration rate for females at 129 per 100,000.[28]

Overall, the rate of growth for female prison inmates exceeded that for males for each of the last ten years. From 2000 to 2006, the male population increased an average of 1.8% per year, and the female population increased by 4.5%. Although the rate of incarceration for females is still considerably lower than that of males (68 per 100,000 females in the nation versus 943 per 100,000 for males), the gap is narrowing.[29] Not all groups of females are incarcerated at the same rate in America. As with males, blacks are incarcerated at a rate eight times that of white females; Hispanics are overrepresented by a ratio of about two to one to white females.

The typical female prisoner is black, non-Hispanic, age 35 to 39, never married, with some high school education and not employed at the time of arrest. She has likely been sentenced for a nonviolent crime (see Figure 17.3), and is a recidivist (either sentenced to probation or previously incarcerated as a juvenile or adult). A third of all female inmates reported they were under the influence of a drug at the time of their offenses. Overall, just over half of the females in prison had been using drugs or alcohol or both at the time the imprisonment offense occurred. An estimated 84% of the females in state prisons had used drugs at some time in their lives prior to admission, fairly close to 80% of the men. Some 40% of the female inmates had participated in a drug-treatment program at some point in their lives.[30]

Female inmates relaxing at Julia Tutwiler Prison, Alabama.
Photo by A. Ramey, courtesy of PhotoEdit Inc.

<table>
<tr><td>table **17.3**</td><td colspan="4">**Prior Abuse Reported by State Inmates and Probationers, 1997**</td></tr>
<tr><td>Abused</td><td>Total</td><td>Male</td><td>Female</td></tr>
<tr><td>Ever abused</td><td>19%</td><td>16%</td><td>57%</td></tr>
<tr><td>Physically abused</td><td>15</td><td>13</td><td>47</td></tr>
<tr><td>Sexually abused</td><td>8</td><td>6</td><td>39</td></tr>
</table>

SOURCE: Caroline Wolf Harlow, *Prior Abuse Reported by Inmates and Probationers* (Washington, DC: U.S. Department of Justice, 1999), p. 1. Information not measured every year.

<table>
<tr><td>table **17.4**</td><td colspan="2">**Specific Conditions Reported by State Inmates, 2004**</td></tr>
<tr><td>Abused</td><td>Male</td><td>Female</td></tr>
<tr><td>Homeless in Year before Arrest</td><td>8%</td><td>16%</td></tr>
<tr><td>Physical/Sexual Abuse</td><td>8</td><td>64</td></tr>
<tr><td>Current Medical Problem</td><td>40</td><td>53</td></tr>
<tr><td>Any Mental Health Problem</td><td>55</td><td>74</td></tr>
<tr><td>Any Substance Abuse Problem</td><td>67</td><td>70</td></tr>
</table>

SOURCE: Lauren Glaze and Laura Maruschak, *Parents in Prison and Their Minor Children* (Washington, DC: Bureau of Justice Statistics, 2008), http://www.ojp.usdoj.gov/bjs/pub/pdf/pptmc.pdf (accessed September 30, 2008).

key term

Abused females
Female victims of usually violent acts that may be physical or psychological in damage, or both.

class activity

Tell students that you are considering submitting a policy paper to the governor on alternatives to imprisonment that the state government could implement to handle female offenders. What major points do they think you should address? If students are not enthusiastic about this portion of the exercise, focus the question on inadequacies of state delivery of medical care for female offenders. One state in which the medical care issues are substantial is California.

class activity

Organize a debate on whether or not the imprisoned female offender is a dangerous criminal.

Prior abuse by spouse, family member, parent, and significant other (boyfriend or girl-friend) creates consequences for the abused.[31] (See Table 17.3.) Childhood and adult victimization of females is frequently a precursor to female criminality. Many **abused females** are left with emotional scars and diminished self-confidence. More than 75% of the female prisoners were mothers, and two in three had children under age 18. Female prisoners reported that more than 80% of their children under age 18 were living with a relative, usually the maternal grandmother. (See Table 17.4.) For male prison inmates, almost 90% of their children under age 18 are living with the children's mothers. This is an important difference that we discuss later.

Female inmates are housed in a variety of facilities. About half of these facilities are penal institutions, known by a variety of names: prisons, reformatories, penitentiaries, correctional facilities, and prison camps. Most are housed in minimum- to low-security units (see Figure 17.5).

This profile of the imprisoned female inmate hardly reflects a dangerous offender for whom incarceration in prison is required. Instead, many such offenders could probably be handled more effectively,[32] less expensively, and more humanely in alternatives to prison. Unfortunately, this situation most likely reflects probable national practice throughout the country. The PEW Trust recently argued that using a broader rage of sanctions can protect communities, punish law violators, and conserve tax resources for other pressing public needs, such as schools or trains.[33]

The health care needs of incarcerated women are inadequately addressed by many jails and prisons.
Photo by Spencer Grant, courtesy of PhotoEdit Inc.

FEMALE INSTITUTIONS

Only 135 training schools and centers, 118 co-gender programs for female juvenile delinquents, 163 institutions for women, and 103 co-gender facilities were listed in the 2007 American Correctional Association's *Directory* report.

figure 17.5

Female Prison Inmates, by
Security Level, 2007

Data from: American Correctional
Association, *2007 Directory*
(Alexandria, VA: ACA, 2007): 56–57.

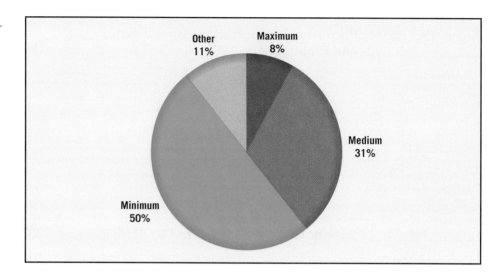

Texas led the way with 17 institutions for females and 13 cogender facilities.[34] The picture with regard to the administration of these female prisons has changed greatly in recent years. In 1966, female correctional administrators headed only ten of the nation's institutions. The 2007 ACA *Directory* showed that 2,008 of the 5,164 correctional administrators of adult and juvenile institutions were females.[35] Female correctional administrators tend to be managing male as well as female and co-correctional institutions, or community and minimum-custody facilities. As a matter of fact, the president of the American Correctional Association from 2004 to 2006 was Gwendolyn Chunn, the seventh female president of that prestigious organization. The first state-level prison exclusively for women was the Indiana Reformatory for Women. The first female warden was Mary Belle Harris at the Federal Correctional Institute at Alderson, West Virginia, when it opened in 1925.[36]

Because conditions in female institutions vary greatly, it would be fruitless to attempt to describe them individually. They are not all horror stories; it is sufficient to state that the best and the worst aspects of the male institution are also in evidenced in the female prison, the only major differences being the variations based on the traits unique to each gender and

Female inmates learn useful
skills in modern prisons.
*Photo by Drew Crawford, courtesy of
The Image Works.*

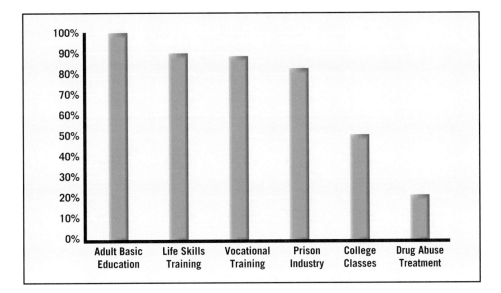

figure 17.6

Vocational Training Programs for Female Offenders

SOURCE: Editors, "Female Offenders," *Corrections Compendium* 23:3 (1998): 9. Most recent national data. See also Stephan LoBuglio, Time to Reframe Politics and Practices in Correctional Education (www.ncsall.net/index.php?id=560, accessed March 3, 2008).

the varied training and education programs available to males. Figure 17.6 lists programs that were available to female prisoners at the end of 2003.

One notable difference between prisons for males and females lies in the fact that many states only have one major facility for females compared to many prisons for males. As a result, a state's female prison will often house every classification level: high, close, medium, and minimum all within one compound. Unlike the male prison where one or two levels may be present, the range of classification levels within female institutions poses unique management issues.

SPECIAL PROBLEMS FOR INCARCERATED FEMALES

Among the many problems female inmates face when in prison are pregnancy, loss of family ties, and aging behind the walls. We start this discussion with the pregnant inmate entering prison. Earlier studies suggest that some one in four adult females entering prison either were pregnant or had given birth to an infant within the last 12 months.[37] In 2003, more than 2,100 pregnant females were imprisoned and more than 1,400 babies were born in prison.[38] Medical care, resources, and programs, while varying across institutions, are thought to be inadequate for such inmates. A primary explanation for the lack of programs has been the relatively small size of the female offender population and the expense involved in special programming for the small segment of prisoners that female inmates represent. The size argument, however valid in past decades, does not hold in current correctional scenes. Although female inmates remain a small portion of the total prison populations, their numbers have increased to the point that new policies are needed.

Pregnant inmates need special diets, lighter work assignments, supportive programs, and a less stressful environment. Programs and resources are needed for miscarriages, premature birth, and deliveries. Until recently,[39] the major options were abortion, placing children with relatives, putting the children up for adoption, or foster care. Not only do such forced separation policy options pose severe emotional anguish and problems for mothers, separation of the newborn child from the mother can create severe emotional and developmental problems for the infant.[40] Many prisons are now starting to provide family services as well as classes in child development and parenting, parental functioning, and stress management. Some female prisons have even started programs that allow young infants to

key term

Pregnant inmates
Female inmates who at time of detention are carrying a fetus or enter that condition while incarcerated.

remain with their mothers. For example, Washington State has a nursery program at its female prison in Gig Harbor that includes an Early Head Start component. Inmate mothers are accountable for the 24-hour care of their children while living in a supervised environment.[41] California operates the California's Community Prisoner Mother Program, which is operated by its Department of Corrections.[42] Other states have policies that permit babies to live with their mother for up to a year, require immediate foster care placement, or do not permit the mother to see the baby.

California Community Prisoner Mother Program

In seven small, community-based facilities throughout California, inmate mothers live with their young children. The Community Prisoner Mother Program (CPMP) is designed to build better parenting relationships and brighter futures while the inmates serve their time.

While in the program, mothers reestablish bonds with their children and prepare to return to the community as working, productive members. The homelike facilities provide a stable, caregiving environment. At the same time, mothers learn valuable skills. In preemployment training, they gain practical information and tips about applying for, landing, and keeping a job.

In specialized parenting classes, they learn how to talk and relate to their children and how to discipline effectively. Both mothers and children also may receive counseling.

Because the majority of the mothers have had some sort of chemical dependency in the past, they also attend drug-education classes geared to keep them from returning to their old habits, make them aware of the dangers of drug addiction, and show them how drugs impair both their lives and the lives of their children.

In addition, research on female inmates documents that females are more family oriented than male inmates and that as many as 80% of imprisoned females are mothers.[43] Evidence of the significance children play in the life of female inmates can be seen in pictures displayed on desks or taped behind prison identification badges, articles in prison newspapers, the frequency with which children are discussed, and general concern about the well-being of their

"Sally" with her son "Bob" in a California Community Prisoner Mother Program facility.
Courtesy of State of California Department of Corrections.

individual children. Many females feel their families and friends have abandoned them when they are sent to prison, just when their needs for support and friendship are highest and inmates are at the lowest point of their lives: ashamed, incarcerated, lonely, depressed, guilt ridden, acutely worried about their children, scared, and with tarnished self-esteem. Family members are particularly central at this time, since they can care for the inmate's children and bring them to visit, send money and special foods, write and call, guard their property, and take up their cause if mistreated by institutional staff. Thus, visiting is of crucial importance to female inmates who sense—if not know—that their role as mother is weak and their incarceration and absence can lead to a child's behavioral problems (obsessive crying, deterioration in relations with peers and schoolwork, withdrawal from relatives and reality, and so on).

Although failure of relatives to visit is a great hardship for most incarcerated mothers, often it results more from physical and institutional barriers than lack of care and concern on the part of relatives. Many institutions are located far away from the urban centers from which most female inmates originate, and travel and related expenses are hurdles to be overcome. Many relatives do not own cars and must depend on the kindness of neighbors for travel. Other discouraging factors include having to submit to searches before visiting, being too poor to afford overnight accommodations, or having work schedules too tight to permit frequent or lengthy visits. Some institutions are not "visitor friendly," with visits limited in frequency to once a month, provision of only one large room for visitations of all families, having no children's toys or a playground, and presenting an unfriendly and hostile setting. Better-managed institutions (such as in Nebraska and New York) have children's nurseries, play areas, and equipment; allow conjugal and family visits; and provide accommodations for mothers to plan, cook for, and feed their children in separate visiting rooms and trailers. Weekend passes, home visits, home furloughs, halfway house placements, and frequent visiting privileges not only ease parenting problems but also lessen the probability that the children will become innocent victims. Clearly there is a need for institutions to establish policies that encourage **family cohesion** and strengthen ties for the mother when she is eventually released. Figure 17.7 lists the types of visitation privileges available to female inmates.

The third major problem is aging in prison. The graying of America is reflected in prison populations, as seen in Table 17.5. This is particularly a problem with the older female inmates undergoing social, psychological, emotional, and physical changes within the institutional walls.[44] Females in America tend to live longer than men (about seven or eight years), and make up about 60% of older Americans. In prison, they are "forgotten" inmates and have been little studied or recognized. Incarceration encourages dependency and passivity, factors that tend to shorten life expectancy under any circumstance. Visual, physical, and muscular impairments pose particular problems for elderly female inmates. Not only will staff have to be specifically trained and programs individualized, but gerontology

figure 17.7

Jurisdictions with Visiting Privileges for Female Prisoners, 2003 (in percent)

SOURCE: Editors, "Female Offenders," *Corrections Compendium* 29:3 (2003): 22–24. Most recent national data.

table **17.5**	Inmates over Age 55, 1988–2012	
Comparison	Males	Females
1988	13,955	511
1990	17,244	709
1992	21,564	875
1994	25,832	1,141
1998	43,258	2,043
2000	38,200	1,900
2004	71,038	3,792
2007	73,134	3,604
2012	74,531	3,478
Change	+534%	+680%

SOURCE: American Correctional Association, *2008 Directory* (Alexandria, VA: ACA), pp. 54–55. Data for 2012 are extrapolated.

consultants and medical programs also will be required that address issues such as dealing with menopause, breast cancer, hysterectomies, eye cataracts, and hip, spine, and back impairments. As the numbers of elderly female inmates swell, physical plants will need to be retrofitted, including color coding of floors and buildings, adding wall handrails and wheelchair ramps, widening door frames and entries, providing rest areas for more challenged inmates, and revamping space to include nursing and convalescent rooms and services. Special diets, medications, nursing patterns, and physical therapy will need to be initiated and expanded. It is clear that a correctional crisis is in the making, and that prisons are not conducive to caring for the elderly (age 65 and over), aged (age 75 plus), or very old (age 85 and over). Alternative sentencing, timely and compassionate release, and community correctional centers are more realistic options for those who pose no threat to the community or self. Correctional action now may avoid costly programming and extensive legal issues and lawsuits in the decades to come. Deliberate indifference to medical needs has been declared a violation of constitutionally guaranteed rights (Eighth Amendment). Indeed, one recent study of medical care in a large jail facility likened the care inmates received to "torture."[45]

THE CO-GENDER CORRECTIONAL INSTITUTION

The **single-sex experience** and long-term deprivation of heterosexual outlets create the same kinds of problems in female institutions as are found in male prisons. The recommendations for co-gender institutions may seem extreme to the uninitiated, but the leavening effect of a system that allows at least nonsexual social contact in daily activity with members of the opposite sex is considerable. Excessive administrative concern about overt signs of friendship that may be indicative of possible homosexual activity conflicts with many standard practices for females outside the walls. If two males were observed holding hands as they walked down the street, they would be suspected of being gay. That same behavior, though not considered at all strange for females (and particularly girls) on the outside, is viewed with great suspicion inside the walls, for girls and adult females alike. Some female inmates were gay or bisexual before entering a correctional institution, and do not change their behaviors under incarceration. Others were heterosexual before imprisonment but enter into romantic alliances within correctional facilities. It is believed that most of the latter return to heterosexual relationships after release, but some continue their lesbian behavior after imprisonment ("jailhouse turnouts"). An inmate graphically describes the situation:

> It's tough to be natural. The thing that most of us are trying to accomplish here, we're trying to get our minds at a point to where we can handle whatever comes our way, to get our emotions balanced, to maybe straighten up our way of thinking. You know, it just makes it hard when you're trying to be a natural person—to react to things normally—when the staff won't let you be normal—when you do a normal thing that being a woman makes it normal, and then have them say no, you can't do that because if you do, that's personal contact and that's homosexuality. So there's our mental hassle.

> I know that when females are thrown together without men or without the companionship of men it makes it pretty rough on them—females being the emotional people that they are. They have to have a certain amount of affection and close companionship. You know, a woman, if she's with a man she'll put her hand on him or maybe she'll reach up and touch him. This is something that a woman does naturally without thinking, and so if a woman has a good friend, or an affair, she does the same thing because this is her nature. The thing of it is—like I have a friend at the cottage—neither one of us have ever played. We're never gonna play. And if somebody tried to force us into it, we couldn't, wouldn't, or what have you. But being a woman and after being here for quite a while, we put our arms around each other, we don't think there's anything the matter with it, because there's nothing there—it's a friendship. We're walking down the hall, our records are both spotless, she's a council girl, I'm Minimum A [minimum custody classification]. I've never had anything on my record that was bad and my god, the supervisor comes out and says, "Now, now girls, you know we don't allow that sort of thing here." And we look at her and say, "What sort of thing?" "This personal contact." And yet this same supervisor, we saw her up at the corner putting her arm around another supervisor the same way we were doing. So this is where part of our mental hassle comes in.[46]

The redefinition of the natural acts just described into something considered evil and proscribed is another reason that institutionalization is so crippling to the long-term female prisoner. As inmates, male or female, learn that simple signs of friendship are prohibited, they learn to repress their impulses toward interpersonal warmth when they get out. The kind of behavior that makes them acceptable on the inside makes them appear hard (unfeeling, unresponsive) on the outside. In the male this kind of coldness can be viewed as "tough" or "macho," but is sometimes considered unattractive when displayed by females.

Until recently, very few studies have been conducted on the homosexuality of female prisoners. Much conjecture is found in the literature, but true scientific research is rare. Even the monumental effort to compile statistics on female offenders in Sheldon and Eleanor Glueck's *500 Delinquent Women*[47] did not consider homosexuality, but gender- and sex-role research is increasing.[48]

The demands of institutional management make it difficult to prevent homosexual activity. There are never enough personnel to watch all of the inmates, so lovers get together despite the staff's efforts. In many institutions the staff adopts the attitude of "looking the other way" with regard to the female inmates' sexual activity. (The same is true in many men's institutions;[49] see Chapter 16.) It is possible that homosexuality and homosociality are even more prevalent in female institutions than in those for men, because a high percentage of the inmates have been so misused by men[50] that they have already turned to other females to fulfill their emotional needs on the outside. In addition, prisons for females are generally less secure and less compartmentalized, making it easier for women to interact. It is also quite possible that the impact of imprisonment is significantly different for females, tending to encourage a homosexual response. Females appear more likely to view arrest, jailing, the court trial, and commitment to prison in highly personal terms. This personalized reaction could harden antisocial attitudes and lead to further illegal behavior. One

lecture note

Using your computer, play the brief videotape of Angela West on "Aging Females" (approximately 3 minutes).

class activity

Organize a class debate on whether or not the pains of imprisonment are greater for female or male offenders.

lecture note

Discuss *homosexuality* in female prisons. Ask why it is so widespread, and point out that most practitioners are heterosexual and will resume heterosexual lifestyles when released.

class activity

Challenge students to describe the advantages of co-gender institutions. What do co-gender institutions tell us about single-sex prisons?

<u>key term</u>

Psychological deprivation
Loss of or failure to develop emotional cohesion, support, or love through failure to provide emotional or physical caring.

<u>key term</u>

Co-gender institution
A co-educational prison housing both male and female inmates interacting under a single institutional administration.

study has identified three **psychological deprivations** that might contribute to homosexual behavior:[51]

1. Affection starvation and need for understanding
2. Isolation from previous symbiotic interpersonal relations
3. Need for continued intimate relationships with a person

It is hard to imagine an incarcerated felon (male or female) who does not suffer these deprivations to some degree.

The co-gender, or co-correctional, prison is a new development in corrections. Two were opened in 1971 in the Federal Bureau of Prisons system. Since that time there have been many coed adult state and federal facilities; 101 state-level and 273 private co-gender facilities existed in 2007.[52] John Smykla and J. Williams defined adult co-corrections (co-gender) as adult institutions, the major purpose of which is the institutional confinement of felons. Each is managed by one institutional administration and has regular programs or areas in which female and male inmates have daily opportunities for interaction.[53] The general concept of **co-gender institutions** is as follows:[54]

1. To reduce the dehumanizing and destructive aspects of confinement by allowing continuity or resumption of heterosexual relationships
2. To reduce the institutional control problems through the weakening of disruptive homosexual systems, reduction of predatory homosexual activity, lessening of assaultive behavior, and the diversion of inmate interests and activities
3. To protect inmates likely to be involved in "trouble" were they in a same-sex institution
4. To provide an additional tool for creating a more normal, less institutionalized atmosphere
5. To cushion the shock of adjustment for releasees, by reducing the number and intensity of adjustments to be made
6. To realize economies of scale in terms of more efficient utilization of available space, staff, and programs

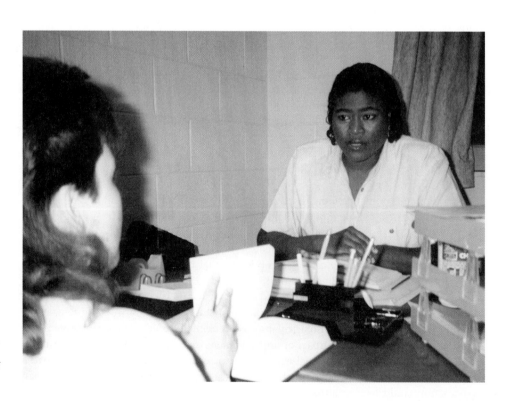

One-on-one counseling works well in a female facility.
Courtesy of New York Department of Corrections.

7. To provide relief of immediate or anticipated overcrowding, sometimes of emergency proportions
8. To reduce the need for civilian labor, by provision of both light and heavy inmate workforces
9. To increase diversification and flexibility of program offerings, and equal access for males and females
10. To expand treatment potentials for working with inmates having "sexual problems," and development of positive heterosexual relationships and coping skills
11. To provide relief from immediate or anticipated legal pressures to provide equal access to programs and services to both sexes
12. To expand career opportunities for females, previously often "boxed into" the single state female institutions, as co-correctional staff

The question of whether these objectives have been met cannot yet be answered, primarily because most evaluations of their effectiveness continue to be weak at best.[55]

lecture note

Describe *co-gender institutions* and problems administrators face in managing them.

COMMUNITY CORRECTIONS AND FEMALE OFFENDERS

Our review of the problems posed by female offenders as well as problems female inmates face due to incarceration has suggested that most female offenders pose little danger to public safety, that substance abuse underlies much of their criminal behavior, and that much damage to inmates and their families may be done through incarcerating those whose basic problem is alcohol and/or drug abuse.

Institutions for females are not known for the long-term effectiveness of their "inside the walls" treatment programs, which tend to be limited in number and occur in an artificial environment, thus reducing their effectiveness.[56] What is needed are more reasonable risk-reduction programs that speak to the underlying problems that have led to criminal behavior and incarceration. Those are, of course, generally found in the community, and include halfway houses, group homes, residential treatment facilities, mental health and substance-abuse programs, probation, and other intermediate sanctions as discussed in more detail in the chapters on probation, intermediate sanctions and parole, and reentry. Such programs have long been recommended for nonviolent offenders, and were strongly advocated by the American Bar Association's Sentencing Project, as well as the National Council on Crime and Delinquency.[57]

There are now more than 906,600 females on probation (23% of adult probationers, up from 21% in 1990), and an additional 108,200 on parole (14% of all parolees, up from 12% in 2000).[58] Unfortunately, gender-specific programs are often lacking, and residential programs specifically designated for females are often found only in the largest urban areas. Because female offenders seldom pose much threat to public safety and are seldom violent, managing them in a community-wide, coordinated correctional system with graduated degrees of supervision in the community is a viable option for this correctional population.

For those females who are incarcerated, it is equally important to develop and expand family-based programming to allow them to maintain contact with their children.[59]

lecture note

Discuss the case disposition patterns for male and female offenders in your state. Emphasize the predominance of community corrections as the disposition of choice for female offenders.

class activity

Challenge students to argue that community corrections should be the sentence of choice for all but the most hardened female offender.

homework

Assign students to locate an article on *elderly female inmates* and submit a one-paragraph statement of the special needs of such offenders.

Summary

This review of the expanding role of the female offender on the correctional scene reveals the overuse of imprisonment as a correctional alternative in sentencing. This policy does not reflect contemporary correctional thought or recommended practice.

The philosophy of the reintegration model is to handle as many causes of criminal behavior as possible in the environment in which it arises—that is, in the local community. Sentencing low-danger/risk female offenders to prisons run by state authorities does little to deal with the causes that have contributed to the criminal events that bring the female offender before a sentencing court. Indeed, imprisonment itself is likely to lessen the ability of the female offender to function when released on parole, because imprisonment ruptures familial, economic, social, and parental ties. Separation from children due to incarceration is a major problem faced by returning mothers.

Local communities and counties, working in conjunction with volunteer and professional organizations (such as the International Community Corrections Association, the National Council on Crime and Delinquency, the John Howard Society, and the National Center on Institutions and

Alternatives), continue to develop and maintain correctional programs that allow the female offender to remain in the local community and support the process of reintegrating offenders by involvement with local agencies. Reintegration is clearly the direction of the future for female offenders.

Now that we have examined the female clients who are sent on different paths from the jail environment, we move on to juvenile offenders and what to do with them in a society that has grown alarmed over and hardened to the superpredator and gang violence on the street that makes headlines. How we have dealt, are dealing, and should deal with juvenile offenders are questions for the next chapter.

Key Words

arrests by gender, 332

preferential treatment, 332

"traditional" female crimes, 333

"victimless" crimes, 334

paternalistic attitudes of judges, 335

women's liberation movement, 336

abused females, 341

pregnant inmates, 343

family cohesion, 345

single-sex experience, 346

psychological deprivation, 348

co-gender institution, 348

Review Questions

1. What are the major crimes for which females are convicted? Explain why.
2. Why have females been treated so differently in the correctional system?
3. What impact does incarceration have on "mothering" of children?
4. Develop a model for handling the female offender that would have differing degrees of social control and offer female criminals an opportunity to stop criminal activity.

5. Describe the typical female inmate.
6. Identify three groups of special-problem female offenders and their specific needs.
7. How has the War on Drugs impacted corrections and specifically female offenders?
8. What should be done with the pregnant female prison inmate? With her baby?
9. What special problems do female offenders who have been victims of prior abuse face when they are imprisoned?

Endnotes

1. Paige Harrison and Allen Beck, *Prison and Jail Inmates at Midyear 2004* (Washington, DC: Bureau of Justice Statistics, 2005), p. 8; and William Sabol, Todd Minton, and Paige Harrison, *Prison and Jail Inmates at Midyear 2006* (Washington, DC: Bureau of Justice Statistics, 2007), p. 5

2. Michael Tonry, "Why Are U.S. Incarceration Rates So High?" *Overcrowded Times* 10:3 (1999): 1, 8–16. See particularly p. 8.

3. Most apprehended drug couriers ("mules") are female. If arrested in New York City's John F. Kennedy Airport, they could be sentenced under New York statutes for a minimum penalty of three years' to life imprisonment,

but the sentence may be reduced to lifetime probation if the mule provides "material assistance" leading to the arrest of a drug dealer or higher-placed drug entrepreneur. Few mules can offer "material assistance" of any prosecutorial value because they are so marginally involved (if at all) with the ongoing criminal enterprise. In 1999, U.S. district courts granted almost 8,000 "substantial assistance reductions" to 44% of defendants in federal courts, most of which were granted to drug offenders. Few were granted to females. John Scalia, *Federal Drug Offenders, 1999 with Trends from 1984–1999.* (Washington, DC: Bureau of Justice Statistics, 2001), p. 10.

4. Federal Bureau of Investigation, *Crime in the United States 2006* (Washington, DC: U.S. Department of Justice, 2007).

5. Ibid.

6. Freda Adler, *Sisters in Crime* (New York: McGraw-Hill, 1975). See also Bernard Schissel and K. Fedec, "The Selling of Innocence," *Canadian Journal of Criminology* 41:1 (1994): 33–56.

7. Federal Bureau of Investigation, "Crime in the United States 2006, Table 32," http://www.fbi.gov/ucr/cius/2006/data/table32_html (accessed March 3, 2008). See also Jacqueline Boles and K. Elifson, "Sexual Identity and HIV: The Male Prostitute," *Journal of Sex Research* 31:1 (1994): 39–46; Thomas Calhoun and G. Weaver, "Rational Decision-Making among Male Street Prostitutes," *Deviant Behavior* 17:2 (1996): 209–227; and Leon Pettiway, *Honey, Honey Miss Thang: Being Black, Gay and on the Streets* (Philadelphia: Temple University Press, 1996).

8. Studies of lifetime prevalence of intimate partner abuse suggest that at least four in ten females will be physically and sexually abused during their lifetimes. There is some evidence that physical and sexual abuse may be highest for females age 18 to 39, with monthly income of less than $1,000, children under age 18 being at home, and those ending a relationship within the last 12 months. Stephen Dearwater, J. Coben, J. Campbell, et al., "Prevalence of Intimate Partner Abuse in Women Treated at Community Hospital Emergency Departments," *Journal of the American Medical Association* 280:5 (1998): 433–438. See also Bureau of Justice Statistics, "Family Violence Statistics," http://www.ojp.usdoj.gov/bjs/pub/pdf/fvs10.pdf (accessed February 28, 2008).

9. Robert Meier and G. Geis, *Victimless Crime? Prostitution, Drugs, Homosexuality and Abortion* (Los Angeles: Roxbury Publishing, 1997); Barrie Flowers, *The Prostitution of Women and Girls* (Jefferson, NC: McFarland, 1998); Karen Stout and B. McPhail, *Confronting Sexism and Violence against Women: A Challenge for Social Work* (New York: Longman, 1998); and Melissa Farley, "Unequal," http://crime.about.com (accessed February 28, 2008).

10. See Ira Sommers, D. Baskin, and J. Fagan, "The Structural Relationship between Drug Use, Drug Dealing and Other Income Support Activities among Women Drug Users," *Journal of Drug Issues* 26:4 (1996): 975–1006; John Potterat, R. Rothenberg, S. Muth, et al., "Pathways to Prostitution," *Journal of Sex Research* 35:4 (1998): 333–340; and Tove P. Tiby, "The Production and Reproduction of Prostitutions," *Journal of Scandinavian Studies in Crime and Crime Prevention* 3:2 (2003): 154–172.

11. Joanne Belknap, *The Invisible Woman: Gender, Crime and Justice* (Belmont, CA: Wadsworth, 2007).

12. Cynthia Seymour (ed.), "Children with Parents in Prison," *Child Welfare* 77:5 (1998): 469–639; James Boudouris, *Parents in Prison* (Lanham, MD: American Correctional Association, 1996); and Ken Gosnell, "Fathers Successfully Returning Home," *Corrections Today* 69:2 (2007): 46–50.

13. Amnesty International, "Mothers behind Bars," http://www.amnesty-usa.org/rightsforall/women/report-101.html (accessed February 28, 2008).

14. As early as 1984, Candace Kruttschnitt and D. Green were debunking the chivalry assumptions in their "The Sex-Sanctioning Issue: Is It History?" *American Sociological Review* 49:4 (1984): 541–551. See also Ellen Steury and F. Nancy, "Gender Bias and Pretrial Release: More Pieces of the Puzzle," *Journal of Criminal Justice* 18:5 (1990): 417–432; Randall Shelden, "Confronting the Ghost of Mary Ann Crouse: Gender Bias in the Juvenile Justice System," *Juvenile and Family Court Journal* 49:1 (1998): 11–26; and Marie Grabe, K. Trager, Melissa Lear, and Jennifer Raush, "Gender in Crime News," *Mass Communication and Society* 9:2 (2007): 137–163.

15. Mark Pogrebin and E. Poole, "Sex, Gender and Work: The Case of Women Jail Officers," in Jeffrey Ulmer (ed.), *Sociology of Crime, Law and Deviance* (Stamford, CT: JAI Press, 1998), pp. 105–126; and Timothy Griffin and John Wooldredge, "Sex-based Disparities in Felony Dispositions before and after Sentencing Reform in Ohio," *Criminology* 44:4 (2006): 893–923.

16. B. Farnsworth and R. Teske, "Gender Differences in Felony Court Processing," *Women and Criminal Justice* 6:2 (1995): 23–44.

17. Meda Chesney-Lind, "Women in Prison: From Partial Justice to Vengeful Equity," *Corrections Today* 60:7 (1998): 66–73.

18. Susan Crawford and R. Williams, "Critical Issues in Managing Female Offenders," *Corrections Today* 60:7 (1998): 130–134; and Editors, "L.A. County Makes Room for Female Prisoners," *Correctional News* 13:3 (2007): 17.

19. Bureau of Justice Statistics, *Prison and Jail Inmates at Midyear 2002* (Washington, DC: BJS, 2003); and William Sabol and Heather Couture, *Prisoners in 2006* (Washington, DC: Bureau of Justice Statistics, 2007), p. 24.

20. Jean Wellisch, Michael Prendergast, and Douglas Anglin, *Drug-Abusing Women Offenders: Results of a National Survey* (Washington, DC: Bureau of Justice Statistics, 1995). See also Jennifer Karberg and Doris James, *Substance Dependence, Abuse and Treatment of Jail Inmates, 2002* (Washington, DC: Bureau of Justice Statistics, 2005).

21. Louise Bill, "The Victimization and Revictimization of Female Offenders," *Corrections Today* 60:7 (1998): 106–112.

22. Donna Kerr, "Substance Abuse among Female Offenders," *Corrections Today* 60:7 (1998): 114–120. See also Michelle Staples-Horne, "Addressing Specific Health Care Needs of Female Adolescents," *Corrections Today* 69:5 (2007): 426.

23. Bureau of Justice Statistics, *Prison and Jail Inmates at Midyear 2003* (Washington, DC: BJS, 2004). See also Bureau of Justice Statistic, "Demographic Trends in Jail Populations," http://www.ojp.usdoj.gov/bjs/glance/tables/jailagtab.htm (accessed March 3, 2008).

24. Doris J. James, *Profile of Jail Inmates, 2002* (Washington, DC: Bureau of Justice Statistics, 2004).

25. Bonnie Green, J. Miranda, A. Daroowalla, and J. Siddique, "Trauma, Mental Health Functioning, and Program Needs of Women in Jail," *Crime and Delinquency* 51:1 (2005): 131–151.

26. Virginia McCoy, J. Inciardi, and L. Metch, "Women, Crack and Crime," *Contemporary Drug Issues* 22:3 (1995): 435–451; and Meda Chesney-Lind, *The Female Offender: Girls, Women and Crime* (Thousand Oaks, CA: Sage, 1997). See also the theme issue "Female Offenders," *Corrections Today* 60:7 (1998).

27. Boot camps, with their requirements of absolute obedience to authority, may be harmful to female offenders who have been in abusive relationships. See Doris MacKenzie, L. Ellis, S. Simpson, et al., *Female Offenders in Boot Camp* (College Park, MD: University of Maryland, 1994).

28. Bureau of Justice Statistics, *Prison and Jail Inmates at Midyear 2006* (Washington, DC: Bureau of Justice Statistics, 2007), p. 15.

29. Ibid, pp. 15, 17.

30. L.I.S., Inc., *Profiles of Correctional Substance Abuse Treatment Programs* (Langmont, CO: National Institute of Corrections, 1994); and Christopher Mumola, *Substance Abuse and Treatment, State and Federal Prisoners, 1997* (Washington, DC: U.S. Department of Justice, 1999), p. 13.

31. Caroline Wolf Harlow, *Prior Abuse Reported by Inmates and Probationers* (Washington, DC: U.S. Department of Justice, 1999). For data on abuse across the nation, see Patricia Tjaden and M. Thoennes, *Prevalence, Incidence and Consequences of Violence against Women* (Washington, DC: U.S. Department of Justice, 1998). See also American Civil Liberties Union, "Words from Prison: Sexual Abuse in Prison," http://www.aclu.org/womensrights/violence/index.html (accessed March 3, 2008).

32. Natalie Pearl, "Use of Community-Based Social Services to Reduce Recidivism in Female Parolees," *Women and Criminal Justice* 10:1 (1998): 27–52.

33. PEW Charitable Trusts, *One in 100: Behind Bars in America 2008* (Washington, DC: PEW, 2008), p. 4.

34. American Correctional Association, *Directory 2007* (Lanham, MD: ACA, 2007), pp. 28–29. Four states did not report the number of their facilities and programs for adults.

35. Ibid, pp. 40–41. Five states did not report on wardens and superintendents in adult institutions.

36. Excellent chronicles of female correctional managers can be found in *Women and Criminal Justice*. See in particular Mary Hawkes, "Edna Mahan: Sustaining the Reformatory Tradition," *Women and Criminal Justice* 9:3 (1998): 1–21; and Joann Morton, "Martha E. Wheeler: Redefining Women in Corrections," *Women and Criminal Justice* 5:2 (1994): 3–20. See also Joann Morton (ed.), "Women in Corrections," *Corrections Today* 54:6 (1992): 76–180; and the theme issues on "Best in the Business," *Corrections Today* (yearly).

37. George Church, "The View from behind Bars," *Time* (September 22, 1990): 20–22.

38. Corrections Compendium Survey Summary Female Offenders. There are no national data, and your authors know of no data on babies born to jail inmates.

39. John Wooldredge and K. Masters, "Confronting Problems Faced by Pregnant Inmates in State Prisons," *Crime and Delinquency* 39:3 (1993): 195–203; and Jessica Pearson and N. Thoennes, "What Happens to Pregnant Substance Abusers and Their Babies?" *Juvenile and Family Court Journal* 47:2 (1996): 15–28.

40. Joann Morton and D. Williams, "Mother/Child Bonding," *Corrections Today* 60:7 (1998): 98–105; and Paula Dressel, J. Porterfield, and S. Barnhill, "Mothers behind Bars," *Corrections Today* 60:7 (1998): 90–94; and Win Sisson, "Don't Forget about the Children," *Corrections Today* 68:7 (2006): 54–57.

41. Washington Correctional Center for Women, "Washington Department of Corrections," http://www.doc.wa.gov/facilities/Washingtoncc-women.asp. See also Jeanne Woodford, "Women and Parole," http://www.ihc.ca.gov/ihcdir/womenparole/woodruffApr04.pdf.

42. Community Prisoner Mother Program (CPMP), California Department of Corrections, http://info.sen.ca.gov/pub/07-08/bill/asm/ab_0051-0100/ab_76_cfa_20070226_094043_asmcomm.html. See also California Department of Corrections and Rehabilitation, "California Department of Corrections and Rehabilitation Opens New Family Foundations Program Facility in Fresno," http://www.cdcr.ca.gov/news/2008_Press_Release/January_25/index.html (accessed March 8, 2008).

43. Joann Morton and D. Williams, "Mother/Child Bonding," and Dressel et al., "Mothers behind Bars."

44. See also Phyllis Ross and J. Lawrence, "Health Care for Women Offenders," *Corrections Today* 60:7 (1998):

122–129; and Susan Crawford and R. Williams, "Critical Issues in Managing Female Offenders," *Corrections Today* 60:7 (1998): 130–134.

45. *Estelle* v. *Gamble*, 97 S. Ct. 285 (1976). See also Michael Vaughn and L. Carroll, "Separate but Unequal: Prison versus Free-World Medical Care," *Justice Quarterly* 15:1 (1998): 3–40; Kristine Shields and C. de Moya, "Correctional Health Care Nurses' Attitudes toward Inmates," *Journal of Correctional Health Care* 4:1 (1997): 37–59. See also Michael S. Vaughn and Linda G. Smith, "Practicing Penal Harm Medicine in the United States: Prisoners' Voices from Jail," *Justice Quarterly* 16 (1999): 175–232; Michael Vaughn and Sue Collins, "Medical Malpractice in Correctional Facilities," *The Prison Journal* 84:4 (2004): 505–534; Paul von Zielbauer, "Private Health Care in Jails Can Be a Death Sentence," *New York Times* (February 27, 2005): A7; and Editors, "California Receiver Issues Status Report on Prison Medical Systems," *Correctional News* 13:7 (2007): 14.

46. David Ward and Gene Kassenbaum, "Sexual Tension in a Woman's Prison," in M. Wolfgang and L. Savitz (eds.), *The Criminal in Confinement* (New York: Basic Books, 1971), pp. 149–150; Candace Kruttschnitt, "Race Relations and the Female Inmate," *Crime and Delinquency* 29:4 (1983): 577–592.

47. Sheldon Glueck and Eleanor Glueck, *500 Delinquent Women* (New York: Knopf, 1934).

48. John Smykla, *Co-Corrections: A Case Study of a Co-Ed Federal Prison* (Washington, DC: University Press of America, 1979). See also Christopher Uggen and C. Kruttsnitt, "Crime in the Breaking: Gender Differences in Desistance," *Law and Society Review* 33:2 (1998): 339–366; and Charlotte Bright, Scott Decker, and Andrea Burch, "Gender and Justice in the Progressive Era," *Justice Quarterly* 24:7 (2007): 657–678.

49. Victor Hassine, *Life without Parole: Living in Prison Today* (Los Angeles: Roxbury, 2002); Robert Johnson and H. Toch, *Crime and Punishment: Inside Views* (New York: Oxford University Press, 2008); Christopher Hensley and Richard Tewksbury, "Warden's Perceptions of Prison Sex," *The Prison Journal* 85:2 (2005): 127–144;

and Editors, "California to Trial Condoms in Prisons," *Correctional News* 14:1 (2008): 32.

50. Patricia Tjaden and M. Thoennes, *Prevalence, Incidence, and Consequences of Violence against Women* (Washington, DC: U.S. Department of Justice, 1998); Bonita Versey, K. de Cou, and L. Prescott, "Effective Management of Female Jail Detainees with Histories of Physical and Sexual Abuse," *American Jails* 16:2 (1998): 50–54; and Shannon Catalano, "Intimate Partner Violence in the United States," http://www.ojp.usdoj .gov/bjs/intimate/ipv.htm (accessed March 8, 2008).

51. Leslie Acoca and J. Austin, *The Crisis: The Women Offender Sentencing Study and Alternative Sentencing* (Washington, DC: National Council on Crime and Delinquency, 1996).

52. American Correctional Association, *2007 Directory*, pp. 28–29; 30–31.

53. John Smykla and J. Williams, "Co-Corrections in the United States of America, 1970–1990: Two Decades of Disadvantages for Women Prisoners," *Women and Criminal Justice* 8:1 (1996): 61–76.

54. Pamela Schram, "Stereotypes about Vocational Programming for Female Inmates," *The Prison Journal* 78:3 (1998): 255–270.

55. Smykla and Williams, "Co-Corrections in the United States."

56. Paul Gendreau, Shelia A. French, and Angela Taylor, *What Works (What Doesn't Work): The Principles of Effective Correctional Treatment.* International Community Corrections Association Monograph Series (LaCrosse, WI: ICCA, 2002).

57. The Sentencing Project. *Women in the Criminal Justice System* (Washington, DC: TSP, 2007); and Christopher Hartney, "The Nation's Most Punitive States for Women" (Oakland, CA: National Council on Crime and Delinquency, 2007).

58. Bureau of Justice Statistics, *Prisoners in 2006.*

59. Family Strengthening Policy Center, "Supporting Families with Incarcerated Parents," http://www .nassembly.org/fspc/practice/documents/brief8.pdf (accessed May 28, 2008).

chapter 18

Juvenile Offenders

Outline

> "The call for a national 'crackdown on juvenile offenders' and the fear of a 'new generation of super predators' is, I believe, an overreaction to one of our weakest emotions—fear."
>
> —James A. Gondles, Jr.,
> *Executive Director,*
> *American Correctional*
> *Association*

Overview

The last two chapters, and the one that follows, describe the variety of "clients" that usually are formed into separate groups for sentencing and incarceration following arrest and detention. In the early history of American justice, the distinctions of sex, age, or personal infirmities were given little thought, and "offenders" were lumped into a single category—prisoners. Institutional inmates needed only be classified as convicted, and even that distinction was often overlooked in society's haste to punish actual or alleged miscreants. Over the decades, many different paths were developed for various categories of offenders; jails were separated into male and female sections and those convicted were sent to different, specialized kinds of institutions to serve out their sentences and meet their special needs. But what about those offenders classified, by age, as juveniles? What became of them in the adult systems?

This chapter digresses somewhat from the general pattern, because the process of handling juvenile offenders has grown into an entirely separate system of justice. Therefore, we develop the history of juvenile justice in more detail than was covered earlier in the text to show how juvenile procedures have developed almost independently from adult justice and are designed to assist wayward youth. The juvenile justice system has now grown into an entirely separate "industry." This is especially timely as we follow the activities of street gangs, children who murder other children, and all the punitive and neoclassical efforts to again try juveniles in adult courts as "superpredators."[1] We hope to provide the student, in this single chapter, with a basic understanding of juvenile justice in relationship to the other clients of corrections. Other texts and other courses have been written and presented on this single offender group. This is not meant to be an exhaustive or complete treatise on

class activity

Using your computer, play the brief chapter overview videotape by Edward Latessa that introduces Chapter 18 (approximately 3 minutes).

key term

Common law
Law based on judges' decisions and custom, as distinct from written laws.

key term

Parens patriae
A Latin term that refers to the duty of the state to protect those unable to protect themselves, particularly juveniles and the mentally disordered.

key term

Ward
A minor subject to wardship or protection by the state; may also refer to other persons protected by court order or legal status.

key term

Chancery court
One of the five divisions of the High Court of Justice of Great Britain, presided over by the Lord High Chancellor, and serves as a legal protector of the rights of minors.

class activity

Ask students if the age of the youth should be the determinant factor in juvenile court, rather than the seriousness of the offenses.

juvenile justice or juvenile offenders, but simply a base on which to build an understanding of the origins and current practices in this separate and unique correctional system.

WHERE DOES THE JUVENILE FIT IN?

How did we go from wayward youth to superpredators in such a short time? Like most of America's criminal justice system, our juvenile justice system derives from the **common law** of England, as brought to the United States by our forefathers. With regard to criminal responsibility, the English common law made three assumptions concerning age and criminal responsibility:

1. Children under the age of seven were presumed to be incapable of holding criminal intent.
2. From the ages of 7 to 14, offenders were not held responsible unless the state could prove they could clearly distinguish between right and wrong.
3. If offenders were 14 or older, they were assumed to be responsible for their acts and therefore deserving of punishment. Here, the burden was on the defendants to prove they were not responsible.

The king was considered the father of his country (***parens patriae,***) who assumed responsibility for protecting all dependent children. *Parens patriae* is a legal philosophy by which the state assumes the role of the parent of the child: *The parent is the state.* In England that responsibility was fulfilled by the chancery court,[2] in which the needful child became a **ward** of the state under the protection of *parens patriae.* The **chancery court** was designed to act more flexibly than the more rigid criminal courts. The main concern was for the welfare of the child; legal procedures that might hamper the court in its beneficial actions were either circumvented or ignored. Thus, there were two concepts under the common law: that children under certain ages were not responsible for their actions and that a certain category of children was in need of protection by the state. It was not until the ages of possible responsibility were raised to 16 and 18 that those two concepts merged into the concept of juvenile delinquency.

CRIMINAL BEHAVIOR DECLINES WITH AGING

Data on the relationship between crime and age indicate that crime is a young person's game. It seems to peak at age 17, before beginning to drop. Younger people may be more likely to be arrested because of inexperience and ineptness in crime. Young people also commit crimes that more easily result in arrest, such as shoplifting, purse snatching, and drug selling. Also, youths tend to commit crimes in groups, and the resolution of a single crime (such as a car theft) may result in several arrests. The decline by age could also be an artifact of incapacitating repeat offenders by imposing longer sentences; such offenders then grow older in prison. Habitual offenders also seem to become less likely to be caught and arrested. Therefore, older prisoners who do return to crime tend to have longer periods before rearrest ("survival periods") and enjoy longer periods of freedom between incarcerations. The most serious offense for which juveniles were arrested can be found in Table 18.1

Although the juvenile crime rate has been declining during the past several years, this could be a result of the shrinking of the population at risk (12- to 18-year-old youths), or it

Table **18.1**	Most Serious Offense for Which Juveniles Were Arrested, 1997–2006	
Most Serious Offense	Total Number of Juvenile Arrests	Percent Change, 1997–2006
Total	1,268,353	−24%
Violent Crime Index	56,467	−20
Murder and nonnegligent manslaughter	710	−42
Forcible rape	2,104	−31
Robbery	19,219	−16
Aggravated assault	34,434	−21
Property Crime Index	237,458	−44
Burglary	49,482	−37
Larceny-theft	165,840	−45
Motor vehicle theft	17,342	−53
Arson	4,794	−22

SOURCE: Federal Bureau of Investigation, "Uniform Crime Report 2006," http://www.fbi.gov/ucr/cius2006/data/table_32.html (accessed February 1, 2008).

could mean that real progress is being made in the juvenile justice system. But, as we will show, juveniles contribute to a significant and alarming portion of the crime problem. Juveniles are persons subject to juvenile court proceedings because a statutorily defined event was alleged to have occurred while their ages were below the statutorily specified limit of original jurisdiction of a juvenile court. A juvenile delinquent, then, has been adjudicated by an officer of a juvenile court for law violations that would be crimes if an adult had committed them.

Because a very large percentage of incarcerated felons were first incarcerated as juveniles in training institutions and schools for delinquents,[3] we look briefly at the development and function of the juvenile court and the juvenile justice system, starting with the philosophy that produced them.

Despite concern for their children's welfare, most communities have a tolerance point for juveniles' disruptive behavior. When children go beyond that point, they can be taken into custody and recorded as delinquents. The mixing of juvenile offenders and adult felons was a practice that had existed for centuries, but in America's early history was looked on as repugnant. In 1899 children in trouble, dependent children, and (finally) delinquent juveniles began to receive differential attention in the courts. The first juvenile court was established in that year in Chicago, and the delinquent joined the dependent and neglected child as a ward of the state. Serious delinquents were the last category to come to the attention of the juvenile court.[4] When the juvenile delinquent was thus placed under the cloak of *parens patriae,* he or she was removed entirely from the formal criminal justice system.

Members of the Culver City street gang use hand signs to communicate membership.
Photo by Alon Reininger, courtesy of Contact Press Images. Inc.

CATEGORIES OF JUVENILE OFFENDERS

Essentially three kinds of children come into contact with the juvenile court system—a significant event in their lives. The children in two of those categories have committed no offense; they are either **dependent** (without family or support) or **neglected** (having a family situation that is harmful to them). The only category that involves an offense is the **delinquent juvenile.**

The care of neglected and dependent children is important, of course, but the juvenile courts were established primarily to handle delinquent juveniles. For judicial purposes, delinquents are divided into three categories:

1. Children who have allegedly committed an offense that would be a crime if an adult had committed it. This group now comprises more than 75% of the population of the state institutions for delinquent juveniles.
2. **Status offenders** who have allegedly violated regulations that apply only to juveniles: curfew restrictions, required school attendance, and similar rules and ordinances. (A "status offender" is generally accepted as a juvenile who has come into contact with the juvenile authorities based on conduct that is an offense only when committed by a juvenile [such as runaway, violations of curfews, and refusal to conform to parental guidance].)
3. **Incorrigible (unruly) juveniles** who have been declared unmanageable by their parents and the court. The second and third groups are often referred to as persons in need of supervision (PINS) or minors in need of supervision (MINS). Thanks to federal intervention, status offenders have been removed from the facilities designed primarily for the first category of delinquent juveniles.[5]

A juvenile institution is intended to provide specialized programs for children who must be under some form of restraint to be treated. Accordingly, it normally houses the more hardened, unstable, or nontreatable youths who fail to meet even the liberal standards for juvenile probation. The institution program attempts to prepare the youth for return to the community.

Despite the vast expansion and growth of community-based facilities, there has been no major decline in the use of juvenile institutions. Spending months or years in confine-

key term

Dependent
Any child without parents or guardians, or whose parents are unable to provide such care, treatment, or custody that should be afforded to a child.

key term

Neglected
General term referring to a child who is not receiving the care that ought to be afforded by parents or guardians.

key term

Delinquent juveniles
Juvenile who has committed a criminal act that if committed by an adult would be a crime.

key term

Status offenders
Juveniles who have committed acts that are law violations by virtue of the child's age but would not be criminal if committed by an adult (such as runaway, incorrigibility, defiance).

key term

Incorrigible juveniles
Unruly juveniles whose behavior is not controlled by their parents.

lecture note

Explain *parens patriae* and detail the assumptions about juveniles leading up to the development of the juvenile court.

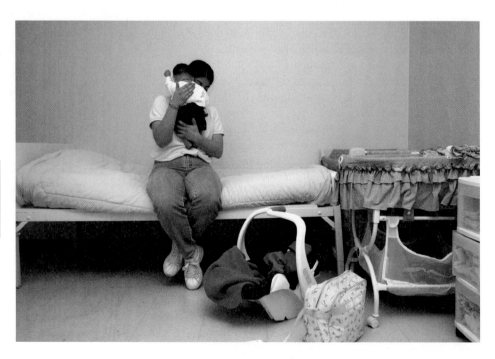

Parenting skills are learned with a mechanical baby in the "Baby, Think Twice" program.
Photo by Spencer Grant. courtesy of PhotoEdit Inc.

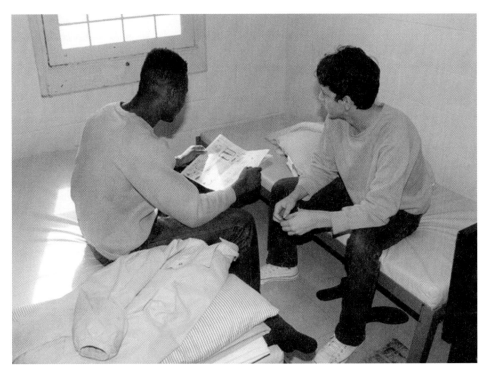

lecture note

Using your computer, play the brief videotape of Francis Cullen on "The Public's Willingness to Save Wayward Youth" (approximately 5 minutes).

lecture note

Explain that criminal offense patterns vary by age, and that a very small proportion of juvenile offenders commit a large part of crimes of violence, and detail those activities. Ask students to explain why this is so.

lecture note

What factors gave rise to the first juvenile court in Chicago? What rehabilitative goals can be identified in the Chicago court?

class activity

Ask students to define *desistance* and identify those social and maturational factors that contribute to general desistance.

ment away from family, friends, and familiar circumstances, however, is an odious prospect for a person of any age. For a young person, the prospect is especially frightening. Compared to the juvenile court's other disposition options, institutional placement of a juvenile in a residential facility is the court's ultimate disposition power. It is the court's most severe and only truly feared disposition.

JUVENILE RIGHTS: THE LANDMARK CASES

Several U.S. Supreme Court cases established many juvenile rights. In the landmark opinions ***Kent v. United States,*** 383 U.S. 541 (1966), and ***In re Gault,*** 387 U.S. 1 (1967), the Supreme Court at long last evaluated juvenile court proceedings and children's constitutionally guaranteed rights. In *Kent* v. *United States,* the Court noted that the child involved in certain juvenile court proceedings was deprived of constitutional rights and at the same time not given the rehabilitation promised under earlier juvenile court philosophy and statutes. It pointed out "there may be grounds for concern that the child receives the worst of both worlds."[6] On May 15, 1967, the Supreme Court rendered its first decision in the area of juvenile delinquency procedure. In the decision, the U.S. Supreme Court ruled that a child alleged to be a juvenile delinquent had at least the following rights:

key term

Kent v. United States
A U.S. Supreme Court decision that courts must provide the "essentials of due process" in transferring juveniles to the adult system.

key term

In re Gault
U.S. Supreme Court decision that juveniles have four basic constitutional rights in hearings that could result in commitment to an institution.

- Right to notice of the charges in time to prepare for trial
- Right to counsel
- Right to confrontation and cross-examination of his or her accusers
- Privilege against self-incrimination, at least in court

The *Gault* decision ended the presumption that the juvenile courts were beyond the scope or purview of due process protection. With *In re Winship,* 397 U.S. 358 (1970), the Supreme Court held that to justify a court finding of delinquency against a juvenile, the proof must be beyond a reasonable doubt that the juvenile committed the alleged delinquent act. *McKeiver* v. *Pennsylvania,* 403 U.S. 528 (1971), implied that the due process standard of "fundamental fairness" applied; the Court rejected the concept of trial by jury for

lecture note

Play the ABC videotape on "Lifers" (approximately 20 minutes).

class activity

Ask students to identify gang pressures and gang problems juveniles face in their local communities. How are juveniles coping with those pressures?

key term

U.S. Office of Juvenile Justice and Delinquency Prevention Act
Act requiring a comprehensive assessment of the juvenile justice system to identify those youth who are victimized or otherwise troubled but have not committed criminal offenses.

lecture note

What are the different categories of children? What other categories, if any, should be added to that list?

lecture note

Why is the institutional placement of a juvenile in a residential facility the juvenile court's ultimate disposition power?

key term

Diversion
The halting or suspension of a juvenile from further involvement with the justice system in return for approved behaviors.

key term

Decriminalization
To remove or reduce the criminal classification or status of a formerly criminal act.

key term

Deinstitutionalization
The return of a patient from a mental hospital into the community.

key term

Decarceration
Process of releasing offenders from institutional facilities, primarily by closing those facilities.

juveniles. The Court contended that the "juvenile proceeding has not yet been held to be a 'criminal prosecution' within the meaning and reach of the Sixth Amendment."[7] Since *McKeiver,* more and more rights have been extended to the juvenile process, while still trying to keep it separate.[8]

The Supreme Court has not been the only source of change in the area of juvenile rights, however. Federal acts and legislation have also played an important role. Until the Uniform Juvenile Court Act of 1968, police or others could still take a child into custody in a situation in which the Fourth Amendment would have exempted an adult. In 1974, the U.S. Congress passed the **Juvenile Justice and Delinquency Prevention Act** (Public Law 93–415). This act required a comprehensive assessment regarding the effectiveness of the existing juvenile justice system. The intent of the act was to clearly identify those youth who are victimized or otherwise troubled but have not committed criminal offenses and to divert such youth from institutionalization. Simultaneously the act was intended to promote the utilization of resources within the juvenile justice system to more effectively deal with youthful criminal offenders.

Thus far, the procedural rights guaranteed to a juvenile in court proceedings are as follows:

1. The right to adequate notice of charges against him or her
2. The right to counsel and to have counsel provided if the child is indigent
3. The right to confrontation and cross-examination of witnesses
4. The right to refuse to do anything that would be self-incriminatory
5. The right to due process, prior to the transfer of a juvenile to an adult court[9]
6. The right to be considered innocent until proven guilty beyond a reasonable doubt

Decisions of the U.S. Supreme Court have led to four major trends in the handling of juveniles: diversion, decriminalization, deinstitutionalization of status offenders, and decarceration.

Diversion is the official halting or suspension, at any legally prescribed processing point after a recorded justice system entry, of formal juvenile (or criminal) proceedings against an alleged offender, and referral of that person to a treatment or care program administered by a nonjustice agency or private agency. Sometimes no referral is given. Diversion programs function to divert juveniles out of the juvenile justice system, encourage the use of existing private correctional agencies and facilities for such youths, and avoid formal contact with the juvenile court. Those programs include remedial education programs, foster homes, group homes, and local counseling facilities and centers. The effectiveness of such programs has not yet been demonstrated, but they are being closely evaluated.

Decriminalization does just what it sounds like it does—it makes the act not criminal anymore. The principal aim in the juvenile and criminal justice systems is to remove from the scope of law and social control certain types of currently proscribed behaviors that pose little perceived danger to society. Those behaviors are frequently seen as "deviant" rather than illegal and thus "not the law's business."[10] The decriminalization movement, then, would delete deviant behavior from juvenile laws and proceedings and leave to social agencies the task of providing assistance if and when requested.

One category of juveniles that falls under the aegis of the juvenile court is the status offender. These youths commit offenses that are based only on the offender's status as a juvenile. These offenses include ungovernability, running away, unruliness, school truancy, disregard for or abuse of lawful parental authority, and repeated use of alcoholic beverages. The nation has moved away from putting status offenders into secure institutional settings (**deinstitutionalization**).[11]

Decarceration removes as many juveniles from custody as possible and treats them in an open environment. This option, given the violent nature of juveniles incarcerated, seems to still be waiting for its time to come. These recommendations reflect the earlier intent of the Juvenile Justice and Delinquency Prevention Act to divert status offenders to shelter facilities rather than juvenile detention centers or jails, as well as not to detain or confine status offenders in any institution in which they would have regular contact with adult offenders. The leading figure in the deinstitutionalization movement is Jerome Miller (1928–), who convinced the governor of Massachusetts to close all but one correctional institution.

WHO IS A JUVENILE TODAY?

The "upper age of jurisdiction" is the key factor in this first decade of the twenty-first century. It is the oldest age at which a juvenile court has original jurisdiction over an individual for law-violating behavior. State statutes define which youth are under the original jurisdiction of the juvenile court. These definitions are based primarily on age criteria. In most states, the juvenile court has original jurisdiction over all youth charged with a criminal law violation who were below the age of 18 at the time of the offense, arrest, or referral to court. Many states have higher upper ages of juvenile court jurisdiction in status offense, abuse, neglect, or dependency matters, often through age 20. All states plus the District of Columbia have at least one provision for transferring juveniles to the criminal court for which no minimum age is specified. Many states have statutory exceptions to basic age criteria. The exceptions, related to the youth's age, alleged offense, and/or prior court history, place certain youth under the original jurisdiction of the criminal court, known as **statutory exclusion.** In some states, a combination of the youth's age, offense, and prior record places the youth under the original jurisdiction of both the juvenile and criminal courts. In these situations where the courts have concurrent jurisdiction, the prosecutor is given the authority to decide which court will initially handle the case. This is known as concurrent jurisdiction, prosecutor discretion, **juvenile waiver,** certification to adult criminal court, or **direct filing.**[12] The number of delinquency cases judicially waived to criminal court grew more than 46% between 1990 and 2007. The trend does vary across offense categories. See Figure 18.1. Data on adjudicated delinquency cases by disposition are found in Figure 18.2.

The most recent national survey of juvenile defendants in crime courts in the largest 40 cities finds that:

1. An estimated 7,100 juvenile defendants were charged with felonies in adult criminal court.
2. Juveniles (64%) were more likely than adults (24%) to be charged with a violent felony.

key term

Statutory exclusion
Principle that requires a category juvenile offender be bound over as an adult, based on the type of offense committed. All such juveniles committing an identified offense must be transferred to adult court.

key term

Juvenile waiver
Juvenile court transfer of alleged delinquents to adult court for more intensive and lengthy punishment.

key term

Direct filing
Prosecutorial decision to refer the case to an adult criminal court rather than to a juvenile court.

figure 18.1
Delinquency Cases Judicially Waived to Criminal Court, 1990–2012

SOURCE: Adapted from C. Puzzanchera et al., *Juvenile Justice Statistics 1999* (Washington, DC: Office of Juvenile Justice and Delinquency Prevention, 2002). Data for 2012 are extrapolated.

figure 18.2

Adjudicated Delinquency Cases by Disposition, 1990–2012

SOURCE: Office of Juvenile Justice and Delinquency Prevention, Statistical Briefing Book, 2006 (http://www.ojjdp.ncjrs.org/ojstatbb/court/ga06501.asp?gadate=2004&text=yes), accessed February 8, 2008. Data for 2012 are extrapolated.

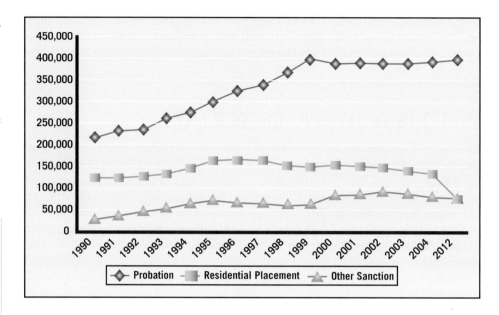

| lecture note

This chapter illustrates many of the problems facing juveniles in our society today: boredom, absent parents, suicide, drug and alcohol abuse, violence, runaways, gangs, gang violence, and inadequate parenting. In your opinion, what can be done to diminish some of these threats to juveniles today?

| class activity

Ask students to describe the procedural rights guaranteed to a juvenile in juvenile court proceedings.

| lecture note

Describe the emerging rights of juveniles since *Kent* v. *the United States.* Why was it necessary for the U.S. Supreme Court to evaluate juvenile court proceedings and the juvenile's constitutionally guaranteed rights?

| class activity

Ask students to compare and contrast decriminalization with decarceration, and to focus on key differences between them.

3. These juvenile defendants were generally treated as serious offenders, as 52% did not receive pretrial release; 63% were convicted of a felony, and 43% received a prison sentence averaging 90 months.[13]

THE JUVENILE CRIME PROBLEM

It has been estimated that approximately 1 of every 6 boys and 1 of every 12 girls in the United States will be referred to a juvenile court before their 18th birthday. The earlier rise in juvenile crime has been considered the most serious aspect of the crime problem in the nation. In 2006, approximately 1.3 million arrests were made of persons under the age of 18.

Gang members holding weapon and flashing gang signs, Long Beach, California.
Photo by A. Ramey, courtesy of PhotoEdit Inc.

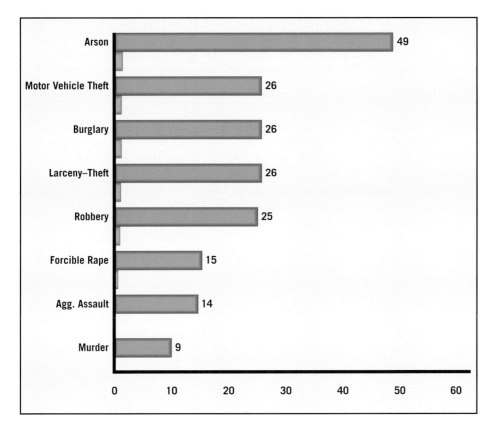

figure 18.3

Percent of Arrests Involving Juveniles

SOURCE: Office of Juvenile Justice and Delinquency Prevention. Juvenile Arrests (http://www.ojjdp.ncjrs.gov/ojstatbb/crime/ga05102.asp?gadate=2005, accessed October 1, 2008).

As shown in Figure 18.3, juvenile arrests have been declining during the past few years, and in 2006 juvenile arrests for property crimes were at the lowest levels since at least the 1960s.

Law enforcement agencies in 2006 made 764 arrests of juveniles for murder and nonnegligent manslaughter; 19,193 arrests of persons under 18 for robbery; 37,135 arrests for aggravated assault; and 2,278 for rape, as reported in the Violent Crime Index (see Figure 18.3). These figures were down from the previous decade. The number of juvenile homicides was 44% below the peak year of 1993 and at its lowest level since the mid-1980s.[14]

JUVENILE VIOLENCE IN DECLINE

As was suggested, across the nation, the amount of violent crime involving juveniles as offenders or victims is on a decline. This is good news, since from about the time of the emergence of crack cocaine in the mid-1980s, the use of violence has become a part of juvenile gang culture, and these crimes seem to have also spread to many youths who are not gang members. Between 1998 and 2006, violent crime for juvenile offenders dropped nearly 19%. Unfortunately, despite the reduction in juvenile crime, the increase in the 1980s and early 1990s, combined with some high-profile cases, has caused society as a whole, and the juvenile courts as well, to develop a "get-tough" attitude toward violent crime by juveniles. Despite the drops, juveniles still account for a significant number of the arrests made in the United States. Juveniles accounted for 15% of all arrests in 2006, more than 15% of all violent crimes, and 23% of the property crimes. Furthermore, while the murder rate has fallen more than 75% since 1993, 9% of all murder arrests in 2006 involved a juvenile under age 18.[15]

lecture note

Describe the diversion process and functions, and the picture of the juvenile that undergoes diversion.

lecture note

Describe the decriminalization movement in the nation and explain the assumptions behind the movement.

lecture note

Describe the variety of upper-age range for transferring the juvenile to the criminal court, and how juvenile waiver can occur. Do juveniles certified to adult court receive more punishment?

class activity

Call student attention to a notorious juvenile case in your state, and ask what the appropriate handling of that case should be. If consensus emerges on waiver and punishment, ask what should be done to prevent recidivism.

class activity

Ask students if they agree with the notion of holding parents accountable for the behavior of their juvenile offspring. Pick a notorious case.

lecture note

Describe the extent of juvenile involvement in crime in your city or state. If it has decreased in recent years, explain what factors have contributed to that decrease.

JUVENILE VICTIMS OF VIOLENCE

Contrary to popular perceptions of the risk of violent crime, teenagers are victimized at higher rates than adults. The following shows some of the findings concerning victimization:

- Between 1980 and 2030, nearly 46,600 juveniles were murdered in the United States.
- The serious violent victimization of juveniles ages 12 to 17 increased from 1985 to 1993, but then dropped substantially until 2006.
- Until their teenage years, boys and girls are equally likely to be victims of murder.
- Between 1980 and 2006, most murdered children younger than age six were killed by a family member, while an acquaintance or stranger killed most older juveniles.
- One in four reported murders of juveniles in 2001 occurred in just five of the nation's more than 3,000 counties (cities in these counties were New York, Los Angeles, Detroit, Chicago, and Philadelphia).
- In one-third of all sexual assaults reported to law enforcement, the victim was younger than age 12.
- Fewer than 50% of teenage homicide victims were shot to death. The overwhelming majority of youth homicide victims in the 10- to 17-year-old age range were male (77%).
- The annual number of juveniles killed with a firearm increased substantially between 1987 and 2001, while the other types of homicides remained constant.[16]

It is important to note that the juveniles who are charged with violent crimes represent 15% of the total crimes committed by juveniles. Despite these relatively small numbers, such crimes of violence as drive-by shootings, casual murder, intrafamilial murder, and senseless abuse of other children create a hard-line attitude in the American public. The courts recognize this perception and are responding with more severe dispositions, including referring those who commit such violent crimes to stand trial as adults (through waiver to adult court).

Violent crime has been and will remain a problem well into this new century. Evidence continues to mount that a small proportion of offenders commits most of the serious and violent juvenile crimes. Decades of research[17] on delinquent careers and prevention have identified the following risk factors as contributing to serious, violent, and chronic juvenile crime:

- Weak family attachments
- Lack of consistent discipline
- Physical abuse and neglect
- Poor school performance
- Delinquent peer groups
- High-crime neighborhoods

On the question of what programs work with youthful offenders, two national assessments of the effectiveness of literally hundreds of intervention programs for treating and handling juvenile offenders found interesting and surprising results.

The most effective approaches are behavioral in nature and include the following types of interventions:

1. Structured learning programs that teach new skills (how to interact with the opposite sex, problem-solving skills, etc.) and reinforce positive behavior and attitudes
2. Cognitive behavioral programs that target attitudes, values, peers, substance abuse, anger, and so on
3. Family-based interventions that train family of appropriate behavioral techniques

Perhaps the most important results dealt with what does not work with youthful offenders. Ineffective programs include Project DARE, drug-education programs, talking cures, self-help programs, targeting non-crime-producing factors, fostering self-esteem, targeting low-risk offenders, correctional boot camps using traditional military basic training, Scared-Straight visits to prisons, home detention with electronic monitoring, and residential programs for juvenile offenders using challenging experiences in rural settings.[18]

The **U.S. Office of Juvenile Justice and Delinquency Prevention (OJJDP)** proposed six strategies for preventing and reducing at-risk behavior and juvenile delinquency:[19]

1. Strengthen families in their role of providing guidance, discipline, and strong values as their children's first teacher.
2. Support core social institutions, including schools, churches, and other community-based organizations, to alleviate risk factors and help children develop to their full potential.
3. Promote prevention strategies that reduce the impact of negative risk factors and enhance protective factors.
4. Intervene immediately when delinquent behavior first occurs.
5. Establish a broad range of graduated sanctions that provides both accountability and a continuum of services to respond appropriately to the needs of each delinquent offender.
6. Identify and control the small percentage of juvenile offenders who are serious, violent, and chronic offenders.

The offending of juveniles is not the only concern. Young people are disproportionately the victims of violence as well. Violence impacts the quality of life for these children in their developing years.

JUVENILE GANGS

The U.S. Juvenile Justice and Delinquency Prevention unit defines a gang as a group of juveniles or young adults in a police jurisdiction that responsible officers would be willing to identify as a "gang." Excluded here are motorcycle gangs, hate or ideological groups, prison gangs (see Chapter 16), and exclusively adult gangs.[20]

It is estimated that in 2004, **youth gangs** were active in more than 2,900 cities with a population over 2,500. (These are the most recent national data.) It is also estimated that approximately 760,000 gang members and 24,000 gangs were active in the United States in 2004. As alarming as these figures are, the good news is that between 1996 and 2004, the number of gangs decreased by over 14%.[21]

The presence of youth gangs and gang problems must be recognized before anything meaningful can be done to address the gang problem. Identifying the manifest and underlying factors contributing to the problem is also important. Promising approaches include the following:

1. Targeting, arresting, and incarcerating gang leaders and repeat gang offenders
2. Referring fringe members ("wannabees") and their parents to youth services for counseling and guidance
3. Providing preventive services for youths who are clearly at risk
4. Crisis intervention or mediation of gang fights
5. Patrols of community "hot spots"
6. Close supervision of gang offenders by criminal justice and community-based agencies
7. Remedial education for targeted youth gang members, especially in middle school
8. Job orientation, training, placement, and monitoring for older youth gang members
9. Safe zones around schools
10. Vertical prosecution, close supervision, and enhanced sentences for hard-core youth gang members (Vertical or hard-core prosecution puts the same prosecutor in charge of all aspects of a case from charging to sentencing.)[22]

key term

Crack cocaine
An illegal drug derived from powder cocaine and consumed primarily by smoking.

lecture note

Ask students to identify some local juvenile gangs and their ethnicities. If the consensus is that they are probably different in ethnicity from other gangs in your jurisdiction, ask if "white" gangs are composed of juveniles with similar ethnicities and backgrounds.

class activity

Ask students to draft a classification policy that would separate dangerous juveniles from other juvenile inmates. This can also be assigned as homework.

lecture note

How was the reality of institutionalization described in the *Gault* case? How have these conditions changed?

key term

RECLAIM
Ohio project designed to reduce admissions to the State's juvenile institutions through grants to local governmental units to underwrite such diversion.

Not until the underlying reasons for belonging to a gang are found will appropriate solutions be developed.

Gangs have been part of the urban scene for decades, but it took the advent of cocaine, especially **crack cocaine,** to create gangs whose only real motivation is money. The law enforcement survey of gangs reports that more than half of the documented gang members in their jurisdiction had migrated from other areas. However, about six in ten agencies reported few or no such migrants. Among agencies that experienced a high percentage of migration, 45% reported that social reasons (such as members moving with their families, and pursuit of legitimate employment opportunities) affected local migration "very much." Drug market opportunities (23%), avoidance of law enforcement crackdowns (21%), and participation in other illegal ventures (18%) were also reported as reasons for migration.[23] Gangs vary in and often are composed by ethnicity and race: white, Asian, Hispanic, African-American, and Pacific-rim gangs abound.

JUVENILES HELD IN INSTITUTIONAL ENVIRONMENTS

In the landmark *Gault* decision, the U.S. Supreme Court emphasized the reality of institutionalization for a juvenile:

> Ultimately, however, we confront the reality. . . . A boy is charged with misconduct. The boy is committed to an institution where he may be restrained of liberty for years. It is of no constitutional consequence . . . and of limited practical meaning . . . that the institution to which he is committed is called an Industrial School. The fact of the matter is that, however euphemistic the title, a "receiving home" or an "industrial school" for juveniles is an institution of confinement in which the child is incarcerated for a greater or lesser time. His world becomes "a building with whitewashed walls, regimented routine and institutional hours. . . ." Instead of mother and father and sisters and brothers and friends and classmates, guards, custodians, state employees people his world, and delinquents confined with him for anything from waywardness to rape and homicide.[24]

An estimated 102,400 juveniles were in correctional institutions and other residential programs at year-end 2006, a 20% increase from 1999.[25] There were more private-sector facilities, but twice as many offenders in public facilities. Figure 18.2 earlier in the chapter shows the disposition of juvenile offenders between 1990 and 2012.

Facilities designated exclusively for juvenile detention are usually not the best examples of how an ideal juvenile correctional facility should be designed and operated. Most of the public-sector structures were originally built for some other purpose and converted to their present use with as little expense as possible. Most are overcrowded before they reach their rated capacities. In the adult institutions the emphasis is on custody, and the same preoccupation with security shapes the programs and general environment in the juvenile facilities. Most are located in urban areas and are virtually sealed off from the community by their physical structure and other security measures. The youths are placed in dormitory-style housing, or single cells in some cases, often with the fixed furniture and dreary interiors that are typical of adult institutions. Most juvenile detention centers lack services and programs that might improve the residents' chances of staying away from future crime.[26] The average cost for juvenile institutional confinement is more than $215 per resident per day, although the cost of small and highly specialized state facilities can easily exceed $600 per resident per day.[27]

One example of an initiative that has successfully reduced the number of youth held in institutions is **RECLAIM** Ohio (Reasoned and Equitable Community and Local Alternatives to the Incarceration of Minors). One of the purposes of RECLAIM was to provide funding to local jurisdictions to develop community programming so that fewer youth

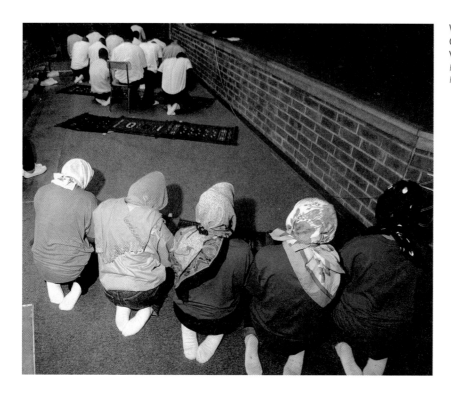

Wards pray in auditorium, California Youth Authority, Ventura, California.
Photo by A. Ramey, courtesy of PhotoEdit Inc.

would be sentenced to state facilities. Since 1995 when RECLAIM went statewide, well over $300 million have been distributed, and the effects on admissions to state institutions have been significant. Figure 18.4 shows the impact of this innovative policy shift on admissions, down over 50% since the program was implemented in 1994. Recently, Illinois began RE-DEPLOY Illinois, modeled after Ohio's program. Only time will tell if it has an impact on that state's juvenile offender population.

An independent evaluation conducted by the University of Cincinnati found RECLAIM Ohio and the Community Correctional Facility (CCF) programs to be cost-effective when compared to placement in any Youth Services (ODYS) institution. To measure effectiveness, juveniles were classified as lower- to moderate-risk youth. High-risk offenders performed better in the program's CCF (estimated cost almost $30,000 per resident year, significantly lower that the ODYS (over $51,000 per resident year). The cost of $1,960 per youth for RECLAIM programming was significantly less than the other two alternatives

figure 18.4

Ohio Department of Youth Services Admissions: 1994–2012

Data from: Ohio Department of Criminal Justice Services (2007). *State of Crime and Justice in Ohio* (Columbus, OH: Ohio Department of Public Safety): pp. 15–17. Data for 2007–2012 are extrapolated.

Male inmate inside cell at Venture School V, California Youth Authority.
Photo by A. Ramey, courtesy of PhotoEdit Inc.

key term
_____

Custody philosophy
Approach to containing juveniles through incarceration programs.

key term
_____

Superpredator
Aggressive juvenile offender believed to engage in frequent and dangerous behaviors.

lecture note
_____

What programs have diminished the number of juveniles in institutions for juvenile offenders?

since RECLAIM provided out-of-home placement, probation, intensive supervised probation, restitution, and county services made available by RECLAIM funding.[28]

Institutions are the most expensive and least successful method of handling juvenile offenders, but until more services needed for supervision and treatment in the community are forthcoming, judges often have no other choice but to commit offenders. The junior prisons are not all bad, but the **custody philosophy** is the prevailing model, which creates the same problems as such philosophies at the adult level.

The New Breed: Dispelling the Myth of the Superpredator

In the past, many of the juveniles in the system were not considered hardened criminals, but simply wayward youngsters who had strayed from the right path. Today, buzzwords such as **superpredator** are used increasingly in the press and by politicians to describe the new type of youthful offender, ruthless young men and women who see crime as a way of life and who are unconcerned about the consequences of their actions, more likely to engage in crime and violence, and less likely to be deterred by the threat of harsh punishment.

Advocates of pursuing a "hard-line" with the "superpredators" were quick to allege "wilding" when "[packs] of bloodthirsty teens from the tenements, bursting with boredom and rage, roam the streets getting kicks from an evening of ultra-violence."

The myth of excessive youth violence has contributed to the public's belief that the juvenile crime rate is increasing and that youth account for a large proportion of overall crime. Yet national data indicate that juveniles account for less than 20% of all crimes; adults make up the other 80%. Youth are decreasingly contributing to the national crime problem.

Governmental units rushed to pass laws to deal with superpredators, but, in fact, they have not emerged. Such laws were touted as benefiting public safety. The evidence today is that treating juveniles as adults increases the probabilities that such young people will continue to reoffend.[29]

As suggested, television news splatters images of heinous crimes perpetrated by youthful offenders. Politicians, eager to look tough on crime and advance their careers, issue promises that they will cure America of this disease by severely cracking down on juvenile delinquency. Although the attacks win political points, not everyone is convinced of their merit. Juvenile justice experts say these attacks can be destructive. Instead of blaming the youth, the media and politicians need to look at the root causes of juvenile delinquency—in particular, the breakdown of the family, child abuse, poverty, and the ready availability of guns. The atmosphere of blame has pressured juvenile justice departments in many states to ignore the causes and concentrate mainly on the crimes. As a result, more youths are being tried in criminal courts and sent to adult prisons (as noted). This is a departure from the way juveniles were handled in the past. Indeed, the prediction of large numbers of juvenile superpredators has not proven true. In fact, juvenile crime, including violent crime, has been declining steadily during the past few years.

Today's Challenges

Adaptations and new programs continue to be developed today. In the 1990s we saw a rise in the number of military-style boot camps designed to drill discipline and coax self-worth into juveniles. Although boot camps were popular with the public and politicians, research on their effectiveness has generally found that they are not effective in reducing recidivism.

Juvenile offenders entering boot camp, Los Angeles Youth Authority.
Photo by A. Ramey, courtesy of PhotoEdit Inc.

class activity

Invite a juvenile court official to speak to your class. Have students prepare questions before the guest arrives that focus on the challenge and rewards of the job. Ask the official to speak to trends in the future. (If you are teaching this class online, use a chat room for discussion purposes).

class activity

Ask students to identify characteristics of a superpredator, and then rank those characteristics by importance. Using notorious but contrasting cases from your local jurisdiction, ask what disposition should be imposed for each.

correctional **brief**

What Works with Youthful Offenders?

Two national assessments of the effectiveness of literally hundreds of intervention programs for treating and handling juvenile offenders found interesting and surprising results.

The most effective approaches are behavioral in nature and include the following types of interventions:

- Structured social learning programs that teach new skills (how to interact with the opposite sex, problem-solving skills, etc.) and reinforce behavior and attitudes

- Cognitive behavioral programs that target attitudes, values, peers, substance abuse, anger, and so on

- Family-based interventions that train family on appropriate behavioral techniques

- Perhaps the most important results dealt with what does not work with youthful offenders:

- Drug-prevention classes focused on fear and other emotional appeals (e.g., DARE)

- Drug education programs

- Talking cures

- Nondirective interventions

- Self-help programs

- Increasing cohesion of criminal groups

- Targeting non-crime-producing factors

- Fostering self-regard (self-esteem)

- Radical nonintervention (doing nothing)

- Targeting low-risk offenders

- Correctional boot camps using traditional military basic training

- School-based leisure-time enrichment programs

- "Scared Straight" programs in which juvenile offenders visit adult prisons

- Home detention with electronic monitoring

- Rehabilitation programs using vague, unstructured counseling

- Residential programs for juvenile offenders using challenging experiences in rural settings

SOURCES: National Institute of Corrections, "Promoting Public Safety Using Effective Interventions with Offenders," http://www.nicic.org (accessed 2001); and Lawrence Sherman et al., *Preventing Crime: What Works, What Doesn't, What's Promising* (Washington, DC: National Institute of Justice, 1998).

|lecture note

Explain how the superpredator failed to emerge in huge numbers. Then ask what special training institutional staff would need to cope with those cases. Finally, ask if the number of special housing units (SHUs) should be increased to accommodate more superpredators.

key term

Restorative justice
System of punishments designed to repair the damage to victims, community, and offender caused by the offender's criminal act.

key term

Teen court
Courts staffed by juveniles who adjudicate juvenile problems and have the authority to enforce those adjudications.

A patient teacher works with a very young offender.
Courtesy of Ohio Department of Youth Services.

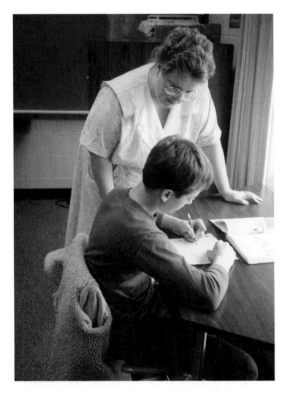

In fact, there is some evidence that juvenile boot camps actually lead to higher failure rates. Some believe this is because the social learning in most boot camps actually teaches and models aggressive behavior.

Fortunately, much research has demonstrated that well-designed treatment programs for youth can be effective in reducing delinquent behavior. Education and restorative justice are two effective ways of successful intervention.[30] Research on effective programs for youth has found that the most effective approaches are behavioral interventions, where offenders learn to replace their delinquent behavior through prosocial modeling and reinforcement. Those programs found not to be effective include, *inter alia,* boot camps, fostering self-regard, home detention with electronic monitoring, and drug education programs.

Restorative Justice

Restorative Justice Online defines **restorative justice** as:

> A theory of justice that emphasizes repairing the harm caused or revealed by criminal justice. It is best accomplished through cooperative processes that include all stakeholders.

> Practices and programs reflecting restorative purposes will respond to crime by:

> 1. Identifying and taking steps to repair harm
> 2. involving all stakeholders, and
> 3. transforming the traditional relationship between communities and their governments in responding to crime.[31]

One example of restorative justice at work in the juvenile delinquency dispositional phase of correcting a juvenile is the **teen court,** also known as the *youth court.* In most cases, the teen court is a diversion program for the first-time unruly and misdemeanor offenses, such as shoplifting, disorderly conduct, destruction of property, and possession of alcohol. In almost all cases, the problem being addressed is a nonviolent crime generally committed by a first-time offender. Volunteer juveniles perform the roles of prosecuting and defense attorneys, bailiff, clerk and jury, with an adult judge presiding. Teen court demands that the delinquents accept responsibility for their actions, and holds them accountable for their offense. Teen-court defendants have already admitted to their personal crime.

Teen jurors hear the case and determine what sentence will be imposed. Sentencing conditions may include performing community service, making financial reimbursement to the victim for the damage the delinquent has inflicted, making a written or oral apology, attending educational programs, obtaining counseling, writing an essay, or performing future teen court service on another case. The jury, of course, may require multiple conditions. Successful completion of all sentence requirements results in the avoidance of a court record and conviction by the juvenile. The restorative justice principles are thus achieved: the offender must make amends to the victim and community, providing opportunities for both victims and community members to participate in the process and provide valuable input in decision making.

The Sioux Falls, North Dakota, teen court, working through Scouting America, indicates national recidivism rates from 3% to 8%. The Anne Arundel (Maryland) teen court reports a 10% recidivism rate; the teen court in Columbus, Ohio, reports a recidivism rate of 4%. If the disposition is not completed in a timely fashion, the case is returned to the referring agency for formal processing.[32]

Although the number of violent juveniles arrested in a given year is still quite small (estimates are 0.5% of youth), the perception of the

Juvenile offenders in Los Angeles, California, work with children with severe disabilities at the El Camino School as part of their jail time and rehabilitation program.
Photo by Tony Savino, courtesy of The Image Works.

dangerous youth remains. This accounts for the pressure to punish juveniles for their crimes by waiving them to criminal courts. People have been looking for a silver-bullet answer to juvenile crime, and the current focus is more on locking them up than on treatment.

Many experts in juvenile justice stress the need to work with families and communities to diffuse problems before they get out of hand:

> Before we put all this money into jails, we must look at education and strengthening the family. Just getting tough and locking juveniles up for long periods will not solve the problem. When values are not being taught and when juveniles have low self-concepts, you are going to get attention one way or another. And attention from the press, politicians and the public is what juvenile delinquents are getting. Many see "Get Tough" as the way to deal with young offenders. They want more jails built and tougher sentences enforced. But many of those who work with juvenile delinquents want more emphasis put on treatment programs so that the interned youth have an opportunity to be rehabilitated. Oliver recounts the tale of a boy who so badly wanted to return to the facility after he was released that he stole a bike and rode back. These stories recounted tenfold over the years beg the question: Do juvenile facilities protect society from the youths under their care, or do they protect delinquent youths from society? Perhaps a bit of both, juvenile experts agree.[33]

lecture note

Point out to your class that about five states hold close to 75% of the delinquents in facilities, but the size of the population in other states has been steeply declining. How can some states have so many delinquents in facilities, while others have facility populations that are dropping? You might want to use Ohio and Texas as sample states.

lecture note

You should give more detail to restorative justice as a legal principle of managing wayward youth. If necessary, search the Internet using the terms "restorative justice" with "juveniles."

TODAY'S APPROACH TO JUVENILE INSTITUTIONS

Directors of early juvenile institutions were concerned chiefly with the protection of society. Youths confined within institutional walls were judged enemies of society, and their custody was looked on as a disciplinary measure. How far have things advanced since then? Has there been measurable progress in the search for an answer to the problem of juvenile delinquency? For the past several decades, juvenile institutions have been subscribing, at least superficially, to a philosophy of social responsibility for the rehabilitation of deviant youth. As a consequence, today's institutions call for greater emphasis on education, vocational training, and personality training, and on the inculcation of socially accepted living habits.

Society has a way of placing its concerns in an order of priority, concerns that are social and technological. One often hears the inquiry, "If we can put a man on the moon, why can't something be done about crime?" In the meantime, the public wants something done about juvenile crime, many urban public schools are barely functioning, and organized and armed youth gangs have emerged as a deadly menace in communities nationwide. A return to the extensive use of incarceration, which stigmatizes youthful criminals as the enemies of society, has not proven effective in solving the juvenile crime problem.[34]

INSTITUTIONAL TREATMENT AND REHABILITATION

Nearly 30 years ago, the Commission on Criminal Justice Standards and Goals offered extensive guidelines and standards to assist the juvenile institutions in their reexamination of educational and vocational training programs. Unfortunately, in spite of those standards and guidelines, actual experience has shown that many youths committed to juvenile institutions are just "doing time."[35] Instead of being a constructive and maturing experience, incarceration in a juvenile institution is likely to be harmful for the juvenile. All juvenile institutions require youth to attend school; but beyond that, the treatment and services offered vary considerably from state to state and facility to facility.

One example of a state that is trying to improve the treatment and services offered to incarcerated youth is West Virginia. There, a pilot program funded by a federal grant has teachers and juvenile correctional staff joining together to improve the treatment of youth in their care. Youth are assessed using a standardized and objective risk/need assessment tool designed to identify those areas of the youth's life that should be targeted for change. Youth then receive a range of programs and services, including school, vocational training, anger management, cognitive behavioral interventions, substance-abuse treatment, and mental health services. While other states are also working to improve the treatment and services offered to incarcerated youth, much remains to be done.

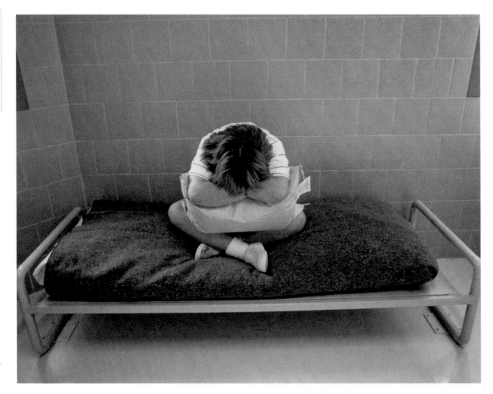

Juvenile teen in cell, Texas.
Photo by Bob Daemmrich, courtesy of The Image Works.

A sixteen-year-old displays the ankle bracelet that restricts her to a 100-foot range from her home.
Photo by AP Wide World Photos.

Prison guards remove shackles from ankles of juvenile offenders at a juvenile hall in California.
Photo by Spencer Grant, courtesy of PhotoEdit Inc.

Summary

It is reasonable to consider that the relatively high proportion of adult felons who were processed through the juvenile treatment delivery systems and training institutions as youths might decrease sharply as alternatives to formal processing, referral, diversion, institutionalization, and labeling are developed for juveniles. Unfortunately, those youth who are left to go through the ever-hardening juvenile institutions are being labeled more like their adult counterparts, and are being referred directly to the adult justice system.[36]

Although there are many examples of programs for our youth that seem to be breaking the patterns of delinquent and criminal behavior, the public seems to have little patience with wayward youth. Gangs and violent acts reinforce that attitude. The number of community-based beds for juvenile programs is shrinking. It is essential that the impacts of poor programming and systems that punish instead of treat our children become known to the general public. Evidence-based programs and changes, while gradually increasing, are needed in the juvenile justice area. Only with informed public support can the patterns of "crime schools" and neglect be broken, so that juveniles will be able to escape the further impact of the adult system. The general public seems to be responding to that kind of logic by making attempts to lower the age of responsibility for criminal remand to adult courts.

It seems that juvenile justice in America will continue at least to give lip service to the ideals of *parens patriae*, but with the Supreme Court watching closely to see that the rights of young citizens are not abused. If we abandon our young people and begin to assume their behavior is adult because it is repugnant or violent, then the jails and prisons of the current century will continue to be overcrowded to the extreme and will become places where it is difficult to provide high-quality programs and services.

Key Words

common law, 356

parens patriae, 356

ward, 356

chancery court, 356

dependent, 358

neglected, 358

delinquent juveniles, 358

status offenders, 358

incorrigible (unruly) juveniles, 358

Kent v. *United States,* 359

In re Gault, 359

Review Questions

1. Explain the concept of *parens patriae*. How does it apply today?
2. Describe and differentiate between the three kinds of children who come into contact with the juvenile courts.
3. What were the major findings in the case of *In re Gault?*
4. What are the major trends in the juvenile justice system?
5. Explain the effect of diversion on the correctional funnel for juveniles.
6. Define *restorative justice* and explain how teen courts implement those procedures.
7. What are five promising approaches to dealing with youth gangs?
8. Debate: Superpredator juveniles should be bound over to the adult courts to be tried as adults.
9. What are the most effective treatment models for juvenile offenders? The least effective?
10. What are the advantages of teen courts?
11. How can restorative justice reduce recidivism?

Endnotes

1. Only about 6% of juvenile gang members in adult and juvenile institutions meet the basic criteria of "superpredator." See George Knox, J. Harris, T. McCurrie, et al., *The Facts about Gang Life in America Today* (Chicago: National Gang Crime Research Center, 1997). See also Liz Ryan and Seth Turner, "New Report Highlights the Impact of Incarcerating Youth in Adult Facilities and Strategies for Reform," *American Jails* 21:2 (2007): 59–65.

2. Chancery courts date back to England's feudal era. They traditionally had broad power over the welfare of children, but exercised that authority almost exclusively on behalf of minors whose property rights were in jeopardy. In America, this authority was extended to minors in danger of both personal and property attacks.

3. Evidence suggests that taking juveniles to juvenile court at first referral may reduce the likelihood of going to prison later in adult life. Wain Brown, T. Miller, and R. Jenkins, "The Human Costs of 'Giving the Kid Another Chance,'" *International Journal of Offender Therapy and Comparative Criminology* 34:5 (1991): 296–302. In addition, about 40% of court referrals in South Carolina were found to have gone on to adult probation and/or prison systems over an 11-year follow-up period. Jan Rivers and T. Trotti, *South Carolina Delinquent Males* (Columbia: South Carolina Department of Corrections, 1995).

4. See Charlotte Bright, Scott Decker, and Andreas Burch, "Gender and Justice in the Progressive Era: An Investigation of Saint Louis Juvenile Court Cases: 1909–1912" *Justice Quarterly* (2007): 657–678.

5. Irving Spergel, R. Chance, K. Ehrensaft, et al., *Gang Suppression and Intervention: Community Models* (Washington, DC: Department of Justice, 1994), pp. 3–4.

6. *In re Gault,* 387 U.S. 1, 27 (1967).

7. *McKeiver v. Pennsylvania,* 403 U.S. 541 (1971).

8. See Christopher Manfredi, *The Supreme Court and Juvenile Justice* (Lawrence: University Press of Kansas, 1998).

9. Robert Meier and G. Geis, *Victimless Crime?* (Los Angeles: Roxbury Publishing, 1997).

10. Philip Secret and J. Johnston, "The Effect of Race in Juvenile Justice Decision-Making in Nebraska," *Justice Quarterly* 14:3 (1997): 445–478.

11. *In re Gault.* See also Adhikain Para and Karaspang Pambata, "Research on the Situation of Children in Conflict with the Law in Selected Metro Manila Cities," http://www.rstorative justice.org/resources/world/asia1/juvjust (accessed January 1, 2008); and *In re C.S.,* 2007–Ohio-4919 (2007).

12. Liz Ryan and Jason Ziedenberg, "The Consequences Aren't Minor: The Impact of Trying Youth as Adults and Strategies for Reform," http://www.campaign4youthjustice.org/Downloads/NEWS/

National_Report_consequences.pdf (accessed February 8, 2008).

13. Bureau of Justice Statistics, "Criminal Case Processing Statutes," http://www.ojp.usdoj.gov/bjs/cases.htm#juvenil (accessed February 8, 2008).

14. Federal Bureau of Investigation, "Uniform Crime Report 2006," http://www.fbi.gov/cius2006/data/table_36.html (accessed February 8, 2008).

15. Howard Snyder and Melissa Sickman, "Juvenile Offenders and Victims: 2006 National Report," http://ojjdp.ncjrs.org/ojstatbb.nr2006/downloads/NR2006.pdf (accessed February 8, 2008).

16. Carl McCurley and Howard N. Snyder, "Victims of Violent Juvenile Crime," *Juvenile Justice Bulletin* (July 2004); Paul Harms and Howard Snyder, "Trends in the Murder of Juveniles: 1980–2000," *Juvenile Justice Bulletin* (September 2004); and *Juvenile Offenders and Victims: 1995 National Report* (Washington, DC: Office of Juvenile Justice Delinquency and Prevention, 1995). The 2006 data are from Office of Juvenile Justice and Delinquency Prevention, "Statistical Briefing Book 2006," http://www.ojjdp.ncjrs.org/ojstatbb/index.html (accessed February 8, 2008).

17. See the excellent review by David Farrington, "Predictors, Causes and Correlates of Male Youth Violence," in Tonry and Moore (eds.), *Youth Violence*, pp. 421–475; National Institute of Corrections, "Promoting Public Safety Using Effective Interventions with Offenders," http://www.nicic.org (accessed September 2001); Lawrence Sherman et al., *Preventing Crime: What Works, What Doesn't, What's Promising* (Washington, DC: National Institute of Justice, 1998); and Margit Weisner, D. M. Capaladi, and H. K. Kim, "Arrest Trajectories across a 12-year Span," *Criminology* 45:4 (2007): 835–864. Evidence-based correctional practices are explored in great detail in the December 2007 issue of *Corrections Today* 69:6 (2007).

18. Lawrence Sherman, *Preventing Crime: What Works, What Doesn't, What's Promising.* Office of Juvenile Justice and Delinquency Prevention, *Highlights of the 2004 National Youth Gang Surveys* (Washington, DC: Office of Justice Programs, 2006).

19. Jeffrey Butts and D. Conners, *The Juvenile Court's Response to Violent Offenders: 1985–1989* (Washington, DC: U.S. Department of Justice, 1993), pp. 14–15.

20. Arlen Egley and Aline Major, *Highlights of the 2002 National Youth Gang Survey,* OJJDP Fact Sheet. (Washington, DC: Office of Juvenile Justice and Delinquency Prevention, 2004).

21. Barbara Allen-Hagen and M. Sickmund, *Juveniles and Violence: Juvenile Offending and Victimization* (Washington, DC: U.S. Department of Justice, 1993), p. 4.

22. Arlen Egley, James Howell, and Ailine Major (eds.), *National Youth Gang Survey Summary: 1991–2001* (Washington, DC: Office of Juvenile Justice and Delinquency Prevention, 2006).

23. *In re Gault.*

24. Michael Tonry (ed.), *The Handbook of Crime and Punishment* (New York: Oxford University Press, 1998). See also Don Gibbons, "Review Essay: Changing Lawbreakers: What Have We Learned since the 1950s?" *Crime and Delinquency* 45:2 (1999): 272–293; and Sharon Levrant, F. Cullen, B. Fulton, and J. Wozniak, "Reconsidering Restorative Justice: Adolescence and Early Childhood," *Crime and Delinquency* 45:3 (1999): 3–27.

25. Melissa Sickmund, *Juvenile Residential Facility Census, 2000* (Washington, DC: Office of Juvenile Justice and Delinquency Prevention, 2002), p. 1.

26. Ibid, p. 1.

27. American Correctional Association, *2007 Directory* (Alexandria, VA: ACA, 2007), p. 24.

28. State of Ohio Office of Criminal Justice Statistics, *State of Crime and Justice in Ohio: Summary* (Columbus, OH: Ohio Department of Public Safety, 2007), pp. 15–16.

29. Ryan and Zeidenberg, "The Consequences Aren't Minor," p. 2.

30. Melissa Sickmund, "Upper Age of Original Juvenile Court Jurisdiction, 1996," adapted from M. Sickmund, H. Snyder, and E. Poe-Yamagata, *Juvenile Offenders and Victims: 1997 Update on Violence* (Washington, DC: Office of Juvenile Justice and Delinquency Prevention, 1997).

31. Restorative Justice Online, "Introduction," http://www.restorativejustice.org (accessed February 16, 2008).

32. Manuel Martinez, "Teen Court," http://www.fccourts.org/DRJ/teenct.html (accessed February 16, 2008). See also Brandi Miller, "Low Recidivism Rate for Teen Court Participants," http://www.siouxempireunitedway.org/NewsReleases/2007/TeenCourt.pdf (accessed February 17, 2008).

33. Stephen Gluck, "Wayward Youth, Super Predator: An Evolutionary Tale of Juvenile Delinquency from the 1950s to the Present," *Corrections Today* 59:3 (1997): 62–66.

34. Stephen Feiler and J. Sheley, "Legal and Racial Elements of Public Willingness to Transfer Juvenile Offenders to Adult Court," *Journal of Criminal Justice* 27:1 (1999): 55–64.

35. But see Michael Hagan, M. Cho, J. Jensen, et al., "An Assessment of the Effectiveness of an Intensive Treatment Program for Severely Mentally Disturbed Juvenile Offenders," *International Journal of Offender Therapy and Comparative Criminology* 41:4 (1997): 340–350.

36. Steven Donziger, *The Real War on Crime* (New York: HarperCollins, 1996), pp. 134–140.

chapter **19**

Special-Category Offenders

Outline

> "The United States currently has more mentally ill men and women in jails and prisons than in all state hospitals combined."
>
> —Chris Sigurdson

Overview

Now we come to the chapter that deals with those offenders who have many more problems than other offenders in the mainstream of criminal behavior. We examine some of the so-called "rejects" of society who are too often found in America's jails and correctional facilities.[1] Many of those individuals are handicapped by their mental processes, and others are labeled by their specific problems, extreme behavior, or personal background.

Of the many categories that could be examined, we have chosen to discuss the mentally disordered offender, the developmentally challenged (retarded) offender, the sex offender, HIV-infected inmates, and geriatric inmates. Although these categories do not constitute an exhaustive list of the possible types of special-category offenders, we feel they are a fair spectrum of the problems faced by correctional administrators and the individual offenders who are in their custody and treatment. We first delve a little into the history and development of categories of mentally disordered (mentally ill) offenders to provide a proper framework for examination of these special inmates.

Since 1970, the closing of 90% of the mental health facilities and centers in local counties and their state-funded counterparts has diverted the mentally disordered into correctional facilities (jails and prisons), a process called **transincarceration.** The increasing and unrestrained overcrowding continues to place these stigmatized offenders into the correctional bureaucratic system, where their special needs are more often ignored than met. What their needs are and how they are met are discussed in this chapter. We also assess the growing numbers of these special-category offenders and how our systems are coping with this problem. The student has now been exposed to most of the clients found in the criminal justice and juvenile justice systems. In Part 4 we delve into the rights of all of these offenders, in or out of the confinement facilities in America, as well as their right to life itself.

THE MENTALLY DISORDERED OFFENDER

What kind of illness would civilized people find so repulsive that they would reject the sufferers in the most barbaric fashion and brand them with a stigma that would remain with them for a lifetime, even if a cure were achieved? Those unfortunates, persons with mental disability (mentally disturbed and disordered), were once scorned, banished, and even burned as evil. But, in more enlightened times, we built backwoods fortresses for them, presumably to protect ourselves from contagion. They have been executed as witches, subjected to exorcisms, chained, or thrown into gatehouses and prisons to furnish a horrible diversion for the other prisoners.[2]

Before the Middle Ages, persons with a mental illness (**mentally disturbed**) were generally tolerated and usually cared for locally by members of their own family, tribal system, or primitive society. However, the advent of widespread poverty, disease, and religious fanaticism seemed to trigger intolerance for any unexplainable deviation from the norm. People who were mentally disturbed were thought to be possessed by devils and demons and were punished harshly because of it. As mentioned in Chapter 1, they were subjected to having "the Devil beaten out of them." At that time, the insane were driven out of society, but later they were confined in asylums, another form of isolation from society.

The first insane **asylum** was constructed in Europe in 1408.[3] From that date until recently, the asylum was a dumping ground for all the mentally disordered people that could be neither understood nor cured. In the United States, one after another of the individual states responded to that compelling method of ridding society of misfits by building numerous institutions during the mid-1800s. The inflated claims of cures for mental illness could not stand up against the process of institutionalization, however, and long-term commitments, often for a lifetime, not cures, became the rule of the day.

Asylums became yet another "invisible empire" in America, with the punitive excesses and lack of care or caring ignored by society. "Out of sight, out of mind" was the catch phrase for these unfortunates. With the discovery of tranquilizing drugs, these "snake pits" became places where patients were put into a controllable stupor, until the "magic bullet," a cure for mental illness, could be found. Longer and longer periods of institutionalization, often ordered at the request of family members, finally got the attention of the courts.

In the 1960s, the rights of all citizens, including the mentally ill and convicts, were being reexamined at every level. The abuses in the back wards of the asylums were brought to light and the counterreaction was extreme. In the early 1970s, state after state adopted policies under the Community Mental Health Act that swept the country. The essential goal was to release (**deinstitutionalize**) all inmates of the asylums who were not a "clear and present danger" to themselves and society.

Although benign in their intents, these acts flooded the central cities of America with tens of thousands of street people with mental impairments and created poorhouses. The response by most jurisdictions has been to transfer the problem to the criminal justice system, filling the jails and correctional institutions of America, a process known as **transinstitutionalization**.[4] In the early 1980s in Seattle, Randy Revelle, a former King County executive, was fond of saying that the King County Jail was the "third largest mental health facility in the state. The first being the Western State Hospital, the second the section of I-5 [freeway] between the jail and the hospital."[5]

Mentally Ill Inmates

From the 1960s to the 1980s, the deinstitutionalization movement demanded that people with mental illnesses be treated in the community, using new drug therapies that appeared to control even the most extreme behaviors of people with mental illnesses. People with mental illnesses suffer from one or more brain dysfunctions that include depression, schizophrenia, and anxiety disorders, which are often successfully treated with such medications as Prozac and Zoloft. This liberation of psychiatric patients was reinforced by court decisions that awarded certain legal rights to people who were emotionally ill. But few community-based programs were developed to treat psychiatric patients effectively. Released to the community without adequate support and treatment services, people with mental illnesses gravitated to criminal confinement facilities for offenders, particularly to jails, but also to the prisons of the United States.

It is estimated that at least 20% of offenders imprisoned at any time have severe or acute mental illnesses, such as schizophrenia, manic-depression illness, and depression. Approximately 10% to 15% of persons with these three illnesses die by suicide. Yet current treatment is extremely effective, if given.[6]

Prisoners tend to be in poor mental health, and about 80% of male prisoners (and 80% of female jail inmates) will, over their lifetime, have at least one psychiatric disorder. The greater the level of disability while in prison, the more likely the inmate is to receive mental health services. In practice, proportionately more female prisoners use mental health services than do males, and whites are more likely to seek or secure prison mental health services than others. At least half of the inmates who need such treatment go without it.

While the U.S. Supreme Court has not found that inmates have a constitutional right to treatment, it has ruled that an inmate's constitutional right to medical treatment includes the right to treatment for serious emotional illness. The corrections system is caught in the middle. Institutions are not required to provide services simply because their clients are criminals, and thus have shifted critical funds to other uses (such as increased security staffing). On the other hand, the threat of potential litigation or having a court-appointed correctional master has meant that some revision and provision of mental health services for seriously ill inmates is necessary.[7]

As people with mental illnesses became a larger segment of the population in jails and prisons, professionals in the mental health field became essential to the correctional administrators. Although the ratio of mental health practitioners to inmates remains much too low, there has been some progress. Because many institutions must deal with mental health issues on a priority basis, few to no services are provided for the majority who do not exhibit violent or bizarre behavior. It is a practical fact that in corrections, "the squeaky wheel gets the grease."[8]

It appears that the relationship between crime and mental disorder (at least in *groups*, as shown in one study) has no real causal effect.[9] It is essential for society to learn more

A unit for mentally disturbed inmates at the Los Angeles County Jail, built in 1998. *Photo courtesy of AP Wide World Photos.*

about distinguishing between different kinds of mental illness and their impacts on safe and secure administration of correctional institutions. It is important to remember that the real link to look for is one that indicates the potential for harm to the mentally ill person and others. It may be a long time before such options are available to the already overcrowded corrections systems in the United States.

Two Ways to Escape Criminal Responsibility

There are two justifications that defendants can invoke in an attempt to relieve themselves of criminal responsibility for a criminal act. The first is **not guilty by reason of insanity (NGRI);** the second is **incompetent to stand trial.** In the first instance, offenders do not deny the commission of the act, but assert they lacked the capacity to understand the nature of the act or that it was wrong. The second instance is based on the common law criterion that defendants must be able to understand the charges against them and to cooperate with their counsel in the preparation of their own defense. The procedures for determining competency vary considerably among jurisdictions, but most make it a court decision based on psychiatric testimony. If defendants are found incompetent to stand trial, then they are usually committed to a mental institution until declared competent.

The Criminally Insane

With the advent of legal insanity and legal incompetence as defenses against criminal conviction came the development of special asylums for the **criminally insane,** in most cases just another form of prison without due process protections. A visiting student from Italy once remarked to the authors, when visiting a hospital for the criminally insane, "How can a person be criminally insane? If you are criminally responsible you cannot be insane, if you are insane you cannot be criminally responsible." That question is difficult to answer directly; such institutions are usually reserved for the following categories of offenders:[10]

1. Persons adjudicated incompetent to enter a plea or stand trial
2. Defendants found not guilty by reason of insanity
3. Persons adjudicated under special statutes (e.g., "sexually dangerous persons," "defective delinquents," or "sexual psychopaths")
4. Convicted and sentenced offenders who have become mentally disturbed while serving a prison sentence and have been transferred to a mental health facility
5. Other potentially hazardous mentally ill persons requiring special security during the course of their evaluation and treatment

In more recent years, those claiming to be NGRI have been the subjects of considerable debate.[11] President Nixon sought to have the NGRI defense abolished. More informed criminologists point to such problems with the insanity defense as excessive media coverage, suspicion of malingering by the defendant, and conflicting and suspicious testimony by mental health professionals testifying for either the defense or the prosecution.

The insanity defense is used in less than 1% of all felony cases, and of those, only one in four are found to be NGRI. One study found only the most emotionally and behaviorally disturbed defendants to be successful in their plea and that the successful petitioners had committed more serious offenses. The decision to acquit is more frequently made in court by prosecutors, defense attorneys, and the judge, and less frequently by jury members. Persons acquitted by NGRI are generally found less likely than their cohort of convicted offenders to commit crimes after release.[12]

Prosecutors often hope that those accused offenders acquitted through the plea of NGRI will be institutionalized for a period sufficient to reduce their dangerousness, and to provide both public safety and some retribution. The debate continues. Perhaps the most

Special-Category Offenders   chapter **19**   **381**

reasonable solution would be to determine guilt first and then shift the issue of diminished capacity (insanity, in this case) to the sentencing or case disposition stage. The American Psychiatric Association, following the attack by John Hinckley on the life of President Reagan, recognized that position.

As a response, by 1986, 12 states abolished the insanity defense entirely, then created **guilty but mentally ill (GBMI)** statutes in its place.[13] Under those statutes, an offender's mental illness is acknowledged but not seen as sufficient reason to allow him or her to escape criminal responsibility. If convicted, offenders are committed to prison. Some states will provide mental health treatment in the prison setting, but others may transfer the offender to a mental health facility for treatment. In Georgia, defendants who entered insanity pleas but were determined GBMI received harsher sentences than their counterparts, whose guilt was determined in trial, suggesting increased punishment for the disturbed offender.[14]

The position of the American Psychiatric Association is that significant changes in the legislation should be made to deal with the disposition of violent persons acquitted by NGRI[15]:

1. Special legislation should be designed for those persons charged with violent offenses who have been found not guilty by reason of insanity.
2. Confinement and release decisions should be made by a board including both psychiatrists and other professionals representing the criminal justice system and akin to a parole board.
3. Release should be conditional on having a treatment supervision plan in place, with the necessary resources available to implement it.
4. The board having jurisdiction over the released insanity acquittees should also have the authority to reconfine them.
5. When psychiatric treatment in a hospital setting has obtained the maximal treatment benefit possible, but the board believes that for other reasons confinement is still necessary, the insanity acquittee should be transferred to the most appropriate nonhospital facility (prison).

While the public remains upset by a seemingly gaping loophole in the net of justice, the courts continue to seek equitable ways to deal with the offender who has diminished mental capacity.

The Problems of Prediction

It is unfortunate that the long indeterminate sentences often given to mentally disordered offenders reflect a fear that those committed might be a problem in the future. It is the expectation that someone is capable of predicting criminal inclination that makes so questionable the programs for treating those who are mentally disordered. Who can **predict potential dangerousness** with any degree of accuracy? Noted psychiatrist Bernard Rubin stated, "The belief in the psychiatrist's ability to predict the likely dangerousness of a patient's future behavior is almost universally held, yet it lacks empirical support." He added, "Labeling of deviancy as mental illness or predicting dangerousness is just a convention to get someone to treatment. Once in treatment the concept of dangerousness is forgotten."[16]

So we see the paradox of requiring psychiatrists to predict behavior and to attach a label to offenders, when that might result in an indefinite, or even lifelong, commitment to a mental institution for someone who is not really dangerous (a false-positive prediction). Further, the individual is then labeled for custody and treatment in a special area within that institution. When we consider the wealth of folklore surrounding mental institutions, it becomes clear that a dreadful lifelong stigma accompanies the label of "criminally insane."

key term

Guilty but mentally ill (GBMI)
Plea entered by the defendant acknowledging guilt but asserting a lack of capacity to understand the nature of the act or that it was wrong.

class activity

Ask an official with the office of the local prosecutor to speak to your class on the subject of "court determination of not guilty by reason of insanity." Have students prepare questions beforehand about the satisfactions and challenges of the prosecutor's job. (If you are teaching this class online, use a chat room for discussion purposes.)

lecture note

Discuss mentally disordered, low functioning, and developmentally challenged offenders. What are the dominant approaches for handling such offenders in a correctional system?

key term

Predict potential dangerousness
Process by which treatment staff assess dangerousness, the offender's risk for future dangerous offenses.

THE DEVELOPMENTALLY CHALLENGED OFFENDER

key term

Developmentally challenged
Another term denoting mental retardation.

lecture note

The prediction of "dangerous" yields four major results: offenders who are predicted dangerous and are; offenders who are predicted not dangerous and are not; offenders who are predicted dangerous but are not ("false positive"); and offenders who are predicted not dangerous but are ("false negatives"). Ask students how prediction can be made more accurate.

class activity

Develop a vignette dealing with a dangerous offender, and ask students to predict if the offender is dangerous, how long between prediction and reoffending, and what correctional program that person should receive. Then present a synopsis of a case of a serial killer, and repeat the process.

lecture note

Play the videotape of Richard Tewksbury on "Mentally Challenged Offenders" (about 6 minutes).

class activity

Ask students to propose a three-phase diversion program for the developmentally challenged offender at point of first arrest.

Within the correctional system are offenders who, though considered legally sane and competent to stand trial, are **developmentally challenged (mentally retarded).** (An IQ score of 69 or below on a standardized test is the generally accepted measure for identifying the developmentally challenged, with exceptions.) Their intellectual level and social adaptability measure well below average, yet they are adjudged legally responsible for their actions. Some 4% to 9% of the prison population is composed of developmentally challenged inmates.

In addition to the developmentally challenged, prisons contain an unknown but larger number of lower-functioning inmates with fewer intellectual abilities (compared to the general prison population) and IQs that may approach 70, but who are not technically retarded. They have diminished intellectual abilities but a diagnosis of mental retardation is not warranted. Unlike mental illnesses, the developmentally challenged and lower-functioning inmates are not treated with medication, but may learn both skills and coping mechanisms that would allow them to lead more satisfactory and productive lives.

In their guidelines for incarcerated developmentally challenged offenders, Santamour and West address the problems encountered:[17]

1. In prison, the retarded [developmentally challenged] offender is slower to adjust to routine, has more difficulty in learning regulations, and accumulates more rule infractions, which, in turn, affect housing, parole, and other related matters.
2. Retarded [developmentally challenged] inmates rarely take part in rehabilitation programs because of their desire to mask their deficiencies.
3. They often suffer the brunt of practical jokes and sexual harassment.
4. Such inmates are more often denied parole, serving on the average two or three years longer than other prisoners for the same offense.

Administrators from both fields (corrections and mental health) have a tendency to regard the developmentally challenged offender as a misfit in their system of services.

Prisoner with learning disabilities working with a computer.
Courtesy of Pennsylvania Department of Corrections.

(People with developmental challenges tend to have higher rates of involvement in violent incidents in prison.[18]) Well-meaning administrators from both systems look to one another to assume responsibility for programming and funding. Because of the few resources available to each system and even more pressing concerns, the result is often very limited programming.

The special needs of the developmentally challenged offender are unique, and the program models are few. Those models that do exist are limited primarily to special education programs geared more to the needs of the individual with learning disabilities other than those of the developmentally challenged person. One promising model concerned with these offenders on a county level focuses on substance abuse, psychological needs, and both vocational and educational improvement.[19]

Historical Perspective

In reviewing historical and philosophical trends in the study of the developmentally challenged offender, it is noteworthy that before the late nineteenth century, little attempt was made to differentiate between the developmentally challenged individual and anyone who committed a crime.

Currently there is less reluctance to associate "retardation" directly with delinquency. Much of the revived interest from the 1960s to date has been generated by the legal community and not by criminologists. Such a phenomenon stems from a growing awareness that the preponderance of developmentally challenged individuals in the criminal justice system may be more an administrative and legal artifact than evidence for a causal relationship between the developmentally challenged and criminality.

The landmark ***Ruiz* v. *Estellez*** decision has also set the tone for judicial consideration of the developmentally challenged inmate.[20] This class-action suit involved issues of overcrowding, medical care, inmate trustees as guards, and other conditions; the federal court declared the Texas prison system to be unconstitutional. Judge Justice found that between 10% and 15% of the Texas Department of Corrections inmates were developmentally challenged and that they were distributed throughout the system. The judge echoed Santamour and West concerning the developmentally challenged inmates' special problems and added the following:

1. They are abnormally prone to injuries, many of which are job related.
2. They are decidedly disadvantaged when appearing before a disciplinary committee.

This raises basic problems of fairness and the special need for assistance.[21] It seems obvious that the issue of the developmentally challenged inmate is slowly coming to the forefront, led by the decisions of the courts.

Recent litigation has determined emerging rights of the developmentally challenged inmate. In 1981, *Green* v. *Johnson* (512 F. Supp. 965) established that mentally retarded inmates under age 22 have a right to receive special education. In *Atkins* v. *Virginia* (536 U.S. 304, 2002), the U.S. Supreme Court ruled that mentally retarded inmates cannot be executed. In 2007, the U.S. Supreme Court decided that incompetent prison inmates could not be executed in *Panetti* v. *Quarterman* [(551 U.S. 2007)] 127 S.Ct.2842, 2007. The Americans with Disabilities Act requires all correctional agencies to establish procedures to screen for developmentally challenged inmates and provide rehabilitation programs specifically designed for them. (See Chapter 15.)

Developmentally challenged offenders are often individuals who have never been accepted by society at large. Becoming a part of the "society of captives" is often their first experience of acceptance and thus has a pervasive impact. At Bridgewater State Hospital and Prison in Massachusetts, personnel commenting on the strengths of the association between developmentally challenged inmates and the prison culture noted that only the developmentally challenged inmates returned to prison for social visits. Are developmentally

class activity

Ask a forensic therapist or psychologist to lecture in your class on managing the developmentally challenged offender in a correctional situation.

lecture note

Discuss the developmentally challenged and the low-functioning inmate. Focus on management issues and treatment programs.

key term

Ruiz v. *Estellez*
U.S. Supreme Court decision that prisons must provide treatment to the developmentally challenged, assessing the conditions in the Texas Department of Corrections.

class activity

Ask students to brief the case of *Ruiz* v. *Estelle* and ask if developmentally challenged inmates have a constitutional right to treatment. If the consensus is "yes," ask what treatment should be provided.

challenged offenders in need of special consideration in regard to criminal responsibility? As noted by Richard C. Allen,

> Historically, society has pursued three alternative courses with the developmentally challenged offender: we have ignored his limitations and special needs; or we have sought to tailor traditional criminal law processes to fit them; we have grouped him with psychopaths, sociopaths, and sex deviates in a kind of conventicle of the outcast and hopeless.[22]

One way to accomplish such consideration would be with a special court, similar to a juvenile court, where the developmentally challenged offenders are handled both for the crime and for their condition.

SEX OFFENDERS

Common Sex Offenses

Any analysis of sex offenses is complicated because state legislatures are often too inhibited to describe specifically the acts they are seeking to punish. Thus, punishment may be decreed for "lewd and lascivious conduct," "acts against nature," "carnal knowledge," "imperiling the morals of a minor," and so on. Almost any sexual activity can be prosecuted under one or another of those vague and overly broad rubrics. The same term, moreover, means different things in different states. Thus, **sodomy,** which in many states would refer primarily to male homosexual acts, might also be applied to heterosexual oral or anal intercourse or to sexual contacts with animals.

Highly misleading terms may be used, such as *statutory rape* for an offense that is not rape at all, but sexual intercourse with a fully consenting female who has not yet reached the age of legal consent (18 in some states). Discussions of **sex offenses** are further complicated by the fact that a man charged with a serious offense such as rape may be permitted, in the course of plea bargaining, to plead guilty to a lesser offense; hence, men who are in fact rapists may be lodged in correctional institutions for such apparently nonsexual offenses as breaking and entering or assault. In the following discussion we consider the actual offenses committed, rather than the vague legal terminology often used or the lesser offenses to which an offender may plead. Trends in reported rape can be found in Figure 19.1.

Until the past few years, the term *sex offense* commonly called to mind a lust-murder of the most irrational and heinous type. More recently, the intense and proper concern of the women's movement with rape and related crimes, such as assault with intent to commit rape, has tended to make rape the predominant sex offense in the minds of many people.

lecture note

Using your computer, play the three videotape segments by Richard Tewksbury on "Sex Offender Registries and Their Implications" (about 7 minutes).

key term

Sodomy
Anal or oral copulation with a member of the same or opposite sex, or copulation with an animal; the U.S. Supreme Court recently struck down sodomy law application to consenting adults in private.

key term

Sex offenses
Violations of laws that control sexual intercourse or crimes of a carnal nature, including attempts at such crimes.

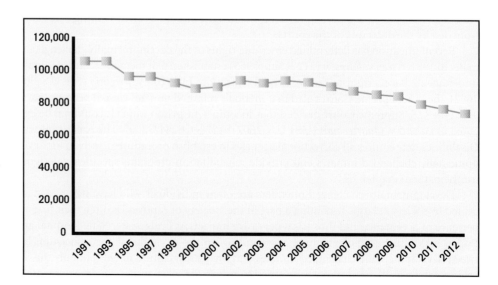

figure 19.1

Reported Female Rapes: 1991–2012

SOURCES: Federal Bureau of Investigation, Uniform Crime Reports 2005, 2006 (http://www.fbi.gov/ucr/05cius/data/table_01.html, accessed January 15, 2007). Data for 2007–2012 are extrapolated.

figure 19.2
Forcible Female Rape: 1991–2012
(rate per 100,000 females)

SOURCE: Federal Bureau of
Investigation, Uniform Crime Report
2006 (www.fbi.gov/ucr/cius2006/data/
table_01.html, accessed January 15,
2008). Data for 2007–2012 are extrapolated.

Data on forcible female rape can be found in Figure 19.2. Many experts believe that heterosexual rape, in its more violent forms, is not a sex crime at all but a crime of power and dominance over women.[23]

By far the most common sex offenses, however, are three that are rarely prosecuted: fornication, adultery, and male homosexual contact:

- **Fornication** is sexual intercourse between persons not married to each other; it remains a crime in most states but is generally ignored by the law enforcement and criminal justice systems.
- **Adultery** is sexual intercourse between two persons, at least one of whom is married to someone else. It also remains a crime in most states, but it is rarely punished and almost never leads to participation in a treatment program.
- **Male homosexual conduct** and other acts classed as *sodomy* were the most common of all sex offenses; the Kinsey reports and more recent data indicate that millions of such sexual contacts are committed each week. In 2003, the U.S. Supreme Court struck down a Texas state law banning private consensual sex between adults of the

key term

Fornication
Sexual intercourse between
persons not married to each
other.

key term

Adultery
Sexual intercourse between
two persons, at least one of
whom is not married to the
second party.

key term

Male homosexual conduct
Sexual contacts between
homosexuals. In 2003, the U.S.
Supreme Court decriminalized
homosexual behavior between
consenting adults.

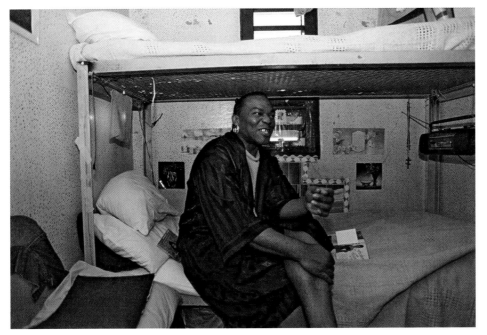

Gay inmate "Jacquie" lives
well at the maximum-security
Buckingham Correctional
Institution in Virginia.
© Shepard Sherbell/SABA/CORBIS
All Rights Reserved.

same sex (Lawrence and *Garner* v. *Texas,* 593 U.S. 558), decriminalizing homosexual behavior between consenting adults.[24] Some correctional facilities continue to view homosexual behavior as an infraction of institutional rules, as they would any sexual behavior between correctional staff and inmates.

Laws governing public indecency and solicitation for prostitution are still enforced in many jurisdictions. But they commonly lead to fines, probation, or short sentences in local correctional institutions. The remaining five categories of sex offenses account for the overwhelming majority of treatment program participants:

1. Rape, attempted rape, assault with intent to rape, and the like[25]
2. Child molestation[26]
3. Incest[27]
4. Exhibitionism and voyeurism
5. Miscellaneous offenses (breaking and entering, arson, and the like) in cases involving a sexual motivation

Child abuse is any act of commission or omission that endangers or impairs a child's physical or emotional health and development. The major forms are physical (such as neglect), emotional (deprivation and abandonment), and sexual. **Child abusers** are found among all ethnic, racial, class, and religious groups. A child abuser is typically a person closely related by blood, kinship, or marriage, such as a parent, stepparent, guardian, other relative, or even a neighbor engaged in a repeated pattern of abuse.

A **child molester** is one who injures or has questionable sexual relations or dealings with a person under the age of puberty or legal age. Victims may be subject to rape, fondling, indecent exposure, sodomy, or murder. In correctional facilities, both child abusers and molesters rank low in the social system and are themselves frequently targets of prejudicial or lethal acts by other inmates.

The majority of sex offenders currently participating in treatment programs are predominantly heterosexual and are there for heterosexual offenses, though some of them, like some heterosexual nonoffenders, have had occasional or incidental homosexual contacts. Most homosexual participants in treatment programs are there for sexual contacts, rarely violent, with children or adolescents. Some are homosexual incest offenders. A few have committed homosexual rape or rape-related offenses.

Almost all sex offenses *prosecuted* in the United States today (except for prostitution-related offenses and offenses involving indecent public performances) are committed by men. The only significant exceptions are the rare cases of child molestation in which a woman is prosecuted along with a man, often her husband, as an accessory, or in child pornography. As a rough estimate, 200 or 300 males are prosecuted for sex offenses for every female prosecuted. It is probable, of course, that the ratio of offenses committed by females is much higher than the ratio of prosecutions.

Most sex offenders in treatment programs are 18 to 35 years of age. A significant minority (mostly child molesters, those offenders whose contacts with children are of a sexual nature) is past 50. How do the sex offenders enrolled in treatment programs differ from the remainder of sex offenders? At least five "sorting processes" distinguish the two groups. Some sex offenses are reported to the police; others are not. Most rapes and a wide range of lesser offenses go unreported. No man ends up in a treatment program as a result of an unreported offense. After an offense is reported, the perpetrator may or may not be apprehended and prosecuted. Those who escape arrest and prosecution no doubt differ in significant respects from those who reach the courts.

Of those prosecuted, a small number are found not guilty and a very large number (mostly minor offenders) receive suspended sentences or are placed on probation without assignment to a treatment program. Of the offenders remaining after those three sorting processes, some are sent to ordinary correctional institutions and others to treatment programs. Who will be sent to treatment programs depends in part on state law, in part on the judge, and in part on the availability of a treatment program.[28]

Finally, most treatment programs can (and do) reject or transfer to other institutions those offenders they deem unsuitable for treatment. The net effect of these five sorting processes is a population of program participants from which most of the very serious offenders and most of the very minor offenders have been screened.

Sex Offenders and Probation

Probation officers are generally underprepared or undertrained to work with sex offenders because such preparatory efforts are complex, expensive, and time intensive. Most officers lack specific training in the required interpersonal and professional skills. Often caseload size inhibits effective supervision; probation linkages with other social service agencies and providers are not optimal. Often female officers feel concerned about their own safety, and most sex offenders are "high-need" cases.

Probation officers, to control sex offenders, increasingly use enhanced probation services, through specialized caseload and electronic monitoring, GPS monitoring, and intensive supervision. Probation and parole agencies also contract with privately run community correctional centers to provide treatment programs for sex offenders as an adjunct to community control (see Chapter 12). As these strategies are more widely implemented across the nation, a smaller proportion of treatable sex offenders will be committed to prison facilities.

It is possible, of course, that tomorrow an alumnus of one of those treatment programs may commit a heinous lust-murder; however, an alumnus of a local high school or a member of a church choir could do the same. Treatment programs are specifically designed to minimize the likelihood that an offender will commit any sex offense following release, either a crime of the grossly offensive type or a lesser offense similar to the ones the offender committed in the past.

Sex Offenders in Prison

Attitudes toward sex offenders widely held by the public[29] as well as by legislators,[30] judges,[31] corrections officers,[32] and others in positions of power are largely influenced by traditional beliefs, and continue to change. The number of sex offenders who are prisoners in state corrections systems continues to climb.

In correctional facilities providing more comprehensive treatment services to sex offender populations, treatment program elements (modalities) are usually combined. Such modalities can include sex education, human sexuality, stress and anger management, social skills, substance-abuse programs, how to identify and avoid high-risk situations, relapse prevention, and coping skills.

Long-term programs generally provide intensive and highly structured programs of at least two years, aftercare (up to a year), and follow-up services. Clients can be returned for refresher treatment ("tune-ups"), if necessary. Treatment with the so-called castration drug (Depo Provera) provides the same effect as castration, without the need for surgery. Although its use is not common, it might be used as an adjunct to supervision.

Initial studies of the effectiveness of combined treatment are favorable. California reports rearrest follow-up rates (for sexual or other offenses) of 6% to 8%. Texas, using Depo Provera as an adjunct to individual and group treatment, showed relapse rates for Depo Provera–treated subjects to be one-third that for comparison offenders not treated, and about 40% less than comparison cases after the drug was withdrawn. The Texas evaluation concludes that maintenance-level Depo Provera drug treatment is beneficial for the compulsive sex offender.[33]

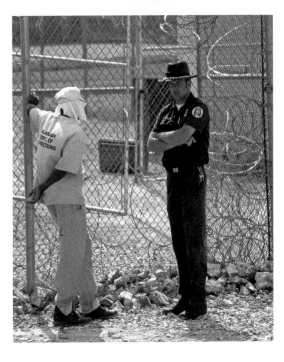

Security guard talks to a "pink-garbed" sex offender at the Limestone Facility, Capshaw, Alabama.
Photo by A. Ramey, courtesy of PhotoEdit Inc.

homework

Assign students to locate an article on sex offender registries and submit a one-paragraph statement on punishment for future crimes.

thematic question

What special management problems do wardens and superintendents face with special-category inmates in their facilities?

One outstanding example of a sensible and apparently successful program for the treatment of the sex offender is the 180 Degrees, Inc., program at a halfway house in Minneapolis. This program involves all prospective members in a men's sexuality group. There seems to be some hope in this program:

> After several years of operation, the program's long-term impact on its participants is not clear. Short-term statistics, however, are encouraging. Of the men who have participated in the sexuality group and who are no longer residents of the 180 Degrees, almost 75 percent successfully completed their stay at the halfway house, 7 percent absconded from the program, and 18 percent were terminated administratively.[34]

The attitude toward the child molester, particularly those who use ritual child abuse and mutilation in cults,[35] has activated many states to legislate extreme increases in the range of punishment for such offenses. The attitudes are reinforced by continued recidivism reported almost daily with regard to these "headline" offenders. The history of the success with sexual offenders was initially poor, and the future is bleak if additional new approaches to this age-old problem are not developed, tested, and tried.

AIDS IN PRISONS

The AIDS pandemic growing in the United States has of course reached prisons, particularly through offenders with histories of injecting drugs, sharing needles, and engaging in unprotected sexual activities. Estimates of the extent of infection vary across states and institutions, but, by 2005, almost 23,000 inmates had been diagnosed HIV positive, almost 2% of the custody population. Almost 25% of HIV-positive inmates had AIDS, and the state of New York accounted for 20% of those. The proportions of inmates carrying the virus that causes AIDS ranged from nearly zero in some prisons to over 7% in New York prisons. The overall rate of confirmed AIDS among the nation's prison population was 0.43%, more than three times the rate in the U.S. population of 0.16%. At year-end 2005, 2.5% of all female state prison inmates were HIV positive, compared to 1.8% of male state prisoners, a rate 30% higher than the male infection rate. Prisoner-to-prisoner (intraprisoner) transmission is also a factor, but the rate appears to be low.[36] One factor

Prisoner with AIDS sits on the floor of his cell, Hamilton Prison, Alabama.
Photo by A. Ramey, courtesy of PhotoEdit Inc.

that may contribute to the low rates of transmission is the availability of condoms and extensive AIDS education programs in some confinement facilities. Three jails in California and at least two state prison systems (Vermont and Oregon) make condoms available to inmates.

AIDS infection has become increasingly problematic for correctional administrators for many reasons. **AIDS** is a medical term describing terminal phases of **HIV infection.** It indicates an acquired immune system in which the human body is progressively unable to ward off common diseases and illnesses that others would quickly overcome. First, the War on Drugs has serious implications for concentration of HIV-positive cases in prisons. As the National Commission on AIDS pointed out, "By choosing mass imprisonment as the federal and state governments' response to the use of drugs, we have created a de facto policy of incarcerating more and more individuals with HIV infection." That trend is shown in Figure 19.3.[37]

HIV-Positive Prison Inmates, by Offense and Prior Drug Use

The percentage of state and federal prison inmates reporting that they were HIV positive varied by level of prior drug use. By type of drug use practice, the following percentages of state prison inmates reported being HIV positive: never using drugs, 1.7% HIV positive; ever used drugs, 2.3%; used drugs in the month before their current offense, 2.7%; used a needle to inject drugs, 4.6%; and shared a needle, 7.7% HIV positive. Like state inmates, federal inmates who used a needle and shared a needle had a higher rate of HIV infection than those inmates who reported ever using drugs or using drugs in the month before their current offense (1.3% and 2.1% compared to 0.7% and 0.3%). Unlike state inmates, federal inmates using drugs in the month prior to their current offense reported a lower rate of HIV infection (0.3%) than inmates who reported ever using drugs (0.7%).[38]

Correctional administrators and investigators usually agree that major problems in prisons include the availability of illicit injectable drugs inside prison, and frequent voluntary and involuntary homosexual activity, including homosexual rape. Despite the clear evidence of the spread of AIDS through sharing dirty needles and anal intercourse, correctional personnel and managers are unreasonably resistant to providing prophylactics and bleach to inmates.

Men in prison who wish to engage in anal intercourse are usually sufficiently capable of bringing that act to a successful completion. If the act is forcible intercourse with a passive male coerced into receiving an unwanted intrusion and the HIV is spread, the matter of liability might mean considerable financial loss for the state, managing officer, and lowest-level

key term

AIDS

Medical term describing terminal phases of HIV infection.

key term

HIV infection

Person who has contracted an acquired infection that compromises the body's ability to arrest or overcome common diseases and other illnesses.

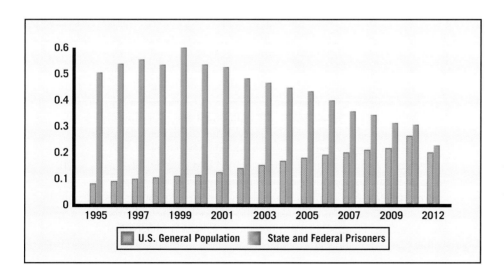

figure 19.3

Population with Confirmed AIDS: 1995–2012 (in percent)

SOURCE: Laura Maruschak, HIV in Prisons, 2005 (Washington, DC: Bureau of Justice Statistics, 2007), p. 3. Data from 2006 to 2012 are extrapolated.

correctional employee. Providing condoms to prisoners will soon be a constitutional right. Dirty needles shared by prisoners can be easily and effectively sterilized by double rinsing of syringe and needle in common household bleach. Institutions with substantial availability of injectable illicit drugs should make distribution of household bleach a routine sanitary procedure.

HIV infection and resulting AIDS cases pose particular problems for corrections in terms of staff and inmates. Staff have been alarmed by the introduction of AIDS into prison, and initially little was done through education or training to reduce levels of irrational fear. Institutional policies need to be developed and reconsidered in the areas of diagnosing, managing, and treating HIV infection.[39] Additional policy development and implementation are necessary in the areas of staff training and education, inmate counseling, pretest and post-test counseling, voluntary (versus mandatory) testing, medical parole, and discharge and aftercare services (for parole and community supervision). Infection control policies are necessary for dentists, nurses, physicians, security staff, and treatment personnel. HIV transmission and risk factors and precautionary and preventive measures are as follows:

- High-risk behaviors for HIV transmission—sex, drug use, sharing of injection materials, and tattooing—occur in correctional facilities.
- HIV transmission among correctional inmates has been shown to occur.
- Comprehensive and intensive education and prevention programs represent the best response to these facts, although the precise content of such programs is controversial.
- Rape and coerced sexual activity also occur in correctional facilities but require a different response, one based on inmate classification, housing, and supervision.
- The implementation of "standard precautions" represents the heart of a correctional infection-control program and the first line of defense against the occupational transmission of HIV.
- Condom distribution and other harm-reduction strategies have not been widely adopted in American correctional systems.
- Experience with harm reduction in correctional facilities in Europe and elsewhere may warrant the attention of U.S. correctional administrators.[40]

AIDS and Custody Staff

Craig identified five communicable diseases frequently found in correctional facilities: hepatitis A and B, HIV, rubella, and tuberculosis. She presented procedures thought necessary to address HIV infection.[41] These include the following:

- Avoid blind pocket searches and reaching into blind crevices to lessen the possibility of needle-sticks and other puncture wounds; instead, use flashlights, mirrors, and other visual aids.
- Protective equipment should be provided and used, including latex gloves, masks, protective eye goggles, and gowns for invasive therapy by dentists or at autopsies, and one-way valve masks for emergency CPR equipment and procedures.
- Handwashing should be required after every contact with potentially infectious materials, and both sinks and disinfectants should be available.
- Infectious waste policies should be implemented that cover bodily wastes, particularly blood or bodily fluids, including used tampons.
- Exposure-reporting procedures should be developed to document possible infection incidents and reduce chains of transmissions of bloodborne and airborne infectious agents (including hepatitis B, HIV, tuberculosis, rubella, and hepatitis A). Such procedures should include after-contact counseling, medical tests of possible

contaminant sources, serial blood tests of exposed staff members, and appropriate medical intervention (such as the hepatitis B immune globulin).

- Comprehensive infection control plans should be implemented, updated, monitored, and revised to maintain a healthy working environment, avoid litigation, and encourage officers to practice universal medical procedures. Adopting these policies will go a long way toward easing staff anxiety and tension in prison settings.

AIDS and Inmates

Perhaps the best single program for managing HIV infections revolves around educational programs to inform inmates of necessary behaviors. Consensus on appropriate medical treatment within prison settings is that prisons should adopt existing community treatment as the standard of care.[42] At a minimum, special infirmaries should be established to prevent AIDS patients from becoming further victims of airborne infections.[43] Infirmaries[44] should also have drug-treatment protocols that specify **antiviral drugs** such as AZT and protease inhibitors (usually taken together and with other antiviral drugs as "cocktails") and drug therapy for such opportunistic infections as tuberculosis and pneumonia. The AIDS death rate is dropping in prisons (see Figure 19.4).

Correctional administrators should propose and encourage a medical-parole mechanism for AIDS patients who are no longer a threat to the public safety, for early release back into the community by paroling authorities. Prerelease counseling[45] well in advance of the proposed release date would help inmates identify resources and service providers in the communities to which they will be released. Ideally, each institution should identify a community-based support group of HIV-positive volunteers for inmate referral and ease of transition.

The cost of HIV and AIDS treatment in prison is unknown, but California approximates its costs as much as $86,000 per inmate per year. Existing Social Security and related medical insurance coverage would pay most of these costs if the offender were in a community setting. By managing medical care, corrections could develop an efficient health care system in prison, lessen stigma, reduce paranoia and staff–inmate tensions, and sharply curtail the potential for costly litigation.[46] Corrections faces a medical challenge unparalleled in American history. Innovation and leadership are required to overcome these problems.

key term

Antiviral drugs
Special antiviral pharmaceuticals used to lessen the levels and virulence of HIV infections.

lecture note

Ask a physician specializing in HIV treatment to guest lecture in your class on the medical needs of HIV patients. Have students prepare written questions beforehand on challenges and rewards of the physician's practice. (If you are teaching this course online, use a chat room for discussion purposes.)

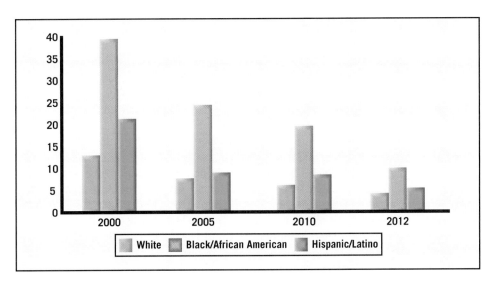

figure 19.4

Rate of AIDS-Related Deaths 2000–2012 (per 100,000 inmates)

SOURCE: Laura Maruschak, *HIV in Prisons, 2005* (Washington, DC: Bureau of Justice Statistics, 2007), p. 5. Data for 2012 are extrapolated.

GERIATRIC INMATES: THE GRAYING OF AMERICAN PRISONS

Robert Lee Lilley, a convicted sex offender, is wheeled into the yard at Territorial Prison (Colorado). The 70-year-old Lilley, who has numerous health problems, requires an inmate attendant. Lilley has been denied parole twice and will likely die in prison. His case highlights the public health costs associated with elderly prisoners throughout the country.
Photo by Sean Cayton, courtesy of The Image Works.

As was mentioned in Chapter 16, the proportion of prisoners in the nation's institutions who are elderly is rapidly increasing, in part due to the tougher long-term sentences inherent in the current "get-tough-on-crime" stance, but also because of the aging of the general population in America. In 2007, a total of 73,135 male and 3,600 female inmates housed in state and federal institutions were over 55 years of age.[47] This trend, which appears likely to continue, will have a significant impact on correctional administration and budgets in this new century. We estimate that by 2010, at least one in ten (over 160,000 inmates) will be age 50 or over. The number of older inmates (age 55 or above) in Florida is now one-third that of prisoners aged 18 to 24.

Elderly inmates are more likely than other prisoners to have committed crimes such as homicide and manslaughter, as well as sexual offenses. They are less likely than younger inmates to be imprisoned for robbery and burglary. Because of their significantly longer sentences, elderly inmates may be concentrated in prisons well beyond their proportions in the civilian population, which will pose problems for them as well as prison administrators. First, they will have health care concerns and need preventive health care programs that, if not provided, could be a source of considerable and, for correctional administrators, substantial litigation costs. At the least, they will suffer from depression and differing nutritional needs (less protein, fewer calories, and more soft food and fiber). Because taste sensations decline with aging, the elderly will request food richer in seasonings and will have a decrease in gastric acid and increase in gas production and constipation. Special diets will be needed.

In addition, growing old in prison will mean having to avoid exploitation and violence by younger inmates, having to adjust new personal needs to prison life, and not having suitable programs (recreational, educational, or housing). Vulnerability to victimization, frailty, and isolation from outside relatives and friends will take their toll, as will fear of death, hopelessness, and being unable to cope when released.

Health care costs will increase significantly for hypertension, diabetes, stroke, cancer, Alzheimer's, and emphysema. Glasses, dentures, kidney dialysis, and heart surgery will be required. It has been estimated that in ten years, annual health care costs for elderly inmates ($69,000 in 1997, and $86,000 in California) will increase by 14-fold.[48] Many smaller prisons will become geriatric centers, or special centers for elderly inmates will be built, and special staff as well as staff training will be necessary to treat this special category of the nation's offenders. Perhaps a nation that can explore space can find the necessary compassion to care for this small but increasing group as we continue into this new century. Executive clemency, including pardons, may become a frequent act, if for nothing else than to save money on prisoners who are probably no longer a danger to society.[49]

State prison expenditure for calendar year 2003 (the last year for which national data were available) totaled $39.2 billion. The Federal Bureau of the Prisons expended $5.1 billion. The average cost of imprisoning a state inmate was $22,650. This translates to a nationwide average operating expenditure exceeding $209 per person. States spent over $3.3 billion for medical care of inmates, averaging $2,625 per inmate. The State of Maine spent the most for medical services for each inmate ($5,600) and Louisiana spent the least ($860). These amount to 12% and 4%, respectively, of their total prison budgets for 2001. The national average percentage for medical care was 12% of operating expenditures.[50]

A geriatric inmate.
Photo by Ron Levine, courtesy of Ron Levine Photography, Inc.

class activity

Ask students what skills should be developed in custody staff working with elderly inmates. How should these skills be developed?

class activity

Structure a debate on the topic of whether or not inmates should be released into community corrections when they reach 76 years of age. In particular, focus on parole and on release mechanisms that "extend the limits of confinement to include residence in the community."

The **geriatric prisoner,** sentenced to life with little hope of parole, could live many years in the prisons of America—long after his or her dangerousness has passed. The courts of the land will be checking carefully to ensure that the person's rights are not violated, and it is certain that imprisonment costs will soar. Geriatric prisoners are "special people" and must be thought of as such when considering sentences that are too long (beyond what is cost effective).

key term

Geriatric prisoners
Older elderly inmates whose physical or mental disabilities require more extensive medical and treatment care.

lecture note

Using your computer, play the videotape by Lawrence Travis on "Geriatric Inmates" (approximately 5 minutes).

class activity

Break students into three groups and present them with a vignette of a confrontation and physical fight between two elderly inmates. Ask how the custody staff will intervene and the potential outcomes of use of force with elderly combatants.

An elderly prisoner in his cell.
Photo by Sean Cayton, courtesy of The Image Works.

Summary

The process of labeling is strong and pervasive in our society. Once labeled as mentally disordered, developmentally challenged, a sex fiend, or just old, a special-category person's lot is rough indeed. Add to those heavy labels the term *offender* and the problems multiply geometrically. Although mental illness is the nation's largest health problem, affecting one of ten citizens, it is still frequently regarded with the snake-pit philosophy of the Middle Ages, especially if some criminal act has been linked to the condition. The developmentally challenged citizen is in a real dilemma if placed in a treatment program that requires measurable improvement as a condition of release. This concept led to laws in the 1930s that essentially gave developmentally challenged persons de facto life sentences if they were placed in an institution until they "improved."

The sex offender is involved in a situation in which society's sexual mores are in transition. Some behaviors that put many in prison just a few years ago are no longer considered criminal. That change has not removed the stigma of the label "sex offender," however, and the tolerance of the outside world is low for those so labeled.

Inmates with AIDS and those who are aging in the prisons also cause problems with special handling procedures and huge medical bills. Both of these categories are unable to avoid transitioning from an HIV-positive situation to AIDS or to continue to stay young forever. Those problems, along with the "right to treatment," seem at constant odds with one another. When treatment programs fail, blame is often placed on the attendant, the overworked and undertrained staff, the legislators, and the courts. In the final analysis, however, it is up to society to decide whether it wants to spend the time and money to provide care and treatment for its bottom-line "losers" and then to attempt to remove the labels and reintegrate those individuals into the mainstream. Without a firm commitment for change, the castoffs of society will continue to return to institutions at great expense and then be released to the public, either with no change or with a decided change for the worse. This nation, long noted for its humanitarian concerns and progressive approach, must not fail in this area.

Key Words

transincarceration, 378

mentally disturbed, 378

asylum, 378

deinstitutionalization, 378

transinstitutionalization, 378

not guilty by reason of insanity (NGRI), 380

incompetent to stand trial, 380

criminally insane, 380

guilty but mentally ill (GBMI), 381

predict potential dangerousness, 381

developmentally challenged (mentally retarded), 382

Ruiz v. *Estelle*, 383

sodomy, 384

sex offenses, 384

fornication, 385

adultery, 385

male homosexual conduct, 385

child abusers, 386

child molester, 386

AIDS, 389

HIV infection, 389

antiviral drugs, 391

elderly inmates, 392

geriatric prisoners, 393

Review Questions

1. What spurred the growth of asylums in America?
2. How can one avoid criminal responsibility?
3. What are the most common sex offenses?
4. What would the American Psychiatric Association do with insanity acquittees?
5. What problems do developmentally challenged offenders pose for correctional administrators?
6. What former sex offense has been decriminalized?
7. What recommendations have been offered for correctional processing of developmentally challenged offenders?
8. Can sex offenders be treated?
9. What can be done to reduce staff fear of AIDS?
10. What should be done with geriatric prisoners?
11. What can be done to reduce AIDS in prison?
12. Why does inmate health care cost more than that of the general public?
13. Debate: Inmates over age 70 should be released to community supervision.
14. Why are there so many mentally disordered offenders in prison?
15. What problems does the prison pose for developmentally challenged inmates?
16. Has the GBMI statute approach solved the dilemma of protecting society while providing treatment to disturbed offenders?

Endnotes

1. Kenneth Adams, "Who Are the Clients? Characteristics of Inmates Referred for Mental Health Treatment," *The Prison Journal* 72:1/2 (1992): 120–141. See also Richard Bembo, H. Cervenka, B. Hunter, et al., "Engaging High-Risk Families in Community-Based Intervention Services," *Aggression and Violent Behavior* 4:1 (1999): 41–58.

2. G. Ives, A *History of Penal Methods* (London: S. Paul, 1914). Exploitation of incarcerated developmentally challenged offenders by more aggressive and stronger inmates remains a problem in all facilities: mental institutions, juvenile centers, nursing homes, jails, and prisons. In 1980, Congress passed the Civil Rights of Institutionalized Persons Act, authorizing the attorney general to intervene in correctional settings if violations of inmates' civil rights are suspected. For an example of juvenile victimization, see C. Bartollas, S. Miller, and S. Dinitz, *Juvenile Victimization: The Institutional Paradox* (New York: Holsted Press, 1976), pp. 53–76. See also Freda Briggs, *From Victim to Offender: How Child Sexual Abuse Victims Become Offenders* (St. Leonards, Australia: Allen and Unwin, 1995). For a study of missed opportunity, see Luke Birmingham, D. Mason, and D. Grubin, "A Follow-Up Study of Mentally Disordered Men Remanded to Prison," *Criminal Behavior and Mental Health* 8:3 (1998): 202–213.

3. J. Wilpers, "Animal, Vegetable or Human Being?" *Government Executive* (May 1973): 3. See also Terry Kupers, "Trauma and Its Sequelae in Male Prisoners: Effects of Confinement, Overcrowding and Diminished Services," *American Journal of Orthopsychiatry* 66:2 (1996): 189–196.

4. Bruce Arrigo, "Transcarceration: A Constructive Ethnology of Mentally-Ill 'Offenders,'" *The Prison Journal* 81:2 (2002): 162–186.

5. Randy Revelle, former King County executive, while accepting the National Association of Counties award for the "6 East" project for mentally ill inmates at the King County Jail, 1982.

6. Chris Sigurdson, "The Mad, the Bad and the Abandoned: The Mentally Ill in Prisons and Jails," *Corrections Today* 62:7 (2001): 162–186. See also Brian Dawe, "Managing the 'Other' Inmates," http://www .corrections.com/news/articles/16946 (accessed January 17, 2008); and Corrections News, "Prisoners in Finland Suffer High Rates of Mental Illness," *Corrections News* 13:6 (2007): 34.

7. Corrections News, "California Receiver Issues Status Report on Prison Medical System," *Corrections News* 13:7 (2007): 14: and Doris James and Lauren Blaze, *Mental Health Problems of Prison and Jail Inmates* (Washington, DC: Bureau of Justice Statistics, 2006), p. 1.

8. In 1999, Los Angles County had to appropriate more than $8 million as a supplemental allocation to improve mental health care in its jail. Chris Sigurdson, "The Mad, the Bad and the Abandoned," p. 72.

9. This is a hotly debated point. First see S. Wessely and P. J. Taylor, "Madness and Crime: Criminology Versus Psychiatry," *Criminal Justice and Mental Health* 1:3 (1991): 193–228. See also Mary Ann Finn, "Prison Misconduct among Developmentally Challenged Inmates," *Criminal Justice and Mental Health* 2:3 (1992): 287–299; Lynette Feder, "A Comparison of the Community Adjustment of Mentally Ill Offenders with Those from the General Prison Population," *Law and Human Behavior* 15:5 (1991): 477–493; and Bruce Link, Howard Andrews, and Francis Cullen, "The Violent and Illegal Behavior of Mental Patients Reconsidered," *American Sociological Review* 57:2 (1992): 275–292. But see Barry Wright, I. McKenzie, J. Stace, et al. (eds.), "Adult Criminality in Previously Hospitalized Child Psychiatric Patients," *Criminal Behavior and Mental Health* 8:1 (1998): 19–38.

10. National Institute of Mental Health, *Directory of Institutions for the Mentally Disordered Offenders* (Washington, DC: U.S. Government Printing Office, 1972); and Anthony Walsh, *Correctional Assessment, Casework and Counseling* (Lanham, MD: American Correctional Association, 1997).

11. Valerie Hans, "An Analysis of Public Attitudes toward the Insanity Defense," *Criminology* 24:3 (1986): 393–413. Among her more interesting findings were that the public wants insane lawbreakers punished, believes that insanity defense procedures fail to protect the general public, and wildly overestimates the use and effectiveness of the insanity defense. See also Bruce Arrigo, *The Contours of Psychiatric Justice* (New York: Garland, 1996); and Caton Roberts and S. Golding, "The Social Construction of Criminal Responsibility and Insanity," *Law and Human Behavior* 15:4 (1991): 349–376.

12. Marnie Rice, Grant Harris, and Carol Lang, "Recidivism among Male Insanity Acquittees," *Journal of Psychiatry and the Law* 18:3/4 (1990): 379–403; and Richard Pasework, B. Parnell, and J. Rock, "Insanity Defense: Shifting the Burden of Proof," *Journal of Police Science and Criminal Psychology* 10:1 (1994): 1–4.

13. John Klofas and Ralph Weisheit, "Guilty but Mentally Ill: Reform of the Insanity Defense in Illinois," *Justice Quarterly* 4:1 (1987): 40–50. The effects of the GBMI statutes are discussed in Kurt Bumby, "Reviewing the

Guilty but Mentally Ill Alternatives," *Journal of Psychiatry and the Law* 21:2 (1993): 191–220.

14. Lisa Callahan, Margaret McGreevy, Carmen Cirincione, et al., "Measuring the Effects of the Guilty but Mentally Ill (GBMI) Verdict: Georgia's 1982 GBMI Reform," *Law and Human Behavior* 16:4 (1992): 447–462; Carmen Cirincione, H. Steadman, and M. McGreevy, "Rates of Insanity Acquittals and the Factors Associated with Successful Insanity Pleas," *Bulletin of the American Academy of Psychiatry and the Law* 23:2 (1995): 339–409.

15. American Psychiatric Association, *Standards for Psychiatric Facilities* (Washington, DC: APA, 1981), pp. 17–18. But see Washington State Department of Corrections, *Mentally Ill Offenders: Community Release Outcome Study* (Olympia, WA: WSDOC, 1997).

16. Bernard Rubin, "Prediction of Dangerousness in Mentally Ill Criminals," *Archives of General Psychiatry* 27:1 (September 1972): 397–407; Robert Prentky, A. Lee, R. Knight, et al. (eds.), "Recidivism Rates among Child Molesters and Rapists," *Law and Human Behavior* 21:6 (1998): 635–659; and Michael Ross, "Reflections from Death Row," in Robert Johnson and H. Toch (eds.), *Crime and Punishment: Inside Views* (Los Angeles: Roxbury, 2000).

17. Miles Santamour and Bernadette West, *Sourcebook on the Mentally Disordered Prisoner* (Washington, DC: U.S. Department of Justice, 1985), p. 70. Petersilia estimates the mentally retarded offender in California as 2% of all probationers and 4% of all incarcerated persons. Joan Petersilia, "Justice for All? Offenders with Mental Retardation and the California Corrections System," *The Prison Journal* 77:4 (1997): 358–380.

18. Finn, "Prison Misconduct," p. 296. See also Allen Beck, Paige Harrison, and Devon Adams, *Sexual Violence Reported by Correctional Authorities* (Washington, DC: Bureau of Justice Statistics, 2006).

19. Severson identifies ten basic services necessary for inmate mental health. Margaret Severson, "Refining the Boundaries of Mental Health Services: A Holistic Approach to Inmate Mental Health," *Federal Probation* 56:3 (1992): 57–63; Rudolph Alexander, "Incarcerated Juvenile Offenders' Right to Rehabilitation," *Criminal Justice Policy Review* 7:2 (1995): 202–213.

20. *Ruiz v. Estelle*, 503 F. Supp. 1265 (S. D. Tex. 1980), *aff'd in part*, 679 F. 2d 1115 (5th Cir. 1982), *cert. denied*, 103 S. Ct. 1438 (1983) at 1344. See Rolando Del Carmen, B. Witt, W. Hume, et al., *Texas Jails: Law and Practice* (Huntsville, TX: Sam Houston Press, 1990); and John Sharp, Behind the Walls: *The Price and Performance of the Texas Department of Criminal Justice* (Austin: Texas Comptroller of Public Accounts, 1994).

21. Joan Petersilia, *Doing Justice: Criminal Offenders with Development Disabilities* (Berkeley: University of California, 2000).

22. Richard C. Allen, "Reaction to S. Fox: The Criminal Reform Movement," in M. Kindred (ed.), *The Developmentally Challenged Citizen and the Law* (Washington, DC: U.S. Government Printing Office, 1976), p. 645. See also Mark Nichols, L. Bench, E. Morlok, and K. Liston, "Analysis of Mentally Retarded and Lower-Functioning Offender Correctional Programs," *Corrections Today* 65:2 (2003): 119–121.

23. Dan Thompson, "Conjugal Visits for Gays, Lesbians OK in State Prisons," *The Desert Sun* (June 2, 2007), p. A3.

24. Cherrel Turner, "Ethical Issues in Criminal Justice Administration," *American Jails* 20:6 (2006): 49–53.

25. See Patricia Cluss et al., "The Rape Victim: Psychological Correlates of Participation in the Legal Process," *Criminal Justice and Behavior* 10:3 (1983): 342–357; and Patricia Mahoney and L. Williams, "Sexual Assault on Marriage: Wife Rape," in Jana Jasinski and L. Williams (eds.), *Partner Violence* (Thousand Oaks, CA: Sage, 1998), pp. 113–162.

26. David Finkelor, "Removing the Child—Prosecuting the Offender in Cases of Sexual Abuse: Evidence from the National Reporting System for Child Abuse and Neglect," *Child Abuse and Neglect* 7:2 (1983): 195–205. But see Philip Jenkins, *Moral Panic: Changing Concepts of the Child Molester in Modern America* (New Haven, CT: Yale University Press, 1998).

27. Jean Goodwin et al., *Sexual Abuse: Incest Victims and Their Families* (Boston: John Wright, 1982). See also Katherine Beckett, "Culture and the Politics of Signification: The Case of Child Abuse," *Social Problems* 43:1 (1996): 57–76; and Joann Brown and G. Brown, "Characteristics and Treatment of Incest Offenders," *Journal of Aggression Maltreatment and Trauma* 1:1 (1997): 335–354.

28. Ross Cheit, R. Freeman-Longo, M. Greenberg, et al., "Symposium on the Treatment of Sex Offenders," *New England Journal of Criminal and Civil Confinement* 23:2 (1997): 267–462. See also Abe Macher, "Pedophiles and the Sexual Transmission of HIV to Children," *American Jails* 11:2 (2007): 33–36.

29. Richard McCorkle, "Research Note: Punish or Rehabilitate: Public Attitudes toward Six Common Crimes," *Crime and Delinquency* 39:2 (1993): 250–252; and Joel Rudin, "Megan's Law: Can It Stop Sexual Predators?" *Criminal Justice* 11:3 (1996): 2–10, 60–63.

30. Timothy Flanagan, P. Brennan, and D. Cohen, "Conservatism and Capital Punishment in the State Capitol: Lawmakers and the Death Penalty," *The Prison Journal* 72:1/2 (1992): 37–56.

31. Anthony Walsh, "Placebo Justice: Victim Recommendations and Offender Sentences in Sexual Assault Cases," *Journal of Criminal Law and Criminology* 77:4 (1986): 1126–1141; and Federal Bureau of Investigation, *Crime in the United States*

1994 (Washington, DC: U.S. Department of Justice, 1995), p. 225.

32. John Weeks, G. Pelletier, and D. Beaulette, "Correctional Officers: How Do They Perceive Sex Offenders?" *International Journal of Offender Therapy and Comparative Criminology* 35:1 (1995): 55–61; and American Correctional Association, *Point/Counterpoint* (Lanham, MD: ACA, 1997).

33. E. Brecher, *Treatment Programs for Sex Offenders,* prepared for the National Institute of Law Enforcement and Criminal Justice (Washington, DC: U.S. Government Printing Office, 1978), pp. 1–12. The material for this section has been extracted from this document and reflects the current literature on the subject. See also Walter Meyer, C. Cole, and D. Lipton, "Links between Biology and Crime," *Journal of Offender Rehabilitation* 25:3/4 (1997): 1–34.

34. John Driggs and T. Zoet, "Breaking the Cycle—Sex Offenders on Parole," *Corrections Today* 49:3 (1987): 124. See also Brian Dixon, "Sex Offender Treatment Services in Australia and New Zealand," Psychiatry, *Psychology and the Law* 3:2 (1996): 179–188.

35. Steven Glass, "An Overview of Satanism and Ritualized Child Abuse," *Journal of Police and Criminal Psychology* 7:2 (1991): 43–50; Ben Crouch and K. Damphouse, "Newspapers and the Antisatanism Movement: A Content Analysis," *Sociological Spectrum* 12:1 (1992): 1–20; and William Bernet and C. Chang, "The Differential Diagnosis of Ritual Abuse Allegations," *Journal of Forensic Sciences* 42:1 (1997): 32–38.

36. Laura Maruschak, *HIV in Prisons 2006* (Washington, DC: Bureau of Justice Statistics, 2007).

37. National Commission on Acquired Immune Deficiency Syndrome, Report: *HIV Disease in Correctional Facilities* (Washington, DC: U.S. Department of Justice, 1992), p. 5. See also James Marquart, V. Brewer, J. Mullins, et al., "The Implication of Crime Control Policy on HIV/AIDS-Related Risk among Women Prisoners," *Crime and Delinquency* 45:1 (1999): 82–98.

38. Theodore Hammett, P. Marmon, and L. Maruschak, *1996–1997 Update: HIV/AIDS, STDs, and TB in Correctional Facilities* (Washington, DC: Bureau of Justice Statistics, 1998), p. xiv; and Laura Maruschak, *HIV in Prisons and Jails, 2002* (Washington, DC: Bureau of Justice Statistics, 2004).

39. Caroline Wolf Harlow, *Drug Enforcement and Treatment in Prisons, 1990* (Washington, DC: U.S. Department of Justice, 1992), p. 1. See also Myer et al., "Links between Biology and Crime."

40. There are no confirmed cases of a correctional officer whose workplace exposure resulted in HIV infection. Jeanne Flavin, "Police and HIV/AIDS: The Risk, the Reality, the Response," *American Journal of Criminal Justice* 23:1 (1998): 33–58.

41. Rebecca Craig, "Six Steps to Stop the Spread of Communicable Diseases," *Corrections Today* 54:7 (1992): 104–109. See also Mary Coplin, "Managing the Challenge of HIV," *Corrections Today* 54:8 (1992): 104–107.

42. Robert Reeves, "Approaching 2000: Finding Solutions to the Most Pressing Issues Facing the Corrections Community," *Corrections Today* 54:3 (1998): 74, 76–79.

43. Abe Macher, "Esophageal Candidiasis in Patients with Primary HIV Infection," *American Jails* 11:1 (2007): 43–46. Abe Macher, "Issues in Correctional HIV Care," *American Jails* 11:3 (2007): 45–48.

44. Joseph Paris, "Why an AIDS Unit?" in *The State of Corrections: Proceedings of the 1991 Annual Conferences* (Laurel, MD: American Correctional Association, 1992), pp. 3–56.

45. Donald McVinney, "Counseling Incarcerated Individuals with HIV Disease and Chemical Dependency," *Journal of Chemical Dependency Treatment* 4:2 (1991): 105–118.

46. Patricia Satterfield, "A Strategy for Controlling Health Care Costs," *Corrections Today* 54:2 (1992): 190–194. But see Margaret Norris and M. May, "Screening for Malingering in a Correctional Setting," *Law and Human Behavior* 22:3 (1998): 315–323.

47. American Correctional Association, *2007 Directory* (Lanham, MD: ACA, 2007), pp. 54–55.

48. Sarah Bradley, "Graying of Inmate Population Spurs Corrections Challenges," *On the Line* 13 (March 1990): 5; and Ronald Aday, "Golden Years behind Bars," *Federal Probation* 58:2 (1994): 47–54.

49. Mari Herreras, "Threw Away the Key?" *Tucson Weekly* (January 17, 2008), http://www.tucsonweekly.com/gbase/Currents/content?oid=oid%3A105444 (accessed January 18, 2008).

50. Kristen Hughes, *Justice Expenditures and Employment in 2003* (Washington, DC: Bureau of Justice Statistics, 2006).

Suggested Readings: Part 4

American Jail Association. *American Jails.* Quarterly publication of the American Jail Association.

Center on Juvenile and Criminal Justice. "California Youth Crime Declines: The Untold Story," http://www.cjcj.org (accessed January 18, 2008).

Center on Juvenile and Criminal Justice. "Crime Rates and Youth Incarceration in Texas and California Compared: Public Safety or Public Waste?" http://www.cjcj.org (accessed January 18, 2007).

Donziger, Steven. *The Real War on Crime.* New York: HarperCollins, 1996.

Harlow, Caroline Wolf. *Prior Abuse Reported by Inmates and Probationers.* Washington, DC: U.S. Department of Justice, 1999.

Harrel, Erica. *Black Victims of Violent Crime.* Washington, DC: Bureau of Justice Statistics, 2007.

Hassine, Victor. *Life without Parole: Living in Prison Today.* New York: Oxford University Press, 2007.

Hayes, Lindsay, and Eric Blaauw (eds.). "Prison Suicide." Special issue of *Crisis* 18:4 (1997): 146–189.

Heidi, Kathleen. *Young Killers: The Challenge of Juvenile Homicide.* Thousand Oaks, CA: Sage, 1999.

James, Doris, and Lauren Glaze. *Mental Health Problems of Prison and Jail Inmates* (Washington, DC: Bureau of Justice Statistics, 2006).

Maruschak, Laura. *HIV in Prisons and Jails, 2002.* Washington, DC: Bureau of Justice Statistics, 2004.

Maruschak, Laura. *Medical Problems of Jail Inmates.* Washington, DC: Bureau of Justice Statistics, 2006.

Mauer, Mark. *Mandatory Minimum Sentencing Laws—The Issues.* Washington, DC: The Sentencing Project, 2007.

Mauer, Mark. "Racial Impact Statements as a Means of Reducing Unwarranted Sentencing Disparities." *Ohio State Journal of Criminal Law* 5:19 (2007): 19–46.

McCoy, Clyde, and James Inciardi. *Sex, Drugs, and the Continuing Spread of AIDS.* Los Angeles: Roxbury, 1995.

Nichols, Mark, L. Bench, E. Morlok, and K. Liston. "Analysis of Mentally Retarded and Lower-Functioning Offender Correctional Programs." *Corrections Today* 65:2 (2003): 119–121.

Ross, Jeffrey Ian. "Supermax Prisons," *Society* 44:3 (2006): 60–64.

Sabol, William, Heather Couture, and Paige Harrison. *Prisoners in 2006.* Washington, DC: Bureau of Justice Statistics, 2007.

Sabol, William, and Paige Harrison. *Prison and Jail Inmates at Midyear 2006.* Washington, DC: Bureau of Justice Statistics, 2007.

Sheppard, David, and Patricia Kelly. *Juvenile Gun Courts.* Washington, DC: Office of Justice Programs, 2002.

Snyder, Howard. *Juvenile Arrests 2002.* Washington, DC: U.S. Department of Justice, 2004.

Snyder, Howard, and Melissa Sickman. *Juvenile Offenders and Victims 2006.* Washington, DC: Office of Justice Programs, 2006.

Stephan, James. *State Prison Expenditures, 2001.* Washington, DC: U.S. Department of Justice, 2004.

The Sentencing Project. *Women in the Criminal Justice System: An Overview.* Washington, DC: The Sentencing Project, 2007.

Thompson, Don. "State Works to Cut Inmate Suicides," *Los Angeles Times,* May 28, 2007: p. A3.

Uzoaba, Julius. *Managing Older Offenders: Where Do We Stand?* Ottawa: Correctional Service of Canada, 1998.

Wahlin, Lottie. "New Restorative Approach to Sex Crimes," http://www.restorativejustice.org/editions/2006/july2006/restore (accessed January 17, 2008).

Wahlin, Lottie. "Victim Offender Mediation in Sweden," http://www.restorativejustice.org/editions/2006/august2006/vomsweden (accessed January 17, 2008).

glossary

Abused females. Female victims of usually violent acts that may be physical or psychological in damage, or both.

Administrative sentencing. Process by which the actual length of the sentence is left up to the administrators of the correctional system, as seen in such processes as good-time credit, probation, parole, and program participation; the actual sentence served is set by the executive branch rather than the judicial.

Administrative-security level. Facilities with special missions that might contain inmates from all custody levels.

Adultery. Sexual intercourse between two persons, at least one of whom is not married to the second party.

Affirm. Appeal court's decision that due processes have not been violated by the government.

Age at risk. Those potential offenders likely to offend, segregated by age categories.

Age of Enlightenment. A philosophic movement of the eighteenth century marked by a rejection of traditional social, religious, and political ideas and an emphasis on rationalism.

Agricultural prison. Any prison whose main products are agricultural and whose institutional value is the foodstuffs and produce grown thereon.

AIDS. Medical term describing terminal phases of HIV infection.

Alcatraz. A supermax island prison for inmates in the San Francisco Bay area and part of the U.S. Bureau of Prisons until its closing; also known as "the Rock".

Alderson. The first federal institution for female offenders.

Alternative to death and flogging. Any correctional punishment less than the death penalty, such as imprisonment, probation, diversion, and so on.

Amnesty. A form of pardon for a class of offenders, such as draft dodgers.

Anger management. Treatment programs within a correctional system designed to help offenders rein in their anger and aggression by understanding how and why anger arises, and rehearsing alternative nonviolent expressions.

Antiviral drugs. Special antiviral pharmaceuticals used to lessen the levels and virulence of HIV infections.

Appeal. Petition to higher courts to reverse procedures and protect offenders based on due process issues.

Arbitrary. Acting without criteria, usually in a discriminatory manner.

Arrests by gender. Comparison of arrest data between male and female offenders.

Asylum. Institution for the care and custody of mentally ill societal members.

Auburn system. Prison model consisting of small individual cells, large work areas for group labor, and enforced silence.

Augustus, John. The "parent of probation" who motivated the creation of probation in Boston, working with alcoholics and appearing before the court to request no further or minimal punishment.

Backfilled. Management strategy to meet minimum critical staffing by asking corrections officers to work the next tour of duty.

Banishment. To remove by authority from a state or country; the sentence to cast out of a local residence or country due to criminal behavior on the offender's part.

Bates, Sanford. First director of the U.S. Bureau of Prisons.

Beccaria, Cesare. The founder of the Classical School of Criminology.

Benefit of clergy. The exclusion of offenders from the death penalty if able to read particular segments of ancient texts.

Bentham, Jeremy. Argued that the crime rate would go down if the amount of punishment were carefully calibrated to deter potential offenders and maximize pleasure.

Black Muslims. American religious offender group based on Moslem theological concepts.

Blood feud. An often-prolonged series of retaliatory, vengeful, or hostile acts or exchange of such acts.

"Blue flu." Ploy used by correctional officers to strengthen their hands in negotiations with command officers.

Boot camp. Modeled after military boot camps, offenders are required to engage in strict discipline and a physical regiment.

Brick-and-mortar solutions. Strategies for reducing overcrowding of prisons by the construction of penal facilities.

Bridewell. A workhouse created for the employment and housing of London's unemployed or underemployed working classes.

Brockway, Zebulon. The first superintendent of the Elmira Reformatory who implemented reduction of recidivism through educational programs.

Bureaucratic control. Predominant public administration format for prison operations.

Capital crimes. Offenses for which an offender can receive the death penalty, usually murder and rape.

Capital punishment. The imposition of a sentence of death by the state.

"Cat-o'-nine tails." Torture device for whipping or flogging.

CCAs. See **Community corrections acts (CCAs)**.

Cell blocks. Multitier living cells usually stacked one atop the other, built within a hollow building and not touching exterior walls.

Chancery court. One of the five divisions of the High Court of Justice of Great Britain, presided over by the Lord High Chancellor; serves as a legal protector of the rights of minors.

Child abuse. Willful action or actions by a person causing physical harm to a child.

Child molester. An adult charged with criminal and civil offenses in which the adult engages in sexual activity with a minor or exploits a minor for the purpose of sexual gratification.

Civil death. The status of a living person equivalent in its legal consequences to natural death; loss of all rights and powers as if dead.

Civil rights. Those rights defined in the U.S. Constitution or accorded through judicial decisions.

Classical School of Criminology. Approach to understanding crime and social policy that looks at the reasons for and consequences of crime for offenders.

Classification. The process of dividing and assigning incoming inmates into meaningful categories for assignment to institutions and programs.

Classification process. The process by which offenders are assigned to types of custody and treatment programs, based on such factors as offense category, escape potential, substance abuse patterns, previous experience with the criminal justice system, and so on.

Clear and present danger. Test used in corrections to justify restricting rights of inmates.

Co-gender institution. A co-educational prison housing both male and female inmates interacting under a single institutional administration.

Cognitive. Mental processes that generally hinder change in prisoners but can be corrected by various thinking, speaking, and conceptual treatments.

Cognitive intervention. A treatment program with the objective to improve behavior through changing beliefs, attitudes, sentiments, and reactions.

Collateral attack. The process of raising additional legal questions in other courts but before case disposition.

Collateral consequences. Disabilities imposed on an offender on the basis of conviction.

Commitment lag. Avoidance of sentencing offenders to imprisonment on the first few offenses.

Common law. Law based on judges' decisions and custom, as distinct from written laws.

Community corrections acts (CCAs). Legislation that funds local community correctional programs designed to divert offenders from prison.

Community Protection Act. Legislation requiring offenders to register and live under public scrutiny.

Community residential center. Any correctional facility existing to provide services and maximize reintegration of the offender back into the community.

Community residential treatment center. Also known as a halfway house, a residential facility that provides room and board as well as rehabilitation programming.

Community work order. Requiring offenders to provide service to the community to help repair the harm they have committed.

Commutation. A reduction of the severity of the sentence by the executive branch of government.

Comorbidity. Two or more occurring medical treatment needs for one inmate.

Conditional liberty. A prisoner release scheme that allows the penitent inmate to be released to the community under specific conditions that can be revoked; a system commonly known as "parole."

Congregate system. Prison modeled on the Auburn system with inmate work and feeding done en masse, in total silence.

Contraband. Any object forbidden in prison.

Convict bogey. Irrational fear of prison inmates who can only be managed through head counts, locking, and recounting.

Convicted offender. Guilty law violator who has exhausted all appeals of conviction and sentencing.

Corporal punishment. Any physical pain inflicted short of death; common methods include crucifixion, whipping, torture, mutilation, branding, and caning.

Correctional chaplaincy. A program of recruiting clergy who minister to the religious needs of inmates.

Correctional officers. Line prison officers working directly with the inmate population.

Corrections Corporation of America (CCA). A private business seeking to provide correctional services to units of government; also known as the "parent of private-sector prison facilities".

Count. Method used to verify that all inmates are present in prison.

Court master. Representative of the court ordered to monitor correctional compliance with a court's orders.

Court of appeals. Any higher court with postconviction authority; any court authorized to treat with contempt decisions made by the lower court.

Court of last resort. The highest appeal court having jurisdiction within that particular geographical area.

Crack cocaine. An illegal drug derived from powder cocaine and consumed primarily by smoking.

Criminal history data. Information related to an offender's prior arrests and convictions.

Criminally insane. Mentally ill inmates who are diagnosed as incompetent to plead or stand trial, not guilty by reason of insanity, became mentally ill while incarcerated, or other potentially hazardous mentally ill persons requiring special security.

Crofton, Sir Walter. Director of the Irish penal system in 1846, he improved on the "ticket-of-leave" system developed by Maconochie; his system also had provisions for supervision by police, the first parole officers.

Cruel and unusual punishment. Prohibited by the Eighth Amendment to the Constitution.

Custody. Term referring to the level of immediate control exercised over offenders within correctional institutions.

Custody philosophy. Approach to containing juveniles through incarceration programs.

Day reporting center. Facility to which offenders are sent for scheduling and monitoring of their activities.

Death penalty. Execution of the offender by the state.

Decarceration. Process of releasing offenders from institutional facilities, primarily by closing those facilities.

Decriminalization. To remove or reduce the criminal classification or status of a formerly criminal act.

Deinstitutionalization. The return of a patient from a mental hospital into the community.

Deliberate indifference. Total deprivation of medical services.

Delinquent juvenile. Juvenile who has committed a criminal act that if committed by an adult would not be a crime.

Dependent. Any child without parents or guardians, or whose parents are unable to provide such care, treatment, or custody that should be afforded to a child.

"Designer" drugs. Analogues of controlled substances manufactured by underground chemists.

Desistance. Ceasing of criminal behavior by the offender; can also imply lessening of the severity of criminal offenses.

Determinate sentence. A flat sentence of punishment imposed by the sentencing court.

Deterrence by sentencing. Discouraging the individual and the public's propensity to commit additional crimes by imposition of harsh punishment; goal is crime reduction.

Deterrent. The hope that a criminal sanction will stop potential offenders by inflicting suffering on actual offenders.

Developmentally challenged. Another term denoting mental retardation.

Direct filing. Prosecutorial decision to refer the case to an adult criminal court rather than to a juvenile court.

Discretionary release. Parole of an inmate from prison prior to expiration of maximum sentence according to the boundaries set by the sentencing body or legislature.

Diversion. Minimizing penetration into the criminal justice system through police, community, or court programs.

Drug court. Problem-solving courts that require drug offenders to participate in court-mandated treatment programs.

Due process. Legal requirement that constitutional rights of the accused and correctional clients will conform to guaranteed constitutional protection minimums.

Eastern Penitentiary. Prison facility designed on the Pennsylvania system with rows of individual cells attached to corridors and outside cells.

Elderly inmates. All prisoners over a specific age, usually 55 years old.

Electrified fence. Barrier to prevent inmate escape through electronic punishment or death.

Electronic monitoring. Tracking of offender whereabouts electronically.

Electronic parole. Community supervision technique that uses electronic devices to maintain surveillance on parolees; can also include GPS surveillance.

Employment restrictions. Denial of employment opportunities due to being an ex-offender.

Equitability. Whether the punishment is applied even-handedly across a jurisdiction.

Escape. The unlawful departure of a lawfully confined person from a confinement facility or from custody while being transported.

Estelle v. Gamble. First U.S. Supreme Court case dealing with prison medical treatment.

Ex-con. Convicted person released from correctional control.

Execution. The killing of an offender by the state.

Executive clemency. A pardon, reduction of sentence, or release of an inmate by the governor, president, or pardoning authority.

Expungement. The sealing or purging of arrest, criminal, or juvenile record information.

External classification. Process leading managers to assign inmates to an institution.

Family cohesion. Term describing the relationship between offenders and their families, as in sticking together tightly.

Family (conjugal) visits. Prison program designed to reinforce family ties through unsupervised contact, usually between husband and wife.

Federal Bureau of Prisons. The federal correctional system located in the Department of Justice.

Fee system. Fees charged to state and federal prison systems to house inmates in local jails.

Felony. A criminal offense punishable by death or incarceration in a state or federal confinement facility for a period of which the lower limit is prescribed by statute in a given jurisdiction, typically one year or more.

Firearms disability. Loss of rights of ex-felons to own, possess, or exercise control over firearms.

Flopped. Inmate term for denial of parole.

Fornication. Sexual intercourse between persons not married to each other.

Frisk search. Process of detecting inmate contraband by manual search of the bodies of inmates.

Front-end solutions. Options for controlling the number of inmates being sent to prison.

Functionally illiterate. Unable to read, write, or spell above the third-grade level.

Furlough. A prison-release program permitting the inmate to pursue education, vocational training, or employment in the community.

Furman v. Georgia. The Supreme Court decision that the death penalty in Georgia was being applied arbitrarily and discriminatorily against minorities; as a result of this case, a moratorium on the death penalty was imposed throughout the United States.

Gagnon v. Scarpelli. U.S. Supreme Court decision that held probation is a privilege, not a right, but, once granted, the probationer has an interest in remaining on probation.

Gaols. Places of confinement in England for persons held in lawful custody; specifically, such a place under the jurisdiction of a local government (as a county) for the confinement of persons awaiting trial or those convicted of minor crimes.

Gatekeeper function. Process by which the criminal justice official exercises authority to move the case to the next higher level.

GED. General equivalency diploma certifying inmate's achievement of the equivalent of a high school diploma.

General population. Prisoners not restricted to tighter controls than other inmates.

GEO Group. A private-sector correctional provider formerly known as the Wackenhut group.

Geriatric center. Correctional facility for elderly inmates.

"Get right with God." Directive that the offender must make peace with God through repentance and atonement.

Goldbrickers. Inmates seeking sick calls for other than medical needs.

Good time. Taking days off an inmate's sentence for good behavior while incarcerated.

Good-time policies. Administrative mechanism reducing sentence length by crediting inmates for good behavior, extra work, or other statutory policies.

Gradualism approach. A "go-slow" approach to design and implementation of new programs.

Graduated release. Programs bridging inmate status from imprisonment to community control.

Gregg v. Georgia. The 1977 case that ended the moratorium on the death penalty.

Grievance board. Organization reviewing inmate complaints of denial of rights.

Growth industry. Any business venture whose volume of work systematically increases over time.

Guilty but mentally ill (GBMI). Plea entered by the defendant acknowledging guilt but asserting a lack of capacity to understand the nature of the act or that it was wrong.

Halfway house. A confinement facility for adjudicated adults or juveniles or those subject to criminal or juvenile proceedings, intended as an alternative to confinement for persons not suited for probation or needing a period of readjustment to the community after confinement.

Hedonistic calculus. Jeremy Bentham's argument that the main objective of an intelligent person is to maximize pleasure while minimizing pain; it was believed that an individual's behavior could be influenced in a scientific manner.

Hepatitis A and B. Viral infections resistant to medical treatments.

High-security level. A classification designation reducing inmate movement and treatment participation within the correctional facility; may also refer to "supermax," security housing units, or "close supervision".

HIV infection. An acquired infection that compromises the body's ability to arrest or overcome common diseases and other illnesses.

"Holdback" jail inmates. Inmates held in jail awaiting transportation to a federal or state prison.

Home detention. Sentence whereby offenders serve at least some of their sentence in their own domicile.

Homosexual attacks. Sexual assaults on potential victim inmates, usually by heterosexual prisoners.

House arrest. Being confined to one's home except when permission is granted to leave.

Howard, John. An English high sheriff who was so appalled by jail conditions that he undertook a crusade to improve places of detention.

Hulks. Abandoned or unusable transport ships anchored in rivers and harbors that confine criminal offenders.

In re Gault. U.S. Supreme Court decision that juveniles have four basic constitutional rights in hearings that could result in commitment to an institution.

Incompetent to stand trial. Legal defense asserting that defendants must be able to understand the charges against them, and to assist legal counsel in the preparation of their own defense.

Incorrigible juveniles. Unruly juveniles whose behavior is not controlled by their parents.

Indeterminate sentence. A period of confinement with specified minimum and maximum length, allowing a parole board to release the inmate when rehabilitation has been achieved.

Indeterminate sentencing. Punishment imposed by a judge that has both a minimum and maximum period (usually of confinement).

Industrial prison. Any penal institution whose main objective is the use of inmate labor to produce marketable products for prison profit.

Initial classification. The initial process by which offenders are assigned to level of custody, work assignment, and treatments.

Inmate grievance. Inmate complaint regarding treatment and custody.

Inquisition. A former Roman Catholic tribunal for the discovery and punishment of heresy; an investigation conducted with little regard for individual rights through a severe questioning.

Institutional needs. Basic and mandatory functions for assigning prisoners to support institutional objectives.

Institutional threat groups. Prison gangs.

Institutional work assignment. Prison industry jobs based on institutional operational needs, community projects, or prison industry programs.

Intent to kill. A legal charge that alleges the offender intended to murder the victim; in contrast to manslaughter.

Intermediate sanctions. Correctional programs that fall somewhere between probation and prison.

Indeterminate sentence. A statutory provision for a type of sentence to imprisonment in which, after the court has determined that the convicted person will be imprisoned, the exact length of imprisonment and parole supervision is afterward fixed within statutory limits by a parole authority.

Internal classification. Process of assigning inmates to types of programs and work and cell locations.

Irish system. A prison management scheme with multiple stages of control, allowing the inmate to earn higher stages until released when penitence was achieved; release was on a revocable "ticket of leave" or conditional pardon.

Isolationism and withdrawal. Implementing programs without a systematic, rational scheme.

Jail. A confinement facility that holds persons detained pending adjudication and/or persons committed after adjudication for sentences of a year or less.

Jail fever. Typhus frequently concentrated in places of detention that will cause large-scale death of inmates and local citizens.

Jail inmates. Offenders housed in a local facility, including those waiting for trial, those awaiting transport to a state or federal prison, and those convicted of a crime, usually punishable by less than one year.

Jailhouse lawyer. An inmate's provision of legal services to another inmate.

Just deserts. Sentencing ideology that stresses that any punishment to be applied must be dependent on the culpability of the offender and the seriousness of the offense.

Justice Department. The unit of the federal government in which the Federal Bureau of Prisons is located.

Juvenile waiver. Juvenile court transfer of alleged delinquents to adult court for more intensive and lengthy punishment.

"Keester." To hide contraband objects within the rectum or vagina of prison inmates.

Kent v. United States. A U.S. Supreme Court decision that courts must provide the "essentials of due process" in transferring juveniles to the adult system.

Lex humana. Laws made by humankind.

Lex naturalis. Legal theory that there are laws that occur naturally and across all cultures.

Lex salica. The custom of atonement for wrongs against a victim by payment to appease the victim's family.

Lex talionis. The act of repaying in kind, such as "an eye for an eye, a tooth for a tooth".

Life certain. Judge's sentence that precludes parole eligibility; order to incarcerate the offender until dead.

Lock psychosis. Term denoting overconcentration of prison administrators with security and community protection, to be accomplished through extensive use of locks, head counts, and internal control of inmates.

Lockdowns. Controlling prison and inmates by not permitting inmates to leave their cells or rooms.

Lockstep formation. Lines of inmates marching closely behind their leader, with hands on top of shoulders or under the armpits; requires shuffling and muteness in march from one area of the prison to another.

Low-security level. A correctional assignment of prisoners permitting limited mobility and program participation consistent with their incarceration.

Maconochie, Alexander. The "father" of parole who developed the concept while overseeing the penal colony at Norfolk Island, off the east coast of Australia.

Male homosexual conduct. Sexual contacts between homosexuals; in 2003, the U.S. Supreme Court decriminalized homosexual behavior between consenting adults.

Malice aforethought. Having the intent to kill prior to the commission of the crime; planned and premeditated.

Mamertine prison. An early place of confinement in Rome using primitive dungeons built under the main sewer.

Mandatory release. The required release of an inmate from incarceration because the statutes mandate the release of any inmate who has served his or her maximum sentence.

Max out. Release after serving the entire sentence.

Mediators. Persons proposing nonbinding solutions to disputed issues.

Medical services. Any treatment programs designed to treat physical or psychological maladies of inmates.

Medium-security level. A correctional classification restricting offenders' movements and privileges while incarcerated.

Megan's Law. Legislation requiring sexual offenders to inform local police agencies of their location and nature of their prior conviction.

Mental health issues. A range of diagnosed mental illnesses that often afflict jail inmates.

Mentally disturbed. Persons with a mental illness.

Minimum-security level. A lower level of custody and freedom to interact with other prisoners and programs consistent with the offender's imprisonment.

Misdemeanor. An offense usually punishable by incarceration in a local confinement facility for a period of which the upper limit is prescribed by statute in a given jurisdiction, typically for a year or less.

Modify. Appeal court order requiring change in the trial court's legal decision on guilt or other rights.

Morrissey v. Brewer. The U.S. Supreme Court decision that spells out the rights of an offender at a parole revocation hearing.

Neglected. General term referring to a child who is not receiving the care that ought to be afforded by parents or guardians.

New-generation jail. Developed in the 1970s, a new-generation jail is a facility designed for maximum interaction between the staff and inmates.

Not guilty by reason of insanity (NGRI). Defense of offenders not to deny the commission of the crime, but to assert they lacked the capacity to understand the nature of the crime or that it was wrong.

Occupational disability. Offender is forbidden to practice designated occupations due to fact of conviction of crime.

Ombudsman. Correctional overseer who investigates reported complaints (as from inmates, prison personnel, and prison staff), reports findings, and helps to achieve equitable settlements.

Outlaw. A lawless person or a fugitive from the law—a person or organization under a ban or restriction; implies the offender is being cast out.

Outside cells. Prison cells attached to a corridor with the back of the cell extending outward toward a peripheral wall.

Paramilitary model. Organization of custody staff into ranks of armed forces.

Pardon. An act of executive clemency that absolves the party in part or in full from the legal consequences of the crime and conviction.

Parens patriae. A Latin term that refers to the duty of the state to protect those unable to protect themselves, particularly juveniles and the mentally disordered.

Parole agreement. Conditions imposed by the paroling authority and offender agreement to those conditions.

Parole board. A correctional person or board that has the authority to release or parole offenders committed to prisons, to set conditions, to revoke parole, and discharge from parole.

Parole, released on. Release of an inmate from confinement to expiration of sentence on condition of good behavior and supervision in the community.

Parole, technical violation. A violation of the conditions of release other than the conviction for a new crime that can result in the offender being returned to prison.

Paternalistic attitudes of judges. Personal sentiments found in a system under which an authority undertakes to supply needs or regulate conduct of those under its control, particularly for female offenders.

Penitentiary system. Prison designed to enforce penitence and prisoner anonymity, with individual manual labor in inmate cells.

Penn, William. Quaker leader who created the state of Pennsylvania and a system of justice that required compensation of victims and repentance to restore the offender to God's grace.

Pennsylvania system. The system of prison discipline using isolation or solitary confinement with both a work requirement and moral and religious instruction.

Podular/direct supervision. With podular/direct-supervision housing units, inmates have interaction with staff and other inmates through day rooms or common areas.

Population at risk. Those offenders more likely to offend, usually expressed as high-level potential for committing a crime.

Predict potential dangerousness. Process by which treatment staff assess the offender's risk for future dangerous offenses.

Preferential treatment. Argument that female offenders receive more lenient treatment at all phases of the criminal justice system.

Pregnant inmates. Female inmates who at time of detention are carrying a fetus or enter that condition while incarcerated.

Presentence investigation (PSI) report. Document that results from an investigation undertaken by a court-authorized officer or agency, designed to provide information on the defendant so the judge can make an informed sentencing decision.

Presentence report. Document prepared by agent of the court that investigates the offender's background for judicial determination of punishment.

Presumption of innocence. Under the U.S. Constitution, those charged with a crime are presumed innocent until convicted in a court of law.

Presumptive sentences. A sentencing mechanism fixed by a sentencing commission or legislature that identifies maximum and minimum sentences for punishment to be imposed by the judge, but permitting adjustment for special circumstances.

Pretrial alternatives. Programs and sanctions designed to release those jail inmates who are awaiting trial; alternatives can include electronic monitoring, supervision, treatment programs, house arrest, and other creative options designed to reduce jail populations.

Pretrial intervention programs. Requiring defendants awaiting trial to report to a supervision officer.

Pretrial jail incarceration. Holding someone accused of a crime who cannot make bail.

Price-tag justice. A term used by inmates to refer to fines imposed as a result of a criminal conviction.

Prison rules. Written documents designed to control inmate behaviors.

Prison stripes. Prison uniforms with horizontal black bands and white stripes, frequently colored to designate inmate classification.

Prisonization. The process of adopting the culture of the prison.

Privatization. The provision of correctional services by private-sector purveyors.

Proactive supervision. Treatment strategy serving to prepare for, intervene in, or control an expected occurrence or situation by offenders on probation, especially a negative or difficult one.

Probation. A court requirement that a person fulfill certain conditions of behavior and accept the supervision of a probation agency, usually in lieu of sentence to confinement but sometimes including a jail sentence.

Probation, broken windows. Concept that the probation officer is asked to communicate with victim(s) and the community, hold the offender accountable, and improve the leadership of probation.

Probation, felony. The offender is placed on probation for committing a felony.

Probation, intensive supervised probation (ISP). Intermediate sanction requiring increased supervision for probationers.

Probation, shock. Designed to give offenders a short "taste of the bars" followed by a period of supervised probation.

Probation, special conditions of. Additional punishments ordered by the courts to probationers, such as fines, electronic monitoring, and house arrest.

Project Newgate. Prison treatment program stressing full-time college work, group counseling, and aftercare following parole.

Psychological deprivation. Loss of or failure to develop emotional cohesion, support, or love through failure to provide emotional or physical caring.

Racial and ethnic groupings. Division of prisoners based on racial or ethnic characteristics.

RECLAIM. Ohio project designed to reduce admissions to the State's juvenile institutions through grants to local governmental units to underwrite such diversion.

Reclassification. The process by which inmate control and programming are changed.

Reentry. Process of inmates' return to the community and their adjustment to society ("free world").

Reentry courts. Specialized courts designed to reduce recidivism and improve public safety through judicial oversight of those offenders released from prison.

Reformatory. An institution for younger offenders that requires education and training, conditional release, and potential revocation of parole.

Registration of criminals. Requirement imposed by government that all offenders be registered with local law enforcement agencies.

Reintegration. The planned transition of an inmate from prison to the community.

Reintegration model. A treatment approach to prevent relapse and recidivism by use of existing community services, often bundled into a reentry plan to lower recidivism.

Remand. To send a case back to the trier of fact for considerations not contrary to the appeal court's order.

Reprieve. A reduction in sentencing severity; sometimes used in death penalty cases, when execution of the offender is at least temporarily stopped.

Restitution. Requirement that offender repay the victim.

Restitution order. Requirement that offender repay the victim.

Restorative justice. System of punishments designed to repair the damage to victims, community, and offender caused by the offender's criminal act.

Retaliation. Act designed to repay (as an injury) in kind, or to return like for like, especially "to get revenge".

Retentionist. Person seeking to retain the death penalty.

Revenge. Seeking retribution for a harm inflicted by the offended.

Reverse. Appeal court's order to cease acting, operating, or arranging in a manner contrary to the usual.

Revocation, probation. Change of sentence from probation to another correctional control status, due to violation of the conditions of probation.

Right of sanctuary. Privilege to avoid punishment by the offender's relocation to a sacred city or location.

Risk and needs assessments. Instruments used to determine the probability of recidivism or future criminal behavior.

Risk management. Strategies designed to provide increased supervision and surveillance for higher-risk offenders and less-restrictive options for those of lower risk.

Ruiz v. Estelle. U.S. Supreme Court decision that prisons must provide treatment to the developmentally challenged, assessing the conditions in the Texas Department of Corrections.

Sally port. Double-gated entry or exit point that restricts movement between the free world and prison.

Sanctuary. Asylum that placed the wrongdoer in seclusion or arrest in cities.

"Screws." Inmate term for correctional officers.

Section 1983. Legal statute for seeking redress regarding deprivation of legal rights of prisoner.

Security-threat group (STG). A prison gang; a criminal enterprise having an organizational structure and internal leadership, acting as an ongoing criminal conspiracy that uses violence and other criminal activity to continue.

Self-efficacy. Ability of offenders to assume direction of their lives.

Self-insured. Government unit whose operations are not covered by external insurers.

Sentencing disparity. Difference between both the types and length of sentences imposed for the same crime or seriousness of crimes when there are no legal bases that can be identified to explain this difference.

Sentencing guidelines. System of sentencing that imposes a predefined sentence length based on prior criminal history and crime severity, which allows judges to depart from the guidelines if warranted by the circumstances.

Sex offenses. Violations of laws that control sexual intercourse or crimes of a carnal nature, including attempts at such crimes.

Shakedown. Cell search to detect and control contraband.

Sick call. Opportunity for inmates to seek medical treatment.

Silence. Absence of speech between inmates within early prisons.

Single-sex experience. Inmate behavior involving other persons of the same sex in either a homogenital, homosocial, or homosexual relationship.

Slaves of the master. Inmates who are compelled to obey correctional managers and their staff.

Social stigma. Mark of dishonor or shame.

Societal protection argument. The argument that once executed, the offender cannot commit another crime, thus protecting society.

Sodomy. Anal or oral copulation with a member of the same or opposite sex, or copulation with an animal; the U.S. Supreme Court recently struck down sodomy law application to consenting adults in private.

Solitary confinement. A punishment program requiring isolation of an inmate in a cell, also known as a "prison within a prison".

Status offenders. Juveniles who have committed acts that are law violations by virtue of the child's age but would not be criminal if committed by an adult (such as runaway, incorrigibility, defiance).

Statutory exclusion. Principle that requires a category juvenile offender be bound over as an adult, based on the type of offense committed; all such juveniles committing an identified offense must be transferred to adult court.

Stigma. A mark of shame and disgrace attached to the offender by virtue of his or her having committed an offense.

Strip search. Process of detecting inmate contraband by visual inspection of the bodies of inmates.

Supermax prison. A free-standing prison or designated area within a prison that functions to control and contain dangerous, violent, disruptive, and other serious behavior in a prison facility.

Superpredator. Aggressive juvenile offender believed to engage in frequent and dangerous behaviors.

Sursis. A suspended sentence in European countries requiring no future punishment provided the offender remains crime-free during a specified time period.

Suspended sentence. Court determination to stop some formal processing of an offender, primarily stopping prosecution, not pronouncing a determination of guilt, or court not requiring a sentence.

Technologies for surveillance. Application of electronic and other programs designed to allow for the identification of locations of offenders.

Teen court. Courts staffed by juveniles who adjudicate juvenile problems and have the authority to enforce those adjudications.

Total institution. Term describing institutional control over inmates and prison operations.

Tourniquet sentencing. When a judge increases the sanctions and conditions imposed on an offender.

"Traditional" female crimes. Those criminal offenses particular to the female gender (prostitution and infanticide, for example).

Transincarceration. Movement of offenders diverted from mental health institutions to prisons.

Transinstitutionalism. Process referring to the transfer of the mentally ill to the justice system facilities, particularly jails and prisons.

Transitional period. Period from parole to rehabilitation and restoration of rights.

Transportation. Legal sentence requiring the banishment of the offender to a different location; the act of transporting that offender to another country.

Treadmills. A mill worked by inmates treading on the periphery of a wide wheel having a horizontal axis and used in prison as a punishment.

Treatment in lieu of conviction. Diversion offered to offenders in which successful completion of probation allows the prosecutor or judge to cease prosecution if treatment program results in no conviction.

Treatment services. Any in-prison program designed to meet an inmate's needs and lower recidivism.

Truth-in-sentencing movement. Begun the 1990s, this movement required inmates to serve a significant portion of their sentence before consideration for release.

U.S. Corrections Corporation (USCC). A private-sector correctional provider.

U.S. Office of Juvenile Justice and Delinquency Prevention (OJJDP). A branch of the U.S. Department of Justice that seeks to improve knowledge about juvenile offenders and evaluate both exploratory and prevention research, and capable of providing grants to researchers and administrators who would focus on solution of a major offense by a juvenile.

U.S. penitentiary. A correctional facility in which offenders are incarcerated to keep them from society and from each other so they can reflect on their crimes, repent, and be rehabilitated.

UNICOR. A wholly-owned federal subsidiary that supports the Federal Bureau of Prisons through the gainful employment of inmates across a variety of work programs.

Unionization. Organization of correctional officers for purposes of improved work conditions or salaries.

Unit team management. Control scheme uniting all staff into a coherent and unified force to attain prison objectives.

Vendetta. Blood feud; an often-prolonged series of retaliatory, vengeful, or hostile acts or exchange of such acts.

Victimless crimes. Offenses in which the victim does not seem to appear, or is equaled to the offender (prostitution and drug abuse, for example).

Violation, technical probation. Probation sentence change due to charges that the offender violated the rules imposed by the court, but not by committing a new crime.

Vocational training. Any training program designed to increase job readiness and skills for inmates.

Walnut Street Jail. First penitentiary created in Philadelphia by the Quakers.

War on Drugs. A criminal justice program focusing on reducing the manufacture, use, sale, or trafficking of drugs.

Ward. A minor subject to wardship or protection by the state; may also refer to other persons protected by court order or legal status.

Weekender. A jail inmate who is allowed to live at home during the week (usually to work) and who must report to jail to serve his or her sentence on weekends.

Wergild. The European word denoting lex salica.

Women's liberation movement. A series of social movements intended to narrow the gaps between rights and privileges accorded to males, and free females from oppressive minority status.

Work camps. A low-security facility organized around work on the exterior of the prison facility.

Work release. A program in which inmates are allowed to work in the community with minimal restrictions, but must return to confinement during nonworking hours.

Workhouse. A house of correction for persons guilty of minor law violations; sometimes referred to as a "poorhouse."

Writ of habeas corpus. A judicial order demanding that another person holding an inmate to produce the same in court, and to justify continued imprisonment.

Writ of mandamus. A judicial order requiring the recipient to conform to the court's decision.

"Yellow card." European identification card, yellow in color, that signifies the carrier has been convicted of a crime.

Youth gang. A continuing criminal enterprise by juveniles and young adults that commits violence and other criminal acts to sustain itself.

author index

r

S

subject index